UNIX® System V Release 4:
The Complete Reference

UNIX® System V Release 4:
The Complete Reference

Stephen Coffin

Osborne **McGraw-Hill**

Berkeley   New York   St. Louis   San Francisco
Auckland   Bogotá   Hamburg   London   Madrid
Mexico City   Milan   Montreal   New Delhi   Panama City
Paris   São Paulo   Singapore   Sydney
Tokyo   Toronto

Osborne **McGraw-Hill**
2600 Tenth Street
Berkeley, California 94710
U.S.A.

For information on translations or book distributors outside of the U.S.A., please write to Osborne **McGraw-Hill** at the above address.

UNIX System V Release 4: Complete Reference

10 11 12 13 14 15 DOC 998765

ISBN 0-07-881653-X

This book is printed on acid-free paper.

For my father, Victor H. Coffin

CONTENTS AT A GLANCE

TABLE OF CONTENTS

Developing this book would have been impossible without the help of a great many people, only a few of whom can be mentioned here. Thanks to Intel Corporation for access to early versions of their 80386/80486 port of SVR4, and to Intel employees Barbara Dawson, Andy Sullivan, and Tim Majne for their excellent support. Bill Corwin, Stuart Goossen, and their team provided an outstanding technical review of the manuscript. Locus Computing and its employee Sassan Behzadi supplied a beta version of the DOS Merge product. Profound thanks to U S WEST Advanced Technologies and its employees Doug Corey, Catherine Marshall and Bud Wonsciewicz for their nonintrusive support. Thanks to Roger Stewart and Jeff Pepper at Osborne/McGraw-Hill. Special thanks to Pat Somers for her patience. And of course, the view from the shoulders of the giants of the UNIX system improves with every new release.

A
C
K
N
O
W
L
E
D
G
M
E
N
T
S

Welcome to the wide world of the UNIX operating system. If you have experience with other microcomputer systems, such as MS-DOS or the Macintosh, you will be surprised by the UNIX system's large, diverse, and very rich environment for computing. If you have no previous computer experience, you will slip easily into the world of the UNIX system without preconceptions.

The UNIX system provides *such* a comprehensive environment that even a large book like this one cannot *completely* cover all its features and functions. But don't worry, the UNIX system and this book are organized so that beginners can start with simple functions, and progress until they learn as much about the system as they need (or wish!) for their purposes. On the other hand, if you are interested in computing theory, or just want to experiment with one of the best operating systems available, you will find plenty in the UNIX system to interest you. Even experts don't know everything about the system. In any case, get access to a UNIX system and jump in; before long, using the UNIX system will seem natural, and you will be reluctant to return to other computing environments.

About This Book

UNIX System V Release 4: The Complete Reference provides detailed coverage of the latest release of the UNIX operating system. This release is widely used as the basis for UNIX systems provided for most computers in the 1990s. If you have access to a microcomputer based on the Intel 80386 or 80486 CPU, a high-performance RISC workstation, a machine sold by Sun Microsystems or by AT&T, or an Apple Macintosh running AUX, the material in this book will be appropriate. Many other machines also use the SVR4 release. These range from the largest supercomputers and mainframes to personal and even portable and laptop machines. Users of other versions of the UNIX system will find most of the material presented here applicable to their release, although some details may differ.

This book starts with the basic concepts and ideas of the UNIX operating system. Beginners without computer experience can learn to use the UNIX system by starting at the beginning of the book with the tutorial, shell, and file system chapters. These chapters also contain a lot of material for experienced computer users, and even for those who are experienced with older releases of the UNIX system.

The book progresses through the user-level commands required to use a system that is administered by someone else, and it also provides extensive coverage of the system administration ideas and tools necessary to configure and use your own personal UNIX system. You can use your UNIX machine as a complete standalone machine, or you can attach it to a Local Area Network and participate in a larger community of users.

This book was written after extensive experience with the original, "standard" release of the SVR4 version from AT&T, as it runs on the 80386 and 80486 machines. This release is known as the *porting base* for the SVR4 system, because all vendors of SVR4 variants start from this base when they adapt the system for their specific hardware. The material in this book is correct for 80386 and 80486 machines, and mostly correct for all other SVR4 machines.

When you have finished this book, you should be able to use any UNIX system on any computer to do most of your computer-related work. You should be familiar with the great breadth of modern UNIX systems, and be able to find any additional information that you need in the *UNIX User's Manual.* If you have your own personal UNIX system, you should be able to maintain and administer the system so it works well for you and for other users you authorize for your machine. In addition, the book should become a friend that will answer your questions about the UNIX system through many years of use. Keep this book near your machine for easy reference!

How This Book Is Organized

It is best to read this book in conjunction with hands-on access to a UNIX system, so that you can try the examples and see the results on your own machine or with your own user identification on a system run by someone else. You can customize the system's operation to meet your needs, and experiment with the commands and functions as your interests dictate. If you try the examples on your own system, you may find bugs in them; if you do, please send them to us!

Each chapter begins with the most generally useful and least complex material on that chapter's topic. You can become a competent user of the UNIX system just by reading the first half of each chapter. However, if you want more information, or need reference material as you become more skilled at using the UNIX system, the second half of the chapters can help you. Each chapter ends with a "Going Further" section that introduces more difficult or esoteric aspects of the topic in question. As your knowledge and experience grow, you can return to the second half of each chapter to pick up additional information that you might not need the first time through.

Remember, the UNIX system is an enormous environment; whole books could (and often do) follow the end of each "Going Further" section.

In general, the first half of the book (through Chapter 11) discusses "traditional" material for users of the UNIX system, including the most important tools and utilities. In the second half of the book, each chapter begins with material of general interest, and then moves on to information that is relevant to administering and operating a UNIX system. The final chapters cover material in special subsystems that may not be available on all UNIX systems.

This book does not describe every command exhaustively, nor every possible option for each command that it does discuss. Use the *UNIX User's Manual* to supplement the information presented here with more detailed and exact reference materials. In addition to learning more about the UNIX system, this will eventually give you a thorough knowledge of the standard reference documentation.

Chapter 1 provides an introduction to the modern UNIX system, including a short history of the system and a discussion of the major new features introduced in SVR4. Chapter 2 is a simple tutorial that will teach you some system basics, including procedures for logging in to the machine, reading your mail, and a few other common functions. Chapters 3, 4, 7, and 8 cover topics considered part of the "classical" UNIX system—material on the file system, the command interface (the shell), and a few of the most common commands. This material is necessary background that is fundamental to using the UNIX system on a daily basis. Chapters 5 and 6 cover the standard editors for the UNIX system. Even if you have a word processing application, knowing the ideas and concepts behind the UNIX editors is important for understanding many of the commands; even the shell uses these ideas. Chapter 9 introduces the *UNIX User's Manual,* the official documentation of the UNIX system. Even a comprehensive book like this one cannot substitute for the *User's Manual,* but often users cannot understand the *User's Manual* without some assistance. Chapter 10 discusses calculation and "number crunching" tools, which most users find useful. The basics of multitasking in the UNIX system are introduced in Chapter 11, and tools for running more than one application at a time are also discussed.

Chapter 12 provides an introduction to system administration. This information is critical if you wish to "drive" your own UNIX system, but most of the real knowledge needed to administer your system is covered in the chapters that follow. Later chapters also introduce more commands and concepts that are key to the UNIX system. Chapter 13 discusses printing; it includes tools for printing your files, and also explains how to install a printer on your machine. Chapters 14 and 15 describe the classical communications tools in the UNIX system, including electronic mail and the **uucp** package. These chapters discuss both how to use these important tools and how to configure them for your own needs.

Chapter 16 covers the two enhanced shells available in SVR4 systems, and Chapter 17 discusses the **troff** word processing package. Chapter 18 discusses the use of magnetic disks and tape, including managing your disk space budget, backing up and restoring data, and installing new disks into the system. Chapter 19 covers the use of MS-DOS tools with the UNIX system. Chapter 20 describes timing and scheduling issues, including the ability to set up regularly scheduled tasks. In Chapter 21, the processes of starting (booting) and stopping (shutting down) a UNIX machine are covered. This information is useful if you have your own machine, and it helps illuminate the "behind-the-scenes" activities of the system. In today's environment, system security is an important consideration, and this issue is discussed in Chapter 22.

Chapters 23 and 24 discuss relatively new features of the UNIX system, which may not be present on all machines. The X Window System, covered in Chapter 23, provides a mouse-and-window environment for the UNIX system. Chapter 24 describes LAN tools and networking issues. Building your own UNIX system and configuring the system software for your environment are discussed in Chapter 25. You should turn to Chapter 25 immediately if you are considering purchasing a computer to run the UNIX system. Finally, Chapter 26 considers some additional issues that can launch you into the community of UNIX users, and some extra "lore" that goes beyond the main scope of this book.

The material in Chapters 17, 19, 23 and 24 may not be useful unless your machine has the add-on hardware and software these chapters discuss. On the other hand, many SVR4 machines do have these features, and they are important parts of the UNIX system.

So, dive in! Maybe you will write the next book on the UNIX system!

Conventions Used in This Book

Usually the concepts and jargon of the UNIX system are printed in *italic* type the first time they are introduced; thereafter they are printed in normal type like the rest of the text. The italic font is also used for words that you should replace with a real value. For example, *hostname* would be replaced with the actual name of your UNIX system.

Command names and filenames are printed in **boldface** letters when they appear in the text, and user input is also printed in **boldface** when it appears in the text itself. Upper- and lowercase characters differ in the UNIX system, so be sure to use the correct case for all characters you type into the system.

Examples of input to and output from the UNIX system are usually set off from the surrounding text, like this:

```
$ cat README
```

Other (longer) examples are given in separate figures. These are all exact interactions with at least one version of the SVR4 UNIX system. Don't worry if your system does not match them *exactly,* or if the material is not *quite* accurate for your specific machine. There is a great deal of variability between releases of the UNIX system, and between versions supplied by different vendors. Try to understand the concepts and maintain a flexible attitude as you explore your system. Remember, your real concern is *your* system and how it acts, not the contents of any book.

UNIX System V Release 4: The Complete Reference is intended for beginning to intermediate users of the UNIX system, people who might be new users of a general-purpose multiuser UNIX system or who might own a personal system. This book will help you learn how to navigate in the UNIX system environment; it will teach you to use the most important commands, and prepare you to go as far as you wish with the UNIX system on your own.

The book assumes that you have some experience with computers and computer operating systems, perhaps with MS-DOS or another microcomputer operating system, or perhaps with a mainframe operating system. However, people with no previous computer experience can use this book to learn the fundamentals of the UNIX system, and then go on to become experts!

If you want to administer your own personal UNIX system, you will find this book to be an invaluable reference in your daily use of the system. It covers all the major administrative issues, and helps you understand not just *how* things work in the UNIX system, but also *why* they work as they do.

This book is oriented toward the System V, Release 4 (also known as SVR4 or 5.4) version of the UNIX system. The descriptions and examples it includes are taken from this release. However, most versions of the UNIX system that are available today act similarly in the basic-to-intermediate level of command usage, so the book will be helpful even if you have an older (or newer!) version.

Introduction

The UNIX operating system has progressed in the last 20 years from its invention as an experiment in computer science to one of the most influential and popular computer environments in the world. Today more than a million computers use the UNIX system, ranging in size from small microcomputers with limited resources to the largest mainframes and supercomputers. This growth is accelerating ever faster as more and more users and application developers are attracted to the system's amazing flexibility, power, and elegance.

Several unique features of the UNIX system have led to this growth:

• *Software Tools* The UNIX system originated a new idea in computing: that problems can be solved and applications created by interconnecting a few simple parts. These parts are usually "off-the-shelf" components designed to do a single job, and do it well. Large applications can be built from simple sequences of commands. This philosophy also extends to the development domain where many libraries of packaged subroutines have been widely adopted, significantly easing the task of creating new executable programs. This basic concept of *software reuse* is one of the major reasons why the UNIX system is such a productive environment in which to work.

• *Portability* The UNIX system has been ported to nearly every midsize or larger computer ever built. Now that microcomputers

3

have the processing power once reserved for mainframes costing millions of dollars, the UNIX system is a natural evolution for these inexpensive but powerful machines. Only a few minor changes and adaptations have been required to make the UNIX system available to microcomputers, and it is now generally agreed that no more portable operating system exists. The value of this portability cannot be overestimated, because software development is expensive and tedious. Creating a major application such as a word processor, database, or a graphics system can consume many years of developer effort. These applications are usually designed for a specific operating environment; if that environment does not survive advances in hardware technology, the investment is wasted and users are abandoned. It is generally acknowledged that the UNIX system provides the required environment: one that allows for easy movement of applications between microcomputers and mainframes, between older and newer machine architectures, and especially between different releases of the UNIX system.

• *Flexibility*   A major attraction of the UNIX system for software and hardware developers is its flexibility. The system has been adapted to applications as divergent as factory automation, telephone switching systems, and personal games and toys. New functions and commands are constantly being added, and most developers prefer to use the UNIX system as a "workbench" for their applications. In fact, it is so easy to extend the basic system that some turnkey application packages are barely recognizable as being based on the UNIX system.

• *Power*   The UNIX system is one of the most powerful operating systems available for any computer. Its clean and terse command syntax allows users to do many things quickly and simply that are not even possible with other operating systems. Users can take advantage of built-in UNIX system services and commands that are often expensive add-ons (if they exist at all) in other systems. No operating system is richer in its capabilities than the UNIX system.

• *Multiuser and Multitasking*   Since the UNIX system is a time-sharing multitasking environment, it can easily do more than one thing at a time. It is common in a personal UNIX system for a user to simultaneously edit a file, print a file to a printer, send electronic mail to another machine, and use an electronic spreadsheet. The UNIX system is designed to handle a user's multiple simultaneous needs effortlessly. The UNIX system is also a multiuser environment that supports the activities of more than one person simultaneously. It is not unusual for large mainframe versions to support several hundred users at once, and each of these users has the same "private" view of the system as does a single user on a microcomputer.

• *Elegance*   The UNIX system is widely regarded as one of the most elegant examples of computer operating systems. Once users understand some of the basic concepts of the system, they can do a great many things in a beautiful and simple way. UNIX system users who move to other operating systems may find themselves wondering why the things that seemed so straightforward under the UNIX system are not even possible in other environments. The developers of other operating systems and applications often borrow ideas and themes from the UNIX system to enrich their own systems.

• *Network Orientation*   Modern releases of the UNIX system are organized for easy and functional network use. The system's built-in communication tools, easy acceptance of additional low-level device drivers, and flexible file system organization are natural for today's network environment, in which users on personal workstations share some centralized resources such as data or communications devices. As computers grow increasingly common in work groups, the networking capabilities of the UNIX system become more and more important. Today networks range from small local area networks (LANs) to worldwide links that allow high-speed data transfers of huge databases. The UNIX system, with its multitasking capability and large base of communication software, makes network computing simple and easy.

All these features, and many others, help to account for the UNIX system's surge of popularity in recent years. Clearly, the UNIX system will continue to grow and develop. Most computer users will eventually encounter it in one setting or another, and many will have their own personal UNIX system on their microcomputer.

The Lore and Controversy Surrounding the UNIX System

The UNIX system is unique since it has attracted both intensely loyal defenders and intensely critical detractors. Almost no one who has used the UNIX system is indifferent to it. Generally, its fans wax profound about its elegance, power, and flexibility, while its enemies wax profane about its terse syntax and strange command names, its sparse documentation, and its complexity to administer. Usually computer experts fall into the "fan" category, while beginners may fall into the "foe" category. We hope this book will help you leap directly over the foe stage to defender status.

Like the pocket calculator, the UNIX system was originally developed by experts for their own use; thus, in the early days, the needs of beginning users were ignored in favor of speed and accuracy for experts. Also like the pocket calculator, the advantages of the UNIX system moved it quickly from the expert to the novice, complete with its expert features and its lack of concern for the beginner.

Happily, recent releases have been aimed at less-skilled users, without detriment to the system's power or other advantages. Now, with SVR4, almost anyone can administer and use their own UNIX system, and take the system as far as they wish. These recent improvements have been primarily in the following areas:

- *Bulletproofing*   The UNIX system has been hardened so that very little routine software maintenance is required to keep it tuned and running at peak performance. Many formerly routine system administration chores, such as periodically deleting log files and rebooting, are now automatic or unnecessary.

- *Consistency*   Most commands have evolved over the years to follow a relatively consistent command syntax, significantly reducing the confusing and inconsistent use of commands. Although there are still plenty of inconsistencies, things are moving in the right direction.

- *User Agents*   Most implementations now provide simplified tools (even some expert systems!) to aid in the configuration and administration of the UNIX system.

- *New Features*   Many new capabilities and commands have been incorporated into the UNIX system in the last few releases. Often, these have been aimed at bringing some of the ideas behind BSD and XENIX into the AT&T System V products. Among other advances, there are new features and a new system organization to support networking; the development environment has been enhanced; and support for shared processing in multiple machines is growing.

• *Interoperability*   The great flexibility of the UNIX system has now been formalized into the *Applications Binary Interfaces* (ABI) and the *Applications Programming Interface* (API). These definitions of standard development environments within the UNIX system ensure that the system will evolve in predictable ways. Thus developers can be confident their investments in software products will maintain their value as the UNIX system software (API) and the machines that use the UNIX system (ABI) evolve in the near future. On a larger scale, the UNIX system is moving toward greater compliance with the POSIX international standard for operating systems. The POSIX standard provides a minimum set of functions that will (eventually) be supported by UNIX-like systems worldwide. Of course, major innovations will continue to appear, but the POSIX standard, the API, and the ABI help to provide a secure footing for users and developers.

• *Operating System Sharing*   Microcomputer implementations allow the machine and its files to be shared between the UNIX system and the MS-DOS system, or between the Apple Macintosh environment and the UNIX system. Operating system sharing means that the multitasking capabilities of the UNIX system can be used to execute the entire MS-DOS system (or the Macintosh Finder) as a process under the UNIX system, thus allowing all the "background" functions of the UNIX system to execute while programs are running in the other operating system.

As a result of these and other changes, many old criticisms of the UNIX system are no longer valid. Make no mistake, the UNIX system is still a powerful and complex operating system, but over time it has become much more regular, controllable, and friendly.

Because of its history as an experts' system, a definite mystique and a great deal of lore have grown up around the UNIX system. Historically, most "gurus" have learned their skills by word-of-mouth — sitting at the feet of an acknowledged expert. Even today it helps to have a more knowledgeable person to answer questions and explain some of the more esoteric aspects of the UNIX system.

The Philosophy Behind the UNIX System

The UNIX system was invented in large part as a reaction to the large and clumsy computer operating systems available in the late 1960s. One of the foremost goals in its design was to make it wide in scope, but using commands that didn't attempt to solve all possible problems. On the contrary, a fundamental principle of the earliest development efforts was to design commands that did only one thing, but did that thing simply, quietly, and very well. For example, a command designed to concatenate and display files should not try to paginate the output or print the files on a printer. Those tasks should be left to other programs that could do those things without the burden of concatenation.

This insistence on a "small is beautiful" philosophy had several major effects. First, a new requirement emerged that was not apparent before: the output of some of these *tools,* as the single-purpose commands were called, must be channeled into the input of other tools. From this necessity came the concepts of command pipelines and standard input and output, which we will examine in detail later. Second, the development of new commands and other applications was much less difficult than it was in other operating systems, so the UNIX system soon began to experience the substantial growth and advancement that still continues today. This ease of software development and maintenance was a direct result of the UNIX system's philosophy of making tools. Third, the UNIX system contains a great number of single-purpose commands. This is a mixed blessing for users, because you must sometimes learn a lot of command names for functions that might be combined into a single command in other operating systems. Nonetheless, most users agree that the difficulty of learning many commands is more than counterbalanced by the flexibility and power the tools approach provides.

The Modern UNIX System—Pro and Con

The UNIX system remains somewhat controversial, though its multi-user and multitasking features are now more widely respected in the microcomputer community than ever before. Compared to MS-DOS, for example, the UNIX system is much larger and more complex; however, in return, it offers many features that are not available in MS-DOS, or even in MS-OS/2.

The original "do one thing well" philosophy of the early commands has been somewhat modified in modern releases, and today's commands offer a great number of options and controls. This fact has both pros and cons; although commands can now be more difficult to use, they can also be adapted to new situations without contortions or inefficiencies. By and large, the key concepts of the early philosophy (such as pipelines) have been retained, while the capabilities of the commands have expanded to meet new needs.

The UNIX system is primarily oriented to *character-based* terminals and devices. Special software called the *X Window System* is required to make the UNIX system work with bit-mapped graphics displays. This historical dependence on and support for ASCII terminals has meant that most tools and procedures are command-line oriented, and mouse-and-menu tools that use the graphics display are just beginning to appear in volume. On the other hand, a user can call a remote machine with an inexpensive terminal, over inexpensive telephone lines. Thus the system is ideal for *server* applications, in which the primary user interface is not associated with the centralized UNIX machine, but executes directly on a remote "intelligent" terminal. This provides a modern architecture for local area network environments; in fact, the standard X Window System is network-capable, meaning that an application can execute on one machine in a network (usually a fast and expensive server machine) while the user interface can run on inexpensive machines located on each user's desk. This scheme can significantly reduce the cost of a computing installation in a networked environment.

The UNIX system runs counter to the current trend of making operating systems "invisible" to the user. Many operating systems have attempted to create user interfaces that hide the operating system from the user's view. The Macintosh Finder, for example, is really an operating system that has relatively simple functions. The window- and menu-oriented user interface helps to conceal the commands, file system, and administrative tools from the user. In the UNIX system, on the other hand, the more aware you are of the system's internal functions, the better you can control them to benefit yourself and improve your productivity. This fact arises mainly from the UNIX system's origin as an expert's system, in which most users were well aware of the system's internal functions as they used it. Now that the UNIX system has been adopted by a larger community, tools such as user agents have been provided to insulate the user from many of the operating system's subtleties and complexities. Nonetheless, even though you can now use the system without a thorough understanding of its complexities, you can still benefit substantially from knowing more about what the system is actually doing when you use a command.

UNIX System History

Even though the UNIX system originated in AT&T Bell Laboratories, one of the largest and most well-funded research institutions in the United States, its history is extremely unusual compared to that of other major computer operating systems. This results from the fact that to a large extent advances have been based on the contributions of individual people with unique creative ideas. A joke among developers that contains more than a grain of truth goes like this: To get a new release of the UNIX system, you lock a bunch of hackers in a closed room (or on a single UNIX machine!); then, every year or so, you take the software more than half of them are using, and call it the next release of the UNIX system. As this story implies, major advances have sprung not primarily from bureaucratic decision making, but rather directly from the needs and creativity of users. This is still true today, making the UNIX system one of the most fertile gardens for the growth of new concepts in computing.

The UNIX system was designed by a group of people who were AT&T representatives on the development team for one of the seminal influences in modern computing, the MULTICS operating system, developed at MIT in the late 1960s. As one of the early *timesharing* systems, MULTICS embodied most of the ideas found in today's multitasking systems. Unfortunately, MULTICS suffered from its innovative role, and was much more complex and clumsy than necessary. In the late 1960s, AT&T withdrew most of its participants from the MULTICS project, leaving a group of talented and frustrated people with plenty of ideas about what a timesharing system *should* be. Without access to the MULTICS system, these people were stranded without a modern operating system, so they created a new one. Ken Thompson and Dennis Ritchie built the system based on a design they worked out with Rudd Canaday. These three were soon joined by several other able computer scientists, including J. F. Ossanna, R. Morris, and others. After a period of discussion and proposals, the group managed to acquire a cast-off DEC PDP-7, and they set to work. Like all the best projects, this one started with the creation of a game: Thompson and Ritchie developed a "Space Travel" game for the PDP-7. With this experience they turned to more mundane pursuits, and soon created a new file system structure and software very similar to the modern file system. A process environment with scheduling was added, and the rest of a rudimentary operating system followed. The name *UNIX* was soon applied to the results, because this system was a simplification of MULTICS. The new system was running on the PDP-7 at the beginning of 1970, and by mid-1970 the group had moved the project to the newly introduced DEC PDP-11. Many of the modern UNIX system's key ideas were present in these earliest implementations, including the file system, the implementation of processes, and the command-line structure still in use today.

Although the original implementation was coded in assembly language, the C programming language was soon developed within the group, beginning in 1971. Almost immediately, C became the language of choice for the continuing development of the UNIX system, and in 1973 the kernel was recoded in C. Today only a very few high-performance kernel subroutines are written in assembly language. This was the first attempt to code an entire operating system in a high-level language, and the portability it provided is widely regarded as a major reason for the popularity the UNIX system enjoys today. Even now, most other operating systems are still written in assembler language, by comparison an expensive and unportable approach.

In these same years, the text-processing tools that later became **troff** were introduced; the first real customer of a UNIX system was the Bell Laboratories patent attorney's office, which began using the **roff** program, predecessor to **troff**, in the fall of 1971.

The UNIX system immediately captured the imagination of the computer scientists at Bell Laboratories, and after only two or three years there were about a dozen UNIX systems running on several different machine types. Major software enhancements followed frequently, and AT&T soon began supporting the system as an internal "product" within Bell Laboratories. The **troff** program appeared during this period, among many other innovations.

The UNIX system came into its own with the development of larger PDP-11 machines, such as the PDP-11/45 and PDP-11/70 in the early to mid-1970s. The UNIX system fitted naturally into the DEC architecture, and has resulted in the sale of many thousands of PDP-11 machines over the years. Developers within Bell Laboratories began using the UNIX system machines for word processing, and Bell System product designers began using PDP-11s with the UNIX system for turnkey products in the telephone business.

Simultaneously, AT&T released numerous copies of the UNIX system to universities around the world, and a whole generation of computer scientists in the late 1970s learned their trade on the UNIX system. This resulted in another fertile wave of innovation, and the widely used BSD (for Berkeley Software Distribution) implementation emerged from the University of California at Berkeley. As AT&T moved to harden the UNIX system and optimize it in the direction of business computing, the BSD releases became dominant in the university and engineering communities. Even today, most users belong to one camp or the other, preferring either a BSD or an AT&T environment for their machines.

In the late 1970s, AT&T introduced a new naming scheme for their version of the UNIX system. Formerly, the major releases had been named for new versions that came out of the research area at Bell Laboratories, and two of the most popular releases were named Sixth Edition and Seventh Edition. Following an internal reorganization of UNIX system support, AT&T changed its numbering to System III and System V. Actually these new releases were direct descendants of the Seventh Edition, and System V superseded System III in the mid-1980s. System IV was used internally at Bell Laboratories, but it was considered a transition product and was not publically supported. Now, in the 1990s, AT&T has standardized on its System V name, and its most recent releases are called System V Release 3 and System V Release 4, often abbreviated SVR3 and SVR4, respectively.

During the late 1970s and early 1980s, either or both the BSD and AT&T releases were ported to nearly every computer with the power to support them. This usually means at least high-speed disk units and built-in memory management support in the CPU, although experimental versions of the UNIX system have been adapted to ROM-based machines with no hard disk at all. Today you can buy versions of the UNIX system for the largest supercomputers, for the more widely used mainframe machines, and for most minicomputers.

The BSD releases were also the dominant platform for experimentation in networking concepts, so some of the best local area networks are available for the UNIX system. The first major experiment in wide-area networking, the ARPANET, was primarily oriented toward the UNIX system. The Network File System (NFS), created by Sun Microsystems, and Remote File Sharing (RFS), created by AT&T, are the end products of this evolution. Both systems are effective networks today, and almost all computing environments provide support for connecting to NFS or RFS. Most PC-based LAN architectures borrowed liberally from these experiences, but the UNIX system still retains a solid lead in networking support. Research in networking remains an active area within the UNIX system, and more innovations are expected as multiprocessing systems gain momentum in the computer industry.

As microcomputers have increased in speed and power, and decreased in cost, these machines have moved into range of the UNIX system. The original 8088 machines were almost powerful enough to support the UNIX system, and a few implementations were able to run on these machines. The original version of the popular XENIX operating system was a streamlined UNIX system designed for the IBM PC, but in fact, it was actually at or over the edge of the machine's capability. XENIX has only come into its own with the 80286 and 80386 machines. Now most XENIX features have been merged with the mainline UNIX system, and XENIX is expected to die out as a separate line in the history of the UNIX system.

When the SVR3 and SVR4 systems became available on PC-AT architecture machines in the late 1980s, the popularity of the UNIX system took a large step forward. The AT-class 80386 machines provided a truly affordable environment for the UNIX system, and well over half the UNIX systems running today use this popular computer.

Another major step has been the rise of the X Window System as a widely accepted part of the UNIX system. X, as it is often called, was prototyped as a research project at MIT in the mid-1980s, and was then adopted by a consortium of UNIX system vendors, who further enhanced and hardened the system to commercial quality. Other mouse-oriented windowing systems were pioneered in the UNIX system environment by Sun and Apollo, but as a nonproprietary industry standard,

X has dominated. Today, most commercial applications packages for the UNIX system run under the X environment.

Recently, AT&T Bell Laboratories has developed a new generic version, called the Tenth Edition, or the Research UNIX System. Although this version is not sold commercially, research releases have been widely distributed to universities, and innovations from the research systems regularly make their way into System V products.

A merger of the three major variants of the UNIX system started with later releases of SVR3, and this merger is nearing completion in SVR4. Now, as a result of agreements between AT&T, Sun Microsystems, and Microsoft, the BSD and XENIX systems are merging into the System V product. Most software designed for BSD or XENIX will run without modification on SVR4 systems, and variants are disappearing as their functions are subsumed into the System V release. This "combined" product also allows object-code compatibility between variants produced for the same machine type.

As the merger of BSD and System V got underway, several other vendors of UNIX systems became worried that a merged system would give market dominance to AT&T and Sun Microsystems. These vendors (primarily IBM, Hewlett-Packard, and DEC) formed a consortium to develop a variant system that would not be under the control of AT&T or Sun. This group, called the Open Software Foundation or OSF, has already developed several important products for the UNIX system, foremost among them being the Motif user interface specification. In response, AT&T and another group of UNIX system vendors have formed their own large consortium, UNIX International, to standardize and publicize System V releases into the 1990s. Some companies participate in both these groups. If the history of the BSD release as a stimulus to the UNIX system is any guide, the competitive tensions between OSF and UNIX International will generate many positive contributions in the future.

In addition, Apple Computer has adapted SVR4 for its Macintosh computer family, and successfully incorporated the Finder and classic Macintosh look and feel within a UNIX system, much as MS-DOS has been incorporated in the Merge and Simultask products.

The UNIX system's power to span differences in hardware is well illustrated by the appearance of the *reduced instruction set computers* (RISC) in the late 1980s and early 1990s. RISCs implement a fundamentally different concept of processor design from that found in the dominant microprocessors, a concept that makes CPU chips much easier and cheaper to design. Thus, in a very short time several different RISC microprocessors have been developed. Because of the difficulties inherent in designing a totally new operating system for each new machine, virtually all RISC machines have adopted the UNIX system. In fact, several RISC machines were designed expressly to perform well with the UNIX system. As a result, the fastest and best microcomputers available today are RISC machines.

As the 1990s progress, the most significant development will be *multiprocessing* features that allow machines to contain more than one central CPU chip. These machines will share resources such as power supply and disk devices, and so provide additional computing resources for much less than it would cost to buy additional machines. In multi-user systems, the additional user processes can be efficiently spread among the different processors, and single-user systems or networked servers can spread the additional load as well. Multiprocessing systems will certainly be a major factor in the lifetime of SVR4.

The history of the UNIX system is still being written, and probably the OSF variant will become a viable alternative to SVR4 in the early 1990s. Successful ideas and tools that originate in one of the systems will eventually be adopted by the other, but probably not immediately, or even in the next system release. Usually add-on software vendors are the first to provide the features of one system to another, so it pays to keep your system administrator informed of new tools and procedures that only exist in variants of your UNIX system.

The same holds true for other operating systems. Innovations in MS-DOS, OS/2, the NeXT, the Macintosh environment, and the IBM/6000 versions of the UNIX system are often available as add-on packages for SVR4. With a little detective work, you can usually find the tools you need.

The SVR4 Release

The SVR4 release is the most up-to-date version of the AT&T UNIX system. It has been ported to most host machines, and is the current standard for the AT&T line. SVR4 has been significantly enhanced over older releases, and numerous changes have been made. Many of the new features are primarily of interest to developers and system administrators, but in most cases the enhancements will eventually make their way to the user level in easier, faster, better, or less expensive applications. Some of the most important enhancements are discussed in the following sections.

Networking Support

The most important enhancement in SVR4 is the addition of full support for local area networks. Both the AT&T RFS system and the industry-standard NFS system for networks are supported, and tools and hooks are provided for other networks to easily mesh with the SVR4 framework. Part of this support has been an extensive reorganization of the file system that enables better file sharing between machines on a net, allowing diskless machines for the first time in System V. Administration of networked machines has been greatly enhanced, and remote administration is now possible across the net. The addition of a new port monitoring system also simplifies the handling of service requests from other machines. Finally, multiprocessing tools (to be added later) will soon allow networked machines to share their workloads.

Unification

SVR4 has taken major steps in unifying the various versions of the UNIX system, especially the popular BSD and XENIX variants. This allows developers to create applications for a single version of the system instead of many separate and different versions. This feature alone will significantly reduce the cost of development for the UNIX system, and will certainly increase the availability and quality of applications.

New Development Environment

The C language development environment has been greatly enhanced and improved in SVR4. There is a new ANSI-compliant C compiler that significantly outperforms older versions. Dynamic linking and shared libraries allow developers to defer many aspects of their programs until the actual time of execution instead of including all subroutines at compile time. The device and kernel interfaces have been documented for the first time, both stabilizing and simplifying developers' access to kernel services. A full-scale deployment of the streams device driver system allows developers to do things that were never before possible with the system.

Internationalization

The entire SVR4 system has been upgraded to support national variations. The language of system messages, time and money conventions, and many other local variations are now included in the system for the first time, so that developers can customize the system for a target environment. In addition, the system as a whole comes much closer to compliance with international standards for operating systems than ever before.

X Window System

SVR4 includes a complete and powerful graphical user interface (GUI), the X Window System. With its user interface standards OPEN LOOK and Motif, SVR4 will stabilize the user's view of the UNIX system, further improving the quality of development and standardizing the environment for users.

Commands

Many new commands and "traditional" UNIX system features have also been added. The **ksh** and **csh** commands are both included, job control features have been added, and multiple virtual consoles can usually be configured. Numerous other small enhancements can be found throughout the system.

Virtual File System

SVR4 supports a new file system organization that allows much improved file operations. Symbolic links allow linking across file system boundaries, memory-mapped files improve buffering and paging in system I/O operations, and memory management as a whole has been significantly improved. The VFS scheme allows numerous different file system types to be used simultaneously, and many enhancements have resulted, including the elimination of the old 14-character filename limit.

Real-Time Processes

Older versions of the UNIX system were unable to respond quickly and predictably to the real-time demands of control applications like factory automation. In SVR4, a new scheduling system allows real-time processes and micro-timers. Thus the UNIX system can now span the full range of applications from multiple-user timesharing systems to high-performance dedicated controllers.

Improved Configuration and Installation

An ongoing project in the development of SVR4 will improve the installation and configuration of the system. In the future, it should be easier to install a new system and to add new hardware and software packages to an existing system. Additions to a system should never clash with its existing parts, or the source of any conflicts should at least be indicated clearly without deranging the machine. It should also be possible to add software without stopping the system or rebooting.

Enhanced Security

Finally, system security has been extensively improved, and the UNIX system now meets many of the U. S. government security requirements. In these days of malicious attacks on computer systems, tightened security is a major feature, the importance of which must not be underestimated.

Going Further

An SVR4 system requires significantly more real memory and a larger hard disk than SVR3 or other releases. In return, SVR4 delivers a state-of-the-art system, new networking features, and better support from administration and development tools.

Microcomputer Requirements

The SVR4 system can run on almost any computer that contains sufficient real memory and a fast hard disk; however, all machines running the UNIX system require much more hardware support than those running MS-DOS, but not much more than those running MS-OS/2. Generally, at least 4MB of real memory (RAM) and at least 80MB of fast hard disk space are required in an SVR4 machine.

A fast disk is required because multiple tasks may need to be stored temporarily while another task uses the real memory. This temporary storage is usually done by *paging* parts of inactive tasks out of real memory to disk, and this can happen many times a second. Implementations of the UNIX system that use only floppy disks usually perform poorly, and are generally viewed as toys.

The large size of the hard disk is due to the very large number of commands and functions the standard UNIX system supports. A fully configured system may contain more than 40MB of stored programs and associated data. There are more than 2000 separate commands, and over 6000 files and directories in SVR4! Of course, many of these can be eliminated when the system is configured for a special purpose; add-on software such as the Standard C Development Environment and the various networking packages consume nearly one-fourth of the total disk space. If you are not doing programming, and you have a stand-alone machine, these files are not necessary. However, it is wise to have at least 80MB of hard disk space before you load an SVR4 system.

The requirement for a large real memory results from some of the powerful, yet subtle, traits of the UNIX system. The lowest level of the operating system, the *kernel*, which resides in memory and mediates all connections between user programs and the machine hardware, takes more than 1MB all by itself. The architecture also includes many *buffers,* which function much as a RAM disk does under a single-tasking operating system. Much of the system's observed speed comes from these built-in buffers, but they also take a great deal of real memory. In addition, executing programs require memory for their own use. Some large UNIX systems configured for high performance with many simultaneous users have more than 40MB of real memory. Of course, smaller personal systems can get by with much less than that, but at least 4MB is required, and 6 or 8MB is generally recommended for faster performance.

Assembling a UNIX System

Most users are not long content with the basic package they purchased from a computer dealer. As with MS-DOS, there are a great many add-on hardware and software products available for UNIX systems. Some of these, such as spreadsheet programs, word processors, or high-quality graphics packages, are geared to specific business needs. Usually, an operating system is chosen on the basis of applications that are available for it; however, the UNIX system environment encourages modifications and enhancements to some of the basic system software, and many software packages are available that substitute for the major subsystems. For example, word processors or spreadsheets and other computational tools are available, as are several additional *shell* programs, which provide the user interface to the operating system.

Also, individual vendors have frequently added to or modified the system either to customize their product, or simply because some command or subsystem could be improved. This most often occurs in three areas: First, because they have grown and changed through the history of the UNIX system, many variants of the commands exist, and individual developers or users tend to "collect" versions of commands that they like better than the standard commands. These custom programs often appear in releases that you can buy. Many times the behavior of a command on a specific release will differ slightly from the SVR4 standards. Second, the file system is frequently reorganized, often in a wholesale manner, to accommodate the specific needs of a release. Different or additional directory trees often appear, the device filenames vary, and other changes may be present. Third, vendors of UNIX systems often provide customized tools for administering the system.

Although these user agents can make the job of managing a machine much easier, they usually do so at a cost: Some of the flexibility and power that is built into the original, manual tools is often lost. These user agents often differ remarkably from each other.

If this is not complex enough, remember that all aspects of the UNIX system change over time as enhancements, modifications, and new features are incorporated into the system. Thus, Releases 4.1 and 4.2 differ in several ways from Release 4.0.

Because it is impossible to cover all these variations in a single book, we will focus on the "official" SVR4 commands and System Administration tools. These are the "vanilla," or standard, tools that appear in the System V, Release 4.0 *porting base,* as shipped from AT&T for PC-AT 80386 and 80486 machines. Where appropriate, the text indicates possible variations or areas that remain volatile between releases. In most cases the variation is in the details of command-line options or command output; few conceptual changes are made between the subreleases of SVR4, and the text of this book will always be helpful even if it is not always exactly correct. Generally, these variations occur in material that is presented in the second half of the book; the material in first half (up to Chapter 12) is usually consistent between nearly all UNIX systems that currently exist.

A Note on BSD and XENIX Compatibility

Historically the BSD releases have been significantly different from the System V releases, and over the years a great many incompatibilities have appeared. SVR4 is making a serious attempt to merge the features of these two releases. By and large this effort has been successful, especially in supporting BSD applications that have been reworked for the SVR4 environment. However, some of the BSD commands and tools provided in SVR4 act slightly differently than a BSD expert might expect. Even though full BSD compatibility is a goal of SVR4, it is still primarily a System V product, and the "intuitions" of its developers are based on System V.

Because of this focus on the System V environment, the BSD and XENIX tools are provided with special *compatibility packages* that allow system administrators to remain in System V or to add the compatibility packages if they wish. On the other hand, many functions and features of BSD and XENIX have been incorporated into the basic SVR4 release, so the compatibility packages are not always required.

Overall, XENIX compatibility has been easier to achieve than BSD compatibility, and the SVR4 system reflects this fact. Most XENIX commands and tools have been merged into the mainline system. The special XENIX compatibility package is much smaller than the equivalent BSD compatibility package.

In this book we will concentrate on the standard ways things are accomplished, without discussing the compatibility packages extensively. If you have experience with the BSD system, and standard SVR4 does not act as you expect it to, you may wish to add the BSD compatibility package to your system, and use its tools in place of the standard ones.

Tutorial

As an introduction to using the UNIX system, we will walk through a short session with the system. Some basic concepts will be introduced, and you will see some examples of how users interact with the UNIX systems. At the end of this chapter, you should be able to get into and out of the UNIX system without difficulty.

We will assume that you have already attached a terminal to a UNIX machine that has been set up by someone else, and is in use by others. Most beginners with the UNIX system start on machines administered by someone else. After learning the basics and exploring an existing system, it is much easier to set up a machine of your own. If you have a brand-new machine, however, you should probably start with Chapter 25, "Configuring a System," and then look at the first few pages of Chapter 21, "Boot and Shutdown." When you have the system up and running, you can return here.

Your terminal might be the system console, a character-oriented terminal attached directly to an RS232 port on the machine, a remote terminal connected via a telephone line and modem, or a terminal connected via a Local Area Network (LAN). It doesn't matter which kind of terminal you have, because the system usually acts the same for all of these terminal types. Terminals and their configuration are discussed in Chapter 12.

In most cases, the initial form of access is completely character oriented; no graphics or icons appear. Since the UNIX system was originally developed for "dumb" printing terminals, much of the system still assumes character-oriented terminals, and the initial stages of system access require such a terminal.

The version of the UNIX system available in English-speaking countries uses the ASCII (American Standard Code for Information Interchange) character set. Thus, IBM 3270-style terminals will not usually work with the UNIX system, and graphics terminals must provide an ASCII mode to be used with the UNIX system. To use the X Window System, the usual window-oriented interface, you must be on the system console or on an intelligent terminal attached to a network.

Logging In

Once your terminal is attached to the UNIX machine, you may have to press the RETURN or ENTER key to wake up the UNIX system. When you do, you will see the *login prompt*, which looks like this:

```
Welcome to the AT&T 386 UNIX System
System name: my_sys

login:
```

If you do not see the **login:** prompt, something is wrong; ask your system administrator for help.

Since the UNIX system is a multiuser system, the first thing you must do is identify yourself so the system can respond to you in an individual way. This gives you access to your files and establishes your session in accordance with the preferences you have selected. A unique *login id* identifies each user who can connect to the system. If you do not know your login id, ask your system administrator for help; the system administrator controls the logins allowed on each machine. Usually your login id will be your name or initials, or some whimsical identification that you choose. The only requirements are that the login id be less than eight characters long and consist only of letters and numbers. In this scheme, uppercase and lowercase characters are distinguished, so that the login id **STEVE** is not the same as the id **steve**. All login id's should have a lowercase character first; if your login id begins with an uppercase character, the UNIX system will think you are calling into the system from a terminal that supports only uppercase, and will treat you accordingly. Each login id must be unique; that is, no two users on the system can have the same id.

If you have established your login id as **steve**, for example, you would respond to the **login:** prompt as follows:

```
Welcome to the AT&T 386 UNIX System
System name: my_sys

login: steve
```

To complete your response, press RETURN. You usually cannot correct typing errors at the login prompt by backing up with the BACKSPACE key as you can during regular text entry under the UNIX system, because at this point the system has not yet identified you. The UNIX system treats the use of the BACKSPACE key to delete a character as a user preference. If you make an error in entering your login id or password, just complete the process anyway; if the login fails, the system gives you another chance.

After you have entered your login id, the UNIX system responds by requesting your individual password, as shown here:

```
login: steve
Password:
```

The system wants you to verify that you actually are the person who is authorized to use that login id. After all, your login id is usually public information, and the UNIX system wants to protect your files and other private data from other people.

Enter your individual password, and then press RETURN. Unlike your login id, the system will not display (*echo* in UNIX system jargon) the characters of your password as you type them. This is an additional security measure that prevents someone looking over your shoulder from discovering your password.

If you enter either your login id or password incorrectly, or if you are not an authorized user of the machine, the UNIX system will respond as follows:

```
Welcome to the AT&T 386 UNIX System
System name: my_sys

login: steve
Password:
Login incorrect
login:
```

The system does not tell you if the login id was entered incorrectly or if the password was wrong, but it does give you a second chance. Start over again by entering your login id, and then entering your password when you are prompted to do so.

When your login id and password pair have been accepted, you will see some initial banners and messages that look something like this:

```
UNIX System V/386 Release 4.0
my_sys
Copyright (c) 1984, 1986, 1987, 1988, 1989 AT&T
Copyright (c) 1987, 1988 Microsoft Corp.
All Rights Reserved

/         : Disk space:  61.31 MB of 144.03 MB available (42.57%).
/proc     : Disk space:   0.00 MB of   0.00 MB available ( 0.00%).
/dev/fd   : Disk space:   0.00 MB of   0.00 MB available ( 0.00%).
/stand    : Disk space:   3.04 MB of   5.22 MB available (58.16%).

Total Disk Space:  64.35 MB of 149.26 MB available (43.11%).

The my_sys system will be down for software installation
from 6:00 to 7:00 PM tonight.   =pat

news: new_user

You have mail.

$
```

The messages will probably differ on your system, but this example is typical of an active multiuser UNIX system. The first message,

```
UNIX System V/386 Release 4.0
```

is simply a banner that identifies the release of the system in use. Next comes the identification of the machine, **my _ sys**. Each UNIX system has a unique identifying name.

Following the system name are some copyright notices for the software that is installed on the machine. These notices may differ depending on who is marketing the specific UNIX system version in use, and what added software is installed on the machine. A long table of disk space and usage may follow, although this is often omitted on larger systems. We will save discussion of this output for Chapter 18.

Next comes a message placed by the system administrator called the *Message of the Day*. Your system may or may not display such a message; usually, it is only used to announce information of current interest.

The next line,

```
news: new_user
```

comes from another UNIX system feature called *news*. News is most commonly used by the system administrator to announce information of longer useful life than messages given by the Message of the Day. Once you've read the news you will no longer see the prompt at login time; the Message of the Day, on the other hand, is displayed every time you log in until the message is changed or deleted by the system administrator. The **news:** prompt also gives the subject of the news, **new _ user** in this case.

Next comes the line

```
You have mail.
```

This is a reminder that mail from another user is waiting in your mailbox. You will see this message each time you log in until you delete the mail. Unlike reading news, reading your mail does not necessarily remove the "You have mail" message from your login screen.

Finally, when the login process is complete, the system turns control over to you by printing the $ prompt. Whenever you see the $, the system is waiting for your input, which will be sent to the command processor, the *shell*.

The X Window System Display

If your login has been configured to start the X Window System when you log in, and you are using a sufficiently intelligent terminal or computer, the display will be very different from the one shown in the previous section. Instead of displaying the $ prompt, your screen will look something like Figure 2-1. Usually, there will be a Workspace menu, which is used to control your session and set your preferences, somewhere on the screen. There may be a File Manager window that looks something like the Macintosh or MS Windows display. The File Manager helps you move around in the file system.

You will probably have one or more **xterm** windows, each containing the $ shell prompt. Each of these *terminal emulator* windows allows you to use the normal UNIX system command line, for which the $ is the prompt. You may also see the Mailbox window (**xbiff**), which shows that mail is waiting with a raised flag on the mailbox icon.

The X Window System is controlled by the mouse and keyboard, and your screen will also have a mouse pointer somewhere on it. You can move the mouse to see the pointer change position. It may also change shape as you move over different areas of the screen. By moving the mouse and clicking the left button, you can make different areas or applications *active*. For example, if you move the mouse pointer to the **xterm** window and click the left button, you *select* that window, and your keystrokes are then sent to it.

The X Window System is discussed in Chapter 23. For the moment, just be sure the **xterm** window is active by moving and clicking the mouse as described. When the window is active, its top border will be highlighted in a color that contrasts with the borders of other windows on the screen. You can then execute normal UNIX system commands inside the active window.

Reading the News

The first thing you might do is read the news, since it may affect your subsequent use of the system. You read the news by entering

```
$ news
```

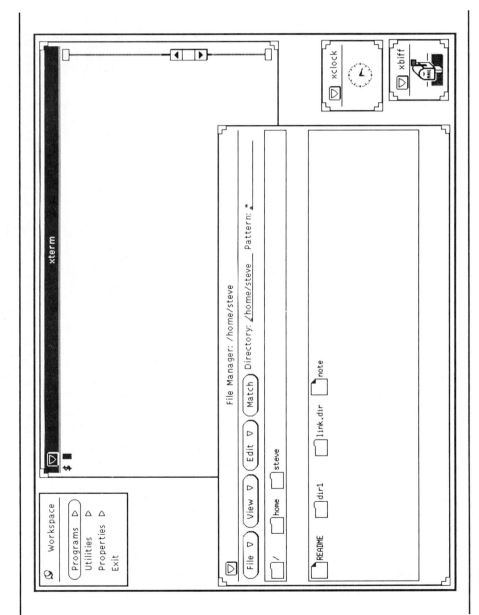

Figure 2-1. Typical startup display for the X Window System

and then pressing RETURN. The system prints the $, so you don't need to type it. Remember that uppercase and lowercase characters are different in the UNIX system; **news** and most other command names are entered in lowercase characters only. You are actually instructing the command processor—the shell—to execute a command called **news**, which looks in a standard place for news items that you have not yet seen, and then prints those items at your terminal. When you enter **news**, the response might be something like this:

```
$ news

new_user (pat) Mon Jun 22 08:26:47 1990

The 'my_sys' system has a new user!  Welcome "steve"....   =pat

$
```

If there are more news items, they will also be displayed. Each item starts with a banner line that tells the name of the news item, the login id of the author (in parentheses), and the date the item was created.

When you've read all the news, the news program ends and control returns to the shell; another $ prompt reminds you that the shell is again listening for your commands.

Listing Your Files

Next, you might look at the files that exist in your private data storage area. The UNIX system has an excellent *file system* for storing files and commands. After you log in, you are at a specific place in that file system, called your *HOME directory*. This is generally where you keep your private files and data. Each user has a personal HOME directory. This segregation of users' data means that different users can give separate files the same names without causing problems. We will examine the file system in Chapter 4.

You can list the names of your private files with the **ls** (for list) command, as shown here:

```
$ ls
note       README
$
```

Again, you enter the command name at the shell prompt $, and the **ls** command executes. When it finishes, control returns to the shell, which awaits your next command. In this case there are two files, **note** and **README**. Recall that upper- and lowercase differ, so **README** is not the same as **readme**. Since you are a new user, this small number of files is not unusual, but neither is it unusual to see up to a hundred filenames when you enter the **ls** command. There is no limit to the number of files allowed in a directory.

In many cases a new user would find no files in his or her HOME directory, and the output from the **ls** command would look like this:

```
$ ls
$
```

In this case, **ls** prints exactly nothing, and returns directly to the shell for your next command, illustrating a rather general feature of the system: if there is nothing to say, the UNIX system usually says nothing. This may seem a bit terse, if not actually rude, but there are good reasons for this silence, as you will see in the next few chapters.

The **ls** command, like most UNIX commands, has several options and features. For example, you might try

```
$ ls -l
```

Adding **-l** (minus-ell) tells the **ls** command to generate a *long* listing, one that gives much more information about a file than the simple version described previously. Usually you tell a command that you want it to do something a little different than usual by giving it an *argument*. Some arguments are signaled by the presence of a - (minus) sign in front of the argument letter. This type of argument is called a *flag,* or *option.* Leave a space after the command name, but no space between the - sign and the argument letter. The result of the previous command might be

```
$ ls -l
total 2
-rw-rw-rw-  1 steve    other        138 Apr  5 19:34 README
-rw-rw-rw-  1 steve    other        227 Apr  5 19:33 note
$
```

This listing reveals several additional facts about the files. The first entry on the left, **-rw-rw-rw-** reveals the *permissions* of the file; **steve** is the *owner* of the file, who belongs to the *group* **other**. The file *size*, in bytes, comes next followed by a *time stamp* for the file, and the last thing on the line is the *name* of the file. These and other attributes of files are discussed in Chapter 4.

Arguments in the UNIX system are similar in purpose to arguments in MS-DOS and other operating systems: they modify the function of the command. In contrast to MS-DOS arguments, however, UNIX command arguments begin with the character - (minus) rather than a / (slash). The / character has another use in the UNIX system.

Most UNIX system commands allow many arguments, and these provide a great deal of the UNIX system's power and flexibility. You can consult the *UNIX User's Manual,* the major reference document for the UNIX system, to learn the exact syntax for all the arguments to every command. Chapter 9 of this book discusses using the *UNIX User's Manual.*

Displaying a File

Now that you know your home directory contains two files, you can display the contents of these files. You use the **cat** (for concatenate files) command to display files, as follows:

```
$ cat note
```

This command illustrates another general aspect of UNIX commands: filenames are usually arguments with no - or other argument marker. This command displays the contents of the file **note** on your terminal, as shown here:

```
$ cat note

Hello, steve, and welcome to the 'my_sys' system.  We all wish
you well in your exploration of the UNIX system, and we hope that
soon you'll be giving us advice on how to better use the
UNIX system                           =pat
$
```

There are several things to notice in this example: first, that the **cat** command displays the file, and then returns directly to the $ prompt for the next command; second, the file is displayed without any extraneous headers or other material that was not in the file itself. Again, this is a characteristic of the UNIX system's terse nature that you will find very handy later.

Deleting a File

The **cat** command did not change the file, so the file is still present. You can now delete it if you wish. Use the **rm** (for remove) command to do this, as shown here:

```
$ rm note
$
```

The **rm** command silently deletes the file, and then returns to the shell for your next command. If you try **ls** again, you will see that the **note** file is gone, and the result now looks like this:

```
$ ls
README
$
```

Under the UNIX system, there is no way to recover a file once it has been deleted with **rm**. Since the **rm** command is so powerful, you might want it to prompt you for confirmation before it deletes a file. You could use the modified command **rm -i note** (the **-i** is for interactive) in place of the previous **rm** command to accomplish this, with the following result:

```
$ rm -i note
rm: remove note: (y/n)?
```

The **rm** command is prompting you to confirm that you really want the file **note** to be deleted. Enter **y** if you want to delete the file, and anything else if you don't want to delete it. In this example we'll enter **y**.

```
$ rm -i note
rm: remove note: (y/n)? y
$
```

Once again the file is deleted. If you are deleting more than one file with a single invocation of **rm -i,** you will be prompted for confirmation before each file is deleted.

You can interrupt execution of the command while it is waiting for your input if you wish to return to the shell directly; to do so, press the DEL or BREAK key on your keyboard. This stops the command's execution and returns you to the shell, as shown here:

```
$ rm -i note
rm: remove note: (y/n)? DEL
$
```

In this situation, any files that you selected for deletion (by answering **y** to the confirmation prompt) before you pressed the DEL key will be removed, but the rest will not.

This *break* action can be taken with almost any UNIX command while it is waiting for your input. You can also use this technique to stop commands that are producing too much output, or that seem to be "hung." What do you think would happen if you pressed DEL while the shell was waiting for your input at the $ prompt?

Reading Your Mail

Recall that when you logged in you saw the message

```
You have mail.
```

This message informs you that another user on the machine has sent you some *electronic mail.* If no mail is waiting, this message will not appear when you log in.

Electronic mail is similar in function to mail that you get from the post office: it allows communication between users, each person has a unique mailing address, and each message has an envelope and contents.

You can read your mail with the **mail** command, shown here:

```
$ mail
```

This instructs the shell to run the **mail** command, which looks in your *inbox* and displays each item of mail in turn at your terminal, as in this example:

```
$ mail
From jim Fri Apr  6 18:24 MST 1990
Hello, steve, welcome to the UNIX system.  Why don't we go out to
lunch today and discuss your new computer system?   -Jim

?
```

The first line of this mail item is known as the *postmark.* It tells you that the message is from **jim**, and that it was sent on **Fri Apr 6 18:24 MST 1990**. You usually won't care what time the message was sent, but the postmark can be useful, as you will see in Chapter 14.

After the message is displayed, the **mail** program pauses for your input, prompting with a **?** to let you know that it is waiting for a decision on what to do with this mail message. You can delete the message, skip to the next message (if there is one), save the message in a file, or take one of several other actions. You can delete the message by entering **d**, and pressing RETURN, or *newline,* to tell the mail program that you're through with the message, as shown here:

```
$ mail
From jim Fri Apr  6 18:24 MST 1990
Hello, steve, welcome to the UNIX system.  Why don't we go out to
lunch today and discuss your new computer system?   -Jim

? d
$
```

The **mail** program silently deletes the message. Since there is no more mail, the program then ends, and you are returned to the shell for your next command. If you had more messages in your mailbox, the next one would have been displayed after you took some action on the first message. Likewise, you can read and dispose of each message in your mailbox in one way or another.

If you are using the X Window System, you will notice that the raised flag on the mailbox window drops soon after the mail message is deleted. Because UNIX is a *multitasking* system, several things can happen simultaneously on your screen. This is normal, and the flag will be raised again soon after any new mail arrives.

The **mail** command includes some built-in help to remind you of all the options available at the **?** prompt. If you have not deleted a mail message, you can try entering **?** instead of **d** to display a list of available options, as shown in Figure 2-2. We will discuss these options in Chapter 14, but as you can see, the **mail** command provides a rich set of operators for dealing with mail messages.

Sending Mail

You may wish to reply to mail that you receive. The **mail** command is used to send as well as to read mail, as shown here:

```
$ mail jim
```

In this case, you give **mail** an argument. Unlike the flag arguments signified by a **-**, this argument tells the **mail** command the major target of the action the command will take. Here, the target is the addressee. The command **cat note** takes a filename as a major argument, because the major function of the **cat** command is to concatenate and display files. The **mail** command, on the other hand, is used to communicate with other users, so its major argument is logically the login id of a user (or users) to whom mail is directed. Most commands in the UNIX system use the login id to refer to users; thus, instead of a user's real name most commands will expect the user's login id.

```
$ mail
From jim Fri Apr  6 18:24 MST 1990
Hello, steve, welcome to the UNIX system.  Why don't we go out to
lunch today and discuss your new computer system?   -Jim

? ?
Usage:
?               print this help message
#               display message number #
-               print previous
+               next (no delete)
! cmd           execute cmd
<CR>            next (no delete)
a               position at and read newly arrived mail
d [#]           delete message # (default current message)
dp              delete current message and print the next
dq              delete current message and exit
h a             display all headers
h d             display headers of letters scheduled for deletion
h [#]           display headers around # (default current message)
m user          mail (and delete) current message to user
n               next (no delete)
P               print (override any warnings of binary content)
P               override default 'brief' mode; display ALL header lines
q, ^D           quit
r [args]        reply to (and delete) current letter via mail [args]
s [files]       save (and delete) current message (default mbox)
u [#]           undelete message # (default current message)
w [files]       save (and delete) current message without header
x               exit without changing mail
y [files]       save (and delete) current message (default mbox)

?
```

Figure 2-2.   Help from the **mail** command

Like most UNIX commands, **mail** allows more than one argument.
You could enter

```
$ mail jim steve
```

to send the same mail message both to the login id **jim** and to yourself.
If you enter this command, the **mail** program will begin executing and
then pause, waiting for you to type your mail message, which might look
like this:

```
$ mail jim steve
Jim-- thanks for your welcome and lunch invitation.
I'd love to join you for lunch.
let's get together around noon.
See you then;  Steve
```

You can type as many lines as you wish. If you make a mistake, you can back up as many characters as needed with the BACKSPACE key, up to the beginning of the current line. Once you've pressed the RETURN key, however, the UNIX system (and, in this case, the **mail** program) will have accepted your input, and you cannot easily erase it. As usual, if you wish to stop the program and return to the shell without sending the message, you can press the DEL key. What do you think happens when you do this?

Assuming you do not abort the **mail** command with the DEL key, you will eventually need to tell the command that you are through entering text. You can do this by entering CTRL-D, that is, by holding down the CTRL key and pressing the lowercase d key. Even though CTRL-D is often printed with a capital letter D, you do not need to hold down the SHIFT key; just pressing CTRL and the lowercase d key is sufficient. This tells the **mail** program that you are through entering the message, as shown in this example:

```
$ mail jim steve
Jim-- thanks for your welcome and lunch invitation.
I'd love to join you for lunch.
let's get together around noon.
See you then;  Steve
CTRL-D
You have mail.
$
```

If there are no errors, the **mail** program silently sends the message and then returns to the shell for the next command. Usually, this silent and terse behavior only holds true if there are no errors in a command's execution. No news is generally good news, and you can usually assume that if a command acts silently and returns to the shell without displaying an error message, it has probably completed successfully.

In the previous example, the shell has given you another prompt: it has repeated "You have mail." Because you sent a copy of the mail message to yourself using your own login id on the **mail** command line, the shell prompts you that new mail has arrived. You will see this prompt only once until you log in to the system again. You can always choose to ignore it and not read the mail immediately (especially if you just sent it!). The "You have mail." message appears on your terminal because the **mail** program sends it before returning to the shell, and the shell looks at your mailbox to determine if any new mail has arrived.

This happens after the **mail** program completes, but just before the shell displays the $ prompt for another command. The UNIX system often provides this kind of service, and you will occasionally see messages from the shell or from other programs that may be running in the system simultaneously. Remember, several other things may be going on in the system at the same time as your session.

The UNIX system has many additional tools for communications, both between users and between different machines. We will discuss these tools in Chapters 14 and 15.

Who's Logged In

Since the UNIX system is a multiuser system, other people may be sharing the system with you, using other terminals attached to the machine. Normally you will not be aware of these other users, since the system makes it appear that each user has the machine to him- or herself. However, there are tools that let you see who else is logged into the machine, and give you some idea what they are doing.

Another theme that runs through the design of the UNIX system is that the users of a machine form a relatively friendly group of people who can easily communicate with each other, and who can share files if necessary. The UNIX system maintains a delicate balance between the freedom of all users to wander around in the machine as a whole, and the restrictions dictated by security considerations. The UNIX system provides excellent tools to identify the security status of user login ids, systemwide administrative files and programs, and individual files. Chapter 22 covers this topic in greater detail.

You can see who is currently logged into the machine by using the **who** command, as follows:

```
$ who
```

Enter the command name as usual at the shell prompt $, and then press the RETURN (newline) key. You'll see something like this:

```
$ who
jim      console      Apr  7 14:05
steve    tty00s       Apr  7 16:41
$
```

The results appear on your terminal, and the **who** command ends, returning you to the shell prompt.

The previous output tells you that two users are currently logged in to the system, **jim** and your own login id **steve.** Some other information is also presented. First is the terminal each person is using. Your terminal, **tty00s,** refers to a remote terminal. The other user, **jim,** is using the system console, which is directly attached to the computer. The remainder of the line tells the date and time that each user logged in to the system. For example, **steve** logged in at 4:41 P.M. local time.

In a large UNIX system, there may be more than a hundred users logged in at one time; in smaller machines there may be only one. It doesn't matter; the system lets each user proceed as if he or she had exclusive use of the machine.

Changing Your Password

You can accomplish one more chore before you end this session by logging out: you can change your password. The login id and password pair form the key to security in the UNIX system. If unfriendly hands get access to these items, they can log in to the system as you, and damage your files. They can even change your password, preventing you from logging in again until the system administrator has patched up your login id; therefore, it is usually desirable to keep your password a secret, and to change it frequently. Of course, you want everyone to know your login id so that they can send you mail, and so on, but your password is like the key to your home: if it falls into the wrong hands, you may be in trouble.

Because you are a new user of this machine, the system administrator probably created your login id with a preassigned sample password. This is already a potential security breach, since most system administrators use a simple rule to generate passwords for new users. Often your login id, or some such easily detected word, will be given as a beginning password; therefore, you should change your password to a more private one as soon as you can.

If your system administrator established your new login id with no password, you probably will not see the **password:** prompt when you log in; you will gain access to the system directly from the **login:** prompt. In this case, you should add a password as soon as possible.

The user password system is designed so that no one can figure out your password unless you tell them. That is, once you've established your own private password, it is not available anywhere in the file system. It is encrypted in such a way that if you forget it, no one can tell you what it is. The only thing the system administrator can do to restore a lost password is to delete the password and assign you a new one. Although you should make every effort to remember your password, some ways of remembering are not as wise as others: for example, you might write your password on a slip of paper and attach it to your terminal, but anyone passing by could read the note and then you could be in trouble.

Think of a password for yourself that you can remember easily, but that is not easy for someone else to figure out. Usually, the system demands that passwords be at least six characters long, and contain at least one digit or other nonalphabetic character. These rules have evolved from years of experience with security considerations, and they provide a range of possibilities that is both large and complex, making it difficult for someone to guess your password.

Once you have decided on a password, you tell the system to use it from now on with the **passwd** command. Note the peculiar spelling of this command name.

```
$ passwd
passwd:  Changing password for steve
Old password:
```

The system will not let you change a password easily. You must first enter your current (old) password to convince the **passwd** program that you really are who you claim to be. Type your current password, and you'll notice that the characters are not echoed as you enter them. The UNIX system treats all passwords this way; they are never echoed as you type them. If you make a mistake, the **passwd** program will exit and return you to the shell for another try. If you enter your current password correctly, **passwd** will let you enter a new one, as shown here:

```
$ passwd
passwd:  Changing password for steve
Old password:
New password:
```

Type your new choice; again it will not be echoed. Here is what you'll see:

```
$ passwd
passwd:  Changing password for steve
Old password:
New password:
Re-enter new password:
```

Now **passwd** wants you to type your new password a second time, just to verify that you've entered it correctly. If the two entries do not match, the **passwd** command will complain, and then let you try again, as shown here:

```
$ passwd
passwd:  Changing password for steve
Old password:
New password:
Re-enter new password:
They don't match; try again.
New password:
```

If this occurs, don't worry; you haven't hurt anything, and you can enter the password again (twice!). If you press DEL now, **passwd** will exit with your old password still in force. If you enter the password the same both times, the **passwd** command will change the system's record of your password, and then return to the shell as usual to await your next command.

Logging Out

When you are through using the system, you should tell it that you are finished. This process is called *logging out*. When you log out, the UNIX system frees the terminal for someone else, or you can log in again immediately if you choose, perhaps with a different login id. Logging out has the added benefit of preventing unfriendly people from using your terminal and user id to cause mischief. It is good practice to log out whenever you leave the terminal, especially if it is in a public place like a business office. The two most important factors for maintaining the security of a UNIX system are keeping the passwords secure, and logging out of the system whenever you are not at your terminal. If your machine is physically secure, in a room that only you have access to, these rules are less important; however, you should learn good security practices early, and continue to observe them as long as you are using the system.

The logout procedure will differ depending on whether your session started in the X Window System or not. If you are in X, select the Workspace menu by clicking on it, and then click on the Exit entry. You may be prompted to confirm the exit with a *pop-up* window. If so, click on the Yes button; the X Window System will collapse, and you will probably be logged out of the system. If not, you will be left at a normal shell.

Entering **exit** within an **xterm** window, will kill the window, and make it disappear. However, the X environment as a whole does not end, and you are not logged off. If you are using X, you must select Exit from the Workspace menu to be certain you are logged off.

The UNIX system provides two ways to log out from the shell. First, the **exit** command will log you off the machine, as shown here:

```
$ exit

Welcome to the AT&T 386 UNIX System
System name: my_sys

login:
```

When you use the **exit** command the UNIX system stops execution of your shell, resets itself, and returns the terminal to the initial login prompt. You can then turn off the terminal or login again.

Instead of using the **exit** command, you can log off the machine by pressing CTRL-D. This is the *end-of-file* mark, and the shell interprets it as a signal to log off. We will discuss the use of the end-of-file mark in Chapter 3.

Some UNIX systems are configured so that turning off the power on your terminal or console also logs you off the system. Usually, terminals connected to the machine through dial-up telephone lines and modems act this way. However, until you are sure about your machine's behavior, you should always log off explicitly before you hang up the telephone line or turn off the power on the terminal.

Going Further

At a terminal, you end commands or other text lines by pressing RETURN. In UNIX system jargon, the symbol used to end a line of text is the *newline* character. For the rest of this book, we will use the term newline to indicate the end-of-line key.

Usually at a terminal the RETURN key acts like newline, but in fact the ASCII character for newline is the *linefeed* character. You can experiment with your terminal and system by ending a line of text with linefeed (CTRL-J) instead of RETURN. Does the system act the same?

Controlling Output to the Terminal

Sometimes you will find that a command's output contains more lines than your screen (or your **xterm** window) can display. In this case, the output will *scroll* off the top of the screen before you can read it. The UNIX system provides two tools that help you control this output. First is the **more** command, which allows you to step through output one screenful at a time. Chapter 7 discusses the **more** command and its use. The second procedure can be used when you have not planned ahead and used the **more** command. Just press CTRL-S to stop output immediately, and CTRL-Q to restart it. You can stop and start the output as often as necessary using this procedure, but be sure that you use CTRL-Q *last*, or your terminal will appear to be frozen.

Introduction to the Shell

**T
H
R
E
E**

The *shell* is the program that listens to commands entered from the terminal, and translates those typed commands into instructions in the system's internal syntax. The name "shell" really describes the function: It is hard material that stands between the core of the system and the outside world, providing a robust *user interface* for the operating system. The shell includes an unusually large number of functions; in fact, it implements some of the most powerful and elegant concepts in the UNIX system. A great deal of development effort has been spent on improvements to the shell and on new versions of the shell for special purposes. The shell is so important that usually it isn't even considered apart from the system as a whole. Many capabilities and functions come from services provided by the shell. In this chapter we examine more functions of the UNIX system, focusing primarily on services provided by the shell.

Commands in the UNIX System

Usually commands are separate executable programs, such as **mail** and **who**, which the shell finds and executes in response to typed instructions. However, the shell is far more than just a means of passing commands to the system for execution; the shell helps you use the machine.

First and foremost, the shell is a *command interpreter* that can expand and change commands, according to the shell's built-in rules, before they are executed. Equally important are wildcard and command connection operators that can make a command line more general and flexible. Also, commands can take advantage of conditions in the current user environment—managed by the shell—to modify the way they work.

Command Structure

When you type a command such as **cat** to the shell, you will frequently add *command-line arguments*. These can be modifying *flags* that usually begin with a - (minus) as well as major arguments like filenames or other user login ids. Commands are of this form:

```
$ pr -d note
```

The **pr** command is used to "print" files. Actually the output goes to the terminal rather than to a printer, so **pr** is something like the **cat** command. The **cat** command is better at concatenating multiple files, while **pr** is better at arranging files in pages and columns.

In the UNIX system command syntax, flags follow the command name, and precede the major arguments. The previous command tells **pr** to copy the file **note** to the terminal, making a double-spaced copy of the input file. A filename is given as a major argument, and the function of the command is modified with a flag (**-d** in this case, to indicate double spacing). Neither the flag nor the filename argument is required for most commands.

You can add a second flag to the **pr** command, as shown here:

```
$ pr -n -d note
```

This command tells **pr** to generate both double-spaced (**-d**) and line-numbered (**-n**) output. All flags precede all filename arguments. An equivalent form of the previous command is

```
$ pr -nd note
```

You can combine flags, using a single - to mark the beginning of the flags.

The previous example produces a double-spaced listing at the terminal with line numbers beginning 1, 2, 3, 4.... You can use the same command to produce output with line numbers 1, 3, 5, 7..., as follows:

```
$ pr -n2 -d note
```

As you can see, the **-n** flag of the **pr** command can have an argument of its own, which determines the interval between the numbers it assigns each line. So, you use **pr -n2** to count lines by two's rather than by one's. You could also use one of these alternate forms:

```
$ pr -n2 -d note
$ pr -d -n2 note
$ pr -d -n 2 note
$ pr -d          -n 2     note
$ pr -dn2 note
```

All of these commands are equivalent, because the system does not care about the order of flag arguments, or whether each flag has its own - sign, or whether there are extra spaces between the flags. The following forms, however, would not perform as you expected.

```
$ pr - n2 -d note
$ pr -nd2 note
$ pr note -nd2
```

You must place the - directly in front of the flag argument, with no intervening space, and you must place the flags (if any) before any filename arguments. Also, you must make sure that the argument modifying a flag, such as the 2 in this example, is next to the flag it modifies.

Generally when you make mistakes such as these, the command responds with a message reminding you of the correct form, but sometimes a mistake is subtle, and the command executes incorrectly. Usually that doesn't hurt anything.

You can add a second filename to the **pr** command as follows:

```
$ pr note README
```

The filenames are listed on the same command line, separated by whitespace characters (or just *whitespace*). Whitespace characters are simply spaces or tab characters. You always need at least one whitespace character to separate arguments, but more than one is also acceptable.

Look at these three commands:

```
$ pr -dl note README
$ cat note
$ pr -d -l 2 README
```

The first has three arguments and the second has one argument. Arguments are counted from the command—**pr** in this case. The **pr** command is said to be *argument zero* of the command entered to the shell, while **-dl** is the first argument, and the two filenames are the second and third, respectively. The third command in the previous set shows **pr** with four arguments, even though the 2 is associated with the **-l** flag. Arguments must be separated by whitespace, so the command

```
$ pr -d -l 2 README
```

is a **pr** command that has four arguments, of which two are flags, one is associated with a flag, and the last is a filename.

Many commands accept multiple filenames as arguments. Compare the output from the command

```
$ pr note README
```

with the output from:

```
$ cat note README
```

The differences arise from the different functions associated with the two commands. The **cat** command is designed to concatenate files, so the two files seem to run together in the output. The **pr** command is intended primarily to paginate files, so the header material it produces is associated with each filename in turn.

Command-Line Expansion

The shell provides tools that make it easy to specify multiple filenames as command arguments. There are three special characters, called *wildcard* operators, that can substitute for filenames or parts of filenames.

In the sample directory containing the files **note** and **README**, the command

```
$ cat *
```

is equivalent to **cat note README**. That is, the asterisk (*) character tells the shell to take all the files in the directory. Actually the shell looks at the filenames, rebuilds the command line with the full names in place of the wildcard operator, and then executes the command.

The * wildcard operator can also be embedded within a partial filename. For example,

```
$ cat RE*
```

will concatenate all files that begin with "RE," and

```
$ cat *AD*
```

will concatenate all files that contain "AD" in their names. Unlike the * wildcard character in MS-DOS filenames, which can substitute for the name section of the filename *or* for the extension section but not for both, the * in the shell can substitute for any character sequence in the command.

The second wildcard operator is the question mark (?). The ? substitutes for any single character in a filename. For example,

```
$ cat ?EADME
```

would display the **README** file, as would the command

```
$ cat ?E?DME
```

However,

```
$ cat R?DME
```

would not find the file, since the **?** can only substitute for a single character.

The third wildcard operator specifies a list of characters that can match a character in a filename. This is like the **?** operator but limits the match to a selected set of characters. Left and right square brackets ([ ]) can enclose a list of characters that can be matched at that point in the filename, as shown here:

```
$ cat REA[BCD]ME
```

This would display all the files REABME, REACME, and README if they exist. The square brackets act like **?** to match only one character in the filename. Multiple characters can be matched with multiple square bracket operators, as in this command:

```
$ cat [RST][Ee]ADM[AE]
```

This example can match quite a few filenames.

You can mix these wildcard operators in the same command, as in this example:

```
$ ls ??A*
```

This command would list the names of all the files that have the character *A* in the third position in the filename.

The previous example would also find a file named **REA**. Actually the wildcard character ***** tells the shell to substitute all strings of zero or more characters. On the other hand, **?** must match a real character in the filename. The command

```
$ ls README?
```

would not find the file **README**, but

```
$ ls README*
```

would find it. Similarly, the square brackets require that exactly one character at that position in the filename match the named list; if no files are found with a listed character at that position in the name, then no files are expanded into the command line.

Environment Variables

Another service provided by the shell is the maintenance of environment variables. *Environment variables* are character strings of the form *name=value*, where *name* can be any character string that does not include a dollar ($) sign and does not have embedded whitespace, and *value* can be any character string including spaces. There are usually many environment variables associated with your login id, although these vary depending on the system, the installed software, and your personal preferences.

   An environment variable is set by giving the *name=value* pair to the shell, as shown here:

```
$ SAMPLE="hello world"
```

The shell recognizes this command as the definition of an environment variable, and it remembers the name and value. Notice that it is a convention to use uppercase characters in spelling the names of environment variables, but this is not required. Immediately after the name, without inserting any intervening whitespace, add an = sign, and then enter the value you wish. Because it includes a space, you need to *quote* the value section of this assignment by surrounding it with the double quote (") character. The use of double quotes is discussed in detail later in this chapter.

   You don't need to predefine or declare the name of an environment variable before you use it. The shell will determine whether or not the name is already in use. If it is in use, the shell will change the value of that environment variable to the new value, and the old value will be discarded. If the name is not already in use, the shell will create it for you.

When you want to use the value of an environment variable, give its name beginning with a $. This lets the shell know that the following string is an environment variable, and tells the shell to take the variable's value; otherwise the shell would interpret the string as a simple character string.

You can use the **echo** command to display the value of an environment variable, as shown here:

```
$ echo $SAMPLE
```

This command tells the shell to write the value of the environment variable to the terminal, as shown here:

```
$ echo $SAMPLE
hello world
$
```

Think about what would happen if you entered the command like this:

```
$ echo SAMPLE
```

You can use environment variables as command names or as command arguments, as shown in this example:

```
$ XYZ="cat note"
$ $XYZ
Hello, steve, and welcome to the 'my_sys' system.  We all wish
you well in your exploration of the UNIX system, and we hope that
soon you'll be giving us advice on how to better use the
UNIX system                           =pat
$
```

Before executing your command, the shell substitutes the value assigned to the name into your command line. You can use this mechanism to link a long but frequently used command with a short environment variable. Be sure to begin the variable with a $ when you use it, so that it is interpreted by the shell.

The **echo** command can also be used to echo arbitrary strings to the terminal, as in this example:

```
$ echo hello $SAMPLE world
hello hello world world
$
```

You could also embed the environment variable inside another character string, as shown here:

```
$ echo hello${SAMPLE}world
hellohello worldworld
$
```

Since the shell doesn't know whether you mean the environment variable $SAMPLE or $SAMPLEworld, you must protect the name SAMPLE when it is not surrounded by whitespace. The *curly braces* do this when they come immediately after a $. The shell usually ignores undefined environment variables; see what happens when you enter

```
$ echo hello$SAMPLEworld
```

There are usually 10 to 30 more-or-less permanent environment variables associated with your login id. These are normally assigned by the system when you log in, and are maintained by the shell until you log off. Some of these permanent environment variables are used directly by the shell, and others may be used by specific application packages for their own purposes. You can examine all your currently assigned environment variables with this command:

```
$ env
```

The **env** command displays a complete list of currently defined environment variables, each in the form *name=value,* as shown here:

```
$ env
LOGDIR=/home/steve
HOME=/home/steve
SHELL=/usr/bin/ksh
MAIL=/var/mail/steve
EDITOR=/usr/bin/vi
LOGNAME=steve
```

```
TERM=xterm
PATH=:/home/steve/lib:/sbin:/usr/sbin:/usr/bin:/usr/X/bin:/usr/ucb
TZ=MST7MDT
$
```

Your list may have many more entries than this one has.

You can add or change environment variables as you wish, but be careful not to change the value of existing environment variables, because they may be used in commands or applications. Before you use an environment variable name for the first time, you should check to see whether it is already in use. If you try to echo the value of a nonexistent environment variable, the shell will display nothing, as shown here:

```
$ echo $ISANY

$
```

This response tells you that you can use the environment variable for your own purposes.

Quoting Command-Line Arguments

The shell will interpret a character string that includes embedded whitespace as multiple arguments, because it uses whitespace as a delimiter to divide up the command line. Here is an example:

```
$ SAMPLE=hello world
world: not found
$
```

The error message that follows the assignment of the environment variable SAMPLE results from the fact that the shell interpreted the string "hello world" as two separate arguments. Since the *name = value* pair of the environment variable assignment requires that the value be a single argument, the shell assigns it the value hello. Then the shell goes on and tries to interpret the next argument, world, as a command to be executed. Since no **world** command exists, the shell complains that it cannot find the command, and the command line is discarded.

You can solve this problem by *quoting* the value—surrounding the string you wish to protect with the double quote (") character, as shown here:

```
$ SAMPLE="hello world"
$ echo $SAMPLE
hello world
$
```

Quoting forces the string to be treated as a single argument. You can use quotes on any argument to a command, since command-line arguments are processed by the shell, and the shell interprets the quote operator.

Environment variables within quoted strings are not protected from interpretation by the shell. You can take advantage of this fact to construct command-line arguments that include both environment variables and embedded whitespace, as in this example:

```
$ SAMPLE="My login id is $LOGNAME"
$ echo $SAMPLE
My login id is steve
$
```

On the other hand, you may wish to prevent the evaluation of an environment variable, but include its name in the command line. The shell allows you to do this by using the single quote (') instead of the double quote. For example:

```
$ SAMPLE='Use $LOGNAME to determine my login id'
$ echo $SAMPLE
Use $LOGNAME to determine my login id
$
```

You can also quote your command-line arguments with single quotes if you wish to have an embedded double quote character, as shown here:

```
$ echo '"hello world"'
"hello world"
$
```

In this example the double quotes are no longer shell operators, because they are protected by the single quotes. Instead, they will be treated as part of the character string that you wish to echo.

PS1

Some environment variables that are used by the shell may not appear in the output of the **env** command. One of these is PS1 (for prompt symbol, level one). PS1 is the value of your shell prompt, which until this point has been a $. You can check the shell prompt's value with the **echo** command, as follows:

```
$ echo $PS1
$
$
```

In this example, the echo command has displayed the value of the prompt, and the shell has printed it to signal that it is ready for the next command.

You can change the value of PS1 just as you can any other environment variable. Here is an example:

```
$ PS1="hello: "
hello:
```

Now the shell prompt is no longer $ but the new value that you just assigned, hello:. You can change your prompt to any character string that you wish.

Environment variables are evaluated when they are entered, not when they are executed. For example:

```
$ SAMPLE="Your command master: "
$ PS1=$SAMPLE
Your command master: SAMPLE=hello
Your command master: echo $SAMPLE
hello
Your command master:
```

Here, PS1 was set to the value of SAMPLE, but when you changed SAMPLE, $PS1 did not change. The shell evaluated the command to set PS1 to $SAMPLE when the value assigned to $SAMPLE was "Your command master: ". Thus, that phrase became the new value of PS1, not the value assigned to SAMPLE when $PS1 was printed.

Standard Input and Output

So far, you have entered commands by typing them at the terminal, and the output of the commands has been displayed at the terminal. Actually most commands take input from any input stream and write their output on an output stream. That is, the commands are implemented such that they read as input a sequence of characters, and produce a sequence of characters as output. These input and output character sequences are called *streams* because they have no internal structure. The command merely sees a long sequence of characters as input. Even the newline character is not treated differently, although some commands (like the shell) take action on character sequences that end with a newline. The input stream for a command is called *standard input* and the output stream is called *standard output.* For example, the command

```
$ echo $PS1
```

writes to standard output.

Usually, the shell arranges things so that the standard input of a command comes from the terminal keyboard and the standard output goes to the terminal display. However, you can *redirect* standard input and standard output to a file, as shown in this example:

```
$ cat note > n.copy
$
```

The right angle bracket (>) is used to tell the shell to redirect standard output to a file, in this case to one named **n.copy**. The shell will create the file if it does not exist, or will empty an existing file before writing the command output to it. You can easily destroy an existing file this way, so be careful when you are redirecting output.

You can also redirect standard input to come from a file instead of from the terminal by using the left angle bracket (<) symbol, as follows:

```
$ mail jim < note
$
```

In this example, the content of the file **note** is used as input to the command **mail jim**. As a result, Jim will receive the file in his electronic mail. This achieves the same effect as executing the command **mail jim** and typing the contents of the file **note** at the keyboard.

You can redirect both standard input and standard output at the same time, as shown here:

```
$ pr < note > n.copy
$
```

This example causes the shell to execute the **pr** command with the file **note** as input, and to send the output to the file **n.copy**. Notice that the shell requires the command name to come first on the line, with the redirection operators following. You could also write any of the following commands:

```
$ pr > n.copy < note
$ pr >n.copy <note
$ pr <note >n.copy
$ pr >n.copy<note
```

However, the form

```
$ n.copy > pr < note
```

is incorrect. It is good practice to separate redirection operators from command names and arguments with blanks, but this is not required. Note that you can also use an environment variable if you wish, as shown here:

```
$ SAMPLE=note
$ pr < $SAMPLE > n.copy
$
```

Standard I/O and stream redirection are among the most general and powerful features of the UNIX system, and they have some important implications. First, most commands are designed to work with simple byte streams as input and output in order to make redirection as powerful as possible. Almost all files are simple streams of bytes, with no internal structure as is seen in record-oriented file systems. The meaning of a file is determined solely by the application or the user who uses the file, and is not enforced by any property of the UNIX system. Since most commands use standard input and standard output, there are consistent and reliable ways of using I/O. In most cases, you can usually interchange the keyboard, files, and hardware devices in your commands.

Some commands allow you to give filenames as arguments instead of requiring you to redirect standard input from a file to the command. This is a property of the commands, and is not enforced by the operating system or the shell, so it does not always work. For example, the two commands

```
$ cat < note
$ cat note
```

are equivalent, because the **cat** command operates on a file or on its standard input. Like many commands, **cat** lets you mix both files and standard input in the same command.

These forms are also equivalent:

```
$ cat note README n.copy
$ cat note - n.copy < README
```

The - (minus) alone as an argument, with no flag letter attached, is often used in commands to signify "take the standard input at this point." In the second example of the previous set, **cat** processes the file **note**, takes the standard input, which was redirected from the file **README,** and then processes the file **n.copy.**

Similarly, the command

```
$ cat note - n.copy > output
```

would process the file **note,** wait for your input from the keyboard, and then process the file **n.copy.** Since you did not redirect the standard input in this case, the shell would leave it attached to the keyboard.

The End-of-File Mark

When you use the keyboard as standard input, you must tell commands like **cat** that you are through entering characters, so the command can continue its work as if the "file" you entered through the keyboard had ended. The UNIX system provides a special character that functions as an *end-of-file* mark when it is the first character on a line.

This character does not appear at the end of a disk file, because the system can tell when a disk file ends. However, when you are using the keyboard as a "file," the system doesn't know when you are through unless you tell it. The CTRL-D character is used as the end-of-file symbol when it is entered from the keyboard right after a newline. You form this character by holding down the CTRL key and pressing the lowercase d key.

Given the command:

```
$ cat note - n.copy > output
```

cat will process the file **note,** wait for input from the terminal, read your typed input until you enter CTRL-D, and then go on to process the file **n.copy.** All three sources of input will be joined in the file **output.**

Appending Standard Output to a File

Because the > operator causes an existing file to be emptied and recreated, the original contents of the file are lost. Sometimes you may want the output of a command added to the end of an existing file. There are several ways to accomplish this. The command sequence

```
$ pr < note > n.copy
$ cat note n.copy > dup.note
$ rm n.copy
$
```

will result in the file **dup.note** containing both the original **note** and the one produced by the **pr** command. Another way to accomplish the same thing is with the operator >>. Like >, >> tells the shell to redirect standard output to a file, but instead of replacing the file's original content, it adds the new characters onto the end of the file. The sequence

```
$ cat note > dup.note
$ pr note >> dup.note
$
```

produces the same result as the previous example, but with one less command. If the file given as a target to the >> operator does not exist, it will be created. Note that no whitespace can intervene between the > characters in the >> operator. There is no equivalent << operator for standard input.

Standard Error

We have discussed standard input and standard output of commands, but the system also provides a third stream: *standard error*. Most commands use the standard error stream to display any error messages or unusual output that shouldn't appear in the standard output stream. You don't want error messages mixed with normal output, so the system writes these messages on another stream. You will see standard error in operation if you intentionally create an incorrect command. For example, if you try to use **cat** on a file that does not exist, you will see the following error message:

```
$ cat no.file
cat: cannot open no.file
$
```

Now redirect the standard output of the **cat** command, as follows:

```
$ cat no.file > output
cat: cannot open no.file
$
```

The file **output** will be created in your directory, but it will be empty. The error message still appears at the terminal, because it is written to the standard error stream. You can redirect standard error by using the operator 2> or 2>>, depending on whether you want to create a new file or to append data to an existing file, respectively. Here is an example:

```
$ cat no.file 2> output
$ cat output
cat: cannot open no.file
$
```

The peculiar notation **2>** is used because standard I/O channels are assigned numbers: 0 refers to standard input, 1 refers to standard output, and 2 refers to standard error. These numbers are primarily used by programmers in developing software, but in this case the number 2 has crept into user-level shell access.

Pipes

You will often find that you wish to use the output of one command as the input to another command. For example, you might use this command sequence:

```
$ cat note README > temp
$ pr < temp > output
$ rm temp
$
```

You may not be interested in saving the intermediate file, but you want the output of the **cat** command to be used as the input to the **pr** command. While the previous command sequence will work, the shell provides a more powerful and elegant operator for this purpose: the *pipe* (|) operator. A command line built with the pipe operator is known as a *pipeline*. Use the | operator to tell the shell that you wish the output of one command to be used as the input to another command. For example, the command

```
$ cat note README | pr > output
$
```

will concatenate the files **note** and **README,** and use the standard output as the standard input to the **pr** command. The standard output of **pr** will go to the file **output,** since it has been redirected.

There are other command lines that accomplish the same function. You could have redirected the input to **cat** with this command:

```
$ cat - README < note | pr > output
$
```

You can read this last example as two commands separated by the | operator: **cat - README < note** and **pr > output**. The standard output of the first command is attached to the standard input of the second. Redirection is local to the part of the pipeline where it appears, so the following command is not equivalent to the previous one.

```
$ cat - README | pr > output  < note
```

In most cases standard input goes into the beginning of a pipeline (reading from left to right on the command line), and standard output emerges from the end, or right-hand side, of the pipeline. However, a command line must always begin with a legal command. This command is incorrect:

```
$ note > cat - README | pr > output
```

Also, note that the | operator only connects commands; you must use the > and < operators to redirect data files. Thus, the command

```
$ note | cat - README | pr > output
```

is also incorrect, unless you have a **note** command in your system!

Filters

The pipeline is not limited to two commands. You can build pipelines of any length, just by attaching the standard output of one command to the standard input of the next. The UNIX system includes many commands that are intended to be used in this way. These commands are often called *filters*, since they pass their input to their output, changing it on its way through the program. The particular changes made by a filter program depend on the program itself.

The **tr** (for translate characters) program is a classic example of a filter. The program takes two arguments, which are interpreted as sets of characters (not as character strings this time). The **tr** program copies its standard input to its output, but replaces each character in the character set given as the first argument, with the character in the same position in the second argument, as shown here:

```
$ echo "hello world" | tr e 3
h3llo world
$
```

The **tr** command is unusual, because it will not take a filename for its input, but can only read its own standard input. This example is a little trickier than the previous one:

```
$ echo "hello world" | tr eo 34
h3114 w4rld
$
```

Fields and Delimiters

A more useful command, which is often used as a filter, is **cut.** The **cut** command copies only certain parts of each line of its standard input to its output. A *field* of a line is a string of characters separated by a fixed *delimiter* character. The UNIX system uses several field delimiter characters in different situations. Three characters that are commonly used as delimiters are the tab, the space, and the colon. The combination \t signifies the tab character in printed text like this book, but to create the tab character you press the TAB key on the keyboard. The way fields are arranged on a line is similar to the way you count arguments in commands to the shell, but in the latter case the field delimiter is always a whitespace character. In other situations, the colon (:) is used as a delimiter.

The **cut** command is used to copy only selected fields of an input line to the output. In creating a command line for the **cut** command, you must tell it which field or fields to copy to the output, and what character to use as a delimiter between the fields on the input line. You might consider the following file as a set of data *records*, with one record on each line.

```
$ cat datafile
123:543:654:234
987:753:123:765
435:765:135:963
$
```

Each record in this example consists of four fields separated by the : delimiter, and the end of a line delimits each record. If you needed to use the : as a character within a field, you would choose a different delimiter character. You must select the delimiter character carefully, to be sure that it will not appear in the data.

You can use the **cut** command to show only part of the data in this simple *database*. If you want to see only the second field on each line, use this command line:

```
$ cut -f2 -d: < datafile
```

The **-d** (for delimiter) argument tells the **cut** command to use the : character as a delimiter, and the **-f** (for field) argument tells **cut** that you wish to copy only the second field to the output. Here is the result:

```
$ cut -f2 -d: < datafile
543
753
765
$
```

Notice that the delimiter character is not included in the output, and that each line of input produces one line of output.

The **cut** command will also let you save more than one field of your input lines, as in this example:

```
$ cut -f1,2,4 -d: < datafile
123:543:234
987:753:765
435:765:963
$
```

Here, fields one, two, and four of the input file have been selected, cutting out field three. The fields are selected with the **-f1,2,4** argument; each field that you wish to copy is listed, and the fields are separated with commas. In the output, the fields are separated with the original delimiter, the colon.

You can also change the delimiter character. What would happen if you used the character 3 as a delimiter? The system will let you do this if you wish, since there is nothing special about any character; using the : as a delimiter in the previous example was simply a *convention,* an agreement to be consistent in some area. Many commands use the : as a delimiter, but you will often find reasons to use different or multiple delimiters, for example:

```
$ cat datafile
123:543:654:234
987:753:123:765
435:765:135:963
$ cut -f2 -d3 < datafile
:54
:12
5:765:1
$
```

The output may look a little confusing, but you can understand it if you read the line

```
123:543:654:234
```

as four fields separated by the 3 character: 12, :54, :654:2, and 4. Again, in the UNIX system, files are just streams of characters; the system does not enforce any special structure on data.

The **cut** command can also cut its input lines based on the columns that a field occupies. The word *column* is a holdover from the days when data was stored on punched cards, each of which had 80 columns (which also accounts for most terminals having 80 character positions on a line). We still refer to lines of input as having columns, even though the system treats data as a stream of characters with no intrinsic column positions. As another convention, we agree that the newline character in the input stream tells us to begin counting columns and continue until we see the next newline character.

You can create a **cut** command that operates on fields in columns. Here is an example:

```
$ cut -c5-8 datafile
```

Notice that the **cut** command can take a filename or list of filenames as a command line argument, as well as reading its own standard input. The previous example uses the **-c5-8** (for column) argument to select columns five through eight of the input file as one field. You mark the range of a field with - (dash). The result of the previous command is shown here:

```
$ cat datafile
123:543:654:234
987:753:123:765
435:765:135:963
$ cut -c5-8 datafile
543:
753:
765:
$
```

Again, the **cut** command is counting column positions in each line of the file, so the : has no special meaning in this example.

Another commonly used filter is the **sort** command. This command is used to rearrange its input lines into an alphabetic or numeric sequence, as follows:

```
$ sort < datafile
123:543:654:234
435:765:135:963
987:753:123:765
```

The **sort** command does not change the content of each line, but it does rearrange the lines into alphabetic or numeric order. By default, **sort** sorts a file using the beginning of the line as the *key field*, the character string that is used to alphabetize the lines. However, **sort** will let you use any field in the file as the key field, and the field detection rules are similar to those for the **cut** command. The **sort** command is discussed in detail in Chapter 7.

You can combine **cut** and **sort** in a pipeline to achieve many purposes. You can use them, for example, to list the names of all your environment variables in alphabetical order, as shown here:

```
$ env | cut -f1 -d= | sort
EDITOR
HOME
LOGDIR
LOGNAME
MAIL
PATH
SHELL
TERM
TZ
$
```

In this example, the = was used as a field delimiter. The **cut** command cut the name part out of each *name = value* environment variable, and then sorted the names into alphabetical order. Since it was not redirected, the output was sent to standard output; that is, to the terminal.

Many filters are intended to be the last element of a pipeline. A good example is the **more** command, which prevents output that is directed to the screen from scrolling off the screen before it can be viewed. The function of the **more** filter is to break the output into screen-sized chunks. It displays a screenful, and then pauses, displaying the message "--More--" at the bottom of each screen. When you press the SPACEBAR, **more** displays another screenful. This process continues until the output reaches its end-of-file, when **more** returns to the shell for the next command. The **more** command was adapted to form another similar command called **pg** (for pager). Your system may have one or both of these commands. To see **more** in action, try to display a file that is longer than a single screenful, as in this example:

```
$ cat /etc/profile | more
```

If you want to stop the **more** program before it has completed, press the lowercase q (for quit) or the DEL key to return to the shell immediately when **more** pauses.

You can make a pipeline as long as you wish. Many pipelines contain more than five or six commands, and a great many commands are designed to be used as filters. You can develop fairly sophisticated applications using only sequences of pipelines, but the major benefit of stream files, standard I/O, redirection of I/O, and command pipelines is that these features allow you to create solutions to file-related or data-related problems easily and quickly at the terminal. The previous example of listing, cutting, and sorting your environment variables, might have required the development of an application program in BASIC, C, or Pascal in another operating system. In the UNIX system, many of your ad hoc questions and problems can be solved with pipelines of commands that operate on data files consisting of character streams and text lines.

Return Values from Commands

In addition to their standard output and standard error, commands return a numeric *return code* to the shell. This return code is not displayed. The value is usually zero if the command completes successfully, and some nonzero value if the command fails for any reason. The nonzero values are command-dependent; they can range from 1 through 255. Usually different possible reasons for the failure of a command are associated with different return codes. You can see the return code's value by using the variable $?, which is reset after each command to be the return value of that command. Thus, if you wish to save the return code value for a command, you must assign it to a new environment variable. This assignment actually causes the value of $? to change, but luckily not until after it has been assigned to your "safe" new environment variable. Here is an example:

```
$ cat no.file
cat: cannot open no.file
$ SAVE=$?
$ echo $?
0
$ echo $SAVE
2
$
```

In this sequence, only the return value from the very last command executed is saved in the $? variable.

Actually, $? is not an environment variable like those discussed previously; it belongs to another class of object called *shell variables.* These variables are not available to executed commands as true environment variables are; rather they are maintained internally by the shell. Shell variables have single character names, but as usual, when you want to see their value you must precede the name with a $. In addition to ?, there are several other shell variables, including the pound sign (#), which gives the number of command-line arguments for this shell, and the $, which gives the process number of this shell. You use $$ to access the value of the shell variable $. Chapter 8 discusses these shell variables in more detail.

The Grave Operator

You can also assign the standard output of a command to an environment variable by using the grave or backquote (`) operator. You must take care when you do this, because the length of the value part of the *name = value* pair that makes up an environment variable is limited, although this limit is usually more than 5120 characters in SVR4. Here is an example:

```
$ SAMPLE=`echo $LOGNAME`
```

This line assigns the standard output of the command **echo $LOGNAME** to the environment variable SAMPLE, as shown here:

```
$ SAMPLE=`echo $LOGNAME`
$ echo $SAMPLE
steve
$
```

Note that the grave character is not the same as the single quote character; it is a separate character, often located in the upper-left corner of the ASCII keyboard.

A good example of how to use the ` operator to advantage involves the command **wc** (for word count). The **wc** command is a filter that reads its standard input (or a filename given as an argument) and produces a count of the number of lines, words, and characters in the input. Words are character strings surrounded by whitespace. Here is an example:

```
$ wc note
      4      44     227 note
$
```

The file **note** contains 4 lines, with 44 words and a total of 227 characters. The command

```
$ wc < note
```

or the command

```
$ cat note | wc
```

would give the same result, except the output would not include the filename because no filename was given as an argument to **wc**. Thus, your result would look like this:

```
$ cat note | wc
      4      44     227
$
```

The **wc** command can take three arguments: **-l, -w,** and **-c,** which limit the output to lines, words, or characters, respectively, as in the following:

```
$ wc -w < note
     44
$
```

You might use this form as the end of a pipeline, and assign the result to an environment variable for later use, as shown here:

```
$ ALLWORDS=`cat * | wc -w`
$ echo $ALLWORDS
73
$
```

In this example you created the pipeline **cat * | wc -w**, and assigned the standard output to the environment variable ALLWORDS. Recall that the * character is expanded by the shell to refer to all filenames in the relevant directory before the command is executed.

Going Further

The functions of the shell discussed in this chapter include most of the fundamental tools that the shell provides to the user. However, the shell is actually a powerful programming language that lets you easily build useful tools from its commands. Shell programming is often practiced by users and is also used to implement key operating system functions. Chapters 8 and 16 discuss using the shell as a programming language.

Command Sequences

The shell offers several more operators for combining commands into a command line. You can use the semicolon (;) operator to put two or more commands on the same command line. Unlike the pipe operator, the ; doesn't connect the commands; instead, it separates independent commands that happen to be on the same line, as in this example:

```
$ ls ; echo hello
README    note
hello
$
```

As you can see, the output of the **echo** command directly follows the output of the **ls** command at your terminal. You could also use this form:

```
$ SAMPLE=`ls ; echo hello`
$ echo $SAMPLE
README note hello
$
```

Here, the environment variable SAMPLE contains a list of the names of your files, and the **echo** command adds a name that is not an existing

file. The return value from a command sequence separated with the ;
operator is the value of the last command entered, in this example the
echo command. There are a great many uses for command sequences,
as you will see in later chapters.

Shell Redirection

The shell is known by the name **sh** (for shell). Since **sh** is a normal
command like any other, you can execute it just as you can any other
command. The instance of the shell that receives your commands as you
type them is called your *login shell,* since it starts when you log in and
ends when you log out. Its standard input is attached to your keyboard
when you log in, and its standard output is attached to your terminal's
display. If you wish, you can execute another instance of the shell as a
command, as follows:

```
$ sh
```

When you do this, you *recursively* create a second copy of the shell that
now receives and executes commands in place of the login shell. However, the login shell is still around, waiting patiently for the current
command (another instance of the shell!) to end so that it can go back to
work. You can end the second shell with the **exit** command, and you'll
be returned to the original shell, or you can end it by pressing CTRL-D as
an end-of-file for the input to that shell. Then you must kill your login
shell when you want to log off. When you have a second shell, it still
prints the PS1 prompt, so it can be very difficult to determine which
shell is in control (unless you change your PS1 prompt). You can take
advantage of this feature if you wish to use a different shell than the one
you get when you log in, perhaps a shell that allows you to edit a
command line before you hit the RETURN key to execute it. We'll see
examples of this technique with the Korn and C Shells.

Another use of the shell as an executable command is very common.
Instead of typing your commands directly to the shell, you can make a
file that contains several commands, perhaps a frequently used sequence
that you execute regularly. You can create this list of commands with a
text editor, or simply by using

```
$ cat > cmds
```

Then you can type commands until you press CTRL-D to signal an end-of-file to **cat**. Instead of being executed as you type, the commands will be saved in the file **cmds,** to which you have redirected the output of **cat.** Now you can take that file of commands and use it as redirected standard input to a **sh** command, as follows:

```
$ sh < cmds
```

This line executes a second copy of the shell, giving it the file **cmds** as input. The shell (remember, this is *not* your login shell) then reads and executes the commands in the file, writing the results to the standard output, which is your terminal. If you redirect the output from this command, you can also save the results in a file, as shown here:

```
$ sh < cmds > output
```

In case something goes wrong, you might also wish to save the standard error output in another file as follows:

```
$ sh < cmds > output 2> errors
```

The shell uses these same concepts, although in a form that is much easier to use, to implement *shell programs.*

# FOUR

The File System

Another major contribution the UNIX system has made to computing technology is the *file system.* File management is extremely flexible and powerful in the UNIX system, so much so that many concepts first introduced in the UNIX system have been widely adopted by other operating systems, notably MS-DOS.

The UNIX system provides a hierarchical directory scheme. A directory acts as a container for a group of files. Directories can be included in other directories, which results in a large, branching arrangement, often described as a *tree structure.* Commands, data files, other directories, and even hardware devices can be represented as directory entries. The UNIX system provides a powerful and simple way to name a specific file or directory within the file system, so that commands can easily locate anything entered as a filename on the command line.

This chapter introduces files and directories, and looks at some of the commands the UNIX system provides for you to manipulate them.

Files and Directories

A *file* is a sequence of bytes of data that resides in semipermanent form on some stable medium like a magnetic disk or tape. Files can contain anything that can be represented as a stream of bytes: executable programs, such as commands; text, such as mail messages or book manuscripts; databases; bitmaps, which might be screen images or pictures; and so forth. If you can store it on a disk or tape and name it, it can be a file.

Although the UNIX system regards all files as simple undifferentiated sequences of data bytes, users or application programs can impose additional structure on the contents of a file to give it more meaning. A text file is a simple example of added structure. In a text file, a special ASCII character called a *newline* is used to delimit lines, which creates a logical structure in the file. Another example is the binary data contained in executable programs like **cat** or **wc**, which you'll find in the file system. You can use the **wc** tool to count the characters in an executable file just as you can in a text file. Usually the **cat** command isn't too useful for files that do not contain text, but there is no reason why you can't use it to display a binary (non-ASCII) file, or any other file. In fact, you will occasionally use **cat** or **wc** in a pipeline when you're doing some operation on a non-ASCII file. For example, you can sometimes **cat** binary files directly to printers or graphics terminals for output.

One type of file that is of special interest is the directory. A *directory* is a file that contains not text or an executable program, but a list of filenames and other information about those files. Although a directory is a file like any other, it serves a different purpose than other types of files do.

A directory is a location within the file system as a whole that contains files. This location is analogous to a file drawer in your desk where you can store things. In the UNIX system you place files in directories. Since the system treats every file as a sequence of data bytes, you can store any type of file in any directory. In fact, you can even put a directory into another directory. This helps explain the file system as a whole, because the system is actually a file hierarchy of directories and subdirectories.

Figure 4-1 shows an example. Here, **steve** is the name of a directory that contains the files **note, README,** and **dir1.** The **note** and **README** files are normal text files, but **dir1** is another directory. The **dir1** directory, in turn, contains the files **hello, goodbye,** and **dir2.** The

dir2 directory contains two more files, **up** and **down**. Directories within directories are called *nested subdirectories*. There is no limit on the depth of nested subdirectories. You can usually think about and draw directories as hierarchies of subdirectories like Figure 4-1.

When you execute the **ls** command to list the names of your files, it does not list the name of every file in the entire system; it only lists the files in a specific directory. You cannot tell from a simple listing of filenames whether a particular name is associated with a file or a

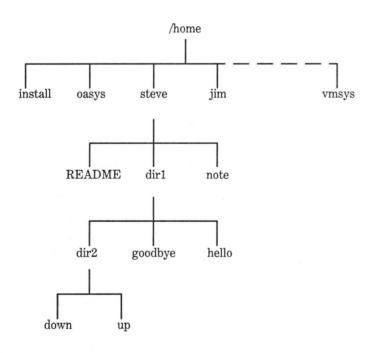

Figure 4-1.   A sample directory hierarchy

directory; you simply see the names of all the entries in the *current* directory. You can add an argument to the **ls** command, as follows:

```
$ ls note
note
$
```

If the argument refers to a file, **ls** only writes the name of that file to the standard output. If the argument refers to a directory, **ls** looks in the directory and writes the names of all the files in that directory, as shown here:

```
$ ls dir1
hello        goodbye        dir2
$
```

As you will see, there are also other ways to distinguish files from directories.

Rules for Naming Files

Directories have names just as other files do, and directory names obey the same rules as normal filenames: any ASCII characters are allowed, but upper- and lowercase characters are not equivalent, so a file named **NOTE** is different than one named **note**.

You can use any characters in filenames, and there is no arbitrary distinction between the name of a file and its *extension*. Many filenames in the UNIX system use extensions, such as **main.c** or **rc2.d**, but these naming rules are conventions that users agree on; they are not enforced by any property of the system.

Although you can use any filenames you wish, it is usually unwise to name a file or a directory so that it includes the shell wildcard operators or other characters that have a special meaning for the shell. For example, avoid the $ (dollar), the ; (semicolon), the \ (backslash), the & (ampersand), the ! (exclamation point), the * (star, or asterisk), and the | (pipe) in your filenames. You can use these characters in filenames if you wish, but doing so may cause confusion, because whenever you mention these names to the shell, you must quote them, or the shell will interpret them as operators instead of normal characters. One character, the /

(slash), is reserved for use in creating filenames, and cannot be used within a name.

In some directories in SVR4 systems, filenames may be limited to a maximum of 14 characters. In other directories you can use longer names (up to 256 characters). Unfortunately, it is not always easy to tell whether a specific directory has the 14-character limit or not. Generally if one directory has the limit, all the subdirectories under it will also have the limit, but even this rule is not absolute unless you create the subdirectory yourself. For each directory you use, you may wish to create a test file that has a name longer than 14 characters. If the name is truncated at the 14-character limit, you must take care not to use longer names in that directory. For example:

```
$ cat /etc/profile > 12345678901234567890
$ ls
12345678901234
$
```

As you can see, this directory has the 14-character limit. If the complete name appears in the **ls** output, it is safe to create filenames longer than 14 characters.

This complexity with respect to filenames results from two important new features in the SVR4 system: file system types (discussed in Chapter 18) and symbolic links (discussed later in this chapter). Soon the 14-character limit will be completely eliminated.

The length rules for directory names are the same as those for filenames.

Naming Directories

You can construct filenames that include a directory as part of the name. The **/** character is used to separate the different components of a filename. For example, the name **dir1/goodbye** refers to the file named **goodbye** in the directory **dir1**, the name **dir1/dir2** refers to the file (a directory in this case) **dir2** in directory **dir1**, and **dir1/dir2/down** refers to the file **down** in directory **dir2**, which is located in directory **dir1**. You can make these names as long as you wish, but each part may be subject to the 14-character limit. Only the last element of a file named this way can be a file; all the intermediate components must be directories. The last component can be either a file or a directory. This type of name is called a *path* or a *pathname*, because the listing of the directories and subdirectories in the name describes a path through the large hierarchy of subdirectories in the system.

You can use normal shell wildcard operators in constructing full pathnames. For example, the form

```
$ cat /home/steve/*/*
```

tells the system to display all the files in all the subdirectories under **/home/steve**. The other shell wildcard operators also work as usual.

The Working Directory

When you give the command **ls** with no arguments, it lists the contents of the current directory. You are always logically located at (or in) a directory. This directory is called the *current* or *working* directory. The current directory is a reference point or base point in constructing pathnames. For example, the pathname **dir1/goodbye** refers to a directory **dir1** that is located in the current directory, and to the file **goodbye** that is located in **dir1**.

The command **pwd** (for print working directory) tells you what directory you are in, as shown here:

```
$ pwd
/home/steve
$
```

The **pwd** command returns the pathname of the current directory on its standard output. You can use this command in an assignment to an environment variable, to help you remember a directory as you move around the file system. For example:

```
$ HERE=`pwd`
$ echo $HERE
/home/steve
$
```

Use the ` (grave) character to assign the standard output of the command to the variable.

Moving Around in the Directory Hierarchy

You can move around in the directory hierarchy using the **cd** (for change directory) command, as follows:

```
$ ls
README     dir1       note
$ cd dir1
$ ls
dir2       goodbye    hello
$ pwd
/home/steve/dir1
$
```

As you can see, the current directory has been changed.

The current directory is also known by the directory name . (dot). You can use the pathname **./note** to refer to the file **note** in the current directory, or **./dir1/goodbye** to refer to the directory **dir1** in the current directory. Here is an example:

```
$ pwd
/home/steve/dir1
$ cd ./dir2
$ pwd
/home/steve/dir1/dir2
$
```

The dot at the beginning of a pathname is usually redundant, since the system begins interpreting a path at the current directory, but there are times when the dot is necessary.

In the previous examples, you have moved *down* through the file system to a subdirectory using the **cd** command. You can also move *up* through the file system to a parent directory of the current directory. You use the special name .. (dot-dot) to refer to the parent of the current directory, as shown here:

```
$ pwd
/home/steve/dir1/dir2
$ cd ..
$ pwd
/home/steve/dir1
$
```

You can move down through subdirectories as far as directories exist. At the bottom of the directory hierarchy there will be no more subdirectories, only files. You cannot go down any further without creating a new directory at the lowest level. What happens if you continue to move upward, toward parent directories? An example follows:

```
$ pwd
/home/steve/dir1
$ cd ..
$ pwd
/home/steve
$ cd ..
$ pwd
/home
$ cd ..
$ pwd
/
$
```

Eventually you reach the top of the directory hierarchy, above which no more directories exist. This top directory is an anchor point for the file system, and it is called the *root* directory, or the root of the file system. The root has a special status, since any file in the system can be found by starting at this directory and working down through more and more subdirectories.

If you construct a pathname that begins with the **/** (slash) character, the system understands that the pathname starts at the root directory. If the pathname has no leading slash, the system assumes that you are starting at the current directory, as this example demonstrates:

```
$ pwd
/home/steve
$ ls dir1
dir2      goodbye      hello
$ ls /home/steve/dir1
dir2      goodbye      hello
$
```

These two commands refer to the same directory, but one begins at the current directory, and the other begins at the root directory. The first type is called a *relative pathname,* and the second type is called a *complete pathname* or an *absolute pathname.* You will use both types of pathnames when you construct filename arguments for commands.

  You can always use a pathname in a command argument in place of a simple filename. For example,

```
$ cat /home/steve/note
```

is equivalent to

```
$ cat note
```

providing the current directory is **/home/steve**. This is a general property of the UNIX system. In fact, the full pathname is the unique identifier for all files. You will often use the simple filename as a form of shorthand, because it is convenient, but the system will always understand a full pathname when you enter a filename.

Changing the Directory Hierarchy

You can create new directories and delete directories that you no longer need. Use the **mkdir** (for make directory) command to create a new directory, as shown here:

```
$ ls
README      dir1        note
$ mkdir new.directory
$ ls
README      dir1        new.directory      note
$
```

The **mkdir** command takes a list of pathnames as arguments, and creates the directory or directories that you name. As usual, if you enter a full pathname, the new directory will be created at the bottom of the specified path. If you enter a simple filename, the new directory will be created as a subdirectory of the current directory. Remember, directory names follow the same rules as other filenames; you cannot create a directory that has the same name as another file or directory in the same parent directory. When a new directory is created, it is empty; it has no files in it.

Use the command **rmdir** (for remove directory) to delete a directory, as shown here:

```
$ rmdir new.directory
$ ls
README      dir1       note
$
```

The **rmdir** command will fail and display an error message if you try to delete a directory that is not empty, as in this example:

```
$ pwd
/home/steve
$ rmdir dir1
rmdir: dir1 not empty
$
```

This prevents you from deleting a directory in the middle of the file system, which could leave some files as orphans from the directory you are attempting to delete. However, you can delete a directory and everything in it, including any subdirectories and the files they contain. Needless to say, this is a very dangerous procedure; you must be very sure that you really want to delete everything below a specific point in the directory hierarchy. You use the **rm** command with the argument **-r** (for recursive) to do this, rather than the **rmdir** command. For example:

```
$ rm -r dir1
$
```

Note that if everything goes correctly, **rm** does its job silently, deleting **dir1** and everything in it. To repeat, this can be a very dangerous operation; take care that you really mean it!

Your Home Directory

When you log in to a UNIX system, you enter the file system at a specific place that is your own private directory. You can freely create files and subdirectories in this directory; neither the UNIX system nor other users will touch them. This starting point is called your *home directory*. Most users usually work in their home directory or in the subdirectories they have created within their home directory. Other users have their own home directories, and these do not conflict with yours.

If your home directory is subject to the 14-character filename limit, any subdirectories that you create will also be subject to that limit. If your home directory allows you to create names longer than 14 characters, all your subdirectories will also allow longer names.

No matter where you are in the file system at any time, you can return to your home directory with the **cd** command. In the examples above, **cd** was used with an argument that gave the full or relative file system location of the directory to which you wished to change. If you give the command **cd** with no arguments, you return immediately to your home directory, as shown here:

```
$ pwd
/home/steve/dir1/dir2
$ cd
$ pwd
/home/steve
$
```

The UNIX system provides a HOME environment variable that contains the pathname for your home directory, and this environment variable is used by a great many commands that create files. For example:

```
$ echo $HOME
/home/steve
$
```

Note that the following two commands

```
$ cd
$ cd $HOME
```

have the same effect.

Every system defines the HOME environment variable for you, and you should not change it. Because certain commands and applications use this variable, some systems may prevent you from changing it to protect the integrity of the system.

File-Oriented Commands

The UNIX system provides many commands that allow you to manipulate files and move them around within the file system. Use the **cp** (for copy) command to make an exact copy of a file, as follows:

```
$ ls
README     dir1     note
$ cp note note.copy
$ ls
README     dir1     note     note.copy
$
```

In this example, the first argument is the existing file, and the second argument is the new file to create. As usual, you can give a pathname instead of a simple filename, as in this example:

```
$ cp ./note /home/steve/note.copy
```

This has the same effect as the previous example. If the target file or pathname already exists, the **cp** command will delete the old file and then make the copy without comment, so you must take care that the target filename is correct.

If the target pathname is an existing directory instead of a filename, the copy is placed in that directory, under the same source filename, as follows:

```
$ pwd
/home/steve
$ ls dir1
dir2     goodbye     hello
$ cp note dir1
$ ls dir1
dir2     goodbye     hello     note
$
```

The **cp** command will also accept a list of filenames as the source, and copy all of those files to the destination. When you give multiple names as the source, you must give a directory and not a filename as the target, or an error will result; **cp** will complain, and refuse to take any action. On the other hand, if the target is a directory, **cp** will copy all the files named as sources into the target directory, as shown here:

```
$ pwd
/home/steve/dir1
$ ls dir2
down      up
$ cp hello goodbye dir2
$ ls dir2
down      goodbye      hello      up
$
```

You cannot use a directory as a source name. If you wish to copy the contents of a directory to a new directory, you must name each file that you wish to copy, either explicitly or with a wildcard operator, as in this example:

```
$ pwd
/home/steve
$ cp dir1/* .
$
```

If **cp** completes its work successfully, it returns to the shell silently. Only when some problem occurs, does **cp** complain on its standard error output.

A command that is similar to **cp** and that obeys the same command line rules is **mv** (for move). The **mv** command does not make a copy of a file, but instead moves the file from one place to another or changes the file's name, as shown here:

```
$ ls
dir1      goodbye      hello
$ mv hello welcome
$ ls
dir1      goodbye      welcome
$
```

You can move a file into an existing directory and keep the same filename, or you can change the name of a file as you move it, depending on whether the target argument is an existing directory or a filename. Here is an example:

```
$ mv note dir1/try
$ ls dir1
dir2    goodbye    hello    note    try
$
```

Again the source can be a file or pathname list, and the target is the last argument you give. In this case, you usually make the target a directory, which must already exist because neither **cp** nor **mv** will create it.

The **mv** command is also used to rename a file or directory. Use the form

```
$ mv oldname newname
```

to rename a file. You can rename either files or directories in this way, and you can also give a different target location if you wish.

The **ln** (for link) command acts in a similar way, but the function of **ln** is to make the same file appear under two different names, as shown here:

```
$ ls
dir1    goodbye    hello
$ ln hello hhh
$ ls
dir1    goodbye    hello    hhh
$
```

In this example, **ln** did not make a copy of the file **hello**; it just created a second filename that refers to the same physical file. If you edited or changed the file **hello**, you would find that the changes also appeared in the file **hhh**. That would not be the case if you had actually made a copy of the file with **cp**. The **ln** command is usually used to make the same file appear in more than one directory.

Like **cp** and **mv**, **ln** can take a list of filenames as source arguments, and a single existing directory as target (the last argument on the command line). You cannot use a directory as the source argument without naming each file to be linked.

When you create another name for a file with **ln**, you give the file an additional link. If you then delete one of the filenames with **rm**, you don't actually delete the file, you just remove the link from the name to the file. A file is actually deleted from the system only when you have removed the *last* link, or deleted the last name that the file was known by in the file system. Once you've done this, the disk space is reclaimed and the file can no longer be recovered.

A file is always a member of a directory. If the file has multiple links, it may be in more than one directory at the same time (with the same or different names); however, this is not true of directories, because you cannot link a directory by name. The file system is a strict hierarchy; directories must have a fixed location within that hierarchy, with a parent directory and possibly some subdirectories. Remember, a file can be in two places at once, but a directory cannot!

Symbolic Links

Actually there is an apparent exception to this strict hierarchy rule in *symbolic links,* or *symlinks,* which are files that *point* to other files or directories. A symbolic link has a name and a location in the directory tree, like a normal file or directory, but unlike a real file or directory, a symbolic link has no *contents*; it simply acts as a pointer to another file or directory. When the system opens a normal file—when you **cat** a file, for example—it reads the contents of the file; however, when the system opens a symbolic link, it only reads a pathname from the link, and then reads the file (or directory) that the link points to. Symbolic links greatly complicate the UNIX file system, and we will reserve discussion of some of the issues they involve until the end of this chapter.

You create a symbolic link with the -s (for symbolic) option of the **ln** command, as follows:

```
$ ln -s note new.link
```

The existing file precedes the name of the link on the **ln** command line. Now, when you specify the file **new.link**, the system will actually work with the file **note**. Symbolic links can be files or directories, as shown here:

```
$ ln -s dir1 link.dir
```

This command creates a new object in the file system named **link.dir**, which acts like a directory, as this example demonstrates:

```
$ ls
README      dir1      note
$ ln -s dir1 link.dir
$ ls
README      dir1      link.dir      note
$ ls dir1
dir2        goodbye   hello
$ cd link.dir
$ ls
dir2        goodbye   hello
$
```

This is the only way a directory can be "in two places at once." You cannot make true links between directory names, but a symbolic link is only a *pointer* to another file or directory, so there is no real connection between the two objects. Thus, it is possible to delete the "real" object without changing the symlink, as shown here:

```
$ cd
$ mv dir1 DIR1
$ cd link.dir
link.dir: does not exist
$
```

This is a common error. Similarly, many commands that traverse the directory hierarchy do not automatically follow symbolic links the way that **cat** and **cd** do. If you use symbolic links in your directories, you need to take extra precautions to make sure that the contents of directories beneath symlinks are backed up or processed as you intend them to be.

Symbolic links are not directories, so you cannot delete them with the **rmdir** command, even though they may point to directories. You must use the **rm** command to delete them, as follows:

```
$ ln -s dir1 link.dir
$ rmdir link.dir
rmdir: link.dir: Path component not a directory
$ rm link.dir
$
```

Remember, when you delete a symbolic link you do *not* delete the real file or directory, just the pointer to it.

Options for the ls Command

In previous examples, when **ls** was used to display the contents of a directory, you saw the files listed in alphabetical order and lined up in columns on the screen. This display format is useful for listing to the terminal, but if the output is intended for a pipeline or for some other purpose, you may wish to see one file (or directory) per line. The **ls** command provides several options that control the display of the output, as well as other options that control what files or directories are selected for display. If you use **-1** (for one column) as a flag to **ls**, the output will be displayed one item per line, as shown here:

```
$ ls
dir1       README      note
$ ls -1
dir1
README
note
$
```

Actually, **ls** uses the one-per-line format if the output is redirected to a pipeline, so you may not need the **-1** option very frequently. At the terminal, the columnar form is likely to be more useful. If you need it, you can force columnar output with the **-C** (capital C, for columns) option. The order of files in the columnar display will vary widely between systems, and the display format may also depend on how many files are listed. Try testing your own system to see how it acts.

Another useful option for **ls** is **-a**. Actually, by default, **ls** does not really list the names of every file in a directory; it does not display any files in the named directory that begin with a . (dot). You can see all the files in a directory as follows:

```
$ pwd
/home/steve
$ ls
dir1       README      note
$ ls -a
.          .profile    dir1
..         README      note
```

Here, several files are listed that did not appear before. Most systems maintain several hidden files in your home directory; the number can vary depending on the system and on what application software you have installed. In any case, the files shown above are of special interest. The . (dot) is the current directory and the .. (dot-dot) is the parent directory. These are real entries in each directory, because each directory includes a link for finding itself and its parent. This is a *linked list* implementation of directories in the file system. In every directory, . and .. directories will be displayed with **ls -a**. What does .. refer to in the root (/) directory, since there is no parent to the root? In fact, the root is a special case, and there the .. and . directories are the same!

The **ls** command will mark the type of each file that it displays in a directory listing if you use the **-F** argument. This option adds a **/** to the end of each directory name, an * to the name of each executable file, and an @ (at sign) to the end of each symbolic link. These extra characters are not part of the filename; they are added by **ls**, as shown here:

```
$ pwd
/home/steve
$ ln /usr/bin/cat .
$ ln -s dir1 link.dir
$ ls -F
README     cat*    dir1/    link.dir@    note
$
```

In this directory **cat** is marked as executable, the subdirectory **dir1** is displayed with the **/** character, and the symlink has the @ after its name.

Another useful option of the **ls** command is **-R** (for recursive). Be sure to use a capital *R* here, because another **ls** option uses a lowercase *r* to reverse the order of output. The command **ls -R** will search through the directory hierarchy from the directory named as argument and display all the files and subdirectories, as shown here:

```
$ pwd
/home/steve
$ ls -RF
README     cat*    dir1/    link.dir@ note
 ./dir1:
dir2/    goodbye   hello
/home/steve/dir1/dir2:
down    up
$
```

This command defaults to the current directory if no argument is given. You can redirect the output to a file or use it as standard input to a file manipulation command.

The UNIX system provides another command, **find,** that is often used when a complete list of filenames in a directory substructure is desired, to back up a portion of the file system to floppy disk, for example. Chapter 7 covers **find** in detail.

File Permissions

Each file and directory in the file system has many attributes in addition to its name. You can see some of these attributes by using **ls -l** (for long listing). For example:

```
$ pwd
/home/steve
$ ls -l
total 3
-rw-rw-rw-  1 steve    other        138 Apr  5 19:34 README
drwxrwxrwx  3 steve    other         80 Apr  5 19:43 dir1
lrwxrwxrwx  1 steve    other          4 Apr  5 19:49 link.dir -> dir1/
-rw-rw-rw-  1 steve    other        227 Apr  5 19:33 note
$
```

The filename appears at the far right, and each name in the directory has its own line in the output. The next entry to the left—for example Apr 5 19:34—is the date and time that the file was last changed. This *time stamp* is often used to compare files, and also comes in handy when you are backing up your data.

The next column to the left gives the size of the file in bytes. A file can be any size, from zero bytes for a newly created file to a full megabyte or more. The UNIX system provides a systemwide variable called **ulimit** to control the maximum file size, but the maximum size is often set at two megabytes. Recall that a directory is a file, so it has a size in bytes too, but this number is usually not very useful.

If the listed object is a symbolic link, like **link.dir** in the previous example, the name field at the right will show the peculiar -> (for points to) form. The name of the link is given first, and it *points to* a second name, which is the "real" object.

File Ownership

Since the UNIX system supports multiple users, files can be created by individual users, who then *own* those files until they delete them or give them to another user. Each user also belongs to a *group,* and can share files with other users in that group, but not with users in different groups. Chapter 22 discusses groups in more detail. In the output from **ls -l,** shown in the previous section, you can see the user who owns the files and the group that user belongs to: **steve** is the file owner, and **other** is the name of the group that **steve** belongs to. When you create a file, the system gives the file to the group of which you are a member; however, you can change the ownership and group assignment of a file independently, so the user listed in the output from **ls -l** may not actually belong to the group listed.

Moving one column to the left in the output from **ls -l,** you see a column of single-digit numbers. These are the number of links that each file has. When you use **ln** to create another name for a file, this count goes up by one. When you delete a filename with **rm,** the count goes down by one. When the count reaches zero, the file is deleted.

Understanding File Permissions

Finally, the leftmost column of the output from **ls -l,** which looks like **-rw-rw-rw-,** gives the *permissions* or *mode* of the file. The leftmost position in the output is a - (hyphen) if the file is a normal file, a *d* if it is a directory, and an *l* (ell) if it is a symbolic link. A letter *b* or *c* can also appear in this position if the file is a special file that is used to control a hardware device. The next three positions give the permissions for the owner of the file, the following three give the permissions for the group that owns the file, and the final three give the permissions for all the other users in the system. Each of these three groups of permissions has three parts: read access, write access, and execute access. *Read access* means that the subject (either the owner, the group, or all others) can read the file (with **cat,** for example). *Write access* means that the subject can write the file (by editing it or redirecting output to it, for example). *Execute access* means that the subject can execute the file as a command (by naming it as we have been doing with **ls** or **rm**). For a directory, the meanings are slightly different: read access means that the subject is allowed to look at the contents of the directory (with **ls,** for example). Write access means that the user can create a file in the directory, and execute access means that the user can pass through the directory searching for subdirectories.

Symbolic links have the permissions of the objects they point to; the permissions of the link itself have no meaning.

These access forms are shown in the output from **ls -l** as **r** for read access, **w** for write access, and **x** for execute access. The output **-rw-r-----**, for example, means that the owner can read and write the file, the members of the group can read the file but not write or execute it, and others have no access to the file at all. The output **-r----x--x** means that the owner can read the file but not write or execute it, while members of the group and all others can execute it but not read or write it.

Changing File Ownership

The UNIX system provides several commands designed to manipulate the ownership and permissions of files and directories. You can give away the ownership of a file with the **chown** (for change owner) command, assuming the file is yours to give. Here is an example:

```
$ ls -l note
-rw-rw-rw-  1 steve     other      227 Apr  5 19:33 note
$ chown jim note
$ ls -l note
-rw-rw-rw-  1 jim       other      227 Apr  5 19:33 note
```

The **chown** command takes a filename or list of filenames as an argument, along with the login id of the user you wish to give the file or files to. The target user is always the last argument. The user to whom you give the file must be a legal login id for someone on the system. Remember, once you have given a file away, you cannot use **chown** to get it back!

Similarly, you can use the **chgrp** command to change the group that owns a file, providing you own the file and you are a member of the group that owns it. For example:

```
$ ls -l note
-rw-rw-rw-  1 steve     other      227 Apr  5 19:33 note
$ chgrp bin note
$ ls -l note
-rw-rw-rw-  1 steve     bin        227 Apr  5 19:33 note
```

Again, once you have given the file to someone else you no longer own it, so you cannot get it back. Of course, if you have read permission on the file you can copy it with

```
$ cat note > my.note
```

or some such command, and then you will own the new file.

Changing Permissions

You can change the file permissions of a file that you own using the **chmod** (for change mode) command. As you know, a file has three sets of permissions: user, group, and other. These are known as **u**, **g**, and **o**, respectively, and they correspond to the three sections of the permissions listed with **ls -l**. Again, each of these three categories of user can have read, write, or execute access to a file, which are represented by **r**, **w**, and **x** respectively. You can use this shorthand to create various **chmod** commands, as shown here:

```
$ ls -l note
-rw-rw-rw-  1 steve     other       227 Apr  5 19:33 note
$ chmod -w note
$ ls -l note
-r--r--r--  1 steve     other       227 Apr  5 19:33 note
$ chmod +w note
$ ls -l note
-rw-rw-rw-  1 steve     other       227 Apr  5 19:33 note
$
```

The first example gives the flag argument **-w** to **chmod**, which tells it to remove write permissions for the file. The second example restores write permissions. The use of **+** (plus) as a flag is an exception to the normal use of **-**, but the meaning is clear: in this case, you use **-** to remove a permission, and **+** to add one.

You can change more than one of the three permissions in the same command, as follows:

```
$ chmod -w+x note
$ ls -l note
-r-xr-xr-x 1 steve     other       227 Apr  5 19:33 note
$ chmod -wx note
$ ls -l note
-r--r--r-- 1 steve     other       227 Apr  5 19:33 note
$
```

In all these examples, **chmod** changes the permissions for all three classes of users. You can also make changes for any class individually by adding a letter before the - or +, as in this example:

```
$ ls -l note
-rw-rw-rw-  1 steve     other        227 Apr  5 19:33 note
$ chmod u-w note
$ ls -l note
-r--rw-rw-  1 steve     other        227 Apr  5 19:33 note
$ chmod go+wx note
$ ls -l note
-r--rwxrwx  1 steve     other        227 Apr  5 19:33 note
$
```

The syntax for **chmod** is user class (**u, g,** or **o**), followed by the action to take (- or +), followed by the permission to change (**r, w,** or **x**). The list of filenames or directory names to change follows at the end of the command line.

The **chmod** command can also take a numeric argument that describes the user class and permission to change as a sequence of bits. For example:

```
$ chmod 0466 note
```

This usage is more error-prone than the previous one, however. The number is an octal representation of the permissions described earlier. With **chmod** you can set permissions **s** and **t** as well as **r, w,** and **x.** The **s** and **t** permissions are used by some executable programs to modify their execution environments, and may appear in **ls -l** output for some system files; they are not used by individuals.

Listing Directory Permissions

There is one more important option for **ls.** If you request **ls -l** for a file, you see the information for that file; however, if you give the same command for a directory, the output is the listing for the files in that directory, as shown here:

```
$ ls -l dir1
total 1
drwxrwxrwx  2 steve     other         64 Apr 18 12:43 dir2
-rw-rw-rw-  1 steve     other          0 Apr 17 17:42 goodbye
-rw-rw-rw-  1 steve     other          0 Apr 17 17:42 hello
$
```

This is normally what you're after because you usually want information about the contents of a directory, but how do you get information about the permissions of the directory itself? One way is to use **cd** to change to the parent directory and then issue the **ls -l** command, as in the above example, which gives information for the directory **dir2**. To get information about directory **dir1** when you're in that directory, you could use

```
$ cd ..
$ ls -l
```

However, **ls** provides the following more efficient way to do this without changing directories.

```
$ ls -ld .
drwxrwxrwx  3 steve     other         80 Apr 18 12:43 dir1
$
```

You can use **ls -d** (for directory listing) to list the name of a directory rather than its contents. Combined with the **-l** option, **-d** also shows you the status of the directory.

Going Further

Many of the file system's most interesting features, such as the **s** permission, are associated with the execution of commands. Some are designed to improve the linkage between a filename in a directory and the actual physical data stored on the disk or other medium. The system allows you to *mount* additional file systems at arbitrary places in the directory tree. You can even configure the system to use a Local Area Network in such a way that a file can reside on a different machine's disk. Most of these capabilities are associated with system administration and configuration, which we will discuss in Chapters 12, 23, and 24.

The X Window System File Manager

If you are using the X Window System, you can use the File Manager instead of the command-line functions discussed in this chapter. To see a sample File Manager display, turn back to Figure 2-1; the OPEN LOOK File Manager appears at the lower-left of the screen. Most X packages include an application similar to this one. If you need more information about window management under X, read the first part of Chapter 23.

The File Manager lets you move around in the file system, select a subset of the files in a directory for an action like moving or deletion, and successively open subdirectories. The contents of directories are displayed in the large area at the bottom of the File Manager window, and the full path needed to get to each directory is given as a line of items in the center of the window (see Figure 2-1).

Each item included in the contents of a directory has an icon next to its name, which hints at the function or nature of the object: Directories look like folders, files have a turned-down corner, and executable programs show a picture of a window with borders. Many other icons may also appear.

If you *click* on an object with the left mouse button, you *select* that object for some action, which is in turn selected from the menus in the upper-left of the File Manager window. By *double-clicking* the left mouse button on an object, you *open* that object. If the object is a directory (folder), the contents of the directory replace the current contents of the large window, and the directory appears in the list at the center of the File Manager window. Other objects cause different actions. New windows appear if you choose to edit a text file or execute a program. When an the application ends (or is killed by the Quit option in the Window menu), its window disappears.

As an alternative to moving around the file system by double-clicking on the icons for folders, the Directory line at the top-right lets you type a pathname, and then click the Match menu item to jump to that directory.

You can select a subset of files in the selected directory by typing a filename wildcard pattern (using the familiar * and ? operators) in the Pattern field, and then clicking on Match.

You can access more complex file system features through the File..., View..., and Edit... menus. These menus allow you to configure the order in which files are displayed, show permissions and other file attributes, and create files and directories. Experiment with some of these choices to see how they respond.

basename and dirname

The UNIX system provides commands that allow you to construct filenames and directory names from complete pathnames, and vice versa. For example, you might have an environment variable that contains a complete pathname, and wish to know only the name of the file, without the path part. You can get this information by using the **basename** command, as follows:

```
$ echo $EDITOR
/usr/bin/vi
$ MYEDIT=`basename $EDITOR`
$ echo "My editor is $MYEDIT"
My editor is vi
$
```

You use the **basename** command to return the last component of a full pathname on its standard output. This usually gives you the name of a file stripped of its directory path. On the other hand, the command **dirname** returns the directory section stripped of the filename, as shown here:

```
$ EDDIR=`dirname $EDITOR`
$ echo "My editor $MYEDIT is in the directory $EDDIR"
My editor vi is located in the directory /usr/bin
$
```

You will learn many additional uses for these pathname manipulation tools when we discuss shell programming in Chapter 8.

Device Files

We have looked at regular files, symlinks, and directories. A fourth type of file called a *device file, special file,* or simply a *device,* can be observed with the **ls** command. The UNIX system provides a standard interface between hardware peripherals and the operating system that acts just like a normal file; that is, all I/O to hardware is done by writing to a file. This is not a disk file such as we have discussed up to now, but a special pathname that refers to an I/O channel to the hardware. Just as you can redirect standard I/O to a normal file, you can redirect output to a hardware device from the shell level without fanfare or confusion. This is a complex subject, primarily of interest to system designers and developers. Only a brief introduction will be given here.

The command **tty** (for teletype, a throwback to the early days of the UNIX system when terminals were slow printers often manufactured by the Teletype Corporation) returns the pathname associated with your terminal, as shown here:

```
$ tty
/dev/tty00s
$
```

Your terminal can be accessed through the file **/dev/tty00s**; in fact, the standard input for the shell that is executing your commands (the login shell) was attached to this file when you logged in to the system. The device pathnames vary on different systems, and change when you log in to different terminals on a system, so always use the **tty** command if you need to determine your login device. The directory **/dev** contains many other device files, in addition to those for terminal devices. You can use this pathname just like any other in the file system. For example:

```
$ ls -l /dev/tty00s
crw-rw-rw-  1 steve  other     3,  2 Apr 19 13:21 /dev/tty00s
$
```

The first character in the output, **c**, tells you that this file is neither a normal file nor a directory, but is a *character special* file. This means that it is designed to move data character by character, as a terminal, modem, or printer does. Another type of special file is the *block special* device, which is marked with **b** in the first position and is designed to move large chunks of data all at once as disk drives and some tape devices do. You can use a block device as a file system.

Device files have permissions just as other files do, and some are owned by the current user. In the previous example, you are allowed to read and write the file, which allows data into and out of your terminal, and other users are allowed to read the file, which allows them to "listen in" on your terminal session. What command line would you use to listen in on the device? This would do it:

```
$ cat - < /dev/tty00s
```

Try this command on your own device, as follows:

```
$ cat - < `tty`
```

Type a few keys and see what happens. You can hit the DEL key to kill the **cat** command and restore your terminal to sanity. Then try this version:

```
$ cat - > `tty`
```

What happens now?

The mesg Command

In the preceding example, you were able to directly read and write to the device file that represents your terminal. If the permissions output from **ls -l `tty`** shows that other users can read and write your device file, others can eavesdrop on your session or write directly to your terminal by redirecting I/O as shown previously. This is a potential security risk, because your I/O can be monitored by other users; however, there are times when the system administrator, or the system itself through software, needs to send a message directly to your terminal. This might occur when the system is being turned off, and the system administrator wants to warn you before the machine goes dead, so you can save your files and log off cleanly. The **wall** (for write to all users) and the **write** (for writing messages between users) commands use this direct I/O to your terminal for communications. Chapter 14 discusses the use of these commands.

You can control the access that other users have to your terminal simply by changing the permissions on the device file. This can be done directly with the **chmod** command, but the system provides another command expressly designed to allow or prohibit messages. The **mesg** (for message) command lets you select whether other users can write to or read from your terminal device. The command takes one argument, which can be **y** or **n** to accept or reject messages, respectively. For example:

```
$ ls -l /dev/tty00s
crw-rw-rw-  1 steve   other      7,  2 Apr 20 18:37 /dev/tty00s
$ mesg n
$ ls -l /dev/tty00s
crw-r--r--  1 steve   other      7,  2 Apr 20 18:38 /dev/tty00s
$ mesg y
$ ls -l /dev/tty00s
crw-rw-rw-  1 steve   other      7,  2 Apr 20 18:37 /dev/tty00s
$
```

As you can see, the **mesg** command just changes the permissions on your device file.

Other Devices

In addition to the **tty** devices, there are many other device files in the **/dev** directory. One of the most interesting is **/dev/null**, which is an infinitely large wastebasket that you can use to redirect output that you wish to discard. For example:

```
$ cat /etc/passwd > /dev/null
$
```

Another interesting device file is **/dev/kmem** (for kernel memory, which is a representation of the real memory in the machine). Special programs, such as debuggers, can read **/dev/kmem** to see how the system is using memory at any time. However, normal users are prohibited from peeking (or writing!) into **/dev/kmem**, because it would violate security if the system's memory were accessible.

In addition, all the hardware devices attached to the system, such as terminal ports, printer ports, and disk drives, have representations in the **/dev** directory. We will discuss these as needed.

More on Symbolic Links

As mentioned earlier, the introduction of symbolic links greatly complicates the UNIX file system. Once you get outside your home directory, you will encounter many symbolic links. Because several symbolic links can point to the same file, and a symbolic link can point out of one file system (such as one with no 14-character name limit) into another (which may have the 14-character limit), the old rules concerning the strict hierarchy of the directory tree no longer apply. In SVR4 the organization of the overall system (i.e., starting at the root directory, /) is very complex. As you move around the file system, you must take note of symbolic links, and treat them with care. Many file system traversal programs, like **find**, do not follow symbolic links by default. Symbolic links require careful handling. For instance, you may have a symbolic link that points to a directory, such as **link.dir** in the examples presented earlier in this chapter. You can use **cd** to move into that directory, and the **pwd** command will report the directory location correctly, as shown here:

```
$ cd link.dir
$ pwd
/home/steve/link.dir
$
```

This gives the impression that the symbolic link is really a directory, and that **link.dir** is your current directory. Actually, one goal of the symlink is to create exactly that impression. In fact, **link.dir** is *not* a directory, and your current directory is actually the **dir1** directory, assuming that is where **link.dir** points; thus, these two commands are equivalent:

```
$ cd /home/steve/dir1
$ cd /home/steve/link.dir
```

Nonetheless, the output of **pwd** will differ, as follows:

```
$ cd /home/steve/dir1
$ pwd
/home/steve/dir1
$ cd /home/steve/link.dir
$ pwd
/home/steve/link.dir
$
```

As this example demonstrates, you can get to a single location in the file system through several different paths. If you are not careful, you may assume that these separate paths lead to distinct places, and make changes to one apparent destination that could wreak havoc with the others.

Actually, the **pwd** command is usually built into the shell, as is the **cd** command. Thus, the shell conspires with the file system to give you the impression that the file system actually has the hierarchy that *you* use to move around in it, even though with symlinks there may be several other versions (since there can be more than one symlink to a file or directory). In most cases this simplifies things, because you always see the version of the file system that you are using. Nevertheless, there is one *real* or *objective* file system representation that follows the strict hierarchy. Since symlinks are pointers, they must point to something real, and that is the objective file system represented by real files and directories.

All the common shell programs (**sh, ksh,** and **csh**) implement **pwd** by reporting the path that you used to get to a specific directory, not by reporting the real path. However, the program **/usr/bin/pwd** is independent of this shell convention, and it always reports the real pathname of the current working directory, as shown here:

```
$ cd link.dir
$ pwd
/home/steve/link.dir
$ /usr/bin/pwd
/home/steve/dir1
$
```

As you browse through the file system, use **/usr/bin/pwd** frequently to be sure what directory you are *really* in at all times.

Browsing the File System

In this chapter, we've focused mainly on your home directory and the files and directories that you create for your own use. Of course, this is only a small part of the file system; as a whole, the file system is a large and complex structure. In fully configured SVR4 systems there are as many as 6500 files and 850 directories, although about one-fourth of the total is in the System Administration tools, and about one-tenth is in the Software Development Set, which may not be installed on all systems.

In addition, there are about 350 symbolic links. About 800 files are commands of various types. Also, individual users and application software can substantially add to the total. Most of these files have specific purposes for the operation of the system, and if they are not present or if their permissions are wrong, something will not work correctly, with extremely variable results. When something like this goes amiss, it can test the skills of the best "guru" to find and fix the problem without reloading the system. You must be very careful when you change or delete a file that is not in your home directory, and even more careful when you change the permissions of an existing system file.

On the other hand, browsing through the file system can be a source of great entertainment and insight into its inner workings. Only a few files are not readable, and those can be made readable for examination if security considerations are not of paramount importance in your machine.

Starting in the root directory, there are several important files and subdirectories, as shown here:

```
$ ls -F /
bin@        export/      lib@          proc/      tmp/       var/
boot/       home/        lost+found/   sbin/      u/
dev/        home2/       mnt/          shlib/     unix*
etc/        install/     opt/          stand/     usr/
$
```

These few directories provide entry into the entire hierarchy that lies below; from here you can see the whole file system. Table 4-1 is an abridged summary of the major files and directories in SVR4 systems. As you wander through the file system, consult this table for information on each directory you encounter.

A Note on File System Reorganization in SVR4

The overall file system organization has changed dramatically from SVR3 and older releases to SVR4. These changes were made primarily due to the requirements of *networked* or *distributed* systems. Some parts of the system are specific to an individual machine, such as certain logs and control files, while others can be shared between different machines of the same type, and still others can be shared by nearly *all* machines regardless of what version of the UNIX system they run. This

Path	Comments
/bin	Symlink to **/usr/bin**
/boot	Boot-time files
/dev	Device special files
/dev/dsk	Disk devices
/dev/fd	Open file descriptor devices
/dev/kd	Keyboard and display devices
/dev/kmem	Memory
/dev/null	Garbage can device
/dev/osm	Kernel error messages
/dev/pts	Pseudo **ttys**; same as **/dev/pts***
/dev/rdsk	Raw disk devices
/dev/term	Terminals, same as **/dev/tty***
/dev/xt	Pseudo **ttys**; for DMD layers
/etc	Machine-specific administration
/etc/Backup	List of directories for backup
/etc/Ignore	List of directories to skip during backup
/etc/X0.hosts	Host allow list for X
/etc/bkup	Control files for backup
/etc/bupsched	Time table for auto backup (**ckbupscd**)
/etc/conf	Kernel reconfiguration material
/etc/cron.d	Control files for **cron**
/etc/default	Control files for boot-time defaults
/etc/fs	Executable tools for all file system types
/etc/group	Group memberships
/etc/inittab	Process setup at boot
/etc/issue	Printed by login "Welcome..."
/etc/lp	Information files and interfaces for **lp**
/etc/mail	Mail control files; configured for **/bin/mail**
/etc/mnttab	Table of currently mounted file systems
/etc/motd	Message of the day
/etc/net	Control files for network services and hosts
/etc/profile	Systemwide login profile
/etc/rc?.d	Directories for boottime scripts
/etc/rfs	Files and commands for RFS
/etc/rstab	Remote mounts
/etc/saf	Control files for SAF
/etc/shadow	Password file

Table 4-1.   The SVR4 File System Hierarchy

Path	Comments
/etc/ttydefs	Control files for SAF
/etc/ttytype	Defaults for login on **tty** channels
/etc/uucp	Control files for **uucp**
/export	Exported on network
/home	User home directories
/home/oasys	OA&M administration support files
/home/vmsys	OA&M administration support files
/home2	User home directories
/install	Add-on packages
/lib	Symlink to **/usr/lib**
/mnt	Mount point
/mnt1	Mount point
/opt	Add-on material
/proc	Current processes
/sbin	Administrative **bin**
/shlib	Shared libraries
/stand	Standalone boot-time files, kernel
/tmp	Temporary files
/u	User home directories
/usr	Files that do not change (can be read-only)
/usr/X	X Window System support tools
/usr/X/bin	X executables
/usr/X/clients	OL support data files
/usr/X/include	X include files
/usr/X/lib	X support data files
/usr/add-on	Support files for add-on packages
/usr/admin	Administration menus for add-on packages
/usr/bin	Executable user commands
/usr/ccs	C Compilation System
/usr/include	System definitions in header files
/usr/lbin	Local **bin**; has some **installpkg** commands
/usr/lib	Libraries and shared libraries
/usr/lib/acct	Accounting tools
/usr/lib/class	Control files for priority classes
/usr/lib/installed	Data on installed packages
/usr/lib/layersys	Control files for layers
/usr/lib/locale	Time- and nation-specific files and directories

Table 4-1.   The SVR4 File System Hierarchy (*continued*)

Path	Comments
/usr/lib/lp	Static **lp** tools
/usr/lib/mail	Control files for **/bin/mail**
/usr/lib/netsvc	Control files for NFS commands
/usr/lib/nfs	Control files and demons for NFS
/usr/lib/rsh	Restricted shell
/usr/lib/sa	Control files for **sa** accounting system
/usr/lib/saf	Services for SAF
/usr/lib/spell	Control files for **spell**
/usr/lib/terminfo	Symlink to **/usr/share/lib/terminfo**
/usr/lib/uucp	Control files for **uucp**
/usr/net	Control files for RFS and **nls**
/usr/news	News files; symlink to **/var/adm/news**
/usr/nserve	RFS administration; symlink to /etc/rfs
/usr/options	Names of installed packages
/usr/sadm	System administration tools for OA&M
/usr/sbin	Executable administrative commands
/usr/share	Shared between machine architectures
/usr/share/lib	Application-specific shared material
/usr/share/lib/spell	Control files for **spell**
/usr/share/lib/terminfo	Terminal control files for **vi**, etc.
/usr/spool	Symlink to **/var/spool**
/usr/src	Source code when present
/usr/tmp	Temporary files during compilation
/usr/ucb	**bin** for BSD Compatibility tools
/usr/ucbinclude	Include file for BSD Compatibility tools
/usr/ucblib	Libraries for BSD Compatibility tools
/usr/vmsys	Tools for admininistration of SVR3 add-ons
/var	Files that change during life of system
/var/adm	Accounting controls; symlink to **/usr/adm**
/var/lp	**lp** logs
/var/sadm	OA&M support files
/var/spool	Temporary files for **uucp**, printing, etc.
/var/uucp	**uucp** logs

Table 4-1.   The SVR4 File System Hierarchy (*continued*)

has led to situations in which many familiar parts of the system—which logically belong together in a single directory subtree according to *function*—now reside in different directories. That is, the file system has changed from a functional organization to one that is determined by which *machine* in a heterogeneous networked environment is responsible for maintaining and using a file.

This reorganization was necessary to fully support a networked version of the UNIX system, but if you have experience with older UNIX systems you will have to relearn the locations of each file and directory. On the other hand, symbolic links throughout the system point the old names to the new locations. As you browse through the file system, take care not to confuse real files with symbolic links that "pretend" to be the real file system. Use **/usr/bin/pwd** frequently to see where you really are in the new organization.

Conventions for Naming Files and Directories

The UNIX system has evolved some relatively standard conventions for naming directories, though many conventions are new in SVR4. Usually different applications, and even individual users, follow these conventions in their own home directories, although the rules are not enforced outside the system directories.

The directory names **bin** (for binary), and **sbin**, **lib** (for library), **src** (for source), **man** (for manual), **home** and **usr** (for users), and **etc** (for etcetera) appear widely. Most executable programs reside in a **bin** directory; most development libraries and other supporting material reside in a **lib** directory; most source code for applications and commands resides in a **src** directory; most documentation resides in a **man** directory; most of the items associated with users reside in a **home** or **usr** directory; and most of the supporting material resides in an **etc** directory.

You can see many of these names in the root directory. The **/usr/bin** directory contains many of the commands, and **/bin** is often a symlink to **/usr/bin**. Most of the remaining commands are in the directories **/sbin** (for standalone bin) and **/usr/sbin**. Usually, the **sbin** directories contain primarily administrative commands, while the **bin** directories contain user commands. Many systems may include another directory, **/usr/local**, or sometimes **/local/bin**, to contain commands that are not part of the official UNIX system, but have been added to that specific machine.

The **/etc** directory contains a large number of files and tools that are used in the administration of the UNIX system as a whole. For example, **/etc/rc2.d** is a directory that contains files used when the system boots, and **/etc/passwd** is a file that contains the list of authorized users on the machine.

The pieces of the UNIX operating system that make up the kernel are kept in **/etc/conf**. These materials are used to build a new kernel when you add hardware that includes device drivers. The actual run-time version of the kernel that is loaded when the machine boots is located in the **/stand** directory, and a copy is retained in **/unix** for compatibility with older software. The **/unix** file is no longer used as the bootable kernel. You should never manually change or delete the contents of these directories, even though they may occupy a considerable amount of disk space. The directory **/shlib** (for shared libraries) contains additional parts of the UNIX operating system, the dynamically loaded software libraries that support most applications.

The Software Development Set resides primarily in **/usr/ccs** and its subdirectories, although parts of the set are also kept in **/usr/include** and **/usr/lib**. Often **/lib** is a symbolic link to **/usr/lib**.

The **/dev** directory contains the files that link to hardware devices, and the **/tmp** directory is used for temporary storage of files by applications, especially during software development. You can use **/tmp** for your own temporary files if you wish. The files stored in **/tmp** are deleted when the system is rebooted. Another temporary directory, **/var/tmp** is also available, and in some systems it is not cleared at boot time.

Home directories for individual users generally reside in the **/home** directory, although some systems may also use **/usr** or **/u** for user directories.

The source code for the complete UNIX system is usually kept in **/usr/src** and its subdirectories, but this is rarely present on microcomputers. Some support for the **uucp** communications subsystem resides in **/usr/lib/uucp**. The **/usr/share/lib/terminfo** file contains descriptions of specific features of different terminals that may be attached to the system. If present, **/usr/man** contains documentation, including the text of the *UNIX User's Manual*.

The **/usr** directory contains numerous other objects, but many of them are symbolic links to directories in **/var** (for variable), which contains objects that are subject to change as the machine is administered. Most logs, spool directories, and other variable data are kept in **/var**.

The **/export** subtree is designed to hold files and directories that are shared, or *exported* to other machines on the network.

The BSD compatibility package, if it is installed, resides in **/usr/ucb**; it contains the executable commands. You can add this directory to your

PATH to pick up the BSD commands. The **/usr/ucblib** file contains support materials for the BSD compatibility package.

The X Window System tools and supporting material may reside in **/usr/X,** but they are often found in **/usr/bin/X11** and in **/usr/lib/X11** instead.

System administration forms and menus are usually stored under **/usr/admin** and **/usr/vmsys.** These subtrees can be large if the machine includes all the administration tools provided in SVR4.

Finally, application developers usually carve out a piece of the directory hierarchy for the exclusive use of their applications. Often **/install, /opt** or **/usr/add-on** are used, but each application may have its own scheme. Thus, your system may have many more directories than have been mentioned here. Browse through your own system and think about its layout; you will meet many of these files and directories again in later chapters.

Basic Editing with vi and emacs

The UNIX system provides several text editors as standard parts of the system. These editors differ greatly, and are generally optimized for a subset of the text editing work you do. None of these standard editors is a true word processor like those found in other small computer environments; word processing or document formatting is performed with a separate set of tools. In addition to the standard editors, many word processors and desktop publishing systems are available as add-on products. You can buy an editor with just about any features that you wish. In this chapter, however, we will discuss only the most popular text-editing tools.

The **vi** (for visual; pronounced "vee-eye" or "vye") editor originated in the BSD release but has been included in all System V releases for many years. The other major editor, **emacs** (for editor from Project MAC at MIT), is widely used and well supported on most systems, but is not included in the standard release. You may have to purchase it separately, but several versions are available free. One of the best is the *gnu emacs* version distributed by the Free Software Foundation. Other editors, such as the venerable **ed** (for editor), and **sed** (for stream editor), are discussed in the next chapter.

Like many other subjects in the UNIX system, text editing introduces many new and powerful concepts. Because text files are streams of characters, many of these concepts involve modifying, or *filtering*, character strings. The most powerful concept involved—the *regular expression*—reaches beyond text editing to influence the entire environment. In this chapter you'll learn basic editing techniques as you use the common editors to create, change, and browse files. The more advanced (and faster) editing concepts and tools are covered in the next chapter.

A Note on Learning to Use the Editors

Text editing tools in the UNIX system are designed for a terse, very fast user interface and operation that favors the skilled expert at the expense of the novice. The best way to learn editing is to experiment extensively on small test files. You cannot learn editing simply by reading a description, because editing must become an automatic skill. Try watching over the shoulders of skilled users, and asking for an explanation when they do something you don't recognize. Even experts progress this way! Short of hiring your own expert, the best way to proceed is to constantly review the editing documentation as you practice, and slowly integrate new features as you master earlier material. Usually, when an editor won't do something that you want it to, it is because you don't know how to do it, not because the editor is unable to do it.

If you are new to the UNIX system, it is probably preferable to start with **emacs** rather than **vi**. Although tastes differ and each editor has its devotees, research suggests that **emacs** is easier to learn and less error-prone than **vi**. In addition, **emacs** is somewhat more configurable. However, the differences in usability are small, so if your local experts are **vi** users or if you don't have **emacs** on your machine, **vi** is perfectly acceptable.

The vi Text Editor

The **vi** editor is a full-screen text editor that manages the entire display, providing a window into the full file that is retained internally in the **vi** *buffer*. The screen cursor is always on the *current line,* and most editing operations take place at that point. As you move the cursor to a new part of the file, the screen is automatically redrawn so that the current line is always on screen. However, **vi** is not a word processor or a publishing system; it does not format text or support integrated graphics. On the other hand, **vi** is terminal independent, so you can use it equally well on the system console or from a remote terminal.

The **vi** editor is a subset of a larger editor called **ex** and some of the documentation refers to **ex** commands. Actually **ex** itself is rarely used, so our discussion will focus on **vi**.

Setting Your Terminal Type

To use **vi** on different terminals, you just have to tell the program what kind of terminal you are using. The *TERM* (for terminal) environment variable handles this chore. The **vi** editor and many other full-screen applications read this environment variable when they start up, and adjust their output to display efficiently for your terminal. Most systems do not automatically define the TERM variable when you log in unless you are on the system console. However, much software uses the TERM variable, so you should be sure it has been defined. You can set the variable directly from the shell, as follows:

```
$ TERM=ansi
$ export TERM
```

The lowercase "ansi" is the correct format for standard ANSI or similar terminals. Most popular terminals are supported under the TERM variable. If you make an error in setting the TERM variable, full-screen applications will display strange character sequences at unexpected times.

The second command in the previous set, **export TERM**, allows all your subshells as well as the login shell to use the TERM variable. You can include these two commands in your **.profile** so that TERM is always set when you log in to the system. Chapter 8 discusses the **.profile** and explains how to set the TERM variable.

The **vi** editor and other full-screen programs read the TERM variable and then look in the **terminfo** database to find a symbolic description of the terminal specified. On SVR4 systems, this database is located in the directory tree under **/usr/share/lib/terminfo** (also known as **/usr/lib/terminfo**). This directory contains subdirectories for each letter or number that can begin a terminal type used by full-screen programs. For example, the directory **/usr/share/lib/terminfo/a** contains a list of terminals that begin with the letter *a*, such as **ansi**. The directory **/usr/share/lib/terminfo/2** contains a list of terminals whose names begin with 2, such as the HP 2626 terminal. You can browse through this database to see if your terminal is included. Older releases of the system may use a different database scheme for the terminals. In this case, all the terminal descriptions will be in the file **/etc/termcap**. If the **/usr/share/lib/terminfo** directory tree is present on a machine, it will be used instead of **/etc/termcap** for **vi** and for most other full-screen applications.

The 80386 and 80486 systems based on the AT bus use the line **TERM = AT386** for logins on the console. Use **TERM = xterm** under the X Window System. From a remote terminal, **TERM = ansi** will often work.

Starting the vi Editor

You can invoke **vi** from the shell with an optional filename list as an argument, as shown here:

```
$ vi old.file
$ vi new.file
$ vi new.file old.file
$ vi
```

All these are acceptable commands. If the named file does not already exist, **vi** will create it. This is the normal method for creating new files in the UNIX system.

If you include more than one filename in the list of arguments, **vi** will edit files one by one, loading the first one into the text buffer when you start the program. Commands are provided to switch files, but **vi** cannot edit multiple files simultaneously. The current filename is accessible with a **vi** command. If you execute **vi** with no filename as an argument, **vi** will work correctly, but you will have to name a file before you write the text buffer back to the file system.

Given the previous commands, **vi** would start with the first line of the file as its current line.

In addition to filenames, **vi** allows several other command-line arguments. You can use the + option followed by a line number to make the specified line current. For example,

```
$ vi +45 old.file
```

will make line 45 of the file **old.file** the initial current line. The command

```
$ vi +$ old.file
```

is used to start **vi** at the end of the file. You can also use the form

```
$ vi +/string old.file
```

to make **vi** search for *string,* and make the first occurrence of *string* the current line. In fact, you can use any **vi** command after the **+**, and it will be interpreted before **vi** draws the screen for you.

Figure 5-1 shows a typical screen during an editing session with a short file. Usually, **vi** fills the entire screen with a text file, allowing only one line at the bottom for special information; however, if a file is short or if you are at the end of a file, **vi** fills the unused portion of the screen with empty lines that begin with a ~ (tilde). The ~ marks an unused line in the **vi** text display. When you load **vi** with a new filename or with no filename, the entire screen will have tildes at the left, since there is no text in the buffer.

Lines in the internal buffer are numbered from one through the end of the file, although the line numbers do not appear on the screen.

The screen cursor appears over one character displayed on the screen. The line it occupies is the *current line,* and the character it rests on is in the *current position* on the line. Most editing operations use the current line or cursor position; **vi** provides commands for moving the cursor and changing the current line.

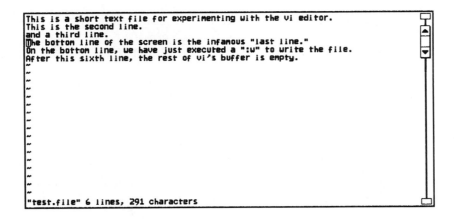

Figure 5-1.   Typical **vi** screen display

Modes in vi

In operation, **vi** has three modes. *Modes* are different states the editor can be in at various times. You switch between modes to perform different editing operations. *Command mode* allows you to enter commands directed at the editor, change the current line, or quit. *Input mode,* or *text mode,* allows you to enter text directly into a file. Normally you start **vi** in command mode, enter input mode to add text, and then switch between command and input modes as you change the text. This can be a source of error, because it is easy to forget what mode you are in. If you enter commands while you are in text mode they become part of the file's contents, and entering text while you are in command mode can cause strange changes in your file. The internal **set** command allows you to display the current mode on the screen. This command is discussed later in this chapter, but for now, you can use the command

```
:set showmode
```

to turn on a display of the current mode.

A third mode, called *last line mode,* allows you to enter line-oriented commands that are displayed on the bottom line of the screen. The : entered from command mode switches to last line mode, so the previous **set** command is an example of using last line mode. You can only enter last line mode from command mode; if you were in text mode the : would be entered into the buffer as text.

When you enter last line mode with : (and some other commands), the cursor jumps to the last line of the screen and **vi** waits for your command. Then you can enter the **set** command to display the current mode.

Switching Modes

Last line mode is used to enter a single command line on the bottom line of the display. When that command completes, **vi** returns you to command mode, so last line mode is short-lived; however, the other two modes stay active until you explicitly switch out of them.

When you are in input mode, you can jump to command mode by pressing the ESCAPE key, which is marked ESC on many keyboards. You enter input mode from command mode by using one of the text commands discussed later in this chapter.

Each mode acts differently, and has its own command set. Last line mode commands are displayed on the last line as you type, but command mode input is not echoed in this way.

Consult Table 5-1 for a summary of the major **vi** commands, which are discussed in the following sections.

Ending your vi Session

To exit from **vi** back to the shell, you can use the command **:q** (for quit). This command only works if you have not changed the file since the last time it was written. You can force **vi** to exit and abandon any recent changes to the file by adding a ! (bang) after the **:q**, as follows:

```
:q!
```

Remember, all changes made since the last time you wrote the file will be lost if you force **vi** to exit in this way.

Writing Files

Last line mode provides commands to read and write files between the internal **vi** text buffer and permanent files in the file system. Use **:w** to write the edited file back to disk. You will usually do this before you end your **vi** session, but remember, the **w** operation will overwrite the file on disk. The internal buffer is not changed by the write operation, so you can write the changes as often as needed. It is usually desirable to write the file frequently as you edit, to prevent editing errors from unexpectedly changing the file. The **vi** editor does no automatic writes or backup as you edit.

You can change the filename during the write operation by giving a pathname after the **:w**, as shown here:

```
:w new.file
```

	Enter Input Mode			Move Cursor	
i	Before cursor		l or SPACEBAR	One space right
a	After cursor		h or BACKSPACE	One space left
I	At start of line		j or +	One line down
A	At end of line		k or -	One line up
o	Open line below		$	End of line
O	Open line above		^	Start of line
			w	Next word
			e	End of word
			b	Previous word
			nG	Line n

	Delete			Change	
dw	Word		cw	Change word
dd	Line		cc	Change line
D	To end of line		C	To end of line
x	Char at cursor		r	Char at cursor
			R	Until ESC

	Other Functions			Screen Control	
u	Undo		CTRL-D	Scroll forward
/	Search forward		CTRL-U	Scroll back
?	Search backward		CTRL-F	Next screen
n	Next occurrence		CTRL-B	Previous screen
.	Repeat last action		CTRL-L	Redraw screen
Y	Yank line			
p	Put below			Last Line Mode	
P	Put above		:w	Write file
ZZ	Write and quit		:q	Quit
ESC	Cancel command		:wq	Write and quit
"	Mark		:n	Next file
			:r	Read file
	When in Input Mode		:e	Edit file
BACKSPACE	Delete char		:f or CTRL-G	Filename
CTRL-W	Delete word		:set	Change options
ESC	Command mode		:!	Shell escape
			:n	Line n
			:addr	Jump to address

Table 5-1.   Major Commands for the **vi** Text Editor

This creates a new file named **new.file** in the current directory, and writes the edited buffer into it. Then, **vi** reports on the size of the file as written. For example:

```
:w new.file
"new.file"  4 lines, 96 characters
```

This message appears on the last line in place of the :w command.

If the file already exists, **vi** will warn you, as follows:

```
:w new.file
"new.file" File exists - use "w! new.file" to overwrite
```

You can force **vi** to write the file anyway and destroy the old contents of **new.file** by adding a ! after the w, as instructed in the error message. If you do not have permission to change the file, **vi** will display this message:

```
:w! new.file
"new.file"  Permission denied
```

In this case, you must change the permissions on the file or write the buffer to a different filename.

You can write a portion of the buffer by giving a range of lines with the **w** operation. Enter the first line you wish to write after the :, followed by a comma, and then the last line you wish to write, as shown here:

```
:3,6w new.file
```

Only lines three through six will be written to **new.file**, and the internal buffer will be unchanged.

You can combine the write and quit operations with the command

```
:wq
```

This writes the file, and then returns to the shell. From command mode, you can also use the command **ZZ** as a synonym for :wq to write your file and exit back to the shell.

Reading Files

The **r** command is similar to **w**, except it *reads* a file into the internal buffer after the current line. Again, **vi** reports on the change.

```
:r old.file
"old.file" 6 lines, 158 characters
```

This command can be used to load a file into an empty buffer or to add the contents of the named file to the current buffer. If you add a line number before the **r**, as in this example,

```
:6r old.file
```

vi will read the file after that line instead of after the current line. The read operation changes the current line to be the last line read.

Changing Files

If you have entered **vi** with a list of filenames, the command **:n** (for next) closes the current file and switches to the next file in the argument list. However, **vi** will not let you edit more than one file at a time; there is always only one current file. As you may have expected, you can force **vi** to switch files with **:n!**, even if the buffer has not been written.

If you need to see which file is current, you can use the last line mode command **:f** (for file), or the command mode operator CTRL-G to display the name and size of the current file.

Redrawing the Screen

If the display gets confused for any reason, the CTRL-L operator from command mode causes **vi** to redraw the screen, updating it to show the current content of the buffer. This is useful if a system message appears and disrupts the display while you are editing.

Escaping to the Shell

The ! has several other uses within last line mode. You can use

```
:!command or pipeline
```

to temporarily suspend **vi** and execute a command in a subshell. When the shell command is completed, **vi** returns. For example,

```
:!ls
```

will run ls on the current directory. To get a full shell, you can use the special case

```
:sh
```

The **vi** editor will be suspended, and you will see your PS1 prompt. When you are through with the shell, end it with **exit** or CTRL-D and **vi** will go back into action.

Editing In vi

Now that you understand the basic operations of **vi**, you can begin using the many commands provided to accomplish real editing tasks. Practice these commands on your own test files.

Undoing a Change

One of the more important commands is the **u** (for undo) operator. The **vi** editor only retains a memory of the *last* change made to the file, but you can restore this last change at any time with **u**. That is, as you make a series of changes, you can always undo the most recent one. Try experimenting with **u** to see how it responds. What happens if you issue two undo commands in sequence?

Entering Input Mode from Command Mode

Many commands will switch you into input mode from command mode. You can move the cursor to a specific point in the file, and then enter input mode. When you are in input mode, you can enter as much text as you wish, including new lines. Remember to press ESC to return to command mode when you are through adding text.

The **o** (for open) command opens a new line of text after the current line, and positions the cursor at the beginning of the newly created line. The uppercase operator **O** (letter *O*) opens a line above the current line. Use **a** (for append) to enter input mode at the next character after the cursor. Material to the right of the cursor will move to the right as you enter text into the line. The uppercase operator **A** enters text mode at the end of the current line. Similarly, the **i** (for input) operator enters input mode just before the current cursor location, and **I** (uppercase letter *I*) enters input mode at the beginning of the current line. Use ESC to return to command mode.

Input Mode

Most of the functions of the **vi** input mode are intuitive. When you are in input mode, all the text you enter goes into the file. Newlines also go into the file, and this is how you add additional lines. If you make an error in typing, the BACKSPACE key lets you back up, deleting characters as you go, until the beginning of the line; however, **vi** will not let you backspace past the beginning of the line. To change a previous line, you must enter command mode, probably reposition the cursor to the error, and then make the change. Pressing CTRL-W deletes the current word without leaving input mode.

A common error is to attempt to enter commands while in input mode, without pressing ESC first. Even **vi** experts make this mistake, or make the opposite error of trying to enter text while in command mode. This second error is more destructive, because you can make multiple changes to the file as you type. These changes usually cannot be corrected with **u**, because the undo command can only repair the last change. To prevent problems associated with these mode errors, be sure to write the file back to disk frequently with the **:w** command when you are sure it is correct.

Moving Around in the Buffer

Command mode is used primarily to move around in the text buffer, and to enter input mode in various ways to change text that you've already entered. You can reposition the current line, which often causes the screen to be redrawn so that the current line is centered on screen. You can also move the cursor on the current line. When you enter text mode or change a portion of the buffer, changes will occur on the current line, at the current cursor position.

The **w** (for word) operator jumps the cursor ahead to the beginning of the next word, moving to the next line if necessary. The **b** (for back) operator jumps the cursor backward to the beginning of the previous word. The SPACEBAR moves the cursor ahead a single character, and BACKSPACE moves the cursor backward a single character. Newline or RETURN moves the cursor to the beginning of the next line, and - (minus) moves the cursor to the beginning of the previous line. The ^ (caret) moves the cursor to the beginning of the current line, and the $ (dollar sign) moves the cursor to the end of the current line. All of these motion operators can take a numeric argument, or *repeat count,* preceding the operator. For example, the command **5w** moves the cursor ahead five words, and **6-** moves the cursor back to the beginning of the sixth line previous to the current line.

The **H** operator moves the cursor to the top line of the currently displayed screen, and **L** moves to the last line displayed on the screen. You can jump to a specific line of the buffer with **G** (for go), preceded by a line number.

The last line of the file is known by the logical name $. Thus, you can use **$G** or simply **G** to jump to the end of the buffer.

Some last line mode commands are also used to move around the file. To move to the first line of the file you can enter :1, and, as expected, to move to the last line of the file you can use :$. The current line in the file is known by the logical name . (dot). You can determine the current line number with the last line mode command

```
:.=
```

(dot-equal). In response, **vi** will display the current line number at the bottom of the screen. Similarly,

```
:$=
```

displays the line number of the last line in the file.

CTRL-F moves forward in the file by one complete screenful, redrawing the screen as it goes. CTRL-B moves backward by one screenful.

Many terminals include cursor control keys on the keyboard. Usually, **vi** will honor these cursor control keys in addition to the motion operators just defined. Since these keys vary from keyboard to keyboard, you will have to experiment with your terminal and your version of **vi** to see what effect they have.

If your terminal does not have cursor control keys, you can use the letters **h** (to move left one character), **l** (ell, to move right one character), **j** (to move down one line at the same cursor position), and **k** (to move up one line at the same cursor position).

Searching for Text

A variant of last line mode allows you to search for text strings in the file. The search begins at the current cursor position, continues through the end of the file, and then wraps around to the beginning of the file. If no match is found, the search ends back at the current cursor position.

You use the **/** (slash) followed by a string to perform a search. This command

`/string`

will search for *string* in the file. When you enter the **/**, the cursor jumps to the last line of the screen (without changing the current line) and the string you enter is displayed. When you press newline or RETURN, the search starts, and if a match is found **vi** redraws the screen with the cursor on the matched string. You can search backward in the file by using a **?** (question mark) instead of a **/**. When you search backward, the search proceeds from the current line upward to the beginning of the buffer, and then wraps around to the end of the file and continues backward until the current line is reached.

After you have found a string with **/** or **?** you can repeat the search to find the next occurrence of the same string just by entering a **/** or **?** and a newline. The same string will be searched. You can switch the direction of a search whenever you wish.

Actually **vi** is storing the search string for you, so if you enter a **/** without specifying a string right after you enter **vi**, it will complain, as shown here:

```
/
No previous regular expression
```

Actually the search string can be much more complex than a simple text string, as you'll see when we discuss regular expressions in the next chapter.

Changing Text

Several operators enter text mode and allow you to change existing text. The command **r** (for replace) followed by a single character changes the character at the current cursor position to the character that you type. This operator leaves you in command mode, since it only changes a single character. The **R** operator allows you to replace as many characters as you wish, starting at the current cursor position. This command leaves you in input mode, but you can replace only to the end of the current line. Any new lines are added to the file right after the current line. When you return to command mode with the ESC key after an **R** operation, any characters left on the current line that you did not overtype will remain as they were. The **C** (for change) command is similar to **R**, but it changes the whole line even if you only change one character before returning to command mode. The **J** (for join) operator merges two lines of text by deleting the newline character that separates the current line from the following line. To split a single line into two lines, simply enter input mode with the cursor where you want the split to occur, and press the newline (RETURN) key.

Deleting Text

The **vi** editor also provides operators to delete sections of text. The **x** operator deletes the current character. You can use **6x** to delete the next six characters from the cursor position. The **dd** operator deletes the current line, and **6dd** deletes the current line as well as the next five lines. You can delete a single word with **dw** or the next five words with **5dw**. Use **cw** to change the current word, and **6cw** to change the next six words. The **cc** operator changes the current line, and **6cc** changes the next six lines.

The **D** command deletes from the cursor position to the end of the line.

You can also use last line mode to delete a range of lines using line numbers. The command

```
:3,5d
```

will delete lines three through five.

Repeating a Change

The . (dot) command applies the last change to the current cursor position. This includes text addition and deletion operations as well as replacements.

Cut and Paste Operations

The **vi** editor can maintain several internal storage spaces, or *buffers*. Blocks of text can be pulled out of the file into a buffer, and then read back into the file from the buffer. There is a single default buffer in addition to the main text buffer, or you can name a buffer with a one-character name. When you perform an operation on a buffer you use the buffer's name to refer to it. These operations work from **vi** command mode, not from the last line mode. They are known as *yank* and *put* in **vi** terminology, but in other environments they are often called *cut and paste* or *copy and paste* operations. All of these operations work on blocks of complete lines; to yank a part of a line you must split the line in two and yank the piece you want.

You can copy a section of text into a buffer with the **Y** (for yank) command. **Y** takes a number of lines to yank. The command

```
7Y
```

will yank the current line and the next six lines into the default buffer. You can reposition the cursor, and then use the **p** (for put) command to paste the lines of text back into the file after the current line. Uppercase **P** puts the lines into the file just above the current line. This is a copy and paste operation, since the yank does not change the text, but makes a copy in the default buffer.

To do a *cut and paste* you can delete a block of lines with a command such as **7dd**. This deletes the current line and the next six lines from the main file. Actually, deletions are placed in the default buffer, so after a deletion like this you can reposition the cursor and use **p** or **P** to paste the material back into the file.

When you do a paste operation, the material is not deleted from its buffer, so you can paste the same material into a file several times. As soon as you make another editing change, however, the material in the default buffer is lost, and the most recent change replaces it. Actually, this is how the undo operation is implemented in **vi**: the content of each change is placed in the default buffer, and **u** simply pastes it back into the file at its original location.

You can store text in a buffer more permanently by giving a buffer a one-character name, preceded by a " (double quote). This command

```
7"aY
```

will yank seven lines into a buffer named **a**. The **vi** editor allows up to 26 named buffers to exist simultaneously. A named buffer can be put back into the text using a command like

```
"ap
```

which pastes the contents of buffer **a** into the file after the current line.

Cut and Paste Using Line Numbers

Last line mode provides commands to move and copy blocks of lines by number. For example, you could use

```
:3,5m9
```

to move lines three through five to follow line nine. Similarly,

```
:3,5t9
```

would copy lines three through five after line nine, but would not delete them from their current position. Use a single number if you only want to move or copy a single line, as shown here:

```
:6t9
```

The line numbers can actually be full regular expression addresses, as you will see in the next chapter.

The emacs Editor

The **emacs** editor is another popular full-screen text editor. It is almost as popular as **vi**, but it is not part of the standard UNIX system. However, **emacs** is widely available for any version of the UNIX system running on any machine; **emacs** is usually the first or second piece of software ported to new machines as they are designed.

The **emacs** editor is very different in its philosophy from **vi**, but like **vi**, **emacs** is not a word processor in the modern sense. Neither editor formats text or allows embedded graphics. Like **vi**, **emacs** allows you to use nearly any terminal, as specified by the TERM environment variable. However, some versions of **emacs** do not use the **/usr/share/lib/terminfo** terminal database, but have their own terminal description file in **/usr/share/lib/emacs/terminals** (or **/usr/lib/emacs/terminals**). Other library material related to **emacs**, such as the text of available macros, may also be in the directory **/usr/share/lib/emacs**. These directory locations may vary in different versions of **emacs**.

Fundamental Concepts of emacs

In operation, **emacs** is fundamentally different from **vi**. There is no input or command mode, and all normal characters typed at the keyboard go into the text file at the cursor position. Thus, **emacs** is always in input mode. In fact, the term *mode* has a different use in **emacs**; it refers not to the command state of the editor but rather to the options that are currently set. For example, when the editor displays line numbers for the file being edited it is in the *line number mode*.

Commands to move the cursor, read and write files, open additional lines, and so on are special keystroke sequences that begin with the ESC or CTRL key. For example, to exit from **emacs** back to the shell, you use the keystroke sequence CTRL-X followed by CTRL-C. In **emacs** terminology, these keys are denoted ˆxˆc (or sometimes C-xC-c), where the ˆ (caret) or **C-** preceding the other characters means to hold down the CTRL key while you press the lowercase **x** and **c** keys. Other commands are invoked with the ESC key preceding the command, such as the sequence ESC-D (ESC followed by the lowercase letter **d** key), which deletes the next word on the screen. In **emacs** terminology, these escape sequences are denoted with an **M** (for meta) preceding the letter; thus, **M-d** would indicate the ESC-D sequence. Remember, any character sequences that do not begin with either ESC or a CTRL character are treated as text to be entered into the file. The **emacs** editor uses nearly all the CTRL keys for various functions, and the key sequences ˆx and **M-x** introduce longer sequences that have specific meanings, such as ˆxˆs (CTRL-X-CTRL-S, used to write the buffer) or **M-x?** (meta-x question, used to list all available commands). We will discuss some of these operators in the following sections.

There is a (loose) logic to the use of the meta and CTRL operations in **emacs**. The CTRL commands generally operate on single lines and characters; the meta commands generally operate on words or sentences, and the CTRL-meta commands are complex combinations of both operations. Table 5-2 summarizes the **emacs** commands.

Many users prefer the modeless operation of **emacs** over the three modes of **vi**, even though the commands used by **emacs** are less mnemonic than the **vi** commands.

Starting emacs

You invoke **emacs** with an optional filename, as shown here:

```
$ emacs old.file
```

Move Cursor

^f	Forward one character
^b	Backward one character
^n	Next line
^p	Previous line
^a	Beginning of line
^e	End of line
M-f	Forward one word
M-b	Backward one word
M-a	Beginning of sentence
M-e	End of sentence
M-[	Beginning of paragraph
M-]	End of paragraph
M-<	Beginning of buffer
M->	End of buffer
^v	Next screen
M-v	Previous screen
M-nM-r	Move down *n* lines
M-x goto-line *n*	Go to line *n*

File Commands

^x^f	Read file into a new buffer
^x^s	Write a buffer to its file
^x^w	Write buffer to a named file
^xi	Add file to current buffer

Region Commands

^SPACEBAR	Set mark at cursor
^w	Delete from mark to cursor
M-w	Copy to kill stack
^x^x	Exchange cursor and mark

Search Commands

^s	Search forward to string
^r	Search backward to string
^M-s	Search forward to RE
^M-r	Search backward to RE

Deletion Commands

^d	Delete forward one character
BACKSPACE	Delete backward one character
^K	Delete to end of line
M-d	Delete forward one word
M-k	Delete forward one sentence
^y	Restore last deleted text
M-y	Swap yanked text with kill stack

Buffer Commands

^x2	Split screen
^x1	One buffer on screen
^xb	Switch to named buffer
^x^b	List buffers
^xo	Switch to another window
^xk	Kill buffer
^y	Yank

Miscellaneous Commands

^x^c	Exit
M-!	Shell escape
^l	Redraw screen
^h	Help
^hw	Key sequence for command
^xu	Undo last operation (unstack)
^o	Insert blank line
^g	Abort partially entered command

Macro Commands

^x (	Start keyboard macro
^x)	End keyboard macro

Table 5-2.   Major Commands for the **emacs** Text Editor

The program will not accept multiple filenames as arguments. The file, if any, is read into the *main* buffer of **emacs**. The optional argument +*n*, where *n* is a number, causes **emacs** to position the cursor on line *n* as it starts. Many additional command-line arguments are available.

After loading, you can read more files into additional **emacs** buffers, and edit up to 12 files simultaneously. The command ˆxˆf (for file) reads a file into a new buffer. This differs from the command ˆxˆr (for read), which reads an existing file into the current buffer and marks it as read-only. The command ˆxi (for insert) reads a file into the buffer at the current cursor position without deleting the current contents of the buffer. All of these commands prompt for the name of the file to read.

Figure 5-2 shows a typical **emacs** display after the program has been loaded with **/etc/profile**. This display may differ slightly on other releases of **emacs**. The top section of the display shows the current line and surrounding lines of the file you are editing. You can change the size of the display with **emacs** commands, using the ˆxˆm (for change mode) command sequence as discussed later. The bottom of the screen contains the **emacs** name, followed by the current file or buffer name, and the modes or options in effect ("Fundamental," in this case). The last part of the line displays the percentage of the the file above the top of the screen. With a small file, "All" is displayed, indicating that the

```
# issue message of the day
        trap : 1 2 3
        echo ""              # skip a line
        if [ -s /etc/motd ] ; then cat /etc/motd; fi

        trap "" 1 2 3
# set default attributes for terminal
        stty erase '^h' echoe

        if [ x$TERM = x -o "$TERM" = 'unknown' ]; then
                LOGTTY=${LOGTTY:='tty'}

                TERM=ansi
                if [ `expr "$LOGTTY" : '.*/\(.*\)'` = "console" ]
                then
                        /sbin/isat386
                        if [ $? = 0 ]
                            then TERM=AT386
                        fi
                fi
        fi
        if [ "$TERMCAP" = "" ]
-----Emacs: profile              (Fundamental )----26%--------------------
```

Figure 5-2.   Typical **emacs** screen display

whole file is on screen. The ----- (dashes) at the left signify that the file has not been changed since you started editing it; this will change to --**- as soon as you have changed the contents of the buffer. The last line of the display is an **emacs** information line, reserved for special messages and commands. Among other messages, many versions of **emacs** will announce on this line that incoming mail is waiting. Most versions of **emacs** include special commands to read your mail into a text buffer or to send the content of a buffer as mail.

Splitting the Screen

The **emacs** editor can split its display screen so that any two buffers can be displayed and edited simultaneously. If you read another file into a second buffer with ˆxˆf, you can then split the screen with ˆx2 (for two windows), and **emacs** will prompt you to select the name or buffer number of the new buffer to add to the screen. Although **emacs** can edit up to 12 buffers simultaneously, many versions can display only 2 at once. You return to a single window display with ˆx1. Again, **emacs** prompts you to select which buffer should remain on the screen. When you display or hide a buffer, it still remains in the internal **emacs** memory, so you have not closed the file or deleted any changes to it. Before you return to the shell, **emacs** prompts you to write each buffer or discard the changes. The editor announces which of the two windows is currently active; the information line at the bottom of the screen displays the name and buffer number of the active window. You can make the other window the active buffer with the ˆxˆo (for other) command, or you can change the displayed buffers completely with ˆxˆb (for buffer).

Writing the File

After you make changes to the buffer, you can write it with ˆxˆw (for write). This message will appear at the bottom of the screen

```
Write file:
```

prompting you to enter the pathname to write. You can enter a newline by pressing RETURN, and the same filename will be used, or, you can enter a different name. You can also enter ˆg to abort the write operation. To write the currently active buffer to its current filename, use the ˆxˆs (for save) command.

Exiting from emacs

The command ˆxˆc (for close) is used to quit from **emacs** back to the shell. If try to quit back to the shell before you have written the file, **emacs** will prompt you for confirmation before returning to the shell.

Getting Help

Most versions of the **emacs** editor provide a lot of help. The ˆh (for help) command enters the large help subsystem. After ˆh you can enter a **?** or a second ˆh to get help on the help system. Alternatively, you can use

ˆhc *key*

to get a short description of the function of any keystroke sequence. A longer description is available with

ˆhk *key*

The inverse — the keystroke needed to perform a function — is displayed by

ˆhw *command*

assuming you know the correct name of the command. It is well worth the time required to learn the **emacs** help system.

Changing the Cursor Position

When the cursor appears *on* a character, **emacs** actually treats the *current point* as just *before* the cursor position, so that when you enter text, it appears just in front of the cursor. Keep this behavior in mind as you use **emacs**.

A rich set of operators is provided for changing the current cursor position, where all text entry takes place. The **^f** (for forward) operates moves the cursor ahead one character, and **^b** (for backward) moves the cursor back one character. The **^n** (for next) operator moves the cursor to the next line, and **^p** (for previous) moves the cursor back one line. The **^a** operator moves the cursor to the beginning of the current line, and **^e** (for end) moves the cursor to the end of the current line. **M-<** moves the cursor to the beginning of the buffer, and **M->** moves the cursor to the end of the buffer. **M-f** moves the cursor ahead one word, while **M-b** moves the cursor back one word. The **^v** operator moves the cursor ahead by one screenful, redrawing the screen to display the new block of text. **M-v** moves the cursor back one screenful.

Most of these commands can take a numeric argument to multiply their action. To enter these arguments begin with the ESC key, followed by the number, and then the argument mentioned previously. For example, to move forward by eight words, enter ESC, followed by the digit 8, and then by another ESC, and an **f**.

Deleting Text

Since any normal characters you type go into the text buffer at the current point, there is no difficulty inserting text with **emacs**. However, to delete text more special commands are needed. The BACKSPACE key deletes the character just to the left of the cursor, and **^d** (for delete) deletes the character directly under the cursor. The **^k** (for kill) operator deletes the rest of the current line after the cursor position, or joins the current line with the next line if the cursor is at the end of the line. If you give an argument of 0, all the text from the beginning of the line to the cursor position is deleted. An argument greater than 0 deletes that number of lines forward from the cursor, while an argument less than 0 deletes that number of lines backward from the cursor.

Marks In emacs

More complex deletion and text movement commands involve *marks*. The **emacs** editor allows up to 12 marks, one for each text buffer. Place a mark at the current cursor position with **M-SPACEBAR**. The mark will not be displayed on the screen in most versions of **emacs.** When you move the cursor, the mark remains in place. Then you can move or delete the material between the mark and the current point. When you switch to another **emacs** buffer, the mark remains in place in the old buffer, and you can set another mark in the currently active buffer if you wish.

Because the marks are not displayed on screen, it is easy to forget where a mark is located. You can swap the cursor and mark position with ˆxˆx. To return to the original cursor position (and replace the mark), just execute ˆxˆx a second time.

Cut and Paste in emacs

When material is deleted from a text buffer, **emacs** maintains the material in a *kill stack.* The last eight deletions are maintained in the kill stack. Usually you move text by marking the beginning of the block, moving the cursor to the end of the block, and then deleting the block with ˆw. The text is not really lost, so you can move the cursor to the location where you want the text to go, and issue the ˆy command to insert the last killed block of text at the cursor position. To delete an area of text, simply move it to the kill stack with ˆw, and then forget about it.

You can also use ˆy to undo errors in deleting text, since the text is retained on the kill stack after a deletion. There is also a separate undo command in **emacs.**

The **M-w** command grabs the text from the mark to the current cursor position, and places it on the kill stack. However, this command does not change the current buffer, so it is used with ˆy to copy blocks of text from one region of the buffer to another, or from one buffer to another.

Searching and Replacing Text Strings

The **emacs** editor has powerful search operators to locate text strings or regular expressions in the current buffer. The command ˆs (for search) starts the action, and **emacs** prompts for a string to locate. The search proceeds forward from the current point to the end of the file. Use ˆb (for backward) to search from the current point back to the beginning of the file. Again, **emacs** will prompt for a string to search. After the search string is found, you can continue to search for the next instance of the same string with another ^s (for search) or ^r (for reverse). If you do not enter a different string, the previous string is reused. You can *wrap* the search from the end of the file back to the beginning by entering another ^s when the end of the file has been reached. To clear a search in progress, use ^g.

A similar procedure is provided to substitute strings after a match. The command

```
M-x replace-string
```

starts the operation. In this case, you type the string *replace-string* after the **M-x** and enter a newline by pressing RETURN; then **emacs** will prompt for the string to replace. Enter the original string and another newline; then enter the new string and one more newline. The **emacs** editor will replace *all* occurrences of the first string with the second, so use this operation with care.

With the command

```
M-x query-replace
```

followed by the same sequence of operations, you can instruct **emacs** to prompt for confirmation before it makes each replacement. Press **y** if you want the substitution to be made on that occurrence of the match, and **n** to skip an occurrence. In either case, **emacs** goes to the next occurrence of the match string, if there is one. You can also enter **R** to instruct **emacs** to replace all the rest of the occurrences of the pattern in the file without prompting, or you can enter ^g to abort the operation and return to normal **emacs** operation.

Escaping to the Shell

Like many other commands, **emacs** allows you to suspend its operation temporarily while you do other work from the shell. Enter **M-!** and **emacs** will prompt for a command line to execute. The **emacs** editor will wait until the command is completed, and then redraw the screen and resume its actions. You can also enter

```
M-x shell
```

to get an interactive shell. When you exit from that shell, **emacs** will resume.

The command **M-|** (meta-pipe), followed by a command line, uses the text between the mark and the cursor as the standard input of the command, and the buffer remains unchanged. You can also capture the output of the shell command to replace the current region, with **^uM-|** followed by a command line. Try experimenting with these operations to see how they work.

Going Further

There is a great deal more to editing under the UNIX system. Here we will mention a few customization features, before moving to a discussion of regular expressions in the next chapter.

A Note on Using the Editors with the X Window System

Figures 5-1 and 5-2 were taken from a display operating under the X Window System. In the default X configuration, *scroll bars* will be present on your screen, as shown on the right of Figures 5-1 and 5-2. However, the **vi** and **emacs** editors are not designed to take full advantage of these scroll bars, which are controlled by the X Window System rather than the editors. Thus, you can move the screen contents by manipulating the scroll bars (as discussed in Chapter 23), but these movements will not change the current line as used by the editors.

In fact, when you change the scroll location, and then enter a keystroke to the editor, X will repaint the screen at the current line as used by the editor. About the best you can do is use the scroll history to copy a region of text into the current point in the editor. To accomplish this in **vi**, enter text mode where you want the material to be copied, move the scroll bar to display the desired text, and then *copy* the material with the X Tools. If you are in text mode in the editor, X will send the material to the current point, and the screen will shift.

Similarly, you cannot resize an X window while either of the editors is running. If you do so, the editors will not adapt to the new size, and your screen will become deranged. The correct procedure is to exit from the editor, resize the window as desired, and then reenter the editor. When the editors start, they adapt to the current window size.

Configuring vi Options

The **vi** editor has many options that change its behavior. These are accessed in one of two ways. The **:set** command, discussed earlier with **:set showmode**, is one example, and there are nearly 50 options in addition to **showmode** that can be set this way. The command

```
:set all
```

displays all of the available options. When you change an option, use the option name after the **:set** command to turn the option on, and put *no* in front of the option name to turn it off. These commands

```
:set showmode
:set noshowmode
```

will turn **showmode** on and then off. Some of the options take an argument. For example,

```
:set window=10
```

makes the logical window size ten rows high. You can experiment with the **vi** options to customize the editor for your taste and terminal environment. Some of the more widely used options are **terse**, which produces a shorter message display, **autoindent**, which starts a new line at the same column as the beginning of the previous line, and **number**, which displays line numbers on the screen. The **tabstop** option changes the number of character positions the cursor moves when the TAB key is pressed. The **ignorecase** option causes both uppercase and lowercase characters to match in regular expression searches. Many additional options are also available.

The options that you set with **:set** are only active for the current editing session. When you exit the editor with **:q** the option settings are lost, and the next time you run **vi** you have to reset them. However, **vi** provides two mechanisms that allow you to set options permanently, so that when the program starts up it configures itself according to your instructions. First, the environment variable **EXINIT** can contain a **set** command that is executed when **vi** begins. For example,

```
$ EXINIT='set number tabstop=4 ignorecase' ; export EXINIT
```

will configure **vi** with **number** and **ignorecase**, and tabs set to four spaces. Normally, you set this environment variable in your **.profile**, so it is active each time you log in to the system. Second, you can put these commands in a file called **.exrc** (for **ex** run commands) in your HOME directory. Then, when **vi** loads, it will read the file and take the actions specified.

Another way to use the **EXINIT** variable and the **.exrc** file is with the **map** command. You can use this command to map any keystroke to any **vi** function or sequence of functions. This allows you to configure **vi** to perform complex actions with only a few keystrokes. Unfortunately, this function uses an obscure and difficult programming language, and is mainly useful to **vi** experts.

Filtering Text from Inside vi

You can add the standard output of any command to your current buffer with

```
:r !command
```

This reads the standard output of *command* into your file at the current line. Similarly,

```
:w !command
```

writes the file into the standard input of *command.*

You can also filter a portion of the current file through a pipeline, as follows

```
:3,56 !command
```

This writes lines 3 through 56 into the standard input of *command,* deletes the lines from the buffer, and reads in the standard output of *command* in their place.

Finally, you can use the simple formatting tool **fmt** to "flow" short text lines together. Try

```
:1,$ !fmt
```

on a test file to see how this works. It provides an easy way to make sure your text has lines of a reasonable length.

Major Modes in emacs

The **emacs** editor includes several independent *major modes* that allow efficient editing of different kinds of text. There are specific modes for C programs, **troff** source documents, LISP programs, and several others. Usually, **emacs** figures out what kind of file you are editing from its filename, and switches modes appropriately. Indentation, nesting, line splitting, and other functions change their behavior based on the current mode. The exact list of available modes depends on the version of **emacs** you are using, and also on how the editor has been customized at your site. Consult your local **emacs** expert to find out what modes are available. Experts find this automatic mode switching very convenient, but beginners may be confused by it.

You can force **emacs** to use a particular mode for editing a file by inserting a special string at the beginning of the file. The mode command must be the first line of the file. Type -*- (dash-star-dash) both before and after the name of the mode that you want to use for that file, as shown here:

```
-*- nroff -*-
```

This line will select a mode suitable for editing **nroff** source documents. Since this string can appear anywhere on the first line of the file, you can surround it with characters that make it a comment in the target "language." For example, you might enter the previous line as

```
\" -*- nroff -*-
```

Minor Modes in emacs

The **emacs** editor also includes *minor modes*, which are used to set various preferences and options. Use the **M-x** command to select a mode. You can enter a name after the command, and that mode will be turned on or off. Here we'll look at a few of the most important modes. Remember, the names of modes differ widely from site to site, so consult your **emacs** expert if you need more information.

The **save** mode tells **emacs** to save your buffer to disk automatically after you enter a number of characters specified by the **savetype** mode. The save file has a different name than the original file, so you need not worry about **emacs** automatically overwriting your file just after you've made an error. If your file is named **file**, the save file will have the name **#file#** in the current directory.

Turn on the **auto-fill-mode** mode when you want to use the *auto-wrap* feature, so that **emacs** will add a newline whenever you type more than **fillcol** characters on a single line. When this mode is active, **emacs** breaks lines intelligently at word boundaries. The **overwrite** mode causes ordinary characters normally entered into the file to *replace* existing characters. This mode is often used to change an existing file more quickly. The **set-number** mode toggles the line number display, and **height** and **width** give the dimensions of the screen display. This is useful if you are using the X Window System. Many other modes are also available, but they differ between **emacs** versions.

The emacs Customization File

When **emacs** starts, it reads the file **.emacs** in your HOME directory. This file contains a set of **emacs** keystrokes that you can also enter directly from the keyboard. The program executes these commands before it draws the screen and turns control over to the user. You can use the **.emacs** file to customize the **emacs** modes and environment to your personal taste.

Macros In emacs

The **emacs** editor also provides excellent extension and customization tools. These *macros* are composed of a series of normal **emacs** commands, and they can contain calls to other macros that have been defined. Most commercial versions of **emacs** include many macros, ranging from automated spelling checkers to tools that remap the keyboard for specific terminals. Nearly unlimited extensions of the **emacs** system are possible; some **emacs** gurus run their entire sessions from within the editor, using so many customized tools that the normal shell and commands are barely visible. Consult the documentation for your specific version of **emacs** if you want to create and use macros.

Keyboard Macros

One form of macro—the keyboard macro—is very easy to create and use. *Keyboard macros* allow you to set up a sequence of keystrokes and name it as a macro. Then, when you use the name, **emacs** executes the entire remembered sequence. This can be very helpful when you have repetitive work to do in an editing session.

To start recording a series of keystrokes as a macro, use the command

^x(

(CTRL-X left parenthesis). All the keystrokes you enter until you end recording with

^x)

(CTRL-X right parenthesis) will stored as part of the macro. Note that the keystrokes are executed as well as recorded in the macro as you enter them.

When you complete a macro definition, you can execute it with **^xe** (for execute). This command can only execute the *last* macro you defined. If you want to have more than one keyboard macro defined simultaneously, you can name the macros with

```
^x name-last-kbd-macro
```

Keyboard macros are lost when you exit from **emacs**, unless you include their definitions in your **.emacs** file.

Keymaps are another useful **emacs** feature. You can *rebind* your keyboard to customize nearly all the keystrokes that are used for commands. Many users make extensive keymap changes in their **.emacs** file to suit their preferences. Consult the specific documentation for your **emacs** version to learn how to set up keymaps.

Regular Expressions and Advanced Editing

S
I
X

Editing under the UNIX system is really based on the regular expression. *Regular expressions* are formal descriptions of text strings that allow extremely powerful matching operations.

The **/** and **?** search operations of **vi** are much more powerful and flexible than indicated in the previous chapter. By using regular expressions in **vi,** you can efficiently search for many different strings in the same command, and match any of them. You can also perform complex search and replace operations using regular expressions as the base.

Regular expressions occur not only in **vi,** but also in all the other standard editors, and even in the shell. You might recognize the shell wildcard operators as a simplified form of the regular expressions discussed here. Unfortunately, the syntax for regular expressions in the shell command line is not identical to the form used in **vi,** so confusion is possible even for expert users.

In this chapter we will introduce the concept of regular expressions, discuss the commands that use them directly, and then return to **vi** and other editors to show how regular expressions make these programs come alive.

Basic Concepts of Regular Expressions

Whenever you can use the operation /*string* in **vi** to search for a matching string, you can use a regular expression instead of a simple string. In fact, a character string is just the least complex form of a regular expression.

Matching Any Single Character

A regular expression is made up of operators that describe single characters to search for. For example, the string **abc** consists of three characters. For each character, you could have substituted a complex expression to describe the character you were looking for in that position in the string. The character . (dot) is one of the regular expression operators, and stands for any single character.

Thus, you could use the string **a.c** to refer to any string that begins with *a*, ends with *c*, and has any character between them. The string **adc** would match, as would **a#c** or **aSc**, but **abdc** would not match, because there are two characters between the *a* and the *c*. You could match **abdc** with the regular expressions **a..c, a...,** or **....**; however, **a...** or **....** would also match many other strings that you might not want. The trick in using regular expressions is to specify the exact set of strings you are looking for and no others.

Matching a Set

The operators [and] (brackets) denote a *set* of characters, any one of which will match. The expression

[abc]

will match any of the single characters *a*, *b*, or *c*. The expression

[aA]

will match either an uppercase or lowercase *a*.

This type of expression—a set of characters enclosed within square brackets—matches only one character in the file you are searching. You can use sequences of these expressions to search for more than one character. For example,

[aA] [bB]

will match any of the strings **ab, aB, Ab,** or **AB,** but will not match **BA.** Since each sequence surrounded with square brackets matches a single character, the previous construction matches a two-character string. In a search command to **vi,** you might use

/[aA] [bB]

to find the first occurrence of any of the four possible two-character matching patterns.

You can build these regular expressions to any level of complexity, but each sequence enclosed in square brackets can only match a single character.

Matching a Range

The square bracket operator can also match on single characters in a range of characters in the alphabetic sort sequence. For example, to find an occurrence of any digit in the file, you could use

[0123456789]

However, a shorter form would be

[0-9]

The - (hyphen) works within the bracket operator to denote a range of characters. To find any alphabetic character, you would use

[A-Za-z]

This expression will find any single alphabetic character, either upper-
or lowercase.

Escaping the Special Meaning of Regular Expression Operators

To search for the character [directly, without having **vi** interpret it as
the beginning of a regular expression, you must *escape* the operator's
special meaning by preceding it with a \ (backslash), as follows:

```
/\[
```

This **vi** command will find the first occurrence of the bracket in the
buffer. You can escape the special meaning of any regular expression
operator in this way.

Special Symbols for the Beginning and End of a Line

You can *anchor* your regular expressions at the beginning or end of a
line so that you can specify the character that must appear in the first
or last position on the line. Use a ^ (caret) to denote the beginning of the
line. For example, the command

```
/^This
```

will match the string **This** only when it appears at the beginning of a
line. Similarly, you can use the $ (dollar sign) to denote the end of the
line. Thus,

```
/This$
```

will only match when **This** is directly followed by a newline. To escape
these special meanings and match the ^ and $ characters literally, you
must escape them with a \. For instance, the expression

```
/\$25
```

will match the string **$25.** Note that using an expression such as

`/hello^goodbye`

or

`/hello$goodbye`

makes no sense, because regular expressions do not span multiple lines. In fact, **vi** will determine that these regular expressions are meaningless, and treat the ^ and $ as literal characters instead of special characters that mark the line ends.

Building Complex Regular Expressions

You can combine single-character regular expressions to match longer strings, as in this example:

`/[0-9][0-9][0-9]`

This line will find the first three-digit sequence of numbers. You can add the * (star) operator to denote zero or more occurrences of the preceding single-character regular expression. For example, to find a sequence of digits of any length you would use

`/[0-9][0-9]*`

Why couldn't you just use

`/[0-9]*`

as your search command? Because * denotes zero or more occurrences of the string, this command would match the beginning of each line, which is not the intended result. The initial **[0-9]** forces at least one digit to appear in the pattern before the optional digits.

To match an entire line of a file, you would use

`/^.*$`

You can read this as, "Start at the beginning of the line (^), and take any character (.) any number of times (*) until the end of the line ($)." You can create very complex and clever regular expressions with these simple building blocks.

The Longest Matching String

One important rule to remember is that regular expressions match the longest matching string. If you have the string

```
abc1234def
```

and use the command

```
/[0-9][0-9]*
```

the expression will match all the digits, or

```
1234
```

because the [0-9]* section tries to find all the digits in the string, and match them all. Thus, complex regular expressions will sometimes match more than you expect, so take care when you are creating and using these powerful tools.

The grep Command

The UNIX system provides a filter that lets you search for strings in files, using regular expressions to specify the match string. The **grep** (for global regular expression and print) command reads its standard input or a list of files given as arguments, and writes to its standard output any lines that contain the matched string. The first argument to the **grep** command is the pattern to find. Use this form

```
$ grep any_pattern files
```

to search the list of files. The search string *any—pattern* can be any regular expression. In its simplest form, the regular expression can be a simple sequence of characters, as in this example:

```
$ grep world old.file
hello world
$
```

Each line that matches the pattern goes to the standard output of **grep**.

You can use any regular expression as the match pattern. For example,

```
$ grep "^[a-z]12" another.file
```

will find any line that begins with a lowercase letter followed by the digits 1 and 2. Quote the regular expression you are searching for to prevent the shell from interpreting the bracket characters before **grep** sees them.

The **grep** command also allows you to select every line that does *not* contain a pattern by using the -v option, as shown here:

```
$ grep -v world old.file
another line
a third line
$
```

This command will display every line that does not contain the string *world*.

The **grep** command also provides many other options. The **-c** (for count) option produces only a count of matching lines, like piping the output of **grep** to **wc -l.** The **-n** (for number) option adds the source file line number to the matching output. The **-i** (for ignore) option ignores case distinctions in matches.

One of the most important uses for **grep** is to search through several files to find a particular string. If you have several files in a directory, and do not recall which file contains some specific material, **grep** or one of its variants is ideal. If you include more than one filename in a list of arguments to **grep**, the command will report the name of the file at the beginning of each line it prints, as shown here:

```
$ grep and *
test.file1:and a third line.
story:It was a dark and stormy night.
$
```

You can usually tell immediately which of the files you want.

The fgrep and egrep Commands

There are two variations on the **grep** command that optimize the search for some special cases. The **fgrep** (for fixed **grep** or fast **grep**) command takes only a simple search string, rather than a regular expression. The **egrep** (for extended grep) command allows a richer set of regular expression operators than does **grep**. Although slower than **grep**, it is optimized for more complex searches. In most situations, the original **grep** proves to be a good compromise between these features.

The **egrep** command provides some additional regular expression operators that differ slightly from the **grep** operators. In addition to the * operator, used to designate zero or more occurrences of a single-character pattern, **egrep** also provides the + (plus) operator, which denotes *one or more* occurrences of the character. For example, in **grep** you would write

```
[0-9][0-9]*
```

for any sequence of digits of any length. This would work with **egrep**, but you could also write

```
[0-9]+
```

to mean the same thing. Similarly, the **?** (question mark) operator denotes *zero or one* occurrence of the pattern. For example,

```
^[0-9]?a|b
```

will match a line that begins with an optional digit, and then contains an *a* or a *b*.

In **egrep**, the | (pipe) operator denotes *either* of a pair of regular expressions. For example,

```
^a|b
```

will match a line that begins with either the character *a* or *b*. The **egrep** command also allows a parenthesis operator to group multicharacter regular expressions. The command

```
$ egrep "([0-9]+ab)*1234" file
```

will find any strings that begin with a sequence of one or more digits, followed by **ab**, followed by a sequence of one or more digits, followed by **ab**, and so on for any number of these patterns, until the string **1234** occurs.

In **egrep,** you can use the **-f file.name** (for file) command-line option, which takes the regular expression from the file specified after the **-f** flag, rather than from the command line. In **fgrep,** the file contains the list of strings to search for.

The **grep** command is widely used, and provides a very quick and powerful mechanism for finding arbitrary character strings in text files. When you use it, try to specify the smallest regular expression that meets your needs, because the output from a large **grep** command can be enormous if the match is too general.

Searching in vi Using Regular Expressions

The last line mode search operators **/** and **?** allow any regular expression to specify the match string. A specific character string is just a simple form of a regular expression. Try using regular expressions when you edit. As you learn how they work, you will find that your editing goes much more quickly and efficiently.

Substitutions in vi

You can perform powerful search and replace operations on strings, using regular expressions to define the matches you are looking for. The last line mode operation **:s** (for substitute) allows you to specify a regular expression for matching, and then a new string to replace the matched string. Following the **:s**, enter the delimiter **/**, the regular expression you want to delete, another **/**, and then the new string you want to substitute, as shown here:

```
:s/powerful/flexible
```

This will substitute the new string, **flexible**, for the first occurrence of the match string (or regular expression), **powerful**, on the current line. You can specify the first part of the substitute command as any regular expression, but the second part must be a specific string to insert on the line in place of the regular expression.

The previous substitute command will replace only the *first* occurrence of the regular expression on the current line, even if the cursor position is past the matched string. That is, these substitution commands work on the line as a whole, regardless of the current cursor position on the line.

To substitute *all* occurrences of the regular expression on the current line, add a trailing **/** to the command, followed by the letter **g** (for global), as shown here:

```
:s/old.re/newstring/g
```

This command will find and substitute all matches on the current line.

To delete a string with this mechanism, simply name an empty string for the target, as follows:

```
:s/the//
```

The trailing **/** is not needed, but it can be added if you wish.

As you might have expected, you can use the special operators **^** and **$** in your regular expressions to designate the beginning and end of a line. To add a string to the end of a line you might give this command:

```
:s/$/new text at end
```

To add a string at the beginning of a line you could use

```
:s/^/new text at beginning
```

A trailing **/** is not required unless you want to add a **g**.

Using the Matched Regular Expression in a Substitution

Sometimes you may want to name a string in the search section of the **:s** command, but not want to substitute it. For example, you might wish to add a word following a string of digits. You cannot use

```
:s/[0-9][0-9]*/new_string
```

because this would delete the sequence of digits and replace it with **new_string**. The special operator **&** (ampersand), when used in the substitution section, allows you to name whatever you matched in the search section. For example, given the string

```
abc1234def
```

and the command

```
:s/[0-9][0-9]*/&newstring
```

The result would be

```
abc1234newstringdef
```

The **&** operator has substituted the matching string in the output line. As usual, you can include a literal **&** character in your output by escaping it with a ****.

Substitutions on a Range of Lines

Normally the **:s** command will only change the first occurrence of a string on the current line. You can specify a range of lines after the **:** and before the **s** to make **vi** take the same action on each line in the range. For example,

```
:3,7s/old/new
```

will substitute the first occurrence of the string **old** with the new string **new** on lines three through seven of the file. To replace all occurrences of the regular expression on those lines, simply add the trailing **g**, as shown here:

```
:3,7s/old/new/g
```

To change every occurrence of a string in the file, use

```
:1,$s/old/new/g
```

Here, the $ is interpreted as the last line of the file. Note the two uses of $ in **vi**: Inside a regular expression the $ indicates the end of the line, while in a line address it indicates the last line of the file. Similarly, the . (dot) indicates any character when it is used in a regular expression, but signifies the current line when it is used in a line address.

More on Line Addressing

You can use one line number instead of a range if you wish to select a single line. The command

```
:34s/old/new
```

will replace the specified string only on line 34 of the file. Using a logical line number such as

```
:.s/old/new
```

will make the substitution on the current line. Similarly,

```
:$s/old/new
```

will make the substitution on the last line of the file.

Simple arithmetic expressions are also allowed. You can specify a range of lines around the current line by giving a *relative address*, as in this example:

```
:.-4,.+6s/old/new
```

This command will make the substitution on a range of 11 lines, starting on the fourth line above the current line and going to the sixth line after the current line. You can also use a $ in these computations, as shown here:

```
:.-4,$-2s/old/new
```

If you make an error in these arithmetic operations, **vi** will complain (assuming the address you've given is not valid). For example:

```
:.,$+6s/old/new
Not that many lines in buffer
```

A *legal* address that is not *logically* correct for your purpose can easily slip through, so be careful; these substitution operators do not prompt you for confirmation before they act.

Context Addressing with Regular Expressions

Actually the $ above is an example of a *context address*. In addition to naming ranges of lines by their line numbers (not so easy, because **vi** does not display line numbers by default), you can specify lines by giving a regular expression. Then, **vi** will search for the first line that matches the regular expression, and use that line as the addressed line. For example, you can replace the first occurrence of a string after the current line with

```
:/old/s//new
```

That is, **vi** will treat the first regular expression as a search operator and position the current line at the line where the first match occurred. Then it will execute the substitution. As you would expect, you can search backward with a command such as

```
:?old?s//new
```

Note that when **vi** has an existing current regular expression, as defined in this case by /**old**/, it reuses that regular expression until a new one is defined. This means that the command

```
s//new
```

does not need a regular expression in its match part; it defaults to the current expression, /**old**/. Of course, if you don't want to replace the current regular expression, you can specify a new one. For example, to find the first line that contains **old**, but then replace the string **hello** on that line, you might use

```
:/old/s/hello/goodbye
```

The current regular expression after this operation will be **hello**, not **old**.

You can also give a range of addresses using the regular expression form

```
:/hello/,/goodbye/s/old/new/
```

In this case, **vi** searches from the current line until it finds the matching string **hello**, and then makes the substitution until it finds a line that contains **goodbye**.

Although this form is more difficult to control than line numbers, it reflects the often-stated fact that all editing can be done without line numbers under the UNIX system. For this reason, **vi** is often called a *context editor*.

The sed Stream Editor

Some of the features of **vi**'s last line mode and **grep** are combined into the **sed** (for stream editor) command. This command is a filter like **grep**, but it lets you make changes to files. On the other hand, it is not interactive like **vi**. The **sed** command reads its input line by line, and writes the lines one by one to its standard output. For each line read in, **sed** applies a substitute operation of the form used with **vi** last line mode. If the match succeeds, the substitution is made and the line is written. If there is no match, the line is written unchanged.

One of the major advantages of **sed** over **vi** or other editors is that lines are read, modified, and written one by one; therefore, there is no buffer of the entire file stored in memory. This means that you can change files of any size with **sed,** even files that are too big for **vi** or another text editor. The **sed** command is often used to edit files that are larger than one megabyte. Most normal text editors cannot handle such large files, and **vi** is often limited to files smaller than 256,000 bytes.

You invoke **sed** with a command line similar to that used for **grep,** except you can use a full substitution operator, as shown here:

```
$ sed "s/hello/goodbye/" in.file
```

This substitutes the first instance of **hello** on each line of the file **in.file** with the string **goodbye,** and writes the line to the standard output, as follows:

```
$ echo "1234hello5678" | sed "s/hello/goodbye/"
1234goodbye5678
$
```

You must quote the substitution command to protect it from interpretation by the shell. As usual, the match string can be any regular expression.

The **sed** command also allows many other operators. You can delete all the lines that contain the string **hello** with

```
$ sed "/hello/d" in.file
```

In this example, the command searches for the string **hello** and deletes the line in which it is found. The previous **sed** command has the same result as

```
$ grep -v hello in.file
```

To delete only the string **hello** from the line, without deleting the line as a whole from the output, you would use this form instead:

```
$ sed "s/hello//" in.file
```

Like **vi**, the **sed** operators can also take a line address or a range of addresses if you wish to restrict your changes to a part of the file. This command

```
$ sed "3,7s/hello//" in.file
```

deletes the first **hello** from lines three through seven of the file, and leaves the rest of the lines unchanged. Furthermore, you can use a context address instead of a line number if desired, as shown here:

```
$ sed "/hello/,/goodbye/s/bad/good/g" in.file
```

This command finds the first instance of the string **hello**, and changes all instances of the string **bad** to **good** until the string **goodbye** is found or the file ends. In this example, if there is another instance of **hello** after the **goodbye** is found, the substitution will begin again and continue until the next instance of **goodbye**.

Complex sed Programs

Actually, **sed** is even more powerful than described so far. If you put the command in a file, instead of on the command line, you can use the **-f** (for file) option to **sed**, as shown in this example:

```
$ sed -f command.file in.file
```

In this command the regular expression operators are in the file **command.file**. Otherwise, **sed** acts as expected. When you only have a single command, as in the previous examples, there is little use for a command file, although complex regular expressions can sometimes be debugged more easily if you keep them in a relatively permanent place. However, the command file has a more important function: it allows you to write multiline scripts for **sed,** so that a series of operations can be performed on each input line before **sed** writes it to the output. For example, you can create a file named **command.file** with the following command list.

```
s/hello/goodbye/
s/good/bad/
```

Then, if you executed

```
$ echo "1234hello5678" | sed -f command.file
```

the output would be

```
$ echo "1234hello5678" | sed -f command.file
1234badbye5678
$
```

The operations specified in the file are executed sequentially on each line of the input until the line is deleted or the end of the file is reached. When the command set is completed, the line is written to the standard output; the next line of the input is then read, and the process is repeated.

There are many other options in the **sed** command set. Using **sed** — and regular expressions in general — is a skill that is best learned by experience and by studying the relevant pages in the *UNIX User's Manual.*

Basic Editing with ed

The original general-purpose text editor that has been a part of the UNIX system since the earliest days is the **ed** (for editor) program. Because **ed** is a line-oriented tool rather than a full-screen display like most modern editors, we will not discuss it extensively; however, **ed** introduced some of the key concepts that were incorporated into **vi,** and so it is the basis for the other editors. Nonetheless, it is not wise to become dependent on **ed.**

You invoke **ed** from the shell with an optional filename argument, like this:

```
$ ed old.file
260
```

If the file already exists, **ed** copies it into its buffer, so that you are not altering the original file as you make changes. The size of the file in characters (260 in this example) is returned to signal that **ed** has read the file. If the file does not exist, **ed** creates it. If you don't give a filename as an argument, **ed** will work correctly, but you will have to provide a filename when you write the new file to disk.

If you name a new file, instead of displaying the count of characters in the file, **ed** will signal that it has nothing in its buffer, as follows:

```
$ ed new.file
?new.file
```

Unlike **vi** or **emacs**, **ed** does not display any of the text in its buffer unless you ask for it, so it can be difficult to keep track of the buffer's current contents. Although this allows **ed** to be used on even the dumbest line-oriented printing terminals, in practice that is rarely required.

Modes in ed

The **ed** program has two modes: input mode and command mode. Input mode is like input mode in **vi**; all the characters you enter become contents of the edited buffer. Command mode is like the last line mode of **vi**; it is used to search for regular expressions, read and write files, and so forth. Note that commands in **ed** do *not* begin with a : (colon). No mode equivalent to the command mode of **vi** exists in **ed**.

Turning on Prompts and Help

By default, **ed** does not tell you which mode you are in, although when you enter the program it begins in command mode. You can enter the command **P** (capital *P*, for prompt) to tell **ed** to display a prompt character, as follows:

```
$ ed new.file
?new.file
P
*
```

Now **ed** will prompt you with * whenever you are in command mode. You turn off the prompt by entering **P** again.

Similarly, when you make a mistake in a command, by default **ed** only displays a terse **?**, as shown here:

```
$ ed new.file
?new.file
XXX
?
```

As you can see, **XXX** is not a valid command. You can get a more informative error message by using the **H** (for help) command, as follows:

```
$ ed new.file
?new.file
XXX
?
H
XXX
? illegal suffix
```

This may not be much better, but it provides some information at least! You toggle help off by entering **H** again.

Reading In Another File

You can read another file into the buffer by using the **r** (for read) command, as shown here:

```
r old.file
```

In most versions of **ed**, this inserts the file **old.file** at the end of the current file (if one exists). You can use a line address if you wish to insert the file in the middle of the file. In this case, the new file will be added *after* the line address given. The command

```
Or old.file
```

will read the file at the beginning of your buffer, at line zero.

Write and Quit

Like **vi, ed** does not change the original file on disk until you explicitly write it out with the **w** command, as in this example:

```
$ ed old.file
260
p
*
w
260
*
```

Note that **ed** does display the number of characters written.

When you are through editing, you can exit from **ed** with the **q** command, as follows:

```
$ ed old.file
260
q
$
```

This ends **ed** and takes you back to the shell. If you try to quit before you have written the file, **ed** will question you; just enter a second **q** to insist. Then **ed** will abandon the changed file and exit as requested.

Working with Lines

Most operations in command mode work on complete lines of the text file. There is no current position on a line as there is with **vi**. You move around in the file by jumping from line to line, and most commands act on the current line as a whole. The current line is called . (dot), and the last line of the file is called $ (dollar). Line numbers are rarely used, but **ed** always knows which line you are currently working with, and you can use line numbers with **ed** commands if you wish.

Displaying the Current Line

The command **p** (for print) is used to display the current line. Note that this is a lowercase **p**, while the prompt command is an uppercase **P**. By default the **p** command prints only the current line, as shown here:

```
$ ed old.file
260
p
see you later          .... steve
```

When you first read a file into **ed,** the current line is the last line of the file, as this example demonstrates:

```
$ ed old.file
260
p
see you later          .... steve
.=
6
$=
6
```

You use **.=** to report the number of the current line, and **$=** to report the number of the last line in the file. As you can see, this file has six lines.

Most **ed** commands can take a line or a range of lines preceding the command. If you don't give this line range, **ed** usually assumes you mean only the current line, . (dot). In the previous example, the command **p** could also have been written **.p, $p,** or **6p.** Because both . and **$** indicate line 6 in this example, all these versions of the **p** command are the same. To specify a range of lines, separate the first and last line numbers with a comma, as you would in **vi** last line mode. For example:

```
$ ed old.file
260
1,2p
hi jim, how was your vacation?  I've been learning
the UNIX operating system recently, and it's a lot of
```

For this to work, the first line number must be smaller than the second line number. You can also use . and $ in these line number addresses. Similarly, you can use simple arithmetic expressions in line addresses, as shown here:

```
$-2,$p
powerful than any other small computer os, and I'm sure
it will help us a lot.
see you later          .... steve
```

To display the entire file, use the short form **,p.**

Changing the Current Line

You can change the current line while in command mode. Simply entering a newline (or pressing RETURN) moves forward one line and displays
the contents of the new current line. The - (minus) command followed by
a newline moves back one line. You can also name a line number
directly, and **ed** will make that the current line, as in this example:

```
.=
6
2
the UNIX operating system recently, and it's a lot of
.=
2
```

The current line has been changed to line 2, and **ed** displays that line.
Simple arithmetic expressions are also allowed.

Input Mode

When you enter input mode from command mode, you always start on a
new line either before or after the current line. Use the **i** (for input)
command to enter input mode just before the current line, and the **a** (for
append) command to enter input mode just after the current line. When
you are in input mode, all the characters you enter at the keyboard go
into the file. To return to command mode after you are through entering
text, use . (dot) on a line by itself, as shown here:

```
$ ed new.file
?new.file
a
hello world
another line
a third line
.
,p
hello world
another line
a third line
```

To correct a line that contains an error, you can use the BACKSPACE key on
the current line, but to repair an error on a previously entered line, you
must return to command mode.

The **i** and **a** commands can also take a line address preceding them; for instance, **14a** tells **ed** to append following line 14 of the file.

Deleting Lines

The **d** (for delete) command deletes lines from the file. By default, **d** deletes the current line, as it does in this example:

```
,p
hello world
another line
a third line
2
another line
d
,p
hello world
a third line
```

This example deleted line 2 from the buffer. The **d** command can also take a line number or range of line numbers if you want to delete more than one line.

Undoing Mistakes

Since **ed** remembers the last command you entered, you can undo the last change you made to a file. Only the most recent change can be recovered in this way. The **u** (for undo) command restores the buffer, as it does in **vi.** If you hit **u** again, the restored line will be deleted once more. The undo feature will successfully undo even very large changes, but remember, only the last operation can be recovered.

Searching for Strings

Like **sed** and **vi, ed** supports full regular expression search and substitute operations. The syntax

```
/match.re
```

finds the next line containing the regular expression **match.re**, and

```
?match.re
```

searches backward in the file to find the first match. Note that no : is used here, since **ed** does not use last line mode. If no match is found, the search will wrap around from the end of the file and keep searching back to the current line. When a match is found, the search stops and **ed** displays the matching line, as shown here:

```
/[0-9]th hello
This is the 45th hello I've sent you; why don't you reply?
```

Although **ed** does not report the line number, the displayed line becomes the current line. Since **ed** remembers the last regular expression, you can continue searching for the next occurrence just by entering / or ? (depending on which direction you wish to search) followed by a newline.

Substituting Sections of Text

The **s** (for substitute) command substitutes one string for another. Its syntax is the same as the last line equivalent in **vi**. Here is an example:

```
p
powerful than any other small computer os, and I'm sure
4,6s/powerful/flexible
flexible than any other small computer os, and I'm sure
```

The changed line is echoed to verify that the change has been made.

This example makes the substitution on the *first* occurrence of the string **powerful** on each of lines 4 through 6. You can use complex regular expressions for the delete part of the substitute operation, but take care to examine the results of the change, because small errors in regular expressions can cause **ed** to match more or less than you intended.

The regular expressions ˆ and $ designate the beginning and end of the line, as you would expect.

Normally the **s** command only changes the first occurrence of a string on a line. You can add a **g** to the end of the substitute command to force the **s** command to make the substitution globally, that is, on every occurrence of the string on the line (or sequence of lines if you give an address range). For example,

```
4,6s/old text to delete/new text to add/g
```

will change every occurrence of the string on lines 4 through 6 of the file.

Moving and Copying Lines

The command **m** (for move) lets you move a line or sequence of lines from one location to another location in the file. This is the familiar cut and paste operation. For example, to move the current line to the end of the file, you would enter

```
.m$
```

Like the other commands, the **m** command can also take a line address or range of lines. For instance,

```
3,5m1
```

moves lines 3, 4, and 5 to a position immediately following line 1.

To copy a line from one place to another without deleting the original, use the **t** command, as shown here:

```
2,4t$
```

This is the copy and paste operation, which in this case copies lines 2 through 4 to the end of the file.

Shell Escapes—The Bang Operator

Finally, you can jump out of **ed** to execute any command from the shell by entering a ! (bang) followed by the command that you wish to execute. For example:

```
!cat old.file
```

When the command is completed, **ed** echoes the ! for you, and then returns to action. To temporarily suspend your **ed** session and create an interactive shell, you can enter

```
!sh
```

When you are through with whatever you are doing in the subshell, you can kill that shell with CTRL-D or **exit** to return to the **ed** session.

Going Further

To reiterate, the way to learn editing under the UNIX system is to practice constantly with your preferred editor. Also, look over the shoulder of an expert, and don't be afraid to ask when he or she does something too complex (or too fast!) for you to follow. Finally, spend as much time as you can browsing through the editing documentation to pick up new ideas.

ed Scripts

The **vi** editor executes with terminal controls different from those used by most programs, so the concepts of standard input and output do not apply to **vi** as they do to other programs. The **vi** editor is totally interactive, and requires that its input and output be directed to a terminal. However, **ed** uses normal standard I/O, and you can take advantage of that fact to create **ed** *scripts*. These scripts can be used to modify files "automatically" if you know the contents of the file and can predict the sequence of **ed** commands that will be needed to make the desired changes. This file contains a simple **ed** script:

```
$ cat ed.script
/findme/
a
hello
```

```
goodbye
.
w
q
$
```

If these commands were entered interactively, they would set the current line to the first line containing the string **findme**, enter append mode after that line (**a**), enter **hello** and **goodbye** in input mode, return to command mode (.), write the file (**w**), and finally quit (**q**) the editor. Then, the command

```
$ ed-s old.file < ed.script
$
```

would execute the commands and change the file without input from the user. This form also appears in several system shell scripts, but it is only useful if you know exactly what changes you wish to make to the file before you create the **ed** script.

You can suppress the various information output produced by **ed** during its processing of a script with the **-s** (for silent) command-line option.

Regular Expression Searches in emacs

The **emacs** editor has additional search operators to locate strings specified by regular expressions. The command **^M^s** (CTRL-meta CTRL-S) starts the action, and **emacs** prompts for the regular expression to find. Regular expression syntax as used in **ed** is accepted, although **emacs** also has some extended regular expression operators. The previous command searches forward in the current buffer; use **^M^r** to search backward. After an instance of the string is found, you can continue to search for the next occurrence of the same string with a simple **^s** (forward) or **^r** (reverse), and the previous regular expression will be reused.

A similar procedure will be provided to substitute strings from regular expressions that are matched. Use the command

```
M-x replace-regexp
```

followed by a newline, and **emacs** will prompt for the regular expression to match, and also for the substitute string. This command replaces *all* occurrences of the regular expression with the substitute string. To make **emacs** query you about each substitution before it is performed, use

```
M-x query-replace-regexp
```

The **emacs** editor will find the first occurrence of the regular expression, and then pause for a command. Press y if you want that substitution to be made, and n to skip it. In either case, **emacs** goes on to the next occurrence of the match string, if there is one. You can also enter **R** to instruct **emacs** to silently replace all remaining occurrences of the pattern in the file, or you can enter ^**g** to abort the operation and return to normal **emacs** operation.

More Useful General-Purpose Commands

S E V E N

By now, you are familiar with the basic style of the UNIX system shell and user interface, and you know some commonly used commands. The UNIX system as a whole includes more than eight hundred executable commands. You'll explore this rich set of tools topic-by-topic throughout the rest of this book. This chapter discusses the common commands that you need almost every day to make effective use of the UNIX system.

Unlike the tools discussed in later chapters, those covered here have little in common with each other, except that they are all generally useful commands that can make your life with the UNIX system a pleasure rather than a chore. In addition, these commands are the fundamental building blocks for *shell scripts,* which allow you to automate your common tasks. Chapter 8 discusses shell scripts in detail.

The Environment Revisited

Recall that when a command is executed, the system establishes an execution *environment* for the command, and passes some of your environment variables to that environment. Commands often rely on this environment. For example, the full-screen editors described in the last chapter depend on the TERM environment variable.

Not all of your environment variables are available to the commands you execute. When a command is executed, the shell gives it a starting environment that can be passed on to its *subprograms*. Only environment variables that are *exported* are available to subprograms through this mechanism, and those are a subset of the full list of environment variables. If you give the command

```
$ export
```

with no arguments, a list of the currently exported environment variables will be displayed. You can add a new environment variable to the export list by naming it as an argument to the **export** command, as follows:

```
$ export TERM
$
```

This command will export the TERM environment variable to your commands and subprograms.

The **export** command also allows multiple variables on the command line, as shown here:

```
$ export TERM EDITOR HISTFILE
```

This technique only works with subprograms; in no case can an environment variable be exported "upward" to the *parent* environment of a command.

Using the PATH Variable

One of the most important environment variables is the *PATH* variable. When you execute a command by naming the full pathname of the command, like this,

```
$ /usr/bin/vi
```

the shell finds the command to execute by following the path from the root of the directory hierarchy. However, if you only give a partial pathname, such as

```
$ vi
```

the shell does not know where to look for the executable program. The PATH variable lists the directories the shell will search to find commands that you name without providing the full pathname. Here is a typical PATH variable:

```
$ echo $PATH
:/home/steve/bin:/sbin:/usr/sbin:/usr/bin:/usr/X/bin:/usr/ucb
$
```

Your PATH may differ, but the syntax is common to all UNIX systems. The PATH variable is a short database, with individual entries that are separated by a : (colon). When you give a command without a full pathname, the shell searches through the directories listed in the PATH, trying each of them in turn from left to right, until it finds a command with the specified name. If no such command resides in any of the directories, the shell reports that information, as follows:

```
$ xxx
xxx:  not found
$
```

If the command is found in one of the directories, the shell executes it.

You can have multiple commands with the same name on a machine, providing they each reside in a different directory. Since the directories in the PATH are searched in order, when commands have identical names the order of directories in the PATH determines which one executes. In the previous example, the directory **/home/steve/bin** appears before **/sbin**, so a command in **home/steve/bin** will be executed instead of a command with the same name in **/sbin**. Another user might not have **/home/steve/bin** in the PATH variable, but most users would have the **/usr/bin** directory. They would execute the version of **vi** in **/usr/bin**, while the user who had our example PATH would get the version in **/home/steve/bin**. Thus, individual users can control the set of commands available to them just by changing their PATH.

Most normal executable commands are located in one of the directories **/sbin**, **/usr/bin**, or **/usr/sbin**, and these will almost always be included in your PATH. You can add other directories as you wish to customize the execution of commands or to hold your personal commands.

If you have installed the X Window System or add-on application software such as a word processor or database management system, the directory location of these applications might also be included in your PATH. Similarly, if you wish to use the BSD tools provided in SVR4, you should add the directory **/usr/ucb** to your PATH. Place it at the beginning if you want the BSD versions of commands to override their System V equivalents, and at the end if you want the System V commands to take precedence.

As noted earlier, the individual entries of the PATH are separated by a :. If there is an extra : in the PATH, as there was at the beginning of the previous example, the current directory is used at that point. The difference between

```
$ PATH=/sbin:/usr/bin:/usr/sbin
```

and

```
$ PATH=:/sbin:/usr/bin:/usr/sbin
```

is that the current directory, whatever it is, will be searched first in the latter PATH, but in the former example, the current directory will not be searched. You can instruct the shell to search the current directory *after* all the other directories with this command:

```
$ PATH=/sbin:/usr/bin:/usr/sbin:
```

Here, an extra : has been added at the end of the PATH. Usually the PATH variable is set and exported for you when you log in to the system; you only need to change it if you want a setup that is different from the default.

The banner Command

The system provides many handy general-purpose commands. Some are more fun than useful, but each has its place in the system. One of the simplest is the **banner** command, which writes its arguments to standard output in a greatly enlarged size, as shown here:

```
$ banner hello world
```

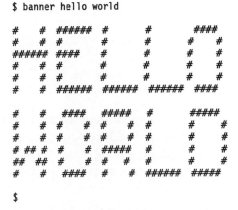

```
$
```

The **banner** command makes separate lines for its output on individual word boundaries to keep the screen display relatively sane. It is often used in output functions such as print spoolers to display various information. For example, this command would display the user id:

```
$ banner $LOGNAME
```

Clearing the Screen

The **clear** command is a simple tool that erases the screen and displays the $ prompt on the top line. You enter **clear** as follows:

```
$ clear
```

This command takes no command-line arguments. It should work correctly on most types of terminals.

The date Command

The UNIX system has excellent timekeeping facilities, and controls time in the system at all resolutions from milliseconds through years. Nearly all systems have built-in clock/calendar chips, and the time is usually set correctly by the kernel when it boots. All files have a modification time-stamp associated with them, as you have seen. In addition, there is a general-purpose command that displays the current date and time, as shown here:

```
$ date
Wed May 30 18:12:56 MDT 1990
$
```

By default, the date is displayed according to your local time and time zone, although **date** can format its output differently. The system can determine the start and end of daylight-saving time, but if the daylight-saving time law changes, the system may become confused.

The **date** command is often used to time-stamp work. It is also used to set the system time. Since much internal system activity depends on the correct time, the date should always be set correctly. Setting the system time and changing the format of the **date** command's output are discussed in Chapter 20.

The cal Command

The **cal** (for calendar) command falls into the category of useful and fun commands. With no arguments, it produces a calendar of the current month on its standard output. Here is an example:

```
$ cal
   May 1990
 S  M Tu  W Th  F  S
        1  2  3  4  5
 6  7  8  9 10 11 12
13 14 15 16 17 18 19
20 21 22 23 24 25 26
27 28 29 30 31
$
```

If a year is given as an argument, **cal** will print a complete calendar for that year. Any year from 1 through 9999 can be displayed. Note that the system interprets the year 92 as early in the Christian era, not as 1992. In addition, **cal** can take a second argument before the year, specifying a month during that year, as follows:

```
$ cal 9 1752
```

This command will display a calendar for the month of September in the year 1752. What is interesting about this month? The **cal** command is not buggy.

The calendar Command

The **calendar** command provides a rudimentary reminder service that you can use to record your appointments. This feature is simpleminded compared to other timing features in the UNIX system, but it can be handy for beginning users. If a file named **calendar** is present in the current directory, the **calendar** command will effectively **grep** through the file searching for lines that contain either today's or tomorrow's date anywhere on the line. In practice, you can edit your **calendar** file, adding new appointments one per line as they come up. Running the **calendar** program once a day keeps you abreast of your current schedule, as shown here:

```
$ calendar
Doctor's appointment on May 28 for checkup
$
```

The **calendar** command can handle several different date formats, including the one used in the previous example. The same date could be displayed as 5/28, but the European date format 28/5 is not acceptable. You might set things up so that **calendar** runs whenever you log in to the system and displays your activities for the day. Usually the **calendar** file is in your home directory.

The more, tail, and head Programs

You have already met the **more** program, which presents output to your display one screenful at a time, and waits for you to press the SPACEBAR before going on to the next screenful. Another command, **pg** (for pager), is similar but is not as widely used as **more**. Usually **more** is placed at the end of a pipeline or used with a list of filenames as arguments, as in this example:

```
$ more /etc/profile /etc/inittab
```

The command pauses after each screenful of output, prompting with **--More--(%)** at the bottom of the screen. To go on to the next screenful simply press the SPACEBAR or f (for forward). If you enter a number before the f, **more** skips forward that many screenfuls. You can also skip backward in a file by entering CTRL-B (for backward). Enter a number before the CTRL-B to skip backward that number of screenfuls. Use newline (RETURN) instead of the SPACEBAR to move forward line-by-line instead of by screenfuls. The newline command can also take a positive argument to specify how many lines to scroll forward. The CTRL-L operator redisplays the current screen.

In addition, **more** can accept many other commands at the **--More--(%)** prompt. You can enter a regular expression following a **/** (slash) in **ed** syntax, and **more** will search forward for that expression. If the expression is found, **more** will display the segment of text surrounding it. A number n preceding the **/** causes **more** to search for the nth occurrence of the expression. For example,

```
6/[fe]grep/
```

will search for the sixth occurrence of the string **fgrep** or **egrep** following the current line.

If there is more than one file in the argument list to **more**, **:n** (for next) will skip to the beginning of the next file, and **:p** (for previous) will skip back to the beginning of the previous file. Both **:n** and **:p** can take a number before the letter to specify the nth previous file, as in this example:

```
:3p
```

Naturally, the **:n** and **:p** commands do not work if **more** is invoked at the end of a pipeline. The **h** (for help) command displays a list of **more** commands, and **q** (for quit) or the DEL key exits back to the shell.

The **more** command uses the TERM environment variable to format output for most full-screen terminals, so this variable must be correct or **more** will not work properly.

Because **more** starts its display at the beginning of the file, you must step through the entire file to see the end. The **tail** command is used to look at the end, or tail, of the file given as an argument. This command can also be used at the end of a pipeline, or even in the middle of a pipeline. It writes the last ten lines of the file to its standard output, as shown here:

```
$ tail /etc/profile
      if [ $LOGNAME != root ]
      then news -n
      fi
      ;;
-su)
      :
      ;;
esac
export PATH;
trap 1 2 3
$
```

The **tail** command can also take a number following the - argument flag, to specify a number of lines other than ten to display. For example:

```
$ tail -1 /etc/profile
trap 1 2 3
$
```

In addition, a letter can follow the number to count in units other than lines. Two possibilities are **-c** (for characters) and **-b** (for blocks) to count in characters or blocks. This command displays the last 20 characters of the file, starting in the middle of a line if necessary:

```
$ tail -20c /etc/profile
rt PATH;
trap 1 2 3
$
```

The **tail** command usually exits back to the shell when it reads the end of a file; however, in many situations when a program is writing to a file, you may want to watch the end of the file as it grows. You could accomplish this by repeatedly executing **tail -3**, for example, but the **-f** (for follow) option to **tail** is more efficient. This option causes **tail** to continue executing, displaying each new line of the file as it is written. The **-f** option looks like this:

```
$ tail -f growing.file
```

Because **tail -f** does not end on its own, you must kill it by pressing the DEL key when you are through viewing the end of the file.

The **head** command acts like **tail**, but it displays the beginning of the file rather than the end. This command takes a filename list as an argument, or reads its standard input if no filenames are given. By default, **head** displays the first ten lines of each input file, but you can change this by adding a number to the command line, as follows:

```
$ head -4 /etc/profile
#ident  "@(#)/etc/profile.sl 1.1 4.0 12/26/89 60576 AT&T-SF"
trap "" 1 2 3
umask 022        # set default file creation mask
. /etc/TIMEZONE
$
```

Obviously, you can't use **-f** to follow the head of a file.

The cmp and diff Commands

It is often desirable to compare two files or directories to see if they are the same. The **cmp** (for compare) command will compare any two files, including binary files. The command takes two filenames as arguments. For example:

```
$ cmp /sbin/sh /usr/bin/ksh
/sbin/sh /usr/bin/ksh differ: char 5, line 1
$
```

This output is somewhat limited; it only reports the first byte number, if any, at which the files differ. The **-l** (letter ell) option causes **cmp** to list the byte number and the differing values for each discrepancy in the two files. Although this is more useful, it can produce substantial output if there are many differences.

The **cmp** command can take an argument of - instead of the first filename, in which case the standard input is used instead of a filename, as shown here:

```
$ cat /sbin/sh | cmp -l - /sbin/sh
$
```

If there are no differences in the files, **cmp** is silent.

A much more powerful tool is available for text files. This is the **diff** (for differences) command. The **diff** command produces a complete index of all the lines that differ between two files, along with their line numbers. It also reports what must be changed to make the files match. Here is an example:

```
$ cat file1
this is a simple file
with only a few lines,
all very straightforward.
This file will show how "diff" works.
$ cat file2
this is a simple file
with only a few lines,
all very easy.
This file will show how "diff" works.
$ diff file1 file2
3c3
< all very straightforward.
---
> all very easy.
$
```

The first part of the **diff** output lists the line numbers that differ in the two files, separated by **c** (for changed). The next lines display the line in the first file, marked with <, and the line in the second file, marked with >. With larger files that have more differences, the output is correspondingly large, but **diff** is a very intelligent search tool that can easily handle large files with many differences and missing lines. Almost always, **diff** successfully finds the smallest set of differences in two files. If one filename is replaced with a - (minus), the standard input is used in that position instead of a named file.

Usually, extra blanks or tab characters in the files cause **diff** to mark lines as different. The **-w** (for whitespace) option causes **diff** to ignore lines that differ only in their whitespace, so that tabs or spaces in a file are considered the same. The option looks like this:

```
$ cat file3 | diff -w - file2
$
```

You can also use the **-i** (for ignore) option to instruct **diff** to ignore the case of characters in its comparison. As usual, if the files are the same, **diff** says nothing.

The output from **diff** resembles **ed** commands that convert the first file into the second. In fact, the **-e** (for ed) option produces a script that **ed** can use directly to convert the files, as follows:

```
$ diff -e file1 file2
3c
all very easy.
.
$
```

This output can actually be used to convert file1 to file2, as shown here:

```
$ diff -e file1 file2 > ed.script
$ ( cat ed.script ; echo w ) | ed file1
109
98
$ diff file1 file2
$
```

This example contains several ideas. You know that **ed** reads your commands from standard input, so you can use a pipeline to send commands to **ed** instead of typing them at the terminal. When **ed** sees an end-of-file from the pipeline, it exits and returns to the shell; thus, if you **cat** the output from **diff -e** into **ed**, **ed** will respond to those commands and exit when the file **ed.script** finishes. For this reason no **q** is required to end the **ed** session. Note, however, that the script from diff **-e** has no **w** command for **ed** to write the file, so by default **ed** makes the changes and then exits without writing them. To have **ed** write the file, you must add the **w** using the **echo w** command.

The **cat** of **ed.script** is separated from **echo w** by the shell operator **;** (semicolon), which separates multiple commands on the line. This is almost what you want, but the end of **ed.script** will signal an end-of-file, so **ed** will exit before it sees the **w** from the **echo** command. You can prevent this by enclosing the entire sequence of commands that you want **ed** to see within parentheses. Using parentheses as a shell operator causes all the commands contained within the parenthesis to be executed in a single subshell, rather than as individual commands. As a result, the output of all these commands is concatenated as input to **ed**, eliminating the undesirable end-of-file normally caused by the **;**. Here is another way to write the same command:

```
$ echo w | cat ed.script - | ed file1
```

The two numbers—109 and 98—in the example before this one, are the standard output from **ed** when it reads and writes the file, respectively. Experiment with these ideas on your own machine. What are the differences between the form with the parentheses and the alternate version of the same command?

The dircmp Command

The command **dircmp** (for directory compare) compares the contents of two directory subtrees. It reports on the files that appear in one directory only, and compares the files (using **cmp**) that appear in both directories. Its output can be voluminous, especially for large directories, but **dircmp** is useful when you need to compare two *versions* of a directory. You give the two directories as arguments to the command, as shown here:

```
$ dircmp $HOME /tmp/copied
```

You can use the **-d** (for diff) option to generate output on file differences that resembles the output of **diff** rather than that of **cmp**.

The sort and uniq Commands

The UNIX system provides two more tools that are often used in pipelines to filter text files in useful ways. The **sort** command reorders a stream of text lines in alphabetical order. It can take a list of filenames as arguments or read its standard input. The **sort** command writes the sorted lines to its standard output, as shown here:

```
$ cat text.file
This is a short file.
Each line begins with a different letter.
each line starts with a four-letter word.
Most lines start with capital letters.
$ sort text.file
Each line begins with a different letter.
Most lines start with capital letters.
This is a short file.
each line starts with a four-letter word.
$
```

The **sort** command sorts all the lines of all the input files together, so it includes what is often called a *merge* function in other operating systems. It can also handle very large files, although its performance is seriously degraded when files of more than about one thousand lines are sorted. It is often faster to sort several large files separately, and then merge them with the **-m** (for merge) option of the **sort** command.

By default, **sort** uses the ASCII *collating sequence* to determine the sort order, starting at the beginning of the line. The ASCII collating sequence sorts whitespace first, followed by most punctuation marks, followed by numbers, uppercase letters, and finally by lowercase letters. When the first character of two lines is the same, **sort** looks at each subsequent character, up to the newline if necessary, to determine the correct order. When you are sorting alphabetical files the result is usually correct, but when you are sorting numeric data, things may not turn out as you expect, as this example demonstrates:

```
$ cat data.file
1
2
10
11
21
$ sort data.file
1
10
11
2
21
$
```

This result occurs because 1 precedes 2 in the collating sequence, so all lines that begin with 1 will precede any line that begins with 2. The **-n** (for numeric) option to **sort** causes the output to appear in the correct order for numbers, as shown here:

```
$ sort -n data.file
1
2
10
11
21
$
```

The **sort** command also allows you to ignore the difference between uppercase and lowercase characters in the sorting comparison. The **-f** (for fold) option is used for this purpose, as follows:

```
$ sort -f text.file
Each line begins with a different letter.
each line starts with a four-letter word.
Most lines start with capital letters.
This is a short file.
$
```

In this case *Each* and *each* are regarded as the same; the first difference in the lines appears in column position 11, where *begins* comes before *starts*. Similarly, the **-d** (for dictionary) option suppresses sorting on embedded punctuation or other special characters; only letters, digits, and whitespace are significant. The **-M** (for month) option causes **sort** to consider the first three characters of the line as months, so that *Jan* will sort before *Feb*, rather than after it as you would otherwise expect.

So far the sort key has been at the beginning of the input line. The *sort key* is the section of the data that **sort** uses to determine whether a line is out of order. The **sort** command allows you to specify any section of the input line as the sort key, but always keeps each line intact. That is, **sort** will not break its input lines, which are regarded as *records*. You instruct **sort** to use some other part of the input line as the key with the +*n* and -*n* arguments, where the *n* is a number specifying a field in the line. A *field* is a sequence of characters set off by a *delimiter*. By default, a whitespace character (a blank or a tab) is the field delimiter, and the beginning of the line starts at *field 0*. That is, **+1** tells **sort** to use the second field as the sort key rather than the beginning of the line, as shown here:

```
$ sort +1 text.file
This is a short file.
Each line begins with a different letter.
each line starts with a four-letter word.
Most lines start with capital letters.
$
```

In this example **sort** begins with *is* or *line*.

Similarly, the -*n* option can make **sort** stop its comparison just before field *n*, as follows:

```
$ sort +1 -3 text.file
```

This command will use only the second and third fields in the sort key. When data is sorted using fields, and some lines differ only in fields that are not included in the sort key, you cannot predict what order those lines will appear in the output. However, you can control sorting in all fields of the file by using more than one field in the **sort** command, as shown here:

```
$ sort +3 -4 +0 -1 text.file
```

This command will sort based on field four as the *primary key*. On lines in which this key compares as equal, the beginning of the line will be used as the *secondary key*. For example:

```
$ sort +3 -4 +0 -1 text.file
This is a short file.
Each line begins with a different letter.
Most lines start with capital letters.
each line starts with a four-letter word.
$
```

Compare this with the following output:

```
$ sort +3 -4 +6 text.file
This is a short file.
Most lines start with capital letters.
Each line begins with a different letter.
each line starts with a four-letter word.
$
```

Can you see what accounts for the difference?

You can change the field separator from the default whitespace using the **-t** option, which takes a character as an argument. For example, to use the : as a field separator, type

```
$ sort -t: /etc/passwd
```

In addition, **sort** allows the **-b** (for blanks) option, which ignores blanks in the sort key, and the **-r** (for reverse) option, which reverses the sort order of output. Of course, all the options and sort keys can be combined to produce sorted output in just about any sequence you desire. It usually takes some experimentation to come up with a **sort** command that produces exactly the output you want.

The **sort** command is often used with **uniq** (for unique) to count the occurrences of a specified line or field in a file. The **uniq** command reports on repeated lines in a file, but its input must be sorted correctly for it to work.

The **uniq** command reads its standard input or a list of filenames, and writes to its standard output. By default, **uniq** writes one instance of each input line that is different from other lines, as shown here:

```
$ cat data2
abc
def
ghi
def
abc
$ sort data2 | uniq
```

```
abc
def
ghi
$
```

Only one copy of each differing line is written; that is, **uniq** produces a list of the *unique* lines in a file. Again, the input to **uniq** must be in correct sort order, or the command will fail.

The **-c** (for count) option of **uniq** is often used. It produces a count of the number of occurrences of each line preceding the unique line, as follows:

```
$ sort data2 | uniq -c
   2 abc
   2 def
   1 ghi
$
```

In this example, there are two instances of the lines *abc* and *def* in the input, and only one instance of the line *ghi.* The **-u** (for unique) option produces as output only lines that are *not* repeated in the input, and the **-d** (for duplicate) option produces only lines that *are* duplicated in the input.

The **uniq** command can also restrict its examination to specific fields of the input. The *-n* option, where n is a number, ignores the first n fields of the line in its comparison. As with **sort**, the fields are delimited by whitespace. The $+n$ option, where n is a number, ignores the first n characters of the line. When *-n* and $+n$ are used together, **uniq** skips fields before characters.

The cut and paste Commands

The **cut** command was discussed in Chapter 3. It is used to split up input lines according to column positions or fields. Like **sort**, it operates on specific parts of the input line, but unlike **sort** it does not usually copy the entire line to its output; **cut** is used to eliminate sections of the line from the output. In addition, **cut** has a companion command that joins lines from two files into its output. The **paste** command takes two or more filenames as arguments, reads a line from each file, combines the lines into a single line, and writes the newly created line to its standard output. Each of the input files is assumed to provide a field in the output line, and by default a tab character is added as a delimiter between the contributions of each file. The **-d** option allows you to specify a different delimiter character. For example:

```
$ cat new.d1
1111
2222
3333
$ cat new.d2
AAAA
BBBB
CCCC
DDDD
EEEE
$ paste -d: new.d1 new.d2
1111:AAAA
2222:BBBB
3333:CCCC
:DDDD
:EEEE
$
```

The **paste** command can take any number of filenames, and in the output it pastes lines together from the input in left-to-right order. If some of the files have fewer lines than others, **paste** just puts in the delimiters with nothing in the field. Any one of the filenames can be replaced by a - (minus), and **paste** will read its standard input for that "file."

In the previous example, a : was used as the delimiter character. In fact, more than one character can follow the **-d** option, and each delimiter in that list will be used in turn to delimit one pair of fields in the output. When all the characters in the list have been used, **paste** circles around and starts the list again. This multiple delimiter feature is occasionally useful for separating different fields with different delimiters. Normally, this option is used when there are as many delimiters in the list as there are fields to separate. For example:

```
$ paste -d123 file1 file2 file3 file4
```

This command takes the first line of **file1**, adds the digit 1 after it, adds the first line of **file2**, adds the digit 2, adds the first line of **file3**, adds the digit 3, and finally adds the first line of **file4.** The resulting line is terminated with a newline, and written to the standard output. The **paste** command will continue to perform this operation on each additional line until the last file is completed.

The Join Command

In contrast to **paste,** which joins corresponding lines from several files, the **join** command joins lines of files that match on a specified field. For example, you might have two files that contain a user name or id in one field, but different information in the other fields. The **join** command allows you to merge the information for each name (the shared field) from the two files, into a single output line, as follows:

```
$ cat file1
name.a:office:phone
name.b:office:phone
name.c:office:phone
$ cat file2
name.a:address:children
name.b:address:children
name.c:address:children
$ join -t: file1 file2
name.a:office:phone:address:children
name.b:office:phone:address:children
name.c:office:phone:address:children
$
```

The **-t** (for tab) option selects the field delimiter; the tab character is used by default. The result of the **join** command comes to standard output. You can also select a subset of fields in the output with the **-o** (for only) option, which takes a list of arguments of the form $m.n$, where m is the file number (one or two) and n is the field number.

The **join** command requires that the two input files be sorted on the common field before the command is issued, but files may contain several lines with the same join field. By default, **join** uses the first field of the line in each file; the **-j** (for join field) option changes this behavior. To join the files using field **n** from the first file and field **m** in the second file use this command:

```
$ join -j1 n -j2 m file1 file2
```

Database Operations for Text Files

The commands discussed in this chapter are extremely useful on their own for processing text files and producing new permutations of their input. In addition, they are frequently combined into pipelines, sometimes using temporary files for intermediate output. With these tools you can perform very complex operations on your files, including cutting, sorting, and counting to produce useful reports and new combinations of the data they contain. In fact, these operators are the basic tools required to perform relatively sophisticated *database* operations. Once you understand the basic commands and their major options, it becomes easy to create complex databases. These databases are usually composed of simple text files consisting of individual lines, or *records*, with each field of the records separated by your chosen delimiter character. The tab and : characters are most often used as delimiters. In practice, you can create several files that contain data, either with your editor or using the output from some application program. Individual files usually contain related data, and different files usually contain unrelated data. If you have separate files that share an identical field, or can be related through two fields of a third file, you can write command lines to implement *relational* databases. By creating new combinations of commands and pipelines as you need them, you can create ad hoc queries on your data without specially written software, such as a database management system. Many large and complex databases have been developed under the UNIX system using just these commands; the possibilities are nearly limitless.

In the example below, we will try only to convey an appreciation of the possibilities. Try these ideas on your own data-related problems. These tools and filters may execute a little slower than a professional database management system, but on the other hand the files are usually in easy-to-read text format, and you can add data, reformat the data, generate queries, and produced complex reports very simply.

For example, it is easy to determine the user ids of all the users allowed on your machine:

```
$ cut -f1 -d: /etc/passwd
root
daemon
bin
sys
adm
```

```
uucp
lp
nuucp
listen
sync
install
sysadm
vmsys
oasys
steve
pat
jim
$
```

Similarly, you can determine the shell these users get when they log into the machine, as this example demonstrates:

```
$ cut -f1,7 -d: /etc/passwd > temp.data
$ cat temp.data
root:
daemon:
bin:
sys:
adm:
uucp:
lp:/sbin/sh
nuucp:/usr/lib/uucp/uucico
listen:
sync:/usr/bin/sync
install:
sysadm:/usr/sbin/sysadm
vmsys:/sbin/sh
oasys:/sbin/sh
steve:/usr/bin/ksh
pat:
jim:/usr/bin/ksh
$
```

Here, the output was redirected to the temporary file **temp.data** for later use.

If you want to add the default shell **/sbin/sh** to the lines that have no shell in the last position, you can take advantage of the fact that **cut** places its delimiter at the end of lines that have no final field, as shown here:

```
$ grep ":$" temp.data | sed 's/$/\/sbin\/sh/' > new.data
$ cat new.data
root:/sbin/sh
daemon:/sbin/sh
bin:/sbin/sh
```

```
sys:/sbin/sh
adm:/sbin/sh
uucp:/sbin/sh
listen:/sbin/sh
install:/sbin/sh
pat:/sbin/sh
$
```

This command will **grep** for all lines that contain a : at the end of each line in your temporary file, and then **sed** adds the string **/sbin/sh** to the end of each line. The **sed** command is used a little differently here than you have seen it used before, since the substitution expression includes the **/** character as a normal character rather than a delimiter. You must escape the special meaning of **/** by preceding it with a **** (backslash) when you use it as a normal character.

At this point, the file **new.data** contains only users who had no shell specified in the **/etc/passwd** file. You can easily add the other users with the command

```
$ grep -v ":$" temp.data >> new.data
```

This simply adds all the lines that do not end in : to the end of the file.

Now, you can ask some questions about the way people use shells on your machine. First, this command determines what shells are in use:

```
$ cut -f2 -d: new.data | sort | uniq
/sbin/sh
/usr/bin/ksh
/usr/bin/sync
/usr/lib/uucp/uucico
/usr/sbin/sysadm
$
```

Next, you can find out how many people use each shell with this command:

```
$ cut -f2 -d: new.data | sort | uniq -c | sort -nr
  12 /sbin/sh
   2 /usr/bin/ksh
   1 /usr/sbin/sysadm
   1 /usr/lib/uucp/uucico
   1 /usr/bin/sync
$
```

The last command in the previous example, **sort -nr,** puts the results in descending numeric order. Many more questions can be answered in this way. Furthermore, there are several other ways to formulate the previous query from the original **/etc/passwd** file. Can you think of some of them?

Writing complex pipelines like these usually requires experimentation. In practice, you build these commands slowly, letting the output come to the terminal until you are sure it is correct. A small test database is often used instead of actual data, especially when the data is voluminous and the commands are complex. It is usually helpful to keep the command line in a file and modify it with your editor as you experiment, rather than retyping the command every time. The command form

```
$ sh cmdfile
```

will execute the command line in **cmdfile,** or you can make **cmdfile** executable directly with the command

```
$ chmod +x cmdfile
```

Then you can execute the command by simply typing

```
$ cmdfile
```

This technique can also reduce long and complex pipelines to easily typed commands, and forms the basis for *shell programming,* as you will soon see.

Going Further

There are a great many commands, and even more clever ways to use these commands. As you experiment, and as you see how other people work, you will soon learn procedures for solving your particular data-related problems. In later chapters, we will discuss many of these techniques.

The sleep Command

An interesting command that has many uses is **sleep**. This command takes a numeric argument that is interpreted as a number of seconds. All it does is delay that number of seconds, and then exit back to the shell, as shown here:

```
$ date "+%r" ; sleep 100 ; date "+%r"
11:18:23 AM
11:20:04 AM
$
```

The **sleep** command can err in its timing up to one second, so the command

```
$ sleep 1
```

may not produce exact results.

One of the simplest ways to use **sleep** is to create an alarm clock to alert you at some time in the near future. This command rings the bell at your terminal and displays a message ten minutes after the command is entered:

```
$ sleep 600 ; echo "\007 Time for lunch! \007" &
```

This command will only work if you do not log off the machine until after the alarm rings, but the command is executed in the background with & so you can continue to do other work while it is running. The string **\007** in the **echo** command shows another way you can specify characters to echo; 007 is the octal ASCII code for the CTRL-G character, which sounds a beep at the terminal. In this context, \007 is very different than \07, 007, 7, or \7. You tell **echo** that this is a single character rather than three digits by escaping it with the \.

Since the UNIX system is a multitasking system, it is desirable to relinquish control of the CPU when you want to delay for an interval. This allows another program, perhaps executed by another user on the machine, to run while your command is delaying. This differs from single-tasking systems like MS-DOS, where a delay can be implemented by actively using the system, and where counting iterations of some active loop is a common practice. This *busy wait* approach is wasteful under the UNIX system, where other programs may be waiting to use the system while your command is delaying. One principle of a multi-tasking system is that other users share the system's resources. When you are idle, even if your command is active in the background, it is your responsibility to use commands that turn system resources over to other users. The **sleep** command does this for you; when a command is sleeping, you are making minimal use of the system's resources. Another benefit of **sleep** is that its timing depends on the internal clock, and not on the system load or basic processor speed; thus its timing is always exact to the nearest second.

The find Command

When you examine the contents of a directory with **ls** or copy files with wildcard expansion as in the command

```
$ cp * $HOME/new.directory
```

you may notice that these commands only act on files in one specific directory. Often you may wish to copy or examine the contents of a directory subtree as a whole, instead of working with each directory separately. The **find** command gives you this capability. Although **find** is one of the most powerful commands, it also has one of the most difficult command-line structures. On the other hand, **find** is so useful that it is well worth the effort required to wrestle with its syntax.

The **find** command descends a directory hierarchy locating all the files that meet special criteria given on the command line. It can take several types of actions on the files that it finds. Its command line is basically

```
$ find path-name-list expressions
```

where *path-name-list* is the list of directories to search. The list can include one or more directories, with either full or relative pathnames. The *expressions* are the operators that describe the selection criteria for the files you wish to locate, and the action you wish **find** to take when a file matches the selection criteria. For example,

```
$ find $HOME -print
```

is one of the smallest **find** command lines. This command will display the names of all the files and directories in your home directory. Additional directories can also be specified in the path-name-list section of the command line, as follows:

```
$ find /home/steve /home/jim -print
```

This command will display the names of all the files and directories under **/home/steve** and **/home/jim**. Wildcard pathnames are also allowed, as in this example:

```
$ find /home/* -print
```

In the **find** command line, all the pathnames immediately follow the command name, and the operators follow at the end of the command. All the operators begin with the - (minus) flag, and none of the items in the path-name-list can begin with minus.

By default, **find** takes no action on the files it finds, so the **-print** operator is required if you want to list the files that **find** locates. The **-print** option instructs **find** to write the items it finds to its standard output, one item per line. This property also lets you use **find** to count all the files and directories on your machine, as follows:

```
$ find / -print | wc -1
8642
$
```

This machine has 8642 files and directories! Large-scale **find** operations like this one, which searches through the entire directory structure, can take a lot of real and CPU time, especially on large machines or those with networked file systems. Take care to limit your use of **find** to the minimum path-name-list that meets your needs.

You can also add other operators to restrict the search to some subset of the files encountered. The **-name** argument specifies that only files with the given name should be found, as shown here:

```
$ find / -name profile -print
/etc/profile
$
```

The specified name can include the shell wildcard characters if they are quoted. For example:

```
$ find / -name "*profile" -print
/etc/profile
/home/jim/.profile
/home/pat/.profile
/home/steve/.profile
/.profile
$
```

The other shell wildcard operators like ?, [and] are also allowed providing they are quoted.

When **find** searches through the directory hierarchy, the order in which it finds files depends on the internal organization of the file system, which you cannot control. Occasionally, you may process the output with **sort** or some other tool to arrange the names in some specific order.

When multiple options are specified for **find**, they are executed in left-to-right order on each file that **find** encounters. The command

```
$ find / -print -name "*profile"
```

is not the same as

```
$ find / -name "*profile" -print
```

because the first example prints the filename and then selects for the name, while the second example selects the matching names first, and then prints the names. Keep this behavior in mind as you add options to **find**. The command searches for each filename in its path-name-list, and then uses the expressions to select or reject the filename until all the expressions have been executed. If a filename is rejected on one of the expressions, the rest of the expressions are not executed. In **find** terminology, the expression evaluates to *true* if the filename is selected, and to *false* if the filename is rejected.

There are many other options for **find**. Several specify files with selected attributes: **-user pat** selects files owned by user **pat**, and **-group sys** selects files belonging to group **sys**. The command

```
$ find / -user $LOGNAME -print
```

displays the names of all the files in the machine that are owned by you.

The **-type** *c* option selects files of type *c*, where *c* is any of the types in the left-most column of the permissions from **ls -l** (**f** for file, and **d** for directory are the most commonly used types). The **-mtime** *n* option selects files that were modified exactly *n* days ago. The expression **-mtime** *-n* selects files modified within the last *n* days, and **-mtime** *+n* selects files modified more than *n* days ago. The **-size** *n* option selects files exactly *n* blocks in size, **-size** *-n* selects files smaller than *n* blocks, and **-size** *+n* selects files larger than *n* blocks. Usually, 1000 blocks, or 512,000 bytes, is a relatively large file. To see all the large files on your machine, use

```
$ find / -size +1000 -print
```

Any of these operators can be negated. If the operator name (such as **-size**) is preceded by a ! (bang) and a space, the operator is made false when it would normally be true, and true when it would normally be false. For example,

```
$ find . ! -print
```

negates the printing of the list. This command is an expensive no-op! A more useful example might be the following, which finds all the files in your home directory that are not owned by you.

```
$ find $HOME ! -user $LOGNAME -print
```

The ! character must be surrounded by whitespace in the command line, and it only negates the operator immediately following it. To see a list of all files in your home directory that are not owned by you, and are also larger than 50 blocks, use this command:

```
$ find $HOME -size +50 ! -user $LOGNAME -print
```

You can also specify one operator *or* another, as follows:

```
$ find $HOME -size +50 -o ! -user $LOGNAME -print
```

The **-o** (for or) operator connects the two expressions that it is between, **-size +50** and **! -user $LOGNAME**, in this case. This command will select a file that has either attribute. By default, adjacent operators that are not separated by **-o** are logically connected by an *and* operation, which selects a file only if both the attributes are true.

The **find** command can select on the type of file. You would use

```
$ find . -type f -print
```

to find all the normal files. To find all the directories you would use **-type d**, and to find all the symbolic links you would use **-type l**. Several other file types are allowed, and **find** can also select based on the file system type that a file belongs to. Note that **find** will not search across symbolic links unless the **-follow** option is specified.

Finally, **find** can execute any command for each file that it finds with its other operators. The **-exec** (for execute) operator takes a following command line. The command can include the name of the current file **find** is processing, using the special syntax **{}** (left and right curly braces). The command line ends with the special operator **\;** (backslash semicolon). This option might be used to change the permissions of all files in a directory subtree, as shown here:

```
$ find . -exec chmod -rw {} \;
```

This command will not print the filenames as they are changed. To print the names you would use

```
$ find . -exec chmod -rw {} \; -print
```

The **-exec** operator will be true if the command it executes returns a zero exit value; otherwise it will be false. Of course, other **find** selectors and operators are also allowed with the **-exec** operation, and as usual the **find** command line is processed left-to-right until an expression evaluates to false.

The stty Command

The last command we'll discuss in this chapter is **stty** (for set tty). This command is used to examine and change the communications parameters associated with your terminal in your current login session. The UNIX system gives you a great deal of control over the way keystrokes and output to the terminal are processed. The **stty** command allows you to set up your terminal options for a specific terminal or communication line.

To look at your current terminal settings, use the **-a** (for all) option to **stty**, as follows:

```
$ stty -a
speed 9600 baud;
rows = 24; columns = 80; ypixels = 318; xpixels = 660;
intr = DEL; quit = ^|; erase = ^h; kill = @;
eof = ^d; eol = <undef>; eol2 = <undef>; swtch = <undef>;
start = ^q; stop = ^s; susp = ^z; dsusp = <undef>;
rprnt = ^r; flush = ^o; werase = ^w; lnext = ^v;
parenb -parodd cs7 -cstopb hupcl cread -clocal -loblk -parext
-ignbrk brkint ignpar -parmrk -inpck istrip -inlcr -igncr icrnl
-iuclc ixon ixany -ixoff -imaxbel
isig icanon -xcase echo echoe echok -echonl -noflsh
-tostop -echoctl -echoprt -echoke -defecho -flusho -pendin -iexten
opost -olcuc onlcr -ocrnl -onocr -onlret -ofill -ofdel
$
```

The options are displayed in a form that could be used to reenter them if necessary. Each terminal option has a name, such as **ixon**, and most can be either *set* or *clear*. If the option name is preceded by a - (minus), the option is clear; if there is no -, the option is set. For example, **ixon** refers to XON/XOFF flow control as controlled by the terminal. If this flow control is enabled, the option displays as **ixon**, as it does in the previous example. If XON/XOFF flow control is disabled, the option displays as **-ixon**.

You can change the value of an option by giving it as a command-line option to **stty**—with the - when you want to turn the option off (clear it), and without the - when you want to turn the option on (set it). For example,

```
$ stty ixon
$
```

turns on flow control, and

```
$ stty -ixon
$
```

turns it off. Multiple options are allowed on the command line, as shown here:

```
$ stty -ixon 1200
$
```

This command sets the terminal to 1200 bps, and turns off flow control.

You can set the character, row, and column extent of your terminal (or window!), as follows:

```
$ stty rows 24 columns 80
```

The new extents will be passed to full-screen applications such as **vi** when they start, overriding the normal defaults. Thus, if you resize a window or log in with an unusual terminal, you can set the screen size manually if it is not correct.

The list of options is long, and you must take care not to make changes that would disrupt your session. Typically, when your terminal is not working correctly, it is completely out of action. Usually no output is displayed or your keystrokes are not read correctly by the shell. In other situations, the newline may display as a line feed with no carriage return, or your typed newline characters may not be read correctly by the shell. Usually the procedure for creating a new login id establishes the **stty** options correctly, and you don't have to make changes in normal use. However, sometimes you might experiment with new terminals or communication channels such as local area networks that may require changes to the **stty** options.

Usually, if the terminal is working normally when you log in to the machine, but then becomes deranged for unknown reasons, the best response is simply to log off and log in to the system again. This causes the system to reset your terminal options to the "good" values they had before. However, a less severe solution is the command

```
$ stty sane
$
```

The **sane** option is actually a collection of **stty** options that seem to work on most types of terminals most of the time. It does not change the speed of the communication channel, but usually has a beneficial effect when the terminal is deranged. The **sane** option will probably not allow full-screen applications like **vi** to work correctly; if you cannot immediately fix any problems after you set the **sane** option, just log off and log in again. If the terminal is not working correctly at login, it is unlikely your login will succeed.

If the terminal becomes deranged in such a way that your newline key is not understood to end your command lines, you can usually use CTRL-J as a substitute newline until you execute **stty sane**. In this case, you terminate the **stty sane** command with CTRL-J to make the system understand it.

There are several other important options for the **stty** command. The **parenb** or **-parenb** option enables or disables parity, while **parodd** or **-parodd** selects odd or even parity, respectively. The **parodd** option is only used if **parenb** is set. The **cs5, cs6, cs7,** or **cs8** option sets a character size of 5, 6, 7, or 8 bits, respectively. The **300, 600, 1200, 2400, 4800, 9600,** or **19200** option sets the named bps rate, and **cstopb** or **-cstopb** sets two stop bits or one stop bit, respectively. The **tabs** option sets the system to use tabs instead of sequences of spaces when this would reduce the amount of output; **-tabs** uses only spaces, and is intended for situations where the tab character is not processed correctly by the terminal.

In addition, **stty** is used to determine what keys you use for some specific control functions. You have used CTRL-D as the end-of-file character; however, some users prefer CTRL-C for this function. You can change it with the command

```
$ stty eof c
```

where *c* is replaced by the specific control character that you want. You can enter control characters directly by preceding the character with a ^ (caret), which is in turn preceded with a \ (backslash). For example,

```
$ stty eof \^c
$
```

will set your end-of-file character to CTRL-C. This syntax is also used to change your erase character (usually BACKSPACE), and your intr (for interrupt) character (usually DEL). To change your erase character to BACKSPACE, use

```
$ stty erase \^h
```

You can also set your session so that when you enter a backspace character, the system responds with the sequence *backspace-space-backspace*, which causes the character that you just backspaced over to be removed from the display. Use the command

```
$ stty echoe
```

to turn on this feature.

You'll find the full list of options for **stty** in the *UNIX User's Manual*; consult the manual and your local communications guru before you stray too far from the instructions given here. Terminal modes and their management are some of the most arcane and difficult topics in the UNIX system. They should be approached with caution.

Shell Programming and More

**E
I
G
H
T**

Now that you are acquainted with many of the most general commands and most of the issues involved with command lines and their construction, you are ready to explore the more interesting features of the shell. The modern shell is a highly functional and flexible environment for users; it provides many tools that make working with the system much easier and less time-consuming than you might have suspected. Most users create some custom tools with the shell. In fact, the shell is really a full-scale programming language something like BASIC or the MS-DOS *batch* language, but it is more powerful and elegant than either of these. *Shell programming* is widely used to capture frequently performed commands and procedures.

Shell programs are often used in the tools and commands needed for system administration. Normally, system designers write an application in the shell programming language when run-time efficiency and speed are less important than making the application easy to understand and change; however, the modern shell provides excellent performance for executing *shell scripts*, as shell programs are often called. In fact, full-scale turnkey application systems have been developed entirely in shell scripts.

In this chapter we will first discuss some additional shell features, and then dive into shell programming. Finally, some more advanced shell features will be introduced. Note that this chapter discusses the "standard" Bourne Shell and basic features of the Korn Shell; C Shell programming is much different. Chapter 16 deals with programming the Korn and C Shells, and discusses more features of these enhanced shells.

Multiline Commands

When you enter a command line at the shell, it may be longer than the width of the terminal. This is often true of complex pipelines that include commands and long filenames. As long as you do not enter a newline character, most terminals will wrap around to the left end of the next display line so you can continue entering the command. When you enter the newline at the end of the command, the shell interprets it as the signal to begin processing the command line, which, in this case, is treated as a single-line command even though it occupies more than one terminal line.

In addition, the shell will actually allow commands to span more than one line. This is useful if you want to segment a command for readability or for some other reason. You can continue a command on a second line (or even on multiple lines) by entering a \ (backslash) as the last thing on the line before the newline character. This *escapes* the newline, so that the shell does not treat it as the end of the command, but instead accepts more input for the same command on the next line. A multiline command can also result if you quote a command argument, and press newline before closing the quotation marks.

In either case, the shell stores the part of the command that you have already entered, and displays a different prompt (instead of $) to remind you that it expects more of the same command, as shown here:

```
$ cat /etc/profile \
>
```

The new prompt is known as PS2 (for second-level prompt string), which follows, because your normal $ prompt is known as PS1. PS2 can be set and exported just as any other environment variable can. Here is an example:

```
$ echo $PS2
>
$ PS2='more:'
$ echo $PS2
more:
$
```

In this case, PS2 is originally set to >.

The appearance of PS2 signals that the command you have entered is not complete for some reason, and that the shell expects more input to complete the command. You can abort the command at the PS2 prompt by pressing the DEL key, which causes the stored command text to be discarded. In this event the PS1 prompt, usually $, returns, signaling that the shell is ready for another command.

here Documents

The shell treats any command that is entered on multiple lines as a single command line; however, the PS2 prompt can appear under two conditions. First, if you escape the newline with a \, or if a quoted argument is not closed before the newline, the shell simply discards the newline and uses PS2 to signal that more input is expected. Second, some shell operators flow across multiple lines, and in this case the embedded newlines provide syntactic information to segment the commands. A good example of this situation is the *here document*, so called because the input data is "here," rather than stored in a file. The shell operator <<*name* introduces a here document. The *name* can be any string of characters, and the << acts much like to the normal redirection operator from a file. No whitespace is allowed in this construction. Following the <<*name* operator, starting on the next line, is the actual data the command will read. A line that contains only *name* ends the here document. For example, the command

```
$ cat - <<MARKER
> hello
> goodbye
> MARKER
hello
goodbye
$
```

defines a two-line section of data as a here document, and the command **cat -** displays the here document as its standard input. When you type this command at the terminal, you press newline after <<**MARKER**. The shell determines that you have begun a here document and displays PS2 for more input. All the lines up to the line that contains only **MARKER** are part of the here document, and the shell stores all the input until it encounters the closing mark. After the shell sees the mark, it executes the command **cat -** using the here document as standard input. Then it returns to PS1 for the next command.

In this example, the shell interprets your newline as a true end-of-line mark, so the output from **cat -** appears on several different lines. However, it does not interpret the newline as the end of the command, because it is waiting for the end of the here document. There are several other occasions where multiline commands will be used in this book. If PS2 appears when you are entering a single-line command, you know you have made a mistake. When it appears in a multiline command, it means the shell is responding correctly.

Using here documents is preferable to redirecting standard input when you wish to use shell variables in data. A redirected file will always be read directly by the target command, but a here document will be processed by the shell, and then fed to the command. For example:

```
$ cat - <<HereDocument
> My login id is $LOGNAME
> HereDocument
My login id is steve
$
```

In addition to using shell variable substitution, you can use the ` (grave) operator to capture the standard output of a command line in the here document. For example:

```
$ cat - <<XYZZY
> There are `ls -1 $HOME | wc -l` files in $HOME
> XYZZY
There are        4 files in /home/steve
$
```

This allows you to merge powerful combinations of shell variables and command output in a text stream.

Storing Shell Commands In Files

You have already seen that any command, or sequence of commands, that can be typed directly at the terminal can be stored in a file and executed from the file. Using commands that are stored in a file is *identical* to typing the commands directly. The shell simply arranges things so that the file rather than the terminal is connected to standard input. One way to execute commands in a file is to give the filename as an argument to **sh**, which executes as a subshell. For example:

```
$ cat cmd.file
echo $LOGNAME
pwd
$ sh cmd.file
steve
/home/steve
$
```

Here, the file **cmd.file** contains the two commands **echo $LOGNAME** and **pwd**. The commands are executed with **sh cmd.file**, and the output comes to standard output, as you would expect. The file **cmd.file** is an example of a short *shell script*. Another way to execute the command is this:

```
$ chmod u+x cmd.file
$ cmd.file
steve
/home/steve
$
```

If the shell script has executable permissions, you don't need to give it as an argument to an explicit subshell. The login shell can figure out that it is a shell script, and once it does, it executes its own subshell to carry out the command. Thus, a shell script can be executed just like a binary program, and there is usually no reason to distinguish between the two kinds of commands.

In the script, new commands begin on new lines of the file, but otherwise they are entered just as you enter them at the terminal. Any function that can be performed directly at the terminal can be included in a shell script. For example, it is often useful to define shell variables whose lifetime is only for the duration of the shell script, as in this example:

```
$ cat cmd2.file
DIR=`pwd`
echo $DIR
$ cmd2.file
/home/steve
$
```

The **DIR** variable is set to the current directory, and then **echo $DIR** echoes it. Shell variables set this way are recognized only within the shell script in which they are defined, and do not remain in force when your login shell resumes after the script completes. Similarly, other commands in shell scripts do not continue beyond the scripts in which they appear, as this example demonstrates:

```
$ cat cmd3.file
pwd
echo Changing directory....
cd /home/jim
pwd
$ cmd3.file
/home/steve
Changing directory....
/home/jim
$ pwd
/home/steve
$
```

You can change directories within a shell script, but the **cd** operation affects only the script, and not the rest of your session.

Since the system does not distinguish between binary executable programs and shell scripts, you can include shell scripts as commands within other scripts. Do not forget to **export** any local environment variables you wish to use in subprograms or scripts.

Commenting Shell Scripts

Shell programs saved in files, especially long and complex scripts, usually need *comments* to remind readers of what they do. The operator # (pound sign) is used to introduce a comment in a shell script (or at the terminal). If your erase character is #, you must escape the # with a \ before using it to mark a comment. The shell ignores everything on the same command line following the # character. Here is an example:

```
$ #cat /etc/passwd
$ echo hello  #this is a comment at the end of a line
hello
$
```

The comment overrides the \ operator that normally escapes the newline for shell commands and files, because all the material after the # is ignored. Comments are very helpful in maintaining shell scripts, and cost nothing in performance, so you can use them liberally.

The If Operator

The shell provides tools that can make many types of decisions based on the current execution environment for a command or shell script. One of these is the **if** operator, which introduces a *conditional* operation. The format of the **if** command is

```
$ if expression ; then commands ; fi
```

This example appears on a single command line, but **if** introduces a multiline command sequence that is not closed until the characters **fi** (for inverse if) are interpreted. The *expression* is any logical expression or a command that returns a value. If it returns a zero, the *commands* following **then** are executed, up to **fi**. For example:

```
$ if true ; then echo hello ; fi
hello
$ if false ; then echo hello ; fi
$
```

These commands are shown with a ; (semicolon) separating the parts, but normally they would be written on multiple lines, with the PS2 prompt reminding you that the command sequence is incomplete, as follows:

```
$ if true
> then
>       echo hello
> fi
hello
$
```

If the newlines are not present, the semicolons are required; one or the other method must be used to delimit the parts of the commands.

The previous example includes a special logical operator that is available to shell scripts: **true**. This operator always returns a value of zero, to ensure that **if** executes the commands following **then**. Also available is **false**, which always returns a nonzero value, as shown here:

```
$ false
$ echo $?
1
$
```

Recall that $? is a shell variable that contains the return value from the last command executed.

You can use as many commands as necessary in the **then** part of the **if** construction, including other nested **if** commands. For example:

```
$ if true
> then
>       echo hello
>       echo `pwd`
> fi
hello
/home/steve
$
```

More complex versions of the expression part of the **if** construct are discussed later in this chapter.

In case a second leg of the **if** construction is required, the **else** operator is available. Commands that follow the **else** operator are executed when the expression part returns a nonzero value, as in this example:

```
$ if false ; then
>        echo hello
> else
>        echo goodbye
> fi
goodbye
$
```

Once again, the contents of the command list following the **else** command can include as many commands as necessary.

Additional **if** constructions can follow the **else**. These are introduced with the short form **elif** (for else if), as shown here:

```
$ if false ; then
>        echo hello
> elif true ; then
>        echo goodbye
> fi
goodbye
$
```

The **then** section after **elif** is required. Again, the whole construction closes with **fi**.

The test Command

So far, only a very simple *expression* has been used with **if**, so simple that the previous examples are probably not very useful. In practice, the expression can encompass almost any kind of logical operation. For example, it would be handy to compare two numbers, and if they were the same have the **then** section execute. Or, you might wish to execute the commands following **then** if a specific file existed. You can perform these and many other operations using the **test** command, which is designed to follow **if** and to provide truth values (or return codes) that **if** can interpret. The **test** command has two forms, which are synonyms for each other. Both forms appear frequently in shell scripts, and which one you use depends on your personal preference; however, your shell scripts will be easier to read if you use the same form consistently. The first form is the command name **test** itself, followed by arguments that are resolved according to specific rules, which we'll explain after this example:

```
$ if test $VAR
> then
>       echo hello
> fi
$
```

Here, if the environment variable **VAR** is not defined, the operation **test** **$VAR** will fail, and **if** will treat the result as false. If the environment variable is defined, the test will succeed, as it does here:

```
$ if test $HOME
> then
>       echo hello
> fi
hello
$
```

The other form of **test** uses the special operators [and] (square brackets). In this form the **test** arguments are enclosed within the brackets, and the word **test** does not appear. Here is an example:

```
$ if [ $HOME ]
> then
>       echo hello
> fi
hello
$
```

Note that the brackets must be surrounded by whitespace or the shell will not interpret the command line correctly. This use of square brackets differs from their use as a wildcard or regular expression operator for filename expansion; however, the shell interprets them correctly because they are used after the **if** operator.

Many tests are possible, depending on the arguments within the brackets. The **test** command provides operations for files and for comparing numbers, strings of characters, and the values of environment variables. In all forms of the command, whitespace must surround the brackets and each of the operators.

The form **-f** **file** (for file) returns true if the *file* exists and is a normal file, as shown here:

```
$ if [ -f /etc/passwd ] ; then echo file exists ; fi
file exists
$
```

Similarly, **-r** *file* returns true if the *file* exists and is readable, **-w** *file* returns true if the file exists and is writable, **-x** *file* returns true if the file exists and is executable, and **-d** *file* returns true if the file exists and is a directory. The test **-s** *file* returns true if the file exists and has a size larger than zero. Although several other file-related operators available, they are not often used.

String comparison operators are provided to test the presence and value of environment variables. This allows you to perform an operation, assign the value to an environment variable, and then test the value of the variable to decide whether to take some further action. For example, you might wish to execute some commands only if you are in a particular directory, as in this example:

```
$ DIR=`pwd`
$ if [ $DIR = $HOME ]
> then
>       echo In home directory!
> fi
In home directory!
$
```

Note that the = (equal) operator is used here to test whether two character strings are identical. The **test** command returns true if the strings are the same, and false if they are not. The form != (bang equal) can be used to return true if the strings are not equal. Again, these operators must be separated by whitespace both from the brackets and from the other arguments within the brackets.

A string or an environment variable can appear alone to determine if the string has been defined, as shown here:

```
$ if [ "$NOVALUE" ] ; then echo hello ; fi
$
```

If the environment variable **NOVALUE** has not been defined, **test** returns false and the **then** section is not executed. The construction **$NOVALUE** is quoted in this example because if the environment variable is not defined, nothing will be substituted in the test and the brackets will be empty, which is an error condition for **test**. The quotes cause the expression's value to be an empty string rather than nothing at all if **NOVALUE** is undefined.

In the previous examples, the = operator is reserved for comparisons of strings; it cannot be used to compare the equality of numbers. The **test** command can also compare integer numeric values, although shell programming is not as good at numeric problems as most other programming tools are. Numeric comparisons within **test** take the form

```
if [ n1 -eq n2 ]
```

where *n1* and *n2* are expressions that resolve to a number. The operator **-eq** (for equals) evaluates to true if the two numbers are equal, as shown here:

```
$ echo $VAL
2
$ if [ $VAL -eq 2 ]
> then
>        echo equal
> fi
equal
$
```

Other numeric operators are **-ne** (for not equal), **-gt** (for greater than), **-lt** (for less than), and **-le** (for less or equal). The inequality operator **-lt** returns true if the first number is less than the second, and the other operators follow this same pattern.

The numeric operators are often used to test the return value of a command or pipeline, and take some action if the return value is a specific number. Most commands return zero if they complete success-fully, as shown here:

```
$ mkdir /tmp/SS
$ RET=$?
$ if [ $RET -eq 0 ]
> then
>       echo "mkdir succeeded"
> else
>       echo "Couldn't make directory"
> fi
mkdir succeeded
$
```

Of course, these examples would be more likely to appear in shell scripts than in commands that you enter directly at the $ prompt, but all of them can be entered directly.

The **test** command also provides tools you can use to combine operators and build complex expressions. The ! (bang) is used to negate an operator, as in this example:

```
$ if [ ! -f file ]
> then
>       touch file      # this creates the file
> fi
$
```

This command creates a file if it doesn't already exist.

Other combination operators available to **test** are **-o** (for or), and **-a** (for and). These are used to separate other operators, as shown here:

```
$ F1=file1 ; F2=file2
$ if [ ! -f $F1 -a -f $F2 ]
> then
>       echo "$F1 doesn't exist, but $F2 does exist"
> fi
$
```

These operators can be combined into very complex expressions, and you can group complex operations within parentheses if necessary; how-ever, in practice you should try to keep **test** commands relatively simple.

The exit Command

You can use the **exit** command inside shell scripts to immediately end execution of the script. The command can take an argument, which becomes the value the script returns to the calling shell, as in this example:

```
$ cat cmd4.file
if true
then
        exit 6
fi
$ cmd4.file
$ echo $?
6
$
```

When you use return values from within shell scripts, you should follow the standard convention: commands that complete correctly should return zero. Nonzero return values should be reserved for various failure conditions.

The expr Command

Although the shell programming language is not optimized for numeric calculations, it does provide commands that do computations. The **expr** (for expression) command is the most useful of these. It takes numbers and arithmetic operators as arguments, and computes the result, returning the answer on its standard output, as shown here:

```
$ expr 4 + 5
9
$
```

Longer commands are also allowed, but each piece of the expression must be surrounded by whitespace, since **expr** treats each individual argument as part of the expression to evaluate. Only integers and the operators + (plus), - (minus), * (multiplication), / (division), and % (for remainder) are allowed. You must escape * and / to keep the shell from interpreting them before **expr** gets to them. For example:

```
$ expr 3 \* 4 + 2 \/ 2
13
$
```

Normal arithmetic *precedence* is used, so in the previous example the 3 * 4 and the 2 / 2 would be evaluated before the +. You can easily change the precedence by performing complex calculations in several separate steps, as shown here:

```
$ VAL=`expr 3 \* 4 + 2`
$ expr $VAL \/ 2
7
$
```

This example shows how **expr** is normally used within shell scripts. Environment variables are usually defined to store numbers, and you can use the value of the environment variables later in other **expr** commands or in **test** operations.

In addition, you can *group* operations inside parentheses providing you escape the parentheses, as follows:

```
$ expr 3 \* \( 4 + 3 \) \/ 2
10
$
```

The **expr** command can also perform *logical operations*. That is, it can determine whether one argument is *equal to, greater than,* or *less than* another. The operators = (equal), != (not equal), > (greater than), < (less than), < = (less than or equal to), and > = (greater than or equal to) are allowed. Note that these must be escaped since most contain characters that are special to the shell. Here is an example:

```
$ X=`expr 4 \< 5`
$ echo $X
1
$ X=`expr 4 = 5`
$ echo $X
0
$
```

If the arguments for these logical operators are numbers, **expr** will do numeric comparisons; if they are strings, **expr** will make comparisons based on the sort order or *collating sequence* of the strings in the ASCII alphabet.

The for Operator

Other operators in the shell programming language provide *looping* constructs, which repetitively execute a section of the shell program. The **for** operator is an example. It uses the form

```
$ for var in item1 item2 item3 ; do commands ; done
```

where *var* is an environment variable that you name, and *items* are a list of character strings, with each item separated from the others by whitespace. For example:

```
$ for VAL in 1 2 3 4 ; do commands ; done
```

When the shell reads this command, it sets **VAL** equal to the first item in the list, and then executes the *commands* between the **do** and its matching **done**. Then the shell sets **VAL** equal to the second member of the list, and executes *commands* again. This procedure is repeated until all members of the list have been processed. The value of **VAL** is available within the command list if it is needed, as shown here:

```
$ for VAL in 1 2 3 4
> do
>         echo $VAL
> done
1
2
3
4
$
```

As usual, the commands within the **do-done** delimiters can be as complex as necessary, and may include **if-fi** expressions or more **for** operations.

The **for** construction is often used with filenames to perform some operation repeatedly on each file. Because the **for** command is interpreted by the shell, wildcard expansion is performed, as in this example:

```
$ for FILE in * ; do echo $FILE ; done
```

Because * is replaced by the names of all the files, this command will echo the name of all the files in the current directory. A particularly inefficient way to count the files in a directory might be

```
$ COUNT=0
$ for FILE in *
> do
>       COUNT=`expr $COUNT + 1`
> done
$ echo $COUNT
14
$
```

As you can see, there is no rule that forces you to *use* the environment variable that follows the **for** command, but it must be present, or **for** won't know how many times to iterate the **do-done** section.

The standard output of a command can also create the list, as shown here:

```
$ for VAR in `ls`
> do
>       echo $VAR
> done
```

This is an acceptable command, because the shell executes the **ls** command, places its output into the **for** command, and then executes the entire command.

The **for** command has many uses, both in shell scripts and directly at the terminal, because it allows you to iterate through a list of objects, executing a (possibly) large number of commands on each member of the list. Not surprisingly, **for** is one of the most frequently used shell operators.

The while Operator

The **while** operator combines some characteristics of both **for** and **if**. It takes a following **test** command, and then a **do-done** section. If the **test** section resolves to true, the **do-done** section is executed; if the **test** section resolves to false, the **do-done** section is not executed and the loop completes. After the **do-done** is executed, the **test** section is executed again, and the loop continues until the **test** section resolves to false, as follows:

```
$ while [ ! -f file ]
> do
>       echo Trying to create file
>       touch file
> done
```

This example keeps trying to create a file until it succeeds.

You will usually include some commands to change the result of the **test** section within the **do-done** section, or the loop is likely to continue forever! The next example creates ten files, named **file1**, through **file10**.

```
$ VAL=1
$ while [ $VAL -lt 11 ]
> do
>       touch file$VAL
>       VAL=`expr $VAL + 1`
> done
```

Here is another way to write the same command:

```
$ for VAL in 1 2 3 4 5 6 7 8 9 10
> do
>       touch file$VAL
> done
```

As usual, any commands—including other **while** operations—can be part of the **do-done** section.

You can substitute **until** for the **while** keyword to reverse the sense of the test. That is, **while** executes the command list as long as the test is true, but **until** executes the command list as long as the test is false.

When you write shell scripts, try to indent each new sublevel of the commands an additional tab stop, as in the previous examples. This helps to organize the program; commands at the same level align vertically, and the whole program is easier to read than it would be if all the commands started at the left margin, or right after the PS2 prompt. Indenting the commands does not affect the way the shell interprets the script, but it definitely improves the way humans interpret it!

The case Operator

The shell provides one additional control operator. This is the **case** operator, which acts like a large **if-elif-elif...elif-fi** command. Given a character string, **case** determines which of several categories the string matches, and then executes a list of commands associated with that category. The other, unmatched, categories are ignored. The format of the **case** operator is

```
$ case $VAR in
>        pattern1 )
>                command-list
>                ;;
>        pattern2 )
>                command-list
>                ;;
>        pattern3 )
>                command-list
>                ;;
> esac
```

There can be as many *patterns* and *command-lists* as necessary, but the command list associated with each pattern must be terminated by the special operator ;; (semicolon semicolon). In addition, each pattern must be different from all others, and the) (right parenthesis) after each pattern is required. *VAR* can be any environment variable, or any expression that resolves to a character string. The whole construct is terminated by **esac** (for case backwards). As usual, any other shell operators can be nested inside the command-list for each case.

The following command prints a special greeting for each user on the machine:

```
$ case $LOGNAME in
>      jim)
>                    echo Hello Jim, welcome back
>                    echo from your vacation
>                    ;;
>      pat)
>                    echo Pat, do not forget to read your mail
>                    ;;
>      steve)
>                    echo Please delete some files, you are using
>                    echo too much disk space....  Thanks!
>                    ;;
> esac
```

Normally a script like this would be executed from a file, perhaps by users as they log in to the machine. This script could be included as part of the **profile** discussed later in this chapter.

The pattern section of the **case** operator allows the use of regular expressions in the shell wildcard format. In the previous example, you could have used **ste***, ***te***, **?teve**, or another pattern to match **steve**. In addition the | (pipe) character can be used to mean *or* in the pattern section, as shown here:

```
$ case $LOGNAME in
>      steve|jim)
>                    echo do not forget the meeting today
>                    ;;
>      *)
>                    echo Welcome to our UNIX system
>                    ;;
> esac
```

The first case is for **steve** or **jim**. The second case, *****, matches any other string. It is used as a catchall default case. Remember, only one of the sections will be executed each time the **case** construct as a whole will be executed, and that will be the *first* pattern that matches the character string. If none of the patterns match, none of the cases is executed.

The printf Command and Output from Shell Scripts

The major tool for getting output from a shell script is the **echo** command, used extensively in the previous examples. It provides a quick and easy way to put simple character strings and the value of environment variables into the output stream.

For more complex forms of character output, the **printf** command is available. This command provides a string-oriented subset of the capabilities of the C language's **printf(3)** subroutine.

The **printf** command takes two kinds of arguments. The first is a *formatting specification*, which is a character string that specifies the general form of the output, and may include special "holes" in which real data can be inserted. The second type of argument to **printf** is a list of strings. There will be as many of these strings as there are holes in the formatting specification. The holes, called *conversion specifications*, define how the variables will be printed. For example:

```
$ printf "this is a string:  %s\n" 1234567890
this is a string: 1234567890
$
```

The first (quoted) argument gives the formatting specification. Normal characters are simply printed, like the *this is a string*: part. The conversion specifications are introduced with the special sequence **%s**. Each string (or command that resolves to a string) given after the formatting specification is replaced in sequence into the conversion specifications. Unused string arguments are ignored by **printf**, but unused conversion specifications will produce unexpected results.

Some special sequences are allowed in the formatting specification. You can use **\n** to generate a newline, and **\t** to add a tab character. However, most versions of **printf(1)** are string-oriented, and other types of conversion specifications, such as **%d** or **%c** will not usually work.

The previous example is just a complex form of the **echo** command; but **printf** shows its usefulness when you need to *truncate* a character string to shorten it, or when you want to put the displayed string into a specific field of the output line. You can add numbers after the **%** but before the **s** in the conversion specification to control the positioning of the string in the output field. You specify a minimum field width with a number, as shown here:

```
$ printf "string in a 20-character field:  >%20s<\n", 1234567890
string in a 20-character field:  >          1234567890<
$
```

To *left-justify* the string, add a - (minus) sign, as follows:

```
$ printf "left-justified string:  >%-20s<\n" 1234567890
left-justified string: >1234567890         <
$
```

You can also truncate the string by adding a *field width* after a dot in the conversion specification. For example:

```
$ printf "this is a 5-character string:  >%.5s<\n", 1234567890
this is a 5-character string: >12345<
$
```

The **printf** command is often used to truncate a string while assigning it to an environment variable, as shown here:

```
$ XXX='printf "%.4s" "hello world"'
$ echo $XXX
hello
$
```

This is an easy way to get *substrings* from longer character strings in your shell programs.

The .profile and /etc/profile

One of the best examples of shell scripts, and one that each user must normally create and maintain individually, is executed by the shell during the login procedure. This script is usually used to configure your login sessions according to your preferences, and to create some of the environment variables that commands expect to find. The *profile* is somewhat equivalent to AUTOEXEC.BAT in MS-DOS systems, except that the profile is specific to your login id; other users have their own versions.

Actually, two scripts are executed when you log in to the system. One is owned by the system, and sets up your environment according to systemwide permissions. This script is located in **/etc/profile**, and is usually readable by all users. As soon as you successfully log in to the system **/etc/profile** is executed. It is not discussed here, but you should browse through it on your own machine. Usually when the system administrator changes the environment for all users by adding a new directory to the default PATH, for example, the change is implemented by modifying **/etc/profile**.

The second profile is executed after **/etc/profile**, but before the shell displays the first $ prompt. This is called **.profile** (dot profile) and is located in your home directory. You do not normally see your **.profile** in your home directory with **ls**, because the leading . (dot) at the beginning of the name keeps **ls** from displaying it. The command

```
$ ls -a
```

will display your **.profile** and any other filenames that begin with a dot. You own your **.profile**, and you can use it to configure your personal environment beyond what the system does with **/etc/profile**. Usually, personalized commands that are always executed on login go in your **.profile**.

A Typical .profile

Normally, the system administrator for your machine gives you a simple **.profile** when your login id is created, but in most cases this is not sufficient. As you gain experience with the UNIX system, you will probably want to customize the environment to your preferences; many users edit their **.profile** soon after they get a login id on a new machine. Figure 8-1 shows a typical **.profile** that suggests the kinds of changes usually made to the environment. Most of these changes are not necessary, but they can make a session more pleasant because your preferences will be used instead of the system defaults.

Let's look more closely at Figure 8-1. First, the PATH variable is redefined to pick up the current directory and a private bin ahead of the system commands. This allows you to override some of the normal commands with your private, custom commands. However, this can be a security risk if the directories are writable by other users, because someone could put a corrupt version of a command into your directory, which you would use instead of the system default. The current directory is usually included in the PATH, either at the beginning or at the

```
# typical .profile
# edit yours to meet your own needs...

# Change PATH to put private directories ahead of system bins
# Note: this can be a security risk
PATH=:$HOME:$HOME/bin:/sbin:/usr/sbin:/usr/bin:/usr/X/bin:/usr/ucb

# reconfigure the terminal for tabs, XON/XOFF,
# and "space-backspace-space" for erase
stty tabs echoe erase ^h ixon ixoff ixany

# change the prompts....
PS1="[!] `uname`> "
PS2=" >> "

# Now special processing for each of the different
# terminals we might use....  If we're on the console,
# we can skip this part....
PORT=`tty`
PORT=`basename $PORT`
if [ $PORT != console ] ; then

        # prompt for the terminal this session,
        # and read it into an environment variable
        echo "\nTERM=\c"
        read TERM

        case $TERM in
            s*)      # AT&T UNIX PC
                     if [ $TERM = ss ] ; then stty cr2 nl1 ; fi
                     TERM=ansi
                     stty -tabs
                     ;;

            pc|2621)        # HP 2621 or terminal emulator
                     TERM=2621
                     tabs -Thp
                     ;;

            ansi|v*)        # DEC VT102, VT200, or term emulator
                     TERM=vt100
                     tabs
                     ;;

            *)       # all others are treated as very dumb terms
                     TERM=dumb
                     stty -tabs
                     ;;

        esac
fi
```

Figure 8-1.   A typical **.profile**

```
# repeat what terminal is really being used
echo "TERM=$TERM"

# this is for the "vi" editor
EXINIT='set ai'

# some software likes to know the name of my preferred editor
EDITOR=/usr/bin/vi
EDIT=/usr/bin/vi

# For "cd" commands
CDPATH=:$HOME:$HOME/bin

# and make sure they are all exported
export PATH TERM PS1 PS2 EXINIT EDITOR CDPATH EDIT

# display the date and time
date

# display any news that we haven't seen yet
news

# prompt if any old mail saved in "$HOME/mbox"
if [ -f mbox ] ; then echo "You have oldmail!" ; fi

# setup for use with the Korn Shell
FCEDIT=/usr/bin/vi
VISUAL=$FCEDIT
MAILCHECK=60
ENV="\${-:+$HOME/.ksh.aliases\${-##*i*}}"
HISTFILE=$HOME/.ksh.history
export ENV HISTFILE FCEDIT VISUAL MAILCHECK

# last, we switch shells from the default to the ksh
exec /usr/bin/ksh
```

Figure 8-1.   A typical **.profile** (*continued*)

end. Next, the **stty** command resets the terminal configuration to enable XON/XOFF flow control, to send tabs instead of spaces when possible, and to make BACKSPACE the erase character. The *echoe* command makes the system send a *backspace-space-backspace* sequence when you press BACKSPACE. This erases your typed characters from the screen as you backspace over them. Next, the script changes the PS1 and PS2 prompts.

The largest part of this sample **.profile** handles different terminals that you might use. First a local environment variable, *PORT*, is used as a target of the **test** command to determine whether you are on the system console or a remote terminal. On the console, the **/etc/profile** sets the TERM variable correctly, so this long **if-fi** section is not executed. When you are not logged in to the console, the **.profile** prompts for the terminal you are using. The command

```
read TERM
```

waits for you to enter a line from the keyboard, and then stores the line in the environment variable TERM. Next, **case** is used to perform different processing depending on what is entered. Usually it simply sets the TERM variable correctly for each of the different terminals. The **tabs** command sends out the proper escape sequences to set the tab stops at the terminal, in case the terminal cannot remember tab settings when its power is shut off. The **tabs** command works with **stty tabs** to reduce the amount of output sent to the terminal by replacing a number of spaces with tabs when it is appropriate to do so.

Since the TERM variable may have changed as a result of the **case-esac** block, the TERM value is echoed back; then a few more environment variables are set. EXINIT is used by the **vi** editor, and the EDITOR and EDIT variables tell some software what the preferred editor is. CDPATH is an advanced feature of the shell that allows you to use a short and intelligent form of the **cd** command. It is discussed at the end of this chapter. Next, the script makes sure that all of your subshells have access to these environment variables by exporting them.

Now a little administrative work is done. The **date** command simply displays the current date and time, while **news** automatically displays any news that you haven't yet read. The short **if-fi** block that follows reminds you that some saved mail exists. Usually you should delete mail when you are through with it, so if the **mbox** file exists, there is probably some unfinished business that may need attention.

Finally, several more environment variables are set up. These are associated with the **ksh**, another shell that is often used instead of the default shell. The last command in the script, **exec /usr/bin/ksh**, actually switches to that shell.

Your **.profile** will probably differ from this example, but remember that most of the customization of the individual user environment and login process belongs in the personal **.profile**.

The . Operator

Normally the **.profile** is executed for you when you log in to the system; however, when you are editing and testing your **.profile**, it is tedious to log off and log in to the machine repeatedly. Since the **.profile** is a normal executable shell script, why can't you just execute it like any other shell script? The answer is a little tricky. Recall that shell scripts are executed in their own subshells, and changes to environment variables within subshells do not propagate back to the parent shells. Therefore, if your **.profile** is executed directly with

```
$ sh .profile
```

any effects that it might have, such as changing your TERM variable, will not make permanent changes to your environment. To get around this problem, the shell provides another operator that effectively causes the shell to execute a script by the current shell, rather than creating a subshell to execute it. This is the . (dot) command, which takes an argument naming the script you wish to execute, as shown here:

```
$ . .profile
```

Any shell script is an acceptable argument, but the dot command is usually used with **.profile** for testing, or to load a profile during execution of another shell script in a subshell. Changes made to the environment with the dot operator permanently alter the current environment, and may affect any subshells that are created later, but they do not change parent or higher level shells.

Command-Line Arguments

There are still several issues related to shell programming to be discussed. One is *command-line arguments*. You can create shell programs that process command-line arguments in exactly the same format as other commands do. In fact, you should usually try to duplicate the normal argument syntax as closely as possible, so that your commands work the way users expect them to. For this reason, operators are provided in shell scripts to process command-line arguments that are constructed in a familiar way.

$#, $*, and Positional Parameters

You have already met the $# and $* shell variables, which the shell interprets as the number of command-line parameters to a shell script, and the values of all the parameters, respectively. In this shell script

```
echo $#
for VAR in $*
do
        echo $VAR
done
```

the shell expands the $* variable to be all the command-line arguments to the script. For example, if the previous shell script were called **echo.args,** you might execute it with a command such as this:

```
$ echo.args first second third
```

The arguments **first, second,** and **third** are passed to the script, as follows:

```
$ echo.args first second third
3
first
second
third
$
```

The 3 in the output is the result of the **echo $#** command in the script, and the other output is the result of the **for-do-done** loop.

In addition, each of the command-line arguments to the script are available individually, with the names **$1, $2, $3,** and so forth, for as many as nine command-line arguments. For example, the previous script could have been written:

```
echo $#
echo $1
echo $2
echo $3
```

with exactly the same results. Each of these command-line arguments can be used to pass filenames or other information into a shell script from its command line.

These command-line arguments are usually useful only in shell scripts that are executed as commands, because the login shell has no arguments associated with it. That is,

```
$ echo $#
0
$
```

No command-line arguments are defined to your login shell, with one exception. **$0** is a legitimate argument just like **$2**, and it returns the command name itself, as shown here:

```
$ echo $0
sh
$
```

The first command-line argument after the name is **$1**.

In addition, the shell provides an operator to *set* these command-line arguments if needed. For example:

```
$ echo $#
0
$ echo $2

$ set hello goodbye third
$ echo $#
3
$ echo $2
goodbye
$
```

The **set** operator assigns its arguments to the *positional parameters* so that scripts can use the names **$2**, and so on, even if no command-line arguments are given. For example, if you write a script that did something with its command-line parameters, but in some instance there were none, the script itself could set them to default values. The **set** command is often used within shell scripts.

Errors and Error Messages in Using Shell Scripts

Developing shell scripts that work as you want them to usually requires some experimentation and testing. The shell provides some diagnostic error messages when it cannot execute a script that is incorrect, but this output is often terse, as shown here:

```
$ for VAR in `ls` do
> hello
syntax error: 'hello' unexpected
$
```

The error here was omitting the ; or newline before the **do** keyword, but the error output from the shell did not provide much information. The shell can provide more diagnostic output, however. Shell scripts are usually put into files and not executed directly from the terminal. You can *trace* the execution of a script by executing it with the -x option, which causes the shell to print each command in the script as it is executed (see Figure 8-2). Each command is displayed with a leading + as it is executed, after the shell has carried out its substitutions and processed any shell operators such as **test**. The trace facility makes it much easier to follow the trail of execution that led to an error. Another aid is the -v (for verbose) flag, which displays much more information about each command in the script. For example:

```
$ sh -v shell.script first second third
echo $#
3
for VAR in $* ; do
        echo $VAR
done
first
second
third
$
```

```
$ cat shell.script
echo $#
for VAR in $* ; do
        echo $VAR
done
$ sh -x shell.script first second third
+ echo 3
3
+ echo first
first
+ echo second
second
+ echo third
third
$
```

Figure 8-2.   Trace (-x) output from executing a shell script

The **-x** and **-v** options can be used together to yield even more diagnostic output. This output goes to standard error so you can save it in a file separate from the normal output.

Going Further

There is much more to writing and using shell scripts than we have touched on here. You learn shell programming by practice, by constant experimentation with short scripts entered directly at the terminal, and by reading and changing other people's scripts.

There are many examples of shell scripts in the commands; usually you cannot easily tell if a command is a binary compiled program or a shell script with executable permissions. In most systems, among many others, the commands **/usr/bin/calendar**, **/usr/bin/spell**, and **/usr/bin/basename** are shell scripts. Examine these on your own system and try to follow what they do. Can you understand their logic?

shar—An Instructive Shell Script

Figure 8-3 shows another example of a moderately complex shell script; in fact, this shell script produces another shell script as its output. Figure 8-3 is an implementation of the **shar** (for shell archive) command. Its job is to produce a single file that contains within it several other files. One file is usually easier to move between machines via electronic mail or **uucp** than several files. Although **shar** is limited compared to some other file-packing tools because it only handles text files and not binary or compiled files, it is widely used to exchange data between UNIX systems. In practice, users often create **shar** archives of several short source files, and send those files to someone else who *unpacks* or *unshars* them to recover the originals. Like all good data communications tools, the **shar** program includes some tests to detect whether anything was lost during the *shar-move-unshar* procedure. The **shar** program is executed as follows:

```
$ shar filename-list > /tmp/out.file
```

The script reads the files in the list, and writes the archived output to its standard output. You would usually redirect this to a different file, in a directory other than the one you are bundling with the **shar** command.

The **shar** archive produced by this shell script is in fact an executable shell script itself. The original files can be unpacked from the **shar** archive with the command:

```
$ sh /tmp/out.file
```

or with this one:

```
$ chmod +x /tmp/out.file
$ /tmp/out.file
```

This simple **shar** mechanism provides a way to pack files into a shell script, and the program in Figure 8-3 rewards extensive study. We will describe it briefly here.

```
#! /sbin/sh
# shar: shell archive shell script
# Runs in  /sbin/sh
# shar:  group files into distribution package in "shar" format
#        suitable for extraction with sh or ksh, not csh.

# there must be at least one cmdline arg
if [ $# -lt 1 ] ; then
        echo "usage: shar file1 file2 file3 ... fileN"
        exit 1
fi

# begin building the output file.
# first is a general header....
echo '#  To unbundle, "sh" this file -- DO NOT use csh'
echo '#  SHAR archive format.  Archive created '`date`

# each file is processed in turn:  "$*" is the list of args
for file in $* ; do

        # if the file doesn't exist, complain, but don't quit
        if [ ! \( -r $file -a -f $file \) ] ; then
                echo shar:  "Cannot archive $file" > /dev/tty
                continue
        fi

        # the file is found, so we put out its name
        echo "echo x - $file"

        # Make a here document out of the file,
        # and write the here document intact to the output

        # count the matching quotes... this is tricky!
        # we're echoing a "sed" command line, not executing "sed"
        echo "sed 's/^X//' > $file <<'+SHAR+MARK+'"

        # Here we execute the "sed" to prefix 'X' to each line.
        # write it to stdout
        sed 's/^/X/' $file

        # now we close the here document
        echo "+SHAR+MARK+"

        # we "ls" the file, then stash the results inside an "echo"
        echo "echo '`ls -l $file`    (as sent)'"
```

Figure 8-3.   **shar** shell script

```
        # this one processes the permissions in the "ls -l",
        # creates a "chmod" command, then writes the
        # "chmod" command to the output
        ls -l $file | sed \
                -e 's/^.\(...\)\(...\)\(...\).*/u=\1,g=\2,o=\3/' \
                -e 's/-//g' \
                -e 's/.*/chmod & '"$file/"

        # now a direct "ls" for the output script
        echo "ls -l $file"

done    # end of the per-file loop

echo "exit 0"   # and an exit command for the output
```

Figure 8-3.   **shar** shell script (*continued*)

The first few lines are comments. Remember, you should use comments extensively in all programming, especially if other people need to understand the program. The next few lines simply determine whether any filenames are given as arguments to the **shar** command. If not, it prints an error message and exits.

The real work begins with the **echo** commands. This script is actually executing some commands, and writing some other commands to its output with the **echo** statements. After echoing a few messages, the main loop begins. The $* shell operator evaluates to the list of command-line arguments for the script. The number of arguments that are produced by $* is the same as the number given by $#. However, $* evaluates to the actual arguments, separated by whitespace, while $# only produces the number of arguments. Within the loop, **shar** tests whether each file is actually present. The **test** section resolves to true if the file is not readable or if it does not exist. The parentheses are used to group the **test** operators, but they must be escaped with backslashes to prevent the shell from misinterpreting them. If the file is not found by these tests, **shar** echoes an error message, but to prevent the error message from going into the archive **shar** is building, the output from **echo** is redirected to the terminal with > **/dev/tty**.

The next several lines are tricky, because they are building some executable commands into the output script. In fact, **shar** is creating a here document in the output, and enclosing the actual file inside it. The

sed commands just add an *X* to the beginning of each line of the here document. The line **echo +SHAR+MARK+** ends the here document.

The next few lines allow error checking on the transferred files. The first, **ls -l** embeds the size of the original file in the output. Then the line **echo ls -l $file** near the end of the script causes the **ls** command to be executed on the receiving side. It's up to the recipient to check whether the two files are the same size. The complex **sed** command transforms the **ls -l** output into a **chmod** command to set the permissions correctly on the receiving file. Can you understand what it is doing? Finally, an **exit** command goes into the output.

When **shar** executes, it embeds the files in its argument list into a new executable shell script. Try this script on your machine. How does it work? This version of **shar** does not handle files in subdirectories well. Can you improve it?

The getopts Command

So far we have discussed arguments to shell scripts that might be names of files or other input arguments. However, the normal command-line syntax allows flags that begin with - (minus) to modify the operation of the command. Shell scripts can also have flags as part of the argument list. The shell operator **getopts** (for get options) is designed to make the job of parsing command-line flags easier when these flags are allowed to be in any order on the command line, and may in turn have associated arguments. The **getopts** operator replaces an older form named **getopt**. In SVR3 and SVR4 systems you should use the **getopts** function, but in older versions you must use **getopt**. The **getopts** operator allows you to create shell scripts that can process command-line arguments like other executable commands. It processes the options and flags in the command-line arguments, and after it finishes, you can **set** the remaining nonflag arguments to $1, $2, and so forth. Figure 8-4 is a sample shell script that shows how to use the **getopts** function. The line

```
while getopts yz:x VAR
```

defines a loop using the **getopts** function, which takes two arguments of its own. The first is a list of acceptable command letters with no

```
#! /sbin/sh
# first we parse the command options, assigning shell
# variables to mark which of the legal flags have been set.
while getopts yz:x c
do
        case $c in
            x)
                    XFLAG=true
                    ;;
            y)
                    YFLAG=true
                    ;;
            z)
                    ZFLAG=true
                    ZOPT=$OPTARG  # OPTARG is the "current" value
                    ;;
            *)
                    echo $USAGE
                    exit 2
                    ;;
        esac
done

# now we've parsed all the flags and options, we just reset
# the argument list to be only what's left after these are
# taken from the input line
shift `expr $OPTIND -1`

# now XFLAG, YFLAG, or ZFLAG may be set, depending
# on what args were on the command line.
# ZOPT is set to "str" if option "-z str" was given
# We can go on now to the rest of the shell script, as needed
```

Figure 8-4.   Use of the **getopts** operator

embedded whitespace. In this list, each letter that requires a following argument has a : (colon) after it. The second argument, *VAR* in the example above, is a temporary environment variable containing the value of the current command-line option, which is set each time through the **while** loop. The **while** loop is executed once for each of the command-line arguments given; when each of the arguments has been processed, **getopts** returns false and the **while** loop ends. The command-line flags **-x**, **-y** and **-z** are allowed, and the **-z** option must have a following argument. Assuming the script is named *script*, these command lines are allowed, among others:

```
$ script
$ script -x
$ script -y -x
$ script -z hello
$ script -x -z hello
$ script -z hello -y
```

The shell variable *USAGE* is defined by the **getopts** function, and reports what options were allowed in the **getopts** command embedded in the **while** command. The shell variable *OPTARG* is also defined by the **getopts** function, and is set to the value of the argument following the current flag option. In this example, OPTARG is only defined when the **-z** option is processed, because the control string for **getopts** only included a : after the **-z** option.

Within the **while** loop, you can process each of the allowed command-line arguments, setting some variables or processing as needed when an argument is given. In addition, for those flags that take their own arguments, such as the **-z** option in the example, you must use an additional environment variable to store the value of the argument, because the **getopts** function will only define the OPTARG variable while a specific command-line option is current in the **while** loop.

After all the command-line arguments are processed using this **while** loop, the **shift** command will change the $* variables to remove the flags that are already processed, so that a new **$1** is defined for the first command-line argument that has not yet been processed. Once all the flags have been processed, the script can continue to do the work for which it was intended.

The trap Command

Usually a *signal* such as a hangup, a CTRL-D (terminate), or some system error signal sent to a shell script while it is executing causes the script to end immediately and returns you to the calling shell. Usually this is what you want, but sometimes the shell may be in the process of swapping some files or taking some other sensitive action. In that case, you would prefer to *trap* the signal, and let the script continue to completion. Or you might wish to *notice* the signal and do some clean-up procedure before the shell exits. The **trap** command is designed for this purpose. It can go anywhere inside a shell script, but do not use it directly from the command line! The **trap** command takes a quoted command line as its first argument, and a list of signal numbers afterward. When one of the listed signals is received, the command line is executed; then the script goes back to what it was doing. If you use **trap** and you want the script to exit, you must put an explicit **exit** in the quoted command. For example:

```
trap "echo signal seen!; exit" 1 2 15
```

The list of available signals and their meanings is given in the **signal(5)** man page, located in the *Programmer's Reference Manual.*

You do not have access to the signal number inside the quoted command list, but you can have as many **trap** commands in your script as you need. To reset a trap, just use another **trap** command with the same signal. If the command string is null, that signal is ignored. For example,

```
trap "" 1 2 15
```

will ignore the three signals, making it hard to kill the script.

The wait Command

Sometimes you might wish to create several background jobs, but stop additional work until one or all are finished. Normally background jobs return immediately to the shell, although they may not complete for a long time. You can use the **wait** command to instruct the shell that even though you have executed the job in the background, you would like to pause until the job has completed. Execute **wait** with the process id of the background job you wish to wait for as its argument, as follows:

```
$ cat /unix >/tmp/ss &
10009
$ wait 10009
```

When the job completes, **wait** will return you to the shell for another command. To wait for *all* your background jobs, execute **wait** with no arguments. The **wait** command provides some of the features of *job control* to shell scripts.

Shell Layers and the shl Command

SVR3 and SVR4 systems provide a tool that allows more than one shell to be active on a single terminal. This is not a windowing system such as the X Window System, but each of the shells takes the full screen. Tools are provided for creating additional shells, for switching between them, and for killing shells when you are done with them. With this *shell layers* procedure, the system treats each separate shell that has been created as an independent session; thus, to the system it appears as if you have logged in to the machine multiple times with separate terminals. Each "session" is treated as a *virtual terminal* called a *layer,* and the different layers do not interact. Because each layer takes up the full screen, special tools are provided to switch to another layer when desired. With the shell layers scheme, you can run several programs simultaneously, and they will all have full-screen access to your terminal. The shell layers system has many uses, but is limited to the **tty** devices, so it cannot be used over some local area networks or under the X Window System. For the system console, the **vtlmgr** (for virtual terminal layer manager) is preferred if your system supports it.

The **shl** (for shell layers) command starts the *layer manager,* which controls access to the different layers that can be created. After the **shl** program executes, a new prompt is displayed to signal that you are not in a normal session but rather under the auspices of the **shl** program. For example:

```
$ shl
>>>
```

At this point, **shl** is waiting for a command. You can create a new layer, kill an existing layer, or close the layer manager entirely. To create a new layer, enter **create** after the >>> prompt, as follows:

```
$ shl
>>> create
(1)
```

The new layer is created, and given a name. The name is usually the number of the layer, from 1 through the maximum number of layers allowed, 7. The PS1 for the layer is changed to the layer name, to help distinguish which layer is currently active on the screen. After the previous example, the login shell is *suspended,* and the layer (1) shell is listening to commands. You can use this layer just as you would any normal shell, and you can kill it with **exit** or CTRL-D. When you kill a layer, you return to the layer manager with the >>> prompt; from there you can instruct **shl** what to do next.

Once the **shl** program is running, no matter which layer is active, you can return to the >>> prompt at any time. The special character CTRL-Z tells **shl** to wake up and listen to your input. When you press CTRL-Z, **shl** immediately displays the >>> prompt and waits for a command. This use of CTRL-Z overrides the use of CTRL-Z for job control (discussed in Chapter 16). You can create another layer as shown here:

```
$ shl
>>> create
(1) CTRL-Z
>>> create
(2)
```

Now you have two layers, and the currently active layer is layer (2). Up to seven layers can be active at any time.

It is possible to create a layer, start an application that produces output in that layer, and then create a second layer. In this situation, output from the first layer (and all active layers!) will come directly to the terminal, overwriting output from the current layer. That is, applications in layers continue to execute and write their output to the terminal, no matter how many layers are active. However, only one layer can listen for your keystrokes, and that is the current layer; the other layers are *nonblocking,* since they continue to run even when they are not active. The **shl** system includes the **block** and **unblock** commands to change this behavior. Use the command:

```
>>> block 2
```

to make layer (2) blocking, and

```
>>> unblock 2
```

to make the same layer nonblocking.

You can return to the **shl** program at any time with the CTRL-Z character. Several other commands are available in addition to **create**. Press **?** (question mark) at the >>> prompt to see the list of available commands.

You can switch freely between layers by issuing the **resume** command at the >>> prompt. More simply, just enter the name of the layer to make current, without the **resume** keyword, as shown here:

```
(2) CTRL-Z
>>> 1
(1)
```

To kill a layer, enter CTRL-D in the layer itself, or use the **delete** command at the >>> prompt, with a layer number as argument. For example:

```
(2) CTRL-Z
>>> delete 2
>>>
```

Finally, **quit** kills the layer manager and returns you to the original login shell. When you use **quit**, all active programs in any layer are killed.

The CTRL-Z command to wake the **shl** program is called the *switch character*. You can change it to suit your personal preference with the **stty** command

```
$ stty swtch c
```

where *c* is the new character to use instead of CTRL-Z.

Virtual Consoles

An important adaptation of the **shl** concept is the *virtual console*. Some releases of SVR3 and SVR4 allow the use of the function keys on the system console to directly switch between layers, bypassing the **shl** command and its CTRL-Z procedure. The virtual console feature is limited to the system console, but **shl** can run on remote terminals as well as on the console.

In some releases, pressing a function key clears the screen and causes a **login:** prompt to appear, allowing you to log in to the machine again. In other releases, the current login is preserved and pressing the function key starts a new shell. Once a session is established, you can immediately switch to that session by pressing the function key associated with it. The screen will usually be redrawn when you switch sessions, which solves one of the major drawbacks of the original **shl** command.

In some releases, the virtual console is always available, and you need not start it with a command such as **shl** before you use it. In other releases, you have to start the virtual console feature with the command

```
$ vtlmgr
```

(for virtual terminal layer manager).

To switch screens when the **vtlmgr** feature is active, press ALT-SYSREQ (hold down the ALT key and press SYSREQ), followed by a function key. The first few function keys are each associated with a specific layer, and pressing a function key causes that layer to become active. Again, you kill a layer by exiting from it with CTRL-D or the **exit** command. The ALT-SYSREQ function key sequence will also create a new virtual console if that one does not already exist. You may also use the **newvt** command to create a new virtual terminal.

On the system console you can start a virtual terminal, run the X Window System or a DOS session in one window, and then switch to a new window to start another DOS session. Thereafter, you can switch between these different sessions as often as you wish.

Consult the documentation for your release of SVR4 to see whether the virtual console feature is available and how many simultaneous sessions are allowed.

Shell Functions

The SVR3 and SVR4 shells provide an additional mechanism for creating scripts, which is slightly more efficient than the script file approach discussed earlier. However, these *shell functions* are more difficult to control than normal shell scripts, because they are defined directly to the shell and do not have a permanent life in a file. When you define a shell function, the current shell reads the definition, and the function is stored inside the currently active shell. You can execute a shell function just like any other command or shell script, but when you log off, the function is lost. Of course, you can put definitions of shell functions in a file and execute the file with the *.filename* mechanism discussed above, which allows the *filename* to be read and interpreted by the current shell rather than by a newly created subshell. Shell functions are *not* exportable or automatically available to subshells; they must be reread by subshells if they are needed.

Shell functions are defined by the form

```
$ name () {
>       command-list
> }
```

where *name* can be any name you choose for the function. The ( ) (left and right parentheses) are required, and the **{** (left curly brace) begins the command-list. Any normal executable commands or shell operators are allowed in the command-list, as you have come to expect. In addition, the **$#**, **$***, and **$1** through **$9** positional parameters are available within the function. Here is an example:

```
$ show () {
>       echo $1
>       echo $2
>       exit 2
> }
$ show hello goodbye
hello
goodbye
$
```

This example defines a shell function named **show** that echoes its first two arguments, then returns the exit value 2 to the calling shell. Shell functions can be as complex as you wish, and frequently used shell scripts can be made into shell functions with potential savings of system CPU resources. However, if you use a set of shell functions routinely, take care to install them in your **.profile** or use some other mechanism to ensure that they will always be available when you want them.

Using The CDPATH Variable

The shell allows you to specify a search path for **cd** operations that works much like the PATH variable. The *CDPATH* environment variable is used to name a list of directories to search when you execute a **cd** command with a relative pathname as argument. The **cd** command looks for its argument in each of the named directories, and changes to the first one that matches the name. The value of CDPATH follows the same syntax as PATH. For example:

```
$ echo $CDPATH
:/home/steve:/home/steve/src
$
```

The leading : (colon) means search the current directory first. Then **/home/steve** will be searched, and finally **/home/steve/src**. If you give a full pathname, **cd** will respond normally. This is very helpful if you change directories frequently.

Command Sequences

One additional shell construct that you may see in scripts occasionally is the *command sequence*. Unlike the ; operator, which just *connects* multiple commands, a command sequence is constructed with the operator **&&** (logical *and*) or **||** (logical *or*) separating individual commands. The **&&** operator executes the second command only if the first command has succeeded (returned zero). The **||** operator executes the second command only if the first command has failed; if the first command succeeds, it does not execute the second. For example,

```
$ touch myfile || echo Cannot create myfile
```

is equivalent to:

```
$ touch myfile
$ if [ $? -ne 0 ] ; then echo Cannot create myfile ; fi
```

Understanding UNIX System Documentation

Most UNIX systems include a copy of the *UNIX User's Manual*, which is usually called simply the *User's Manual* or the *UNIX Manual*. In some systems, the *User's Manual* is provided only in paper form but it may be available on-line in others. In addition, many implementations of SVR4 contain an on-line help facility that can assist you in determining the correct command for an application and in selecting the right option for a command. This chapter discusses these documentation tools.

The UNIX User's Manual

The *User's Manual* is the official documentation for the UNIX system, and has had as much development and modification over the years as the system software itself. All the commands, arguments to commands, subroutine libraries, file formats, utilities, and tools are documented completely in the *User's Manual,* and it is the next-to-final authority on all issues regarding the UNIX system. The final authority, of course, is direct empirical testing of a system attribute on your own machine.

Unfortunately, although the *User's Manual* is a complete reference document, it is not as accessible as you might wish. It is not uncommon to see several users or developers poring over a single sentence of the *User's Manual*, discussing (even arguing) about the meaning or implication of a word or phrase. Invariably the *User's Manual* is correct, but sometimes it is not easy to understand.

The *User's Manual* is a reference document. It is designed to be as concise as possible, to bring the great scope of the UNIX system into a form that experts and near-experts can use to find out any of the many specific details of the system. It is very difficult, if not impossible, to learn to use the system from the *User's Manual*, but it is equally impossible to become an expert user without the manual.

If you do not have a *User's Manual* readily available, you should immediately get one from your vendor, preferably one provided specifically for your release of the system and your computer hardware. While the *User's Manual* does not differ very much between versions, at some point you will probably be led astray if you use the wrong version.

The Layout of the User's Manual

Originally, the *User's Manual* was published as a single small volume that included all the information that was available for the operating system at that time. The original document contained eight major sections, which are still preserved today:

1. Commands and Application Programs

2. System Calls

3. Subroutines

4. File Formats

5. Miscellaneous

6. Games

7. Special Files

8. System Maintenance Procedures

These eight sections are often referred to by number: Section 1 is the commands, Section 3 is the subroutine section, and so on.

Most of the commands discussed in this book are documented in Section 1. Although some related issues are dealt with in sections 4, 5, 7, and 8, you will find user commands such as **cat** or **uux** documented in Section 1 of the manual.

Sections 2 and 3 are primarily of interest to software developers, since they describe subroutines that a developer would use in a C or Fortran language program. Some of the names of the functions in Sections 2 and 3 are similar to the names of Section 1 commands, so you must take care that you have the correct manual section when you use the *User's Manual.* Although Sections 2 and 3 both contain information on subroutines that developers can use, the two sections differ: the *system calls* in Section 2 are entry points into the kernel, similar in function to MS-DOS interrupts; on the other hand, the Section 3 items are real subroutines or *functions* that are provided with the system. Many, but not all, of the subroutines use system calls internally. System calls and functions usually *look* the same, but the distinction between them can be important for system designers and developers.

Section 4, "File Formats," documents the way data is stored in the files the system uses. It includes a description of the file **/etc/passwd**, as well as information on the format of an executable file and the format of the terminal description files used by the **terminfo** system.

Section 5, "Miscellaneous," contains useful information that would not be appropriate in other sections. For example, it includes a table of ASCII character codes, comments on the shell environment variables, descriptions of the country-specific character codes, a discussion of terminal tab settings, and much more.

Games and toys are described in Section 6. Some systems will not include this section if the implementation does not include games, but add-on software for games will usually include documentation that should be filed under Section 6.

Section 7 includes the formats of the *special files* that reside in the directory **/dev**. This material is of greatest interest to software developers who wish to use these special device files from their programs. Section 7 includes discussions of disk and tape formats, synchronous and asynchronous terminal interfaces, and local area network interfaces.

Section 8, on maintenance procedures, includes procedures for booting the system, diagnosing hardware failures, and other low-level aspects of system administration. The material in Section 8 is often somewhat outdated, and it may be of minimal use for a microcomputer-based SVR4 system; in fact, some versions of the SVR4 manual no longer include Section 8.

While the basic format of the documentation has stayed the same, the rapid growth of the UNIX system soon made the single manual unwieldy, and it is now published in three parts: the "User's Manual," the "Programmer's Manual," and the "Administrator's Manual." Each of these parts includes some of the material in each of the 8 sections, resulting in a situation in which a Section 1 command might not appear in the User's Manual, but rather might be in the Administrator's Manual. Unfortunately, it is not always obvious which of the three manuals will cover a particular command, so you must often search for a command that you wish to read about.

In SVR4, the manual is usually further subdivided into several separately bound volumes. Sometimes as many as 25 volumes make up the manual as a whole. Usually the volumes are organized by general topics, so that a particular volume contains all the information relevant to development, networking, the X Window System, and so forth. Often portions of all eight sections of the manual will appear in one of these books, but the book as a whole will be of most interest to X users, networking gurus, or some other group.

Except for the "Permuted Index" and some of the introductory material, the *User's Manual* as a whole is organized according to topic; each command or subroutine is documented separately, and each item is called a *manual page* or *man page*, even if it spans several printed pages in the document. This organization is excellent for a reference document, because each man page is independent of the others. As the system has grown and developed, the modular nature of the *User's Manual* has made it very easy to update. You can replace outdated man pages with new ones as you modify your system. Furthermore, most of the material about a specific topic is collected in a small area, making it easy to locate, providing you know what to look for.

Developers creating new software or new tools usually write man pages for their applications. These man pages are then used by documentation writers to produce glossy user documentation or on-line help. Since the original developer of an application usually writes the man page, these pages often describe the behavior of applications more accurately than other documentation.

Referring to the Manual Section of a Command

When you name a command or other item in the UNIX system, you may wish to indicate the manual section the command comes from. Usually the manual section is included in parentheses following the name. For example, **uname(1)** refers to the user command **uname**, which is documented in Section 1 of the manual, while **uname(2)** refers to the developers' system call documented in Section 2 of the manual. Sometimes there will be an additional letter following the section number, such as **df(1M)**. The additional letter identifies the subsection of the manual with which the command is categorized. For example, **1M** is a Section 1 command that is associated with the "System Administrator's Manual"; **3C** is a C language subroutine; and **3E** denotes a subroutine related to the **elf** object-file format.

Each command, subroutine, or file type that has its own man page is filed alphabetically within its section, although some man pages may be in the "User's Manual" while others may be in the "Administrator's Manual" or the "Programmer's Manual." In addition, the documentation includes an excellent indexing system, which we will discuss later in this chapter.

A Typical Man Page

Figure 9-1 shows a sample of a short but complete man page, for the **du(1M)** command. This man page comes from the "User's Manual," since **du** is a general user command that appears in Section 1 of the manual. However, this command is of most interest to system administrators, as the **1M** identifier tells you.

The name of the command appears at the top of the page, on both the left and right sides. This name is used to alphabetize the page in the manual as a whole.

Usually some special additional release information appears in the middle of the page heading, such as "Essential Utilities" in this example. The SVR4 version of the system is divided into several different software *sets*, or separately loadable units. These sets can be installed

---

NAME

  du – summarize disk usage

SYNOPSIS

  du [-sar] [*name* ...]

DESCRIPTION

  The du command reports the number of blocks contained in all files and (recursively) directories within each directory and file specified. The block count includes the indirect blocks of the file. If no *name*s are given, the current directory is used.

  The optional arguments are as follows:

  -s   causes only the grand total (for each of the specified *name*s) to be given.

  -a   causes an output line to be generated for each file.

  If neither -s or -a is specified, an output line is generated for each directory only.

  -r   will cause du to generate messages about directories that cannot be be read, files that cannot be opened, etc., rather than being silent (the default).

  A file with two or more links is only counted once.

NOTES

  If the -a option is not used, non-directories given as arguments are not listed.

  If there are links between files in different directories where the directories are on separate branches of the file system hierarchy, du will count the excess files more than once.

  Files with holes in them will get an incorrect block count.

SEE ALSO

  The *File System Administration* chapter in the *System Administrator's Guide*.

Figure 9-1.   A typical *User's Manual* page (Reprinted with permission of AT&T)

separately on a machine and can sometimes be purchased separately. If a particular command is not available on your machine, probably the software set that includes it was not loaded. In the example **du(1M)**, the command is included in the Essential Utilities set. Other software sets are C Compilation set and the Text Preparation set.

Sometimes there is a date at the bottom of the man page that tells the last date that the page was changed or the date it was printed. The page number is relative to the beginning of that man page, not to the document as a whole. This makes it easy to remove an outdated page and replace it with a newer version without having to discard the whole manual.

Within the body of the man page, the material is divided into several subject headings. The name of the command is first, along with a short summary of the command's function. This is the primary command that is given at the top of the man page. In some cases secondary commands will be documented with the primary command. These are commands that are closely related to the primary command, and do not rate their own separate man page. Secondary commands do not appear on the page heading, so you may not find a command if you simply look at the alphabetical page headings. Even common commands may not have their own man page, though in SVR4 manuals most do. For example, the restricted and job control versions of the shell, named **rsh(1)** and **jsh(1)**, respectively, are listed as secondary commands under the man page for **sh(1)**. Look up commands in the index to avoid this potential problem. The command names and summary lines are indexed word by word in the manual's Permuted Index, which is discussed later in this chapter.

Synopsis

The Synopsis briefly summarizes how you invoke the command from the command line. The synopsis is presented in a condensed format in which each character is significant, but you usually don't enter the command in the form given in the Synopsis. Once you understand this format you can determine how to enter the command according to your needs. Items printed in boldface type, such as **du** in the example, are typed on the command line just as they appear in the Synopsis, or are not included in the command line at all. The material printed in italics on the man page represents argument prototypes that can be substituted on your command line. The string *name* in the example is not entered as printed; instead you use the name of the file system you are interested in. When an element is enclosed in square brackets, like **[-sar]**, the element is optional and you only include it in your command line if you need it. For example, the **-a** option is only used if you want the total listing. When several elements are separated by a | (pipe), your command line can contain any *one* of the elements separated by the | character. You do not enter the square brackets or the | character (unless you want the shell to create a pipeline for you). The entry ... (ellipsis) signifies that the synopsis element just preceding the ellipsis can be repeated as often as desired. For example,

```
cat [ -u ] [ -s ] [ -v [ -t ] [ -e ] ] file ...
```

means that you can have one or more files. This example also demonstrates another feature: these synopsis elements can be nested. The **-v** argument is optional, as are the **-t** and **-e** arguments; however, **-t** and **-e** are embedded within the square brackets for **-v**. This means that **-v** is optional, but if you give **-t** or **-e**, you must also give the **-v** option. The **-u** and **-s** arguments are independent, and can be used either with or without the **-v** argument. This nesting of arguments is common in the UNIX system and in the man page Synopsis. Finally, the modifier arguments given with command-line flags are included in the same scheme, as follows:

```
ed [ - ] [ -p string ] [ -x ] [ -C ] [ file ]
```

All the arguments are optional here, although if you give the **-p** argument you must also include a prompt string.

Description

The Synopsis is intended to serve as a quick reference when you understand the command usage for the most part, but wish to check on a specific component for your command line. When you need a more detailed description of the command, its arguments, and its intention, read the Description section of the man page, which follows the Synopsis. The Description explains the use of the command as well as the purpose of all the options. This section differs widely on different man pages; however, it always provides a complete if terse description of the command. You may need to read and reread the Description to fully understand all the details and implications of the command and its arguments. Usually, every sentence in the description is *exactly* correct, but often it helps to examine the command output along with the man page to understand the material thoroughly.

Other Parts of the Man Page

Several other man page sections usually follow the Description. These are not as well defined or standardized as the Name, Synopsis, and Description sections, and one or more may be omitted.

The Note section provides footnote information that is considered important but does not fit within the description for some reason. Similar to the note section is the Warnings section, which indicates potential pitfalls to avoid when using the command. Generally, you should understand the warnings, if any are listed, before you use the command.

The See Also section lists related commands or relevant material in other manual sections. You can use this section to find other commands that might fit your needs better than the one documented, or that have related functions. In the example in Figure 9-1, you can see that the **du** command is reviewed in the *System Administrator's Guide*.

The Files section gives the pathnames of databases and other files that are used or changed by the command. Frequently, the connection between the command and the listed files is not discussed in the Description section. It would be useful if these files were indexed so that if you ran into a file while browsing the file system you could look up the purpose of the file, but this has not been done.

The Diagnostics section gives a short description of the possible error messages or return values for the command. This is not usually a complete list of the diagnostic messages that a command can produce, but it does provide some clues when a command does not act as you expect it to.

The Bugs section lists a few of the conditions under which the command does not act as expected. Usually, this section does not discuss the *real* bugs in the command, because they would be fixed if developers knew about them. The items included as bugs are actually more like limitations, where you might wish the command could do more than it actually does.

Some manual pages, especially those produced for add-on software or application packages, may include additional sections, such as Author or Limitations. These are usually easy to understand.

The Permuted Index

The *Permuted Index* is the most effective way to enter the *User's Manual* when you have a specific question or problem. You cannot assume that a command or function will be listed under its own man page, and in any case, the key concepts associated with commands are not usually apparent from the name. Luckily, the Permuted Index almost always provides the needed information.

The Permuted Index alphabetically indexes each word of the Name section of each man page. Since the short summary given with the command name consists mainly of conceptual *keywords,* this index is quite effective. The Permuted Index is also known by the name KWIC (for keyword in context) in other computer settings. Each of the three parts of the manual (user's, programmer's, and administrator's) has its own Permuted Index, so sometimes you must consult more than one index to find what you need. Unlike most indexes, the Permuted Index usually appears at the front of the bound manual rather than at the end.

Figure 9-2 is an example of a page from the Permuted Index of the "User's Manual." As you can see, the alphabetical listings appear down the middle of the page, and the man page containing that alphabetical item appears at the far right. You look up a word by finding it in the middle of the page, and then turning to the man page listed at the extreme right.

The Permuted Index is constructed by taking each word of the Name section of the manual, and placing it in the center of the page. The following words in the Name are printed at the right of the particular word in question, and the words preceding it in the Name

	join relational database operator	join(1)
control, and restricted/ sh,	jsh, rsh shell, the standard, job	sh(1)
terminal	jterm reset layer of windowing	jterm(1)
	jwin print size of layer	jwin(1)
makekey generate encryption	key	makekey(1)
	kill terminate a process by default	kill(1)
command and programming/ ksh, rksh	KornShell, a standard/restricted	ksh(1)
standard/restricted command and/	ksh, rksh KornShell, a	ksh(1)
awk pattern scanning and processing	language	awk(1)
bc arbitrary-precision arithmetic	language	bc(1)
command and programming	language /a standard/restricted	ksh(1)
pattern scanning and processing	language nawk	nawk(1)
at, batch execute commands at a	later time	at(1)
jwin print size of	layer	jwin(1)
shl shell	layer manager	shl(1)
terminals layers	layer multiplexor for windowing	layers(1)
jterm reset	layer of windowing terminal	jterm(1)
rename login entry to show current	layer relogin	relogin(1M)
windowing terminals	layers layer multiplexor for	layers(1)
ar maintain portable archive or	library	ar(1)
line read one	line	line(1)
nl	line numbering filter	nl(1)
cut cut out selected fields of each	line of a file	cut(1)
	line read one line	line(1)
col filter reverse	line-feeds	col(1)
comm select or reject	lines common to two sorted files	comm(1)
fold fold long	lines	fold(1)
uniq report repeated	lines in a file	uniq(1)
head display first few	lines of files	head(1)
of several files or subsequent	lines of one file /merge same lines	paste(1)
subsequent lines/ paste merge same	lines of several files or	paste(1)
ln	link files	ln(1)
ls	list contents of directory	ls(1)
available on/ uuglist print the	list of service grades that are	uuglist(1C)
listusers	list user login information	listusers(1)
xargs construct argument	list(s) and execute command	xargs(1)
information	listusers list user login	listusers(1)
	ln link files	ln(1)
finger display information about	local and remote users	finger(1)
ruptime show host status of	local machines	ruptime(1)
rwho who's logged in on	local machines	rwho(1)
newgrp	log in to a new group	newgrp(1M)
rwho who's	logged in on local machines	rwho(1)
relogin rename	login entry to show current layer	relogin(1M)
listusers list user	login information	listusers(1)
logname get	login name	logname(1)
attributes passwd change	login password and password	passwd(1)

Figure 9-2.   A typical Permuted Index page (Reprinted with permission of AT&T)

appear to the left. The end of the text is marked with the **/** (slash) character. Sometimes the material to the right of the current keyword is too long to fit on the line, so it is wrapped around to the beginning, as in the **paste(1)** example in Figure 9-2. Similarly, there are sometimes too many words to the left of the current command, and the extra words are then wrapped to the right of the line.

For example, if you know you want to manipulate lines of a file, you can look up the keyword *lines* and find several entries. By reading the rest of the summary—paying attention to the location of the **/** that marks where the summary begins—you can pick the command that does what you want.

Once you understand the format of the Permuted Index, and have some feel for the jargon in the Name section of the man pages, the index becomes a very useful tool. However, if you do not hit exactly the correct keyword, and you cannot find the command that you need, it is often useful to look at the man page for a similar command, and consult the See Also section of the page. The command you want will often be listed there.

The On-line man Command

Many large machines include the entire contents of the manual on-line, usually including man pages for locally installed software as well as the standard *User's Manual*. The complete text is usually two to three megabytes in size, so smaller machines do not always include the on-line manual.

These on-line manual pages can be displayed with the **man** (for manual) command, which writes the requested man page to its standard output. It is called with an argument that specifies the man page you wish to display. For example,

```
$ man diff
```

will display the man page for **diff(1)**. If there is an entry under the specified name in more than one section of the manual, all the man pages will be displayed, one after the other. You can redirect the output to a file or to a printer for later examination. The man pages are usually formatted with **nroff** when they are displayed, so the **man** command may take a relatively long time to produce output, often up to one or two minutes on a heavily loaded machine.

The **man** command takes several options. To restrict the output to a man page in a single manual section, you can give a section number before the name of the page. Thus, the command

```
$ man 1 man
```

will produce the man page for the **man(1)** command only. To format the output for a specific terminal, use **-T** (for terminal), followed by the terminal type. The command

```
$ man -Tvt100 1 man
```

produces **man(1)** formatted for the DEC vt100 terminal or its clone such as **xterm**. If you don't include the **-T** option, your **TERM** environment variable will be used for the terminal type.

There are several other options to the **man** command. The **-d** (for directory) option changes the default search path to the directory given as argument, and **-c** (for col) produces a form of the output without reverse line-feeds, which is suitable for most simple printers.

When present, the man pages are located in the directory **/usr/man** and its subdirectories. Usually there are several immediate subdirectories of **/usr/man**, the major ones being **u_man** (for user's manual), **p_man** (for programmer's manual), and **a_man** (for administrator's manual). Each of these directories contains subdirectories for each manual section included in that part of the manual: **man1** (for Section 1 commands), **man2** (for Section 2 commands), and so forth through **man8** (for Section 8 commands). Usually the man pages are stored in their original **troff** source format, and have to be formatted using the **troff -man** or **nroff -man** text preparation tools before they will resemble the printed manual. The pages are kept in source form so that they can be formatted for any printer or terminal. In addition, some systems maintain a set of the man pages in preformatted files, so they can be accessed on-line without the delay and CPU usage involved in formatting the pages on demand. If so, the directories **man?** are usually named **cat1** through **cat8** in the **u_man**, **p_man**, and **a_man** directories.

Response time for the **man** command is much shorter when the man pages are preformatted, but the preformatted pages are usually prepared by the system administrator for the least powerful printer or terminal on the system.

On-line help Command

In addition to the indispensable *User's Manual*, SVR4 also provides an on-line help facility that can often substitute for the *User's Manual* in a pinch. This facility takes a lot of disk space, so it may not be present on small machines. However, for novice users, it is often worth the disk space it requires.

The name "help" was first given to a small part of the *SCCS* (for Source Code Control System) software development tool. Releases of the UNIX system prior to SVR3 retain this usage, but the SVR4 help facility discussed here is a completely new package that has very little in common with the older version.

You can enter the help subsystem with the command **help**, which displays the following menu to prompt you for your next action:

```
$ help
help:  UNIX System On-Line Help

        choices             description
           s                starter:  general information
           l                locate:  find a command with keywords
           u                usage:  information about commands
           g                glossary:  definitions of terms
           r                Redirect to a file or a command
           q                Quit

Enter choice >
```

You are still in the help subsystem, and can take further action as indicated by the prompts. To exit back to the shell, enter **q** at the "Enter choice >" prompt. You can also copy the contents of the screen to a file, or use it as the standard input to a command, by entering **r** at the prompt, as follows:

```
Enter choice > r
Enter > file, | cmd(s), or RETURN to continue >
```

At this point, you can enter > followed by a filename, or | followed by a pipeline to redirect the current screen to a file or command, as shown here

```
Enter choice > r
Enter > file, | cmd(s), or RETURN to continue > >/home/steve/help.menu
Enter choice >
```

In this example the output was redirected to the file **/home/steve/help.menu**. After the action is taken, the help system returns to the current level for another menu selection. Only the current topic is saved, usually a single screenful. Each of the help submenus allows this redirection, so it is easy to grab data for later use.

The top-level menu provides access to all the other help capabilities. If you enter **s** here to display starter information, the system prompts with another menu, shown in Figure 9-3. The starter section is an excellent way for new users to familiarize themselves with the UNIX system. To access the most basic material, select **c**, which displays information about the simplest commands and features of the system. The **d** selection provides a bibliography of useful documents, though the things listed in this output may be difficult to locate. The **l** selection provides information about capabilities and features local to this specific

```
Enter choice > s

 starter:  General UNIX System User Information

    starter provides general information for  system  users. Enter
    one of the choices below to proceed.

       choices          description

          c              Commands and terms to learn first
          d              Documents for system users
          e              Education centers for UNIX System training
          l              Local UNIX System information
          t              Teaching aids available on-line

          r              Redirect to a file or a command
          q              Quit
          h              Restart help
```

Figure 9-3.   Screen display for help starter menu selection

machine. Your system administrator can add this section using the **helpadm** command, discussed later in this chapter. The **t** option lists other teaching aids available on-line. This is usually only the Instructional Workbench package, which may not be available with all SVR4 implementations. The Instructional Workbench is a full-fledged *Computer-Aided Instruction* system that provides powerful tools for development of on-line training for many topics, not just for the UNIX system. You can return to the top-level menu at any time by entering **h** from any menu within the help system.

If you select **l** from the top-level menu, the help system lets you locate commands by entering keywords that describe the action you wish to perform, as in Figure 9-4. Select **k** from this submenu if you wish to have the system search for keywords that you enter. In Figure 9-4, *print* has been entered as a keyword, and the help system has located several commands associated with printing files. The help system uses keywords different from those used in the *User's Manual*, so you may see different commands here than you see in the manual.

Not all the capabilities of the system are included in the help facility. For example, the test with the keyword *print* did not reveal anything about the **lp** printer subsystem. Although it can be useful, the help system cannot substitute for the *User's Manual*.

If you select **u** from the top-level menu, you get specific information about how to use a command, including help on the available arguments and how they are used, as shown in Figure 9-5. You can enter the name of a command if you know it, and the system will prompt you to select the kind of information you are interested in; select **d** for a description of the command, **e** for some examples, or **o** for a listing of the command options. If you select **d** for a description, the result might look like Figure 9-6. This material is not identical to the contents of the *User's Manual*, so you may find that it provides some additional ideas about how to use a command or its options. The **o** (options) and **e** (examples) menu selections provide additional information that can also be helpful.

Frequently the material in these sections extends over more than one screen; you can select **n** (for next page) when you see "More" at the bottom of the display. As usual, you can also redirect the material to a file or command for later examination.

```
Enter choice > 1

  locate: Find UNIX System Commands with Keywords

      Give locate one or more keywords related  to  the  work
      you  want  to  do. It  will print a list of UNIX system commands
      whose actions are related  to  the  keywords.

      For example, you enter the keywords print file

     locate could produce the list:    The cat (concatenate) command
                                        The ls (list) command
                                        The pr (print) command

      Enter a k to use locate.

          choices            description

            k                Enter a list of keywords

            r                Redirect to a file or a command
            q                Quit
            h                Restart help

Enter choice > k
Enter keywords separated by blanks > print

Commands found using print:

The cat (concatenate) command
The echo command
The line command
The ls (list) command
The pcat (concatenate packed file) command
The pr (print) command
The pwd (print working directory) command
The tail command
_____
Choices:    UNIX_command ,  k (new keywords),  r (redirect),  h (restart help),
 q (quit)
_____

Enter choice >
```

Figure 9-4.   Screen display for help **locate** command

```
Enter choice > u

 usage:  Information about Commands

        usage provides information about specific UNIX System commands.

               Within usage, double quotes " " mark options or literals,
        and angle brackets < > mark argument variables.

               You should see starter for basic UNIX system commands and
        terms before going on to anything else.

        Enter one of the choices below to proceed.

           choices              description

        UNIX_command            Obtain usage information for a command

             p                  Print a list of commands

             r                  Redirect to a file or a command
             q                  Quit
             h                  Restart help

 Enter choice > cat
 Enter  d (description),  e (examples),  or  o (options) >
```

Figure 9-5.   Screen display for help **usage** command

The **g** selection from the top-level menu provides a glossary of terms and special characters. You can enter a term or character, and the help system will return a short but useful definition of the term. This material is not available in the *User's Manual*.

Using Help from the Command Line

Instead of selecting an option from the top-level menu of the help system, you can enter a command directly from the shell to access one of the help subsystems. Use

```
$ locate [ keyword ]
```

to enter the locate subsystem directly. If you give the command with no arguments, the locate menu is presented so you can enter a keyword. If you give the keyword as an argument for the locate command, the help system will produce the results only for that keyword. Similarly, you can use

```
$ glossary
```

or

```
$ glossary [ term ]
```

to enter the glossary subsystem directly, and

```
$ starter
```

or

```
$ usage [ -d ] [ -e ] [ -o ] [ command_name ]
```

for the other top-level options. The additional arguments for the **usage** command start the help system at the submenus for description, examples, and options, respectively.

Going Further

The help subsystem is a flexible tool that can be adapted or expanded as desired. This section discusses tools by which a system administrator,

```
Enter  d (description),  e (examples), or  o (options) > d
cat:  Description

Syntax Summary:  cat [ -u ] [ -s ] [ -v [ -e ] [ -t ] ] [ file_name ... ]

        where:  file_name  is the name of a file.

Description:
    cat is  shorthand  for "concatenate". Use cat to send the
    contents of a file to standard output. If more than one file name is used,
    cat prints each file in sequence on the standard output. cat
    echos standard input if you do not list a file name or if you use "-" as an
    argument. See also:  cp(d1), pg(d1) and pr(d1) for commands with functions
    similar to cat.

Choices:   o (options),  e (examples),  UNIX_command ,  p (print list),
 r (redirect),  h (restart help),  q (quit)

Enter choice >
```

Figure 9-6.   Screen display for help **description** command

logged into the machine as **root,** can change the database. In addition, a few more SVR4 tools are described.

The Help Directory Structure

Most of the help system commands reside in the directory **/usr/bin.** The help data files are kept in the directory **/usr/lib/help** and its subdirectories, as shown here

```
$ cd /usr/lib/help
$ ls -F
HELPLOG*    checklen*   default    ge           lib/        un
ad          cm          defnlen*   glossary*    list*       ut
admgloss*   cmds        delete*    he           locking*    vc
admstart*   co          editcmd*   helpclean*   prs
bd          db/         extract*   interact*    rc
cb          de          fetch*     keysrch*     replace*
$
```

The files that have short names, such as **cm, he, un,** and so on, belong to the older part of the help system associated with the SCCS system. The executable commands are the basic executable components that comprise the new part of the system. **HELPLOG** is associated with a help activity logging feature. The directory **lib** contains more executable parts of the help system. The **db** directory is the major directory that contains the displayable **help** text materials, as listed here:

```
$ ls -F db
descriptions.a   glossary.a    screens.a
examples.a       options.a     tables/
$
```

The files that end in **.a** are the actual text of the parts. The subdirectory **tables** contains more information for the help displays, in a more compact form than the ***.a** files. These files are read by software, so you should not edit them directly.

Changing the Help Database

The on-line help facility provides its own tools to customize the output, and to add information on new commands and keywords. You must be superuser to access these materials. The command **/etc/helpadm** (for help administration) is used to administer the help database. This command will prompt you through all the changes needed to install a complete entry. As you respond to the **helpadm** prompts, the system will often execute an editor on your behalf. To get your favorite editor, you should be sure that you have the EDITOR environment variable set correctly, as follows:

```
$ echo $EDITOR
/usr/bin/vi
$
```

If this variable is not set, the default editor **ed** will be executed.

The **/etc/helpadm** command will prompt you for the information it needs to update the help database, as shown in Figure 9-7. The menu format is similar to that used in the normal help displays. You can select either **starter, glossary,** or **commands** to update that section of the help system. In addition, you can turn the help usage log on or off, and

```
# /etc/helpadm
          helpadm:  UNIX System On-Line help Administrative Utilities

These software tools will enable the administrator to change
information in the help facility's database, and to monitor use of
the help facility.

          choice              description

            1                 starter

            2                 glossary

            3                 commands

            4                 prevent recording use of help facility

            5                 record use of the help facility

            q                 quit


Enter choice>
```

Figure 9-7.   Help administration menu

use **q** to exit back to your shell. When you descend to the next menu level, you are prompted for the specific materials the help system needs, as in Figure 9-8. When you make a selection at this point, **helpadm** executes your EDITOR with the text material as its content. You can then change the material as you choose.

Each of the other menu selections of the **helpadm** system allows you to add to or change the material. This is self-evident for the most part, but only the superuser is allowed to change the help database.

Other Sections of the Manual

The format of man pages in manual sections other than Section 1 differs slightly from the Section 1 standards discussed previously. The differences are primarily in the Synopsis section, but you'll also notice a few other differences. Most users will have very little reason to refer to these manual sections, but you should understand their layout in case you do need them. In Sections 2 and 3, the Synopsis gives the C language programming conventions and the subroutine arguments

```
Enter choice> 1
        helpadm:  starter

Which screens of starter do you want to make changes to?

        choice          description

          c             commands screen

          d             documents screen

          e             education screen

          l             local screen

          t             teach screen

          q             quit

Enter choice>
```

Figure 9-8.   Help administration submenu

needed to call the functions documented. These pages also include a Return Value section that is useful for developers. In Sections 4 and 5, the Synopsis (if present) usually gives information for the programmer about how to include the material in software that is under development. Section 6 man pages are similar to those for Section 1, since they cover commands that are available to all users. The man pages for Sections 7 and 8 usually do not include a Synopsis, since there is no concise way to represent the contents of these sections.

Command-line Generators

A few SVR4 systems include a new front-end for command execution called *command-line generators*. Using a combination of menus, forms, and on-line documentation, these tools help you create complex command lines by providing significant error-checking and assistance. One of these tools is the appropriately named AT&T Assist system, and several others exist, some of which will run under the X Window System. These tools are not yet well known, and only a few SVR4 implementations include them.

Most of these tools provide all the features of the help system discussed earlier, including keyword search, command syntax summaries, and a menu orientation. In addition, they can execute commands after their form- and menu-oriented user interface generates them. This helps to create commands with arguments that are syntactically correct. These tools are usually not shells, but application programs that sit in front of the shell, reading your input and passing the correct commands to the login shell for execution. They are designed to be self-training; you can usually use them successfully without much documentation or instruction. They include their own on-line help; however, there are usually many gaps in their coverage of the Section 1 commands. Consult your system's documentation to see whether you have one of these tools, and for details on its features.

Computation and Number Processing

An important area of computing that most people use regularly is *computation*. Number processing is one of the original reasons for the development of computers, and though word processing and graphics have overtaken "number crunching" in small computers, computers can ease your work with numbers.

The UNIX system provides many tools for computation. At the simplest level the **expr** command, discussed in Chapter 8, can do simple arithmetic computations, but its power is definitely limited. On the other hand, at the most sophisticated level, the C Programming Language allows just about any computation that can be imagined. Between these two extremes several tools are available to help you work with numbers.

Most of the computation tools available in the standard SVR4 release are line-oriented tools that resemble programming languages more than they do full-screen "pocket calculator" simulations like those seen in other personal computer systems and in the X Window System. Under X, full-screen calculators are available for use with bit-mapped displays. In this chapter we will focus on the tools provided in the standard system, which can be used on remote ASCII terminals as well as on the system console.

If you are running the X Window System, you may prefer the **xcalc** (for X calculator) or **hexcalc** (for hexadecimal calculator) applications that are usually provided with X. These calculators provide an intuitive mouse-oriented user interface, but they lack the programmability of the traditional UNIX system calculation tools.

A Note on Electronic Spreadsheets

The standard release of the UNIX system does not include an electronic spreadsheet like LOTUS 1-2-3 or Microsoft Excel. Although several spreadsheets have been developed for the UNIX system, none has been included in the standard release; however, add-on spreadsheets are available from several sources. In fact, most popular spreadsheets for the Apple or MS-DOS environment are available in UNIX versions, including LOTUS, and some of these run under X. If you have learned a spreadsheet in the past, you can probably get the same product in a version designed for the UNIX system.

Shell Reprise

You have seen that the filter and pipeline orientation of the shell is very useful in processing large blocks of characters, whether they are text files or databases. With the shell programming tools and the **expr** command, you can perform some quite clever computations; however, these tools are inefficient for numeric operations, and without some assistance from executable programs they can be tedious to use. Several programs designed for use in shell pipelines have been developed for numeric computing, but few of these have survived. One example is the **stat** package, which is oriented toward statistical computations. This package is not included in many SVR4 implementations, but it can often be purchased separately as part of the Graphics Utilities Set.

The dc and bc Calculators

Two powerful line-oriented calculators are provided with the standard system. These are the **dc** (for desk calculator) and **bc** tools. Although **bc** is actually a preprocessor for **dc**, these two tools implement the two user interface models for modern calculators. The **dc** tool uses *postfix notation*, the so-called *reverse polish* notation, in which computations are entered by typing two numbers, and then the operator, as follows:

```
$ dc
2
3
+
p
5
```

Here you would enter **2** and **3**, followed by the arithmetic operator **+**, and then type **p** to display the result. The **dc** command prints the answer, **5**. On the other hand, **bc** uses *infix notation*, which is similar to the normal arithmetic operations taught in elementary school. Here is an example:

```
$ bc
2+3
5
```

Here, you enter **2+3**, and **bc** prints the result. You can use either command depending on your preference, but the features of the two calculators differ slightly, and one may be more convenient for some operations than the other. Both commands allow any *precision*, and can do computations in any number base, or *radix*, as well as in normal decimal. While **dc** is *stack oriented*, which means all operations take place on a single variable stack, **bc** is *procedure oriented*, so you can define local *subroutines* and assign values to variables as part of the computation. In addition, **bc** includes logical operators and statements, which make it more of a programming tool than **dc**.

The dc Command

After the **dc** command is executed, it reads instructions in its internal command language from standard input. Alternatively, you can name a single file on the command line, in which case **dc** reads that file until it ends, and then **dc** switches to its standard input for more commands.

Input from a file is treated identically to instructions from standard input, except that an end-of-file instruction (CTRL-D) from the keyboard ends execution of **dc**, while the end of the input file does not. The **q** (for quit) command will end **dc** from either input source.

An instruction to **dc** can be a number, which is immediately pushed onto the **dc** stack. Numbers can contain decimal points, and negative numbers are preceded not by a - (minus), but by the _ (underscore) character. For example, these are acceptable numbers for **dc**:

```
123
123.5
123.45678901234455
_23.4
```

The **dc** command recognizes the arithmetic operators **+** (addition), **-** (subtraction), **/** (division), ***** (multiplication), **%** (remainder), and **^** (exponentiation). Each of these causes the appropriate action for the top two numbers on the stack, and the result of the operation goes on the stack, in place of the two numbers. In addition, many special commands allow you to further control operations. The **p** (for print) command causes the top value on the stack to be displayed, but does not change the stack. For example:

```
$ dc
3
4
*
p
12
q
$
```

In the preceding examples, each command has been shown on a separate line of input, but **dc** can accept several commands on a single line. Numbers must be delimited by whitespace, but other commands can run together. The previous operation could also have been written as follows:

```
$ dc
3 4*pq
12
$
```

In addition, **dc** can perform several operations in a row when several numbers are on the stack. Because **dc** puts the result of an operation on the stack in place of the numbers used in the operation, the next operation uses that value and the next number below it on the stack. For example:

```
$ dc
3
4
7
+ - p
-8
```

In this example, the **+** operator adds the top two numbers, **7** and **4**, to produce **11**, which goes onto the stack. Then, the - operator subtracts **11** from **3**, producing the result -8.

By default, computations retain as many decimal digits as are needed. Although the **dc** man page suggests that all computations are performed on integers unless the *scale factor* is changed with the **k** command, this is not completely correct. The addition and subtraction operators work on all digits included in the input numbers; only multiplication and division operations return results that depend on the scale factor.

Other stack-oriented commands are **c**, which clears the stack, **d**, which duplicates the top element of the stack, and **f**, which prints all elements of the stack in order.

Variables in dc

Although **dc** does not provide an operation that simply pops the top stack element and discards it, it does allow *register* variables, which are named variables that can contain a value. Stack elements can be popped into registers, and register variables can be pushed onto the stack. Register names must be single lowercase characters, so 26 register variables are allowed at any time. The **s** (for save) command takes a following register name, and pops the top of the stack into the named register. The **l** (letter ell) command is the inverse; it pops the value out of the named register, and pushes it back onto the stack. For example:

```
$ dc
2.34
4.56
p
4.56
st
p
2.34
lt
p
4.56
```

To discard a value from the top of the stack, just use **s** to place the value in an unused register. You can also use this intermediate register procedure to *reverse* the order of elements on the stack.

The **s** and **l** commands will also work with *auxiliary stacks*. If the register name is an uppercase character, it is treated as a stack. If the command is **s**, the top value on the main stack will be pushed onto the auxiliary stack, as shown here:

```
2.34
sT
p
empty stack
5.44
sT
p
empty stack
lT
p
5.44
lT
p
2.34
```

If a stack is empty or does not contain enough numbers to complete an operation, **dc** prints the "empty stack" message.

A character string surrounded by [and] (square brackets) is treated as an ASCII string and pushed onto the stack, as follows:

```
[hello world]
p
hello world
```

This ability to store ASCII strings is an unusual feature for a calculator. Although you cannot use these strings for numeric operations, the **x** (for execute) command will take a string from the top of the stack and execute it as a **dc** command. The string must be explicitly popped from the stack after the command is executed. In addition, the **!** (bang) command is a shell escape that causes **dc** to execute the rest of the line in a subshell. When the command is finished, **dc** resumes operation.

The **dc** command allows several other commands, including **v**, which replaces the top element of the stack with its square root, and several commands that change the number base, or radix, for further computations. The **i** (for input) command causes **dc** to use the number at the top of the stack as the radix for input numbers, and **o** (for output) causes **dc** to use the top of the stack as the radix for output. This allows base conversion and computations in bases other than the default base 10. For example:

```
2
i
1001
p
9
2
o
p
1001
```

Of course, when the input radix is changed, all numbers entered after that point must be consistent with the new radix.

Users familiar with HP pocket calculators or the FORTH and PostScript programming languages will recognize that this relatively small command set is more than sufficient for any computation that computers normally do, even iterative solutions to integrals and transcendental functions. However, if you are not familiar with postfix notation, **dc** can be confusing. In this case, the **bc** program may provide a friendlier environment.

The bc Calculator

Although **bc** is really a preprocessor for **dc**, and uses **dc** to do its work, **bc** contains many more functions than **dc** does, including named functions, logical operators, and mathematical functions such as **sqrt** (square root). The overall command language looks something like the C language, but is much simplified in accordance with its interpreted nature. The **bc** command is simple to execute and its interactions with **dc** are not visible to the user. It looks like this:

```
$ bc
```

Once executed, **bc** starts silently and waits for your input. To exit from **bc**, use the **quit** command, or enter CTRL-D to signal an end-of-file. The **bc** command reads its standard input and writes to its standard output, so redirection from a file is allowed. When the file ends, **bc** exits, as shown here:

```
$ cat cmd.file
/* comments begin with slash-star, and end with star-slash as here */
6+5
$ bc < cmd.file
11
$
```

In addition, **bc** can take a filename as an argument, as follows:

```
$ bc cmd.file
```

This procedure differs from redirecting a file to the standard input of **bc**. When a filename is given as an argument, **bc** reads the file, processes its commands, and then switches to the terminal for its input. This allows complex commands and functions to be stored in a file, and then used directly from the keyboard.

bc Notation

The **bc** command uses an *infix* notation, and the end of the input line signals that the command should be evaluated.

In **bc**, numbers can be as long as necessary, and they may contain a decimal point and an optional - (minus) sign to mark a negative number, as shown here:

```
-3.45667
```

The normal arithmetic operators are allowed for computations. For example:

```
$ bc
3.45 + 2
5.45
```

Variables are also allowed, and can have lowercase, one-character names. Values are assigned to variables with the = (equal) operator, as follows:

```
w = value
```

Here, the *w* can be any lowercase letter. Variables are used to store numbers temporarily for later use; they can be referenced like numbers, as in the example:

```
$ bc
y=4
3+y
7
```

A variable retains its value until it is reused in another assignment statement.

In addition, **bc** understands *arrays* of numbers, if the array operators [and] (square brackets) surround the array index, as they do here:

```
s[2]=3.3
```

Array indexes start at zero, so this example sets the third element of the array named **s** to **3.3**. The array index can be any expression **bc** can resolve to a number.

By default, **bc** performs many calculations as if the numbers were integers, but the scale factor can be changed by assigning a number to the **scale** variable. The number is the number of digits to the right of the decimal point that you wish **bc** to retain in its calculations. For example:

```
$ bc
6.456/5.678
1
```

```
scale = 3
6.456/5.678
1.137
```

In addition, the **ibase** and **obase** variables can be used as they can in **dc** to set the input number radix and the output number radix, respectively, as shown here:

```
$ bc
ibase=2
1001
9
obase=8
1001
11
```

These features can be used to perform base conversions or to do arithmetic in number systems other than decimal.

The **bc** command allows many operators in addition to the normal arithmetic operators understood by **dc**. The **+ +** (plus plus) and **--** (minus minus) operators increment and decrement the value of a variable, respectively, as follows:

```
s=4
s
4
--s
3
s
3
```

These operators change the value of the variable and return the value that was set, so that the following operation will work:

```
s=4
t[--s]=3.3
t[3]
3.3
```

In this example, **t[4]** is not defined and **s** is 3 after the operation. The **+ +** and **--** operators can be used before or after the variable name. When they are used before the name, the value is changed before it is returned; when they are used after the name, the value is changed after the value is returned. For example:

```
s=4
t[s--]=3.3
t[4]
3.3
```

In both of the two previous cases the final value of **s** is 3, but the array **t** differs.

bc Statements and Operators

The following additional *assignment* operators are also allowed. They act by changing the named variable according to the operator.

```
=-
=+
=*
=/
=%
=^
```

That is,

```
s =- 3
```

is the same as

```
s = s - 3
```

Sequences of operations can be grouped inside the { and } (curly braces). All commands bracketed in this way are treated as a single object by **bc**, and can be used as a single *statement*. Here is an example:

```
{ s=3 ; y=4 }
```

This statement as a whole will return whatever value the *last* component part returns, as shown here:

```
{ s = 3 + 2 ; s }
5
```

This grouping operation is useful when you wish to take advantage of the *logical operators,* which evaluate the material within the brackets to determine whether some test operation is true.

The **bc** command supports the logical operators **if, for,** and **while.** Although these have the same meaning as they do in the shell programming language, they differ in the way they are used. For example, the test part of an **if** statement is included within (and) (parentheses), and if the test is true, the statements within curly braces are evaluated, as follows:

```
s=3
if ( s == 3 ) {
        s =+ 2
}
s
5
```

This example reveals a great deal. First, **bc** constructs can span multiple lines if a grouping operator like (or { is opened but not closed. Although **bc** does not prompt for continuation as the shell does with PS2, if a command is entered incorrectly **bc** displays a terse error message, such as this:

```
syntax error on line 4, teletype
```

The source of the input is identified along with the line number. In this case, the input is from the terminal, known to **bc** as the *teletype.*

The logical operators $==$ (is equal to), $<=$ (is less than or equal to), $>=$ (is greater than or equal to), $!=$ (is not equal to), $>$ (is greater than), and $<$ (is less than) can be used within the test part of the **if** to specify a test to perform. If the answer to the test is true, the material within the curly braces is executed. If the test is not true, the material within the curly braces is not executed. Note that the **if** command has no **else** part, so if you want to take some other action should the first test fail, the test must be repeated with its sense reversed. The test is only executed once, and the material within the braces can only be executed once if the test succeeds. When you are writing constructions like this, it is best to indent each line within a block, as in the preceding examples, to make it easier to understand the logical relationship between the commands.

The format of the **while** operator is similar to that of **if**, except it begins a *loop* in which the material within the braces is executed repeatedly until the test fails. Thus, the material within the curly braces must include commands to change the values of the test variable, as in this example:

```
s=4
while ( s > 0 ) {
        s
        s =- 1
}
4
3
2
1
```

If the test variable is not modified by the operation of the **while** loop, the loop will continue forever!

The **for** operation is like a more complete version of **while**. Three parts are included within the parentheses, each separated by a ; (semicolon). The first part sets the value of some test variable, and the third part modifies it. The middle part is the test operation like that used in the **while** command. For example, the previous command could also have been written:

```
for ( s = 4 ; s > 0 ; --s ) {
        s
}
```

The result is the same, but the logical grouping of the index-related operations within the **for** statement makes this command easier to understand than the equivalent **while** command. The **for** command is usually used when the index variable is relatively self-contained; **while** is used when some complex or external factor causes the test variable to change. As many commands or nested **for** and **while** constructs can be included within the { and } as you wish.

To exit from a loop before the condition tests false, you use the **break** statement, as shown here:

```
for ( s = 4 ; s > 0 ; --s ) {
        if ( s <= 2 ) break
        s
}
```

```
4
3
```

The **break** statement simply ends the loop and causes the next command after the end of the loop to be executed. If there are multiple nested loops, **break** just exits from the innermost loop; no single operator breaks out of all the nested loops. The **quit** command is executed immediately when it is read from the input, so it cannot be used inside **bc** programs.

bc Functions

Finally, **bc** allows the construction of *functions*. A function is a procedure that has a name, can take arguments, and returns a value when it is used. You define a function with the **define** command, which takes a following name, named arguments enclosed in parentheses, and then the body of the function enclosed in curly braces. For example:

```
define x ( a, b ) {
        for( s=a; s<b; ++s ) {
                s
        }
        return( 22 )
}
```

Like variables, functions have single-character names. The arguments in the function definition are formal names that can be used as variables inside the function. As many arguments as necessary are allowed, but you should keep the number of arguments as small as possible. In addition, other external variables can be used inside the function. In the previous example, s is such an external variable, and its value will have changed after the function is executed. Local variables, known only within the function, are also allowed if they are *declared* as local variables within the function using the **auto** statement. This example uses a local s variable:

```
define x ( a, b ) {
        auto s
        for( s=a; s<b; ++s ) {
                s
        }
```

```
        return( 22 )
}
```

The value of any externally defined variable named **s** will not have changed after this function is executed.

To execute a function, name it with the correct number of arguments enclosed in parentheses and separated by commas. The actual values of the arguments, as given when the function is *called*, will be used in place of the formal arguments specified when the function is *named*. For example, the previous function might be called with

```
x( 3, 6 )
```

and the result would be

```
x( 3, 6 )
3
4
5
22
```

The numbers **3** through **5** come from the evaluation of the expression **s** each time through the **for** loop, and **22** is the return value from the function.

The return value can be assigned to another variable to save its value, as follows:

```
w = x( 3, 6 )
3
4
5
```

Now the variable **w** contains the value 22. This is how functions are normally used, to hide a complex or repeatedly used section of the program in a simple name that can be called when it is needed. Functions are usually defined as part of longer programs that are stored in files, and read into **bc** when they are required.

Some mathematical functions are predefined for **bc**, and can be included when **bc** is loaded. The **-l** (for library) command-line option loads the math library. It looks like this:

```
$ bc -l
```

The functions included in the math library are **s(x)**, which returns the sine of x; **c(x)**, which returns the cosine of x; **e(x)**, which returns the exponential of x; **l(x)**, which returns the log of x; **a(x)**, which returns the arctangent of x; and **j(n,x)**, which returns the Bessel function of x. When the math library is loaded, you must take care not to redefine these function names.

The **bc** command is an excellent tool that can be extremely useful for creating simple sums and products, as well as for more complex computations; the possibilities are limited only by your imagination. Because it can make calculations at an arbitrary level of precision, **bc** has a great many uses. Also, since **bc** reads its standard input for expressions, it can be used in shell programs and with the grave operator in assignments to shell variables. Neither **bc** nor **dc** is very good at reading data from files, although either can readily read in programs that have been saved in files. Input to **bc** and **dc** is expected to come from the terminal, or to be given at run time as arguments to function calls.

The awk Command

One tool that is very useful for computation, is also excellent for *pattern processing* tasks. This is the **awk** command, with its associated control language. The name **awk** is an acronym composed of the last initials of the command's three developers, Aho, Weinberger, and Kernighan; however some users complain that the command has earned its name by being awkward to use. In fact, though, **awk** is a very powerful and elegant programming language that has never lived down its extremely terse and arcane documentation. (A recent book on **awk** by its three developers may help). The **awk** command has a great many uses, and can do things that no other tool can accomplish without extreme contortions.

SVR3 and SVR4 systems offer two versions of **awk**, called **nawk** (for new **awk**) and **oawk** (for old **awk**). One or the other of these tools will be linked to the name **awk** in the **/usr/bin** directory. Which one is used as **awk** may vary between implementations; check your machine to be sure. The **oawk** tool is the venerable old version that has been included with UNIX systems for many years. It is quite slow and inefficient in operation, but many **awk** *scripts* have been written for it. The **nawk** tool is a greatly enhanced and optimized version that first appeared in SVR3. It runs much faster and has more powerful internal commands and operators than **oawk**, but the real reason for its existence is its support for international character sets. Unfortunately, **nawk** is not 100 percent compatible with **oawk**, so some **oawk** programs will not run correctly with **nawk**. The discussion of **awk** in this section applies to *both* versions; some **nawk** enhancements are discussed at the end of this chapter.

Basic awk Concepts

The **awk** command scans a list of input files for lines that match a specified set of *patterns*. For each pattern that is matched, a specified set of *actions* is performed. These actions can involve field manipulations within the line, or arithmetic operations on the values of the fields. Actually, **awk** is a programming language that has features of the shell programming language, the **bc** language, and the C programming language. It is completely interpreted like **bc**, contains field variables from each input line named like the shell's **$1, $2,** and **$3** arguments, and contains printing and control operators similar to those used in the C language.

To use **awk**, you must create a *program* that specifies a list of *pattern* and *action* sections; **awk** reads the input files, and for each input line that matches a pattern, it executes the associated action. The **awk** command is executed with this command line:

```
$ awk -f prog filename-list
```

The set of patterns and actions is given in a file named after the **-f** (for file) option. Any additional filenames are the text files that **awk** reads to get its input. If no filename list is given, **awk** reads its standard input. In addition, standard input can be inserted in the middle of a filename list with the special argument - (minus). For example:

```
$ awk -f prog file1 - file2
```

Here, **awk** will read the program from the file **prog**, process **file1**, read its standard input until an end-of-file is reached, and then process **file2**.

The **awk** command also allows the program to be included directly in the command line, if the **-f** option is not used. In this case, the program appears literally, following the **awk** name but before the file-name list. Even **awk** experts take several tries to debug an **awk** program, however, so the in-line form is rarely used except in carefully prepared shell scripts. The in-line usage can save an additional file in an application, but be sure the program is working correctly before you remove the **-f file** form.

How awk Reads Input Lines

Each line **awk** reads from the files or from standard input is treated as containing fields separated by whitespace. The field delimiter can be changed to any other character if the **-F** (for field) option is given on the **awk** command line with a new delimiter as argument. For example, to make **awk** use the : (colon) as a delimiter, you might use the command line

```
$ awk -F: -f prog files
```

You refer to each field in the input line with the names **$1, $2, $3,** and so forth. The first field on the line is **$1**. The special variable **$0** refers to the input line as a whole, without the division into fields.

awk Patterns and Actions

The pattern-action pairs define the operations that **awk** performs on the lines and fields that it reads. The format of these pattern-action pairs is

```
pattern { action }
```

As you can see, the action portion is separated from the pattern by enclosing it in { and } (curly braces). A missing action part will cause the line to be printed, and a missing pattern part will always match the line; thus, if the pattern is missing, the action applies to every line. The action may include a complex series of operators, including variables and logical operators much like **bc**, with the field variables **$1**, **$2**, and so on, used as the input data. One common operator is **print**, which writes its arguments to the standard output. The action

```
{ print $2, $1 }
```

will reverse the first two input fields, and write them out. If the input data is

```
$ cat in.file
hello goodbye again
111 222
thirty forty
$
```

and the **awk** program is

```
$ cat awk.prog1
{ print $2, $1 }
$
```

the output will be

```
$ awk -f awk.prog1 in.file
goodbye hello
222 111
forty thirty
$
```

In this example, the arguments to **print** are separated by a , (comma), which causes the **print** command to insert the current field delimiter between the output data. If the comma were omitted, then **$1** and **$2** would run together in the output.

Remember, when the pattern matches the input line, the action is taken. In the previous example there is no pattern section, so the action is taken on each input line.

A pattern is a regular expression, or sequence of regular expressions separated by the operators **!** (not), **||** (logical or), **&&** (logical and), or parentheses for grouping. Each regular expression must be enclosed by the **/** (slash) character, as in **ed**. For example, the **awk** program

```
/hello/ { print $2, $1 }
```

will process the **in.file** used in the last example as follows:

```
$ awk -f awk.prog2 in.file
goodbye hello
$
```

Only one line of the input file matched the pattern **/hello/**, so only one line was printed by the action part. Since no action was specified for the other lines, no action was taken and nothing appeared in the output. However, multiple pattern-action statements are allowed to handle different cases, as in this example:

```
/hello/ { print $2, $1 }
/thirty/ { print $1, $2, "and more" }
```

This program produces different results, as shown here:

```
$ awk -f awk.prog3 in.file
goodbye hello
thirty forty and more
$
```

The entire **awk** program, including all the different pattern-action pairs, will be processed for each input line. This example illustrates another feature of the **print** command: literal strings surrounded by quotation marks that appear in the arguments to **print**, will appear in the output as expected.

The patterns can be joined with logical operators to broaden the range of possible tests. For example, the program

```
/hello/||/111/ { print "hit", $1, $2 }
```

will produce

```
$ awk -f awk.prog4 in.file
hit hello goodbye
hit 111 222
$
```

The ‖ operator tells **awk** to perform the action if *either* of the regular expressions match the input line. The **&&** operator tells **awk** to perform the action only if *both* of the regular expressions match the input line, and the **!** operator tells **awk** to perform the action only if the regular expression *does not* match the input line. The **!** operator precedes a regular expression and does not separate two expressions, as shown here:

```
!/hello/ {
      print "not hello"
}
```

Of course, more complex regular expressions are allowed. For example,

```
/^[Hh1]/ { print "hit", $0 }
```

will produce

```
$ awk -f awk.prog5 in.file
hit hello goodbye again
hit 111 222
$
```

Note the use of **$0** to display the original input line in its entirety.

The action part of an **awk** command can span as many typed lines as you wish, with each additional statement in the action on a separate line. The entire action is enclosed within curly braces, as follows:

```
$ cat awk.prog6
/hello/ {
      print $2
      print "another"
      print $1
}
$ awk -f awk.prog6 in.file
goodbye
another
hello
$
```

Each **print** statement causes a new line of output, but all the output is produced by the one line in the input file that matches the pattern **/hello/**.

Numeric Operations with awk

As the preceding simple examples demonstrate, **awk** has excellent facilities for matching and juggling strings. In fact, one of **awk**'s major uses is to reformat text data according to rules specified in the program. Although **awk** allows reformatting operations that are too complex for **sed** or other tools, its real power is in the logical and arithmetic operators that can be used in the action portion of the command; **awk** is very intelligent in its use of numeric variables, and provides automatic conversion between character strings and numbers. Using **awk** for arithmetic is different from using **bc** in that **awk** can use the pattern section to pick up a subset of the lines in an input file. This allows some fields to be index, or *key*, fields, and other fields that contain data to be processed by **awk**. Also, **awk** can readily convert input between character and numeric format, and it offers better tools for formatting output than **bc** does. On the other hand, **bc** can be more efficient than **awk** in operation, allows greater precision, and is somewhat easier to learn. Both tools have their place in the UNIX system.

One of **awk**'s friendliest features is that it automatically interprets character string input fields as either strings or numbers, depending on the context. For example, the built-in **awk** function **length** returns the length of an input field taken as a character string, while numeric variables can be assigned the value of the field taken as a number. For example:

```
$ cat awk.prog7
{
    s += $2
    print $2, "length=" length($2), "s=" s
}
$
```

This example adds up the numeric values in the second field of each input line. The *type conversion* is done automatically by **awk**; you neither have to declare the variable **s** in advance nor worry about its type. Here are the results of executing the previous program:

```
$ awk -f awk.prog7 in.file
goodbye length=7 s=0
222 length=3 s=222
forty length=5 s=222
$
```

Strings that cannot be converted to numbers take the value zero, so that things work as expected. The string *thirty* is of this form, and cannot be converted, but **awk** can convert the string 222 correctly. By default, a form such as 222 is treated as a number, but you can force **awk** to treat it as a string by enclosing it in quotes.

The **awk** command allows values to be assigned to variables, as in **s = 0**. Variables in **awk** are treated much like variables in **bc**, except that **awk** variable names can be more than one character long. In fact, variable names can be any length, as long as they begin with an alphabetic character. Array variables are allowed, and the array index must be enclosed in square brackets, as it must in **bc**. These are legal **awk** variables:

```
s
S
SS
S1
qwerty[42]
```

Variables need not be declared or initialized before they are used. The **awk** command initializes a variable to an empty string, but a variable can be used to store a string or a number without difficulty. In fact, a single variable can change its type as it is used in an action. For example,

```
/hello/ {
        SSS = 34
        print "SSS is", SSS
        SSS = hello
        print "SSS is", SSS
}
```

might produce this output:

```
$ awk -f awk.prog8 in.file
SSS is 34
SSS is hello
```

Automatic variable typing makes **awk** variables easy to use. If you try to use this power inappropriately, **awk** will display an error message.

Special Patterns for the Beginning and End of Processing

In addition to the regular expression patterns **awk** uses to decide whether to apply an action to an input line, two special patterns are always executed. These are the *BEGIN* and *END* actions. BEGIN is executed at the beginning of an **awk** program, before any input lines are read. END is executed at the end of the program, after the last input line. The BEGIN pattern is usually used to initialize variables, and so forth, while the END pattern is used to make final calculations and produce summary output. Neither the BEGIN nor the END pattern is required in the **awk** program, but either can be included if it is needed. For example, this program will produce the mean or average of a list of numbers:

```
BEGIN {
          print "Beginning to process the input data...."
       }
       {
          s += $1
          n++
       }
END    {
          print "mean of these", n, "data items is", s/n
       }
```

The action associated with the BEGIN pattern is executed at the beginning of the program; in this case it just displays a message, because **awk** automatically sets the count (**n**) and the sum (**s**) variables to zero without explicit initialization. Then, each input line is read. Since no pattern is associated with the action, the action is executed for each input line. This action adds the first field of the input line to variable **s** and increments the count by one. Finally, the action associated with the END pattern is executed after all the input has been read. In this case, END prints the results of the computations.

awk Statements

The **awk** command provides a great variety of actions, allowing you to write complex programs that can combine numeric and string actions. The basic form is the statement. A *statement* is a single operation that is defined by **awk**. A statement is terminated by a newline or a semicolon. For example, these are both **awk** statements:

```
s += $1
print $2 $1
```

Any sequence of statements enclosed in curly braces is treated as a single statement by **awk**. All the action parts of the pattern-action pairs presented earlier are statements, because they are all enclosed in curly braces.

Many logical constructs are also statements. For example, **if** is used in **awk** much as it is in **bc**, that is,

```
if ( conditional ) statement
```

This causes **awk** to execute the statement if the value of the *conditional* part is true (nonzero). Of course, many **awk** statements can be included in the statement part if the entire construct is enclosed in curly braces, as shown here:

```
{
        if ( s < 2 ) {
                ++s
                print s
        }
}
```

This entire example is a single **awk** statement that is composed of several other statements.

Many simpler statement forms are also allowed. Assignments of arithmetic expressions to variables are the most common. The format is the same as in **bc**, and the common mathematical operators are allowed. For example, these are all valid assignment statements:

```
x = 3
n += 3
n++
w = 14 / 4 + 32 - ( 14 * 6 ) / 5.2
```

The **awk** command converts all numbers to floating point before doing its computations, so integers and floating point numbers can be mixed freely in **awk** statements.

Looping operators are also supported by **awk**. The **while** operator takes the form

```
while ( conditional ) statement
```

where the *conditional* is any expression that resolves to a zero (false) or a nonzero (true) value. If the conditional is true, the statement is executed. For example:

```
{
    while ( s < 10 ) {
            s = $1 / 32.3
            ++m
    }
}
```

Here, the two statements within the curly braces are executed if **s** is less than ten. The **for** command is similar, except it takes three parts, as shown here:

```
{
        for ( s = 0 ; s < 10 ; ++s ) {
                s = $1 /32.3
                ++m
        }
}
```

Each of the three parts within the parentheses is separated from the other parts by a ; (semicolon). The first part can be used to initialize any local variables. The second part is the conditional, and the statement following the **for** is executed if the middle part resolves to true. The third part is executed after the statement has been executed, but before the conditional is tested again for another pass through the loop. The third part is usually used to change some variable that appears in the conditional part; the statement is executed repeatedly, until the conditional resolves to false. Of course, any of these operators may be further embedded inside the statement part of the action. For example, this is a complete action:

```
{   for ( s = 2; s < 10; ++s ) {
        print "outer loop:  s is now", s
        if ( s > 3 && s < 6 ) {
            print "inner loop:  s is now", s
        }
    }
}
```

You can use the **break** statement inside a **for** or **while** loop to cause an early exit from the loop, even though the conditional part may still be true. After the **break** statement is processed, execution begins at the first statement after the end of the **for** or **while** loop. For example:

```
{   for ( s = 2; s < 10; ++s ) {
        print "In loop:  s is now", s
        if ( s == 4 ) break
    }
    print "loop finished, s is", s
}
```

This causes the **for** loop to end when **s** is equal to 4, even though the **for** conditional (**s < 10**) is still true. Again, **break** causes the immediately executing loop to end. If there are nested loops, **break** only ends the innermost loop; the outer loops continue to execute.

Similarly, the **continue** operator starts the next iteration of a loop at the top, even though all the statements in the loop may not have been executed. For example, the **awk** program

```
$ cat awk.prog9
BEGIN { for ( s = 2; s < 6; ++s ) {
            if ( s == 4 ) continue
            print "s is now", s
    }
}
```

will cause this output:

```
$ awk -f awk.prog9
s is now 2
s is now 3
s is now 5
$
```

In the conditional

```
if ( s == 4 )
```

the $==$ operator is a logical "if equal" test that returns true or false. The conditional

```
if ( s = 4 )
```

is an assignment within the conditional that will return the value 4, which is evaluated as nonzero (true). In addition, the second form assigns 4 to the variable **s**, while the former does not change **s**. Misuse of the $=$ and $==$ operators within conditional expressions is a very common and hard-to-detect error. Take care when you use these conditionals!

Two other operators that control **awk** program flow are **next** and **exit**. The **next** operator causes the current action to end; then **awk** immediately reads the next input line and restarts with it. Similarly, **exit** causes **awk** to stop processing the current action, discard all remaining input lines, and proceed to an END section if it exists. If there is no END section, **awk** exits back to the shell when it sees the **exit** command.

Formatting Output with awk

The **print** command can be very useful for producing simple output, as in the examples presented earlier; however, for more complex printing tasks the **printf** (for print function) command is available. This command differs from **print** in that it allows complete control over the way output is produced. In fact, **printf** implements the complete set of functions available in the C language's **printf(3)** function, and performs a function similar to that of the **printf(1)** command discussed in Chapter 8. The **awk** version supports a powerful and complex list of conversion specifications; here we will cover only the major forms.

The **printf** command takes two kinds of arguments. The first is a *formatting specification* that is a character string. This specifies the general form of the output, and may include special "holes" in which real data will be inserted. The second type of argument to **printf** is a list of variables. There will be as many of these variables as there are holes in the formatting specification. The holes are called *conversion specifications*, and they define how the variables will be printed. For example,

```
printf "this is a number %d and a string %s\n", 333, "333"
```

produces

```
this is a number 333 and a string 333
```

The first argument after the **printf** command is the formatting specification. It includes several words that are printed as they appear, and two conversion specifications. The arguments are separated by commas.

Conversion specifications begin with the % (percent) character, and the specification is made with the characters immediately following the %. The major formats allowed are **d** (for decimal), **s** (for string), **c** (for a single character), **o** (for octal), **x** (for hexadecimal), and **f** (for float). In the previous example, %d displays the variable as a decimal integer, and %s displays the variable as a character string. The variables given after the formatting specification, **333** and "**333**", are displayed according to the conversion specification, with type conversions to the correct format made internally.

By default, **printf** selects an appropriate length for the conversion, acting intelligently where possible. As many digits as necessary are used to make the conversion, and you do not have to worry about the length. However, you can force a conversion to be a specific length by placing a number that represents the desired number of digits, after the % and before the conversion type. For example,

```
printf "one= >%1d<, two= >%2d<, three= >%3d<\n", sss, sss, sss
```

will use *at least* one, two, or three digits to format the variable **sss**; however, **printf** will use *more* digits if they are required. That is, if **sss** has the value 42, the previous **printf** statement will produce the result

```
one= >42<, two= >42<, three= > 42<
```

When more digits are specified in the conversion specification than are needed in the conversion, **printf** *pads* the format with whitespace on the left, so that digits are *right-justified* in the field. If a - (minus) follows the % and precedes the field width, the output is *left-justified* within the field. For example,

```
printf "one= >%1d<, two= >%2d<, three= >%-3d<\n", sss, sss, sss
```

will produce this output

```
one= >42<, two= >42<, three= >42 <
```

These field size specifications let you control columnizing output, but remember, **printf** will not truncate a number if the field specification is too small for the value to be printed; instead, it will expand the field specification to fit the value.

For floating point numbers that will contain a decimal point on output, **printf** recognizes a more complex length specification. The length is given as two numbers separated by a . (dot). The number to the left of the decimal point is the total field width desired, and the number to the right of the dot is the number of digits after the decimal point in the output. For example,

```
printf "short= >%6.1f<, longer= >%6.4f<\n", 6.345678, 6.345678
```

will produce this output:

```
short= >   6.3<, longer= >6.3457<
```

Note that the results are rounded correctly to fill the field. With **printf**, this kind of truncation of the output occurs only to the right of the decimal point. The **printf** command will use as many digits as necessary to correctly represent the part of the number to the left of the decimal point. With floating point output the - can also be used after the % to left-justify a number within the field. However, the precision will dominate and the right will be padded with whitespace. Thus,

```
printf "short= >%-6.1f<, longer= >%-6.4f<\n", 6.345678, 6.345678
```

will produce this output:

```
short= >6.3   <, longer= >6.3457<
```

In addition, **printf** recognizes two special control characters: **\n** outputs a newline, and **\t** outputs a tab character. The command

```
printf "hello 12\t%c%c\ngoodbye", 3, 4
```

will produce this output:

```
hello 12       34
goodbye
```

Although **printf** supports several more operators and conversion specifications, the ones described here will be sufficient for the great majority of your work with **awk**.

Going Further

There are, of course, many more tools for computation, including the several *programming languages* developers can use to write programs. Generally not part of the foundation software included with the UNIX system, these require purchase of the C Compilation System. Nonetheless, serious programs are almost always written with one of these programming languages. A short discussion of these development tools is included in Chapter 26. Here we will continue our discussion of **nawk**.

The New awk Program

The **nawk** command includes many enhancements over **oawk**, and eventually it may fully replace the older version. When all the old applications have been ported to **nawk**, **oawk** may be eliminated from the UNIX system. Athough this probably won't occur for several years, new programs should be developed in **nawk** unless you are porting to a system that only has **oawk**. It is easy to write **nawk** programs that are incompatible with **oawk**.

The major enhancement in the **nawk** language is a larger set of built-in functions and variables. You have access to the command-line arguments, the name of the current input file (or standard input), the number of fields in the current line, the sequence count of the current line, and other variables. Taken together, these new operators merge many of the features of **oawk** and **sed**.

In addition to using the **-F** (for field) command-line argument to specify a single character field delimiter, **nawk** allows you to specify a complete regular expression (in the format of **egrep**) after the **-F**. Whenever the specified regular expression matches a string in the input file, **nawk** uses that string as the delimiter. This allows you to write much more powerful (though complex) field operations on complex input files. For example:

```
$ nawk -F "^[Hh]ello" -f prog filenamelist
```

Be sure to quote the regular expression if it contains any shell wildcard operators.

The **nawk** command includes many more built-in variables than does **oawk**, and these greatly enhance **nawk**'s programmability. The most important of these variables is **FILENAME**, which always contains the name of the file **nawk** is currently processing. Thus, you can include the name of each file in your output when it is needed, as follows:

```
$ cat prog8
/Hello/ {
     print "file", FILENAME, "contains the string", "Hello"
}
$
```

The **RS** variable contains the current *record separator*, which is usually newline, as in all the previous examples. That is, each line of the input file is usually treated as a separate record, but if you change the **RS** variable, you can process files that contain multiline data records. If you do this, your input files must contain the new **RS** value at the end of each record. If **RS** is changed, **nawk** will read multiple lines from the input and concatenate them before it begins to process the record. Usually the BEGIN section of the program will set **RS** to the desired value. To produce multiline records as output, you can set the **ORS** (for output record separator) variable, and **nawk** will write that value to end each record it outputs. Be sure that you write correct **print** or **printf** commands, or the **ORS** value will not be correct.

The **NR** (for number) variable contains the *count* of records that have been read since the **nawk** program started. The count spans input files if more than one is given on the command line. Several other built-in variables are also included in **nawk**.

In addition, a large number of built-in functions allow various substring and character indexing operations on input records, and there is a **getline** operation that will discard the current record and read the next input record. Thus, you can read (or discard) data records without leaving the current pattern-action operation.

You can also write to files instead of to the normal standard I/O. For example, you may wish to keep a log of **nawk**'s operation as it processes data, but without merging this output into your normal output. To do so, simply write a **print** or **printf** command as usual, but add >*filename* at the end, as shown here:

```
print "Output to another file" > "/tmp/log.file"
```

This will write a string to the file **log.file** without interrupting the normal I/O streams. If the filename is a full pathname, it must be quoted or **nawk** will display an error message. You can combine this feature with the **getline** function to read a line from another file, as follows:

```
getline < in.file
```

This statement will change the current value of **$0** to the first line in **in.file**, discarding the old value, and subsequent use of this input operation will read additional lines from **in.file**. If the entire input file is read before the **nawk** program finishes, the **getline** operation will not succeed. In this case, **nawk** will not complain, and the current record will not change. This is a common source of errors, so take care when you use the **getline** command.

Finally, **nawk** allows user-defined functions. You can use these functions just as you would use regular built-in functions, but they are defined at the beginning of the program, replacing a pattern-action pair, as in this example:

```
$ cat awk.prog9
function putout( x, y ) {
    print "x is >>" x "<<"
```

```
        print "y is >>" y "<<"
}
{
        putout( $0, $1 )
}
$
```

You begin a function definition with the keyword **function**, followed by the name and (in parentheses) as many formal arguments as you need. The function itself must be enclosed in curly braces. You can continue with a BEGIN section or a normal pattern-action pair, and the action part can include calls to the function you have defined.

Once you understand the basics of **awk** programming, you can use the new features of **nawk** to great advantage. Consult the **nawk(1)** man page for more information.

The Process

The multitasking aspects of the UNIX system are generically grouped under the topic of the *process*. A process, or *task*, is an instance of an executing program. Your login shell is a process while you are logged in, because it is always present until you log off. If you execute a command from the $ prompt, that command is a process while it is executing. Processes have many properties, and there are many commands for manipulating processes and their properties. In this chapter we will discuss the issues associated with multitasking, and consider how you can control the execution environment to your advantage.

Before we go on, let's look at a few examples. The command

```
$ cat /etc/passwd
```

generates one process that lives until the **cat** operation is completed. If you create a shell pipeline using the | operator, each of the command components becomes a separate process. The command line

```
$ cat /etc/passwd | wc
```

generates two processes, one for each command. These two processes communicate with each other through the pipe. How many processes are created by the next command?

```
$ SIZE=`cat /etc/passwd | wc -l`
```

The answer is two, one for the **cat** and one for the **wc**. The assignment to the environment variable SIZE is handled internally by the shell, and no additional process is created for that operation. Similarly, some commands are executed directly by the shell and do not create a new process. The **cd** command, and usually **pwd** and **echo**, are built-in shell commands that do not involve a separate process. For the most part, however, each of your commands, and many more commands that the UNIX system creates for its own purposes, are processes.

Timesharing in the UNIX System

Because most UNIX systems have only a single *central processing unit* (CPU) that executes programs, only one program can actually be executing at any time. One of the major purposes of the *kernel,* the portion of the UNIX system that manages the system as a whole, is to control and support the many programs that need to use the CPU at any one time. If you are sharing a machine with other users, each user's shell is a process, as are any applications or commands each person uses. Several of these programs may request access to the CPU at once, and it is the kernel's job to grant access to one application (or to keep control itself) at any given time; thus a process executes for a short time, and then control passes to another process.

Because these changes of task, or *process switches,* occur at least once every second, and usually more often, each user has the impression that he or she "owns" the whole machine. This is why multitasking operating systems are called *timesharing systems*—the single CPU is a resource that is shared by all users and processes. The kernel also creates the impression that each individual process has the whole machine, even though it may actually control the machine for less than a second at a time. Since a process only has to wait for a short while to gain control again, the user at a terminal generally does not even notice that the system is being used by other people and programs.

Of course, the system can become more heavily loaded than was expected when it was configured; when this happens noticeable delays may result for users running commands and applications. In fact, once you are familiar with the speed at which a specific UNIX system tends to work most of the time, you can use extreme delays in *response time* to detect problems and errors in the system. You should not interpret any specific delay as a system error, however, because different commands naturally take more or less time to complete, depending on how much processing each one requires. It is only a definite change in the system's normal behavior that may indicate something is amiss.

Again, a process is an instance of an executing program. A command that is stored on disk may be executable, and you may be able to invoke it with a command name, but unless it is running or waiting for access to the CPU it is not a process. Processes describe the *current* status of the machine.

A Note on Priority Classes

Usually, most processes have equal *priority*. That is, they all have an equal claim on the CPU. However, the UNIX system provides tools for modifying the priority of a process that you create. In SVR4, there are two entirely separate classes of processes whose priority can be manipulated separately. The *timesharing* priority is the normal class for user applications, and we will discuss this class first. But a new *real-time* priority is also allowed. Real-time priority finally allows the UNIX system to be used in applications that demand a rigid and fast response. You can separately manipulate the priority of processes in each class, but real-time processes always get CPU time before timesharing processes. We will discuss real-time processes and the **priocntl** (for priority control) command at the end of this chapter, but here we assume a "normal" UNIX system that is running nearly all timesharing processes.

Controlling Process Priority Within the Timesharing Class

Usually, increasing the priority of a process causes it to complete more quickly at the cost of other processes in the machine. Because the other processes do not get as much CPU time, they complete more slowly. On the other hand, lowering process priority makes a process demand less CPU time during each interval, so it takes longer to complete. In this case, other processes in the machine benefit, since they get a bigger share of the system's resources.

Unless you are the superuser, you cannot increase the priority of a process; after all, it might be viewed as unfriendly if you set your process to such a high priority that other processes had little or no access to the CPU. However, you can always lower the priority of a command with the **nice** (for nice and friendly) command. To use this command, begin your normal command line with **nice**, as shown here:

```
$ nice cat /etc/passwd
```

The command line or lines that you wish to execute serve as the argument or arguments to the **nice** command. The previous command will reduce the priority of the command **cat /etc/passwd** by 10, the default value. The number is actually an arbitrary scheduling value that can range from 0 to 19. You can reduce a command's priority more or less by giving the numeric increment you wish to make as an argument to **nice**. Here is an example:

```
$ nice -14 cat /etc/passwd
```

This will reduce the priority of the **cat** command line by 14 units. Generally if you have an application that consumes a large amount of CPU time, you can run the command at a low priority, so that it *soaks* idle CPU time but does not interfere with higher priority work that is going on in the machine.

The superuser is allowed to increase process priority, but this privilege should be used with discretion. Give the **nice** command with a negative priority argument to increase the priority of a command. For example,

```
# nice --14 cat /etc/passwd
```

will increase the priority of the **cat** command by 14 priority units.

The **nice** command is actually an interface to the general process priority features of SVR4, but **nice** is much easier to use than the more general **priocntl**, which is discussed at the end of this chapter.

Background Processes

You will usually use the **nice** command in association with commands that you run from the shell, but in the *background*. This means that your shell remains available while the program is executing, so you can run other commands at the same time. The shell provides the **&** (ampersand) operator to let you run commands in the background. To use the **&**, add it to the end of your command line, like this:

```
$ cat /etc/passwd &
```

In this example, the **cat** command is executed in the background, but its output still comes to your terminal, because you have not redirected it. When you run a command using **&**, the shell returns immediately for your next command, even though the process that you just created is still executing in the system. The shell returns a *process number* or *pid* (for process id) so you can refer to the background job, and then returns to your prompt for another command, as shown here:

```
$ cat /etc/passwd &
1536
$
```

We will discuss the meaning of the process number later in this chapter.

Generally, you will redirect the input and output of commands that execute in the background as follows, so your terminal session is not interrupted by their output:

```
$ cat /etc/passwd > file.copy &
1540
$
```

You may wish to redirect the standard error output as well, or it will come to your terminal even though the standard output is redirected. This command redirects both the standard output and the standard error:

```
$ cat /etc/passwd > file.copy 2>error.out &
1544
$
```

On the other hand, you may want the standard error to come to the terminal, so you get immediate notification of errors in your background processes.

The UNIX system lets you create as many background jobs as you wish, although system performance suffers noticeably if you create too many. When a background process completes, the system does not give you any notification. You can monitor the status of background processes with the **ps** command, discussed later in this chapter. If you have redirected output to a file, you can examine the output at your convenience.

Logging Off While Background Processes Are Running

If you have created background processes during your session, they will be killed when you log off, because they are associated with your login shell. The UNIX system provides a tool that allows background processes to continue running after you log off. This is the **nohup** (for no hangup) command, which can be very useful for long jobs that might run all night (or all week!). Use **nohup** as you would **nice**; put it at the beginning of your command line, as shown here:

```
$ nohup cat /etc/passwd &
```

This example tells the **cat** command to ignore your logging off the system, and to continue running until it completes. Usually, **nohup** is used with background commands, because you can't log off if you don't have a prompt.

When you use **nohup** with a pipeline, you must begin each element of the pipeline with the **nohup** command, as shown here:

```
$ nohup cat /etc/passwd | nohup wc > out.file &
```

If you don't do this, the members of the pipeline without the **nohup** command will be killed when you log off, and the whole pipeline will collapse.

If you do not redirect your output, **nohup** creates an output file for you, because if you log off the machine there will be no terminal for output to go to. For example:

```
$ nohup cat /etc/passwd &
1565
Sending output to nohup.out
$
```

Here you get the identifying number from the shell because you used the & operator, and the "Sending output..." message comes from **nohup** as it creates an output file. The file **nohup.out** in the current directory will contain the results of commands executed under control of **nohup**. Take care to handle standard error output separately if you don't want it to appear in the **nohup.out** file.

Parents and Children

When you log in to the system, it creates a shell process for your use, and this process disappears, or *dies,* when you log off. Thus, you always have at least one process associated with your session, and frequently more than one.

Processes are said to be *born* when they start, and to *die* when they end. Many processes come and go in this way, depending on how the system is being used. Although some processes start when the system is turned on and live until the system is powered down, more often a process has a relatively short lifespan that corresponds to the duration of a command entered at the terminal.

The only way for a new process to be born is for another process to start it. The "older" process is known as the *parent* process, and the new one that it creates is called the *child* process. A parent process can *spawn* multiple children, but a process can have only one parent. Similarly, a process can spawn a child, which can in turn spawn another child, and so on. You don't speak of a "grandparent" of a process, but in fact you can trace the parentage of any given process all the way back through its intermediate parent processes to the moment when the system was turned on. Although these intermediate processes may or may not continue to exist, each process still has a definite parent.

If a process spawns a child, and that child spawns its own child process, the intermediate process may die. Usually when a parent dies all its children die, but you can arrange things so that the child does not die. When this occurs, the original parent *inherits* the children of the process that died. Thus, every process always has a parent.

When you use **nohup** to execute a command, **nohup** listens for you to log off. When you do, **nohup** reassigns the parent of your process to be process 1, so it is no longer associated with your login. Normally, processes that you create from your shell are children of the shell that die when the shell dies.

All users on the machine have processes associated with their current login. In addition, there are systemwide processes that the system creates. Some of these systemwide processes are created for a specific purpose, and once that purpose is accomplished, they die. For example, a process is created to send your electronic mail to another machine, and when it has done so it dies. Other processes, such as the *spooler* for the **lp** printer subsystem, are likely to live for the entire time the machine is running.

The ps Command

As mentioned earlier, you can examine the processes that are currently alive in the machine with the **ps** (for process status) command. This command displays information about processes that are alive when you run it. If you run the command more than once, the output is likely to be different each time; that is, **ps** produces a "snapshot" of machine activity.

If you execute the **ps** command with no arguments, it shows you information about processes associated with your login session. For example:

```
$ ps
   PID TTY      TIME COMMAND
  6756 tty00    0:01 -sh
  6760 tty00    0:02 ps
$
```

This output reveals that you have two processes running: one for the shell, which is born when you log in to the system, and dies when you log out, and the other for executing the **ps** command. Each process that is listed has an execution time associated with it—two seconds for the **ps** command in this example. This is not elapsed or "clock" time, but the total amount of CPU time the process has used since it was born. A process may also have an associated terminal that it reads from and writes to listed in a column of the output. A process that is associated with your login is usually, but not always, attached to your terminal. Some processes are attached to no terminal, in which case the TTY column of the output contains a **?** (question mark). Finally, each process has a unique *pid* that identifies it within the system. Pids start at 0 when the system is turned on, and each new process gets the next number until the maximum, usually 32,767, is reached. In this example the **ps** process was the 6760th process born since the system was turned on. When the maximum number is reached, the count starts again from 0; however, a pid assigned to a process that is still alive will not be reassigned to a new process. Children usually have a higher pid than their parents, but if the parent pid is near the maximum, a child may have recycled back to a lower number.

Actually there is much more information associated with each process, and some of this information is available with the -**f** (for full) option of **ps**, as shown here:

```
$ ps -f
     UID    PID PPID  C    STIME TTY      TIME COMMAND
   steve   6756    1  6 13:04:57 tty00    0:01 -sh
   steve   6761 6756 23 13:05:19 tty00    0:01 ps -f
$
```

The command name, time of execution, tty, and pid are displayed in this output, and some additional information is also available. On the left is the user id, which reveals the owner of the process, since each process is owned by the login id that created it. The PPID column lists the pid for the parent of each process. Because the system created the shell for you when you logged into the machine, its parent pid will be a very low number, the pid associated with part of the kernel. The parent of most processes created by the system is usually pid 1. When you executed the **ps** command, the shell created that process, so the parent pid of the **ps** process is the pid of your shell. You can trace chains of parents and children by looking at their pid and ppid.

The next column of the output, C, lists the amount of processor resources the process has used recently. The kernel uses this information to decide which of several processes gets access to the CPU next. The kernel will let a process with a low C value have control of the CPU before one that has a high number. The **nice** command works by changing the internal algorithm by which this number is computed. Generally, this column is not very useful except to developers who are working on kernel improvements and drivers.

Finally, STIME gives the time of day when the process started. You can use this information to track old or rogue processes that should no longer be in the system.

Listing the Activity of Other Users

The **ps** command can also provide you with information about what other users are doing on the machine at any time. If you know that a specific user is logged in to the system, you can display the status of that user's processes with

```
$ ps -u user
```

where *user* is the login id of the user you are interested in. On a small system it is usually easier to list the activity of all users at once. To do this, use the **-a** (for all) option of **ps**, as follows:

```
$ ps -af
     UID    PID  PPID  C    STIME  TTY      TIME COMMAND
    root     82     1  0  Apr  9  console  0:05 -sh
   steve   6756     1  3 13:04:57 tty00    0:01 -sh
   steve   6762  6756 21 13:05:28 tty00    0:00 ps -af
$
```

Several items are of interest here. First, note that another user is
currently logged into the machine. This login id, **root**, is reserved for a
system administrator, and can only log in from the main system console,
as indicated in the TTY column. Apparently the **root** user logged in soon
after the machine was turned on, because a relatively low pid is associated with that login. If you examine the STIME column you can see
something more: the start time of a process is expressed in *hh:mm:ss*
format for *today's* times. However, for processes that were born on
previous days, only the month and day are given. This format is only
used to reduce the size of the output; the UNIX system keeps all times
exactly.

System Processes

We have examined the processes associated with each user, but there
are also long-lived processes that support the activities of the system,
and other transient processes that are born and then die as the system
goes about its business independently of individual users. The **ps** option
-e (for every) displays information about all the processes active in the
machine. This **ps -e** output is very useful for examining what the machine does "behind your back," and is vital for diagnosing problems. The
exact output depends on what software is installed on the machine, and
on what hardware I/O devices are attached to the system. Also, different
versions of the UNIX system organize the system processes very differently. When you move to a new version on a new machine, try to
understand what processes are normal, so that you can identify problems or errors in the **ps** output when things go wrong. Try **ps** commands
frequently on your own system, to get a feel for what is normal.
    If you run the command

```
$ ps -ef
```

on an SVR4 system based on the Intel 80x86, this output might be typical:

```
$ ps -ef
    UID   PID  PPID  C    STIME TTY      TIME COMD
   root     0     0  0   Mar 31 ?       0:00 sched
   root     1     0  0   Mar 31 ?       0:01 /sbin/init
   root     2     0  0   Mar 31 ?       0:00 pageout
   root     3     0  0   Mar 31 ?       0:00 fsflush
   root     4     0  0   Mar 31 ?       0:00 kmdaemon
   root   173     1  0   Mar 31 ?       0:00 /usr/lib/saf/sac -t 300
   root   245   173  0   Mar 31 ?       0:03 /usr/lib/saf/ttymon
   root   174     1  2 09:16:14 console 0:01 -sh
   root   184   174  8 09:16:48 console 0:00 ps -ef
   root   163     1  0 09:16:10 ?       0:00 /usr/sbin/cron
$
```

This output is from a "basic" system configured without many optional software packages.

The first process executed when the machine boots is the *scheduler*. This is the key to the timesharing features of the UNIX system, and is responsible for determining which of the processes that are ready to run actually gets access to the machine's resources. This process is named **sched** and assigned pid 0. In turn, **sched** starts **init** (for initialization), which keeps standing system processes running. The **init** process is assigned pid 1. (We will discuss **init** in Chapter 21.) Next comes **pageout**, which manages the virtual memory of the machine, and swaps parts of active processes between disk and real memory as they are run or pushed aside temporarily. The **pageout** process is responsible for most of the administrative work the system does to manage processes in the multitasking environment. The **kmdaemon** (for kernel memory demon) process handles the same chore for parts of the operating system itself. The **sched**, **kmdaemon** and **pageout** processes work closely together, and make up the core of the kernel. The **pageout** process gets pid 2, and **kmdaemon** gets pid 4.

Next is **fsflush** (for file system flush), which manages the disk I/O for the system. Because the system contains many internal data buffers that act much like a RAM disk acts on other operating systems, there is a possibility that the data in the buffers will not match the disk if the system fails unexpectedly, or *crashes*. To prevent this, **fsflush** periodically writes all the buffers to disk by causing a **sync** operation. How often this occurs is a system-dependent parameter, but on many small machines it happens once every 20 seconds. Only things that have changed are written to disk each time. The **fsflush** process gets pid 3.

Except for **init,** these system processes are stored on disk within the file **/stand/unix,** which represents the kernel. There is no disk file that contains the executable **sched, pageout, fsflush,** or **kmdaemon** process.

These processes are created when the system boots, and they stay alive until the system is shut down. For this reason, the TIME column of the **ps -ef** output may show a great deal of apparent CPU time allocated to these processes. This figure is not always accurate, because some implementations arbitrarily assign all idle CPU time to **sched** or another of the kernel processes. This is not usually a cause for worry; if these kernel processes were not working, the system would probably not even be sane enough to execute **ps**!

All the rest of the processes in the system can trace their parentage back to **init,** because **init** is responsible for maintaining the system processes according to the contents of the file **/etc/inittab.** The terminal controller and other standing processes arise from **init.** As processes are born and die, the pid count keeps rising, but all processes that have no living parent are ultimately inherited by **init.** Notice that the ppid of many processes in the system is 1.

The rest of the processes in the output from **ps -ef** belong either to users or to special applications that you are running. For example, if you have the **lp** print subsystem running on the machine, there will be a line in the **ps -ef** output for its demon (sometimes spelled *daemon*). A *demon* is a system process that acts without a user requesting it. This can be either a standing system process like **fsflush;** an application process that is always running, like **lpsched** (and **lpNet**) for the **lp** subsystem; or a process that executes under control of the timing subsystems, like **uuxqt.** Usually these scheduled processes do not live very long, but you might see some of them when you run **ps,** and of course they increase the pid count.

With SVR4, several new processes are associated with terminal port management under the *Service Access Facility.* The **sac** (for service access controller) process is the master process for incoming services, and it creates **ttymon** (for tty monitor) to manage serial ports (tty), and possibly several other processes such as **listener,** which handles local area network activity.

If you are using the X Window System and the Ethernet (TCP/IP) networking package, several other demons are also present, as shown in Figure 11-1. The **xntad** process controls network access, and **mousemgr** controls the mouse. These processes are demons that live

```
$ ps -ef
    UID  PID  PPID  C    STIME  TTY      TIME  COMD
    root    0     0  0 21:02:15  ?        0:00  sched
    root    1     0  0 21:02:15  ?        0:01  /sbin/init
    root    2     0  0 21:02:15  ?        0:01  pageout
    root    3     0  0 21:02:15  ?        0:01  fsflush
    root    4     0  0 21:02:15  ?        0:00  kmdaemon
    root  256     1  0 21:03:32  ?        0:00  /usr/lib/saf/sac -t 300
    root  257     1  0 21:03:32  console  0:01  ksh
    root  161     1  0 21:03:18  ?        0:00  /usr/sbin/rpcbind
    root  185   175  0 21:03:23  ?        0:00  lpNet
    root  157     1  0 21:03:15  ?        0:00  /usr/sbin/cron
    root  163     1  0 21:03:18  ?        0:01  /usr/lib/netsvc/rwall/rpc.rwalld
    root  165     1  0 21:03:18  ?        0:01  /usr/lib/netsvc/rusers/rpc.rusersd
    root  167     1  0 21:03:19  ?        0:00  /usr/lib/netsvc/spray/rpc.sprayd
    root  175     1  0 21:03:22  ?        0:01  /usr/lib/lpsched
    root  259   256  0 21:03:36  ?        0:01  /usr/sbin/inetd
    root  251     1  0 21:03:31  ?        0:00  /usr/X/lib/xntad
    root  267   266  0 21:03:43  vt01     0:19  X :0
    root  253     1  0 21:03:31  ?        0:00  /usr/lib/mousemgr
    root  266     1  0 21:03:43  pts/1    0:00  olinit
    root  270   266  0 21:03:47  ?        0:02  olwsm
    root  309   308 43 21:06:31  pts/9    0:02  ps -ef
    root  273     1  0 21:03:53  ?        0:04  olwm
    root  285   277  0 21:04:28  pts/5    0:00  ksh
    root  277     1  0 21:03:53  ?        0:01  xterm -geometry 80x24+10+0
    root  278     1  0 21:03:53  ?        0:03  xterm -geometry 80x24+1-1
    root  286   278  0 21:04:28  pts/9    0:00  ksh
$
```

Figure 11-1.   Larger process environment for init state 2

even while the X Window System is not running. Other processes
associated with X are **olinit**, which starts the OPEN LOOK system;
olwm, the OPEN LOOK window manager; **olwsm**, the Workspace manager; and **olfm**, the OPEN LOOK file manager. If you are running
additional applications, such as **xclock**, under your X session, these will
also appear in the **ps** output.

Other demons are associated with networking. The **inetd** process is
the basic listener for network activity, and **rpcbind** listens for *Remote
Procedure Call* requests. The **rpc.walld**, **rpc.rusersd**, and **rpc.sprayd**
processes support various user-level functions in the networking system.
If you are running the machine as a server on a LAN, even more
networking demons will be present.

There are many more options for the **ps** command, but these are
primarily for the use of system designers and application developers.
Try **ps -l** for a cryptic example!

Diagnosing Problems with Processes

By frequently examining the output from **ps -ef** you can develop your intuition about what is normal on your machine. Usually, on a small system relatively few processes will be active at any time, although the number will vary depending on the time of day. If any process seems to have accumulated an inordinate amount of time in the TIME column, or is the parent of a large number of other processes, or if the machine's response time suddenly becomes very slow, you can suspect that a process is not working correctly. You must understand what is normal in your machine before you can detect what is abnormal, and this varies widely between machines. Also, diagnosing the *source* of a problem may not help you much when you're trying to *repair* a problem. Most problems are related to a specific command or application, and many are related to missing files or directories, or to incorrect permissions on existing files. Because the UNIX system is a multiuser and multitasking operating system, a single problem can affect the entire machine. Although this may cause the machine to slow down significantly and act very abnormally, it usually doesn't damage other programs, users, or files on the machine. In pathological failures this may not be true, so it is always wise to back up your data and files to floppy disks or tape regularly, especially when you are experimenting.

An application that is not acting the way it was designed to will usually show one of the following failure modes.

1. *Its process will die prematurely.*   If the application is a command, the system will usually return to the shell unexpectedly. If it is a demon, **init** may try repeatedly to spawn the application. In the former case, you will not find any process associated with the application in the output from **ps**, and the application will appear to execute much more quickly than usual. In the latter case, the system will slow down dramatically, and it will usually take several minutes for any command to start, although the machine's disk will be working full time. Sometimes rebooting will repair this type of problem, but more often you will have to uninstall the application, or even remove the entry that refers to the program in **/etc/inittab**.

2. *The process will spawn many children.*   Occasionally a program will fail in such a way that it repeatedly spawns more and more child processes. You can detect this problem if the machine slows

down dramatically, and there are many more processes than usual listed in the output from **ps**. Usually these unexpected processes will all have the same parent pid, and this parent is likely to be the cause of the problem. Sometimes this type of failure results in a single stray process being created each time the offending application is run. When this happens, you will see several copies of the stray process, but the parent is usually no longer active, so the parent pid of the stray process will not be meaningful. This case is difficult to diagnose, but you can try to execute the suspected culprit and see if a new stray process results. Sometimes the TTY or STIME column of the **ps -ef** output can help you determine where or when the stray process was born.

3. *The process will consume inordinate amounts of CPU time.* Occasionally a single process will go astray and take all the CPU resources that the machine can grant it. You can detect this problem if the machine slows down noticeably, and a single process in the **ps -ef** output has accumulated a lot of CPU time, usually several minutes worth or more. If you execute **ps -ef** repeatedly, you will see that the offending process is getting almost all the CPU time in a system that might otherwise be close to idle. This problem is most difficult to detect, because you must be certain that a real-time application doesn't have legitimate use of all the CPU time. Usually timesharing processes that are running correctly will take longer to complete if they need a lot of CPU resources, but will not slow the machine noticeably.

Again, the key information for detecting process-related problems is a noticeable change in response time, or unusual disk activity that has no apparent cause. As you become more experienced with the machine, you will learn to detect changes in its performance, and with **ps** you can usually determine the source of the problem.

Killing a Process

When you detect a process that has gone astray, or if you have simply started some large job that you wish to stop before it completes, you may wish to *kill* the process. The UNIX system provides tools for killing processes, and you are allowed to kill any process that you own. The superuser can kill any processes in the system except for pids 0, 1, 2, 3, and 4; however, regular users are prohibited from killing any processes that they do not own.

You use the **kill** command with a pid as an argument to kill a process, as shown here:

```
$ kill 4314
$
```

If the kill succeeds, the process disappears from the **ps** output, and the **kill** command returns silently. Unfortunately, many things can cause **kill** to fail, so you should always check the **ps** output after you kill a process to make sure it has actually been killed. Usually, you will also want to check that the system has not immediately started the process again (with a new pid!). When you kill a process, its children may be inherited by **init**, and in this case the children will not be killed. Therefore, before killing a process you should determine whether it has children, and kill all the children at the same time as the parent. You can give multiple pid's as arguments to the **kill** command, as follows:

```
$ kill 4320 4326 4356
```

Killing processes can be dangerous, especially when you are logged in as **root**, because you may interrupt an important function in the system. Usually if you kill a process that should not have been killed, you must reboot the machine to straighten things out.

Signals

In killing a process, you are actually instructing the system to send the process a *signal.* Signals are used to communicate between processes, and many different signals can be sent. There are usually 31 signals in SVR4; the complete list is given in the **signal(5)** man page. These signals usually refer to various error conditions within the system. For example, if a process tries to access system memory outside its "authorized" memory area, the UNIX system will send it signal number 11, a memory segmentation violation. Other signals are sent when you turn off power at the terminal, when you press the DEL key, when a child process dies, and when an internal "alarm clock" goes off. It is the job of the application to respond appropriately to the signal, either by dying or by taking some remedial action so that the condition that led to the signal does not recur.

When you execute the **kill** command, by default the system sends signal 15 to the pid or pids that you've specified. This is a software termination signal that usually causes the process to die. However, the process need not honor this signal, so an unconditional kill signal is provided, which will always work immediately. Signal number 9 causes an unconditional, immediate kill of a process. You can give the signal number to the **kill** command as a flag. For instance:

```
$ kill -9 4367
```

You can also use a *logical* signal name as listed in **signal**(5) with the SIG part removed, as shown here:

```
$ kill -HUP 4369
```

Again, you must take care not to kill any process unnecessarily.

Going Further

Processes and their management can be a confusing part of the UNIX system, but careful observations of the **ps -ef** output can be very helpful in determining the cause of a problem. In addition, there are several more issues to consider with respect to processes.

Processes that Respawn

The UNIX system provides a facility to restart processes if they die. Occasionally a wayward process will automatically restart after you've killed it. If this happens, you must tell the system not to restart the application in question. The information about what processes to restart is kept in the file **/etc/inittab**. This file contains a great deal of important information, so when you change it take care not to make any mistakes. You must be superuser to change **/etc/inittab**.

You'll see a sample of a typical **/etc/inittab** file in Figure 21-5. The **/etc/inittab** file is one of the key files that supports system operation; Chapters 21 and 25 discuss it in detail. Here we will only review the issues involved in changing **/etc/inittab** to control wayward processes that respawn under control of **init**.

Note that direct changes to **inittab** such as those discussed in this section may not survive after you add or delete software packages, because this file is recreated by the kernel *build* procedures. The information presented here is for emergencies only.

The **/etc/inittab** file is a simple database in which each record is a line that has four fields, and each field is separated by the : (colon) character. The **init** program uses each line to control one process that may respawn according to rules established for the file. If field two of the record contains the digit 2 or 3 (for example, 1245 contains 2 but 145 does not), and field three contains the string *respawn,* **init** will automatically restart the process whenever it dies. The last field of the line contains the command that is executed and its arguments.

If you diagnose a problem with a specific process based on your machine's behavior and the output of **ps -ef,** and you note that the program immediately restarts when you kill it, look for the name of the program in the last field of a record in **/etc/inittab**. If the name is there, check field two of the record for a 2 or 3, and field three for the string *respawn.* If all these are present, you can turn off the offending process while you determine why it is going astray. You may lose the use of the application while it is shut off, but the rest of the system should remain available.

To turn off such an application, you can edit the file **/etc/inittab**, assuming you are logged in as **root**; simply change the contents of field three of the line of the file you are interested in from *respawn* to *off,* and then write the file and leave your editor. Now you must signal the **init** process that you have changed its instructions, so it will reread the file **/etc/inittab** for the new information. Use the command **telinit** (for tell init what to do), with the argument **q** (lowercase *Q*) to accomplish this, as shown here:

```
# telinit q
#
```

The program that is associated with the altered line in **/etc/inittab** will no longer restart automatically; however, if an instance of the program is still running, you may have to kill it manually by finding it in the **ps -ef** output, and then using **kill** with its pid as argument. The **telinit** procedure will not kill an existing process, but it will stop it from respawning.

When you are ready, it is easy to reverse this process. Simply change the contents of field three of the line in **/etc/inittab** from *off* back to *respawn,* and run **telinit q** again. Of course, you should be sure that the original problem does not return when you do this.

Why the First ps Takes Longer

To do its work, the **ps** command needs information about the in-memory executing kernel. It reads the internal process tables to build its output for each process. This is a time-consuming task, and may take 7 to 10 seconds of CPU time for a small system, and much longer for a large system that has hundreds of processes. To reduce this delay, the SVR4 **ps** command maintains a table of some of this data in the file **/etc/ps_data**, which is a binary file kept in data format suitable for **ps**. Having this intermediate data available speeds up the execution of **ps** noticeably.

Remember, however, that the kernel information in the **/etc/ps_data** table may differ after a reboot of the system, so the **ps** command may automatically rebuild the table the first time you run **ps** after a reboot, or whenever the file **/etc/ps_data** is not present. Consequently, the speed of **ps** depends on whether it has been executed recently; it may be very slow or very fast at different times. You can test this by deleting the file **/etc/ps_data** and executing **ps**. Does the file reappear?

Waiting and Defunct Processes

When a process spawns a child, it will usually wait for the child to complete before resuming its activities. Normally the login shell operates this way when you execute a command at the terminal. When the child completes, the kernel recognizes this fact and sends signal 18, death of a child process, to the parent. The parent acknowledges the death, and the system goes about its business. The scenario differs slightly when you run a process in the background with the **&** operator, because in this case the shell does not wait for the child to complete, and may not even be the parent of the background process.

If the parent of the dying child is busy doing something else, it may not acknowledge the death of the child. In that case the system refuses to let the child die a normal death, and puts the process into a *zombie* or *defunct* state, in which the process is not really dead, but neither is it executing or using any CPU time. As soon as the parent acknowledges the death of the child, the defunct process disappears from the system.

When you run **ps**, you may occasionally see a defunct process in the output, marked by *<defunct>*. This is not usually a problem, unless the defunct process lingers for an hour or more, or the number of zombie processes grows as time passes. Because the parent of the zombie must acknowledge the death of the child, the presence of defunct processes usually points to some problem with the parent. The parent is probably blocked for some reason so that it cannot act to acknowledge the death of its children. You can usually kill this wayward parent process to restore the system to sanity.

Session Groups

In studying the creation of processes in the UNIX system, you have seen that process number 1, **init**, is responsible for spawning most of the major system processes. In turn, these major processes spawn most of the children that do the real work. Your login shell is an example of such a "superparent," as are many other processes whose parent is process 1. These processes can (and often do) produce whole families of related subprocesses. These families are known as *process groups* or *sessions,* and the superparent process is the *process group leader* or *session leader.* Every parent is not a session leader, since these processes have a special status. Usually a session leader is a child of process 1, but this is not required, because a program can change its own session group without changing its ppid (for example, shells often do this during job control procedures).

The **ps** command will not display *only* session leaders, but it will display all processes that are *not* session leaders. Try **ps -df** to see all these processes. Can you tell what distinguishes the session leaders?

You can use **kill** to send a signal to all the processes in a session instead of just to a single process. For example, the command

```
$ kill 0
```

will send signal 15 to all the processes in your terminal session. Of course, you cannot kill any other sessions this way unless you are superuser.

Your login shell is usually set to ignore signal 15, the software termination signal, so **kill 0** might not have much effect unless you have some background processes running. But what if you execute **kill -9 0**, which sends all processes in your session the unconditional kill signal? When you log off the system, the system effectively uses **kill -1 0** to send the *hangup* signal to all the processes in your session. This kills all your processes unless you have made special arrangements by invoking some programs with the **nohup** command.

/proc

SVR4 includes a new directory that contains the name of each process executing in the system. This is the **/proc** directory. The contents of **/proc** change as the processes change. Use this command to list the current processes active in the machine:

```
$ ls -l /proc
total 7824
-rw-------   1 root     root          0 Apr  5 18:49 00000
-rw-------   1 root     root      77824 Apr  5 18:49 00001
-rw-------   1 root     root          0 Apr  5 18:49 00002
-rw-------   1 root     root          0 Apr  5 18:49 00003
-rw-------   1 root     root          0 Apr  5 18:49 00004
-rw-------   1 root     root     274432 Apr  5 18:49 00153
-rw-------   1 root     root     671744 Apr  5 18:49 00161
-rw-------   1 root     root     557056 Apr  5 18:49 00171
-rw-------   1 root     root     659456 Apr  5 18:49 00237
-rw-------   1 root     root     229376 Apr  5 18:49 00239
-rw-------   1 root     root     450560 Apr  5 18:49 00242
-rw-------   1 steve    other    323584 Apr  5 18:49 00243
-rw-------   1 root     root     512000 Apr  5 18:49 00245
```

```
-rw-------   1 steve   other     249856 Apr  5 18:49 06514
$
```

Actually the "files" in **/proc** are the virtual memory images of the processes active in the machine, mapped into a file system representation. The size field in the **ls** output is the actual memory size used by that process, and the time is the current time, not the time the process started. The user and group fields provide the usual information. These memory images can be accessed by debuggers and other special tools. The **/proc** innovation is very powerful, and will come into its own as the idea of memory-mapped file systems further penetrates the UNIX world, but currently **/proc** is of little value for end-users.

Real-Time Processes

In addition to the "normal" timesharing processes discussed previously, SVR4 introduces a new concept of *priority classes.* You can configure a machine to include multiple classes of processes, and the processes in each class will be executed with a *scheduling policy* specific to their class. Different classes can have different policies, making it easier to customize a machine for some special purpose like factory automation or high-performance data acquisition.

The default SVR4 configuration includes three classes: a *system* class, a *timesharing* (TS) class and a *real-time* (RT) class. The timesharing class receives the UNIX system's "normal" treatment: the system *fairly* allocates CPU time to each process so that none becomes *starved* for resources. The real-time class behaves quite differently. First, it implements a *fixed priority, preemptive* scheduling policy, which means that each process is assigned a priority, and a process with higher priority will always run before a process with lower priority. This is only true if a process is *ready,* or "wants" to run; sometimes a process is waiting for an external event like a keypress or the end of another process. In any case, *all* ready processes in the real-time class will execute before *any* process in the timesharing class. The system priority class is used only by the kernel; it is not available to users.

With this new priority capability, you can completely specify the system's behavior, although it is easy to make errors and cause the system to malfunction. Only the superuser can configure and manipulate priority classes, and this should always be done with extreme care. It is probably best to leave priority management to experts, but if you want to experiment, be prepared to reboot the machine frequently!

The **priocntl** (for priority control) command assigns processes to a priority class, and lets you manage process priorities within a class. It has several modes, corresponding to different actions you might wish to take. You must select one of these modes on each **priocntl** command line. After you've selected a mode, you can select a process or list of processes for the command.

Use the **-l** option to list the priority classes currently configured in the system, as follows:

```
$ priocntl -l
CONFIGURED CLASSES
==================
SYS (System Class)
RT (Real Time)
        Maximum Configured RT Priority: 59
TS (Time Sharing)
        Configured TS User Priority Range: -20 through 20
$
```

In addition to listing the three classes, this reveals the *ranges* available within each class for fine-tuning the relative priorities of individual processes. A lower number means that the process will have *lower* priority in the system.

Use **-d** to display the priority class of processes:

```
$ priocntl -d
TIME SHARING PROCESSES:
    PID    TSUPRILIM    TSUPRI
   6620       -1          -1
$
```

This command displays only the parameters that are associated with the **priocntl** command itself. While this is not particularly useful, it does show the output format of the **priocntl** command. Each selected process is listed by its pid, and two other columns report the execution priority of the process (TSUPRI or RTPRI) and the maximum priority allowed for TS processes (TSUPRILIM). For RT processes, the TQNTM column shows the number of clock ticks the system will allow that process to execute before transferring control to another RT process at the same (or higher) priority. Note that RT processes (if they are ready) will always run before TS processes, and that RT processes with higher RTPRI values will always run before RT processes with lower RTPRI values.

To select some of the active processes for display, add a list of processes, or use **all** to select all processes in the system. In addition, you must use the **-i** option to tell **priocntl** what format the process list is in. If you provide a list of processes, you must also specify the **-i** option. The process list is last on the command line. The **-i** option can take several different values. Use **pid** to select a list of processes by pid. The command

```
$ priocntl -d -i pid all
```

will display information for all processes in the system. Use **class** followed by RT or TS to see all the processes in the selected class, as shown here:

```
$ priocntl -d -i class RT
REAL TIME PROCESSES:
    PID    RTPRI      TQNTM
   6714      0        1000
$
```

To see all the processes associated with a named user, use **-i uid** followed by a numeric user id, as in this example:

```
$ priocntl -d -i uid 104
```

Other types are also available.

The **-s** option sets the priority class of an existing process. It uses the **-i** format as well, so you can set the priority of several processes simultaneously. Normal users can reduce the priority of their own processes, but only the superuser can increase process priority or change processes that belong to other users. In addition, **priocntl -s** can take several options that are specific to the RT or TS class, so you must take care when you use this format. For example, to change an existing TS process to a RT process, use

```
# priocntl -s -c RT 6714
```

This changes pid 6714 from a TS process to an RT process, using the default RT priority values. You can also change priorities within a class.

Finally, you can execute a new process at a specified priority level, using the **-e** option. A command line to execute follows the **priocntl** options, as shown here:

```
# priocntl -e -c RT cu -s9600 -1/dev/tty00s
```

This command line executes a **cu** command at RT class, using the default RT scheduling values. You must have superuser privileges to do anything significant with the **-s** and **-e** options.

# TWELVE

UNIX System Administration

System administration is the routine maintenance required as a system grows and changes. Adding and deleting user login ids, installing new software, cleaning up log files, formatting floppy disks, and backing up files are all tasks that fall into the category of system administration. One user of a UNIX machine is usually designated as the system administrator, and it is the administrator's job to keep the system up and running in the service of the other users. This function is vital, even in a single-user UNIX machine.

While administration chores are significantly greater on a multiuser system than they are on an MS-DOS machine, recent releases of the

UNIX system have introduced greatly improved tools that can ease these chores. Most implementations, including most SVR3 and SVR4 systems, provide a *user agent* for administration. This agent is usually a menu-oriented tool that prompts the administrator through the functions, and a lot of complicated work is done by the tool without much detailed attention from the user. Most user agents include full-screen menus and forms for data entry, with good error-checking facilities.

These tools can make running a UNIX system much easier than it has ever been before. Even experts tend to use the tools instead of the manual methods. However, most user agents are actually designed for users who understand the ideas and jargon behind the manual procedures. Although the user agents can ease a task that involves several steps, and provide lists of choices and some error-checking for each step, they do not eliminate the need for understanding the underlying concepts.

In this chapter we will review the basics of system administration, including some discussion of the user agents and some of the most commonly used administrative procedures. More detailed analyses of the individual topics introduced here are given in the following chapters. As you learn more about the UNIX system, you can delve deeper into the many options and procedures supported by the user agent. Experiment with both manual methods and the user agent to learn how to control your machine most effectively.

The Superuser

The system administrator is usually an individual user who is responsible for keeping the system running correctly. Long experience has shown that a single person can maintain system consistency much better than several users. This person becomes the contact point for other user requests, and holds final responsibility for keeping the machine running. In a small, personal UNIX machine, the owner is normally the system administrator who gives access to other users, backs up the disk files, and so on. In a multiuser system the administrator must also act as a policeman and fireman, keeping the machine sane for the benefit of other users.

The UNIX system provides a special login id, **root**, for the system administrator. The **root** id has its own password, and also has special privileges, including full access to all system files and resources; thus, the **root** login is called the *superuser*. This login id should *always* have a password, and this password should be known only by the system administrator and possibly a backup person. The **root** user has the ability to cause great damage to the system software and files, so this login should be used with care. Even if you are the system administrator, you should reserve the **root** login id for system administration tasks, and use another login id for your routine work on the machine. This provides some measure of protection, because the system will usually complain if a normal user tries to make changes that are reserved for the administrator.

The Superuser Environment

The shell provides a special PS1 prompt to remind you that you are the superuser. This is the # (pound) prompt, and it should act as a warning to remind you that you have extra access to the system.

The rest of the system environment is also very different for the **root** login id than it is for a normal user. The home directory for **root** is the **/** (slash or root) directory, and the default PATH will probably differ as well. In addition, some commands act differently when they are issued by the superuser. These differences almost always provide expanded capabilities, so all the command lines that you might use as a normal user will also work when you are **root**. The **root** login id gets profile services just as a normal user does, and you can create or change the file **/.profile** to customize the superuser environment.

On modern UNIX machines, use of the **root** login id is limited to the system console unless special arrangements are made in **/etc/default/login**, so normally you cannot use it from a remote terminal. From the console, you should log out from your normal login id and log in again as **root** when you want to do administration tasks; then immediately log off and go back to your normal login id when the administrative work is complete.

The su Command

The UNIX system also provides a tool that lets you switch your login id temporarily, without logging out. This is the **su** (for switch user or superuser) command. The **su** command is accessible from a remote terminal, so in an emergency you can log in to the machine remotely using your normal login id, and then switch to **root** with the **su** command. When you are finished, you should exit from the **su** privileges as soon as possible.

You can use **su** to change to any other login id in addition to **root**, but **root** is the default login id for **su**. You execute the **su** command like this:

```
$ su
Password:
#
```

You must enter the correct password for the **root** login id, and then the prompt will switch to the root PS1. As usual, the password is not echoed as you enter it. If you do not have the correct password, the **su** command will fail, as shown here:

```
$ su
Password:
Sorry
$
```

On some systems the **su** command requires a full pathname, as in

```
$ /sbin/su
```

Not using the full pathname can be a security risk, for reasons you'll learn in Chapter 22. It is good practice to use the full pathname whenever you execute **su**.

While the **su** command is running, you have full system administration privileges. When you wish to exit back to your normal login id, just press CTRL-D or use the **exit** command as follows:

```
$ /sbin/su
Password:
# exit
$
```

Actually, the **su** command provides a subshell on top of your normal login, and when you finish with **su** you are returned to your normal environment.

The su Environment

Invoking **su** provides a shell environment that is like your normal environment, except with **root** privileges. That is, your normal PATH is active, your home directory is the same, and so forth. To switch completely to the **root** environment, and temporarily abandon your normal environment, you can execute the **su** command with the - (minus) option, as shown here:

```
$ /sbin/su
Password:
# echo $HOME
/home/steve
# exit
$ /sbin/su -
Password:
# echo $HOME
/
# exit
$
```

In fact, the **su** command provides **.profile** services for the **root** user when the - argument is given, but does not use the **.profile** when the - is not given. This difference is sometimes confusing, so take care to use the - when you want a full **root** environment.

Switching to Another Login

You can also use **su** to change to another user instead of **root**. Just give the user id as the last command-line argument, like this:

```
$ /sbin/su - jim
Password:
$
```

As usual, you will be prompted to enter the correct password for the user you wish to change to. The - argument acts as you would expect to create that user's login environment. Also, the new PS1 for the named user will be presented rather than the #, which is reserved for **root**.

Finally, you can use **su** to execute a single command as if you were the named user. When the command completes, the superuser privilege is revoked and you are immediately returned to your normal environment. For example:

```
$ /sbin/su - root -c "chgrp sys /etc/passwd"
Password:
$
```

With this form, you must give the user id, and the command to execute must be enclosed in quotation marks. Use the - argument to get the user's environment. The **-c** (for command) argument is required before the command you wish to execute. It tells **su** to use a subshell for the command. You can use **-r** (for restricted) instead of **-c** if you want the command to execute in a *restricted shell* rather than a full shell. The restricted shell is discussed in Chapter 22.

When you are logged into the system as **root**, and you run **su** to change to another user, **su** does not prompt for the password. This is because the **root** user already has full privileges, so **su** acts without an additional password. Furthermore, if the user has not specified a password, **su** will not prompt for it. In all other cases you are required to know the correct password before you can change to another user.

The **su** command is often used to execute commands in shell scripts when special privileges are required.

Creating News and the Message of the Day

One of the system administrator's responsibilities is to create most of the system's *news*. If there are other users on the machine, it is polite to announce scheduled downtime, new software, and other current information. The **news** command is often used for this purpose, because users usually get news announcements when they log in to the machine.

Another feature that is often used for higher priority news is the **motd** (for message of the day), which is automatically displayed for each user when they log in to the machine. The system administrator can edit the file **/etc/motd** to create the message, and that is all that is required. Keep in mind that the message cannot be avoided when a user logs in to the machine, so it is best to use this feature sparingly, and delete out-of-date messages as soon as possible.

For very high-priority announcements, the **/usr/sbin/wall** (for write all) command can be used. The **wall** command reads its standard input for a message, and immediately writes the message directly to the terminal of all users who are currently logged in to the machine. This command should only be used for messages of immediate concern, such as imminent system shutdowns.

Chapter 14 covers these features in detail.

System Mail Sent to the Administrator

Many systemwide demon processes and other special administrative functions are configured to send electronic mail to the system administrator when they run. Normal **uucp** cleanup demons, printer failures, and even installation of new software cause mail messages to be created and sent to an administrator. Usually these messages are addressed to different users, depending on the sending program. For example, messages concerning the **uucp** system are sent to the user **uucp**, while messages associated with software installation are sent to the **root** user. Other messages commonly go to the **lp, adm,** and **sysadm** users.

In most cases, these are just informational messages, which report that the system took some action, but in some cases they provide useful data about partial system failures such as printer problems, or even report some types of security violations. In any case, these messages are important clues for the correct functioning of the system, and they should not be overlooked. After the machine has been up and running for a week or two, examine the contents of the mail directory **/var/mail**, and establish mail forwarding (discussed in Chapter 14) for the system logins that have received this type of mail. Normally the system administrator will forward these messages to the **root** login, or to the administrator's personal login id if **root** is not used frequently.

Again, be sure that you understand and act on these messages as they come in; they are really quite helpful in keeping the machine running correctly.

Solving Unusual Problems

After the initial configuration of the machine, the UNIX system is usually very stable. Most administrative tasks are relatively routine. The most common problem is lost files, deleted by mistake or as a result of hardware failure. Other disk-space issues also come up frequently, especially as the hard disk fills up. Printer maintenance tends to be the next most common concern, followed by managing user login ids. Electronic mail and **uucp** setup may also require increased attention as your list of mail correspondents changes. These activities should all be treated as routine tasks, not as system problems.

Other problems, although rare, can arise unexpectedly and cause the machine to malfunction. Serial ports can stop working, processes can appear or disappear unexpectedly, and all manner of gremlins can invade the system. In these cases, your first reaction should always be to reboot the machine. Amazingly, most software malfunctions in the UNIX system disappear after a reboot. If a reboot does not solve the problem, and if no hardware has obviously failed, your next response should almost always be to reload the system software (after backing up the local files!). Even experts have difficulty finding and repairing the more complex and confusing malfunctions.

System Administration User Agents

You can handle most routine system administration chores through the user agent provided by the software vendor. The standard SVR4 release provides the OA&M (for Operations, Administration, and Maintenance) system, but you must consult the specific documentation for your machine to determine how your administrative subsystem works.

Only the superuser should use these tools, though some releases of the UNIX system allow you to delegate system administration privileges to other users. Usually when you establish a new user id you can choose whether or not to give the user these powers. However, best security is maintained if only one or two users on the machine are allowed to perform administration tasks.

On most releases, the system administration tool is called **sysadm** (for system administration). If you have this command, it should be executed from the **/** (**root**) directory, the home directory for the system administrator, as shown here:

```
# cd /
# sysadm
```

If you are not logged into the machine as **root**, or your current directory is not **/**, the **sysadm** tool may not work.

Other releases may use the names **sysviz** (for visual system administration) or **adm** (for administration) instead of **sysadm**. The **sysadm** and **adm** commands are strictly for administration, but the **sysviz** menus include some user functions, such as displaying files and directories, sending mail, and executing installed applications.

These user agents are generally large menu systems with many prompts and several different subsystems for various administration chores. Although they differ substantially in appearance and details between vendors, all of them include similar functions, because all UNIX systems require the same basic administration tasks. We will review the most common functions in this chapter, but the specific prompts and menu selections on your system may differ from these examples. You can match the functions with the menu items available on your machine. Whichever user agent you have, take time to explore its features!

Table 12-1 is a list of functions that are usually available within the user agent. We will discuss these functions one by one in the following sections.

Controlling the User Agent

The standard user agent for "vanilla" SVR4 systems is the OA&M (Operations, Administration, and Maintenance) system. OA&M is in turn based on FMLI (Form and Menu Language Interpreter) tools. To use these tools, you must install the appropriate software packages.

If you have the OA&M system, after you've executed the **sysadm** command the screen will look something like Figure 12-1. The *main menu* is at the upper-left of the figure, and you can move the highlight (caret) around the menu by pressing the TAB key, or by typing the first few characters of a menu item. Menus can contain more entries than are allowed on the screen at once, so if you tab past the bottom of the menu, additional items will sometimes appear. If not, the highlight will return to the top of the menu.

Main Operation	Subfunctions
Backup and restore	Backup history
	Schedule backup
	Personal backup
	System backup
	Personal restore
	System restore
Disk operations	Add device
	Remove device
	Erase disk
	Floppy-to-Floppy copy
	Format disk
File system operations	Check file system
	Create file system
	Display disk usage
	Find files
	List mounted file systems
	Mount file system
	Unmount file system
Networking	**uucp** management (mail)
	Distributed file system configuration
	Network addresses of machines
Printer operations	Printer setup
	Filters setup
	Forms setup
	Printer restart
	Printer status
	Remote printing
Schedule jobs	Add
	Delete
	Display schedule
Service access facility	Port monitors
	Port services
	Terminal setup
Software management	Check
	Install
	Remove
	Display
	Application dependent

Table 12-1. Administration Functions in Most SVR4 User Agents

Main Operation	Subfunctions
System configuration	Display configuration
	Machine name
	Date and time
	Root password
	Reboot
	Shutdown
	List users
User Logins	Add
	Delete
	Display
	Reset passwords
	Set defaults

Table 12-1.   Administration Functions in Most SVR4 User Agents (*continued*)

At the bottom of the screen is a row of labels that assign functions to the first eight function keys on the keyboard. For example, F1 is the Help key. Pressing it at any point brings up a short text description in a

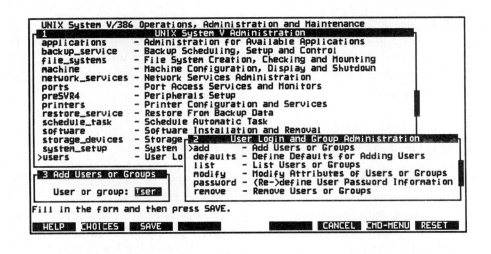

Figure 12-1.   Sample screen from the OA&M administrative user agent

window. You dismiss the Help window by pressing the Cancel (F6) key. F6 is used to dismiss all windows except the main menu.

To exit the OA&M system and return to the shell, press CMD-Menu (F7). This brings up a menu of commands. Select Exit to return to the shell. The other function keys offer additional functions, but a key label is not present on the screen unless that function is currently available.

You can select an item when it is highlighted on the main menu by pressing the save or enter (F3) key. Although the newline on the keyboard may work, F3 is the correct way to select menu items or save the contents of forms. When an item is selected, the system presents a submenu or a form, depending on the current function. The new windows will appear on top of the main menu, as shown at the lower-right section of Figure 12-1.

At the bottom of the series of menus, there will usually be a form with fields for information such as user name, directory or device name, and so on. You can move between fields on the form by pressing TAB, but some fields require an entry, and you must fill in those items before you can continue. Usually, the system will prompt you with instructions or error messages on the last line of the screen, just above the row of key labels.

Forms often have a prespecified set of items that a field will accept. In this case, the choices (F2) key will be available. If you can press F2, and select an item off that menu, it will be entered into the current field. You can see a simple (one-item!) form at the lower-left of Figure 12-1. To make the system take action on a form, press F3; to dismiss the form and abandon the work in progress, press F6.

There are usually several more functions available in the OA&M system, and other user agents may differ in their functions and user interface. You should experiment on your own system to get a feel for its capabilities.

When In Doubt, Take the Default Values

The majority of user agents provide access to most of the UNIX system's complexity, and there are often many menu items and forms associated with each function. On the other hand, these forms and menus usually provide defaults for most of the data. If you do not understand the exact meaning and use of these data items, it is best to let the system choose them for you. In the following discussion, we assume that unmentioned data items will default to correct values.

Handling Floppy Diskettes

The entry marked Storage Devices or Disk Operations is intended for *media management,* for formatting and copying floppy disks.

Usually you create a usable floppy disk by *formatting* it, creating a *file system* on it, and then *mounting* the disk at a location in the file system. After all these steps have been accomplished, the floppy disk can be used just like a normal directory. You can **mv** or **cp** files to the disk, change the modes of the files, or use the directory pathname in your commands and shell scripts. When you are through with the disk, you can *unmount* it and remove it from the floppy drive. In addition, there is a second mode of accessing disks, which is used for the *backup* and *restore* functions. Chapter 18 discusses media in detail.

Formatting Floppy Disks

Select the appropriate option from the Storage Devices menu to format a floppy disk. The system will format both 3 1/2-inch and 5 1/4-inch disks if your machine has the correct drives, and you can usually select the *density* of the disk (usually 1.4MB and 1.2MB, respectively). You will be prompted to insert the floppy and close the drive door before the procedure starts. You cannot format *write-protected* disks, so be sure that the tab has been removed from the notch in the diskette before you insert it in the drive.

Usually the system will provide some error messages if the format operation fails for any reason. If it fails once, try the format again, but if it fails after two tries, you should probably discard the diskette. Diskettes are always cheaper than the data stored on them; don't take chances with bad floppies!

To erase a disk, just reformat it.

Making a File System on a Formatted Diskette

After formatting a diskette, you must create a file system on the floppy before it can be mounted. If you are using a floppy for backup, you do not need a file system; the format step alone is sufficient. However, if you wish to use the floppy like a normal directory within the file system, you must add a file system to the formatted disk. This procedure is handled in the File Systems menu. Insert the formatted disk, and then select the Create File System option from the user agent.

In SVR4, you must select a *file system type*. The choice is not important if you always mount disks through the user agent, but the **ufs** type is preferable to **s5** unless you plan to mount the disk on SVR3 or older systems, which require the **s5** type.

After you've selected the type, you must specify the number of *blocks* for the new disk. If you have no default value from the user agent, use the capacity of the disk divided by 512. For example, a 1.2MB disk will have 1440 blocks available. If you choose a value that is too large for the disk, the operation will fail, and if you choose a value that is too small, the extra space will be unusable.

You will also be prompted to enter the file system name, which determines the place in the file system where the diskette will appear when it is mounted. This means you can **cd** to that directory to access the contents of the floppy. Mounted diskettes are treated just as normal directories are; each one has a place in the file system when it is mounted. When a diskette is unmounted it disappears from the file system. Usually the floppy disk will be at the directory location **/install** or **/mnt**, and any files or subdirectories of this directory will be on the floppy. You can use any directory location you wish, but if it doesn't already exist you must create it.

You can also *label* a diskette if you wish to provide some identification for the floppy, but this is not required. The label can be up to six characters long. In addition, some releases require you to choose the maximum number of files and directories allowed on the disk. Usually the default is sufficient.

After you've started the Create File System option, do not remove the diskette from the drive until the system prompts you to do so. Many systems will automatically mount the diskette as part of the file system creation.

Mounting a Diskette

In addition, you can mount a diskette whenever you wish to use it; however, the disk must have a file system before it can be mounted. The mount option is usually in the File Systems menu. Once the disk is mounted, you can exit from the user agent, use normal commands to refer to the disk under its directory location (usually **/install** or **/mnt**), and use it as you would any normal directory. To unmount the disk before removing it from the drive, you must reenter the system administration tool. You can seriously damage the contents of a disk if you remove it without first unmounting it.

When you mount a disk, you have to specify the file system type that you selected when the disk was created. You must get this correct, but many systems will detect the file system type and mount the disk correctly for you.

You must also give the location where the contents of the disk will appear. This will usually be the file system name that you specified when you created the file system on the floppy, but you can mount a disk at a different *mount point* if you wish.

You can usually choose to mount a disk as *read-only* or both readable and writable. If you mount the disk as read-only, you cannot change any of the files on the disk, but you can use write-protected disks. On the other hand, the diskette must be write-enabled if you mount it with read and write access.

When you first mount a disk after creating the file system, it will be empty. Files or subdirectories that you create in the directory at the mount point will be on the disk, and they will appear again at the mount point the next time you mount the diskette. If you change the mount point for a subsequent mount, the files will appear under the new mount point, rather than the old one. To copy a file to the floppy from the hard disk, you can use the **cp** or **mv** command, but the **ln** command will not work.

To unmount a diskette, you have to name the device or mount point you used to create it. You have to get this correct, or you might unmount some important system files! Before unmounting, you must also exit from any application that may be using files on that disk, and **cd** out of any directory at or below the mount point. That is, the disk must be completely idle before it can be unmounted.

Copying a Floppy Disk

You can copy a floppy disk from the Storage Devices menu. Before copying, you must have a formatted disk with the same format as the source disk. Be sure to format the new disk first. You do not need to make a file system on the disk you are copying to, because the tool will copy the file system from the source disk.

The disk copying tool first prompts you for the drive to use, (usually *diskette1* or *diskette2*), and then tells you to insert the original disk. Next, it reads the disk and prompts you to remove it. Finally, it prompts you to insert the new disk, and completes the copy.

You can usually make multiple copies of the same source disk. The user agent will prompt you to insert another formatted blank disk after a copy is completed.

The copy will be a complete and exact copy of the source disk, with all file systems, directories, and time stamps preserved. You can copy mountable, backup, or bootable disk formats without trouble.

Disk Backup and Restore

The backup and restore options are used to back up the system files and directories from the machine's hard disk to a removable disk or tape. This can save your valuable data when the hard disk finally fails, or if you delete some important file by mistake. Normally you should take care to keep your backups current with your use of the system. Backups cannot be performed too often, and the risk of losing your valuable data as a result of a system failure is *never* acceptable. Failures may be rare, but they always seem to occur at the most inconvenient times. *Back up your data early and often.*

Four backup procedures are usually supported. First is a *full backup*, which can be performed soon after you install the system software. Second, you can do regular, smaller *incremental backups* to save only the files that have changed since the last backup. You must do a full backup before an incremental backup is allowed. Third, you can usually do a *personal backup*, which saves all the files within a specific home directory. Finally, you can usually configure a *selective backup* to save a list of files from anywhere in the file system. In addition, you can usually get a display of the *backup history* for the machine. This tells you when the last backups were performed, and what was included.

Backups are often made onto a floppy disk, or a series of disks if necessary. You can use magnetic tape instead of disks if your machine has a tape unit. Be sure you have enough formatted disks or tapes on hand to complete the backup, because the backup procedure will prompt you to change disks when one is full. Format a large number of disks before beginning the backup procedure; you will soon learn how many diskettes you need to back up the specific files you select. Some releases will compute the approximate number of disks required, but this can be a time-consuming process.

You should carefully mark each disk with its sequence number immediately after removing it from the drive, because disks must be inserted in the same order when you restore their contents to the machine's hard disk.

When you do a system backup, you must usually select the individual file system to back up from a list of available file systems. The list will vary depending on your configuration and on how many hard disks are installed in the machine. Back up each file system separately, since the fewer diskettes you use in a backup, the less the chance there is of a floppy going bad and causing problems in restoring the data. You can usually bypass a bad floppy when you restore the files, but this procedure can be prone to problems. When a disk goes bad, some data will always be lost. It is better to do multiple, short backups than large infrequent backups.

The first time, you have to do a full backup. On subsequent occasions, you can do incremental backups, but do not reuse your original set of disks from the full backup. In addition to your files, a full backup copies all the system files, so you should have a large pile of formatted floppy disks before you start a full backup, which can take as many as 40 1.2MB floppies in a typical system. Finally, you must select the device to use for the backup, and the device must match the floppy disks that you have.

You can also back up a specific list of files and directories. After selecting the appropriate menu item, usually Selective Backup, you can enter a list of files and directories to store in the backup. You can edit the list, add to it, or display it at any time. When you specify a directory name, all of that directory's files and subdirectories will be included in the list. When you are satisfied with the list, you can back up the files.

Again, the backup may overflow onto additional disks, so be sure you have enough formatted disks on hand before you begin.

Restoring Files from Backup

Should it become necessary to restore the backed up data, select the Restore Service option. You will be prompted to load the disks in the order they were created. Be sure to select the same device that you used when you made the backups.

In case of a catastrophic system failure, you can recover an exact image of your system at the time of the last backup. To do so, reload the system software from the original floppy disks, restore your full backup, and then restore each incremental backup in the order in which it was created. Although this is a time-consuming procedure, it can guarantee the integrity of your system; however, experienced system administrators usually back up their data directory by directory, using manual procedures or the selective backup procedures in the administrative user agent. This method is usually much faster, and it requires many fewer floppy disks. Unfortunately, the manual procedures are more difficult to work with than the user agent.

Displaying Hard Disk Usage

Most user agents provide a tool for displaying the amount of disk space used on the system's hard disk and on any file systems that are mounted when the command is executed. This is usually part of a System Information prompt, or it may be in the File Systems subsystem.

The disk space is usually listed as megabytes of free space, with the total space available also given. The numbers are often expressed in a percentage as well, and some systems list the space in 512-byte blocks within the file system.

The disk usage data is very important in managing your system. Normal operations of the UNIX system require some temporary files that may demand disk space without warning, and then free the space soon after. If your system has less than ten percent free space, your disk may fill up unexpectedly, and when this happens the system can fail.

Disks always tend to fill up over time, so you should examine the disk usage data regularly and take steps to back up and delete unnecessary files when the occupied disk space approaches 90 percent.

Setting the Date and Time

The user agent also provides a tool for setting the system's clock/calendar hardware. This is usually called Date and Time or datetime, and is often part of the System Setup menu. The UNIX system uses the current time in many ways, and you should keep the system time correctly set. Many small computers do not keep good time, even with built-in clock hardware, so you should regularly examine the system time, and reset it if it is more than a few minutes off. Be sure the time zone and the daylight-saving time prompts are answered correctly.

Shutting Down the Machine

The user agent often includes an option for shutting down the machine. The UNIX system differs from MS-DOS and other single-tasking operating systems in this area. You should *never* simply turn off the power to the machine while it is running, because damage to the files on the hard disk can result. *Always* use the shutdown procedure in the administrative user agent, or execute the **shutdown** command while you are logged in to the machine as **root**.

Before starting the shutdown procedure, check to be sure no critical operation is in progress. Once it starts, the shutdown procedure will warn other users that the machine is about to be shut off, and give them time to log out. Then it will bring the machine down cleanly to a point where you can turn off the power. When you see the message

```
Reboot the system now.
```

or

```
Reset the CPU to reboot.
```

you can turn off the power, but *not before* the message is displayed. Boot and shutdown are discussed in detail in Chapter 21.

Adding and Removing User Login Ids

The Users menu is used to add or delete users' login ids from the system. Every user should have an individual login id; users should not share login ids. This is important both for system security and to keep users from damaging each other's files by mistake. However, all users can be in the same group if you wish, or they can belong to different groups. Recall that groups are used in the middle set of permissions for file access, as shown in the output from **ls -l**.

When you create a new login id, you should give the user a starting password, which they can change when they log in to the system. In addition, when users leave the machine permanently, you should immediately remove or disable their login ids to prevent security problems from occurring later.

The Users menu may include many options, but generally only a few are used regularly. List displays information associated with the users known to the system. You can add a new user with Add, and delete a user id with Remove.

To add a new user to the system, you must enter the login id and the user's name. The login id must be different from any other id on the machine, and the user agent will test to see whether your entry is unique. Most users wish to select their own login id, so you should consult the user before you add the id. Be sure you enter the user's name correctly in the *Comments* field, because it may be used by some software that can read it from the **/etc/passwd** file where it is stored.

On many systems you must also select the user's *id number* and *group name,* which are representations of the user and group ids, and are used by much system software. It is almost always best to let the system choose these, because this guarantees there will be no errors. On some systems, you are not asked to select these ids, and you cannot change the defaults. The default puts all normal users into the same group, which is usually fine for small systems. Only if you have more than one distinct interest group among your users should you explicitly select a group, and in this case you must create a new group using the Add Group option if you have it, or by manually editing **/etc/group**. Groups are discussed in Chapter 22.

Next you must select the pathname for the user's home directory. Again, unless there is some special reason not to, you should let the system select and create the home directory.

Often you can assign an *expiration date* for a login. This is recommended for temporary users, but your regular users may become annoyed if their login id magically disappears one day.

Finally, you may be able to grant system administration privileges to the new user. If these are granted, the user will have access to the administrative user agent, and will be able to add or change login ids and grant system administration privileges to other users. Because this is a security risk, it is usually preferable to limit system administration privileges to a very short list of trusted users.

When you add a new user, you must usually assign password information. You can set up *password aging* data that requires users to change their password periodically. You can specify a minimum and maximum interval (in days) that the password is acceptable. A minimum of a few days and a maximum of 180 days are good choices. *Never* create a login id with no password; assign a beginning password to each user, and request that the user change it as soon as possible. If you set the password status to *lock,* the user cannot log in; this is probably not your intention.

After all this material is entered, the system echoes the information back and gives you the option to install the user or cancel the operation. Do not install the entry if there are any errors, because this can introduce security risks into the system.

The other options on the Users menu act similarly. To remove a login id, select Remove. The Modify option allows you to change the attributes of a current login without requiring you to remove and re-create the login id. The Password menu lets you change a user's password or lock a user out of the system temporarily without removing all their files and directories. Then you can change the password once more, allowing the user to log in again. Select the lock option in Password Status to do this. Be sure to reenable or delete the login id as soon as the status changes.

Installing Software Packages

Tools are usually provided to install application software packages into the system and to remove them from it. These tools usually reside under the Software menu.

Not all add-on software will be supported, because the application developer must make the application fit within the scheme. However, if an add-on software package is compatible, you can install it, remove it, and list its attributes. Follow the installation instructions that came with the application software.

The Package Location item selects the source of the package to install. The spool entry is used if the package was delivered by electronic mail, but usually you will want *Ntape1* or *diskette1* for cartridge tape or a floppy disk, respectively.

In addition, you can usually list installed packages, check packages for some types of internal consistency and for accuracy of installation, and remove installed packages. Chapter 25 provides more information about software installation and system configuration.

Setting the Machine Name

You can change the *nodename*, or *uname* (for UNIX name) of the machine from the System Setup menu. The uname is the identifying name for the machine. This value must be unique, at least within the *domain* of machines that you communicate with via **mail**. Once the name is chosen, it is not easy to change because the remote machines that send you mail all have to change as well. Select a nodename when you first install the system, and stick with it. Do not allow your machine to keep its default nodename, which is definitely *not* unique.

If your user agent includes a Mail Setup option, the entry for Mail Name of this System changes the uname. Otherwise, the option will be in the System Setup menu.

The machine name should have eight or fewer characters, and begin with a lowercase letter (a through z). Numbers can be used after the first character, but you should avoid special characters.

Mail Setup

Along with the uname of *this* machine, you can also specify information about other machines that will be sending you electronic mail. At installation, the SVR4 system is usually configured such that the system will refuse incoming mail from unknown machines. Thus, if your machine is attached to a modem and phone line, you must list all the machines you expect to send you mail. Alternatively, you can examine Chapter 15, and then configure your system to relax this restriction if you have correspondents on unknown machines.

In general, you must distinguish machines that use modems (and phone lines) or direct connections from those that are connected via a LAN. Here we will discuss adding machines that might contact you via phone lines; consult your network administrator for more information about LAN access. In some systems, these functions are divided between a Mail Setup menu item and a separate Network Services menu. In other releases, the mail configuration is part of a Basic Networking menu item under the Network Services menu.

To send mail between your machine and another machine, you must inform the UNIX system of the unique name of each remote machine you wish to contact (or that will contact you). You must give the login id and password for data communications access, which you get from the system administrator of each machine. Finally, you must instruct your machine about how to call the other machine, including the *device* and the communications speed to use. You can also restrict calling to some hours of the day or days of the week, if you wish. You cannot send mail to another system if you have not set this data correctly, though sometimes other systems can call you even though you cannot call them.

The login id that other machines use to call you when they wish to send you mail is usually **nuucp** (for new uucp), and you should not change it unless you have a very specific reason. You can specify whether the **nuucp** login id will have a password. Because the data communication tools contain excellent internal security, you usually do not need a password here, and you should probably not specify one. If you do, any machine that sends you mail must know the password. Thus, you are effectively putting a password on the login id, and then immediately distributing the password to all your friends (and usually to their friends). It is better not to have a password on the **nuucp** login id, unless you have a very specific reason to restrict mail to a short list of machines. Some releases may not allow you to change this login id or password through the user agent.

The Add System menu usually prompts you for the unique uname of the other system, for its login (usually **nuucp**), and for the password associated with that login id, if it has one.

If the connection will be made via a modem and dial-up telephone line, you will need to know the telephone number. It is the telephone number that connects to the dial-up modem on the other machine.

Associated with each system is a device for calling that machine. Usually you will choose between *modem* and *direct*. After you make this choice, you must select the type of modem in use for that device.

Some user agents only support adding systems that can be called via a telephone line (modem device), and in this case you cannot add systems that are accessible over a LAN or direct connection. Other user agents support the selection of several different connection methods in addition to dial-up calls. The connection control tools in the data communications subsystems are very powerful, and can quickly get confusing. You should review Chapter 15 before adding systems that use any connection method other than dial-up calls.

Next you must select the data communications speed for the link. Your modem must be capable of the same speed as the modem at the other machine, or you will not be able to communicate with it. Most dial-up modems can be set for 300, 1200, or 2400 bps. Consult the system administrator at the remote machine to agree on a communications speed.

When you select a device, you must specify which *port* the device is attached to. This is usually **/dev/tty00s** or **/dev/tty01s**. Some user agents will expect you to enter the device without the leading **/dev/** part; experiment with your system to be sure.

You can usually restrict calls to specific days or times of day. That is, the data communications software will only call the other machine when permitted. This feature forces electronic mail to be sent when the remote machine is available, or during late-night hours when the work load and the telephone rates are low. You can also specify *Never*, which means that the other machine must call you to pick up mail queued for that machine. If you want quick delivery of your electronic mail to the other machine, do not restrict calling times. This menu entry does not prevent other machines from calling you during the restricted hours.

Several other options are usually available on the Basic Networking or Mail Setup menu, including polling and other features. Examine Chapter 15 before trying most of these.

Scheduling Automatic Tasks

The Schedule Task menu allows you to set up jobs that are executed regularly at specific times on specific days of the week or year. Usually, you create a task as a shell script and test it carefully before scheduling it. Then the scheduling form allows you to select the times and days that you wish the task to run. Give the full pathname of your shell script in the Task field. If the machine is down when the scheduled time arrives, that time is skipped.

Scheduling can be error-prone, especially if you move or delete the script without removing the task from the schedule. Be sure to test your scripts *carefully* before you schedule them. In addition, some users may be prohibited from scheduling jobs. Examine Chapter 20 for more information on scheduling in the UNIX system.

Printer Management

The UNIX system includes a powerful *print spooler* that manages the printers installed on the system. You can send output to any installed printer by giving the name of the printer when you want to print a job. To install a printer, you must give it a name, assign it to a parallel or serial port, and specify the printer type. Most SVR4 systems will allow you to name a printer attached to another machine that your machine can contact, either by mail or on a LAN.

Once a printer is installed, you can manage the *queue* of jobs waiting to be printed, delete jobs from the queue before they are printed, change the printer on which a job is destined to print, and remove a printer from service.

Installing a Printer

The Printer Services menu allows you to install a new printer on either a *parallel* (i.e., LPT1 or LPT2) or *serial* (i.e., COM1 or COM2) port. A specific printer can only attach to one or the other type of port. The device files associated with these physical ports are listed in Table 13-1. (Printing is discussed in detail in Chapter 13, and you should examine that chapter before you install a new printer.)

First, you must select a name for the printer. This is used in print requests to specify which printer will receive your job. The printer type must also be given. Usually a large list of known printers is included in the menu, and you can select your printer from the list. If your printer is not on the list, try the entry for dumb. If none of the listed printers work, you will need to set up the printer manually.

Together, the name and type define various *defaults,* or standard settings for other attributes of the printer. You can accept the defaults or change them through additional submenus. Usually you will only see the submenus if you reject the defaults in the main Printer menu. Experiment with changing these attributes carefully; a printer will often stop working if the attributes set in the **lp** system conflict with the printer itself.

One of the defaults for serial printers is the communication speed. Be sure to set the switches on the printer correctly for the communication speed you select in the menu. Parallel printers do not use a communication speed selection.

You must enter the *device* used for that printer, which is a full pathname of the form **/dev/lp0**. Be sure to enter the correct device name from Table 13-1 that corresponds to the port where the printer is attached.

Finally, you must name one printer as the *system default*. Jobs with no printer name will be printed on that machine. Only one printer can be the system default.

Unless you have a special reason to use them, it is best to ignore the Filters and Forms menus until you understand their purpose.

The Printer menu often contains an entry to establish a remote printer attached to another machine on a LAN as a destination for printing. Consult your network administrator before trying to configure a remote printer since network policy determines how remote printing is used. Also, you can usually select a printer that is accessible by a dial-up link. In the Basic Networking Address field, give a remote name that is known to your **cu** system. Usually this will be a standalone printer with an autoanswer modem, not the **lp** service on another UNIX system.

Managing an Existing Printer

Once a printer is installed and running, you can send output to it with the **lp** command. Several jobs may be queued at once, and the **lp** system will manage the spool correctly.

The Printer Operations menu includes options for looking at the current spool of unprinted jobs, and you can usually delete an unwanted job from the spool through the Printer Requests or Printer Queue menu item.

The Printer Status menu lists the printers configured into the **lp** system, and reports whether they are currently accepting requests for printing. This means that you can add new jobs to the print queue, even though the printer might not be actually printing them. If the printer runs out of paper, or its power is turned off then turned on again, it will no longer print, but will be listed as accepting requests; there may be several jobs on the print spool, but the printer will be idle. When this happens, you must restart the printer with the Printer Restart or Enable option in the Printer Operations menu. When you restart the printer, it should immediately begin printing if any jobs are queued. If a printer is listed as not accepting requests, you may need to remove and then reinstall the printer in the Peripherals Setup menu to get it working. Most SVR4 systems include an Accept menu item that lets a printer accept jobs, even though it may not be enabled. A printer must be both enabled and accepting requests to function normally.

Network Services

In addition to printing, you can usually configure other network services, such as access to remote files and net addressing parameters, through the administrative user agent. Again, the best procedure is to consult your network administrator before venturing into this area. Incorrect network setup caused by experimentation can have a detrimental effect on the overall performance of your network. Once you understand the configuration of your LAN, you can use the networking menu items to configure your machine on the net.

You may need to establish *services* as part of network configuration. If so, these are usually included under the Service Access Facility, discussed next.

Port Management

Finally, the most difficult topic in the administrative user agent is ports or peripherals setup. This task may be distributed across several menu items in some versions, or it may be collected under one menu item. The major tasks involved are *terminal setup, port monitors,* and *port services.* Some systems include options for setting up other peripheral devices such as a second hard disk or tape drives. This menu item will usually change when you add new hardware devices to your machine, so that you can administer the new devices.

The configuration of ports is completely new in SVR4, and most older information about **getty** processes is no longer applicable. The new organization is called the *Service Access Facility,* for it provides a general concept of service for all types of ports that allow incoming calls. This includes serial ports that may be connected to a modem or to hard-wired terminals, and also high-performance ports that may be attached to a LAN. Ports that are only outgoing, such as printer ports, do not have services associated with them.

You must establish an entry in the system for each type of port you wish to use for incoming calls. Serial ports and LAN ports are the most common, but many other types of incoming connections are allowed. Each type of port has its own *listener* or *port monitor* to handle incoming calls. These port monitor processes can listen for traffic on more than one port simultaneously. For example, several serial ports can be monitored by a single monitor process, called **ttymon** (for tty monitor) in SVR4. You must tell the port monitor which ports to listen to, and what to do when a call arrives.

When a call does appear on a port, the call is "answered" by the monitor, which then executes the appropriate service for that call; then the port monitor steps out of the picture until the call ends and the service returns control to the monitor to listen for the next call.

You must establish all these procedures through the Port Management menu item.

Quick Terminal Setup

The simplest way to add services on serial ports is through the Quick Terminal Setup menu. This item will handle all the complexity of monitors and services, but it is very limited and can only deal with the simple setup of serial ports. With it, you can select the port to add based on the ports that are configured in your system, and choose the speed for that port. You should choose the highest speed possible. For example, if a 1200 or 2400 bps modem is attached to the port, select a speed of 2400. Calls that arrive at a lower speed will also be accepted if the incoming caller sends a *break* signal before logging in. For directly connected terminals, 9600 is usually a good choice. The Quick Terminal Setup menu cannot configure the port for computers that are connected directly.

Port Monitor Management

The complete setup procedure allows more flexibility, but it is also more complex. The first step is to establish port monitors. Each port monitor has a name, or *tag*, to identify it. You can choose this name, but it should describe the type of port. For best results, use the same name as the port monitor type. The port monitor type is usually **ttymon** for a serial port, **inetd** for an Ethernet link, or **listen** for a StarLan link. The associated command is the pathname to execute for this monitor: **/usr/lib/saf/ttymon** for serial ports, **/usr/sbin/inetd** for Ethernet, and **/usr/lib/saf/listen** for StarLan. Consult your particular documentation for other types of ports supported under SAF.

You can also select whether the monitor should be *started*, and whether it should be *enabled*. You can usually stop port monitors through another menu item if necessary, so it is easier to start the monitors immediately. Then, add a comment that describes the monitor, and save the screen. The new monitor should be in service.

As with printer services, if the monitor does not appear to be working you must verify that it is both started and enabled. Use the List Port Monitors menu item to check these conditions.

If you select a Terminal Setup or LAN Setup menu item instead of Port Setup, the **sysadm** package will start the correct port monitor for you; then you can list the existing monitors to get a feel for what the correct data items will be.

Port Service Management

Once the port monitor is running, you must select the specific ports that it will cover, and the name of the command or service that will be executed when an incoming call arrives. Often you must specify several communications parameters and *flags* as part of the setup process. These determine the specific behavior of the port when it answers calls. The Port Services menu handles these chores. Start with this menu by entering the tag you used in the previous step to name the port monitors; this selects the monitor to which you will add new services. Then, give a new tag for the service, and assign a login id (the *service invocation identity*) that will execute the service. This will be **root** in almost every case, since most services such as login switch to the correct id as needed. Again, you must enable the service, and make a descriptive comment for later use.

At this point you may jump to a second form, which includes the real data for the service. This form will probably differ depending on the port monitor. You must always select the port id by giving the full pathname of the device in the **/dev** directory. This will be **/dev/tty00s** or **/dev/tty01s** for serial ports one and two, respectively. Other port types and network connections will have different device paths.

For serial ports, you must select the *label* for the terminal configuration information. Usually you can select the label that corresponds to the highest speed of the device attached to that port. For example, use 9600 or 19200 for a directly connected terminal or computer, and 2400 or 1200 for a modem. These are names in the **/etc/ttydefs** file, discussed later in this chapter. Many other possible labels are usually available, but these are for special needs. The system will *cycle* to a lower speed when an incoming call does not match the label, so a setting of 2400 will accept both 2400 and 1200 bps calls.

Next, you must select the *service command* that will handle the call. This will usually be **/usr/bin/login**, since the login service uses the **/etc/passwd** file and thus provides the best password protection. Select bidirectional if you wish to share the port between incoming login calls and outgoing **uucp** or **mail** traffic. Accept the default values in the rest of the fields.

When you save this screen, the port should be available for incoming calls. If it is not, be sure the speed (label) is correct, and that you have started the monitor and enabled the service.

Going Further

UNIX system administration can be a complex topic, and the rest of the chapters in this book address it in one way or another. As your understanding of the UNIX system grows, you will find that the administrative user agent is quite helpful in many situations. Stick with the automated tools where possible, because they are less prone to error than manual methods. Use manual methods for increased speed or other special needs.

The uname Command

The user agent provides tools for setting the machine's unique identifying name, or *uname*. In addition, a regular command called **uname** is available for reporting or setting the uname from the shell. It looks like this:

```
$ uname
my_sys
$
```

By default, **uname** displays the system name only. Use the **-a** (for all) option to display other information about the machine, as shown here:

```
$ uname -a
my_sys my_sys 4.0 1 i386 386/AT
$
```

The six items displayed in this output are the system name; a *node-name*, which may differ from the system name if the machine is a server on some types of network; the operating system release number (4.0); the version number of that release; the type of CPU the machine uses (i386); and finally, the machine type. The **uname** command also has options to display any one of these items alone, and it is often used in shell scripts whose behavior depends on some of this data.

The **uname** command can also be used by the superuser to set the system's name. Use the **-S** (for set) option to set the machine name, followed by the new name you wish to use. For example:

```
# uname -a
my_sys my_sys 4.0 1 i386 386/AT
# uname -S steve
# uname -a
steve steve 4.0 1 i386 386/AT
#
```

Remember, other machines may be using your **uname** to send you electronic mail, so take care to inform them when you change your machine's name.

More on Terminal Modes

Like all the tools in the administrative user agent, the Ports menus have analogues in manual procedures. Whenever a communications port is enabled to accept incoming calls, a monitor process is listening to the port. This process is called **/usr/lib/saf/ttymon** (for tty monitor), and it waits for the *carrier detect signal* on a list of RS232 ports. When the signal is asserted on a line, **ttymon** sets that line to some initial **stty** values (the *initial line settings*), and then turns control over to the **login** program, which prints **login:** for the user. When the user finishes the session and logs out, **ttymon** wakes up and begins listing for another login.

The line settings, which **ttymon** reads to determine how to set up the RS232 port, are stored in the file **/etc/ttydefs** (for tty definitions). In SVR4, the **ttydefs** file replaces the older **gettydefs** equivalent, but the **gettydefs** file may still be present in some releases. The **/etc/ttydefs** file consists of a series of line settings, one per line of the **ttydefs** file. Here are two sample lines from the **ttydefs** file:

```
9600: 9600 opost onlcr tab3 ignpar ixon ixany parenb istrip echo echoe
echok isig cs7 cread : 9600 opost onlcr sane tab3 ignpar ixon ixany
parenb istrip echo echoe echok isig cs7 cread ::4800
4800: 4800 opost onlcr tab3 ignpar ixon ixany parenb istrip echo echoe
echok isig cs7 cread : 4800 opost onlcr sane tab3 ignpar ixon ixany
parenb istrip echo echoe echok isig cs7 cread ::2400
```

These are actually only two very long lines, even though they have more than 80 characters each, and print on multiple lines. Each line contains five separate fields, delimited by a : (colon). The first field is the name of the line setting. These two lines are called 9600 and 4800 respectively. The next field consists of all the initial **stty** values for that setting, and the third field contains the final **stty** values. The initial values are used on the line when the call is answered and until **ttymon** executes the login service; the final values are set just before the login service is started. The distinction between the two is subtle, and usually the same values appear in both fields. Each **stty** parameter has a name, and these names are separated by whitespace within the field. The fourth field is blank.

The last field is the name of another **ttydefs** line setting. If **ttymon** detects a break signal on the line before the user responds to the **login:** prompt, it will cycle to the line setting in the last field, and try again with that setting. This cycling can continue as long as breaks are received. This feature allows a single incoming tty port to receive calls at several different speeds or **stty** values, without constant intervention by the administrator. If you don't want the port to cycle to a new line setting, you can use the name in the first field again in the fifth field, which causes **ttymon** to reuse the same setting after a break signal.

Starting a Port Monitor

Port monitors such as **ttymon**, which controls login on serial ports, are managed from the **/usr/lib/saf/sac** (for service access controller) process. This process starts at boot time and should always be running. The **sac** demon consults the file **/etc/saf/_sactab** (for service access controller table) for a list of monitors to manage, as shown here:

```
# cat /etc/saf/_sactab
# VERSION=1
inetd:inetd::0:/usr/sbin/inetd#internet daemon
ttymon:ttymon::0:/usr/lib/saf/ttymon #
#
```

The content of each line is the key data from the Port Monitor setup menu in the user agent. You can interpret these fields with the **sacadm** (for sac administration) command, as follows:

```
# sacadm -l
PMTAG     PMTYPE   FLGS RCNT   STATUS     COMMAND
inetd     inetd     -    0     ENABLED    /usr/sbin/inetd #internet daemon
ttymon    ttymon    -    0     ENABLED    /usr/lib/saf/ttymon #
#
```

The -l (for list) option lists the currently active monitors.

The **sacadm** command is the actual program that gets executed by the user agent to reconfigure the port monitors. It has many options. You can use **sacadm** to start and stop port monitors, reconfigure the **_sactab**, and take other actions.

Starting a Service Within a Port Monitor

After a port monitor is configured, it will read the file **/etc/saf/pmtag/_pmtab** (for port monitor table), where the *pmtag* is the tag used to name the port monitor. Like the **_sactab**, the **_pmtab** contains a list of services under the control of its port monitor. Here is an example:

```
# cat /etc/saf/ttymon/_pmtab
# VERSION=1
00s:u:root:reserved:reserved:reserved: /dev/tty00s:bhr::/usr/bin/login
::9600::tty00  login: :: # this is a comment
01s:u:root:reserved:reserved:reserved: /dev/tty01s:bhr::/usr/bin/login
::9600::tty01  login: :: # COM2 setup
#
```

These are just two long lines in the **_pmtab.** Line 00s is for the COM1 or tty port 0, and line 01s configures login service on the COM2 or tty port 1.

Use the **pmadm** (for port monitor administration) command as follows to understand the meaning of the separate fields.

```
# pmadm -t ttymon -l
PMTAG   PMTYPE   SVCTAG FLGS ID    <PMSPECIFIC>
ttymon  ttymon   00s    u    root  /dev/tty00s bhr - /usr/bin/login
- 9600 - tty00  login:  -  # this is a comment
ttymon  ttymon   01s    u    root  /dev/tty01s bhr - /usr/bin/login
- 9600 - tty01  login:  -  # COM2 setup
#
```

The **pmadm** command has many options. Use **-t** (for type) to specify the monitor type, and **-l** to list the currently active monitors.

Again, the previous output is just two long lines. The first five fields are generic to the **ttymon** monitor, and the last few are specific to the serial ports. They specify the device pathname (/dev/tty00s), the flags (bhr), the service pathname (/usr/bin/login), the label from **ttydefs** (9600), the device tag (tty00), the greeting message (login:), and the comment. The several - (hyphen) characters define unused fields in this example.

The flags define the behavior of the port under certain circumstances. The **b** defines a *bidirectional* port that can allow both incoming calls and outgoing (mail) traffic, and the **h** flag suppresses an automatic *hangup* immediately after an incoming call is received. The **r** flag forces **ttymon** to wait until it receives a character from the port before it prints the **login:** message. This flag is needed if you are connecting two computers that both have login service. If one computer wishes to connect to the other, it sends a character or newline, and this alerts the other computer to print **login:** on the port. Without this flag, each machine would constantly try to send **login:** to the other, and each would think the other was trying to log in. Since this is probably not what you want, it is almost always correct to use the **r** flag.

If an *inactive* message is given in the last field before the comment, and then the service for that port is stopped, incoming calls will receive the inactive message instead of the **login:** message. This is sometimes useful for announcing that a port is unavailable.

These **_pmtab** lines are generated by commands that are specific to each monitor. Examine the **ttyadm(1)** man page for more information about possible fields for the **ttymon** services.

Installing New Terminal Descriptions

When your TERM environment variable is used by a program such as **vi**, the application looks up a *terminal description* based on the value of the TERM variable. These terminal descriptions are kept in the directory **/usr/share/lib/terminfo** and its subdirectories. The terminal capabilities are kept in a compiled form in this directory tree, and are not directly readable by humans. In older releases of the UNIX system (before SVR2), the terminal descriptions were kept in text form in the file **/etc/termcap**. In addition, the format of the descriptions changed between the **termcap** and **terminfo** versions. To support these changes, three new tools have been provided.

The **tic** (for terminfo compiler) program takes a filename as argument. For example:

```
# tic termdesc.ti
```

The file contains a terminal description in source form. The **tic** program compiles the description, and puts the result into the **terminfo** database.

The **infocmp** (for terminfo compare) program can compare compiled **terminfo** descriptions, or display the source form from the compiled form. Used without an argument, it displays the source form for the terminal currently set in the TERM variable. The **infocmp** program is a powerful tool that includes many options and features. It can also produce a source form of a terminal description that can be edited and then run through **tic** to produce a modified entry.

Finally, the **captoinfo** program helps convert terminal descriptions written in the older **termcap** form into the **terminfo** form.

These are all sophisticated tools that are difficult to use correctly unless you have some experience with terminals and the *curses* software package. Examine the manual pages for these commands before you begin experimenting with them.

Using Color Monitors

Many terminals and system consoles in today's machines support color displays; however, the monochrome TERM entry 386AT-M is often the default value for AT-class machines. Be sure to set **TERM = 386AT** if you have a color console.

The UNIX system does not provide a standard command to manage the color of material displayed on the screen (except for the X Window System!), but many releases do provide special commands to change the background and the color of the ASCII characters displayed. In addition, experts can often use the **terminfo** feature to highlight specific displays in specific colors. You might highlight the PS1, command lines as a whole, or messages from shell scripts. The results may differ between the console and remote terminals, but you can usually set up **terminfo** description files that allow some use of color on both types of display.

Many SVR4 releases include the **setcolor** command for setting the default background and foreground colors on the console. This command usually takes two command-line arguments that specify the background and foreground colors, respectively. The arguments are color names or numbers; consult the man page for your release of the UNIX system. For example:

```
$ setcolor blue white
$
```

This produces white characters on a blue field. In some releases, the **setcolor** command can take additional flags to specify a light or dark shade, or can use coded numbers to specify colors instead of color names. Some releases allow you to completely flood the background with the background color, while others color only a small box around each character. You can experiment to get a pleasant display, and then add that command to your **.profile** to make it permanent.

In addition, you can add the *escape sequences* for color to the **terminfo** database to change the color of specific messages on the display. That is, most terminals and consoles respond to special sequences of characters that begin with the ESC character and contain codes for different colors. You can use this feature to display character strings in color, and you can usually get colors on the command line by adding the escape sequences to your PS1 or shell scripts. Try this command line if you have a color monitor:

```
$ echo "\033[34mHello world\033[0m"
```

What is the result?

You can also modify the **terminfo** file for your terminal so that full-screen applications such as **vi** display messages in color. Add the escape sequences in the different types of highlighted strings defined in the **terminfo** entry. The codes vary in different implementations of the UNIX system (and on different monitors), so some experimentation is usually necessary.

Printing

T
H
I
R
T
E
E
N

The UNIX system provides extensive tools for controling printers and for *spooling* output to hard-copy devices. The software can be configured for a single simple printer that you can use for all paper output, or a UNIX machine can act as a central print server driving dozens of hard-copy devices of different types. Many users can direct output to a printer simultaneously; the software will queue the output correctly and add banner pages to the printout so individual users can find their own output.

Printer support is especially powerful under the UNIX system because of the multitasking nature of the system. Unlike many operating systems, the printer software in the UNIX system runs as a user-level application, with no exotic device drivers or RAM disks visible to the user. The print tools do an excellent job of hiding hardware dependencies.

The printing tools are generically called the **lp** (for line printer) subsystem. They are so general and so powerful that no other printing software is usually provided in UNIX systems. Because the UNIX philosophy favors tools that do only a specific job, functions like pagination of output and hardware-specific formatting are not done by **lp**, but rather by special-purpose applications and filters. This allows the **lp** subsystem to specialize in print queue management and efficiently driving the hardware.

An additional, but very similar, printing subsystem that originated in the BSD release is also included in the BSD Compatibility Package in SVR4. This **lpr** system acts very much like the **lp** tools in most respects, although the standard **lp** system is better for larger print centers. If your machine is configured to use **lpr**, you can spool jobs to the printer with the **lpr** command, and get a status report of the spool with **lpq** (for **lp** queue). Ask your system administrator for more information about the **lpr** subsystem.

Using the lp Command

In the standard SVR4 print system, you request printing with the **lp** command. The command will place either the file named on its command line, or its standard input, onto the queue for a printer. The **lp** command returns to the shell after the job has been queued, not when the printing has been completed.

The **lp** command is frequently used as the termination of a shell pipeline, as in this example:

```
$ cat /etc/lp/model/standard | lp
```

However, it can also take a pathname as argument, like this:

```
$ lp /etc/lp/model/standard
```

The **lp** command specializes in printing; if you want paginated output with special headers on each page, use an additional tool in the command line, as shown here:

```
$ pr -h "my_sys printer model" /etc/lp/model/standard | lp
```

The **lp** command allows several options that can modify the printing process. The **-m** (for mail) flag will provide notification by electronic mail after a file has been printed. Since the print queue is limited only by disk space, and the printing may take a considerable amount of time, this option can be useful. The **-n** (for number) option allows you to print more than one copy with one **lp** command. To print six copies of a file, with notification by mail when the job is complete, you could use this command:

```
$ lp -m -n6 /etc/lp/filter.table
```

In addition, **lp** will print a *banner page* at the beginning of each output job. You control the contents of this banner with the -t (for title) option, as follows:

```
$ lp -t"This file owned by $LOGNAME" /etc/lp/printers/*/configuration
```

This title appears only on the **lp** banner page, not on each page of the output. You can also eliminate the banner entirely with the **-o nobanner** option. Use the **-h** option of **pr** to put a header on each page.

When the **lp** command queues a print job, it returns a *request id* to its standard output, as shown here:

```
$ lp /etc/lp/model/standard
Request id is ATT470-78  (1 file)
$
```

You should note this job number, because you can use it to track or cancel the job. Some versions of **lp** on some machines do not return the request id, but you can still track your job with the **lpstat** command discussed later in this chapter.

If you have several printers attached to the machine, you can direct **lp** to use one specific printer, using the **-d** (for destination) option. The **-d** option takes the name of a specific printer as argument. For example:

```
$ lp -d ATT470 file1 file2 file3
```

The **lp** command has several other options that allow you to make copies of files before printing (**-c**), write a message to your terminal when the printing is completed (**-w**), and pass printer-specific options directly to the actual program that controls the printer (**-o**).

Canceling a Job

You can cancel a print job before it has been printed with the **cancel** command. This command takes a printer request id, or list of request ids, and removes the named jobs from the print queue as follows:

```
$ cancel ATT470-78
request "ATT470-78" cancelled
$
```

This command will cancel a job even if it has already started printing, so if you start a large job by mistake, you can stop it without tying up the printer until it completes.

The **cancel** command can also take a printer name as an argument, in which case it will cancel the job currently printing on the device. For example:

```
$ cancel ATT470
request "ATT470-78" cancelled
$
```

This will not affect other jobs on the queue that have not yet started printing.

Printing on Forms

In larger computer centers, there may be several printers set up with special *forms,* such as letterhead paper or invoices. If your installation supports different forms, you can either specify that a print request go specifically to the printer that contains the form you want, or you can name the form in the print request, and the **lp** system will spool the job to the correct printer. The latter is usually the preferable procedure, because the system administrator may move forms around on printers as required. It is easier to keep track of the form rather than the printer.

To take advantage of this feature, the system administrator must first establish form names that are known to the system. This process is discussed later in this chapter. Then the administrator publishes the list of known forms, and when you wish to use a specific form, you can simply add its name to the **lp** command line following the **-f** (for form) option, as follows:

```
$ cat letter | lp -f letterhead
```

If you ask for a specific printer with the **-d** option on the same command line with the **-f** option, and the form is not available on that printer, your request may be rejected. On the other hand, this is quite an intelligent procedure; it can verify that the form is available and route the request to the correct printer. In some cases, it may spool the request, and then send mail asking the system administrator to *mount* the named form on one of the available printers. When the correct form is mounted, the job will be printed.

Content-Types and Print Filters

The **lp** system is able to print many different types of output files. For example, if a printer accepts output in the PostScript language, a preformatted PostScript file can be printed directly. A text file, on the other hand, must be converted to PostScript format before printing. Many other format conversions are also necessary in routine printing tasks. This is the function of the *filter* subsystems in the **lp** package. You can specify a desired format conversion, or filter, for different *content-types* of files on the **lp** command line. The file will be passed through that filter and the file contents will be converted to the appropriate format before the file is printed.

Several standard filters are supported in most systems, and additional filters can be installed and configured by the system administrator. Ask for a list of supported content-types (and filters) on your machine, or use the **lpfilter** command (discussed later in this chapter) to display the available list.

You can name the content-type of a file on the **lp** command line, after the **-T** (uppercase T, for type) option, as shown here:

```
$ lp -T postscript myfile.ps
```

If a printer has been configured to accept that content-type directly, the job will be spooled to that printer. Otherwise, **lp** will invoke a filter to process the file, producing output in a format the printer can accept. After the filter has processed the file, it will be sent to a printer that can handle the output format from the filter.

Most text files have a content-type of **simple**, and these can be printed directly on typical text-only printers such as dot matrix or daisy wheel. If no content-type is specified on the **lp** command line, **lp** will look at the file to determine its content-type. If its content-type cannot be determined, type **simple** will be assumed. Only a few common content-types can be recognized by **lp**, so it is preferable to name the content-type explicitly if you know it.

Additional Print Options and Defaults

The **lp** system allows many more options and controls. The administrator can authorize individual users or prohibit them from making requests to a specific printer, form, or filter. Several types of *special handling* are allowed with print requests. If authorized, a user can request that a job be held or printed immediately on a printer. Specific pages of a document can also be printed, and unusual page sizes or print *modes* can be requested.

In addition, a user can specify additional printer-specific controls following the **-o** (for option) argument on the **lp** command line. For example,

```
# pr file | lp -o nobanner
```

will print the file without the normal banner page at the beginning. The **nobanner** option may be required to print to a PostScript printer. Other options control the page width, page length, special **stty** controls used by the interface script to configure the data link to the printer, and other attributes. Consult the **lp(1)** and **lpadmin(1)** man pages for details of these advanced features.

Determining Printer Status

Information about the overall state of your **lp** system is provided by the **lpstat** (for **lp** status) command. If you execute this command without arguments, **lpstat** lists information about your own spooled jobs, as shown here:

```
$ lp /etc/profile
Request id is ATT470-79 (1 file)
$ lpstat
ATT470-79          steve          1092    Apr 27 19:07
$
```

The request id comes first, followed by the user who spooled the request, the output size in bytes, and finally the date and time of the request. You can use **lpstat** in this way to determine the request ids of your jobs if you forget them.

When a job has started printing, that information is also included in the output of **lpstat**:

```
$ lpstat
ATT470-79          steve          1092    Apr 27 19:07    on ATT470
$
```

When the job has finished printing, it is removed from the queue and there is no longer any way to track it. However, if you know the job was spooled, then its disappearance from the spool is an indication that the job has been printed.

You can use the **-u** option with a user id to see spooled requests for other users:

```
$ lpstat -u jim
ATT470-80          jim            4822    Apr 27 19:09
$
```

Command-Line Options for lpstat

The **lpstat** command provides many other options that can tell you much about how the printer is configured. The **-d** (for default printer) option reports which printer is the default, as follows:

```
$ lpstat -d
system default destination: ATT470
$
```

The **-r** (for request) option tells you whether the printer system is in operation. For example:

```
$ lpstat -r
scheduler is running
$
```

If the **lp** system is not available, **lpstat -r** will report that fact, as shown here:

```
$ lpstat -r
scheduler is not running
$
```

You must take administrative action to turn on the **lp** system, as discussed later in this chapter.

You can determine the status of an individual printer with the **-p** (for printer) option, followed by the name of the printer, as follows:

```
$ lpstat -p ATT470 -l
```

When the **-l** (ell, for long) option is given with **-p**, a full listing of printer information is displayed. Use the **-D** option with **-p** to produce a short summary instead.

The **-t** (for total) option for **lpstat** tells you everything about the printer system, as this example demonstrates:

```
$ lpstat -t
scheduler is running
system default destination: ATT470
members of class Parallel:
        ATT470
device for ATT470: /dev/lp0
ATT470 accepting requests since Apr 19 18:58
Parallel accepting requests since Apr 19 18:58
printer ATT470 now printing ATT470-85.  enabled since Apr 27 21:03.
        available.
ATT470-85        steve        1092   Apr 27 21:15 on ATT470
ATT470-86        root          526   Apr 27 21:19
$
```

This output shows the system default printer (ATT470 in this case), the hardware device pathname (**/dev/lp0**) for that printer, whether or not the printer is accepting print jobs, whether the printer is enabled, and the spool of current jobs.

Printers can be grouped into *classes,* so that several printers of the same type are grouped together, but distinguished from printers of another type. This allows more than one output device to share the workload, and also allows you to force output to one type or another as your needs dictate. The **lpstat -t** command displays class membership of printers, and whether the class as a whole is accepting requests. We discuss printer classes in more detail later in this chapter.

The **-t** option is one of the most useful of the **lpstat** options for a small system, because all the output can usually fit easily on a single display screen. When a system includes many printers of several classes, and there are many users requesting print output, one of the more limited **lpstat** options may work better.

lpsched, the lp Demon

The **lp** system is controlled by a demon process called **lpsched** (for lp scheduler) that runs whenever the **lp** system is up. When you execute the **lp** command to spool a file to the printer, **lp** communicates with this demon, telling it that a new job is ready for the queue. The **lpsched** command handles queue management to prevent multiple jobs created at the same time from competing for printer resources. It also drives the printer devices, sensing when a printer is idle or nonfunctional.

You can see the **lpsched** program with the **ps -ef** command, shown here:

```
$ ps -ef
    UID   PID  PPID  C   STIME TTY       TIME COMD
   root     0     0  0 14:24:22 ?        0:00 sched
   root     1     0  0 14:24:22 ?        0:03 /sbin/init
   root     2     0  0 14:24:22 ?        0:01 pageout
   root     3     0  0 14:24:22 ?        0:14 fsflush
   root     4     0  0 14:24:22 ?        0:00 kmdaemon
   root   256     1  0 14:26:58 ?        0:01 /usr/lib/saf/sac -t 300
  steve   262     1  0 14:26:58 console  0:02 ksh
   root   154     1  0 14:26:38 ?        0:00 /usr/sbin/cron
```

```
root    259   256  0 14:27:00 ?        0:01 /usr/lib/saf/ttymon
root    396     1  0 14:43:43 ?        0:02 /usr/lib/lp/lpsched
steve   656   262 19 16:42:48 console  0:00 ps -ef
$
```

The parent of the **lpsched** process is **init**. The process is owned by the user **root**. In some systems there is a special user id associated with the **lp** system, and you can use the **lp** login as a target for print jobs spooled from remote machines. Usually, you won't try to log in as **lp**, and it is desirable to disable the password for the **lp** login in **/etc/shadow** for security reasons.

Starting and Stopping the Scheduler

You can determine whether **lpsched** is running on your machine with **lpstat -r** as discussed earlier, or the **lp** command will warn you if the scheduler is not running. If it is not, you cannot queue jobs to the printer. The command

```
# /usr/lib/lp/lpsched
```

will start the scheduler if it not running, but the scheduler is usually started automatically at boot time. The **lpsched** command and other **lp** administrative commands are reserved for the superuser. If **lpsched** is not running, it is usually a sign that something is wrong with your **lp** system.

You turn off **lpsched** with the command

```
# /usr/sbin/lpshut
```

This method is safer than simply killing the **lpsched** process, because it stops the printing process in an orderly way.

Connecting a Printer

Basically there are two types of printers: *serial* and *parallel*. These terms refer to the way data is transmitted through the cable that connects the computer to the printer. Serial printers usually attach to the computer through an RS-232 port, or possibly through a serial modem, while parallel printers attach to the computer through a unique parallel interface connector, or sometimes with a DB-25 connector much like an RS-232 connector. You cannot attach a parallel printer to a serial port or vice versa, so it is important to discuss printer cables with the printer manufacturer or with your hardware vendor. Printer cabling is usually specific to an individual printer, and attaching "unknown" printers to a computer, even if you know whether the printer is serial or parallel, can be difficult and tedious. It is generally preferable to purchase the correct cable for the connection when you acquire your printers.

PostScript printers often provide only serial access, while dot-matrix and letter-quality printers may be either serial or parallel. The HP LaserJet series (and compatibles) may include both interfaces. When connected to a serial port, PostScript printers usually require a *null modem* cable.

Most printers include a large number of switches to configure the printer's behavior. This is another area that can be very frustrating; again, consult the printer manufacturer or retailer for advice.

You can use both serial and parallel printers with the **lp** system without difficulty, but you must specify the *port* that the printer will use. Table 13-1 is a list of ports and their associated device files for AT-class

PC Name	Device File	Type
LPT1	/dev/lp	Parallel
	/dev/lp0	
LPT2	/dev/lp1	Parallel
LPT3	/dev/lp2	Parallel
COM1	/dev/tty00s	Serial
	/dev/term/tty00s	
COM2	/dev/tty01s	Serial
	/dev/term/tty01s	
COM3	/dev/tty02s	Serial
	/dev/term/tty02s	
COM4	/dev/tty03s	Serial
	/dev/term/tty03s	

Table 13-1.   Printer Devices for Small SVR4 Systems

UNIX systems. Many small machines are configured with only one parallel port. If you have more than one, device file **/dev/lp1** or **/dev/lp2** might be present depending on how many parallel ports are available. It is often easier to add additional serial ports than it is to add parallel ports, so you are likely to configure multiple printer systems with serial printers, using device files **/dev/tty02s, /dev/tty03s,** and so on.

Serial printers usually default to a communications speed of 9600 bps, and you should accept this default if the printer provides flow control. Many serial printers (including PostScript printers) can run at 9600 bps, but can only print at a speed of less than 1200 bps; thus, without flow control the printer will not work correctly. Set the printer communications speed with the printer switches, and set the speed at the UNIX system side in the printer defaults, as discussed later in this chapter.

If you have a serial printer, be sure no terminal port monitor is also configured on that port.

If you wish to attach an unusual or new type of printer, you may need to know quite a lot about its behavior. The **lp** system works by passing the output file through an *interface* program that is usually a shell script. This script prepares the banner page, configures the I/O port (using **stty**), and writes the data to the correct device file. Unlike older releases, SVR4 uses a single interface script, called **standard**, for most common printer types. You may need to modify this interface for unusual printers. Sometimes printer manufacturers supply an interface script if the standard one will not work.

Installing a Printer Into the lp System

There are several steps involved in adding a new printer: First, you must verify that the printer is correctly attached to the machine and is working. Second, you must examine the interface script, verifying that it does what you expect it to do. In rare cases you may need to modify the script to make it fit the printer's requirements. Next, you must establish a set of *defaults* for the printer so the **lp** system can communicate with it when the user specifies no special command-line options. You may also establish a set of filters to convert files to the correct output format for the printer. Then, you must inform the **lp** system that the printer is available. Finally, you have to *enable* the printer so the **lp** software will begin spooling your print jobs to it. The following sections discuss each of these steps in turn.

Testing Your Printer Configuration

You can usually test your printer hookup by redirecting some output to the device file to which you think the printer is attached. You can write directly to the device file, as follows:

```
$ cat /etc/lp/model/standard > /dev/lp
```

If the output does not appear at all, the cabling or printer configuration switches are probably set incorrectly, or the printer itself may be non-functional. If output appears but is garbled, the printer configuration switches are set incorrectly.

The previous test will work for most printers that accept normal character streams (i.e., content-type *simple*), such as dot-matrix printers. However, printers that speak the PostScript or another *page description language* need to receive an executable program in their control language before they will print anything. If you have a PostScript printer, try this test and see if anything prints.

```
$ cat testfile.ps
%!
/Times-Roman findfont 14 scalefont setfont
300 400 moveto
(hello world) show
showpage
$ cat testfile.ps > /dev/tty00s
```

If the string *hello world* appears on your printer, it is functioning. If this **cat** procedure does not work with a PostScript printer, try connecting to the printer port at the configured speed (usually 9600 baud) using the **cu** command, and then enter the printer's interactive mode. If you still cannot talk to the printer, something is configured incorrectly.

Printer Interface Models

The directory **/usr/lib/lp/model** contains shell scripts that interface between the **lp** user command and the device file that actually drives the printer. These scripts are responsible for setting the printer device attributes, such as data communications rate and flow control, for formatting and printing the banner message that separates the different output jobs, for preparing multiple copies of the output, and so forth. Generally, when you add a new printer, you must select one of these scripts, or models, to use with it. In most SVR4 systems, the single *standard* model will work for almost all common printer types, both serial and parallel.

The models are shell scripts, and you can read them to understand how they interface between the **lpsched** demon and the printer hardware. They take a number of command-line arguments, and produce output on their standard output. In operation, the **lpsched** program will execute the script with its output redirected to the appropriate device file.

If you need to create a new interface script, start by copying the standard script into a separate directory, and then edit the copy. You must place your interface in a separate directory because the **lp** administrative tools have a glitch that requires you to distinguish between the standard model and your own scripts. Set the permissions and ownership of new scripts to the same settings used in the standard model.

Configuring the lp Software

The command **/usr/sbin/lpadmin** is used to set up and change the printer configuration. This command is used to add printers, define the printer type to the **lp** system, assign printers to classes, and set printer defaults. You can use it after you are sure the printer is correctly configured, and the model script is correct. The **lpadmin** command is a sophisticated program that can take many options; it is reserved for the superuser.

In SVR4, you must be sure that the **lpsched** program is running when you use **lpadmin**. Verify with **lpstat -t** that the **lpsched** program is running before you attempt to administer the **lp** system.

You can name a printer anything you wish, but since this is the public name used in your commands, it is usually best to give it a name that indicates what type of printer it is. In the following examples, the new printer will be called PS; there is already an existing printer in the system called ATT470. You can refer to a printer with **lpadmin** following the **-p** (for printer) option, as follows:

```
# lpadmin -p PS ....
```

Other options for **lpadmin** give instructions on how to administer the specified printer.

In adding a new printer, **lpadmin** takes options that define the model script and the device, in addition to the printer name. Here is an example:

```
# lpadmin -p PS -m standard -v /dev/tty01s
```

The **-m** (for model) option takes the name of the model script, and the **-v** option takes the full pathname of the device file you wish to use. This command will add a printer named PS to the system. Unfortunately, the **-m** option only works with predefined models that are delivered with the system. If you change a model for a new printer type, you must use the **-i** (for interface) option instead, giving it the full pathname of your edited interface script, as shown here:

```
# lpadmin -pPS -i/home/steve/lpscript -v/dev/tty01s
```

The Printer Type

You must also specify the printer *type*, which is usually the product name of the printer, or an alias for the product name. In SVR4, printer types are maintained in the **terminfo** database with the list of acceptable terminals. The **terminfo** entry contains information specific to the printer, such as how to generate a form feed, and the "natural" page length and width for the printer. Often the correct printer type is difficult to determine, but if you browse through the **terminfo** database (using the **infocmp** program), you can usually find a name that represents your printer. For example, the type of the ATT-470 printer is **att470**, and the Apple LaserWriter has type **lw** or **postscript**. Give the printer type following the **-T** (for type) option on the **lpadmin** command line when the printer is installed, or use a command of this form:

```
# lpadmin -p PS -T lw
```

A correct printer type is essential to the correct operation of the **lp** system.

Specifying the Printer Content-Type

When you add a new printer, you must also specify the format of data that it can print directly. By default, content-type **simple** is assumed. This is correct for most dot-matrix and letter-quality printers, but is not correct for PostScript printers, which usually will not print simple text files properly. To set the content-type that is acceptable to a printer, give a list of content-types after the **-I** (uppercase *i*, for interface) option on the **lpadmin** command line, as shown here:

```
# lpadmin -p PS -I postscript
#
```

Acceptable printer types are also allowable content-types, so if the printer can only handle one content-type, you can omit the -I option.

More than one content-type is allowed if the different types are separated by commas after the -I option. If you establish a content-type list in this way, you must explicitly include **simple** if the printer can handle simple text files.

If a printer can handle an output type, and if the user specifies one of the printer content-types as the content-type of a print request, the **lp** system will print the job directly on the printer. Otherwise, filtering is required as discussed later in this chapter.

Additional Print Options and Defaults

If the user does not specify any options with **-o** on the **lp** command line, default values will be used for the print job. Normally, these defaults are drawn from the **terminfo** entry for the specific printer type, and they rarely need to be changed. If necessary, however, you can change the default options when you install the printer by using **a -o** option on your **lpadmin** command line. For example, to set the communications speed for a serial printer to 1200 bps, you would use a command like this:

```
# lpadmin -p ATT470 -o stty='1200 cs8 ixon -ixany opost'
```

The specified **stty** values become the normal defaults for that printer. Similarly, you can suppress the printing of a banner page with

```
# lpadmin -p PS -o nobanner
```

Note that the **nobanner** option is usually required to install a PostScript printer, or another device that uses a page description language, because most versions of the **lp** system print the banner in content-type **simple**.

You can change several other defaults as well. These are documented in the **lpadmin(1)** man page.

The Default Destination

If you are adding the first printer to the machine, you will usually want to make it the *system default destination,* so you can use the **lp** command without a printer as an argument. If you have more than one printer, you only want one default printer. Usually either the lowest quality or the most commonly used printer will be the default, depending on user preferences. After you have installed the printer, use the **-d** (for default) option to **lpadmin** followed by the printer name, as shown here:

```
# lpadmin -d PS
```

This makes PS the default destination. If you do not select a default destination, none will be assigned, and you will have to explicitly name a printer for each use of the **lp** command.

Checking the Installation

You can execute **lpstat** to verify that a printer has been added to the system, as follows:

```
$ lpstat -t
scheduler is running
system default destination: PS
members of class Parallel:
        ATT470
device for ATT470: /dev/lp
device for PS: /dev/tty01s
ATT470 accepting requests since Thu Apr 19 18:58 MDT 1990
Parallel accepting requests since Thu Apr 19 18:58 MDT 1990
PS not accepting requests since Mon Apr 30 19:00 MDT 1990 -
        new destination
printer ATT470 is idle.  enabled since Thu Apr 30 18:58 MDT 1990.
        available.
printer PS disabled since Mon Apr 30 19:00 MDT 1990. available.
        new printer
$
```

This output tells you that the printer has been added, and also provides some additional information. It lets you know that the printer is not accepting requests, and that it is disabled. If the output does not look something like this after you add a printer, the command has failed and you should try again.

Removing a Printer

You can remove a printer from the system with the **-x** (for exterminate) option, using this form:

```
# lpadmin -x PS
```

Accepting Print Requests

When a new printer is added, it is installed but not activated. Two more features of the **lp** system are of interest here. You can configure a printer to *accept* or *reject* requests for printing without removing it from the system. As a result of this action, the **lp** command will refuse to spool a job when the device is not accepting print requests. Use the command **/usr/sbin/accept** to allow a printer destination to accept requests, as shown here:

```
# accept PS
destination "PS" now accepting requests
# lpstat -t
scheduler is running
system default destination: ATT470
members of class Parallel:
        ATT470
device for ATT470: /dev/lp
device for PS: /dev/tty01s
ATT470 accepting requests since Thu Apr 19 18:58 MDT 1990
Parallel accepting requests since Thu Apr 19 18:58 MDT 1990
PS accepting requests since Mon Apr 30 21:02 MDT 1990
printer ATT470 is idle.  enabled since Thu Apr 19 18:58 1990.
        available.
printer PS disabled since Mon Apr 30 18:58 MDT 1990. -
        new printer
#
```

PS will now accept requests for printing.

You use the **/usr/sbin/reject** command to tell a printer to reject requests. This command is normally used when a printer will be out of service for a relatively long time, but when you don't want to eliminate it from the system permanently with **lpadmin -x**. The **reject** command takes a printer destination as an argument, and optionally a reason for the printer's being disabled, following the **-r** (for reason) option. For example:

```
# reject -r"Down until Fri. for Repairs" PS
destination "PS" is no longer accepting requests
#
```

The reason will be displayed in the **lpstat -t** output, and will also appear if a user tries to spool to the device with the **lp** command.

Enabling the Printer

Once a printer begins accepting requests, it is still not completely functional; although it accepts requests, the jobs are just placed on the spool for that printer. As you can see from the previous **lpstat -t** output, the printer is still *disabled.* You must *enable* the printer before it will actually begin to print your jobs. Unlike the *accept/reject* condition the **lp** software will automatically disable a printer if it tries to print to it unsuccessfully. If a printer runs out of paper, or if the power to the printer is turned off, the device will be automatically disabled. You can enable the printer with the **/usr/bin/enable** command, as follows:

```
# enable PS
# lpstat -t
scheduler is running
system default destination: ATT470
members of class Parallel:
        ATT470
device for ATT470: /dev/lp
device for PS: /dev/tty01s
ATT470 accepting requests since Thu Apr 19 18:58 MDT 1990
Parallel accepting requests since Thu Apr 19 18:58 MDT 1990
PS accepting requests since Mon Apr 30 21:02 MDT 1990
printer ATT470 is idle.  enabled since Thu Apr 19 18:58 MDT 1990.
        available.
printer PS is idle.  enabled since Mon Apr 30 21:06 MDT 1990.
        available.
#
```

The printer is now fully functional.

A printer will be disabled automatically by the **lp** command when the command thinks the printer is malfunctioning, but you must enable it manually when you have fixed the problem. Often, when a printer seems to be incorrectly configured, it is only disabled. Check the output from **lpstat -t** to assess the state of a printer that is not working. The **lp** system will usually send warning mail to the administrator when a printer is disabled. Several other types of *alerts* are also sent to the administrator via mail when the **lp** system needs attention. Be sure to check this mail regularly, or forward it to a login id that is used more often than **lp** or the administrator's id.

You can disable a printer manually using the **/usr/bin/disable** command, shown here:

```
# disable PS
```

The **disable** command can take three optional arguments. Use **-c** (for cancel) if you wish to cancel any jobs that are currently printing before the device is disabled, or use **-W** (for wait) if you wish to disable the printer after any current job is completed. You can also give a reason for disabling the device with the **-r** (for reason) option. For example:

```
# disable -c -r"Out of Paper" PS
```

Usually, **disable** is used to stop output to a printer temporarily while you add paper, or turn the printer off for some reason. Because **lp** is still accepting requests for that printer, you must get the printer back on-line relatively quickly or the spool of jobs may get large.

Moving Jobs from One Printer to Another

When a printer malfunctions or a spool to a single device gets too large, you may wish to distribute the jobs among several printers. The **/usr/sbin/lpmove** command gives you this ability. The **lpmove** command takes as arguments a list of request ids followed by a destination id, and moves the requests to the new destination. Here is an example:

```
# lpmove ATT470-87 ATT470-88 daisy
```

This command will move requests ATT470-87 and ATT470-88 to the new printer. In SVR4, you must be sure that **lpsched** is running before you move jobs between devices. A second form of the **lpmove** command, shown here, moves *all* the jobs on one device to another printer:

```
# lpmove ATT470 daisy
```

This will put all the jobs queued to ATT470 on the spool for daisy. Note that you cannot usually move jobs between incompatible printer types; for example, you cannot move jobs spooled on a dot-matrix printer to a PostScript printer. Instead, you must cancel the jobs and respool them with **lp**.

Going Further

The previous discussion provides sufficient information for administering simple printers on smaller systems. However, a UNIX machine can make an excellent *print server* that can be dedicated to controlling many printers of various types. You can attach a print server to a local area network (LAN) to serve a large organization efficiently. Network-based printing can substantially reduce the costs associated with hard-copy output, since the highest quality (and most expensive) devices can be shared among a large user group. The **lp** features discussed here will be most useful in larger installations that have several printers.

Printer Classes

First, a printer can be assigned to a printer class. A *class* is a group of printers that shares a single spool queue. That is, when a printer becomes idle, the next job it prints comes off the shared queue. When another printer in the same class becomes idle, it takes the next job off the same queue. The **lp** software manages the queue, passing jobs to individual printers as they become idle.

In practice, printers of the same or similar type are assigned to one class, and printers of a different type are assigned to another class. For example, laser printers may all be in one class, and dot-matrix printers may be in another class. If you don't really care which device produces the output, you can put all the devices in the same class.

You can refer to an entire printer class with a single destination id. With the printer configured as it was in the preceding examples, the command

```
$ lp -d ATT470 /etc/lp/filter.table
```

will produce the same results as

```
$ lp -d Parallel /etc/lp/filter.table
```

This is because the printer ATT470 belongs to the class Parallel. Printer classes are displayed in the output from **lpstat -t**. Wherever you use a printer destination in the **lp** system commands, you can use a printer class instead.

The **-c** (for class) option is used with **lpadmin** to assign a device to a printer class, as follows:

```
# lpadmin -p PS -c typeset -m standard -v /dev/tty01s
# accept PS
destination "PS" now accepting requests
# enable PS
printer "PS" now accepting requests
#
```

This example will assign PS to class typeset. You must use the **-c** option when you initially install the printer with **lpadmin**. To change the class of an existing printer, completely remove it from the system with **lpadmin -x**, and reinstall it with the new class. The class name you assign can be either an existing printer class or a new class. If you use a new class name, **lp** will create a new class consisting of only that printer. After the previous command is executed, the **lpstat -t** results are different, as you can see here:

```
# lpstat -t
scheduler is running
system default destination: ATT470
members of class Parallel:
        ATT470
members of class typeset:
        PS
device for ATT470: /dev/lp
device for PS: /dev/tty01s
ATT470 accepting requests since Thu Apr 19 18:58 MDT 1990
Parallel accepting requests since Thu Apr 19 18:58 MDT 1990
PS accepting requests since Mon Apr 30 21:40 MDT 1990
typeset not accepting requests since Mon Apr 30 21:40 MDT 1990 -
        new destination
printer ATT470 is idle.  enabled since Thur Apr 19 18:58 MDT 1990.
     available.
printer PS is idle.  enabled since Mon Apr 30 21:06 MDT 1990.
     available.
#
```

A new class has been established, and the printer PS is a member of that class. The **accept** command is used here to allow PS to accept requests for printing, but the new class, typeset, is still rejecting requests. With the current configuration, you could spool jobs to PS but not directly to the class typeset. If you wish it to be a destination, you must also use **accept** for the class name. For example:

```
# accept typeset
destination "typeset" now accepting requests
#
```

Using Forms

The SVR4 version of the **lp** system allows the user to specify that a print job be printed on a specific *form* or printed with a special character set, or *printwheel.* These are printer-specific resources that must be *mounted* before they can be used. That is, you must install a form (such as a letterhead or preprinted paper of some sort) on a printer before the job can be printed. You can mount a specific form on a printer, and then tell the **lp** system that the form is available, and which printer it is mounted on. Subsequently, when users request that form, the **lp** system will print the job on that printer. If the form is not mounted, the job will be queued but not printed until the form is mounted. Jobs intended for unmounted forms will cause an *alert* message to be sent to the administrator, requesting that the form be mounted.

A similar procedure is supported for *printwheels,* which are alternative replaceable character sets allowed on some printers, usually letter-quality printers that have removable print heads (daisy wheel or print ball). A user may request a specifically named character set, and if that character set is not available, an administrator will be alerted and the job will be saved on a special queue. When the resource is mounted, the job will be printed.

Usually these mechanisms are reserved for larger printing sites that have several printers, a full-time administrator, and many users requesting different types of print jobs. In smaller systems with only a few users and no professional administrator, it is much easier to avoid complexity by personally verifying that the desired form or printwheel is mounted before you spool the job.

Each form and printwheel established within the mounting and alerting mechanism has a name and some attributes associated with it. To make a specific form available, the administrator must add the form to the known list, and set the correct attributes for that form. Then the administrator must inform the **lp** system which forms are currently mounted on each printer in the system. User print requests may specify a form following the **-f** (for form) option, and a printwheel following the -S option, as follows:

```
$ lp -f letterhead -S elite my.letter
```

The administrator must mount the resources and inform the **lp** system of the change before the job will be printed.

Creating Forms

The **/usr/sbin/lpforms** command is used to establish new forms. First you must create a control file that lists the attributes of the form, including the page length and width, the number of pages in each form, and so forth. Here is an example:

```
# cat letter.form
Page length: 66
Page width: 80
Number of pages: 1
Character set choice: any
#
```

The full list of possible attributes is given in the **lpforms(1)** man page, but a subset of the total is allowed in the control file; defaults are used for missing items.

Once the control file is established, you can add the form to the available list, as follows:

```
# lpforms -f letterhead -F letter.form -A mail
#
```

The command returns silently if the action succeeds. The name of the form follows the **-f** (for form) option, and the attribute file follows the **-F** (for file) option. Both are required, although you can use a - (minus) alone instead of the **-F** option if you want **lpforms** to use standard input instead of a file.

The **-A** (for alert-type) option allows you to specify the type of alert to be sent when a particular form is requested but is not mounted. Use **mail** to have electronic mail sent to the login id who executed the **lpforms** command; use **write** to write a message directly to the administrator's console. There are also several other possibilities.

When a set of forms has been installed, you can list the attributes of form *name* with this command:

```
# lpforms -f name -l
page length: 66
page width: 80
number of pages: 1
line pitch: 6
character pitch: 10
character set choice: any
ribbon color: any
#
```

The **-l** (ell, for list) option is used to list attributes. You can also list the attributes (and names) of all forms with

```
# lpforms -f all -l
```

To delete form *name,* use the **-x** option, as follows:

```
# lpforms -f name -x
#
```

Allowing and Mounting Forms

Next you must *allow* the form for each printer that you wish to mount it on. To do this, use the **lpadmin** command, shown here:

```
# lpadmin -p ATT470 -f allow:letterhead
```

The special keyword **allow** comes after the **-f** option, followed by a colon and the form name. This step is required before you can mount a form.

Once a form is established, and you have physically set up the form on a printer, you can mount the form with **lpadmin**, as shown here:

```
# lpadmin -p ATT470 -M -f name
#
```

As usual, the printer name is given after the **-p** option. The **-M** (for mount) option specifies mounting, and the form name appears after the **-f** option. Mounting a new form unmounts the previous form on that printer. You can force an unmount using the special name *none,* as follows:

```
# lpadmin -p ATT470 -M -f none
```

You must specify the **-f** option with the **-M** option to mount a form.

Using Character Sets and Printwheels

A similar procedure is provided to mount different character sets or printwheels as required by user print requests. Two forms of alternative character sets are provided in SVR4. First, there are *software* character sets for printers that can download them. This procedure usually requires a relatively intelligent printer, but providing the procedure is supported, the **lp** system can manage the user request without administrator intervention. The second type of character set is physically mounted on a printer when it is needed. This is usually a removable daisy wheel or print ball.

Software character sets supported by a printer are listed in the **terminfo** entry for that printer, and a user request such as

```
$ lp -S elite file.to.print
```

(uppercase *S,* for set) will be printed correctly with the named character set if that set is allowed. The **lpstat -t** command lists available character sets for each printer defined in the system. The **lp** system will logically mount a character set as it is needed, without additional effort by the administrator.

Physically mounted character sets are treated much like forms: the administrator must announce the names of available printwheels to the **lp** system. Then, when a user requests a particular character set with the **lp -S** command, an alert is sent to the administrator and the job is placed on a queue. When the administrator mounts the correct printwheel and informs the **lp** system of the change, the job is printed.

The **lpadmin** command is used to name available printwheels, as shown here:

```
# lpadmin -p printername -S elite,math,graphics -A mail
#
```

Be sure to leave no whitespace in the comma-separated printwheel list after the -S option. The previous command allows the use of three printwheels on the *printername* printer. Note that the printer must be configured to allow printwheels in its **terminfo** entry.

To delete a set of printwheel names, use

```
# lpadmin -p printername -S none
```

The special keyword *none* removes the list of printwheels and restores the default behavior.

After a user requests a printwheel, and the administrator responds to the alert message by mounting the correct printwheel on the printer, the **lp** system must be informed of the change, as follows:

```
# lpadmin -p printername -M -S elite
#
```

The mounted printwheel will remain in force until a new character set is mounted, or until the unmount command is given, as shown here:

```
# lpadmin -p printername -M -S none
#
```

If the printer cannot take printwheels, the command will be rejected and an error message will be displayed.

Using Filters

You can also configure *print filters* that allow one or more input content-types and reformat the print request for a specific printer. For example, a PostScript printer cannot print most types of files correctly, because the input must be reformulated in the PostScript page description language. Many other types of input files may need similar filtering before they can be printed, and this is the purpose of print filters. Usually a standard set of print filters is provided with the **lp** system to handle the most common content-types and printer types. A user can specify that a print request is a specific input content-type by using the **-T** (for type) option on the **lp** command line. The **lp** system will try to match that content-type with the content-type for the available printers. If there is a match, the file can be sent directly to the printer. If no match is found,

lp will attempt to match the content-type of the file with the input content-type of available filters, and the output type of the filter with the content-type of the printer. If both match, the print request is passed through the filter before being sent to the printer.

The **/usr/sbin/lpfilter** command is used to manage the list of available filters. You can list the data on a filter with

```
$ lpfilter -f postprint -l
```

The filter name is given after the **-f** (for filter) option, which is required in all **lpfilter** command lines. The **-l** (ell, for list) option displays the control data associated with that filter, as shown here:

```
$ lpfilter -f postprint -l
Input types: simple
Output types: postscript
Printer types: any
Printers: any
Filter type: slow
Command: /usr/lib/lp/postscript/postprint
Options: PAGES * = -o*,COPIES * = -c*,LENGTH * = -l*,MODES
portrait = -pp,MODES landscape = -pl,MODES group= * = -n*,MODES
x= * = -x*,MODES y= * = -y*,MODES magnify= * = -m*,MODES
ptsize= * = -s*,CHARSET * = -f*
$
```

The **postprint** filter is the standard filter used to convert simple text files to the PostScript language. Other common filters are **dpost**, which prints **troff** output on a PostScript printer, and **postio**, which prints files already in PostScript format on PostScript printers. If no content-type is specified on the **lp** command line, the file is assumed to be of **simple** content-type. You can see the full list of available filters and their attributes with the command

```
$  lpfilter -f all -l
```

The information displayed by the **lpfilter -l** command tells how each filter operates. The list of input types for the filter is compared with the content-type of the user's request. Then, the list of printer types for that filter is matched with the content-types acceptable to each printer (or with the printer destination selected by the user). If both parts match, the filter is appropriate for the job and the user request is passed through it. Finally, the *Command* is executed, taking account of the *Options* listed at the end of the output.

Adding new filters is not easy, and generally requires extensive experimentation. Creating the Input types, Output types, and the Command (usually a shell script) may not be difficult, but the filter system allows complex Options that provide a language to process users' command-line arguments within the filter. First, create a file containing the fields shown in the output of the previous **lpfilter -l** command, and then create a processing command to implement the filter. Next, use **lpfilter** to add that filter to the system, as follows:

```
# lpfilter -f newname -F path
#
```

The filter name follows the **-f** option, as usual, and the pathname of the file containing the filter data follows the **-F** option. Consult the **lpfilter(1)** man page for more information about the Options needed to make the filter work, or experiment by copying the options from an existing filter.

Server Machines

A UNIX system with the **lp** software makes an excellent print server. Because printer support consumes a relatively small amount of CPU resources, a single machine can support many printers without difficulty. Machines that are configured primarily as print servers can usually support some other activities simultaneously, such as user logins or data communications. It is a good idea to test a specific configuration to see how much load printers put on the system, but a rule of thumb might be that three or four active printers use about the same amount of CPU resources as a normal user; however, this estimate may vary considerably if the server is configured to do most of the processing of a print job, such as formatting output via **troff** before printing.

One issue that must be carefully considered when you are configuring a print server is the disk space it will use. Queued files take space on the machine's disk, and the rate of new jobs coming into the queue or queues should be weighed against the maximum print speed of the attached devices. Naturally, you will need enough printers to keep up with the print requests from the users; however, if a printer fails, the queue can grow quickly. There is usually no control over disk usage for spooled jobs, so a disk can fill without the knowledge of a system administrator. You must be vigilant when you are working with print servers to be sure that the printers are always enabled and that the spool of waiting jobs does not overflow the available disk resources.

Remote Access to Printing via LAN

The **lp** system allows you to send print requests to a central print server machine that is connected to your machine by a LAN. This feature makes it possible for networked machines to share printers, reducing the overall cost of a network. From the user's perspective, remote printers are the same as local printers: each one has a name or a destination id. The user specifies this name after the **-d** option on the **lp** request, or you can make a remote printer the default on the local machine so the **-d** option is not needed. The **lp** system takes care of sending the job to the destination, where it is processed normally, according to the rest of the specified command-line options. If return mail is requested, the mail is sent back across the LAN and delivered to the requesting user. All alerts, filters, and other features act as expected.

Configuring remotely accessible printers involves two steps. First, the **/usr/sbin/lpsystem** command is used to identify remote machines that are accessible from the local machine, as follows:

```
# lpsystem yoursys
"yoursys" has been added.
#
```

The additional command-line option -t (for type) identifies the remote system as a System V UNIX system (with the **s5** option) or as a BSD system (with the **bsd** option), as shown here:

```
# lpsystem -t bsd yoursys
```

The default is **s5**. If the print server is an SVR4 system, you will need to run the **lpsystem** command on the server as well as the client machine, or the server will refuse print requests from the client.

Other options allow you to specify *timeout* and *retry* parameters so that the **lp** system will keep trying if the remote machine is unavailable. Usually the defaults are adequate and these options are not necessary.

To delete a remote system from the **lp** availability list, use the **-r** option, as follows:

```
# lpsystem -r yoursys
Removed "yoursys".
#
```

You can list the attributes of **lp** access to remote systems with the **-l** (ell, for list) option to **lpsystem**.

Once the remote system is available, you can add a printer on that machine to the local machine's printer list with **lpadmin**, as shown here:

```
# lpadmin -p printername -s machinename!printername
#
```

The **-s** (lowercase s, for system) option takes a machine name and printer name as arguments, separating these two elements with a **!** (bang), as in a **mail** address. This aliases the remote printer to the new name. If you omit the **!printername** section, the default printer on the remote machine will be used to service the requests, and if you omit the **-p** option, the remote name will be used. This **lpadmin** command must be given with a *new* printer name; you cannot use a printer that has already been configured in the system.

After the name has been assigned, you must configure the local name as usual to specify the printer type, the class, the forms available, and other information. If you wish, you can make the remote printer the default destination for the local machine.

Remote Access to Printing via uucp

In addition to these LAN-based tools, you can also spool print jobs to other machines using the **uucp** system. You can write a simple command using **uux** to invoke **lp** remotely. For example:

```
$ cat myfile | uux - "yoursys!lp -t$LOGNAME -s"
```

This command will **cat** the file to the **lp** command on the remote machine **lpserve**, suppress the request id with the -s option, and place your login id on the banner that **lp** produces. You must administer the **uucp** system on your machine so that it can send files to the server, and also administer the server so that it allows **uux** jobs to be executed there.

In an actual remote printer script, there will usually be additional error checking of the input file. In addition, there may be the ability to pass a destination id from the local command line into the **uux** command and the remote **lp** command, and it may also be possible to include the local machine's uname on the banner line. You might create an executable shell script, perhaps called **rlp**, to handle these chores. You could also allow this local script to accept filenames for printing as well as (or instead of) the standard input, and to send electronic mail back to the user when a print job completes.

The **lp** system directly supports printing on standalone printers that are attached to autoanswer modems. When a job is spooled to such a destination, **lp** will call the printer and print the job. You can select this option when you configure the printer if you use the -U option to select the printer device, and omit the -v option. The -U option takes a machine name or telephone number in a form acceptable to **cu**; if you can **cu** to a printer, you can print to it. For example:

```
# lpadmin -p daisy -c letter -m standard -U cuname
```

Here, *cuname* is as a **cu** destination such as a remote machine name or telephone number. Note that the -U form will not spool a job on a remote **lp** system, but it will print a job on a dial-up printer.

The lp Directory Structure

The **lp** tools are distributed within the file system. The simple user commands **lp** and **lpstat** are located in the directory **/usr/bin**, and the rest of the administrative commands are located in **/usr/sbin**. The spool of unprinted jobs for each printer is kept in **/var/spool/lp**, and the tables of filters and other administrative data is stored in **/etc/lp**. Several tools, tables, and filters reside in **/usr/lib/lp/bin**, and some symlinks for **lp** commands may be in **/usr/lib**. You can easily examine the commands that are available, since they usually begin with **lp**, as this example shows:

```
$ ls /usr/sbin/lp*
/usr/sbin/lpadmin
/usr/sbin/lpfilter
/usr/sbin/lpforms
/usr/sbin/lpmove
/usr/sbin/lpshut
/usr/sbin/lpsystem
/usr/sbin/lpusers
$
```

In addition, you will find that the following commands, **/usr/bin/enable**, **/usr/bin/disable**, **/usr/sbin/accept**, and **/usr/sbin/reject**, are part of the **lp** package.

The spools for the **lp** system are contained in the directory **/var/spool/lp** and its subdirectories, as shown here:

```
# cd /var/spool/lp
# ls -F
SCHEDLOCK   bin@        requests/   temp@
admins/     fifos/      system/     tmp/
#
```

The directory **fifos** contains communication paths between the user command **lp** and the **lpsched** demon. **SCHEDLOCK** is a *lock file* that **lpsched** uses to prevent multiple **lpsched** demons from running simultaneously. When **lpsched** is turned off, **SCHEDLOCK** should not be present; if it is, **lpsched** cannot be started correctly. The **lpsched** command will return silently, but **lpstat** will report that the scheduler is still not running. If this happens, simply delete **SCHEDLOCK** and restart **lpsched**; however, you must be careful not to delete **SCHEDLOCK** when **lpsched** is running.

The directory **requests** contains subdirectories for each of the printers established on the machine, and for printers available on remote machines. The **lp** command will put the text of files that are spooled for printing into one of these directories. After the job is printed, the file will be deleted from this queue.

The **/etc/lp** directory contains information about the specific printer configuration on this machine, including tables of existing printers, forms, filters, and classes. For example:

```
# cd /etc/lp
# ls -F
Systems          filter.table     interfaces/     printers/
classes/         filter.table.i   logs@           pwheels/
default          forms/           model@
#
```

The file **default** contains the name of the default printer used when no **-d**, **-f**, or **-T** options are given on the **lp** command line. Available forms appear in the **forms** directory, and configured printer classes are in the **classes** directory. The **printers** directory contains tools used to manage each of the configured printers. **Systems** contains information related to printing on remote machines, and the **filter.table** files hold information needed to control configured filters.

Printer Drivers

The device file associated with a parallel printer is usually **/dev/lp**. In older UNIX system releases, the *device driver* that processes the data written to this file may sometimes add additional page ejects and possibly even banners to the output. Even if you **cat** a file directly to the device file, you may see extra material in the output. In addition to **/dev/lp**, a second device file, **/dev/rlp** (for raw lp device), which does not process the output, is often present. If you want to change the output that is produced by **/dev/lp**, you can usually edit your interface script, and assign the output to **/dev/rlp** rather than **/dev/lp**. This may require experimentation, because **/dev/lp** and **/dev/rlp** often behave differently in different systems. Notice that **/dev/lp** and **/dev/rlp** both refer to the same physical I/O port on the machine, so you cannot use both of them at the same time without corrupting the output. Serial printers that usually use a tty port such as **/dev/tty01s** do not have a raw device associated with them, so all manipulation of the output is done in the interface script.

When you attach a high-performance print device to your machine, it may include an interface board that has its own plug and cable for attaching a printer. Some plotters or other graphics devices may require a plug-in board. These devices will use neither the parallel nor serial models discussed earlier, nor will they use the **/dev/lp** or **/dev/tty??** device files. Associated with this special hardware will be a device driver supplied by the board manufacturer, along with instructions for installing the hardware and software. If a device is intended for the **lp** subsystem, a model interface script is usually included with it, and a new device file will be created in the **/dev** directory. By using the special interface script and the new device file, you can install the device into the **lp** system with **lpadmin**. You may need to create or modify the interface script, but you won't encounter any major conceptual differences from normal printers. Almost any type of hard-copy device can be readily attached to a UNIX machine using the **lp** tools.

Basic Communications

Some of the richest commands in the UNIX system involve *communications* between users who share a machine, or who reside on different machines. It is generally agreed that the UNIX system provides some of the most robust and error-free tools for data communications of any popular operating system. Reliable, secure, and error-free communications across inherently noisy and unreliable communication channels such as telephone lines create definite complexities and potential problems. The UNIX system provides tools that allow you to enter this complex topic at any level, from the simple **mail** command to the sophisticated administration of queuing and security needed in the **uucp** subsystem and in high-performance *local area networks*.

The communications tools in the UNIX system have a reputation for complex and arcane features. In a sense, this reputation is deserved; however, compared to communications software offered by most other computer operating environments, the tools in the UNIX system are a model of clarity and trouble-free operation. Indeed, many other applications have liberally borrowed from the rich communications tools available in the UNIX system, but implemented them less successfully. Over the years these tools have steadily improved in reliability, in the features they offer to users, and in security. Today, many designers with communications-related problems will choose the UNIX system to solve these problems. This is especially true as local area networks grow in popularity, making communications more important than ever.

411

This chapter discusses the basic communications tools, which are primarily oriented toward ASCII files and messages, and also discusses terminal emulation. The administrative issues associated with communications and the **uucp** file transfer subsystem are discussed in Chapter 15. Local area networks are discussed in Chapter 24.

The news Command

The most basic communications tools have already been introduced in previous chapters. First is the **news** command, which allows a user to read messages "published" by the system administrator. You can execute **news** to display all news items created since the last time you executed the command, but not news items that you have already seen. Here is an example:

```
$ news

meeting (pat) Mon Jun 18 08:26:47 1990

    9:00 AM on Monday is the marketing review.  Expect everyone
    to be there with their comments on the proposal.   thanks!  -pat
$
```

After you seen the messages once, they will not be redisplayed if you execute **news** again; instead **news** will return silently, as shown here:

```
$ news
$
```

News items are usually short, but you can break out of a news item if desired. Pressing the DEL key causes **news** to stop displaying the current news item, and begin displaying the next item if there is one. Pressing DEL a second time within one second of the first press causes **news** to exit, returning you to the shell.

The **news** command includes several options for changing this default behavior. The **-n** (for names) option causes **news** to list only the names of news items that have not yet been seen. It looks like this:

```
$ news -n
news: meeting lunch welcome
$
```

The **-s** (for show) option gives you a count of the unread news items, without listing their names, as follows:

```
$ news -s
3 news items.
$
```

One of these options is often used in your **.profile**, so that any unread news is displayed each time you log in to the machine.

The **-a** (for all) option causes **news** to display all the available news items, whether they have been read previously or not. This option can produce a lot of output on a large installation. Remember, both old and unread news items are displayed with the -a option.

Any other options to the **news** command are assumed to be the names of specific items that **news** is to display, as in this example

```
$ news lunch
lunch (jim) Mon Jun 18 08:25:31 1990
   Don't forget, today is the big luncheon and party
   See you there...                      =jim
$
```

The **news** command works by maintaining a zero-length file named **.news_time** in your home directory. The modification time (displayed by **ls -l**) of **.news_time** is set to the time the **news** command is executed. When you run **news** again, only files *newer* than this file are displayed, except when the -a option is used. If **.news_time** does not exist, it is created when **news** executes.

News items available to the **news** command are kept in the directory **/usr/news**. Each news item is a separate file in this directory, and the name of the file is the name of the news item, as shown here:

```
$ ls -l /usr/news
total 3
-rw-r--r--   1 jim     other        74 Jun 18 08:25 lunch
-rw-r--r--   1 steve   other       125 Jun 18 08:26 meeting
```

```
-rw-r--r--  1 pat     other      32 Jun 18 08:24 welcome
$
```

The system administrator is usually responsible for maintaining this directory by deleting out-of-date news items. In this case the news directory may only be writable by the superuser, but it should be readable and executable by all users. However, on some systems the **/usr/news** directory is publicly writable, so that all users can create news items by leaving files in the directory. In any case, files created in the directory must be publicly readable or the **news** command will fail.

The Message of the Day

Another facility with a similar function is the *message of the day*. Although there is no command for this, most systems include the facility. The message of the day is generally used for higher priority messages than those displayed by **news**, such as expected downtime or last-minute system changes. In practice, the system **/etc/profile** includes the line

```
cat /etc/motd
```

(for message of the day). Since the system profile is executed when users log in to the machine, the contents of the **motd** file are displayed. Unlike **news**, this file is displayed each time the user logs in, so out-of-date messages in the **motd** file get tedious very quickly when users log in repeatedly. The **/etc/motd** should be readable by all, but maintained (and thus writable) only by the superuser, as follows:

```
$ ls -l /etc/motd
-rw-r--r--  1 root    sys       421 Jun 14  1990 /etc/motd
$
```

The write Command

The **write** command provides direct communications between two users, by sending messages directly to their terminal devices. It is similar to the line

```
$ echo message > /dev/other-tty
```

where *other-tty* is the actual device name the person you wish to communicate with is using. These messages will interrupt any display on the terminal of the recipient. The **write** command is a little more sophisticated than the previous example, and provides several additional services. First, **write** takes the login id of the recipient as an argument, so that you can **write** to another user without knowing the tty device they are using, as shown here:

```
$ write jim < message
$
```

The **write** command will determine the user's terminal device and send the message there. When the message has been written, **write** will exit back to the shell. The **write** command will return an error message if the specified user is not logged in. For example:

```
$ write pat
pat is not logged in.
$
```

Users can disable this kind of direct communication to their terminal by setting

```
$ mesg n
$
```

(for no messages). Messages can be turned on again with

```
$ mesg y
$
```

(for messages yes). The **mesg** command works by changing the permissions on the device file associated with a terminal. If a user has set messages off, **write** will return a different error message, as shown here:

```
$ write jim
Permission denied.
$
```

Often, **write** access is disabled when high-quality output is directed to the terminal, as it is in some printing tasks.

Using write Interactively

Because **write** reads its standard input for the message to send, it can be used in a more direct mode. If the command is simply

```
$ write pat
```

with no redirection of input, **write** will make the connection to the recipient, and send two "beeps" back to signal that the connection is open. Then you can type your message directly at the keyboard, and **write** will send it to the recipient line by line.

Once you have established a connection with **write**, it is held open until you break it with CTRL-D, the end-of-file operator. Until then, everything typed at your terminal will appear at the recipient's terminal. However, the communications channel is one-way; there is no way for the recipient to send messages back. To communicate with you, the original recipient must also use the **write** command with your login id as argument. Then there are actually two **write** paths open, one from your terminal to the recipient, and another from the recipient back to you. Each of the two connections must be broken individually by its creator before things will be completely back to normal.

When someone uses **write** to call you, a banner is displayed on your terminal, and then the caller's message is displayed line by line, as shown here:

```
Message from pat on my_sys (console) [ Mon Jun 18 08:29:58 ] ...

hi steve, how are you today?
```

You must **write** back to answer the message. Often there is a noticeable delay between each line of the received messages, both because the other user must type in the line before it is sent to you, and because the UNIX system must then handle the line. In a heavily loaded machine, communication with **write** can be relatively slow. Furthermore, it is easy for the communication to become confused because both users can send messages to each other simultaneously, and you might try to answer a comment before the other user has finished typing it. Consequently, users have evolved a simple protocol for using **write**. Usually it works like this: The original sender creates a connection to the recipient, which may include a one-line greeting. Then the recipient writes back, signaling a readiness to communicate. Next, the first user sends a multiline message, ending it with **o** (for over). The recipient usually waits for the **o** to be sure the message is complete, and then responds, using as many lines as necessary and adding the **o** to signal that the message is complete. After that, the original caller has another chance, and so on. One person will eventually end the conversation with **o-o** or **oo** (for over and out). The other person can continue, until he or she is ready to enter **o-o** also. Finally, both users might enter CTRL-D to exit from **write** back to the shell. Remember, both sides must break out of **write** with CTRL-D to break their end of the two-way connection. This CB-like protocol is not enforced by the **write** program; it is only a convention that most users follow. Thus, it is possible to become quite confused during two-way writes, and for this reason **mail** is preferred over **write** for most communications. Nevertheless, **write** is a fun command that has a definite place in interuser communications.

The wall Command

The **write** command only allows communications with a single user named as its command-line argument. Occasionally you need to send a message to all the users logged into the machine. For example, system shutdowns should be announced to all users to warn them to secure their sessions before the system goes down. Rather than making you **write** to each user individually, the UNIX system provides the **wall** (for write all) command, which is located in **/usr/sbin/wall**. The **wall** command is usually executable by all users, but it is used routinely only by the system administrator. Like **write**, **wall** reads its standard input for the message to send, as follows:

```
# wall < message.file
```

It then sends the message to all users who are currently logged in, including the originator. The message is preceded by the same header **write** produces, and these messages can also be refused by the recipient with the **mesg n** command. There is no facility that allows **wall** recipients to write back to the originator.

The mail Command Revisited

The most widely used tool for interuser communication is the *electronic mail* facility, discussed briefly in Chapter 2. Mail is used by nearly all users, and several electronic mail programs are available offering different features and functions. These packages range from very simple and easy to extremely feature-rich and complex. Because the UNIX system is so good at communications, electronic mail has always been one of the most fertile areas of development, and the mail tools provided with alternate versions of the system sometimes differ in major ways.

A Note on Versions of the Mail Service

The standard mail program supplied with SVR4 is much enhanced over the older System V *mailers*. It can send binary files, such as executable programs or documents from advanced word processors, as well as ASCII text. It can create *multipart* messages that contain several independent components. In addition, mail addressing conventions have been adapted from the BSD UNIX and AT&T Mail systems. These new and enhanced features can be used to send mail between users on a single SVR4 system, or between users on different SVR4 machines that are connected by a local area network. However, most other mail programs can only accept text messages; that is, only normal ASCII files acceptable to the standard editors are allowed. This means you must take care to include only data formats allowed by the mail tools your correspondents use when you create mail messages. In addition—and this is much more difficult—you must be sure the *intermediate* machines that may handle a message on its way to delivery also support all the mail features you use. To be totally safe, restrict mail to recipients that you do not know well to simple, text-only messages. There are other tools you can use to transfer nontext files, unless you are sure the recipient will be able to read the files you send. However, mail messages can be of any length, so long text files, documents, or **shar** archives can be transferred safely by mail if desired.

Mail Concepts

All mail programs process the *incoming mail* and store it in a special *mailbox* or *inbox* owned by the recipient. Mail remains in the mailbox until the recipient reads the message and deletes it from the mailbox. In most systems, incoming mail is stored in the directory **/var/mail**, with one file per user. This mail file is generally called your mailbox, but additional mailboxes can be created as you read and save mail into them. The mail tools will concatenate multiple messages sent to a user into this single file, but will display the individual messages separately when the mail is read.

The standard electronic mail command is called simply **mail**. It is used both to send electronic mail to other users and to retrieve mail that has been sent to you.

Sending Mail

To send mail, use **mail** with a list of user ids as command-line arguments. The **mail** command then reads its standard input for the message. When multiple users are given as command-line arguments, the same message is sent to all the named users. For example:

```
$ mail jim pat < message.file
$
```

In addition, **mail** will accept its standard input from the terminal if redirection is not used. In this case, the CTRL-D end-of-file character ends the message, as follows:

```
$ mail jim pat
here is a short test message.
see you at lunch....  =steve
```

```
CTRL-D
$
```

You can also end the message by entering . (dot) on a line by itself. This feature prohibits you from generating a mail message that contains a legitimate dot on a line by itself.

Sending Binary Files in Mail

With the input redirection method of creating mail, you can send non-text files in mail between SVR4 systems. The form

```
$ mail jim < binary.file
```

will send **binary.file** to user **jim**. Be sure that your recipient, and all intervening machines, can handle binary data before you try this form. Some releases of SVR4 require that you enable binary mail before you can use it; if so, this is handled in the file **/etc/mail/mailsurr**. Experiment with binary mail before depending on it.

Reading Your Mail

When new mail is delivered to your inbox, the shell displays this announcement at the terminal:

```
You have mail.
```

This message can appear just after a command exits, but before the shell displays the PS1 prompt. You can ignore it, but it will not be redisplayed unless more new mail arrives.

Executing the **mail** command with no arguments opens your mailbox and displays the first message, as shown here:

```
$ mail
From jim Mon Jun 18 08:37 EDT 1990

don't forget to return my book.... thanks.    -jim
?
```

After a message is displayed, **mail** pauses and prompts with a **?** for a command. It expects you to take some action—to skip over the message, save it, delete it, and so on. To display a complete list of the possible actions, enter **?** (for help) at the prompt (or see Figure 2-1). You can respond to the **?** prompt with **d** (for delete) to delete the message, **+** (for next) to skip the message without removing it, **q** (for quit) to exit from the **mail** program, or **s** (for save) to remove the message from the mailbox and save it in a file. There are also many other options. If you respond by moving to a new message, that message will be displayed, and **mail** will pause again with the **?** waiting for your response. When there are no more messages, **mail** exits back to the shell.

The **s** operator can take a filename as an argument, which is the name of a file to be used for the message. If you enter **s** with no argument, the default file will be **mbox**, in your home directory. When mail is saved into an existing file, it is appended, so several mail messages can reside in a save file.

If the incoming message is binary (or any nontext data), **mail** will not try to display it, but will issue a warning message instead, as shown here:

```
$ mail
From root Mon Jun 18 14:45 EDT 1990
Content-Length: 31940

Message content is not printable: delete, write or save it to a file
?
```

You cannot display nontext files, so you must save them and use the intended application to read them.

The **mail** command can take the **-f** (for file) argument with a filename to specify another mailbox rather than the system's normal inbox. This allows you to reread mail that has been saved in different files. The command

```
$ mail -f mbox
```

will open the file **mbox** rather than the inbox. If the named file is a proper mailbox created by the **s** option from reading your mail, all the normal functions of the **mail** program will work as expected on the named file.

mail Message Structure

The first lines of each message are known as the *postmark*. On messages sent from users on the same machine as the recipient, the postmark will contain only one line, but if a message has been forwarded from another user or from another machine, the postmark can contain more lines, one for each step the message took on its way to your incoming mailbox. The postmark is not created by the sending user, but is added by the **mail** delivery software, and as you will see, it can be valuable.

Other lines at the beginning of the message, before the message text, are usually called the *message headers*. The headers will usually be of the form

```
name: value
```

where *name* is the name of a specific header, and *value* is the specific contents associated with that *name* keyword. Many **mail** programs may produce voluminous headers including **To:**, **From:**, **Date:**, and up to 20 or 30 other lines. Again, these are not usually created directly by the sender, but are added by the **mail** program before it sends the message.

Creating Messages with Headers

The standard SVR4 **mail** program always adds one header, the **Content-Length:** header that gives the size (in bytes) of the message to follow. In addition, it can produce two optional headers, a **To:** line and a **Message-Type:** line, but these are not added by default. The **-t** command-line option will add the **To:** header if it is given when the message is created, as shown here:

```
$ mail -t steve jim
```

In addition to the postmark, this message will include a **To:** line that names the intended recipients. The **To:** line can be helpful if the message is sent to more than one recipient, and you wish each person to know who else has received the message. Similarly, the **-m** option followed by a message type, can be added to the command line. Note that message type is user-defined, and is not the same as content type.

You can also create a **Subject:** header line by entering

```
Subject: subject text follows here
```

as the *first* line of your message text. The **mail** program will move this **Subject:** line from the body of the message into the headers.

Displaying a Summary of Mailbox Contents

Each mail message you receive will include some postmarks and headers. The **mail** program can be instructed to display these headers in a formatted list, allowing you to peruse the mailbox contents without reading each message. Then, a specific message can be individually picked from the display for reading, deletion, or other action. The **-h** (for headers) option for reading mail will display this header summary when **mail** begins. It looks like this:

```
$ mail -h
```

Alternatively, the **h** option is available from the **?** prompt within **mail**, as shown here:

```
? h
2 letters in /var/mail/steve, 0 scheduled for deletion, 2 newly arrived
>   2   250    pat         Tue Jun 19 14:37 EDT 1990
    1   556    jim         Mon Jun 18 08:37 EDT 1990
?
```

The messages are listed in inverse order, so that the most recent message is at the top of the list. The *current* message is marked with a > in the leftmost column, and many of the available commands, such as **s** or **d**, operate on the current message by default. Each message has a *message number,* in the column after the >, and this number can be used to refer to the message. If you enter a message number after the **?** prompt, that message will be displayed. For example,

```
? 2
```

will display message number 2. In addition, the message number can be given after some other commands. For example, to delete message number 1, you could use

```
? d 1
```

regardless of which is the current message. The sender is listed next, and finally the time stamp from the message postmark. This information is often helpful if you've received a lot of mail.

When deleted, messages are not actually eliminated from the mailbox until the **mail** program ends. The message is only *marked* for deletion, although it is no longer displayed in the header list. Deleted messages can still be read until you've exited from the **mail** program; then they are physically removed from the mailbox and discarded. The **ha** (for headers of all messages) command displays deleted as well as current messages, as shown here:

```
? h a
2 letters found in steve, 1 scheduled for deletion, 0 newly arrived
    2    250     pat         Tue Jun 19 14:37 EDT 1990
>   1  d 556     jim         Mon Jun 18 08:37 EDT 1990
?
```

In this example, message number one has been marked for deletion, as the presence of the **d** indicates. It can be undeleted before you exit **mail** with

```
? u 1
```

(for undelete). The named message will be undeleted unless no message number is specified, in which case the current message will be undeleted.

Replying to a Mail Message

Often when you receive a message, you wish to answer it. The **mail** command provides an option you can use after the **?** prompt to *reply* to a message. The **r** (for reply) command handles this task by deducing the name and mailing address of the person who sent the message and then spawning a new **mail** program to accept your text for the reply. When the reply operation is completed the sending **mail** program exits, returning you to the mail reading program. The reply operation can be tricky, however, especially if the original message was received from a remote machine, so treat the reply function with care. The process of interpreting the postmark is sometimes very difficult, and the reply option does not always work as you would expect. You may need to address the message manually, as discussed in the next section.

Addressing Mail to Other Users

In the preceding examples, the *addressee* for the message was a login id on the same machine. In this example

```
$ mail jim pat
```

jim and **pat** must be login ids for users on your machine. However, the **mail** facility can also send messages to users on other UNIX machines. This is usually called *remote mail,* because the addressee is a user on a machine that is remote from yours. It is even possible to send mail to a user on another machine *through* a third machine. This *multi-hop* mail is very common, especially in environments with local area networks. In fact, there are several international networks of UNIX system users who communicate worldwide with these multi-hop mail features. Several address formats exist to support these different network types.

The simplest form of addressing specifies a complete *path* for the message to take from your machine to the destination. In this form, mail is addressed to remote users on the **mail** command line by giving the unique name of their machine, followed by their unique user id on that machine. The **!** (bang) character separates the two items, with no whitespace allowed between them, as follows:

```
$ mail other!user
```

Multiple recipients can also be specified in this way, as shown here:

```
$ mail other!user remote!friend
```

In this example, *other* and *remote* are the names of machines, and *user* and *friend* are the user ids of the people to whom you might send mail.

In fact, there can be more than one other machine in the path the mail takes to reach the recipient, as in this example:

```
$ mail other!remote!user
```

Here, the message will be sent to the machine *other*, and the **mail** software there will receive it and forward it to the machine named *remote*, where it will be delivered to *user*. Up to 20 such *hops* are allowed with this kind of addressing.

Domain Addressing

A second address format is often used with mailers that can support it. This style is called *domain addressing,* and it allows you to give a *logical* address rather than a complete path to the destination machine. Mail of this form is usually handed off to a *mail server* process on a *gateway* machine, which consults a table of known addresses, and sends the message to a machine given as a target for that address. The target machine then repeats the process until the message finally reaches its destination. The standard SVR4 **mail** program can handle domain addressing, but some older mailers cannot.

With domain addressing, you send a message to a user *at* a destination domain. The usual form is

```
user@gateway.domain
```

where the user id is followed by an @ (at sign), which is followed by the gateway machine for that domain, and then by a . (dot) and the domain name. For example, you might write

```
$ mail steve@yoursys.com
```

Sometimes you can add additional machine names after the @ to indicate a specific machine within that gateway. For example:

```
$ mail steve@my_sys.yoursys.com
```

Here, **yoursys** may be a *subnet,* and **my_sys** may be a gateway or the target machine. Domain addressing can be very complex; take care to get the address exactly right for your correspondents. Some addresses may use a % (percent sign) instead of one of the dots, or a dot instead of the @ symbol.

Only a few domains have been defined, although many gateways can be in a domain, and many individual machines can be supported by a gateway. The most common domains are **com** (for commercial), **edu** (for education), and **gov** (for government).

With domain addressing, the mailer (or the gateway server!) checks a local database of domain names to *resolve* the logical address and find the most efficient way to pass the message to the next machine. In SVR4, this database is located in the **/etc/mail/mailsurr** (for mail surrogate) file, but changing it correctly can be very complex. Consult your network administrator before you modify **mailsurr** or other domain files.

Bang-style addressing in the remote mail tools rests on the **uucp** data communications subsystem, which is discussed in Chapter 15. However, you must note here that unless a remote machine is known to your **uucp** system or to your domain database, you cannot send mail to it, although it may be possible to receive mail from it. Thus, when remote or multi-hop mail fails to be sent from your system, the likely culprit is the **uucp** list of known remote machines or the domain database. With multi-hop mail, each intervening machine must know about the next machine in the delivery path. You must be very sure that the path is valid before you send a message, or the message may not be delivered as expected. In fact, an intermediate machine may discard a message without returning an error to the original sender if the next machine in the path is unknown to it.

Forwarding Mail

You can specify that mail addressed to you be forwarded to another addressee. That is, **mail** supports the concept of a *forwarding address,* which means that incoming mail is not necessarily delivered to the intended recipient but may be resent to another addressee. In SVR4 systems, the **mail** command can take a command-line option to specify a forwarding address. To use the **-F** (for forward) option, you must delete or save all the mail in your incoming mailbox; an empty mailbox is required to use mail forwarding. The command

```
$ mail -F new!address
```

will establish forwarding to the *new!address* specified. All the rules given above for message addressing also apply to the new address. For example, you can specify a local addressee, as shown here,

```
$ mail -F jim
```

or a remote address, as in this example:

```
$ mail -F other!steve
```

The first form is often used when you use more than one login id on a machine, or when someone else is covering your incoming mail. The remote form is usually used when you have login ids on more than one machine, and one id is preferred. Most users forward mail from the less used login id to the more often used id or machine.

   Once it is established, forwarding stays in force indefinitely, and all incoming mail is *bounced* to the forwarding address. To remove forwarding, a null argument is given with the **-F** argument, as follows:

```
$ mail -F ""
```

The empty quotation marks instruct the shell to reserve an empty command-line argument after the **-F**. This turns forwarding off, and incoming mail is again deposited in your inbox.

   When mail is forwarded, your attempts to read your mail will fail; thus, you can test whether or not mail is being forwarded, as follows:

```
$ mail -F jim
Forwarding to jim
$ mail
Your mail is being forwarded to jim
$
```

In older releases before SVR3 the **mail -F** command is not present, and a different mechanism is required to establish forwarding: First, you delete or save all your mail, and then you send a dummy mail message to yourself. Next you edit the file **/var/mail/login** with your favorite editor, where *login* is your user id. Once you are in the editor, delete the entire contents of the file, and add the line

```
Forward to address
```

at the beginning of the file. The capital **F** at the beginning of the line is required, and *address* is the forwarding address as discussed previously. Finally, write the file and quit from the editor. Forwarding will be enabled until you edit the file again and remove the "Forward to..." line. Do not create the file manually; make **mail** do it by sending a message to yourself. This ensures that the inbox will have the correct ownership and permissions, so the **mail** program will treat it correctly.

Automatically Answering Incoming Mail

If you are unavailable for some reason, such as a vacation, you can configure SVR4 **mail** to automatically answer incoming messages with a stock reply. Your mail will be saved, and your correspondents will get an immediate response. You can specify the text of the reply, or use a default response provided by the system. When you return, you can restore normal **mail** service.

Use the **vacation** command to establish autoanswer service, as follows:

```
$ vacation
Forwarding to |/usr/lib/mail/vacation2 -o %R
$
```

You must delete or save all your mail, or **vacation** will complain, as shown here:

```
$ vacation
mail: Cannot install/remove forwarding without empty mailfile
$
```

If you do not like the canned message given in the **vacation(1)** man page, you can create an alternate message file and give its name following the **-M** (for message) option, like this:

```
$ vacation -M my.reply
```

By default, **vacation** saves your incoming messages in the file **$HOME/.mailfile**. You can change this by naming another file after the **-m** (for mailfile) option to **vacation**. When you return, you can read this saved mail easily, by issuing the command

```
$ mail -f $HOME/.mailfile
```

Be sure to reestablish normal **mail** service when you return, as follows:

```
$ mail -F ""
```

As you may have realized, **vacation** is just a smart form of mail forwarding.

The rmail Command

There is an additional executable program associated with the mail facility, but it should never be executed directly. This is the **rmail** (for remote mail) command, which is used internally in the operation of the mail facility. The **rmail** command usually handles domain address resolution and the *queuing* of mail for **uucp** or LAN-based mail systems. It must be present in the **/usr/bin** directory or the mail system will not work correctly.

Terminal Emulation with the cu Command

The UNIX system provides a standard *terminal emulation* program called **cu** (for call up). This command is often called "call UNIX" by users, but its use is not limited to connecting to another UNIX system.

The **cu** command can connect to almost any machine that provides asynchronous ASCII communications, including MS-DOS machines, bulletin board systems, and most *protocol converters* that convert from IBM 3270 type terminals to asynchronous ASCII format. Of course, some additional functions are available with **cu** if the remote machine is also running the UNIX system.

The **cu** command is actually part of the **uucp** data transfer system, and it uses the **uucp** control files and any external or built-in *modem* attached to the machine. Usually an autodialing modem is required to use terminal emulation functions, but in a small machine it may be possible to manually dial a telephone attached to an external modem providing the **cu** program is executed first, and then the call is dialed.

You execute the **cu** command with a machine name as argument, as shown here:

```
$ cu remote
```

The command consults the **uucp** control files to determine how to set up a connection to the named machine, and then places the call to that machine. The call can be made over dial-up telephone lines, through a hard-wired permanent data link, or across some types of local area networks. If no communications path is specified in the **uucp** databases, **cu** will fail, because communications parameters such as transmission speed and calling scripts are located there.

When the connection is made, **cu** returns the following message.

```
$ cu remote
Connected
```

If the connection fails for some reason, **cu** returns an error message. The possible error messages are the same as those for the **uucp** system. Once the connection is made, **cu** waits for your keystrokes, which it will pass unchanged to the remote machine. There you can log in, or take whatever action is appropriate. All characters sent by the remote machine to the local machine will be passed through **cu** to your terminal; thus, you use the same TERM variable on the remote machine that you use on the local machine, and full-screen functions will work as expected on the remote machine.

In addition, **cu** allows the remote connection to be specified as a telephone number; however, this form only works if an autodial modem is attached to the system. For example,

```
$ cu 5559876
```

will call the given telephone number. The telephone number can be as long as necessary, but it should be all digits, except for some additional characters that have special meanings. The - (minus) character signals a delay of about four seconds, so **cu** can dial though telephone networks that have long-latency switches or connection delays. The = (equal) character causes **cu** to wait for a secondary dial tone. For example, in a business office you might dial 9 to get an outside line with a dial tone, followed by 1 and a long-distance number. At the far end, a remote PBX might answer with another dial tone, and you would then dial an extension number. In this situation, the following command might be appropriate:

```
$ cu 9=13035559876=1234
```

Such complex telephone numbers must be tested to be sure that they work correctly, because the sequence of dial tones and delays must usually be worked out on a case-by-case basis.

Disconnecting from a cu Session

After you have completed your terminal emulation session at the remote host, log out of the remote machine normally. Then you can signal **cu** to hang up the call and exit to the shell. The ~. (tilde dot) command tells **cu** to exit. It must be entered on a line by itself, directly after a newline. Furthermore, a newline must immediately follow it, as shown here:

```
$ cu remote
Connected

~[uname].
Disconnected
$
```

The **cu** command prints the name of the local machine within the square brackets, after you enter the command. This is an example of an *internal command*, discussed later in this chapter. You should log off the remote machine correctly before you enter ~., because some remote machines will not respond correctly if the communications line is hung up abruptly. There is no other way to end a session with **cu** short of unplugging the cable from the communications port, because **cu** passes all other characters to the remote machine, including the CTRL-Z job control character.

cu Command-Line Options

By default, **cu** expects the connection to be *full-duplex*, with character *echo* provided by the remote system. Usually the connection *baud rate* (or speed) is determined by the **uucp** data files, or it defaults to 1200 bps when a telephone number is specified; however, these defaults can be changed by command-line options to **cu**. The -s (for speed) option takes as its argument the desired speed, which can be 300, 1200, 2400, 4800, or 9600 bps. For example,

```
$ cu -s 2400 2345678
```

calls the telephone number, and sets the communications speed to 2400 bps. The -s option will also override the setting in the **uucp** data file if it is used. The command

```
$ cu -s 9600 sysname
```

will connect to machine *sysname* at 9600 bps. Of course, the speed you select must match the capabilities of the modem and the remote system.

If the remote system does not echo characters sent to it, the -h (for half-duplex) option to **cu** can be specified. This option causes **cu** to immediately echo all characters typed at your terminal. This is not a true half-duplex communications channel, because characters typed at the keyboard are immediately sent to the remote machine even if it is sending characters to your machine. In addition, you can specify one of the **cu** options -o (for odd), or -e (for even) to set the communications parity appropriately for characters sent to the remote machine. By default, no parity is used.

The -l (for line) option can be used to specify a specific tty port to use for the communications. This option is handy when you wish to override the **uucp** data for some reason, or when a communications device is directly attached to a serial port. For example, if an intelligent modem with a stored database of telephone numbers is attached to the COM2 port, the following command will allow direct access to the modem through **cu**.

```
$ cu -l /dev/tty01s
```

When the modem answers by setting its *carrier detect* signal, **cu** will return the "Connected" message, and your keystrokes will be read by the modem. You can reprogram the modem or use its built-in command set to dial out from there. The **-l** option also works when one machine is hard-wired to another over a serial port.

The **-d** (for debug) option instructs **cu** to display a trace of its progress in making a connection. The **-d** option is very useful for diagnosing problems with the connections **cu** tries to make, and for learning more about the way **cu** works. Debugging **cu** connections is discussed in Chapter 15, since it is really a part of the **uucp** subsystem. In addition, **cu** can take several other options, but these have more limited usefulness.

Going Further

The **cu** command is much more useful than you have seen so far. Its real power comes from its internal commands and its ability to read and write command output across the communication line to the remote system. We will discuss these features of **cu** next, and then turn to some additional **mail** issues.

cu Internal Commands

The **cu** command includes several *internal commands* that provide more features. These commands are signaled by starting the command with a ~ (tilde), at the beginning of a line (right after a newline). The ~ signals **cu** that a command is coming next, and **cu** then reads the rest of the typed line rather than passing it to the remote machine. For example, to exit from **cu** back to the shell, you use the command ~. (tilde dot), as discussed earlier. When **cu** recognizes the ~, it immediately echoes it to the terminal. When it recognizes the dot, it displays the name of the system within the brackets, and then tilde echoes the dot. The system name is always displayed for all tilde commands, but not until the next character is recognized.

The **cu** command provides many more tilde commands. You can escape temporarily to a local subshell while keeping the **cu** connection active, with ~! (tilde bang). Any commands can be executed from this subshell without hanging up the connection to the remote machine. When you are finished with the local shell, kill it as usual with CTRL-D or **exit**. Then **cu** will echo a ! to signal that it is back in control, and will resume sending your typed characters to the remote machine. For example:

```
~[my_sys]!
$ echo $HOME
/home/steve
$ exit
!
```

The **cu** command will not redraw the display screen after it regains control, because it immediately begins passing characters through to the remote machine. Any screen-refresh operation must be handled at the remote machine.

A single command can be executed on the local machine with the tilde command ~!**cmd** where *cmd* is any command line or pipeline. In this case, **cu** temporarily suspends communications to the remote system and executes the command line in a local subshell. When the command completes, **cu** will echo the ! and return to action.

ASCII File Transfer with cu

When communication is between two UNIX systems, **cu** has built-in tilde commands for passing data in either direction. These are ~%**put** (tilde percent followed by *put*), and ~%**take** (tilde percent followed by *take*). These commands send a file from the local to the remote machine, and from the remote to the local machine, respectively. Each takes a filename as an argument, as follows:

```
~[my_sys]%put my.file
```

The remote machine must be waiting at the PS1 prompt for these commands to succeed. The previous example will create a file named **my.file** on the remote machine, and copy a local file named **my.file** to it. While the transfer is in progress, **cu** will display a digit on the local machine marking each 1000 character chunk transferred. When the copy is complete, **cu** will display a final byte count and a completion message, as shown here:

```
~[my_sys]%put my.file
stty -echo;(cat - > my.file)||cat ->/dev/null; stty echo
1234+
247 lines/4257 characters
$
```

The first output shows how **cu** implements the **put** and **take** operations. This is a command that is sent to the remote UNIX system. Echo is turned off, and the standard input is redirected to the filename. When **cat** ends, echo is turned on. The **cu** command on the local machine sends the file, echoing a digit 1, 2, 3, and 4 as each chunk of data is sent. Finally, the total byte and line count is displayed, and **cu** returns to displaying the PS1 at the remote machine. These actions are reversed for the **take** operation.

It is possible to change the name of the transferred file between the local and the remote machine, if the second filename is given as another argument to the **put** or **take** operations, as shown here:

```
~[my_sys]%take from.file to.file
```

In this example, **from.file** is copied from the remote machine into **to.file** on the local machine. The **put** operation is similar, as this command line demonstrates:

```
~[my_sys]%put from.file to.file
```

In this case **from.file** is the local filename and **to.file** is the new file created on the remote machine.

Remember, no error checking is provided by **cu** during these file transfer operations, so you should always confirm that the target file is the same size as the source file. The **wc** command can provide this information, but sometimes **cu** replaces tab characters in the source file with the appropriate number of spaces in the target file, so usually only the line and word counts from **wc** are helpful; the character counts may not match.

Transferring Binary Files with cu

The **cu** program is designed for ASCII terminal emulation only. It can transfer ASCII files from one machine to another, but it *cannot* directly transfer binary or other nontext files between machines. The **cu** command includes no error-checking file transfer protocol such as KERMIT or XMODEM. Usually **uucp** is used to transfer binary files; however, **cu** allows execution of a program on both sides of the data link, with input and output redirected through the ASCII communications channel provided by **cu**. Thus, it is possible to add application software at both ends of the data connection that can convert binary data to ASCII form, transfer it to the other side, and then convert it back to binary form.

One **cu** internal command can support this function. This is ~**$cmd** where *cmd* is any command line. The *cmd* is executed on the local machine, but the output of *cmd* is sent over the communications line to the remote system, rather than to the local display. This allows you to create a script on the local machine that can *drive* the remote machine. A login script is one example of how this feature might be used. Also, a file-transfer application might be developed in which you execute one side of the application on the remote system, and then use the ~$ command to execute a matching command on the local machine.

The scenario is as follows: the remote application reads its standard input, so that data crossing the communications channel is seen by the remote application. Then the ~$ command causes the output of the local *cmd* to be sent, so that it is read by the remote application. The remote application can then send the string ~>:*filename* where *filename* is the name of a file on the local machine. After this command, all data sent from the remote machine will be redirected to the file. When the remote system sends a line consisting only of ~ >, the *filename* is closed and **cu** begins sending received data to the terminal. This provides a general-purpose mechanism for transferring data between machines. The application programs on each side have the responsibility of converting the data to ASCII form, and then reconstructing the original binary data after the transfer. You might try **uuencode/uudecode** or **btoa/atob** to convert between ASCII and binary data; one of these is usually present on SVR4 machines.

Other Internal cu Commands

Several other useful tilde commands are provided by **cu**. For example, ~**%cd** will change the current directory on the local machine to the argument given to the **cd** command, as follows:

```
~[my_sys]%cd /usr/src
```

This command will change the directory that **cu** thinks is current. The command

```
~[my_sys]!cd /usr/src
```

would not work, because it would will be executed in a subshell, rather than directly by **cu**. When the subshell completed, **cu** would still have the same current directory that it had before the ~! command was executed.

Finally, the command ~**%b** will send a *break* signal to the remote machine. This is usually not needed, because on most machines **cu** can detect the BREAK key and correctly send a break signal to the remote machine. The command ~**%d** toggles debugging output on and off, while ~**%ifc** (for input flow control) and ~**%ofc** (for output flow control) toggle input and output CTRL-S/CTRL-Q flow control on and off. Several other tilde commands are available to **cu**, but they are designed for debugging, and are rarely used.

The mailx Command

There is one additional mail program available in the standard SVR4 system. This is the **mailx** (for experimental mail) command. The **mailx** program is a front-end processor for **mail** that provides advanced user-interface features much like those in the BSD **sendmail** facility. Mail messages created by **mailx** are actually sent by the **rmail** program, and **mailx** reads incoming mail from the same **/var/mail/login** directory used by **mail**. In practice, most users settle into using either **mail** or **mailx** (or some other advanced package!), based on their individual preference, and then rarely use the other program.

Although **mailx** is executed like **mail**, there are many differences in the acceptable command-line options. For example,

```
$ mailx
```

is used to read mail, and

```
$ mailx addressee-list
```

is used to send mail. The **-H** (for headers) option causes **mailx** to print only the message headers, and then exit.

The basic operation of **mailx** is very much like **mail**, but **mailx** provides a great many enhancements and convenience features. In addition to sophisticated tools for listing message headers, **mailx** includes a profile facility. When **mailx** is executed, it starts by looking for two files: **/etc/mail/mailx.rc**, which is a systemwide profile for all users, and **$HOME/.mailrc** (for mail run control), which is a user-specific control file. These two files can contain commands in a special format defined for **mailx** that effectively make **mailx** a mail-oriented programming language, and allow extensive customization of its operation. We will not describe the details of this control language here, but you should know that they can significantly change the appearance of the header display for incoming messages. In addition, the control language allows you to create a semipermanent set of message headers that can be added to each message you create, without reentering the headers each time. A wildcard expansion facility, with substitutions controlled by variables, allows you to add information such as the current date or the current **To:** list to the message. In addition, a *signature* facility lets you predefine a block of lines that are then added to the end of each message as it is created. Many more capabilities are provided by the **mailx** control file. The **mailx** program is a very powerful electronic mail utility, although it can be quite slow in operation, especially on a heavily loaded machine.

The ct Command

Finally, you can instruct your machine to dial an outgoing call not to another UNIX machine but to a remote terminal. This allows you to make a login connection to a terminal *from the host,* forcing the host's account to pay telephone charges. The **ct** (for call terminal) command is designed to do this, but in many releases it does not work correctly. Experiment on your system to see if **ct** works for you.

The **ct** command takes a telephone number or machine name as a command-line argument, and other arguments in the same form as those used with **cu**. For example:

```
$ ct -s2400 5556789
```

The **ct** command dials the number, and if it answers with a modem tone, **ct** will execute a **login:** on the terminal, so that you can log in just as though you had called the host from the terminal. When the session ends, **ct** detects the hangup and cleans up after itself.

You might use **ct** within a scheduled **at** job to call a number at a specific time. You could even schedule a morning wake-up call using this procedure!

The uucp Data Communications Subsystem

The uuto Command
The uupick Command
A Note on uucp Security
The uucp Command
The uux Command
The uustat Command
Administration of the uucp Subsystem
Going Further

In addition to the many communications tools already discussed, the UNIX system includes a very powerful and sophisticated *background* data communications facility that allows files to move between machines, without much attention from the user. The **uucp** (for UNIX to UNIX copy) subsystem is a complete data-movement package that can transfer both ASCII and binary files between machines, and can control execution of commands on a remote machine. It can queue jobs for later transfer and automatically retry when a transfer fails for some reason. The **uucp** subsystem includes many user commands and functions, as well as complete customization facilities for different communication networks. In addition, the **uucp** subsystem offers strong security features, complete logging and debugging tools, and several different data transfer *protocols* that match error checking to the network type.

Intermachine electronic mail uses this facility, and the **uucp** subsystem provides many more capabilities. The **mail** program handles many of these interactions, so the user need not know much about the **uucp** subsystem itself. Since SVR4 **mail** can transfer binary as well as ASCII files, you can usually avoid learning much about the **uucp** system if your correspondents reside on other SVR4 machines. But if you must exchange files with non-SVR4 machines, **uucp** will be the main communication tool available to you. Because the **uucp** subsystem is so powerful and sophisticated, it can be quite difficult to administer and set up correctly. The subject of **uucp** administration is discussed later in this chapter; in the first few sections we assume that a working **uucp** subsystem already exists on your machine.

The uuto Command

The easiest way to move files between machines is with the **uuto** (for UNIX to UNIX "to") command for sending files, and the **uupick** (for UNIX to UNIX pickup) command for retrieving files sent from another machine. The **uuto** command takes a filename list and a remote address as arguments, as shown here:

```
$ uuto data1 data2 remote!login
```

The address is the last argument; it follows all the filenames. The address takes the same form here as it does for **mail**: a remote machine name and login id separated by a ! (bang) character. Unlike **mail**, **uuto** allows only a single destination, so you cannot send the same file to several recipients with a single command line. As many filenames as required can follow the **uuto** command, but the address must be the last argument.

The **uuto** command does not actually transfer files, but rather *queues* them for transfer by the **uucp** system when it can. The **uucp** subsystem can delay transfer for hours or days, so the files may not reach their destination for some time. If the transfer is queued correctly, **uuto** will return to the shell after a second or two, and you can continue with your session.

The **uuto** command can accept two command-line options. The **-m** (for mail) option causes **uuto** to send electronic mail to the sending user as well as the recipient when the data transfer is complete. The **-p** option causes **uuto** to make a copy of the file during the queuing process. If the **-p** option is not used, **uuto** requires that the file retain the same name, and that it not be deleted until after the transfer is complete. If the file is changed between the time it is queued and the time it is sent, the changed version will be sent. If the **-p** option is used, the contents of the file at the time it was queued will be sent, and the original file can be moved, deleted, or changed. Because the **-p** option causes the file to be duplicated, it uses some additional disk space. This may be a consideration if many large files are being transferred.

Unlike the **mail** command, **uuto** does not allow multi-hop addressing. If there is no direct path between the source and destination machines, use **uuto** to move the files to a third machine that knows about both, and get a friend there to forward the files to their final destination.

The uupick Command

When the files have been transferred, the **uucp** system on the receiving machine will send electronic mail to the recipient, announcing that the files have arrived from the other machine. When that mail is received, the recipient can use the **uupick** command to copy the files from the directory where **uucp** left them, into the recipient's current directory. The **uupick** command is usually used with no arguments. It will locate the files sent via **uuto**, and then prompt for a disposition of each file, as follows:

```
$ uupick
from system uname: file data1 ?
```

The remote machine's **uname** is displayed along with the filename **data1**, and then **uupick** waits for a command. The * (star) command will cause **uupick** to display a summary of its available commands. Most useful is **m** (for move), which moves the named file to another directory. The **m** command can take a directory name as argument, in which case the file is moved to that directory instead of to the current directory. For example:

```
$ uupick
from system uname: file data1 ? m /tmp
642 blocks
from system uname: file data2 ?
```

The file size is displayed, and then **uupick** goes on to any other files. If all the files have been transferred, **uupick** will exit back to the shell. Use **m .** (m dot) to move a file to the current directory.

The **a** (for all) command is similar in function to **m**, but it causes all the files sent from a remote machine to be moved at once. This can be faster than **m** if many files have been transferred. The **d** (for delete) command causes a file to be deleted rather than moved, and a file can be displayed with **p** (for print). The **p** option must be used carefully, because binary files can be transferred with **uuto**. The **q** (for quit) command causes **uupick** to end; any files that have not been moved or deleted remain in the spool directory until **uupick** is executed again. Finally, the command !*cmd* (bang *command*) is a shell escape that will execute *cmd* in a subshell, and then return to **uupick**. This command is often used to create directories or change permissions before moving files.

The **uupick** command can take one command-line option, **-s** (for system), followed by a specific system name. This restricts the **uupick** search to files transferred from the named machine. Both **uuto** and **uupick** are usually shell scripts, so you can browse through them in **/usr/bin** if you want more information on how they work.

A Note on uucp Security

Security is an important consideration for the **uucp** subsystem, because file transfer from one machine to another can be extremely risky to the machines and to the privacy of their files. The **mail** and **uuto** commands are preferred for most data transfers between machines, since they only allow transfers *from* the local machine *to* the remote machine, and all files are moved into "safe" public directories owned by the appropriate subsystem. However, the **uucp** subsystem as a whole is much more powerful, in part because it allows remote execution of arbitrary commands. Consequently, there are extensive security protections within the **uucp** subsystem, and many of the command forms and actions discussed below will be allowed on some machines, but prohibited on others. Chapter 22 discusses the administration of **uucp** security in detail. Here it is important to be aware that many of the most powerful **uucp** features may be disabled in specific systems or networks for security reasons. Over the years, **uucp** security has become more and more restrictive, as a result of bitter experience within the UNIX system community. Only in the friendliest machine environments, where there is no access to public telephone lines or dial-up modems, can the most powerful **uucp** features be trusted.

The uucp Command

The **uuto** command provides the easiest access to the **uucp** subsystem for most file transfers. However, the **uucp** command can provide more control over data transfers in specific situations. Unlike **uuto**, the **uucp** command allows you to request that a file from a remote machine be copied to the local machine.

The **uucp** command format is

```
$ uucp source.files destination.file
```

The **uucp** command will copy the *source.files* argument list to the *destination.file*. These filenames are actually addresses in the familiar *machine!target* format, except that the *target* is not a user login id, but rather a pathname of the file or directory to copy. In the syntax of **uucp**, the *machine!* part can be omitted if it refers to the local machine. For example,

```
$ uucp /etc/profile yoursys!/var/spool/uucppublic/profile
```

will copy the file **/etc/profile** on the local machine to the file **/var/spool/uucppublic/profile** on the machine named **yoursys**. Multiple files are allowed if the target is a directory. This command

```
$ uucp $HOME/* yoursys!/var/spool/uucppublic/xfer.dir
```

will transfer all the files in your $HOME directory to the **/var/spool/uucppublic/xfer.dir** directory on the remote machine.

In addition, **uucp** can copy files from the remote machine to the local machine if the *machine!* part is included in the source file list, as shown here:

```
$ uucp "uname!/tmp/hello/*" /var/spool/uucppublic/xfer
```

This will move all the files in the directory **/tmp/hello** on the remote system to the directory **/var/spool/uucppublic/xfer** on the local system. The source list is quoted to prevent the local shell from expanding the * character; it will be expanded on the remote system. You can also include the *machine!* part on both the source and destination file list, as follows:

```
$ uucp machine1!file machine2!file
```

In this case the **uucp** command will perform a third-party transfer, from one machine to another. Neither machine need be the local machine providing **uucp** security is administered to allow this usage!

Logical Path Names

Usually, **uucp** security is administered so that file copies are allowed only from specific *public* directories on the machines, such as the **/var/spool/uucppublic** directory. Thus, the pathname mechanism will not usually work exactly as described previously. To get around these security limitations, the **uucp** command allows some forms of *logical* path naming. If the filename portion is ~*user*, (tilde user) where *user* is a login id on the target machine, **uucp** will create the file in that user's home directory. For example, many systems allow each user to create a public directory called **rje** (for remote job entry) within their home directory. The **uucp** command

```
$ uucp local.file my_sys!~steve/rje
```

will write the file **local.file** into the **rje** directory of user **steve** on the machine named **my_sys**. A filename that begins with ~**/** (tilde slash), such as ~/*destination* will write the file into the directory *destination* in the standard **uucp** public directory on the remote machine. This public directory is usually **/var/spool/uucppublic**, so the command

```
$ uucp local.file my_sys!~/steve
```

will copy **local.file** to **/var/spool/uucppublic/steve** on the machine named **my_sys**. This will work for transferring single files, but if more than one file is being transferred, the ~/*destination* should end with a final **/** (slash), which instructs **uucp** to create a directory with the given name, and to copy all the source files into that directory, retaining their original names. For example:

```
$ uucp $HOME/* system!~/steve/
```

This command is actually very much like the **uuto** operation, except that **uuto** uses a more complex naming convention for the target directory, built up from the local machine name and the recipient's login id on the target system.

Command-Line Options for the uucp Command

uucp allows many command-line options that modify its function. Many of these are used mainly by **uucp** experts to fine-tune the operation of the **uucp** data transfer, but some are of general utility. The **-m** (for mail) option instructs **uucp** to send mail to the user who requested the transfer when the transfer is complete. The **-n** (for notify) option takes a login id on the remote machine as an argument, and sends mail to that user on the remote machine when the copy is complete. The **-C** (for copy) option copies a file into the **uucp** public directory before it is transferred, so you can delete or change the original file. If this option is not used, the file cannot be deleted or renamed until the transfer is complete.

By default, **uucp** is silent if a job is successfully queued for transfer. However, the **-j** (for job) option causes **uucp** to display a unique job identification number as it queues the job. This number is useful for tracking the success or failure of the transfer, as discussed later in this chapter. The **-x** option takes a digit between 1 and 9 as an argument, and causes debugging information to be displayed at the terminal; the larger the number, the more debugging output will appear.

Finally, you can prevent **uucp** from immediately trying to send a job after it has been successfully queued. When you do not wish the connection to the remote machine to start immediately, use the **-r** option; it will cause the job to be queued, but will not start the transfer. Instead, **uucp** will try to send the file during its next regularly scheduled cycle, which usually occurs about once an hour. The **-r** option might be used when you know that the target machine is not running, or that the connection is inoperable for some reason.

The uux Command

The most powerful command available within the **uucp** subsystem is **uux** (for UNIX to UNIX execute). The **uux** command allows the generation of command lines that will be executed on a remote machine. It can collect files named on the command line from various machines, and then assemble the command on the target machine and execute it there. Because of these outstanding capabilities, **uux** is a very dangerous security risk, and its use is usually severely crippled on most systems. When allowed, it can be very useful in network environments where movement of files between machines is quick and efficient.

The **uux** command takes a normal command line as argument, with one exception: the command name and any filenames given as arguments can be preceded with the *machine!* form. This form instructs **uux** to execute the command on the specified machine, or to collect the named files from the machine given. For example, the command

```
$ uux "sys1!cat sys2!/etc/profile sys3!/etc/rc2 > !/tmp/output"
```

will collect the file **/etc/profile** from machine **sys2** and the file **/etc/rc2** from machine **sys3**, and move them to machine **sys1**, where the **cat** command will be executed. Output is redirected to the file **/tmp/output**, on the local machine. Any part of the command line that has only a **!**, without a named machine, is interpreted as the local system. The entire command line is quoted to prevent the local shell from interpreting the redirection character > before **uux** sees it.

In multicommand pipelines, commands that come after the first one cannot have the *machine!* part, because **uux** requires that all parts of the pipeline be executed on the same machine. For example, given the command

```
$ uux "sys1!cat !/etc/profile | grep HOME > !/tmp/out"
```

uux will take the file **/etc/profile** from the local system and move it to machine **sys1**, where the pipeline **cat | grep** will be executed. The output will be redirected to the file **/tmp/out** on the local machine.

You can use the special character - (minus) within the **uux** command as a filename part, in which case **uux** will read its standard input for that file. The previous command could also have been written as follows:

```
$ cat /etc/profile | uux "sys1!cat - | grep HOME > !/tmp/out"
```

Full pathnames are preferred in **uux** commands, but the special operators ~*user* and ~*!path* will work in the filename parts of **uux** commands just as they do in the **uucp** commands discussed earlier. The **uux** command will fail if any of the files are not found as expected, or if the commands are not permitted within the constraints of the **uucp** security rules on the target machine. When **uux** fails, it sends mail to the user who requested the action, on the original machine where **uux** was executed.

The **uux** command can take several command-line options. The -C (for copy) option causes **uux** to copy local files to the spool directory. This allows you to move or delete any named files before the data transfer is complete. The **-n** (for notify) option causes **uux** to *not* send notification mail if the command fails. This is useful for background or *automatic* **uux** jobs, such as regularly collecting data from the machines on a local area network. The **-j** (for job) option causes **uux** to display a job id as it queues the action, and the **-r** option causes the job to be queued but not immediately started. The **-z** option sends mail to the originator of the job if it succeeds; normally **uux** is silent if the job succeeds. Finally, the **-x** option takes a digit between 1 and 9 as an argument, and produces the corresponding level of debugging output as the job is queued.

The uustat Command

Since the **uucp** subsystem does its file transfer activities in the background, there is no immediate way to tell if transfers are succeeding or failing. Therefore, the **uustat** (for UNIX to UNIX status) command is provided to report the status of the **uucp** file transfer queue. The **uustat** command will provide a short summary of spooled but unsent jobs, or of the communications status of the machines with which your machine communicates, among other possibilities. By default, **uustat** reports only on jobs created by the user who executes the **uustat** command. This command

```
$ uucp /etc/profile my_sys!~/root/
$ uustat
my_sysN74d6      06/27-18:58  S  my_sys  root 4290 /etc/profile
$
```

reports that there is one job queued. It has the job id my_sysN74d6, and it was queued at 6:58 P.M. on 6/27. This job is directed to machine **my_sys**, and it was created by user **root**. The file size is 4290 bytes, and the file to transfer is **/etc/profile**. The **S** signifies that the request is to send a file. Also possible is **R**, which denotes that a file is to be received.

A queued job may have more than one part under the same job id, as in this example:

```
$ uustat
my_sysN74d7      06/29-17:47  S  my_sys   root 62 D.tune2317f15
                 06/29-17:47  S  my_sys   root  rmail jim
$
```

This request is the result of a **mail** command with a remote addressee. In fact, the **mail** command sends the mail message as one data file, which is the first file in the **uustat** output. The second file is a **uux** command to execute **rmail jim** on the target machine to deliver the message. If multiple files are sent via **uuto** or **uucp**, they will also result in multiple files per job id. If more than one **uucp** command is queued, there will be more than one job id in the **uustat** output.

When the data transfer is complete, the job id is removed from the **uustat** list, and if no more jobs are outstanding, **uustat** exits silently. Thus, no output from **uustat** is good news; it tells you that all queued jobs have been sent.

By default, **uustat** reports only on jobs queued by the user who initiates the **uustat** command. The -a (for all) option instructs **uustat** to display all the queued jobs on the machine, no matter who created them. In addition, the -u (for user) option takes a user id as an argument, and produces a list of queued jobs scheduled by the named user only. For example:

```
$ uustat -u steve
```

This is the same as **uustat** alone, executed by user **steve**.

Reporting on Specific Machines

The **uustat** command can display the queue for a specific machine with the -s (for system) option. A machine id is required after the -s option, as shown here:

```
$ uustat -s my_sys
```

This command will produce the listing of queued jobs for machine **my_sys**.

The **uustat** command can also produce a report on the communications status of transfers from the local machine to any remote machines that have been contacted recently. Use the -m (for machine) option for this purpose, as follows:

```
$ uustat -m
my_sys      1C          06/29-17:47 SUCCESSFUL
sys2        1C          06/29-18:20 TALKING
$
```

In this example, two machines have been contacted recently. The machine **my_sys** was last contacted at 17:47 on 6/29, and the connection was successfully completed. The machine **sys2** is currently connected to the local machine, and data is being transferred. Other conditions may be reported in the status field at the end of the line, as discussed later in this chapter. The **uucp** weekly administrative script is responsible for deleting the status log, so after the weekly script executes, there will usually be no output from **uustat -m** until some machines have been contacted.

Deleting a Queued Job

Finally, the **uustat** command is used to delete an unsent job from the **uucp** queue. This might be necessary because you've changed your mind about a data transfer, or because a connection is not completing correctly. All **uucp** transfers are available from **uustat**, including those created by **mail** or **uux**. To delete a job, you must know the job id, which is displayed when the job is originally queued or by **uustat**. To kill a job, use the **-k** (for kill) option with **uustat**. This option takes the job id as argument. For example:

```
$ uustat -k my_sysN74d7
Job: my_sysN74d7 successfully killed
$
```

Only one job id is allowed per invocation of the **uustat -k** command. If a job has already been completed, it cannot be killed, and **uustat** will return an error, as shown here:

```
$ uustat -k my_sysN74d7
Can't find Job my_sysN74d7; Not killed
$
```

Furthermore, **uustat** cannot kill a job that is in progress.

Administration of the uucp Subsystem

The **uucp** subsystem is a powerful and extremely flexible data communications tool. However, all this flexibility has its cost; you pay for it when you must *administer* the **uucp** subsystem. The task of **uucp** administration has a reputation for extreme complexity that requires arcane skills on the part of the administrator. This can be true, especially when the machine must be adapted to new communication networks, or when it just isn't working properly. However, **uucp** administration is definitely possible for ordinary users on personal systems, and unless there is some pathological failure the **uucp** subsystem will function correctly without much attention.

A Note on Versions of uucp

The version of the **uucp** subsystem included with SVR4 is formally known as the *BNU* (for Basic Networking Utilities), or informally as the *HDB* or *HoneyDanBer* version, after the login ids of its three developers. This version differs significantly from older releases, and from BSD versions. The following discussion focuses on the HDB version, which is far superior to other versions, due to its elimination of bugs, its great flexibility, and its freedom from derangement.

uucp Directory Structure

Four directory structures are primarily owned by the **uucp** subsystem: **/etc/uucp** contains the control files **uucp** uses to figure out how to connect to a specific machine; **/usr/lib/uucp** contains some executable commands and tools used by the system; **/var/uucp** contains temporary files for transfers that are not yet completed, as well as log and status files used by **uustat** and other commands; and finally, **/var/spool /uucppublic** is the directory used for public transfer of files between machines. The **uuto** and **uupick** commands move files to and from this directory. The last two directories have large subdirectory structures that are maintained by the **uucp** administrative tools; these should never be manually changed or deleted. The **/etc/uucp** directory contains the control files, which you will edit when you add new remote systems or change the modem or network setup of your machine.

The directory **/var/spool/uucppublic** contains the public spool for all normal **uucp** transfers. There can be many subdirectories within it, which are usually created with the command

```
$ uucp files target!~/dir/
```

This command will cause the directory *dir* to appear in the **uucppublic** directory on the target system. The **uuto** command uses **/var/spool /uucppublic/receive**, and each target user has a personal subdirectory within **receive**. Within this per-user directory there will be an additional subdirectory named for each source machine, and the actual transferred files will appear in that directory. That is, the command

```
$ uuto file1 my_sys!steve
```

if sent from machine *uname*, will cause **file1** to appear in the directory **/var/spool/uucppublic/receive/steve/uname** on the **my_sys** system. This complex directory structure is designed to prevent files that have the same name but are sent from different machines from overwriting each other.

The directory **/var/uucp** contains **uucp** *log files* and queued files. For example:

```
$ ls -aF /var/uucp
./      .Admin/    .Log/    .Sequence/   .Workspace/    my_sys/
../     .Corrupt/  .Old/    .Status/     .Xqtdir/
$
```

These materials are all subdirectories, most of which begin with a . (dot), so that **ls -a** is needed to see them. The normal directories contain temporary information about unsent queued jobs for the machine given in the directory name. These spool directories are created as needed by the **uucp** system, and are deleted during the weekly cleanup procedure. The logs and other **uucp** administrative records are kept in the other directories, especially **.Log**. You can browse through them if you are interested. The file **/var/uucp/.Admin/xferstats** contains a listing of the communications efficiency of all data transfers in bytes per second of connect time. A 1200 bps telephone link will average about 105 characters per second, which is a very high efficiency rate compared to that of many other data transfer algorithms. A faster data link has correspondingly better performance.

The directory **/usr/lib/uucp** contains the executable programs owned exclusively by the **uucp** subsystem — that is the administrative demons for cleanup and other chores, as shown here:

```
$ ls -F /usr/lib/uucp
Config@          Permissions@     bnuconvert*       uudemon.hour*
Devconfig@       Poll@            remote.unknown    uudemon.poll*
Devices@         SetUp*           uucheck*          uugetty@
Dialcodes@       Sysfiles@        uucico*           uusched*
Dialers@         Systems@         uucleanup*        uuxqt*
Grades@          Teardown*        uudemon.admin*
Limits@          Uutry*           uudemon.cleanup*
$
```

In SVR4, the control files that instruct the **uucp** programs how to connect to other machines have been moved to **/etc/uucp**, but symbolic links remain in **/usr/lib/uucp**. The contents of **/etc/uucp** are listed here:

```
$ ls -F /etc/uucp
Config      Dialcodes    Limits       Sysfiles
Devconfig   Dialers      Permissions  Systems
Devices     Grades       Poll
$
```

The demons are named *uudemon. . . .* Since these are shell scripts, you can browse them to see their functions. The **uucico** program is the heart of the **uucp** subsystem; it makes the connection and transfers the data. The **uugetty** program is a version of the **getty** program, and it can replace **getty** in **/etc/inittab**. In SVR4, **uugetty** is obsolete; it has been replaced with the Service Access Facility, which supports bidirectional communications. Although **uugetty** has been retained in the system for reasons of compatibility, its use is not recommended.

Most of the other files — those really in **/etc/uucp** — are **uucp** control files that specify *how* to make a connection to a remote machine. They are discussed later in this chapter.

All the materials in the directories **/usr/lib/uucp**, **/etc/uucp**, and **/var/uucp** are owned by the administrative login id **uucp**, and have group **uucp**. It is very important that these ownerships be maintained, and that the permissions of any file not be changed from the values set when the files were created. If changes are made to the permissions or ownership of these files or directories, the **uucp** subsystem will begin to fail in mysterious ways. When this occurs, the best solution is to reload

the system software from the original disks or tape, restoring everything to its default state. You should usually back up the control files
before reloading to save the material in them, but be careful not to
rewrite the old files over the newly restored files, or the incorrect
permissions will follow. Extreme care is required when editing anything
in the **uucp** subsystem. Only the superuser can edit the files, and the
superuser is responsible for maintaining the correct permissions and
ownership.

One additional directory is used by the **uucp** subsystem. This is
/var/spool/locks, where the system's *lock files* reside. Lock files are
created when the **uucico** and **cu** programs are using a device or port.
The **uugetty** program also creates a lock file when a user calls into the
machine. The presence of a lock file signals other programs in the **uucp**
subsystem that a port is in use. Other programs will respect the lock
files, and will not contend for a device when it is already in use. When
the programs finish with a device, they remove the lock file, freeing the
device for other uses. Lock files are deleted during system reboot so
that failed **uucico** jobs that might leave a lock file will not block a port
permanently.

uucp Subsystem Architecture

When a job is queued for transfer with **mail** or one of the **uucp**
programs, the **uucp** utilities look in a list of known remote machines. If
the desired remote system is found, the programs will create a new
directory tree under **/var/uucp** to hold the data transfer request. If no
data transfer to that machine is currently in progress, the **uucp** utilities
will cause the execution of **/usr/lib/uucp/uucico** (for uu copy in copy
out). The **uucico** program will use additional control files to determine
the best way to connect to the target system, and will attempt a
connection to the remote machine using that pathway. If the connection
succeeds, **uucico** will execute the transfer. In fact, instances of **uucico**
will be executing at both ends of the communications link, and one can
often be seen in the output from **ps -fe**. When the transfer is complete,
the control files in **/var/uucp** are deleted.

If a connection fails, **uucico** may try several communications paths
before it gives up. This feature depends on the administration of the
control files.

If the transfer fails for any reason, the job will stay on the queue. In most systems, a regularly scheduled **uucp** demon, scheduled via the **cron** timing facility, executes once each hour. This demon searches **/var/uucp** and its subdirectories for queued jobs that have not been sent, and it will execute **uucico** to transfer any jobs it finds. The scheduling algorithm is variable, so jobs that have recently been queued will be retried more frequently than jobs that have failed repeatedly. Finally, if a job fails repeatedly for a week, the weekly **uucp** cleanup demon will send a warning message via mail to the sending user. Usually **uucp** will succeed before this happens, unless the target machine is not in operation or the communications channel is inoperative.

Specifying a Connection Method to a Remote System

Each remote machine that you can access via **uucp** or **mail** must be specified in a **uucp** control file. When a transfer is queued with the **uucp** tools, they will examine the contents of a control file to see if the remote machine is included. If it is not, the **uucp** commands will fail and will display an error message. For example:

```
$ uucp file1 nosys!~/user/
bad system: nosys
uucp failed completely (11)
$
```

You can determine the complete list of available remote systems with the **uuname** command. It produces a list of machine names, one per line. You might want to **grep** through this list to find a specific machine, since the output may be voluminous. To do so, use

```
$ uuname | grep nosys
$
```

The list of known machines may differ between **uucp** and **cu**; the -c (for **cu**) option of **uuname** lists the machines that are known to **cu** instead of **uucp**.

The list of known machines is kept in a complex interlocking file structure in the **/etc/uucp** directory, so administrators have flexibility in administering the list of systems that are available in different situations. The file **/etc/uucp/Sysfiles** gives a table of these files, along with some additional information, as shown here:

```
$ tail -7 /etc/uucp/Sysfiles
service=cu      systems=Systems \
                devices=Devices \
                dialers=Dialers

service=uucico  systems=Systems.cico:Systems \
                devices=Devices.cico:Devices \
                dialers=Dialers.cico:Dialers
$
```

The first part of **Sysfiles** is usually a long comment section that describes how to use the file. Browse this on your machine for more information. The information in **Sysfiles** is divided according to the different *services* available on the machine. These are usually **cu** and **uucico**, as indicated previously, although additional services may be present if your machine is part of a LAN. The keyword *service =* starts the description of the available services. Each service description starts on a new line, although more lines are allowed if the newline is escaped with a \ (backslash), as in the previous example.

Each service provides three kinds of information the software needs to make the connection: first is *system* information, second *devices* information, and third *dialers* information. Each of these types has a keyword in **Sysfiles** that specifies one or more additional files in **/etc/uucp** where that information can be found. Thus, there may be multiple files that hold each type of information. These files are named after the appropriate keyword following the *service* keyword. Different files are separated with a : (colon) in these lists, and the keywords are separated from each other with whitespace. Each service has its own list of control files.

In the previous example, the *systems =* sections of **Sysfiles** give the names of files that contain lists of remote machines that **uucico** (or **cu**) can access. The files **Systems.cico** and **Systems** contain these tables for the **uucico** service. When **uucico** executes, the file **Systems.cico** is consulted; if it does not contain the requested machine, the file **Systems** is consulted next. All these files must be in the directory **/etc/uucp**.

The Systems Files

The contents of the **Systems** files determine *how* the service will attempt to connect to the remote machine. With different networks, different types of modems, hard-wired data links, and different login-password sequences for different machines, a great deal of information must be encoded in the **Systems** entry for a machine. Normally, the file **Systems** contains a comment section to explain the meaning of the various fields in the file, and you should browse through this for more information. Here is an example:

```
$ tail -3 /etc/uucp/Systems
my_sys Any ACU 1200 5300548 "" \d ogin:--ogin:--ogin: nuucp
packet Any DIR 9600 - "" \d ogin:--ogin:--ogin: nuucp
another Any D2 4800 - "" \d ogin:--ogin:--ogin: nuucp
$
```

Each remote machine has one or more lines in the **Systems** file. The machine name is the leftmost field on the line. The next field gives a range of times when calling is allowed. *Any* means a call can be placed at any time. The device to use for the connection is given in the third field. The name listed here is a pointer to a device descriptor in the **Devices** file. The fourth field in **Systems** gives the requested speed of the data link, which is matched with the capabilities of the device. *Any* is often used for the speed in the **Systems** file to force the **Devices** logic to make the decision on connection speed. The fifth field contains the telephone number if a dial-up modem is used, or a dialer name if a network is desired. The - (hyphen) is a dummy placeholder if this field is unused. The rest of the line constitutes a *chat* sequence that gives a series of handshaking strings.

The chat script works like this: While the connection is being made, the local machine waits to hear the first string (*""* is a null value that means *wait for nothing*). When that string comes across the data connection, the local machine sends the next string, then waits for the next one, and so on in alternating sequence. This allows the service to traverse complex login sequences in making connections to remote machines. The last part usually waits for **login:** at the remote machine, and then sends the login id for the **uucico** program: **nuucp**. If the remote machine requires it, the chat script may wait for the **passwd:**

prompt, and then send the password for that machine. Many machines do not use a password for the **nuucp** login, since the **uucico** program will get control instead of a normal shell.

In addition to these normal character strings, the chat script can also include some special keywords that have functions such as delaying for a while, sending a break signal, and others. These special keywords are documented in the comments for the **Systems** file.

A single remote machine may have more than one entry in the **Systems** file, if there is more than one way to reach that machine. For example, a machine might be accessible over a local area network or by a dial-up connection. When **uucico** attempts to connect to such a machine, it tries the first **Systems** entry; if that one fails it tries the second, and so on. Thus, a busy data link need not prevent data transfer if another route is available.

The Devices File

As part of the connection, the service (usually **cu** or **uucico**) may need to understand some details of how the local communications devices are configured. A *device* is usually a modem or a network link that has a specific port on the local machine, and a chat may be required to activate it. For example, an autodialing modem with the AT command set will be attached via RS-232 connection to a specific tty port on the machine, and the correct AT command must be sent to turn on the autodialing feature along with the telephone number to dial. The modem responds with ASCII strings after each command. This information is logically associated with the modem, and not with the specific system that you access using that modem. Therefore, this chat and other device-specific information is kept with the device data, but the information that is specific to the system, such as the login sequence, is kept with the system data. The latter is kept in the **Systems** file, as discussed earlier, and the former is kept in one of the **Devices** files, as specified by the **Sysfiles** list. **Devices** usually contains a long comment section giving instructions on the usage of the file; you can browse through it for more information.

During the processing of the **Systems** file entry for a machine, the third field names a device for making the connection. The service will search **Sysfiles** to find a *devices=* entry for the service, and will then search the named files. If it finds a line whose leftmost field matches the third field in **Systems,** it will perform the processing specified in the line.

The other fields in the **Devices** files specify other device-specific information, as shown here:

```
$ tail -3 /etc/uucp/Devices
ACU tty01s - 1200 hayes
DIR tty00s - 9600 direct
STARLAN,eg starlan - - TLIS \D
$
```

This example illustrates three commonly used **Devices** entries. The first is for a modem with the AT command set, the second is for a machine directly connected via RS232 link on **/dev/tty00s,** and the third is an entry for the StarLan local area network.

If there is more than one device for a specific connection strategy, there can be more than one line in **Devices** with the same name. For example, two modems might be attached to the machine on different ports. Usually you don't care which modem is used to make a call, so there might be two ACU entries in the **Devices** file, naming the port for each modem separately.

As mentioned previously, the first field is a *token* that names a device. These tokens appear in the third field of a **Systems** entry. ACU (for automatic calling unit) is usually used for dial-up modems, and **DIR** (for direct) is usually used to name directly connected machines. The second field gives the **/dev** file or port used for the connection. The name is given without the **/dev/** part. In the **ACU** entry in the previous example, the modem is attached to the COM2 port, which is named **tty01s** under the UNIX system's naming scheme. The third field can name a dialer device, if the dialer differs from the connection device. This field is rarely used in modern hardware, and it contains a - (hyphen), the dummy placeholder, in these examples.

The fourth field gives the connection speed. If the speed field in the **Systems** file contains *Any,* the speed will be determined from the **Devices** entry. Since the speed is usually a function of the device, *Any* is usually used in the **Systems** entry. Otherwise, the **Systems** speed must match the **Devices** speed, or the service will not use the line. The fifth field gives the name of a line in a **Dialers** file, which usually specifies an additional chat script that is unique to that device. In the **ACU** entry in the previous example, the dialer entry is *hayes*. Sometimes the dialer name specifies a *built-in* dialer that is specifically associated with some special hardware. The STARLAN entry is of this type, because **TLIS** specifies a dialer based on the *streams* I/O mechanism. These built-in dialers will not appear in the **Dialers** file. Consult your network administrator for more tips on configuring LANs, especially using Ethernet and the TCP/IP protocol.

A device-specific chat can follow these five required fields, such as the **\D** operator in the STARLAN line. This chat is described in the comments in the **Devices** file; however, the device-specific chat is usually included in the **Dialers** file entry, rather than the **Devices** entry.

The Dialers File

The **Dialers** file is also specified through the **Sysfiles** list, so that dialers can differ depending on the service. The dialer is the chat script that causes the device to "dial" the connection. Actually the term *dial* may give the wrong impression, since not only dial-up modems use **Dialers**. Many local area networks use complex login sequences to pass network security and address a remote machine on the network, and the control for these connections is also included in the **Dialers** file. The file **/etc/uucp/Dialers** contains comments describing the format and operators available with dialers.

The fifth field of each line in the **Devices** file usually contains a name that matches the first field of the **Dialers** line, as shown here:

```
$ grep hayes /etc/uucp/Dialers
hayes   =,-,    "" \dAT\r\c OK\r \EATDT\T\r\c CONNECT
$
```

The second field lists tokens that appear in a telephone number in the **Systems** entry, giving a translation to the tokens required by the dialer. For example, the *hayes* entry instructs the **uucico** program to translate = and - into , . The = has historically been used to specify a wait for secondary dial tone, while the - has been used to specify a two-second delay. In this example, both of these characters are converted to the AT-style modem's delay operator, the comma. The rest of the line specifies a chat script that is used to communicate with the modem.

In summary, communication services make connections by consulting **Sysfiles** to determine what files to use for the other operations. Then they consult the appropriate **Systems** file to find out what kind of connection to use for the call, when calls are allowed, and so on. Next, they follow the device name (third field of **Systems**) into the **Devices** file, where they determine what hardware implements that connection method. Then they follow the fifth field of **Devices** into the appropriate **Dialers** file (or use a built-in dialer), to determine how to talk to that specific device. When the call is made using the devices and dialers information, and those chat scripts complete successfully, **cu** returns control to the keyboard, or **uucico** goes back to the **Systems** entry and logs in to the machine using the chat given there. When all these steps are complete, the connection is made and data communication begins.

Going Further

The **uucp** subsystem is a very powerful and flexible communications system that can handle a great many kinds of networks and devices; therefore, a great many potential problems and pitfalls are associated with it, especially when you are trying to install a new type of connection. Here we can only mention some of these issues and discuss some additional tools that are available in SVR4.

Debugging uucp Connections

The **uucp** subsystem includes excellent *debugging* tools that can trace the progress of a connection and diagnose failure modes and errors in your chat scripts. The **cu** command includes the **-d** (for debug) option, which displays a trace of the connection as it is made. For example:

```
$ cu -d yoursys
conn(yoursys)
Trying entry from '/etc/uucp/Systems' - device type HAYES.
Device Type HAYES wanted
Trying device entry from '/etc/uucp/Devices'.
processdev: calling setdevcfg(cu, HAYES)
fd_mklock: ok
```

```
fixline(6, 1200)
gdial(hayes) called
Trying caller script 'hayes' from '/etc/uucp/Dialers'.
expect: ("")
got it
sendthem (DELAY
AT^M<NO CR>)
expect: (0^M)
0^Mgot it
sendthem (ECHO CHECK OFF
ATDT5551239^M<NO CR>)
expect: (1)
1got it
getto ret 6
device status for fd=6
F_GETFL=2,iflag=`12045',oflag=`0',cflag=`2651',lflag=`0',line=`0'
cc[0]=`177',[1]=`34',[2]=`43',[3]=`100',[4]=`1',[5]=`0',[6]=`0',[7]=`0',
call _mode(1)
Connected
_receive started
transmit started

login:
```

After the connection is complete, the debugging output stops and
you can use **cu** almost normally. However, more debugging output will
appear when you disconnect, as this example demonstrates:

```
~[my_sys].
call tilda(.)
call _quit(0)
call _bye(0)

Disconnected
call cleanup(0)
call _mode(0)
```

Similarly, the **uucp** subsystem includes a debugging tool in
/usr/lib/uucp/Uutry, that also produces debugging output, as shown in
Figure 15-1. **Uutry** takes the machine name as argument. Figure 15-1
shows a connection over a dial-up line supported with an AT-style
modem (running in numeric mode rather than character mode). In the
figure, two files are transferred during the connection. Can you follow
each step of the communications process?

Uutry is an excellent tool that you should execute frequently on
your machine to start your **uucp** data transfers. When **Uutry** is executed, it will appear to hang the machine; no PS1 prompt will reappear.
This is normal, because **Uutry** uses **tail -f** to display its log file. To

```
$ /usr/lib/uucp/Uutry yoursys
Uucico limit 5 -- continuing
mchFind called (yoursys)
name (yoursys) not found; return FAIL
attempting to open /var/uucp/.Admin/account
stat /var/spool/uucp/yoursys/Z
ulockf name /var/spool/locks/LCK..yoursys.Z
Job grade to process - Z
conn(yoursys)
Trying entry from '/etc/uucp/Systems' - device type HAYES.
Device Type HAYES wanted
Trying device entry from '/etc/uucp/Devices'.
processdev: calling setdevcfg(uucico, HAYES)
gdial(hayes) called
Trying caller script 'hayes' from '/etc/uucp/Dialers'.
expect: ("")
got it
sendthem (DELAY
AT^M<NO CR>)
expect: (0^M)
0^Mgot it
sendthem (ECHO CHECK OFF
ATDT5551239^M<NO CR>)
expect: (1)
1got it
getto ret 7
expect: (in:)
yoursys login:got it
sendthem (nuucp^M)
expect: (word:)
 nuucp^M^JPassword:got it
sendthem (^M)
Login Successful: System=yoursys
msg-ROK
 Rmtname yoursys,  Restart NO, Role MASTER,  Ifn - 7, Loginuser - root
rmesg - 'P' got Pge
wmesg 'U'g
Proto started g
*** TOP *** - Role=1, setline - X
Request: my_sys!D.my_sy4d9dfe9 --> yoursys!D.my_sy4d9dfe9 (root)
setline - S
wrktype - S
 wmesg 'S' D.my_sy4d9dfe9 D.my_sy4d9dfe9 root - D.my_sy4d9dfe9 0666 root
rmesg - 'S' got SY
 PROCESS: msg - SY
SNDFILE:
-> 109 / 0.060 secs, 1816 bytes/sec
rmesg - 'C' got CY
 PROCESS: msg - CY
RQSTCMPT:
mailopt 0, statfopt 0
*** TOP *** - Role=1, setline - X
```

Figure 15-1.   Sample output from **Uutry**

```
Request: my_sys!D.yoursys4d9be23 --> yoursys!X.yoursysA4d9b (root)
setline - S
wrktype - S
 wmesg 'S' D.yoursys4d9be23 X.yoursysA4d9b root - D.yoursys4d9be23 0666 root
rmesg - 'S' got SY
 PROCESS: msg - SY
SNDFILE:
-> 144 / 0.390 secs, 369 bytes/sec
rmesg - 'C' got CY
 PROCESS: msg - CY
RQSTCMPT:
mailopt 0, statfopt 0
*** TOP *** - Role=1, setline - X
Finished Processing file: /var/spool/uucp/yoursys/Z/C.yoursysZ4d9b
stat /var/spool/uucp/yoursys/Z
ulockf name /var/spool/locks/LCK..yoursys.Z
Job grade to process -
wmesg 'H'
rmesg - 'H' got HY
 PROCESS: msg - HY
HUP:
wmesg 'H'Y
cntrl - 0
send 00 0,exit code 0
Conversation Complete: Status SUCCEEDED


$
```

Figure 15-1.   Sample output from **Uutry** (*continued*)

return to the shell at any time during or after the execution of **Uutry**, press DEL. Your terminal will immediately return to the shell, and the **Uutry** output will end; however, the data connection established by **Uutry** will continue until it ends normally. This allows you to watch the **Uutry** output during the connection phase, and then to abandon the display while the files (possibly many of them) are transferred.

In the two previous examples, the majority of the output describes the chat sequence that was executed in completing the connection. These chats look basically similar in the two examples because the requested devices are the same. Both used an AT-style modem connected to **tty01s**, with the **Systems** entry,

```
yoursys Any HAYES 1200 5551239 in:--in: nuucp word: any4pw
```

and the **Devices** entry,

```
HAYES tty01s - 1200 hayes
```

and this **Dialers** entry:

```
hayes   =,-,     "" \dAT\r\c 0\r \eATDT\T\r\c 1
```

The example output describes the selection of the HAYES device, and shows the successful access of the device, through the line *getto ret 6*. More sophisticated networks will show different sequences. Then **cu** displays its terminal settings for this connection, in a terse debugging format. Finally, the output announces that the **cu** transmit and receive processes have been started.

In the **Uutry** output shown in Figure 15-1, more details of the chat are available, so **Uutry** is usually preferred for debugging over **cu -d**. Note that the **Sysfiles** scheme allows different chats for **cu** and **Uutry**, so some connections may work with one connection but not with the other. **Uutry** will make a connection even if no files are queued for transfer to make it easier to debug the chat scripts. However, successful file transfer is more than just the connection, so be sure to test the link by sending a few files in both directions.

The first part of the **Uutry** output shows the **uucico** command that it is executing, and then the selected device (from the **Systems** and **Devices** files). A detailed description of the chat follows, with lines that begin *sendthem...* displaying output from the local machine, and lines that begin *expect...* displaying the things the local machine is expecting from the remote machine. This continues until the local and the remote machines are talking together, when "Login Successful" is displayed. Next, the file transfer begins (after the TOP display). Each file gets a *Request* and *SNDFILE* section. When all transfers are complete, the two sides of the connection signal completion with **H**, and the connection is completed.

When a connection fails, the output will change. Usually the cause of failure is an incorrect chat script, in which case the *expect* section will not be fulfilled and the display will show a "Timeout" message, followed by "Status FAILED." The location of the message will tell you where the chat went wrong. In addition, many other types of error codes may be displayed by **Uutry** to indicate various other kinds of failures. Some of the most important are "No Device" and "Can't Access Device," which mean that the **Devices** file entry is incorrect, or the physical device is not operating properly. In some cases, "Permission Denied" will appear in the output for a file transfer. This means that the directory locations for the files, either on the sending or the receiving side, do not allow the requested operation. This is under control of **uucp** security, but the public directory **/var/spool/uucppublic** should always allow access. Although most of the other error codes are relatively self-evident, a **uucp** expert may be required to debug complex network connections.

The uulog Command

Even when debugging is not selected explicitly with **Uutry**, the **uucp** subsystem retains a log of some information for all systems that have been contacted since the last weekly cleanup of **uucp** data. The **uulog** command displays this information, giving a full history of all accesses to a machine. This information is stored on a per-machine basis, so the **uulog** command requires a system name as an argument, as in Figure 15-2. This example shows the log from local machine **my_sys** for traffic with remote machine **yoursys**. Three calls are represented in Figure 15-2, the first two of which were initiated by **yoursys**. The first failed ("CAN'T ACCESS DEVICE") because the modem was not connected. The others succeeded, and each of these resulted in the transfer of two

```
$ uulog yoursys
uucp yoursys  (4/11-18:56:13,357,0) TIMEOUT (generic open)
uucp yoursys  (4/11-18:56:13,357,0) CONN FAILED (CAN'T ACCESS DEVICE)
uucp yoursys  (4/11-19:20:32,381,0) SUCCEEDED (call to yoursys - process job
grade Z )
uucp yoursys  (4/11-19:20:36,381,0) OK (startup)
root yoursys yoursysZ4d9b (4/11-19:20:37,381,0) REQUEST (my_sys!D.my_sy4d9dfe9
--> yoursys!D.my_sy4d9dfe9 (root))
root yoursys yoursysZ4d9b (4/11-19:20:38,381,1) REQUEST (my_sys!D.yoursys4d9be23
--> yoursys!X.yoursysA4d9b (root))
uucp yoursys  (4/11-19:20:40,381,2) OK (conversation complete tty00s 57)
uucp yoursys  (4/12-18:15:05,321,0) OK (startup)
uucp yoursys  (4/12-18:15:06,321,0) REMOTE REQUESTED (yoursys!D.yoursys0d75e46
--> my_sys!D.yoursys0d75e46 (root))
uucp yoursys  (4/12-18:15:07,321,1) REMOTE REQUESTED (yoursys!D.my_sy2636c80
--> my_sys!X.my_sysN2636 (root))
uucp yoursys  (4/12-18:15:08,321,2) OK (conversation complete tty01s 4)
$
```

Figure 15-2.   Typical output from the **uulog** command

files. The call begins with "SUCCEEDED," which indicates the connection was made correctly; then "startup" indicates that the **uucico** programs are communicating. The call ends at "conversation complete." The third call in Figure 15-2 was a call *from* the remote machine *to* the local machine. In this case, the SUCCEEDED line is omitted, and the log begins with the "startup" line. The remote machine is asking to send two files to the local machine ("REMOTE REQUESTED").

The log can be very long if two machines converse actively, but it is deleted during the weekly **uucp** cleanup. With luck, a long log for a suspected machine will provide a great deal of information that can be very helpful in understanding why your files did not reach their destination as expected.

The uucp Administrative Demons

Much of the work of the **uucp** subsystem is done on a *schedule,* and is not under direct command of the user. This is because the **uucp** subsystem has the responsibility for file transfer and message delivery. Once a job is on the queue, **uucp** will keep trying to deliver it until it succeeds or until someone removes the job from the queue by killing it. No user action is required when a target machine is down or the local machine is rebooted, because the queue stays active indefinitely. Therefore, the **cron** facility is employed to stimulate the **uucp** subsystem into action on a regular basis. The **uucp** tools will search for any queued jobs, and will try to send them if any are found. In addition, the logs are cleaned regularly, and the **uucp** subsystem can be administered to *poll* a remote machine regularly to see whether any jobs are to be sent from the remote to the local machine.

All these activities are managed by the **uudemon** scripts in the **/usr/lib/uucp** directory. They are scheduled from the **crontab** facility, and each demon runs on a different schedule, depending on its function. The **uudemon** tools are usually shell scripts, and you can browse through them for more information about their actions.

The **uudemon.hour** script is executed once each hour while the machine is up. It executes the **uuxqt** (for uuexecute) program, which looks for any unsent jobs and starts sending any it finds. Usually **uuxqt** includes a good algorithm for determining if any specific job should be started on its regular schedule. If a job has failed repeatedly, **uuxqt** will not try as often. A commonly used algorithm tries once each hour for the first day, once every two hours for the second day, once each twelve hours for the third day, and once a day for the rest of the first week. If the job still has not succeeded, **uuxqt** will send a mail message to the user who created the job. Generally, if the job fails for a whole week, either the target machine is nonexistent or the chat is wrong for connecting to that machine.

The **uudemon.admin** script is executed once or twice each day, usually in the small hours of the night. It creates a daily administrative report concerning that day's **uucp** activity that lists job transfers, machines contacted, suspected security breaks, and disk space used by the **uucp** queues. The script sends mail containing its report to the **uucp** login id. Many system administrators forward mail for the **uucp** login to their own id.

The **uudemon.cleanup** script executes up to once a day. It performs cleanup duties, including deleting old log files, informing users of unsent files, and other tasks.

Because of the administrative nature of these demons, it is important that they be set to execute at a time of day when the machine is usually up and running. If the machine is turned off during the nights and weekends, the schedule for these demons should be changed in the **crontab** to move them to a time when the machine is usually active.

Polling Other Machines

The **uucp** subsystem can call another machine on a schedule. This is called *polling* the other machine. Polling might be used when the local machine is able to contact the remote machine, but for some reason the remote machine cannot call the local machine; thus, any jobs queued on the remote to the local will never be delivered unless the local machine calls the remote. The script **uudemon.poll** is often included in the **crontab** to cause regular polling. It is generally scheduled to execute once each hour, a few minutes before **uudemon.hour** runs. The script **uudemon.poll** consults the file **/etc/uucp/Poll** for a list of the systems to poll and the times to poll them. It then sets up a dummy job in the regular **uucp** queue. When **uudemon.hour** runs, it finds the dummy job and calls the machine. If **uucp** security is administered properly, the remote machine will send any queued jobs for the local machine during this call. The **Poll** file contains a line for each machine to be polled, and a list of hours at which to poll that machine. You can set up the file to poll a remote machine as often as desired, from once a day up to once an hour. Naturally, it is best to call a machine as rarely as possible to reduce traffic on the connection network and on the two machines.

Changing the Data Transfer Protocol

The **uucp** subsystem supports several data communications *protocols* for moving data across different types of networks. The default is the **g** protocol, and all **uucp** versions support it. The **g** protocol is an effective error-correcting protocol that has served well for many years; however, faster networks that include their own error-correcting procedures get better performance if another protocol is used. The **e** (for error-free) protocol is often used with local area networks. When more than one protocol is available, the **uucico** program will automatically *negotiate* with the other end of the connection to choose a protocol that both ends speak. The protocol can be specified in the **Devices** files for a specific network type. Following the first field in the **Devices** file you are using for **uucico** (as specified in **Sysfiles**), add a , (comma) and the names of the protocols you wish to use on that device. No whitespace is allowed before the comma. For example,

```
STARLAN,eg starlan - - TLIS \D
```

will use the **e** protocol when the remote can support it; otherwise it will use the **g** protocol. No changes to the **Systems** or other control files are required. Since the protocols are included when the **uucico** program is configured, not all versions of the **uucp** tools can support alternate protocols. Note that you should test your network to be sure it will really produce error-free data transfer before you depend on the **e** protocol.

Grades of Service

The SVR4 **uucp** system includes the ability to select a specific *grade of service* for data transfers. With this facility you can specify that some jobs have priority over other jobs. You can prioritize individual jobs, users, and systems to create a complex pecking order of **uucp** activity. This can be useful for priority transfers on a heavily loaded machine, but it is only required in unusual situations. The file **/etc/uucp/Grades** controls service grades, and contains comments that describe how to use the grades. The **uuglist** command displays the currently configured service grades on a machine. Use the **-g** command-line option on your **uucp** commands to select a grade for your transfers. You can only use grades for which you are authorized in the **Grades** file.

The Devconfig File

There are many other features of the **uucp** subsystem that are just too complex to discuss in detail here. One of these is the **Devconfig** (for device configuration) file, which is a recent addition to **uucp**. **Devconfig** is used for data communication dialers based on the *streams* device driver scheme. When **uucp** wants to use a streams-based device, it consults the **Devconfig** file to determine what streams *modules* must be attached to the data path that leads to the device. Among others, the StarLan and Ethernet local area networks use the streams mechanism in their software.

Using **Devconfig** can be difficult and confusing; consult your network administrator for details specific to your network.

Using uucp on TCP/IP Networks

You can run the **uucp** system across an Ethernet link as well as a StarLan or dial-up link, though this is not usually done. Most Ethernet users prefer the **rcp** command instead of **uucp** for moving files. To run the **uucp** system across a link, you must be running the HDB version of **uucp** on both ends of the connections. Some experimentation is often required to get the system working correctly. Setups for SVR3 and SVR4 machines will also differ. This section is only intended as an example; consult your network administrator for more information.

For each machine you wish to call via TCP/IP, you need a special **systems** entry that includes the Internet address of the machine, as shown here:

```
anysys Any TCPDEV - \x00020401ff003f00
```

You must define a special device entry such as TCPDEV in this example. The long string of digits following the \x is the fixed part 00020401 followed by the Internet address of the machine in hex format (255.0.127.0 in this example). Note that there is no chat here, so *anysys* is expected to provide **uucico** service directly without going through **login**.

The **Devices** entry for TCPDEV will look like this:

```
TCPDEV,eg ip - - TLI \D nls
```

The *ip* is the device file for the TCP link, and *nls* points to the following entry in the **Dialers** file:

```
nls "" "" NLPS:000:001:1\N\c
```

When this **Dialers** entry is executed, it requests service code 1 at the destination machine. You must configure the listener at the destination to respond to this service code with commands like this

```
# nlsadmin -1 \x00020401ff003f00
# nlsadmin -a 1
# nlsadmin -s
```

Use the hex equivalent of the Internet address of the receiving machine after the 00020401 part in the previous example to listen for incoming traffic for this machine.

You may also need to add a line to **Devconfig** at the receiving side to push the tirdwr module onto the stream, as shown here:

```
service=uucico device=ip push=tirdwr
```

Finally, don't neglect the appropriate changes to the systems and permissions files on each machine.

rje and IBM 3270 Emulation

Historically, the UNIX system has been able to connect well to the IBM SNA network, allowing RJE (for remote job entry) access between mainframes and the UNIX machine. Now packages for UNIX systems allow IBM 3270 emulation as well. However, both of these features require add-on hardware and special device drivers. Although these packages are available from several sources, they are not part of the standard UNIX system.

The Korn and C Shells

S
I
X
T
E
E
N

The shell is a user-level process like any other command. It has no special relationship with the kernel, nor any special privileges that are not enjoyed by other commands. Thus, the shell can be changed at the discretion of the user, and many alternative shells are available that look different or are optimized for different functions.

The "standard" shell, the one we have discussed so far, is known as the *Bourne* shell for its developer, Steve Bourne of AT&T Bell Laboratories. This is a small, relatively efficient shell, designed for general-purpose use. The Bourne shell was introduced about 1978. Over the years, features and improvements, such as shell functions, have been added to keep it current with the rest of the UNIX system; however, it has several disadvantages for expert users. First, it doesn't provide a *command history*; there is no way to repeat a command line without completely retyping it. Another desirable feature the standard shell lacks is *aliasing,* the ability for users to customize the command names that they use frequently. You can solve both of these problems with the Bourne shell by creating new commands as shell programs, saving them in a file, and giving the file the name you wish. This solution is inefficient, however, because a subshell is required to read the shell program and execute its contents. Also, there is no quick and easy way to edit commands on the fly, since the shell program is relatively permanent in the file.

These considerations and others motivated the development of two popular enhanced shells that are included with the SVR4 system: the *Korn* shell and the *C* shell. Both of these shells can replace the Bourne shell for interactive user-level sessions or for executing shell scripts. The C shell was originally developed by Bill Joy as part of the BSD version, and the Korn shell was developed by David Korn of AT&T Bell Laboratories as a response to the C shell. The C shell is older, and thus in many ways the Korn shell has improved on its features and methods. The C shell is also relatively inefficient compared to either the Bourne or Korn shells. Nonetheless, it has many devotees, especially among fans of BSD systems. Although the Korn shell is larger than the Bourne shell, it is noticeably more efficient because it has more *built-in* functions that can be performed directly by the shell and do not require a separate subshell.

Neither the C shell nor the Korn shell can completely replace the Bourne shell. That is, neither can be named **/sbin/sh**. While the Korn shell was originally intended to replace the Bourne shell, and to be fully compatible with it, there are still a few differences that always seem to surface at the worst times. The C shell, on the other hand, was never intended to replace the Bourne shell and is quite different from it.

These two shells provide many improvements over the Bourne shell, including more shell programming operators, built-in arithmetic operators to replace the **expr** command, and better string-handling features. However, the most important advantages of both the Korn and the C shells are *command editing, command history,* and *aliases.* Command history and editing work together so that you can recall a previously executed command with the history feature, change it slightly for a new invocation (using the editing features), and then execute the edited command as if you had retyped it. Aliases provide an efficient way to customize the command lines that you commonly use.

Selecting an Enhanced Shell

Most users, once they graduate from the novice stage, find that the standard shell slows down their use of the system, and thus hampers their productivity. When this happens, it is time to move to either the Korn or the C shell. Most users select one or the other of these shells, and use it exclusively. That is, very few people are comfortable in a mixed environment in which they use both shells.

In general, the Korn shell offers a larger set of enhanced features than the C shell, and the command editing and history features are easier to learn and use in the Korn shell. Also, the Korn shell is exactly like the Bourne shell in its basic features, and is significantly faster and more efficient than the C shell. For shell programming, the Korn shell is a superset of the Bourne shell, while the C shell differs significantly. On the other hand, the C shell is more widely available on different UNIX versions, especially older BSD systems. Also, many UNIX sites have a large group of users with C shell experience who can help support a new user. If other users you know are C shell devotees, or if you use a system that only offers the C shell, then perhaps you should use it. Otherwise, the Korn shell is preferable.

The Korn Shell

The Korn shell is intended to be a *superset* of Bourne shell features. That is, any shell script or command line that is acceptable to the

Bourne shell should also work with the Korn shell, including shell functions and other programming features. The converse, however, is not true: Korn shell scripts may not work correctly under the Bourne shell.

Starting the Korn Shell

From your normal login session, you can start the Korn shell like any other command. That is,

```
$ ksh
$
```

The Korn shell uses the PS1 and PS2 environment variables for its prompt, so it may appear that nothing has changed when you execute the Korn shell in this way. Thus, many users set up a distinctive prompt when they are using the Korn shell. There are many possibilities, of course, but the Korn shell allows the operator ! (bang) in the **PS1**, which **ksh** interprets as the number of commands that have been executed since the **ksh** history was last cleared (this is often done at login). For example:

```
$ PS1="[!]$ "
[!]$ ksh
[1]$ echo $PS1
[!]$
[2]$
```

Notice that the prompt keeps changing under **ksh**, while the Bourne shell does not give the ! any special treatment.

When you invoke **ksh** in this way, it runs as a normal command under the usual shell, so when you exit from **ksh**, you are returned to the regular shell, as shown here:

```
[!]$ ksh
[1]$ exit
[!]$
```

You can also exit by entering CTRL-D at the prompt, instead of using the **exit** command.

Another way to enter **ksh** is with the **exec** (for execute) command, which *replaces* the current shell with the new one, as follows:

```
[!]$ exec ksh
[3]$
```

In this case, the original shell is lost, so when you exit from **ksh** you are logged off the system, as shown here:

```
[3]$ exit
my_sys login:
```

This **exec** form can be placed at the end of your **.profile** so that you get **ksh** as your normal shell when you log in to the machine.

When you start **ksh**, it looks for a file similar to the **.profile** from which to read setup commands that are specific to the **ksh**. This *environment file* allows you to configure the **ksh** session to your needs. Since you will often run **ksh** after you log in, many commands that are only understood by **ksh** cannot appear in your **.profile**. The environment file allows you to create a set of commands that will be executed for each **ksh** you start, but not for other shells.

This special environment file is a normal *ksh script*, or list of commands understood and interpreted by **ksh**. To use this file, set the *ENV* environment variable to point to the file, and then export ENV, as follows:

```
[!]$ ENV=$HOME/.kshrc
[!]$ export ENV
```

When **ksh** starts, it will look for the ENV variable; if it exists **ksh** will try to execute the contents of the file in a manner similar to the way the Bourne shell executes the **.profile**.

You can execute **ksh** to interpret a shell script as well. For example,

```
[5]$ ksh script
```

or

```
[6]$ ksh < script
```

will cause **ksh** to execute the file script as a shell script. You can use this form whether or not you are using **ksh** to interpret your command lines.

Command History in ksh

When you have **ksh** as the shell for your session, you can take advantage of its command history and command editing features. As you enter command lines for execution, **ksh** stores each command in a *history list*. Commands in the history are numbered in sequence, and the sequence number of each command is displayed by the ! operator in the PS1 prompt. By default, your most recent 128 commands are kept in the history list, but the value of ! will grow beyond 128 as you enter more commands. When this happens, **ksh** discards the older commands from the history list and keeps the newer ones, and at that point you can no longer retrieve the discarded commands. It is possible to change the history list size by setting and exporting the *HISTSIZE* environment variable, as shown here:

```
[8]$ HISTSIZE=400
[9]$ export HISTSIZE
```

This will instruct **ksh** to retain the 400 most recent commands in the history list. To clear the history list and restart the count, you can delete or truncate the history file before you start **ksh**.

By default, **ksh** uses the file **$HOME/.sh_history** to hold the history list. You can change the file by setting and exporting the environment variable *HISTFILE*, as follows:

```
[!]$ HISTFILE=$HOME/.ksh.history
[!]$ export HISTFILE
[!]$
```

If you have done this, you can enter

```
[!]$ rm $HISTFILE
[!]$
```

right after you log in, and before you start the **ksh**. This will start a new count for each login session. These history-related commands are often placed in the **.profile** to restart the count anew for each login session. Otherwise, the history will be retained across login sessions.

ksh Command Editing with the vi Mode

You can access the history list, and retrieve previously executed command lines, by using the command editing features. Command editing allows you to edit command lines as you enter them, as well as to recall and edit previously executed commands that are stored in the history list.

The Korn shell provides two methods for editing command lines. These follow the editing conventions of the **vi** and the **emacs** text editors. Users familiar with **vi** will probably select **vi** mode, while **emacs** users will prefer the **emacs** mode. You can select which mode to use by setting the value of the *VISUAL* environment variable, and exporting it. The value is the name of the editor you wish to use. Thus, you would select the **vi** editing commands, as follows:

```
[9]$ VISUAL=vi
[10]$ export VISUAL
[11]$
```

To select the **emacs** command mode, you would use

```
[12]$ VISUAL=emacs
[13]$ export VISUAL
[14]$
```

These commands are usually placed in your **.profile** so that you don't have to enter them manually.

Once you have selected an editing mode, you can use that command set to edit your command lines. The **ksh** treats the history list as an editable "file." Normally, you are in input mode in that file (to use **vi** terminology); each line you type is added to the end of the file when you complete the command line with a newline, and the command is also executed as expected.

To jump to command mode when VISUAL is set to **vi**, use the ESC operator. After you press ESC, instead of adding your typed characters to the command, **ksh** allows you to edit the command using **vi** operators. For example, to move the cursor back two words on the current line, you can type **b2w**. Any other normal **vi** command is also acceptable. Then you can reenter input mode with **i** or **a**, add some text, and escape back to command mode with ESC to change three words with **c3w**. You can jump back and forth between input and command modes in this way as often as necessary. You can also use normal **vi** search and replace operators; even **u** works to undo a change.

When you enter a newline, **ksh** assumes you have finished editing the line, and it executes the command line and adds the command to the history list.

You can use the **vi** move and search operators to retrieve commands from the history list. For example, if you want to retrieve a previously entered **grep** command for reexecution or editing, you can press the ESC key, and then enter **/grep** to search for the next previous line in the history list that contains the string *grep*. The **ksh** will then display that command line for further editing, leaving you in command mode so you can continue to edit the command line. When you enter a newline, the command (as edited) will be executed. If you wish to search for another string, or find another command line in the history list, you can do so. These history list search operators will not accept complex regular expressions; only simple strings are allowed.

The last line mode is not supported in the **ksh** editing commands, so the **vi** operators that begin with : (colon) will not work. This means it is not easy to refer to the history list by the command numbers displayed by the ! in your PS1. These numbers are used by the **fc** command, discussed later in this chapter. The full set of **ksh** editing operators, for both **vi** and **emacs** modes, is given in the **ksh(1)** man page.

Normally you would expect the **vi** command **/** to search *forward* in the current file, and the **?** command to search *backward* in the current file; however, **ksh** treats these operators inversely. That is, the **/** operator searches from the current command backward in the history list to find the most recent command line that contains the search string. This is really not a problem, because most users find this behavior to be intuitive.

ksh Command Editing with the emacs Mode

When you have selected the **emacs** editing mode with

```
[17]$ VISUAL=emacs ; export VISUAL
```

you can use the normal editing commands of the **emacs** editor to edit your commands. Since **emacs** does not have true input or command modes, you must specify **emacs** CTRL and meta commands to edit the command lines. Recall that CTRL commands are created by holding down the CTRL key while you enter a command character. We use the form ˆk to signify the CTRL-K keystrokes. The meta commands are generated by pressing the ESC key followed by another key; in **emacs** usage, ESC followed by the k key would be denoted **M-k**. Normally, all your typed characters are interpreted as text and added to the command line at the current cursor position.

Unfortunately, the **emacs** command set used by **ksh** is not identical to the command set used by the popular Gnu emacs, discussed in Chapter 5; however, most **emacs** users will have no difficulty with the **ksh** syntax.

To move the cursor back one character, use ˆ**b** (CTRL-B), and to move it forward one character, use ˆ**f**. To move the cursor forward by a word, use **M-f**, and to move it back by a word, use **M-b**. To move the cursor forward by several words, use **M-nM-f**, where n is a digit setting a repeat count for the operation. That is, establish an argument with **M-n**, and then enter the command you wish to repeat. Unlike most **emacs** editors, the **emacs** editing mode does not support the direct use of arguments within a command; however, most of the normal **emacs** editing commands including text deletion, yank-and-put operations, marks, and search operations will work as expected. You can experiment to get a feel for how the **ksh** responds.

To recall the previous command from the history list, use **ˆp**, or use **ˆn** to recall the next command when you are not at the end of the history list. That is, **ˆn** makes no sense when you have not executed a **ˆp**. As you might have expected, you can recall a command further back on the history list with **M-*n*ˆp**, where *n* is a count of how far back on the list to search for the command.

Similarly, you can search for a string in the history list with **ˆr***string*. If the string occurs in the history list, the command in which it occurs will be displayed on the command line for editing or execution. If an argument or count of zero is given, the search will be forward in the history list; otherwise, it will be backward. That is, normally you will give no argument to find the most recent occurrence of the string in the history list. Use the form **M-0ˆr***string* to search forward when you are not at the bottom of the history list.

Again, **ksh** allows most of the **vi** or **emacs** editing commands, except that a newline is understood as the signal to execute the current command. You need not have the cursor at the end of the command line when you press newline, because **ksh** will execute the entire command line as it exists after editing. To abort the current command without executing it, press the DEL key. This will cause **ksh** to discard the current command line and display a new prompt. In addition, if you add a # (pound sign, the shell comment operator) as the first character on the current command line, and then press newline, **ksh** will add that command line to the history list, but will not edit it. This allows nonexecuted commands or comments to appear in the history list.

Aliases in ksh

Another important **ksh** feature is *aliasing*. Aliases allow you to change your **ksh** environment so that command names you enter on the command line are changed by **ksh** to other, aliased, commands before they are executed. Thus, you can permanently modify your command "world" to use personalized commands, but still use the normal command names. This substitution of aliases for command names is called *alias expansion*. For example, the **rm** command will silently delete files, while the **rm -i** command will interactively prompt you for confirmation before deleting a file. Many users have been burned by the silent behavior of **rm**, but do not want to enter **rm -i** each time they use the command. You can alias the **rm** command to **rm -i** so that whenever you enter

```
[20]$ rm file
```

the command

```
rm -i file
```

will actually be executed by **ksh**. There are many other uses for aliases as well.

To establish an alias, use the **alias** command, as shown here:

```
[21]$ alias rm="rm -i"
[22]$
```

The **ksh** will then replace the **rm** command with its alias whenever it is used on the command line.

Several rules apply to aliases. An alias can have as many words as you wish, providing you enclose it in quotation marks in the **alias** command. The aliasing replacement happens only on the *first* word on the command line, and the first word of each element of a pipeline. For example,

```
[23]$ alias grep="fgrep -i"
[24]$ grep hello file | grep grep
```

will cause the command line

```
fgrep -i hello file | fgrep -i grep
```

to be executed. In addition, when a command begins with a **/** (slash) to specify a full pathname, the alias is not applied. Thus, to get the unaliased form of a command, you should use its full path.

You can remove a previously established alias with the **unalias** command. For example:

```
[25]$ unalias rm
```

will restore the original meaning of the **rm** command. The **alias** command alone with no arguments gives a list of current aliases, as shown here:

```
[26]$ alias
autoload=typeset -fu
cat=/bin/cat
cd=_cd
cls=clear
del=/bin/rm -rf
dir=/bin/ls -F
false=let 0
functions=typeset -f
hash=alias -t -
history=fc -l
integer=typeset -i
ls=/bin/ls -F
mail=mail -v
nohup=nohup
p=enscript -2 -G -r -Plw
r=fc -e -
rm=/bin/rm -i
space=df -a
stop=kill -STOP
suspend=kill -STOP $$
true=:
type=whence -v
vi=/usr/ucb/vi
[27]$
```

Although aliases that contain whitespace must be quoted when the alias is created, the **alias** command will display them without quotes.

Many of these aliases are set automatically by **ksh** and are used to improve internal performance as **ksh** executes. The aliases **suspend, stop, type,** and several more are of this form. Others are known as *tracked aliases,* and these are automatically set to the full pathname of the command by **ksh** when a command is first executed, which reduces the time required to search the PATH for the command. The **vi** and **cat** aliases are of this type. Other aliases are set for the user's individual session, such as **rm, space** and **ls.** Many users with MS-DOS experience configure aliases so that MS-DOS commands entered at the keyboard by mistake are translated to their UNIX equivalents. In the previous list, **cls** and **del** are examples of this practice.

You can create as many aliases as you wish, but since aliases are managed internally within **ksh,** they do not survive across logins as shell scripts do. Thus, most users add **alias** commands to their ENV file so that aliases are set whenever **ksh** is executed.

The whence Command

The **ksh** also includes several convenience features. You can use the **whence** command, followed by a command name, to locate the exact form of the command that is used by **ksh** when you enter it. For normal commands, **whence** shows the full pathname by searching your PATH to find the command. For example:

```
[25]$ whence ksh
/usr/bin/ksh
[26]$
```

If the command is a built-in or a shell function, **ksh** will give the name without a path, as follows:

```
[27]$ whence echo
echo
[28]$
```

Finally, **whence** performs alias expansion, so that you can see what command is actually executed, as shown here:

```
[28]$ whence ls
/bin/ls -F
[29]$
```

The **whence** command is surprisingly useful for identifying "lost" commands and aliases. It can take several arguments to control its behavior.

The fc Command

One of the few uses for the command number given by ! in the prompt is **fc** (for fix command). The **fc** command lets you select a range of commands from the history list, edit this range of commands with your favorite editor, and then execute the edited commands just as if you had created a shell script with them. For example,

```
[30]$ fc 20 35
```

will execute an editor with commands 20 through 35 listed, one per line. You can edit the commands, and when you write and quit from the editor the commands will be executed. By default, **fc** uses a private temporary file for the editing session, but if you wish to save the commands yourself, you can write them to your own file while you are inside the editor.

The **fc** command uses the editor named in the *FCEDIT* environment variable. Since you will wish to use your normal editor with **fc**, you should use a command like

```
FCEDIT=$EDITOR ; export FCEDIT
```

in your **.profile** to set FCEDIT correctly.

The **fc** command has several options. If you specify

```
[31]$ fc -l
```

(ell; for list), **fc** will display the contents of the history list. To list a range of commands, use

```
[32]$ fc -l 20 35
```

You can use **fc -e**, followed by an editor name, to override the FCEDIT variable. If you give the **-e** option, but specify a - (hyphen) as the editor name, **fc** will assume that you simply wish to execute the command list without editing. For example, to reexecute command number 14 from the history list, you can use

```
[33]$ fc -e - 14 14
```

You must give both ends of the range, or **fc** will execute all the commands from the number given to the last command in the history list.

Instead of giving a number as the argument to **fc**, you can give the first character or characters in the command. If you had the command

```
grep -v "^[a-z]hello[1-9]*" file | pr | lp
```

in the history list, you could reexecute it with

```
[34]$ fc -e - gr
```

In this situation, you don't have to give both ends of the range.

Finally, **ksh** uses these features to predefine the alias **r** so that executing **r** alone will reexecute the immediately preceding command, and

```
[34]$ r gr
```

will have the same effect as the previous example.

Tilde Substitution

Another useful **ksh** feature is *tilde substitution*. When **ksh** sees the ~ (tilde) character at the beginning of a pathname, it tries to interpret the next string, up to a **/** (slash), as a user login id. Then, if it finds that user, it will replace the ~ string with his or her home directory. For example,

```
[35]$ cd ~steve
```

will change the current directory to the home directory of user **steve**, and

```
[36]$ cat ~jim/lib/script
```

will display the file **lib/script** located in the home directory of user **jim**.

Changing Directories under ksh

The **ksh** also provides features for enhanced directory changing operations. The form **cd -** will change your directory to the previous directory you were in, as shown here:

```
[37]$ pwd
/home/steve
[38]$ cd /tmp
```

```
[39]$ pwd
/tmp
[40]$ cd -
[41]$ pwd
/home/steve
[42]$
```

The **ksh** supports the CDPATH variable just as the Bourne shell does.

The set Command

The **ksh** includes many options that change its behavior and customize it to your preferences. These options are examined and changed with the **set** command. There are a great many options, which are all documented in the **ksh(1)** man page; this section discusses only the most useful ones.

Two different types of **ksh** behavior can be modified with the **set** command. First, a group of options changes the way shell scripts are treated. For example,

```
[44]$ set -n
```

instructs **ksh** to read commands in shell scripts and check them for errors, but not to execute the commands. This instruction is ignored for interactive shells such as your login session. To restore the shell's original behavior, use

```
[45]$ set +n
```

This example illustrates a general property of the **set** command: an option is set if the argument begins with - (minus), and cleared if the argument begins with + (plus).

The command

```
set -a
```

causes all subsequently defined environment variables to be exported. With this command you can avoid using **export** after you define each environment variable. The

```
set -v
```

(verbose) command causes **ksh** to display each command of a shell script as it is read. Finally, the command

```
set -m
```

instructs **ksh** to inform you when each of your background jobs completes. For example:

```
[38]$ sleep 5 &
[1] 18165
[39]$
```

Here, **ksh** reports the job id of the background job, and then returns another prompt. After the job completes (five seconds later for this simple job), **ksh** will echo

```
[1] + Done           sleep 5 &
```

before displaying a prompt. This notification is often quite useful, but if you wish, you can disable it with **set +m**. Notification is enabled by default.

The second type of **set** function sets options that control your interactive sessions. These commands have the form

```
set -o option
```

where *option* is one of the supported types. Here again, you use

```
set +o option
```

to turn off the option.

The command

```
set -o ignoreeof
```

instructs your current shell to ignore CTRL-D characters, thus preventing **ksh** from unexpectedly logging you off if you enter CTRL-D by mistake. When **ignoreeof** is set, you must use the **exit** command to end your session. The command

```
set -o noclobber
```

prevents the redirection operator > from truncating an existing file. This is very useful for catching mistakes and saving files that might otherwise be lost. You can use

```
set -o emacs
```

or

```
set -o vi
```

to override the VISUAL environment variable and change your command-line editing mode. Finally, use

```
set -o bgnice
```

to run all your background jobs (created with **&** at the end of the command line) at a lower priority than usual. The **bgnice** option is set by default, so you will need to use

```
set +o bgnice
```

to execute background jobs at normal priority. As mentioned earlier, there are several other options controlled by **set -o.**

ksh Enhancements for Shell Programming

In addition to these convenience features, **ksh** includes enhancements for improved shell programming. There are several new operators that provide better logic within scripts, and several operators that improve the performance of shell scripts; however, using these new operators means your shell scripts cannot be executed by the Bourne shell, so use them with care. In general, **ksh** supports all the normal Bourne shell programming operators.

Arithmetic Operators

One of the most important enhancements in **ksh** involves arithmetic operations. In the Bourne shell, you must use the **expr** command to evaluate numeric expressions. This can be quite slow and inefficient, because **expr** is a standalone command that is executed as a separate process. In **ksh**, however, many arithmetic operations are built in, so they execute more quickly.

Use the **let** command to set or change the value of an environment variable. For example:

```
[38]$ let x=42
[39]$ echo $x
42
[40]$
```

Then you can use normal arithmetic operators to update or modify the value, as shown here:

```
[40]$ let x=42
[41]$ let x=$x*3-11
[42]$ echo $x
115
[43]$
```

Note that normal *arithmetic precedence* is followed. To change the order of evaluation, you must use intermediate assignments, as follows:

```
[43]$ let x=42
[44]$ let y=3-11
[45]$ let x=$x*$y
[46]$ echo $x
-336
[47]$
```

You cannot include whitespace within **let** commands, but you can use shell positional parameters or other environment variables as required. You can also omit the **let** operator, because the = sign tells **ksh** that you desire an arithmetic operation.

Arrays

The **ksh** also allows one-dimensional arrays, which are identified with a *subscript* following the variable name. The subscript is a number enclosed within square brackets, as in this example:

```
[48]$ x[3]=20
[49]$ x[4]=30
[50]$ x[5]=${x[3]}+${x[4]}
[51]$ echo ${x[5]}
50
[52]$
```

Note that when you *set* the subscripted variable you can refer to it directly, but when you *use* the subscripted variable it must be enclosed in curly braces, or **ksh** will not interpret it correctly.

By default, the arithmetic operations are performed in normal decimal (base ten) arithmetic, but **ksh** allows you to do arithmetic in other bases as well.

Improved Prompting, Input and Output

The **ksh** includes several built-in commands that make it easier to prompt a user for input and to read lines of data from a file. The **print** command substitutes for **echo**, printing lines of output to the terminal (default), to the history list (with the **-s** option), or to several other targets. The **read** command is used to read a line of input. The input that is read is assigned to the environment variables named as arguments to **read**. For example:

```
[50]$ read a1 a2 a3
are we having fun yet
[51]$ echo $a1
are
[52]$ echo $a3
```

```
having fun yet
[53]$
```

If the input contains more words than the number of arguments to **read**, the last argument catches all the extra words. If there are fewer words in the input than there are arguments to **read**, the extra arguments remain undefined. If the first argument to **read** contains a ? (question mark), the characters *after* the ? are printed as a prompt, and the word *before* the question mark is the name of the environment variable that takes the first word of input. For example:

```
[54]$ read a1?"how are you today? " a2 a3
how are you today? not bad how are you
[55]$ echo $a1
not
[56]$ echo $a2
bad
[57]$ echo $a3
how are you
[58]$
```

This allows you to efficiently prompt for user input in a **ksh** script.

Environment Variable Processing Under ksh

The **ksh** supports an enhanced form for processing environment variables, which allows the use of a default value for a variable that is not defined at run time, the printing of an error message if a variable is not defined, or the use of only a substring of a variable's value. The inverse of all these operations is also supported. These forms can get very complex; see for example the definition of the ENV variable later in this chapter.

The basic form is

```
${parameter op word}
```

where *parameter* is the usual environment variable name, *op* is a special operator, and *word* is the desired default value, substring, and so forth. For example,

```
VAR=${OVAR:-word}
```

sets VAR to the value of OVAR if OVAR is defined, but sets VAR to *word* if OVAR is undefined. Here are two additional forms:

```
VAR=${OVAR#word}
VAR=${OVAR%word}
```

These compare the string *word* with the beginning (#) or end (%) of OVAR, and if it is the same, they delete the matched portion. For example, you can convert the name **file.o** to **file.c** with

```
OLD=file.o
NEW=${OLD%.o}.c
```

While this can be very useful, it can also be very confusing; the full set of operators is given in the **ksh(1)** man page.

The C Shell

The C shell, so named because its programming syntax is supposedly something like that of the C language, is the third major shell in use today. In fact, the C shell probably has more users than the Korn or Bourne shells, because of its long history as part of the BSD version of the UNIX operating system. On the other hand, the C shell is different in many ways than the other shells, and many of the shell-related ideas presented so far are not appropriate to it. The C shell does not support shell functions.

Starting the C Shell

You can start the C shell from the command line as follows:

```
$ csh
my_sys%
```

Normally the prompt for **csh** is the system name followed by % (percent), but you can change the prompt, as you'll see in a moment. You can end your **csh** session with **exit** or CTRL-D. When you do, you will be returned to your previous shell. Alternatively, you can use

```
$ exec csh
```

so that when you end your **csh** session, you will be logged off of the machine.

When **csh** starts, it reads the file **.cshrc** (for csh run commands) in your home directory. The **.cshrc** file is a **csh** script that can contain any commands. Normally **.cshrc** contains startup commands that customize your **csh** environment. You can instruct **csh** to bypass much of its setup overhead (including reading the **.cshrc** file) with the **-f** (for fast) option. Since most variables and other **csh** material are usually exported by default, the fast option is a great timesaver when you are testing **csh** scripts.

The csh Command Line

The **csh** uses some wildcard characters different from those used by **sh** or **ksh**. Thus, you may have to be alert for *escaping* characters on the command line. The ! (bang) is an important example. For instance, you might try addressing mail as follows:

```
% mail yoursys!pat
pat: event not found.
%
```

To use such a command line, you need to escape the !, as shown here:

```
% mail yoursys\!pat
```

Watch for other differences between shells; they can bite!

Setting csh Variables

The **csh** differs from **sh** and **ksh** in many ways. One of the most important is the way it treats environment variables. The value of PS1 is not used by **csh**. Instead, the **prompt** variable serves the same function. Use the **set** command to change your prompt, as follows:

```
my_sys% set prompt="hello: "
hello:
```

Note that the variable names in **csh** are usually lowercase names. Other important **csh** variables are **home** and **term**, which replace the HOME and TERM variables used in the Bourne shell.

You can change the equivalent of PATH by setting the **path** variable. The value is a list of directories, separated by whitespace, and enclosed in parentheses. For example:

```
hello: set path = ( /usr/bin /bin /usr/ucb/bin . /usr/local/bin )
hello:
```

You need not **export** variables set within the **csh**; the **csh** handles this automatically. This form is also used to set the **cdpath** variable, which is equivalent to CDPATH in the Bourne and Korn shells. Here is an example:

```
my_sys% set cdpath = ( $home . /usr/src )
```

Note the use of the **home** variable here. To use a **csh** variable, you must precede it with the $ operator. These commands are often placed in the .cshrc file so that they are set when the **csh** starts.

Many other variables are supported by **csh**, and managed with the **set** command. Some of the most important are **noclobber**, which prevents the **csh** from overwriting an existing file, **ignoreeof**, which inhibits logoff from the CTRL-D character, and **cdpath**. Try this command:

```
my_sys% set
```

to see the currently active list. For more information on these variables, consult the **csh(1)** man page.

Command History and Editing in csh

The **csh** includes support for command history and for the editing of commands from the history list. However, it is difficult to edit a command that you are currently entering, one that is not yet on the history list. The **csh** variable **history** sets the size of the history list, as follows:

```
my_sys% set history = 40
```

Since the **csh** maintains the history list internally, there is no history file as there is in the **ksh**. To display the history list, execute the **history** command.

You can refer to commands stored on the history list by number. Use the ! (bang) operator in your **prompt** to display the *event number* of each command, as shown here:

```
my_sys% set prompt="`hostname`{`whoami`}!: "
my_sys{steve}36:
```

Once you know the event number for your commands, you can use the ! anywhere in your command lines to choose a specific command in the history list. For example:

```
my_sys{steve}36: echo !35
echo set prompt="`hostname`{`whoami`}!: "
set prompt=my_sys{steve}!:
my_sys{steve}37:
```

When you use ! in your commands, the **csh** will echo the command after the ! gets substituted but before it is executed. Use the form !*n* to refer to the *nth* command on the history list.

You can also use ! to reexecute a command from the history list, as follows:

```
my_sys{steve}37: !35
set prompt="`hostname`{`whoami`}!: "
my_sys{steve}38:
```

Again, the command is first echoed, and then executed.

Instead of using the event number to refer to a previous command, you can also use a string. The form !*string* refers to a previous command that begins with *string*. The string must be the first characters on the command line in the history list, and **csh** will find the most recently executed command beginning with that string.

A simple form of the ! command refers to the *immediately preceding* command. Use the **!!** (bang bang) operator to refer to the last command you entered, as shown here:

```
my_sys{steve}39: echo just a test
just a test
my_sys{steve}40: !!
echo just a test
just a test
my_sys{steve}41:
```

Note that when you use the **csh**, you cannot use the ! character as a normal character in your command lines, without *escaping* it; otherwise, **csh** will always assume that you mean the history list. When you don't want ! to refer to the history list, precede it with a \ (backslash), as follows:

```
my_sys{steve}41: echo \!36
!36
my_sys{steve}42:
```

The **csh** provides a complete, though somewhat cumbersome, mechanism for editing commands retrieved from the history list. After selecting a command with the ! operator, you can substitute parts of the command with search-and-replace operators to modify it before it is executed. Use a : after the event identifier, followed by the normal s/*oldstring*/*newstring*/ form to substitute in the command as retrieved. For example:

```
my_sys{steve}42: !39:s/test/hello/
echo just a hello
just a hello
my_sys{steve}43:
```

Only simple string substitutions are allowed; complex regular expressions will not work.

You can also refer to individual words in commands retrieved from the history list. Place a digit after the : to indicate the *position* of the word you wish to use (the command name is word number zero). Here is an example:

```
my_sys{steve}43: echo !39:3
echo test
test
my_sys{steve}44:
```

You can combine these forms with additional colon operators whenever you wish, as shown here:

```
my_sys{steve}44: echo !39:3:s/es/XX/
echo tXXt
tXXt
my_sys{steve}45:
```

In addition, $ (dollar) refers to the last word on the retrieved command line (often a filename), and # (pound) refers to the entire command line. Several other similar operations are allowed. You can use as many of these *modifiers* as you wish, anywhere on the command line, to reconstruct and change your commands.

In handling the history list and substitutions, **csh** performs these steps: First, the event is retrieved from the history list, and then the replacement or subpart is applied. Next, the modified string is substituted into the current command line. Then the completed command is echoed, and finally it is executed.

Hashing

When the **csh** starts, it finds all the commands in directories named in the **path** variable and builds an internal table of their full pathnames. Then, when a command is executed, the **csh** uses the table rather than directly searching the path. This *hashing* technique is designed for performance, but if you change your **path** or add a command to one of the directories, **csh** will not see the changes. In this case, you can force **csh** to rebuild its *hash table* by executing the **rehash** command.

Aliases

The **csh** also provides an **alias** facility to allow commands to be changed before they are executed. You create an alias with the **alias** command, followed by the name of the alias, and then by a (quoted) string to substitute. For example:

```
my_sys{steve}45: alias xx "echo hello"
my_sys{steve}46: xx
hello
my_sys{steve}46: xx sunshine
hello sunshine
my_sys{steve}47: /xx
/xx: Command not found.
my_sys{steve}48:
```

Alias substitution only applies to the *first* word of your command line within each element of a pipeline, and then only when the command name is given as a relative pathname that does not begin with a **/** (slash).

You can eliminate an alias with the **unalias** command, shown here:

```
my_sys{steve}48: unalias xx
my_sys{steve}49: xx
xx: Command not found.
my_sys{steve}50:
```

Aliases are very useful for customizing your command line environment. They are usually defined in the **.cshrc** file.

I/O Redirection with csh

The **csh** format for redirecting standard error differs from that used in the other shells. You can use **>** to redirect standard output as you would expect, but instead of the **2>** form used by the Bourne and Korn shells, you use **>&** to merge standard output and standard error to the same file. For example:

```
my_sys{steve}59: cat /etc/passwd >& outfile
```

If the **noclobber** option is set, you must use >! and >&! to force the **csh** to overwrite an existing file. Similarly, use >>! or >>&! to *append* your output to an existing file, without truncating the file before the output is written.

Although it is not easy to direct standard output and standard error to *different* files, it can be done by using a subshell, as follows:

```
my_sys{steve}60: (cat /etc/passwd > outfile ) >& errorfile
```

Shell Programming with csh

The **csh** supports shell programming, but its programming language differs significantly from that used in the other shells. Still, the same basic functions are provided. Instead of the operation

```
for var in list
do
done
```

the **csh** provides the **foreach** operator, which is terminated by **end**, as shown here:

```
my_sys{steve}50: foreach var ( hello goodbye )
? echo $var
? end
hello
goodbye
my_sys{steve}51:
```

There are several points to note in this example: first, the list is surrounded by parentheses (you can use the output of a command instead of a "literal" list if you wish); second, the **csh** equivalent of PS2 is a **?** (question mark); and third, there is no **do...done** command.

You can perform a test and execute commands if the test is true, with **if...then...endif**. The **then** must be on the same line as the **if**, and the test must be enclosed in parentheses, as follows:

```
my_sys{steve}51: cat isfile
if ( -e $1 ) then
        echo file $1 exists
else
        echo file $1 DOES NOT exist
endif
my_sys{steve}52: csh -f isfile /etc/passwd
file /etc/passwd exists
my_sys{steve}53:
```

There are many test operators in addition to **-e,** which returns true if the file exists. The complete list is given on the **csh(1)** man page, but some commonly used operators are **-r,** which returns true if you have read access to the file; **-f,** which returns true if the file is an ordinary file; and **-d,** which returns true if the file is a directory. You can also compare numeric values within the parentheses, using normal arithmetic operators, as shown here:

```
my_sys{steve}53: cat numtest
set x=20
if ( $x - 20 ) then
        echo TRUE or non-zero value
else
        echo FALSE or zero value
endif
my_sys{steve}54: csh -f numtest
FALSE or zero value
my_sys{steve}55:
```

The **csh** supports numeric operations within the parentheses without the **expr** command.

On the other hand, the ` (backquote or grave) operator is *not* supported in the **csh;** in its place, use **{** and **}** (curly braces) to test the exit code of a command, as follows:

```
if { command args } then
```

Here, the curly braces replace the parentheses in the **if** test.

In addition, simple numeric operations can be handled within **csh** scripts, but not when the same command is given on the command line. Use the **@** (at sign) operator in your scripts instead of **set** when you want to perform an arithmetic operation on a variable. For example:

```
my_sys{steve}62: cat foo
set x = 5
echo $x
@ x++
```

```
echo $x
@ x+=32
echo $x
@ x = $x + 32
echo $x
my_sys{steve}63: csh -f foo
5
6
38
70
my_sys{steve}64:
```

You must surround the elements of *assignment statements* with whitespace, just as you do with the **expr** command. Normal arithmetic operations are allowed, but remember that the @ operator does not work for interactive C shells.

In **csh**, the Bourne shell **case...esac** form is replaced by **switch ...endsw**. Mark each separate case with **case**, and end each case with **breaksw**, as follows:

```
my_sys{steve}51: cat csh_prog
switch ( $1 )
case 43:
                echo hello
                breaksw
case 34:
                echo goodbye
                breaksw
default:
                echo none!
                breaksw
endsw
my_sys{steve}52: csh -f csh_prog 20
none!
my_sys{steve}53: csh -f csh_prog 34
goodbye
my_sys{steve}54:
```

The parentheses after the **switch** operator are required, and they can contain an expression that evaluates to a string. If they do, each **case** is compared to the string, and the subsequent commands are executed up to the **breaksw** command, which breaks out of the **switch**. If no case matches, the **default** case is executed. The **switch** statement ends with **endsw** (for end switch).

You can create loops with the **while...end** pair. Enclose the test part in parentheses, as in this example:

```
my_sys{steve}56: cat ss
set x=1
while ( $x < 5 )
```

```
        echo $x
        @ x = $x + 1
end
my_sys{steve}57: csh -f ss
1
2
3
4
my_sys{steve}58:
```

There is a great deal more to **csh** programming. Although the **csh** is similar to the Bourne shell in many ways, it also differs significantly. This fact causes a great deal of confusion, even among **csh** experts. The best way to learn the **csh** is by studying existing **csh** scripts and experimenting with your own scripts.

Identifying a Command with csh

The **csh** includes no built-in command equivalent to the **ksh whence** operator, which identifies the full pathname (or alias) for a command; however, the **which** command performs the same function. In SVR4 systems, **which** is located in **/usr/ucb/which**. This directory is installed as part of the BSD compatibility package, so it may not be present on all SVR4 systems.

Use **which** to identify the location of a command, as follows:

```
my_sys{steve}58: /usr/ucb/which csh
/usr/bin/csh
my_sys{steve}59:
```

Selecting a Shell to Execute a Shell Script

When you execute a script, by default the shell that is running when you give the command interprets the script; that is, the interactive shell creates a copy of itself to interpret the script. Naturally this will cause problems if a script is written in the **csh** language, but the **ksh** attempts to execute it. This might happen if you use **csh** to write a script for yourself, and then give the script to another user who prefers **ksh**. In this case, your script will fail.

To solve this problem, SVR4 includes a special capability borrowed from the BSD version that allows you to specify *inside* a script which shell you want to interpret the script. Thus, the correct shell will always read the script, regardless of which shell is used to enter the command line.

To use this facility, include the line

```
#! /full/path
```

as the first line of your scripts. For example, you could use

```
#! /usr/bin/csh
```

for a **csh** script, or

```
#! /sbin/sh
```

for a Bourne shell script, or

```
#! /usr/bin/ksh
```

for a Korn shell script. The system will look for this line before it starts the subshell. Since a line that begins with the # (pound sign) is treated as a comment by all three shells, adding these lines will not affect the operation of the script *after* the system has selected the correct shell.

Going Further

The Korn and C shells are designed by UNIX experts, for experts. Thus, they are much more powerful and versatile than the Bourne shell; but along with these extra features comes greater complexity and difficulty, especially when the shell meets the UNIX system. In this section we will discuss some of these interfaces.

Selecting a Login Shell

Normally the Bourne shell is started by the system when you log in to the machine. The Bourne shell interprets your **.profile** when it starts, and eventually displays a PS1 for your command entry. The shell that is listening is known as a *login shell* because it is created by the system when you log in. If you use a command such as **ksh** or **exec csh** in your **.profile** or at the command line, you start a subshell which is *not* a login shell. If you always use the **csh** or **ksh**, you can improve system performance and reduce the number of commands in your startup procedures by changing your login shell to your preferred shell. To do this, you either need *superuser* privilege on your machine, or you need to ask your system administrator for help. You can change your login from the administrative user agent, or follow the simple procedure outlined here.

The last field of the **/etc/passwd** line for your login gives the full pathname of the shell to be started as the login shell. For example:

```
[42]$ grep steve /etc/passwd
steve:x:102:1:Steve:/home/steve:/usr/bin/ksh
```

In this case, the **ksh** is started, and the Bourne shell is not used. You can start **csh** if you wish, with a line something like this:

```
steve:x:102:1:Steve:/home/steve:/usr/bin/csh
```

Do not copy these lines; edit the line in your *own* **/etc/passwd** file to add the preferred shell.

When **ksh** is a login shell, you can continue to use your existing **.profile**, and ksh will read it. Next, **ksh** will read the file named in the ENV variable, as discussed earlier. When the **ksh** is *not* a login shell, it does not read **.profile**; it only reads the ENV file.

The **csh**, on the other hand, does not use the **.profile**. Instead, **csh** reads a file called **.login** in your home directory, and interprets it as a **csh** script. This is necessary because the **csh** programming language is so different from the Bourne or Korn shell language, that the **.profile** will not be executable under the **csh**. After reading the **.login** file, the **csh** reads the **.cshrc** file as discussed previously. If a **csh** is not a login shell, it skips the **.login** file.

When you use the **csh** as a login shell, you can create a file named **.logout** in your home directory. This file will be read and executed by

csh when you log out of the machine. Users often place some cleanup or "housekeeping" commands in the **.logout** file, such as commands for deleting temporary files, logging the duration of the session, or whatever else is needed. The Bourne and Korn shells do not provide a **.logout** feature.

Filename Completion

The Korn and C shells provide a feature that allows you to *partially specify* a filename in a command line; the shell looks in the named directory to find files whose names begin with the string you've entered, lists all those filenames on the terminal, and then returns to the partially entered command. This allows you to see the filenames your command will act on, or to select a subset of those files for your command. When you are typing a filename in a **csh** command, just enter CTRL-D, and the **csh** will list matching filenames. For example:

```
my_sys{steve}70: ls
ball            cribbage        go          greed        tetris
chess           gnu.go          gotool      netgo
my_sys{steve}71: ls g CTRL-D
gnu.go/ go/     gotool/ greed/
my_sys{steve}71: ls g
```

When you enter the CTRL-D, the **csh** suspends what it is doing, lists all the matching filenames, and then returns to the same command line. You can continue to enter the filename, add a * (star) to choose all the listed names, or abort the command.

In the **ksh** the same feature is available in the **vi** or **emacs** editing modes. If you are using the **vi** mode, enter command mode with ESC, and then press the = (equal) key. The currently matching filenames will be displayed, and **ksh** will return to the command line in progress, as shown here:

```
[66]$ ls g ESC =
1) gnu.go/
2) go/
3) gotool/
4) greed/
[163]$ ls g
```

If you are using the **emacs** editing mode, use the **M-=** (ESC followed by equal) command.

In the **ksh**, you can disable these filename completion features with

```
[72]$ set -o noglob
```

(for no global). In the **csh,** use

```
my_sys{steve}71: set filec
```

(for file completion) to enable the filename completion features, or

```
my_sys{steve}71: unset filec
```

to disable them.

More on the ksh ENV File

When the ENV variable contains the name of a readable file, the **ksh** will read and interpret that file when it starts. Usually the file will contain aliases and other customizations for your interactive session. On the other hand, you do not usually want those aliases to be used when you are executing a shell script, because the script writer probably did not have your aliases in mind when the script was developed. Thus, it is desirable to set things up so that the ENV file will be used for *interactive shells* (including the login shell), but not for *subshells.* You can accomplish this by setting the ENV variable as follows:

```
[73]$ ENV="\${-:+$HOME/.ksh.aliases\${-##*i*}}"
```

Don't forget to **export** the ENV variable after you've set it. This complex **ksh** operation sets the ENV variable to **$HOME/.ksh.aliases** on interactive shells, but leaves it undefined on subshells; thus, the startup file will only be read when the shell is interactive. This command line uses **ksh** features that we have not discussed; consult the **ksh(1)** man page to figure out how it works.

Setting the Current Directory in your PS1

Many users like to have the current directory displayed in their prompt, so that when they use the **cd** command, the prompt will change. This is not possible under the Bourne shell, but it is easily accomplished with the SVR4 version of **ksh**. Simply use

```
$ PS1='$PWD: '
```

Note that the single quotes are required. The PWD variable is maintained by **ksh** just for this purpose.

In the **csh**, the job is a little more difficult. You have to redefine the **cd** command with an alias that contains an explicit call to the **pwd** command. Can you write the alias?

Job Control

In SVR4, both the **csh** and the **ksh** include job control. *Job control* is the ability to move currently executing commands into the foreground or background, and to stop or restart them as needed. Job control has been somewhat superceded and duplicated by the *shell layers, virtual console* and *X Window System* features included in SVR4, but many users still find job control the most convenient way to manage long-running jobs started at the terminal. The Bourne shell supports job control if it is executed under the name **jsh** (for job shell) instead of the normal **sh**.

When you execute a command line or start a job in the foreground, terminal input is blocked until that job completes, and you cannot enter additional commands. It is often desirable to push that job into the background to get control of your terminal again. Similarly, you might wish to bring a background job to the foreground so you can control it or enter data from the terminal. Job control allows you to do these things within the current layer or window. Note that in many SVR4 releases, **csh** job control will not work under the X Window System, but **ksh** and **jsh** will work as described here.

When you have a foreground job running, you can press the CTRL-Z key sequence to *suspend* or *stop* execution of that job, and return control to the shell, as shown here:

```
[80]$ sleep 40
CTRL-Z
[1] + Stopped            sleep 40
[81]$
```

The job is stopped, and a message is printed that includes the *job number* (**1**, in this case, since this is job number one), its status (**Stopped**), and the command line (**sleep 40** in this simple example). Then the shell returns for more commands. Note that while the job is stopped, the timer in the **sleep** command is not stopped, so if you restart this job after 40 seconds have elapsed, the job will complete immediately. At this point, you can enter more commands, start new jobs, kill the stopped job, or restart the stopped job either in the foreground or in the background.

To examine the current list of jobs, including all background jobs and all stopped jobs, use the **jobs** command. It lists your jobs in the same format shown in the previous example. That is,

```
[81]$ jobs
[1] + Stopped            sleep 40
(82)$
```

Now you can use the job number to control these jobs.

Use **bg** (for background) to restart a stopped job as a background job, and **fg** (for foreground) to restart a job as a foreground job. These commands take a job number preceded by a % (percent) sign, as an argument. For example:

```
[82]$ fg %1
sleep 40
```

Here, the command line is echoed, and the job takes over the terminal as the foreground job. The **bg** command is similar, except that it pushes the job into the background, just as if you had used **&** at the end of the command line.

You can use the form *%string* instead of *%digit*, where the string is any command line in the job list that begins with the string, or the form *%?string*, which will match any command line that contains the string.

You can stop an executing background job with the **stop** command, and restart it with **fg** or **bg** as desired. Here is an example:

```
[83]$ (sleep 40;echo hello)&
[1]     12032
[84]$ jobs
```

```
[1] + Running              (sleep 40;echo hello)&
[85]$ stop %?sleep
[1] + Stopped (signal)     (sleep 40;echo hello)&
[86]$ jobs
[1] + Stopped (signal)     (sleep 40;echo hello)&
[87]$ fg %1
(sleep 40;echo hello)
hello
[88]$ fg %1
ksh: fg: no such job
[89]$
```

If you try to log off your session while you have stopped jobs, the shells will complain, as shown here:

```
[90]$ jobs
[1] + Stopped (signal)     (sleep 40;echo hello)&
[91]$ exit
You have stopped jobs
[92]$
```

If this happens, you should examine the job list and dispose of the stopped jobs by completing or killing them. If you immediately try to exit a second time, the **csh** or **ksh** will kill the stopped jobs and log you off. You can kill jobs with the form

```
kill -signal %digit
```

where *signal* is the signal you wish to send (normally omitted), and the *%digit* refers to the job number.

Coprocesses under ksh

The **ksh** provides support for *coprocesses,* or interacting processes that run simultaneously and can communicate and synchronize with each other. This allows some very sophisticated shell programs that can work efficiently in parallel computing environments. Only a simple example is given here.

You can start a coprocess by ending the command line with **|&** (pipe ampersand). By default, the standard input of a coprocess is connected to the standard output of its parent shell, and its standard output is connected to the standard input of the parent shell. These arrangements can be changed within the script, if necessary. A common way to access the input and output of coprocesses is with **read -p**, which reads a line from the standard output of the coprocess, and with **print -p**, which writes a line to the standard input of the coprocess. Several other possibilities are also supported.

For example, it is often useful in a shell script to write a **while** or **for** loop that reads a file line by line, and takes some action on each line, much as the **grep** or **sed** commands do. If you code a script as follows,

```
while [ $x < 10 ] ; do
        read FLINE < infile
        (additional processing)
done
```

you will find that the **read** line reads the first line of the file each time—not exactly what was desired. Actually, there is no way to accomplish this goal within **/sbin/sh** or **csh**; however, the coprocess feature meets this need perfectly. The following script will do the job.

```
cat /etc/passwd |&
while true ; do
        read -p FLINE
        if [ -z "$FLINE" ] ; then
                exit 0
        fi
        echo $FLINE
done
```

The coprocess

```
cat /etc/passwd |&
```

is started first, but its output will be blocked until the current shell reads it. This is done with the

```
read -p FLINE
```

command, which reads a line from the coprocess into the FLINE variable. When the entire file has been read, the **read** returns a null string, and the **if** test causes the script to exit. Although this script is just an expensive form of **echo**, this use of coprocesses to read files is very common in **ksh** programs.

# SEVENTEEN

Word Processing

The spell Command
The troff Document Preparation Package
The troff Command Line
The troff Command Language
Macro Packages for troff
The mm Macros
The man Macros
Going Further

The UNIX system was one of the first general-purpose computer systems to include a fully functional *word processing* or *document preparation* subsystem. For years, during the 1970s, the UNIX system was used primarily for word processing. The **troff** (for typesetting run off) package provided very powerful tools for the times. Users could create documents ranging from simple business letters to printer-ready copy for entire books. Indeed, most books on the UNIX system were and are produced entirely on the UNIX system. The *UNIX User's Manual* is always produced entirely with the **troff** tools and a phototypesetter.

Even today the **troff** tools are unsurpassed for large, complex documents like books. However, with the rise of the personal computer in the 1980s, and the recent emergence of *desktop publishing* and sophisticated word processors for personal computers, many of the older word processing tools for the UNIX system have become somewhat dated, especially for smaller documents. Nevertheless, the **troff** package and associated tools are still widely used among professional writers; **troff** experts never seem to switch to another word processor!

The major drawback (and one of the major advantages!) of the **troff** package is a result of its design philosophy: it is a *programming language* for manipulating text and driving an output device. It does not use a *WYSIWYG* (what you see is what you get; pronounced "wis-ee-wig") model for its user interface. Rather, text is created with a normal text editor such as **vi**, and **troff** commands are interspersed with the text to produce an ASCII file containing both the contents (the text) and the form (the commands) of the document. In a separate operation, the text file is processed (or *compiled*) by the **troff** program to produce the final output. This two-step process is not necessary in modern word processors. Like many programming languages, **troff** is very powerful. On the other hand, it can be difficult to learn, and several tries are usually needed to get the exact result you want.

In many versions of the UNIX system, the document preparation tools are sold as a separate add-on software package. If you don't need the specific capabilities of **troff**, or if you already have a favorite word processor, you will not need to purchase this *Documenter's Workbench* software. (In versions of SVR4 that include the BSD compatibility package, you can often find an older version of **troff** in the **/usr/ucb** directory.) Most popular word processors for other operating systems are also available for the UNIX system, and they are adequate for most types of text processing. In fact, modern word processors can outdo the **troff** package in many areas, such as graphics. On the other hand, recent versions of **troff** can produce output to drive printers that speak the PostScript formatting language, and will allow separately produced graphical objects to be embedded in a document.

Of course, the basic concepts of filters and tools readily lend themselves to processing words. Many tasks normally associated with word processors can easily be done with filters and shell scripts.

The spell Command

Usually included with the basic system, the **spell** command is an intelligent and powerful spelling checker. It includes a large database of *root words*, and has sophisticated algorithms for producing plurals and other endings for the English language. In addition, it includes a facility for creating personal word lists, lists of words that you define as correctly spelled. Acronyms, peoples' names, and unusual technical terms can be defined on a per-user or per-system basis, to reduce the list of misspelled words **spell** finds. The **spell** command ignores case in producing its output, treating uppercase and lowercase characters as equivalent. The command is usually a shell script, kept in **/usr/bin/spell**, and it is an instructive script to browse.

The **spell** command will read its standard input or a list of files named as arguments, and produces a list of the words it thinks are incorrectly spelled on its standard output. The basic command looks like this:

```
$ spell file
```

The input must be a normal ASCII file, so **spell** will not work with most WYSIWYG word processors, which usually encode formatting information in non-ASCII form. The **spell** command breaks up the input into a list of words, and looks up each word in a spelling list. The command will ignore the **troff** formatting commands, and it uses an excellent algorithm for determining whether a word is correctly spelled. For example:

```
$ echo behavior behaviour | spell
behaviour
$
```

American spelling rules are used by default, although the **-b** (for British) option instructs **spell** to use British spelling rules, as shown here:

```
$ echo behavior behaviour | spell -b
behavior
$
```

In addition to the built-in list of words, **spell** allows you to add a personal spelling list from the command line. The **+** (plus) option precedes a filename that includes a list of words to be *eliminated* from the **spell** output, as follows:

```
$ cat local.spell
behaviour
$ echo behavior behaviour | spell +local.spell
$
```

The local file contains one word per line. You can add as many words as necessary to a local file, but only one **+** option is allowed in a **spell** command. If you need more, you can use a pipeline, as in this example:

```
$ spell +local.spell in.file | spell +second.local
```

Here, the second **spell** command will filter the misspelled list from the first **spell** command to eliminate the words in both local files.

The **-v** (for verbose) option will display many of the rules **spell** uses to make its decisions. It shows all the words that are not explicitly in the **spell** word list, and the rules that **spell** uses to build derivative words. For example:

```
$ echo derive derivate derivative deriving | spell -v
-e+ion-ion+ive    derivative
-e+ing    deriving
$
```

The root words *derive* and the more obscure *derivate* are in the **spell** word list, so they cause no output. *Derivative* is constructed by removing the *e* from *derivate* (*-e*), and adding *ion* (*+ion*). Then, the *ion* is removed (*-ion*), and *ive* (*+ive*) is added to produce the target word *derivative*. Similar rules are used for *deriving*, but it is based on the root *derive*.

The troff Document Preparation Package

The major word processing tool used with the UNIX system is the **troff** package. The name *troff* refers both to the programming language as a whole, and also to the command in the UNIX system that processes the source documents. The **troff** package produces output that can directly drive most popular phototypesetters and modern laser printers. Actually, **troff** is a programming language optimized for typesetting. It takes an ASCII input file that contains formatting commands interspersed with the text, and *compiles* this *source code* into an instruction stream for a specified printer device. Usually, the output is no longer in ASCII format, since it consists of commands in the control language of the printer device.

The **troff** language cannot produce ASCII output for dot-matrix or other ordinary printers, because it produces control data for typesetters. A separate tool called **nroff** (for nontypesetting runoff) formats its input files for terminals or simple printers. The output quality is necessarily poorer than that produced by **troff**, but **nroff** can take the same input files as **troff**, and most of the same command-line arguments. Unknown or impossible **troff** commands are ignored by **nroff**. The **nroff** command is often used to *preview* a document at the terminal before printing. Furthermore, ASCII printer devices are still much more common than laser printers, so **nroff** has an important place in the **troff** family. Some smaller computers may only support **nroff**.

The troff Command Line

The **troff** command reads the input source text from its standard input, or from a filename list given as argument, as follows:

```
$ troff source.text
```

The **troff** output comes to standard output, but it is not very useful because it is in a typesetter format. Usually the output is redirected to a file or piped to another command that controls the printer device. The **lp** command can be used if the printer can be attached to a serial or parallel port.

The **troff** command can take many command-line options, the most important of which specifies the printer type. Modern versions of **troff** use a filter scheme in which output is sent to a device-specific program that converts generic typesetting commands to specific commands for a particular device. This version of **troff** is known as **ditroff** (for device independent **troff**), but the command-line options are the same for most versions. The **-T** (for typesetter) option takes an argument that names the device, as shown here:

```
$ troff -Tps source.file
```

In this example, the **ps** names a PostScript printer. The filtering is done directly by the **troff** command, from the **-T** option, so users need not create the pipeline directly. Other command-line options allow you to specify the value of some of the **troff** registers, and can limit the output to some part of the true document. The **-a** (for ASCII) option causes an

ASCII approximation of the real output. This option is useful for previewing the document on a terminal before you send it to the typesetter. These command-line options are also used for **nroff**, although the devices named in the **-T** option will differ between **troff** and **nroff**.

The troff Command Language

In general, the function of **troff** is to *fill* or *flow* multiple lines of input text across multiple output lines to fill a page or column, using the character fonts and sizes specified. Larger or smaller characters, different fonts, different spacing, and so on, will change the amount of text that flows onto an output line from the input file. Commands are provided to block the filling functions of **troff**, and these are used to create *breaks* between paragraphs and to make headings in a document. In addition, **troff** does an excellent job of *hyphenation* and of both left and right *justification* of output lines for an optimal page layout.

The **troff** program includes a powerful *macro* capability, which allows complex but frequently used functions to be coded in a simpler form. In fact, several popular macro packages have been developed, and few people now use the raw **troff** commands directly. We will discuss these macro packages after a tour of basic **troff** functions.

Basic troff Concepts

Most **troff** commands begin on a new line in the source document. The command lines are interspersed with lines that contain text. The **troff** commands are identified by a . (dot) as the first character on the line. All **troff** commands are lowercase characters immediately following the dot, and some of these commands can take additional arguments on the line, with each argument separated from the command and from other arguments by whitespace.

For example, to cause a blank line to appear in the output, you can use the **.sp** (for space) command where you want the space. If you want three spaces, you can use the command

```
.sp 3
```

instead. Most of the **troff** commands are listed in Tables 17-1 through 17-3.

troff Units

The previous command instructed **troff** to leave three blank *lines* in its output. The **troff** package understands three different forms of measurement: lines, inches, and points. A *point* is 1/72 of an inch. Points are normally used to specify font sizes; a 12 point font is 12/72 of an inch high. You specify these alternative measures by adding one of the suffixes—**i** (for inches), **p** (for points), or **l** (ell, for lines)—after the numeric argument, with no intervening whitespace. For example, when you are using a 12-point line spacing, these commands are all equivalent:

```
.sp 2i
.sp 144p
.sp 12l
```

The **troff** commands differ as to which unit is the default, so it is good practice to get in the habit of specifying the units when you use these distance measurements.

The units allow decimal points, so you can specify a 6 1/2-inch space with

```
.sp 6.5i
```

However, all these measurements are converted internally into **troff** *basic units,* so measurements of small distances (less than a point) may not be exact.

Page Layout

The **troff** program provides commands for controlling the overall dimensions of your page, and these are normally placed at the beginning of your document, although changing the page boundaries in the middle of a document is allowed. The **.ll** (for line length) command sets the length of your text line on the page, and the **.po** (for page offset) command sets the width of the left margin. Together these determine the horizontal

Command	Initial Value	If No Arg	Causes Break?	Explanation
.ps N	10 pt	prev	n	Set point size
.ss N	12/36 em	ign	n	Set space-character size
.cs F N M	off	-	n	Constant character space width mode
.bd F N	off	-	n	Embolden font F by N-1 units
.bd S F N	off	-	n	Embolden special font when current font is F
.ft F	roman	prev	n	Change to font F
.fp N F	R,I,B,S	ign	n	Font named F mounted on postion N (1-4)
.pl N	11 in	11 in	n	Set page length
.bp N	N = 1	-	y	Eject current page; next page number N
.pn N	N = 1	ign	n	Next page number N
.po N	0	prev	n	Page offset
.ne N	-	N = 1V	n	Need N vertical space (V = current vertical spacing)
.mk R	none	internal	n	Mark current vertical place in register R
.rt N	none	internal	n	Return (up) to marked vertical place
.br	-	-	y	Break

Table 17-1. Basic **troff** Commands: Spacing, Page Control, Filling

Command	Initial Value	If No Arg	Causes Break?	Explanation
.fi	fill	-	y	Fill output lines
.nf	fill	-	y	No filling or adjusting of output lines
.ad c	adj,both	adjust	n	Adjust output lines with mode c
.na	adjust	-	n	No output line adjusting
.ce N	off	N=1	y	Center the following N input text lines
.ll N	6.5 in	prev	n	Line length
.in N	N=0	prev	y	Indent
.ti N	-	ignored	y	Temporary indent
.vs N	12 pt	prev	n	Vertical base line spacing (V)
.ls N	N=1	prev	n	Output N-1 V's after each text output line
.sp N	-	N=1V	y	Space vertical distance N in either direction
.sv N	-	N=1V	n	Save vertical distance N
.os	-	-	n	Output saved vertical distance
.ns	space	-	n	Turn no-space mode on
.rs	-	-	n	Restore spacing; turn no-space mode off

Table 17-1.   Basic **troff** Commands: Spacing, Page Control, Filling (*continued*)

Command	Initial Value	If No Arg	Causes Break?	Explanation
.ta Nt	0.5 in	none	n	Tab settings; left unless t = R (right) or C (centered)
.tc c	none	none	n	Tab repetition character
.lc c	.	none	n	Leader repetition character
.fc a b	off	off	n	Set field delimiter a and pad character b
.de xx yy	-	.yy = ..	n	Define or redefine macro xx, end at call of yy
.am xx yy	-	.yy = ..	n	Append to a macro
.ds ss string	-	ignored	n	Define a string xx containing *string*
.as xx string	-	ignored	n	Append *string* to string xx
.rm xx	-	ignored	n	Remove request, macro, or string
.rn xx yy	-	ignored	n	Rename request, macro, or string xx to yy
.di xx	-	end	n	Divert output to macro xx
.da xx	-	-	n	Divert and append to xx
.wh N xx	-	off	n	Set trap location, negative means from page bottom
.ch xx N	-	off	n	Change trap location
.dt N xx	-	off	n	Set a diversion trap
.it N xx	-	off	n	Set an input-line count trap
.em xx	none	none	n	End macro is xx

Table 17-2.   troff Macros, Registers, and Translations

Command	Initial Value	If No Arg	Causes Break?	Explanation
.nr R N M	-	-	n	Define and set register R to N; autoincrement by M
.af R c	Arabic	-	n	Assign format to R (c = 1,i,I,a,A)
.rr R	-	-	n	Remove register R
.ec c	\	\	n	Set escape character
.eo	on	-	n	Turn off escape character mechanism
.lg N	on	on	n	Ligature mode on if N > 0
.ul N	off	N = 1	n	Underline or italicize N input lines
.cu N	off	N = 1	n	Continuous underline in **nroff**, like .ul in **troff**
.uf F	italic	italic	n	Underline font set to F
.cc c	.	.	n	Set control character to c
.c2 c	'	'	n	Set nobreak control character to c
.tr abcd...	none	-	n	Translate a to b, etc. on output

Table 17-2.   **troff** Macros, Registers, and Translations (*continued*)

Command	Initial Value	If No Arg	Causes Break?	Explanation
.nh	yes	-	n	No hyphenation
.hy N	yes	yes	n	Hyphenate; N = mode
.hc c			n	Hyphenation indicator character c
.hw word	-	ignored	n	Exception words
.tl 'left'center'right'	-	-	n	Three-part title
.pc c	%	off	n	Page number character
.lt N	6.5 in	prev	n	Length of title
.nm N M S I	-	off	n	Number mode on or off; set parameters
.nn N	-	N = 1	n	Do not number next N output lines
.if c any	-	-	n	If condition c is true, accept "any" as input
.if !c any	-	-	n	If condition c is false, accept "any" as input
.if N any	-	-	n	If expression N > 0, accept "any"
.if !N any	-	-	n	If expression N < 0 or N = 0, accept "any"
.if 'string1'string2' any	-	-	n	If string1 identical to string2, accept "any"
.if !'string1'string2'any	-	-	n	If string1 not identical to string2, accept "any"
.ie c any	-	-	n	If part of **if-else**; all above forms
.el any	-	-	n	Else portion of **if-else**
.ev N	N = 0	prev	n	Environment switch (push down)
.rd prompt	-	BELL	n	Read insertion from stdin

Table 17-3.   **troff** Hyphenation, Three-Part Titles, Conditionals, and Miscellaneous

Command	Initial Value	If No Arg	Causes Break?	Explanation
.ex	-	-	n	Exit from **troff**
.so file	-	-	n	Take input from file
.nx file	-	eof	n	Next file
.pi program	-	-	n	Pipe output to program (**nroff** only)
.mc c N	-	off	n	Set margin character c and separation N
.tm string	-	newline	n	Print string on stdout
.ig yy	-	.yy=..	n	Ignore until yy called
.pm t	-	all	n	Print macro names and sizes (if t, total only)
.fl	-	-	n	Flush output buffer
\!	-	-	n	Pass line through to output

Table 17-3.   **troff** Hyphenation, Three-Part Titles, Conditionals, and Miscellaneous (*continued*)

spacing of your text line. For example,

```
.ll 6i
.po 1i
```

produces six-inch text lines with a one-inch left margin. You can set the vertical page length with **.ps** (for page size), but this is not usually necessary, because it defaults to eleven inches.

You can override these line length values for a portion of your document by *indenting* a line or block of text. This changes the effective left margin, but not the right. Use **.in** (for indent) followed by a measurement to indent the text lines following the command. You can also use a minus value if you wish. For example,

```
.in 1i
text is indented one inch.
.in -1i
will return to previous left margin.
```

Use **.ti** for a *temporary indent;* only the line following the **.ti** command will be indented. You can specify more than one line by giving a number after the **.ti**. For instance,

```
.ti 5
```

will indent the next five lines, and then return to the previous left margin. Note that these indenting commands cause a break, so **troff** will start a new output line when it sees them.

You can center the next line or group of lines on the page with **.ce** (for center). Like **.ti**, this can take an argument to specify the number of lines to center. Similarly, the **.ul** (for underline) command will *italicize* the next line or group of lines in the input. In **nroff**, the **.ul** command produces underlining instead. **.ce** causes a break, but **.ul** does not.

You can *suppress* the break caused by many dot commands by using the character ' (single quotation mark) instead of a dot in the commands. For example,

```
.ce
```

will cause a break, while

```
'ce
```

will not. This leads to some interesting effects. See what happens if you center some text with **'ce**.

You can add comments to your **troff** source documents by placing the string \" (backslash quotation mark) at the beginning of a line or after a dot command. Everything that follows this string up to the end of the line will be ignored. You can insert a larger comment after the **.ig** (for ignore) command; all lines up to the next **..** (dot dot) command will be ignored. Comments are very helpful in documenting your **troff** programs; it is a good idea to use them liberally.

Font and Character Control

You can set the size of your character font with **.ps** (for point size), and the interline spacing with **.vs** (for vertical spacing). For example, to select a 12-point font with 14-point interline spacing, use

```
.ps 12p
.vs 14p
```

Note that the **vs** value should be larger than the **ps** value, or your lines will overlap and be difficult to read.

The **.vs** command provides fine control of the interline spacing. You can also use **.ls** (for line spacing) near the top of your manuscript to leave blank lines (of the current size) between text lines. Use

```
.ls 21
```

or

```
.ls 31
```

to produce double-spaced or triple-spaced text, respectively.

You can select the font to use with **.ft** (for font). Normally four fonts are available; however, you can *mount* other fonts as you need them. The command **.ft R** produces a normal roman font (also known as font 1; thus, **.ft 1** will also work). The command **.ft B** produces a boldfaced font (font 2), and **.ft I** produces an italic font (font 3). Finally, **.ft CW** produces a constant-width font that is useful for displays of UNIX command lines and terminal output (font 4). You can switch *back* to the font you used last with **.ft P** (for previous). This allows you to temporarily switch fonts without keeping track of the previous as well as current font.

Fill Control

Normally **troff** fills each line before it starts a new line, executing changes in font, character size, and so forth as it goes. When it reaches the end of the line (specified with the **.ll** parameter), it skips down the vs value, and then starts filling on the new line. However, the **.sp** command causes a break, so **troff** will start a new line (after spacing down the correct amount) when it sees this command. To cause a break without spacing, use the **.br** (for break) command. You can disable filling with **.nf** (for no fill), and restart filling after any number of text lines with **.fi** (for fill). This allows you to lay out a section of your document manually without worrying that **troff** will try to reorganize it. The **.bp** (for break page) command skips the rest of the current page and starts a new one.

You can instruct **troff** to *right-justify* your text, so that each page has a smooth right margin, with **.ad b** (for adjust). It does this is by padding the characters and words with whitespace, spreading the contents of the line to fill the available space. Without this command, **troff** produces a *ragged* right margin, filling each line until the next word will not fit in the remaining space. You can restore the ragged right margin with **.ad l** (for adjust left margin) or with the equivalent **.na** (for no adjust). When right-justification is enabled, you will get a better line layout if you enable automatic hyphenation of long words by using **.hy** (for hyphenation). To disable hyphenation, use **.nh** (for no hyphenation).

These few commands will suffice to produce many simple documents, allowing you full control over the page and the fonts used. Figure 17-1 shows a short text file that contains a **troff** source document. After processing with **troff**, the output will look like Figure 17-2. Consult the listing of **troff** commands in the tables to understand how this result was achieved.

When executed, most of the dot commands make permanent changes in the **troff** *environment*, such as those that change the font style or the character size. However, some commands refer only to the next line after the command, and only affect the processing of that line. The **.ul, .ce** and **.ti** commands are of this type.

In addition, some commands can be embedded in a line to affect text in the middle of the output line. These are identified by special *escape sequences* that begin with the \ (backslash) character to distinguish them from normal text. Many dot commands have in-line equivalents, so that some changes can be made in the middle of a word, without causing spacing or a break. These in-line commands are not often called for in simple documents, and they are not discussed further here, although many of the examples in this chapter use them in various ways.

```
.sp 12
.ll 5i
.ps 14
.vs 16
This is a sample of \fBtroff\f source text
.ps 6
and its output.
.ps 14
\fItroff\f is actually
a \s+6programming language\s-6 that
.ul
fills
text automatically,
and can completely specify \fBfonts\f and spacing.
Here is a simple equation:
.ps 11
\(*S(\*a\(mul\(*b)\(->\(if
.sp 4
and some other stuff:
\s8\z\(sq\s14\z\(sq\s22\z\(sq\s36\(sq
\b'\(lt\(lk\(lb'\b'\(lc\(lf' x
\b'\(rc\(rf'\b'\(rt\(rk\(rb'
.sp 3
.ps 8
\fItroff\f can produce multicolumn output, number pages
correctly with headers and footers,
.de bx
\(br\|\\$1\|\(br\l'|0\(rn'\l'|0\(ul'
..
.br
.ce
.bx "and can even put words in a box."
.vs 14
.br
\fItroff\f allows extension through
.ps 24
macros
.ps 8
and the box is created by a macro definition.
.ps 10
Here are some more special characters:
\(34   \(ct   \(co   \(bu   \(dg
.ps 6
.br
The \fBtbl\f and \fBeqn\f tools allow professional
formatting of tables and mathematical equations, respectively.
```

Figure 17-1.   Source document for a **troff** "sampler"

This is a sample of **troff** source text and its output. *troff* is actually a programming language that *fills* text automatically, and can completely specify **fonts** and spacing. Here is a simple equation: Σ(×lβ)→∞

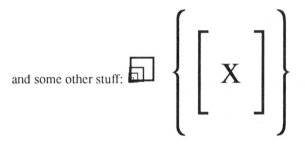

troff can produce multicolumn output, number pages correctly with headers and footers,

and can even put words in a box.

troff allows extension through macros and the box is created by a macro definition. Here are some more special characters: ¼ ¢ © • †

The tbl and eqn tools allow professional formatting of tables and mathematical equations, respectively.

Figure 17-2. troff sampler output

troff Registers

While it is executing, the **troff** program keeps track of numeric and string information in *registers*. For example, the current date, the page number, and a lot of other information is available in registers for your use. Some registers are *read-only*, which means that you can use the value but you cannot change it. For example, you can read the value of the current point size with the **.s** register, but you cannot change the register directly; you must use the **.ps** command to do so. Other registers are predefined by **troff**, but you can change them as required. For example, the current page number is stored in the % register, and although **troff** keeps this number correct as it fills pages, you can always set its value as needed. In addition, **troff** provides many unused registers that you can set and use as you wish.

If you do use your own private registers, you must take care not to use the *predefined* registers, but to establish your own from the unused pool. Table 17-4 lists the full set of predefined registers.

Name	Read Only?	Description
%	n	Current page number
ct	n	Character type (set by ct)
dl	n	Maximum width of last completed diversion
dn	n	Vertical size of last completed diversion
dw	n	Current day of week (1-7)
dy	n	Current day of month (1-31)
hp	n	Current horizontal place on input line
ln	n	Output line number
mo	n	Current month (1-12)
nl	n	Vertical position of last printed text baseline
sb	n	Depth of string below baseline (generated by width function)
st	n	Height of string above baseline (generated by width function)
yr	n	Last two digits of current year
.$	y	Number of args at current macro level
.A	y	Set to 1 in **nroff**, and **troff** if -a arg
.H	y	Available horizontal resolution in basic units
.T	y	Set to 1 in **nroff** if -T option; always 0 in troff
.V	y	Available vertical resolution in basic units
.a	y	Post-line extra linespace most recently used with \x′N′
.c	y	Number of lines read from current input file
.d	y	Current vertical place in current diversion; equal to nl if no diversion
.f	y	Current font (1-4)
.h	y	Text baseline high-water mark on current page or diversion
.i	y	Current indent
.l	y	Current line length
.n	y	Length of text portion on previous output line
.o	y	Current page offset
.p	y	Current page length
.s	y	Current point size
.t	y	Distance to the next trap
.u	y	1 in fill mode, 0 in no-fill mode
.v	y	Current vertical line spacing

Table 17-4.   **troff** Predefined General Number Registers

Name	Read Only?	Description
.w	y	Width of previous character
.x	y	Reserved version-dependent register
.y	y	Reserved version-dependent register
.z	y	Name of current diversion

Table 17-4.   **troff** Predefined General Number Registers (*continued*)

Registers have one- or two-character (lowercase) names. You can refer to a register by the special sequence **\nx** (backslash n name) when the register name is a single character, or **\n(xy** (backslash n left parenthesis name), when the register name is two characters. Use the **.nr** (for number register) command to *set* the value of a register. For example, to set register xx to the current page number you would use

```
.nr \n(xx \n%
```

The register name is the first argument to **.nr,** and the value you wish to use is the second argument. The **troff** language allows arithmetic operations in the **.nr** command, so to set xx to the current page number plus two, you could use

```
.nr \n(xx \n% + 2
```

Most *integer* arithmetic operations are supported, including increment and decrement, but arithmetic operations are processed left-to-right as they appear, *not* using normal arithmetic precedence. You can use parentheses as necessary to force precedence.

To set a register value from the **troff** command line, you can use the **-raN** option, where the **a** is the (one-character) register you wish to set and *N* is the value to use. For example, you can set the starting page number of your document to 40 with

```
$ troff -r%40 file
```

This option is most useful if you are using your own registers in your **troff** source document.

Macro Packages for troff

The direct use of the **troff** formatting commands is actually relatively rare. The command language is so difficult, and it deals with documents at such a detailed level, that it is only used by a few experts. Instead, most users rely on *macro packages* that encode blocks of **troff** commands. The macro packages are themselves based on the **troff** *macro definition* feature, which is discussed at the end of this chapter. Macros can be read by **troff** when it begins executing, and whenever a macro name appears in a document, **troff** replaces the name with the full list of **troff** commands associated with that name. For example, document *headings*, which may involve chapter numbering and font changes, take many commands in **troff**. In the macro packages these can be encoded in a few simple-to-use commands. Most users learn the macros for their specific document type, and never need to use **troff** commands directly.

Many macro packages have been developed for special purposes, but only three have gained wide popularity. The **mm** (for memorandum macros) package produces business letters and business memos. The **me** (for macros for education) macros are used for technical writing in universities. Finally, the **man** (for manual) macros are used to produce the *UNIX User's Manual* and associated documents. A fourth macro package, the **ms** macros, was widely used in the past but has now been replaced by **mm**. Each package defines a command set that can be used instead of the direct **troff** commands, but actual **troff** commands can be interspersed with the macros if necessary. Macros are usually named with capital letters, whereas basic **troff** commands have all lowercase names. This convention can distinguish a **troff** source document from one that uses a macro package.

You can specify one of these macro packages in a **troff** command line. The name of the package is preceded by - (minus) in the **troff** command line, as follows:

```
$ troff -man cmd.1
```

This example selects the **man** macros for formatting man page *cmd.1*. The macros in the packages differ substantially, and only one package can be selected for a single execution of the **troff** or **nroff** command. In addition, commands from the different macro packages overlap significantly, so it is easy to confuse commands from the various packages.

The mm Macros

The best macro package is the **mm** (for memorandum macros) package. It allows easy generation of page headers and footers, section or chapter headings, lists, and displays. A *display* is a block of material that can *float* through the text until **troff** decides to output it. That is, you can specify that a display not cause an immediate break in the text but rather appear where it will look most attractive. This feature can be used to place tables and figures on left-hand pages, to make them take up a full page, or to position them at the top of a page. The **mm** package also supports memo and business letter addressing, abstracts, cover pages, and tables of contents.

The **mm** package is complex and rich in features. A full listing of the **mm** macros and strings is given in Tables 17-5 and 17-6. A simple *template* for the most important **mm** features appears in Figure 17-3.

Basic Commands

The **mm** macros allow you to specify the beginning of a paragraph with .P (for paragraph). You can create an empty line with .SP (for space), or use .SP *n* to skip *n* empty lines. Use .SK (for skip) to start a new page.

You select the *type* of paragraph you wish to use by setting the .Pt (for paragraph type) register, as shown here:

```
.nr Pt 1
```

This setting chooses an indented paragraph. Use the argument 2 to indent each paragraph *except* the first paragraph following a heading. The default, 0, results in paragraphs that are not indented.

Name	Description
.P [type]	Paragraph
.H level [heading text]	Heading — numbered
.HU heading text	Heading — unnumbered
.HM [arg1] ... [arg7]	Heading mark style (Arabic or Roman numerals, or letters)
.HX dlevel rlevel heading text	Heading user exit X (before printing heading)
.HZ dlevel rlevel heading text	Heading user exit Z (after printing heading)
.ND new date	New date
.TL [charge case] [file case]	Title of memorandum
.AF [company name]	Alternate format of "subject-date-from" block
.AU name [initials] [loc] [dept] [ext] [room]	Author information
.TM [number]	Technical memorandum number
.AS [arg] [indent]	Abstract start
.AE	Abstract end
.OK [keywords]	Other keywords for TM cover sheet
.MT [type]	Memorandum type
.SG [arg]	Signature line
.NS [arg]	Notation start
.NE	Notation end
.CS [pages] [other] [total] [figs] [tbls] [refs]	Cover sheet
.TC [slevel] [spacing] [tlevel] [tab] [head1] ... [head5]	Table of contents
.TX	Table of contents user exit
.PH 'left'center'right'	Page header
.OH 'left'center'right'	Odd page header
.EH 'left'center'right'	Even page header
.PF 'left'center'right'	Page footer
.OF 'left'center'right'	Odd page footer
.EF 'left'center'right'	Even page footer
.BS	Bottom block start
.BE	Bottom block end
.PX	Page header user exit
.TP	Top-of-page macro
.I [italic arg] [previous font arg]	Italic (underline in **nroff**)
.R	Return to roman font
.B [bold arg] [previous font arg]	Bold (underline in **nroff**)
.SP [lines]	Space vertically
.SK [pages]	Skip pages

Table 17-5.   Basic **mm** Macros

Name	Description
.OP	Odd-numbered page start
.2C	Two-column output
.1C	One-column output
.SA [arg]	Set right-margin adjust
.HC [hyphenation indicator]	Hyphenation character
.S [arg] [arg]	Set point size and vertical spacing

Table 17-5.   Basic **mm** Macros (*continued*)

Choose point size and vertical spacing with the **.S** (for size) macro. The first argument is the point size and the second is the vertical spacing. For example,

```
.S 12 14
```

is equivalent to

```
.ps 12
.vs 14
```

Select right-justification with **.SA 1**, or a ragged right margin with **.SA 0**. You can switch fonts with **.B** (for bold), **.R** (for roman), **.I** (for italic), **.CW** (for constant-width), or **.P** (for previous).

Predefined mm Memo Formats

The **mm** package provides a set of macros for memo headings and other material that appears at the beginning of most documents. The author, title, abstract, and cover pages fall into this category. These macros, if they are present, must appear at the beginning of the **mm** source document, with the correct arguments in the proper order. For example, the letter in Figure 17-4 contains **mm** source code. The result after processing by

```
$ troff -mm letter
```

Name	Description
.AL [type] [text-indent]	Autoincrement list start
.BL [text-indent]	Bullet list start
.DL [text-indent]	Dash list start
.ML mark [text-indent]	Marked list start
.RL [text-indent]	Reference list start
.VL text-indent [mark-indent]	Variable-item list start
.LI [mark]	List item
.LE	List end
.LB text-indent mark-indent pad-type [mark]	List begin
.LC [list-level]	List status clear
.DS [format] [fill]	Display start
.DF [format] [fill]	Display floating start
.DE	Display end
.FG [title] [override] [flag]	Figure title
.TS	Table start
.TE	Table end
.TB [title] [override] [flag]	Table title
.EQ [label]	Equation display start
.EN	End equation display
.EC [title] [override] [flag]	Equation caption
.FS [label]	Footnote start
.FE	Footnote end
.FD [arg]	Footnote default format
*(BU	Bullet
*F	Footnote numberer
*(DT	Current date
*(HF	Heading font list (up to seven codes for levels 1-7)
*(HP	Heading point size (up to seven point sizes for levels 1-7)
*(RE	MM release level

Table 17-6.   mm Lists, Displays, and Strings

is shown in Figure 17-5. The **.TL** macro must appear before the **.AU** or **.MT** macros in the document, although basic **troff** commands may precede it. On the same line as the **.TL** command, you can include one or

```
command line args: -rC3  "DRAFT" and date in footer
                   -rA1  simulates .AF macro (print on letterhead)
                   -rB1  get Table of Contents [and need .TC at end]

.so /usr/share/lib/tmac/tmac.m   (or use "troff -mm" command line)
.ND "October 2, 1990"   (gives current date if omitted)
        (use    \*(DT     to put date in text somewhere)
==========
These are not for memos, but good page header and footer setup:
.PH "'''SC* \\\\n(mo/ \\\\n(dy/ \\\\n(yr'"
.PF "''- \\\\nP -''"
==========
.AF "string for logo"   (Prints "AT&T" in upper right if omitted)
.TL "ZW52040" ""  (first "" is changing case, second is filling case)
A short but sweet memo    (Title of memo)
.AU "Steve" SC USWAT 9040301 555-1234 329 steve@my_sys.com
.SA 1 (causes left and right justification for filled text)
.nr Df 4
.nr De 1  --These two registers are used to make floating displays
                act rationally.  They force displays to take exactly
                one page each (or more, if longer), and to be printed
                in rational places.
.nr Hb 3
.nr Hs 3  -- These two registers set the lowest heading level that is
                not embedded in the following text line (default is 2)
.ds HF 3 3 2 2 2 2   --this sets font type for each heading level
                  1= roman
                  2= italic (underline)
                  3= bold
.PM      -- for proprietary mark:
                .PM P    Restricted; reproduction is prohibited
                .PM N    Proprietary; director's signature
                .PM BP   Proprietary; Affiliated Companies
                .PM BR   Registered; cover sheet restrictions
.AS 2
   this puts an abstract page at the beginning;
   abstract text is placed here
.AE (ends abstract)
.NS "Abstract Only"            [for Copy (abstract only) to]
  or .NS                       [for "copy to" line]
  or .NS 1                     [for "Copy (with att.) to"]
  or .NS 2                     [for "Copy (without att.) to"]
name1
name2
.NE        (to finish copy to listing)
.MT "Memorandum for file"  (memo type, exactly as typed)
                .MT    is memo for file
                .MT "" is no memo type (and internal letter)
                .MT 3 is engineers' notes
                .MT 4 is released paper style
                .MT 5 is external letter
```

Figure 17-3.   mm crib sheet

```
TEXT HERE AS USUAL
.H 1 "heading title here"
In text, footnotes (and bibliography refs on same page) can be
automatically generated and numbered by using this \*F
.FS
footnote text here
.FE
The "\*F" is where the footnote number should appear in the
text. Use ".FS *" to start the footnote with a "*" instead of
a number, and the footnote character is used in the text
just like any other text character. . . .
also, use \*RF
.RS AA
text here
.RE
to make a reference that gets forced to the end of the output.
"AA", "AB" etc. are sequence indicators for the order of the
refs in the list at the end.
.SP  (adds a blank line)
Also, user can access number registers like so:
.nr X 1  (for register named X, initially set to 1)
          (watch out for reusing predefined register names,
                and for using names of more than one letter)
then refer to register in text as \nX (this prints the value)
and change its value soon after by
.nr X \nX+1  (i.e. this sets the value of reg X to be X+1; other
                arithmetic operations are also allowed.)

.SG unix   (signature line -- arg is typist)
```

Figure 17-3. **mm** crib sheet (*continued*)

two numbers, to be used as the *charging case number* and the *filing case number*, respectively. If present, these numbers cause additional lines to appear in the output. If you do not include these case numbers, you can omit the arguments on the **.TL** (for title) line. The next line after the **.TL** line contains the memo (or letter) title.

Next, the **.AU** (for author) line specifies the author's name, initials, location, organization number, telephone number, room, and up to three additional arguments. If present, these values appear in various places throughout the memo, especially on the cover sheet, the memo heading, and in the signature area. The name is required, but the other arguments may be omitted.

Third, the **.MT** (for memo type) line specifies the general format **mm** will use to organize the document. This is printed at the beginning of the memo. If the argument to **.MT** is the empty string (""), no memo type will be printed, but the **.MT** macro must *always* be present if **.TL**

```
.AF "GV Computing"
.S 12
.TL
Why My Bill Remains Unpaid
.AU "Steve" SC USWAT 9040301 329 555-1234 steve@my_sys.com
.SA 1
.MT ""
.SP 2
Ms. Super Friendly
.br
Friendly Finance Company
.br
1545 Walnut St.
.br
Mytown, Colo.  80302
.SP 2
Dear Ms. Friendly:
.SP
Here are the reasons:
.AL
.LI
My dog ate the bill.
.LI
The check is in the mail.
.LI
I don't have the money.
.LE
.SP
I'll get it to you asap, I promise.
.SP
Better luck next time!  Thanks again for your patience.
.SG svr4
```

Figure 17-4.   Simple **mm** source document

and .AU are present. If you include a string after .MT, that string will
be printed as the memo type. In addition, you can use the numbers 1 to
print "Memorandum for File," 2 to print "Programmer's Notes," 3 to
print "Engineer's Notes," 4 to use a *released paper* memo style, or 5 to
use an *external letter* style. Each of these choices creates a memo or
letter with a very distinctive look; experiment to familiarize yourself
with the various possibilities.

   Within the text, you can use the .P and .SP macros, or any other
mm macros or **troff** commands that you need to lay out your document.
If you wish, you can omit the .TL .AU .MT sequence, and format the
beginning of the document manually with basic **troff** or **mm** commands.

GV Computing

subject: **Why My Bill Remains Unpaid**

date: **July 26, 1990**

from: **Steve**
USWAT 9040301
555-1234 x329
steve@my_sys.com

Ms. Super Friendly
Friendly Finance Company
1545 Walnut St.
Mytown, Colo. 80302

Dear Ms. Friendly:

Here are the reasons:

1.   My dog ate the bill.

2.   The check is in the mail.

3.   I don't have the money.

I'll get it to you asap, I promise.

Better luck next time! Thanks again for your patience.

USWAT-9040301-SC-svr4   **Steve**

Figure 17-5.   Simple **mm** output

This was done in Figure 17-5 to produce an inside address from breaks and line spacing. It is usually preferable to use one of the memo formats whenever possible, because they reduce errors and provide useful services.

When you have used the **.TL**, **.AU**, and **.MT** macros, you can insert **.SG** (for signature) at the end of a memo to add a signature line. The **.SG** macro can take the typist's name as an argument.

Abstract and "Copy to" Notation

You can surround a block of text with **.AS** (for abstract start) and **.AE** (for abstract end) to produce a separate block titled **Abstract**. Abstracts often appear at the beginning of scientific and technical documents. The **.AS** macro can take several arguments that determine whether the abstract appears on page one of the document, on a cover sheet, or on both. This argument (**0**, **1**, or **2**) interacts with the **.MT** macro in a complex way. Usually, no argument is required for **.AS**.

Surrounding a list of names with **.NS** (for notation start) and **.NE** (for notation end) produces a "Copy to:" heading followed by the list of names. If you give **.NS** an argument, you can vary the heading. Use an argument of **1** to produce "Copy (with att.) to:" or **2** to produce a "Copy (without att.) to:" block. You can also code

```
.NS "string"
```

to produce "Copy (string) to:" instead. Several other arguments are also allowed.

Headings

Within the body of a memo, **mm** helps to format headings such as chapter or section titles. The **mm** macros can automatically number headings, so that you can reorganize a document without renumbering the sections manually. The system also allows you to establish font and character size conventions at the start of a document that will be honored when each heading is printed.

Use the **.H** (for heading) macro to identify a heading in your document. The **.H** macro takes a digit as an argument, followed by a quoted text string that is the text of the heading. For example:

```
.H 1 "Word Processing"
.H 2 "The troff Command Language"
.H 3 "Basic troff Concepts"
.H 3 "troff Units"
.H 2 "The troff Command Line"
.H 2 "Beginning a Memo"
.H 2 "Going Further"
.H 3 "troff Directory Structure"
.H 3 "The Writer's Workbench"
```

Of course, you will usually include text between these section headings. This example produces a hierarchy of subheadings, each one numbered as to level. For example, if these headings are in Chapter 17, the "troff Units" line in the previous example will look like this after formatting:

```
17.1.2 troff Units
```

Headings are hierarchically organized, with the most important being *first-level* headings. Under the first-level headings may be second-level subheadings; under those, third-level headings may appear, and so forth down to seventh-level headings. All headings at the same level are sequentially numbered, and subheadings within that level are numbered sequentially from one until the next **.H** command at a lower number.

You can specify the format of each level of heading by setting the values of several of the **mm** registers, as shown here:

```
.nr Hb 3
.nr Hs 3
.ds HF 3 3 2 2 2 2 2
.ds HP 14 12 12 12 12 12 12
```

The **Hb** and **Hs** registers work together to set the lowest heading level that is separated from the surrounding text; lower level headings will be embedded in the next text line. The **HF** register is used to specify a font type for each of the seven possible heading levels: 1 sets the roman font, 2 sets italic or underline, and 3 selects boldface. The **HP** (for heading points) register sets the point size for each of the heading levels; 14 is used for the first level in this example.

Use the **.HU** macro to specify an *unnumbered heading*. This type of heading takes the quoted heading text as its only argument.

Displays

A *display* is a section of a document that must be kept together as a block, but that will not *necessarily* appear in the output at the exact place where it is defined in the input. Typically, you want **troff** to fill lines correctly both above and below the display, without causing a break at the display itself. Similarly, a display should appear on a single page, and should never be broken across two output pages. The **mm** package allows you to define several types of displays.

Surround displays with **.DS** (for display static) or **.DF** (for display float), and **.DE** (for display end). The material between the two commands will be kept together on a single page in the output. The **.DS** macro defines a *static* display that is output as soon as possible. That is, a static display appears in its same relative position in the input document. Since a display will not be split across page boundaries, this may result in empty space on the bottom of a page if the display does not fit on the current page. The **.DS** command can take several arguments that determine the format and indent of the display. Use

```
.DS [format] [fill]
```

where *format* is a number: **0** produces no indent, **1** produces a standard indent, **2** centers each line in the display, and **3** centers the entire display as a block. The *fill* argument can be **0** for no-fill mode inside the display, or **1** for filling.

The **.DF** macro starts a *floating* display that may allow text that comes *after* the end of the display to appear *before* the display in the output, depending on the arguments to **.DF** and on **troff**'s computation of space on the current page. You use the same *format* and *fill* arguments with **.DF** that you do with **.DS**, but the behavior of **.DF** depends on two additional registers that are usually set at the beginning of the document. For example, you would use

```
.nr De 1
.nr Df 4
```

to specify that each display should appear alone on a separate page, with no text on the same page. Set the **De** register to 1 if you want a page eject *after* each display, or to 0 for no special behavior. The **Df** register can be set to 0, which holds all displays until the end of the section (first-level heading); to 2, which outputs the display at the top of the next page; to 3, which outputs the display on the current page if there is room, or at the top of the next page if there is not; or to 5, which outputs as many displays as will fit on the current page.

Any material, including text, tables, or graphics can be included between **.DF** and **.DE** pairs. In addition, **troff** can *hold* as many displays as necessary, and output them in sequence according to the rules above, without any special effort by the user.

Lists

The **mm** package includes excellent support for lists, including the ability to maintain list formatting and list item numbering without your attention. This means you do not have to number or format lists manually; you can add or delete items, and **mm** will automatically adjust the lists as required.

Start a list with **.AL** (for alphabetic lists), **.BL** (for bulleted lists), or **.DL** (for dashed lists). The different types refer to the mark that appears in front of each list item: an alphabetic character or number, a bullet, or a dash. A typical *outline* is an example of a numbered or alphabetic list. End each type of list with **.LE** (for list end). Each element within the list must be separated with **.LI** (for list item). For example:

```
.AL A
.LI
A list item -- a list item can have as many source lines as needed.
.LI
Another item -- mm will fill the lines within the list item.
.LI
Yet another list item -- and any normal troff commands or macros can
appear within the list item.
.LE
```

The **.AL** macro takes an argument specifying the *type* of marking; the argument indicates the first element of the sequence desired. In the example above, the first element will be marked with *A,* the second with *B,* and so forth. If the argument to **.AL** had been **6,** the first list element would have been **6.** If the type argument is omitted, **1** is assumed. The **.BL** and **.DL** macros do not take a mark argument, but can take an argument that specifies the indent of the list. The **.LI** macro can also take an argument to override the normal mark. For example,

```
.LI +
```

will mark that list item with **+,** regardless of the list type.

Footnotes, References, and Table of Contents

The **mm** macros manage footnotes and references similarly to the way they manage displays. As each footnote or reference appears in the body of the text, **mm** keeps the count in a register, outputting the body of the footnotes at the bottom of the same page, and saving the references for the end of the document. The ***F** form is used to retrieve the current footnote number, and this string can also be used in the text to refer to a footnote. Then you can place the footnote text within the normal **troff** source document by surrounding it with **.FS** (for footnote start) and **.FE** (for footnote end). The **.FS** macro can take an argument specifying the *label* that will appear at the beginning of the footnote. If no label is present, the current footnote number will be used. The **.FS** and **.FE** pair with the footnote text should immediately follow the label or footnote number in the source text (starting on the very next line), to ensure that the footnote will be handled correctly if it happens to fall near the bottom of a page in the output document.

References are treated similarly, except they are saved until the end of the document, and then output as a group in the correct order. Surround the reference text with **.RS** (for reference start) and **.RF** (for reference finish). Each reference is automatically numbered, and you can refer to the next reference number with the string ***(Rf.** Type the text of the reference immediately after you mention the reference in the document text.

As **troff** processes each heading in a document, it can maintain a list of headings as a *table of contents* for the document. You can request that the table of contents be printed by including the **.TC** macro at the end of your document. You must also give the **-rB1** command-line argument on your **troff** command to set things up so the headings will be saved. The **.TC** macro can take several arguments that specify the format and spacing of the table of contents, but these are rarely useful. By default, **.TC** saves *all* the headings in your document, but you can control this by setting the **Cl** (for contents level) register. For example,

```
.nr Cl 3
```

will save all third-level and higher headings for the table of contents.

Page Headers and Footers

You can easily control the contents of page headers and footers with the **mm** macros. Use the **.PH** and **.PF** macros to select page headers and footers, respectively. Also available are **.EH** (for even-page header), **.OH** (for odd-page header), **.EF** (for even-page footer), and **.OF** (for odd-page footer).

Each of these macros takes an argument in three-part format. The three parts set the contents of the left, middle, and right sections of the header or footer. The left part is left-justified on the page, and the middle part is centered, the right part is right-justified. Each part is separated by a ' (single quotation mark) in the argument to the header or footer macro. For example:

```
.EH 'Chapter \n(H1'' YABU'
.OH '\n(mo/\n(dy/\n(yr''Revision 2'
.PF '' - % - ''
```

Here, the left part of the header on even-numbered pages will be **Chapter** *n*, where *n* is the current chapter number; recall that the **mm** string **\n(H1** retrieves the value of the **H1** register, which contains the current value of the first-level heading. The middle part of both page headers is blank, but the middle part of the page footer contains the current page number; **%** retrieves the current page. The left part of the odd page header contains the current date. Do you understand why?

The man Macros

Traditionally, the entire *User's Manual* has been produced with the **man** macro package. Nearly all new software for the UNIX system, both professional and public-domain, includes at least one *man page* to describe its function. When this software is installed on a machine, these man pages are frequently placed on the hard disk, usually in the directory **/usr/man** or one of its subdirectories. Usually these man pages are in **troff** source form, although some thoughtful developers also provide versions that can be read with **cat**. The **troff** package and the **man** macros are required to print this source-form documentation. If you have man pages on your machine, but do not have the **troff** package, you can delete the man pages and save the disk space that they occupy.

The traditional way to learn the **man** macros is to start with an existing man page as a template, and then modify it to meet your needs. A listing of the **man** macros is given in Table 17-7.

Going Further

Like most programming languages, **troff** provides the opportunity for you to develop tremendous skill. To learn **troff** well, you will need to study the detailed user's manual provided with the *Documenter's Workbench* package, and then practice and experiment extensively on your own. This section will just mention a few more issues associated with word processing.

The tbl Command

The *Documenter's Workbench* package includes several additional tools. The **tbl** (for tables) command is a preprocessor for **troff** that produces high-quality tables embedded in documents. Tables can be multicolumn and enclosed in boxes. The **tbl** command automatically produces the correct column positioning for the table, so you don't have to lay out tables manually. A special control language has been defined, and the **tbl** command is a filter that reads these controls from the source file,

Command	If No Arg	Causes Break?	Explanation
.TH n c x v m	-	y	Begin page named n of chapter c. x=center page footer text; v=left page footer text; m=center page header text
.TX t p	-	n	Resolve title abbreviation t; join to punctuation p
.SH t	next line	y	Subheading
.PD d	.4v	n	Set interparagraph distance to d
.PP	-	y	Begin paragraph; set indent to .5i
.LP	-	y	Same as .PP
.RS i	indent	y	Start relative indent
.RE	-	y	End of relative indent
.TP i	indent	y	Set indent to i; begin indented paragraph
.HP i	indent	y	Set indent to i; begin hanging paragraph
.IP x i	" "	y	Same as .TP with tag x
.DT	.5i	n	Restore default tabs
.SM t	next line	y	Print text t two points smaller
.SB t	-	n	Print t in smaller bold
.B t	next line	n	Print text t in bold
.I t	next line	n	Print text t in italic
.BI t	next line	n	Print t in alternating bold and italic
.BR t	next line	n	Print t in alternating bold and roman
.IB t	next line	n	Print t in alternating bold and italic
.IR t	next line	n	Print t in alternating italic and roman
.RB t	next line	n	Print t in alternating roman and bold
.RI t	next line	n	Print t in alternating roman and italic

Table 17-7.   **man** Macros

figures out the best table layout, and produces **troff** commands to create that layout.

The output of **tbl** is fed to **troff** or **nroff** for printing, as follows:

```
$ tbl source.file | troff -mm -Tps | lp
```

The **tbl** commands are included in **troff** source files; **tbl** reads only its own commands, and passes the rest of the source document through to **troff**. Because **troff** can effectively use only one macro package at a time, **tbl** is a separate command, rather than a macro package. The separate **tbl** filter is used so that **tbl** commands need not be embedded in every macro package.

If you are using **mm**, you will typically place tables inside a display to control their position in the output document. The **mm** command set provides the **.TS** (for table start) and **.TE** (for table end) macros to improve handling of tables, especially those that may span several pages in the output. Thus, you will wish to code tables

```
.DF 2
.TS
(tbl contents here)
.TE
.DE
```

if you are using the **mm** macros; however, these macros do not actually invoke **tbl**, so you still need to use the **tbl** command line shown earlier.

Tables are defined by an *options section* that gives global options for the table, a *format section* that specifies the layout of the table, and a *data section* that contains the contents of the table. The options section comes first. The format section contains commands for defining how many columns appear in the table, whether the data elements are left-justified, and so forth. The data section contains a line for the contents of each *row* in the table. Each individual data element on that row (or the contents of each *column* in the table) is separated by a tab character. The number of columns is declared in the format section, and this declaration must match the number of elements in each row of the data section.

Using tbl

Table 17-8 lists the complete set of **tbl** commands, and Figure 17-6 shows the **tbl** source code for a simple three-column table. You specify the *style* of the table by setting options such as **center** or **box** to specify that the table should be centered on the page or enclosed in a box. The possibilities are listed in Table 17-8. You can use as many of these

Name	Type	Description
allbox	Options	Draw box around all items
box	Options	Draw box around table
center	Options	Center table on page
doublebox	Options	Doubled box around table
expand	Options	Make table full line width
tab(x)	Options	Change data separator character to x
		Format	Vertical line
| |	Format	Double vertical line
^	Format	Vertical span
\^	Format	Vertical span
a A	Format	Alphabetic subcolumn
b B	Format	Boldface item
c C	Format	Centered column
e E	Format	Equal width columns
f F	Format	Font Change
i I	Format	Italic item
l L	Format	Left adjusted column
n N	Format	Numerical column
nnn	Format	Column separation
p P	Format	Point size change
r R	Format	Right adjusted column
s S	Format	Spanned item
t T	Format	Vertical spanning at top
v V	Format	Vertical spacing change
w W	Format	Minimum width value
T{ T }	Data	Text block
.xx	Data	**troff** command
=	Data	Double horizontal line
_	Data	Horizontal line
\ _	Data	Short horizontal line

Table 17-8.   tbl Commands and Words

options as necessary to specify your table, but they must all appear on a single line following the **.TS** command. You can omit the options if you are satisfied with the defaults, but if it is present the option list must end with a semicolon.

```
.TS
center box;
c s s
c s s
c s s
cb | cb | cb
1 | 1 | 1.

tbl Commands and Words

=
Name    Type     Description
=
allbox  Options  Draw box around all items
box     Options  draw box around table
center  Options  Center table on page
=
a A     Format   Alphabetic subcolumn
b B     Format   Boldface item
c C     Format   Centered column
=
T{ T }  data     Text block
.xx     data     troff command
.TE
```

Figure 17-6.   Sample **tbl** source code

The *format* section determines the layout of the table. Here you specify the number of columns, the point size, whether the items are left-justified or centered within the columns, and so forth. In this section, you use a code to specify each element in your table, row by row. That is, if the table contains three columns, the format section will consist of lines that contain three codes. In addition the rows may include separators that tell **tbl** whether to *rule* the column boundaries with vertical lines, or to use only whitespace between columns. Each line in the data section of the table has a line in the format section, although the *last* line in the format section is used for all *remaining* lines in the data section if there are fewer format lines than there are data lines. You end the format section with a dot at the end of the last line.

The format section allows a wide variety of formats. You can specify that a data element be *left-justified* in its column by coding **L** or **l** (ell) in its position in the format section. (Upper- and lowercase are equivalent in the format section.) Use **c** to center the element in its column, and so on. You can combine different types of codes if necessary. For example, use **cb** for a data element that you want to be centered and boldfaced. Similarly, you can specify point size changes using the **p** code followed by a point size. For instance, you might specify **cp14** for a 14-point centered data element.

Use **s** (for spanned) when you want a data element to *span* more than one column. In Figure 17-6, the title "tbl Commands and Words" is controlled by the lines

```
c s s
c s s
c s s
```

In the data section this title is surrounded by empty lines, which explains why *three* format lines are needed. The **c** specifies that the text be centered within the column, and the two **s** characters instruct **tbl** to span the next two columns, resulting in a title that is centered across the entire table, and surrounded with blank lines.

You can separate the elements in the format section with **|** (vertical bar) or **||** (double vertical bars) to instruct **tbl** to draw single or double vertical lines between the columns. If these characters are omitted, the columns will be separated with whitespace.

Each data item in the table appears in the data section, and each line in the data section specifies a row in the output table. On each line, individual data items are separated by tab characters. Each tab character on the data line tells **tbl** to place the next item in the next column, so you must take care that each data line contains exactly the number of columns you specified in the format section. In addition to data lines, the data section can also include lines that contain an = (equal sign) or _ (underscore). These characters cause **tbl** to draw a double or a single horizontal line at that point in the table. These characters are often used to separate sections of the table. You can include normal **troff** commands within the data section to control spacing, and so forth, as necessary. Also, you can specify a block of text as a table entry by starting it with **T{** (T left curly brace) and ending it with **T}** (T right curly brace). This allows you to treat something as a table entry that will not conveniently fit between tabs in the normal form. These *text blocks* are processed by normal **troff** commands before they are processed by **tbl**. You can include complex font or spacing changes within a text block.

Each data element in a row of the data section is separated from the others by a tab character, although you can use a different delimiter if you use the **tab(x)** command in the options, where x is the new delimiter you wish to use.

Much more complex tables are possible under **tbl**, including sub-tables within a data position, multiline data elements, and so forth. For example, you can interrupt the processing of data entries, and change the table format, by including the **.T&** (for table continue) command. Following **.T&** you can add a new format section, and then another data section. This changes the table format in the middle, but maintains the same options.

Formatting Mathematical Equations and Graphics

The **eqn** (for equations) command provides a tool that is similar to **tbl** for producing high-quality mathematical equations. The **eqn** command is another special-purpose preprocessor for **troff** that has its own set of commands. Although **eqn** is still widely used for equation-intensive documents, it is quite difficult to control, and only a few experts have mastered its use.

The **troff** program was not designed to support embedded graphics within a document; however, some phototypesetters and laser printers allow the installation of a special graphics font, and **troff** can use such a font to produce *line graphics* that allow you to draw moderately complex block diagrams and flow charts. The **pic** (for pictures) and **grap** (for graphs) tools are additional special-purpose preprocessors that let you produce such pictures. Like **eqn, pic** and **grap** have their own command sets.

In addition, if you are using a PostScript printer you can embed any PostScript code into your **troff** source document using the **.so** (for source) command. The **.so** command takes a file or a pathname as an argument, and reads that file at the current location in the document. The **.so** command allows you to add *any* **troff** source material that is in a separate file into your document.

Any line that begins with the string **\!** (backslash bang space) is passed through **troff** untouched and unfilled. Thus, you can include PostScript programs (or other material!) within your documents, to be interpreted directly by the printer device. Usually you will want to place these programs in a separate file, and use the **.so** command to bring them into your documents. For example, this input will draw a single line within a display:

```
.DF 2
.ne 50l     \" ask for enough space on the current page
\! /inchXX { 72 mul } def
\! % draw a simple straight line
\! /dolineXX {     % hstart vstart hend vend dolineXX -
\!    newpath moveto lineto stroke
\! } def
\! gsave
\! 3 inchXX 3 inchXX 6 inchXX 7 inchXX dolineXX
\! grestore
.DE
```

Take care that any PostScript functions you define have unique names that are not already being used internally by the **ditroff** system; use unusual or complex names if you are not sure.

troff Directory Structure

The commands and files associated with **troff** reside in several directories within the file system. The macro libraries are located in **/usr/share/lib/macros**. Frequently, however, **troff** does not access this library directly, but through short linkage files in **/usr/share/lib/tmac**. The reason for this indirect linkage is unclear, but if either directory is corrupted the **troff** tools will probably not work correctly. In addition, the printer and terminal descriptions used by **troff** reside in **/usr/lib/term** or **/usr/lib/nterm**, depending on which **troff** version you are using. In any case, only one of these directories will be present. Note that the **troff** terminal description files are unrelated to the **terminfo** database used by full-screen applications like **vi**.

Conditionals and Macros in troff

The **troff** system is really a full-scale (though difficult) programming language that includes test and branch operations, and the ability to create *subprograms*. Macros such as **mm** and **man** use these capabilities to greatly enhance the basic **troff** commands.

The **.if** (for if) and **.ie** (for if-else) commands are used to test the value of some expression, and take some action depending on the result. For example, the line

```
'if o 'tl '\n(mo/\n(dy/\n(yr'- % -'\n(H1'
```

is interpreted as follows: If the current page is odd-numbered, set the three-part title to the date, the current page, and the current chapter. Similarly,

```
'ie o 'tl '\n(mo/\n(dy/\n(yr'- % -'\n)H1'
'el 'tl "- % -"
```

sets the title to one thing *if* the page is odd, or *else* it sets the title to something else. You can use conditionals to test the value of any string or register, and take action as appropriate. Arithmetic and logical operations are allowed in the test parts of the **if** and **ie** commands.

A common use for conditionals is within macro definitions. Use **.de X** to define a macro named X (you can use one or two character names). Any **troff** commands (or other macros) can follow. End the macro definition with **..** (dot dot) alone on a line. After the macro is defined, you can use it just as you can any other **troff** command. For example, Figure 17-7 shows a simple macro definition for processing at the bottom of a page. It includes several **troff** features we have not discussed. Basically it switches to a separate *environment,* sets the point size and title, and then spaces a few lines for a bottom margin. The **troff** program uses separate environments to allow two or more processing threads to be used simultaneously. For example, displays are processed in a different environment than normal text. In Figure 17-7, the **BP** macro asks for a new page, which causes the current title to be printed in the current font and point size. Then the macro spaces down a few lines at the top of the page and restores the environment, allowing **troff** to return to filling the text. The **.wh** (for when) command tells **troff** to trigger this **BP** macro when it gets 9.25 inches from the top of each page, causing the instructions within the macro to be executed.

Macros can take arguments if necessary, and you can refer to the values of the arguments within the macro definition by using **$1** for the first argument, **$2** for the second argument, and so forth.

Note that within conditionals, three-part titles, and macros, you may need additional **** (backslash) characters when you are using the value of registers. You must experiment to find the right number for each situation.

```
.de BP
.ev 2
.ft B
.ps 12
'if o 'tl '\n(mo/\n(dy/\n(yr'- % -'\n(H1'
'if e 'tl ''- % -''
.br
.ft P
.ps
'sp 21
.bp
'sp 1.5i
.ev
..
.wh |9.25i BP
```

Figure 17-7.   A simple bottom-of-page macro definition

Logos in mm

The **mm** package includes the ability to print a company logo on letters and memos. The original **mm** package as shipped from AT&T only includes the AT&T logo, and often the macros are unchanged in releases from other vendors. If you wish to print memos with the AT&T letterhead, this is appropriate; however, you will probably wish to omit the AT&T logo. If your version of **mm** always produces the AT&T logo on your memos, add **.AF** *string* (for alternate form) *before* the **.TL** in your source document. If it is present, the string will be printed in a large font; **.AF** alone will leave a blank space for printing on your own letterhead.

The Writer's Workbench

One of the most interesting add-on tools available with **troff** is a full-scale *critic* for documents written with **troff**. The *Writer's Workbench* package, which is based on **troff**, **spell**, and filters, provides tools for analyzing sentence construction, word usage, prose style, sexist references, and many other factors in documents. Its output is quite readable, and can actually help teach writing skills to students or even professional writers. It can operate in tutorial mode (voluminous) or summary mode (terse). Table 17-9 lists some summary data for this

Measure	Bell Laboratories Technical Memos	AT&T Training Documentation	This Book
Kincaid readability grade	grade 10.1 to 15.0	7.8 to 12.4	10.2
Average sentence length	16.7 to 25.3 words	12.3 to 20.2	20.1
Average length of content words	5.8 to 7.0 letters	5.5 to 6.8	5.25
Percentage of short sentences	29.2% to 38.0%	23.1% to 31.4%	35%
Percentage of long sentences	11.7% to 18.9%	7.3% to 12.8%	12%
Percentage of simple sentences minus the percentage of complex sentences	-24.2% to 30.1%	-28.4% to 56.0%	-2.0%
Percentage of compound sentences plus the percentage of compound-complex sentences	5.7% to 35.2%	4.7% to 25.7%	24%
Passives should be fewer than	28.6%	28.7%	18%
Nominalizations should be fewer than	4.2%	3.4%	2%
Expletives should be fewer than	5.7%	7.2%	2%

Table 17-9.   Readability Analysis of Some **troff** Documents

book from the **style** analysis program, one of the tools in the *Writer's Workbench* package. In the table you can compare these numbers against typical values for good technical memoranda or training documents.

The spell History File

Whenever **spell** executes, it adds all the misspelled words it finds to a log file. The file **/var/adm/spellhist** contains this log. The log is a mixed blessing: on the one hand a system administrator can use it to update the word list so that commonly used acronyms and words are added to the list. Also, the history file allows statistical analysis of misspelled words, a useful feature in an educational setting. However, the history list can also grow very large, since there are no automatic administrative tools for truncating it. It is the system administrator's responsibility to keep the **spellhist** file from becoming too long. You can regularly truncate the spelling history manually, add the operation to a regularly scheduled cleanup script, or change the **/usr/bin/spell** script to prevent it from building the history.

Building a New spell Database

If you use **spell** for documents that contain specialized jargon, you may need to update the **spell** word lists. Also, you can screen out many control commands from word processors other than **troff** by adding these codes to the **spell** database. Browse through the **spellhist** file to determine what words should be added for your use of the **spell** tools.

The word list used by **spell** is stored in an efficient, *hashed* database of word roots. This database is in the directory **/usr/share/lib/spell**, shown here:

```
$ ls -F /usr/share/lib/spell
compress*    hlista    hlistb    hstop
$
```

The spelling lists are **hlista** and **hlistb**; however, these cannot be browsed since they are binary files. The file **hlista** is the American word list, and **hlistb** is the British list. The **hstop** file contains a *stop list* of misspelled words that would otherwise pass the spelling rules, such as *thier.*

The actual executable spelling checker program called by **/usr/bin/spell** to do the work is **/usr/lib/spell/spellprog**. The rest of the **/usr/lib/spell** directory contains tools for updating the word lists. The **hashmake** program reads a list of words from its standard input, and writes a list of hash codes to its standard output. The **spellin** program reads a list of hash codes from its standard input, and writes a compressed spelling list to its standard output, while the **hashcheck** program does the opposite; it reads a compressed spelling list from standard input, and writes a list of hash codes to its standard output. The **spellin** command takes a numeric command-line argument, specifying the number of hash codes in its input.

To add a new set of words to the **hlista** file requires several steps: first, the list of new words must be prepared, one word per line; second, the list must be given to **hashmake**; third, **hlista** must be unpacked with **hashcheck**; fourth, this output and the hashed list for the new words must be sorted together; finally, the hash lists must be compressed with **spellin**. These commands will do the job:

```
$ PATH=$PATH:/usr/lib/spell
$ hashmake < new.list | sort > new.hash  # make hash file for new list
$ hashcheck < hlista | sort -mu - new.hash > h.out  # make final list
$ NUM=`wc -l < h.out`                     # count needed below
$ spellin $NUM < h.out > hlista          # and make new hlista
$
```

Be sure to save the original files until the new versions are tested!

Media

Disk management is important in any operating system. You will be working with *media* such as disks and magnetic tape from the first time you load the operating system onto the hard disk. Media are used in managing your disk space, and in the routine *backup* procedures that protect your data. The UNIX system provides two basic modes of handling media, and you can use many types and sizes of disks with UNIX systems.

The issues involved in disk management can be complex, and there is really no quick way through them. UNIX systems differ markedly in

563

the way disk devices are named, and it is always a challenge to figure out the scheme used in a new release. In SVR4 there are now several *file system types* that behave very differently from each other. All of these may appear on a single machine; they may even share the same disk, although some are *virtual* file systems that do not actually represent space on a physical disk. When you take an action on a disk, you must usually specify the file system type in the command line. Magnetic tape usually obeys a different set of rules.

In this chapter we will review manual access to the disk management tools, and discuss some of the issues associated with using disks and tape in your normal activities. Simplified menus for disk management are usually present in a system administration tool, as discussed in Chapter 12.

Disk Blocks and Inodes

The UNIX system manages disk space in units called *blocks*. In SVR4, blocks are 512 bytes each. All file-related operations work with blocks. That is, you cannot create a file or a directory smaller than one block, even if it only contains a single byte. A file of 510 bytes will use exactly the same disk space as a file of 1 byte. On the other hand, if a file contains 514 bytes, it will use two disk blocks. Most disk-related commands report disk activity by counting blocks. Only a few, such as **ls**, report file size directly in bytes. Directories also use disk blocks, and again the minimum size of a directory is 1 block, even if only a single file (or none!) is listed in the directory.

In addition to disk blocks, the file system contains a list of names of all the files on the disk, matched with a pointer to the first disk block associated with each name. Each name and the associated blocks are stored in an entity called the *inode* (for identification node). One of the elements in the data table that forms each directory is the inode used for each file. Whenever a file is updated, the system updates the inode. The list of inodes is fixed when a file system is created. Usually, you will have no reason to deal with inodes, but the inode list can fill up, especially on floppy disks, and you cannot create a new file if there is no inode available.

File Systems

The list of disk blocks, inodes, and other information associated with disk usage is maintained separately for each *file system* on the machine. Each physical disk attached to the machine must have its own file system, but it is possible to create more than one file system on a disk. The reverse is not possible; a file system cannot span more than one disk. When your UNIX system was installed, either one or two file systems were probably created on the disk; these initial file systems are usually named **/** (root) and **/usr** (user). As you'll learn later in this chapter, floppy disks and magnetic tapes can also have file systems, although this is not required.

Separate file systems are handled separately within the UNIX system, and you cannot **ln** or **mv** files across file systems, unless you use *symbolic links*. You must **cp** a file to move it to another file system. If one file system fills up or fails for some reason, its failure will *not* affect other file systems on the machine.

Hard Disk Management

Since the primary activity of the UNIX system occurs on the machine's built-in hard disk, you should be especially concerned with its management. Disk space always fills up in time, and there is a natural tendency not to delete material from the hard disk. Understanding your disk space budget can help you keep your machine running better, and can guarantee that enough space will be available when you need it.

Disk Free Space—The df Command

You can determine the amount of disk space in each file system on the machine, including both free space and space in use. The **df** (for disk free) command provides this information, as shown here:

```
$ df
/                    (/dev/root   ):  140331 blocks   63540 files
/proc                (/proc       ):       0 blocks      75 files
/dev/fd              (/dev/fd     ):       0 blocks       0 files
/stand               (/dev/dsk/0s10 ):   7307 blocks      97 files
```

For each file system on the machine, the file system location is reported in the leftmost column. The second column gives the device name of the file system, usually in the **/dev** directory. The number of free blocks comes next, and the number of free inodes is reported in the last column. You may have some *virtual* file systems that are designed for special purposes, such as **/proc** and **/dev/fd**. These are used as objects in some file-related software, but are not designed for storing files. Thus, the block and file values for these file systems will not be relevant.

The inode, or *files,* count gives the total number of new files that you can create before the file system is full. If you created 63,540 more files in this root file system without deleting any, it would be full even though there might still be some free blocks.

The **df** command will also report on the *total* amount of disk space in the file system if you use the **-t** (for total) option, as follows:

```
$ df -t
/                    (/dev/root    ):  140323 blocks   63540 files
                            total:   294986 blocks   73632 files
/proc                (/proc        ):       0 blocks      75 files
                            total:        0 blocks     102 files
/dev/fd              (/dev/fd      ):       0 blocks       0 files
                            total:        0 blocks      66 files
/stand               (/dev/dsk/0s10 ):   7307 blocks      97 files
                            total:    10710 blocks     104 files
$
```

You can easily compute the percentage of disk space used, and see how fast the disk space is being consumed. In fact, most SVR4 systems include a **dfspace** (for disk free space) command that performs this computation for you. Its output is often seen during the login procedure. For example:

```
$ dfspace
/          :  Disk space:  71.84 MB of 144.03 MB available (47.57%).
/proc      :  Disk space:   0.00 MB of   0.00 MB available ( 0.00%).
/dev/fd    :  Disk space:   0.00 MB of   0.00 MB available ( 0.00%).
/stand     :  Disk space:   3.56 MB of   5.22 MB available (68.23%).
```

```
Total Disk Space:  75.40 MB of 149.26 MB available (48.29%).
$
```

The **dfspace** command can take a list of file system names on its command line if you wish to restrict the report to a subset of the total file systems present.

Disk Space Used—The du Command

The **df** command reports on disk space available in the file system as a whole. In addition, you can determine how much space any file or directory is using. The **du** (for disk usage) command reports this figure for directories listed as arguments. For example:

```
$ du /var/spool/cron
1        /var/spool/cron/atjobs
4        /var/spool/cron/crontabs
6        /var/spool/cron
$
```

Here, **du** reports the number of 512-byte blocks used for each of the subdirectories. To determine the true disk usage, you must multiply the output from **du** by 512, as you did for **df**.

By default, **du** will not take a filename as an argument, but only a directory name. It reports on all the subdirectory trees within the named directory. The **-a** (for all) option causes **du** to generate an output line for each file and directory in the named list, instead of just for the directories. The **-s** (for summary) option causes only a grand total for each of the named directories to be displayed, as shown here:

```
$ du -s /etc
9159    /etc
$
```

You can get much shorter output by using this option when you want a quick summary of disk usage.

Finally, by default **du** silently ignores files and directories that it cannot open. Use the **-r** (for report) option to make **du** complain when it cannot open a file or directory.

These commands—**df**, **dfspace** and **du**—are invaluable tools for managing your disk space. You should execute these commands frequently, either manually or in a regularly scheduled demon, to track the disk usage on your machine.

Size of Files and the ulimit

Most files under the UNIX system are relatively small; a file of a megabyte or larger is unusual. However, internally the system allows programs to use as much disk space as they need. Thus, it is possible for rogue processes or failing applications to incorrectly take all the disk space on the machine. To prevent this, the **ulimit** (for user limit) variable and the **ulimit** command are provided. The value of the **ulimit** is the size in blocks of the largest file that can be created by the user. In most UNIX systems the default **ulimit** is quite small. For example:

```
$ ulimit
4096
$
```

When you try to create a file larger than the **ulimit**, the file's growth will stop at the **ulimit**, and the command that is creating the file will fail with an error. In the previous example, the maximum file size is 2MB.

The default **ulimit** is systemwide, but it can be changed for an individual login session. Naturally, you cannot *increase* your **ulimit**, but you can reduce it. Only the superuser can increase the **ulimit** for a session. You set the **ulimit** by giving the new value as an argument, as shown here:

```
$ ulimit
4096
$ ulimit 1000
$ ulimit
1000
$
```

This change only remains in effect for your current session. Furthermore, when the change is made in a subshell it does not affect the parent session. Often the system administrator will set the **ulimit** in the system **/etc/profile**, so that it is set to some reasonable value when you log in to the machine. Frequently the **ulimit** is set to one or two megabytes in small machines, but if you use large databases or other large files, you should be sure that the **ulimit** is not too small for your needs. Configuring the system default value for the **ulimit** is handled through **/etc/default/login**, as discussed in Chapter 25.

Never Fill the Hard Disk

Hard disk space is always limited, and it always seems to get filled up, usually faster than you expect. If the space available for files becomes full, the machine will stop working, either with a painful crash, or by slowing down so much that the system is finally inoperative. Should this happen, you will have to boot the machine from a floppy disk and remove unneeded files from the hard disk manually, which can be a difficult and complex procedure. Alternatively, you may have to reload the system software, in which case you will lose all the files on the hard disk. As you can see, it is an important administrative chore to maintain at least *ten percent* free space on the machine's main hard disk. You should examine the **dfspace** output regularly to determine how much disk space is available, and take steps to delete unnecessary files and directories.

You can use some routine procedures to reduce disk space usage. First, back up little-used files and directories to floppy disk or tape, and only reload the floppies when they are needed. Second, use the **/tmp** directory to store temporary files and intermediate data from your shell scripts. The files in the **/tmp** directory are deleted every time the machine boots, so its contents will not remain in the file system for an excessively long time. Third, you can routinely use **find** to search for files that are larger than a selected size, and then delete files that are growing. For example,

```
$ find / -size +200 -exec ls -l { } \;
```

will display the name and size of all files larger than 200 blocks. If you do this, be careful not to delete files that are legitimately larger than the cut-off size, such as **/stand/unix** and many others. You should look for files that continue to grow over a period of days and weeks. Usually files in the directories **/sbin, /lib, /usr/sbin, /usr/bin** and **/usr/lib** are legitimate, while others may be suspicious. Fourth, you should watch for the accumulation of files named **core** in the system, with

```
$ find / -name core -print
```

Core files are produced when a command or application fails for some reason. Core files are often large, and are almost never useful. In fact, the presence of core files signals some pathological condition in the machine that may need attention. Sometimes the directory location of core files can be a clue to the cause of the failure. Finally, check user areas such as home directories and subdirectories for cases of "disk-hogging" by users. Users should be considerate of the machine's resources and of other users. In some situations you can use a **quota** tool to limit the disk consumption of individual users. This technique is discussed at the end of this chapter.

File Compression

You can reduce the size of rarely used data files by *compressing* them. Compression often saves as much as 30 to 50 percent of the original space, but compressed files must be *uncompressed* before they can be used. Thus, it is not safe to compress a file unless you are sure it is not being used by the system or by another user.

SVR4 offers two programs for compressing files. They differ in the algorithm they use for compression, but otherwise they act similarly. The **compress** program takes a filename list as an argument and produces a compressed version of each file. By default, **compress** returns silently, as shown here:

```
$ compress test.file
$ ls -l
-rwx------  1 steve        30202 Mar  8 16:23 test.file.Z
$
```

You can get a report on the amount of compression by adding the **-v** (for verbose) option.

The **compress** program changes the name of the file by adding the suffix **.Z** (uppercase *Z*) to the filename. Thus, if you have the 14-character filename limit, you can only **compress** files with names of 12 characters or less.

To unpack a file produced by **compress**, use the **uncompress** command, as follows:

```
$ uncompress -v *Z
test.file.Z:  -- replaced with test.file
$ ls -l
-rwx------  1 steve       72465 Mar  8 16:23 test.file
$
```

The time-stamp on the file is unchanged by the **compress** and **uncompress** operations.

The second tool is older than **compress**, but is still occasionally used. The **pack** program takes a filename list as an argument, and produces a packed version of each file. For example:

```
$ pack test.file
pack: test.file: 40.9% Compression
$
```

The **pack** program changes the name of the file by adding the suffix .z (lowercase *z*) to the filename. Again, if you have the 14-character filename limit, you can only **pack** files with names of 12 characters or less. By default, **pack** reports the savings for each file it compresses. The **unpack** program acts like **uncompress** to restore a file to its original form.

The **compress** program usually produces a smaller output file than **pack**, so **compress** is generally preferred.

You can also produce an uncompressed version of a file on standard output, rather than replacing the packed file with its normal version. The **zcat** program works like **cat** to unpack files produced with **compress**. It looks like this:

```
$ zcat test.file.Z | wc
   2195   12844   72465
$
```

Here, the compressed file is unchanged. Use **pcat** to achieve the same result on files compressed with **pack**.

File System Types

SVR4 introduced a new mechanism for handling file systems, which allows developers to create new types of file systems with special and exotic features. The **/proc** directory and the ability to mount MS-DOS file systems under the UNIX system are common examples. In addition, "real" file systems that show up in the normal directory tree can take advantage of this feature. In SVR4 there are two major types of file systems and these act very differently. You must understand their nature to deal effectively with floppy disks.

The old-style System V file system, which has been used for many years in AT&T UNIX systems, is one of these important types. It uses a fixed-size inode table to allocate files and their disk blocks, and limits file and directory names to 14 characters. In SVR4, this file system type is called **s5**. On some machines the basic user-level file systems on the hard disk are **s5** type systems, depending on how the machine was configured when the UNIX software was loaded.

The other major file system type is adapted from the BSD version of the UNIX system. It uses a flexibly configured inode table for directory entries, and allows file and directory names up to 256 characters long. In addition, it is much faster in performance, and more robust in several ways than the **s5** type. In SVR4, this file system type is called **ufs** (for UNIX file system).

Because of complexities in the way the UNIX system can be configured, any specific directory that is visible to the user can be of either type. Because any directory can be a symbolic link to some other place in the overall directory tree, you cannot assume that a subdirectory is the same type as its parent directory, although system administrators normally try to make a disk contain *only* **s5** or **ufs** file systems. In most cases **ufs** is preferred, because it allows longer names, does not suffer from inode shortage, and performs better than **s5** file systems. SVR3 and older systems use the **s5** type exclusively, so floppy disks exchanged with older systems must be **s5**.

The **df -n** (for name) command, shown here, will report the file system type for any directory.

```
$ df -n $HOME
/home/steve      : ufs
$
```

The differences between file system types immediately become important when you try to create file systems on floppy disks.

Floppy Disk Management

Before you can use a floppy disk it must be *formatted.* Formatting prepares the disk for use, and all new disks must be formatted after you buy them. In addition, you can format an old disk to delete all its contents and prepare it for reuse.

How a diskette is formatted depends on the type of disk it is. A 5 1/4-inch *double-sided, double-density* disk has a capacity of 360K of data. This is the common diskette used in older PC-compatible machines. In addition, 5 1/4-inch *high-density* diskettes have a capacity of 1.2MB of data. These disks are used in AT-class machines. 3 1/2-inch plastic-cased disks can usually hold 720K (double-sided, double-density) or 1.4MB (high-density). These are the most common disk types, and you must specify the type when you buy disks.

Even though the physical disks are equivalent, floppy disk *formats* for the UNIX system are not the same as those for MS-DOS or other operating systems. Most SVR4 systems allow you to read and write MS-DOS floppies within the UNIX system, but special tools are required. The discussion here is *only* relevant for diskettes used totally within the UNIX system. Access to MS-DOS diskettes is discussed in Chapter 19.

Once a diskette has been formatted, the UNIX system provides two different ways of using it. One is to create a *file system* on the floppy, which allows you to use it like a hard disk. For example, you can create directories on the disk, **cd** around in these directories, and **cp** files just as you do on the hard disk.

To use this form of access, you must create a file system on the disk, and then *mount* it into the hard disk file system at a specific position, or *mount point*. When you have done this, you can use the floppy just as you can any other directory in the system.

In addition, the UNIX system provides a second form of access to a floppy diskette. This second form is called *raw access*. Disks used in the raw form will not have file systems associated with them, and you cannot use these floppy disks in the same way you use a hard disk. On the other hand, the raw form of access allows you to create more than a disk-full of data, because when one disk fills up you can simply go on to a second disk. The raw form of diskette access is usually used for backing up, or *archiving*, data.

Another complication arises if you want to be able to *boot* the machine from a floppy disk, rather than from the machine's hard disk. Bootable floppy disks are not often used with UNIX systems, but the first disk of the System Installation Set is an example of a bootable disk. Bootable disks must contain a *boot block* and an executable kernel, since the entire operating system must run from the floppy. These additional requirements substantially reduce the disk space available for your data, so unless you have a real need for bootable floppies you should not use them. The decision as to whether a floppy disk should be bootable must be made when the disk is formatted, but the normal formatting tools do not create bootable disks. To create a new bootable disk, you must usually copy the first disk of the Installation Set, or sometimes the first two disks, and then edit their contents.

Device Files for Disks

Diskettes (and hard disks as well!) are managed through the *device file* that names that disk type. These device files specify what disk drive to use for an operation, and also the type of format that disk has. When you use a floppy disk, you name the device file that refers to that type of disk on that drive. Tables 18-1 through 18-3 list disk and tape device files for SVR4 systems, including both hard disks and floppy disks. Refer to Table 18-1 for information about device files for various forms of floppy disk access.

Raw Device File	Block Device File	Device	Size	Comment
/dev/rdsk/f0t	/dev/dsk/f0t	FD 0	*	Whatever drive is installed; entire disk
/dev/rdsk/f0	/dev/dsk/f0	FD 0	*	Whatever drive is installed; all but boot block
/dev/rdsk/f1t	/dev/dsk/f1t	FD 1	*	Whatever drive is installed; entire disk
/dev/rdsk/f1	/dev/dsk/f1	FD 1	*	Whatever drive is installed; all but boot block
/dev/rdsk/f0d8dt /dev/rdsk/f05d8t	/dev/dsk/f0d8dt /dev/dsk/f05d8t	FD 0	320KB	Entire disk
/dev/rdsk/f0d8d /dev/rdsk/f05d8 /dev/rdsk/f05d8u	/dev/dsk/f0d8d /dev/dsk/f05d8 /dev/dsk/f05d8u	FD 0	320KB	All but boot block
/dev/rdsk/f1d8dt /dev/rdsk/f15d8t	/dev/dsk/f1d8dt /dev/dsk/f15d8t	FD 1	320KB	Entire disk
/dev/rdsk/f1d8d /dev/rdsk/f15d8	/dev/dsk/f1d8d /dev/dsk/f15d8	FD 1	320KB	All but boot block
/dev/rdsk/f0d9dt /dev/rdsk/f05d9t	/dev/dsk/f0d9dt /dev/dsk/f05d9t	FD 0	360KB	Entire disk
/dev/rdsk/f0d9d /dev/rdsk/f05d9	/dev/dsk/f0d9d /dev/dsk/f05d9	FD 0	360KB	All but boot block
/dev/rdsk/f1d9dt /dev/rdsk/f15d9t	/dev/dsk/f1d9dt /dev/dsk/f15d9t	FD 1	360KB	Entire disk
/dev/rdsk/f1d9d /dev/rdsk/f15d9	/dev/dsk/f1d9d /dev/dsk/f15d9	FD 1	360KB	All but boot block
/dev/rdsk/f0q15dt /dev/rdsk/f05ht	/dev/dsk/f0q15dt /dev/dsk/f05ht	FD 0	1.2MB	Entire disk
/dev/rdsk/f0q15d /dev/rdsk/f05h	/dev/dsk/f0q15d /dev/dsk/f05h	FD 0	1.2MB	All but boot block

Table 18-1.   Floppy Disk Device Files for SVR4 UNIX Systems

Raw Device File	Block Device File	Device	Size	Comment
/dev/rdsk/f1q15dt /dev/rdsk/f15ht	/dev/dsk/f1q15dt /dev/dsk/f15ht	FD 1	1.2MB	Entire disk
/dev/rdsk/f1q15d /dev/rdsk/f15h	/dev/dsk/f1q15d /dev/dsk/f15h	FD 1	1.2MB	All but boot block
/dev/rdsk/f03ht	/dev/dsk/f03ht	FD 0	1.4MB	3 1/2-inch; entire disk
/dev/rdsk/f03h	/dev/dsk/f03h	FD 0	1.4MB	3 1/2-inch; all but boot block
/dev/rdsk/f13ht	/dev/dsk/f13ht	FD 1	1.4MB	3 1/2-inch; entire disk
/dev/rdsk/f13h	/dev/dsk/f13h	FD 1	1.4MB	3 1/2-inch; all but boot block
/dev/rdsk/f03dt	/dev/dsk/f03dt	FD 0	720KB	3 1/2-inch; entire disk
/dev/rdsk/f03d	/dev/dsk/f03d	FD 0	720KB	3 1/2-inch; all but boot block
/dev/rdsk/f13dt	/dev/dsk/f13dt	FD 1	720KB	3 1/2-inch; entire disk
/dev/rdsk/f13d	/dev/dsk/f13d	FD 1	720KB	3 1/2-inch; all but boot block

Table 18-1.   Floppy Disk Device Files for SVR4 UNIX Systems (*continued*)

All the disk devices are included in the directories **dsk** (for disk) for the mountable disk types, or **rdsk** (for raw disk) for the raw disk types. Both are within the **/dev** directory. Each file in these directories refers to a specific type of device.

The names of the files encode a specific device for that type of access to the disk. For example, the name **f0q15dt** refers to floppy disk drive zero (**f0**). The name **f1** is used for floppy drive 1 if it is installed on your machine. The **q15** specifies a quad density disk with 15 tracks per cylinder, and **d9** refers to a double density disk with nine tracks per cylinder. For 3 1/2-inch disks the names are usually **d** for 720K double-density disks, and **h** for 1.4MB high-density disks.

In addition, the **dt** or **ht** specifies a disk with no boot block, while **d** or **h** specifies a disk with a boot block. Normally you should use the **dt** (or **ht**) format, becuse it allows more space on the floppy for your use. However, some application software is shipped on disks in the **d** format,

Raw Device File	Block Device File	Device	Comment
/dev/rdsk/0s0	/dev/dsk/0s0	HD 0	Entire disk
/dev/rdsk/1s0	/dev/dsk/1s0	HD 1	
/dev/rdsk/0s1	/dev/dsk/0s1	HD 0	**root** file system
/dev/rdsk/1s1	/dev/dsk/1s1	HD 1	First additional file system
/dev/rdsk/0s2	/dev/dsk/0s2	HD 0	Swap area
/dev/rdsk/1s2	/dev/dsk/1s2	HD 1	
/dev/rdsk/0s3	/dev/dsk/0s3	HD 0	**usr** file system
/dev/rdsk/1s3	/dev/dsk/1s3	HD 1	Second additional file system
/dev/rdsk/0s4	/dev/dsk/0s4	HD 0	**home** file system
/dev/rdsk/1s4	/dev/dsk/1s4	HD 1	Third additional file system
/dev/rdsk/0s5	/dev/dsk/0s5	HD 0	DOS-only partition
/dev/rdsk/1s5	/dev/dsk/1s5	HD 1	
/dev/rdsk/0s6	/dev/dsk/0s6	HD 0	Dump device
/dev/rdsk/1s6	/dev/dsk/1s6	HD 1	
/dev/rdsk/0s7	/dev/dsk/0s7	HD 0	Boot device
/dev/rdsk/1s7	/dev/dsk/1s7	HD 1	
/dev/rdsk/0s8	/dev/dsk/0s8	HD 0	Alternate sectors
/dev/rdsk/1s8	/dev/dsk/1s8	HD 1	
/dev/rdsk/0s9	/dev/dsk/0s9	HD 0	Alternate tracks
/dev/rdsk/1s9	/dev/dsk/1s9	HD 1	
/dev/rdsk/0s10	/dev/dsk/0s10	HD 0	**stand** file system
/dev/rdsk/0s11	/dev/dsk/0s11	HD 0	**var** file system
/dev/rdsk/0s12	/dev/dsk/0s12	HD 0	**home2** file system
/dev/rdsk/0s13	/dev/dsk/0s13	HD 0	**tmp** file system

Table 18-2.   Hard Disk Device Files for SVR4 UNIX Systems

Device File	Type	Comment
/dev/rmt/c0s0	Streaming	Rewind after I/O operation
/dev/rmt/c0s0n		No Rewind after I/O operation
/dev/rmt/c0s0r		Retension tape before I/O; rewind after I/O
/dev/rmt/c0s0nr		Retension tape before I/O; no rewind after I/O
/dev/rmt/f1q80	Floppy	Rewind after I/O operation
/dev/rmt/f1q80n		No rewind after I/O operation
/dev/rmt/f1q80r		Retension tape before I/O; rewind after I/O
/dev/rmt/f1q80nr		Retension tape before I/O; no rewind after I/O

Table 18-3.   Tape Device Files for SVR4 UNIX Systems

and to read these you will need to use that format. If you cannot read a disk in one format, try experimenting with other formats.

Thus, **f0q15dt** is a 1.2MB disk in drive 0, while **f13ht** is a 3 1/2-inch, 1.4MB floppy in drive 1. Usually disk drives that can use 1.2MB disks can also format and read 360K disks, but drives that are marked 360K cannot use 1.2MB disks. Similarly, 3 1/2-inch drives that can use 1.4MB disks can also use 720K floppies, but drives marked double-density cannot use 1.4MB floppies.

Hard disk devices follow the same basic organization, though a single hard disk will usually have several different *slices,* or independent file systems. Each slice has a raw and a block device file associated with it.

There are several naming schemes for these slices. The most commonly used is the form */dev/dsk/nsm* where *n* gives the disk number (**0** for the first hard disk, **1** for the second), and *m* gives the slice number within that disk. Table 18-2 lists these names for all the slices, although what slices exist on a specific system depends on the machine's configuration. All of the devices listed in Table 18-2 will not appear on most machines, because if you do not install a file system at configuration, its device (and its slice on the disk) will not appear in the **/dev/dsk** directory.

An alternative naming scheme, primarily used with SCSI disks, uses the form *c0t0d0s0,* where the *c0* refers to controller number **0** and the *t0* is target id **0** within that controller. The *d0* refers to the device number on that target id, and the *s0* refers to slice **0** on that device. The slice number, and the function of the file system on that slice, will correspond to the *s0* part of the name in Table 18-2. With this scheme, the name may not always include the *t0* part, so you may see file systems with the name **c0d0s3** or **c0t0d0s3**. A specific release of SVR4 will use only one of these naming schemes, not both.

Having presented this introduction, we can now discuss the use of these device files.

Formatting Floppy Disks

To format a disk manually, use the **format** command. This command takes the complete pathname of the device you wish to format as an argument. For example:

```
$ format /dev/rdsk/f0q15dt
```

A high-density diskette and a 1.2MB drive are required to use this format. Insert the disk into the drive, and close the drive door, before executing this command. Be sure that the write-protect tab on the side of the disk has been removed. The floppy will be formatted, erasing any data that is already on the disk.

The *raw* device (**/dev/rdsk/...**) is always used in formatting floppies, because formatting is a low-level operation that requires basic access to the disk below the file system level.

The **format** command will format the named disk type, and verify that the format is correct, as follows:

```
$ format /dev/rdsk/f0q15dt
formatting...............
Formatted 160 tracks: 0 thru 159, interleave 2.
$
```

Other diskette devices will sometimes give slightly different output from that produced by **format**, because the number of *tracks* on the disk may differ.

The **format** command will complain if a disk is defective or is not the right type, and the format operation will fail. If this occurs, verify that you are using the correct disk type, in the correct drive for the device filename you are using. If you cannot format a disk after two or three tries, discard the disk. Don't take chances with bad disks, because the data you could lose is always much more valuable than the diskette.

Once a disk is formatted, you don't have to reformat it unless the contents are damaged for some reason, or you wish to erase the disk completely. Part of the formatting operation is a verification step that will find bad blocks on the floppy and mark them as unusable. Occasionally you will find that a questionable disk can be improved by reformatting it, since the procedure creates a new bad block table on the floppy.

Making a File System on the Disk

After a disk is successfully formatted, you can use it for raw access, or you can make a file system on it. The **/sbin/mkfs** (for make file system) command will place a file system onto a newly formatted diskette. A file system is required to mount a disk.

When you create a file system, you must select the file system type. Use the **ufs** type unless you have some specific reason to select **s5**. The file system type must follow the **-F** (for file) option on the **mkfs** command line.

You must also specify the device file as an argument to **mkfs**, as follows:

```
$ mkfs -F ufs /dev/rdsk/f0q15dt 2400
```

Use the raw device for creating a file system on a floppy disk. Creating a file system erases the disk, because it reconstructs the table of directories and files.

Specifying File System Size

In addition to the device file, **mkfs** requires you to specify the number of 512-byte blocks to use for the file system. This number follows the device name in the **mkfs** command line. Normally you will use the entire disk, so you can compute the number of blocks from the disk size: 1.2MB divided by 512 bytes per block will give you 2400 blocks for a 5 1/4-inch high-density disk, as in the previous example. You can specify fewer blocks if you wish, but this will waste the disk space that is not in the file system. If you specify too many blocks, the **mkfs** operation will fail with an error.

The **mkfs** command reports on the values it is using in its creation operation, as shown here:

```
$ mkfs -F ufs /dev/rdsk/f13dt 1440
Warning: 18 sector(s) in last cylinder unallocated
/dev/rdsk/f13dt:   1440 sectors in 9 cylinders of 9 tracks, 18 sectors
        0.7Mb in 1 cyl groups (16 c/g, 1.33Mb/g, 256 i/g)
super-block backups (for fsck -b#) at:
 32,
$
```

The **mkfs** output will differ slightly if you choose to create an **s5** file system instead of a **ufs** file system.

Be sure to check the device name again as you enter it. You can destroy your hard disk or another file system and lose your valuable data if you mistakenly give the wrong device name.

Mounting a Floppy Disk

Once the disk is formatted and the file system has been created, you can *mount* the disk. Mounting a disk links its file system with the normal file system on the machine's hard disk. When a floppy disk (or any other file system) is mounted, you can **cd** into it, **cp** files to and from its directories, and use all the normal file system commands. In many systems superuser access is required to mount a floppy disk.

You can think of a file system as a part of a directory hierarchy that extends below a specific directory. Each file system has its own root directory, and all its subdirectories fan out from this root. When you mount a floppy disk, you are actually inserting the root directory of the floppy disk into a specific place in the normal file system. This place is called the *mount point,* and it is a normal directory in the hard disk file system. That is, you can create a directory on your hard disk, and mount the floppy at that point; then you can **cd** into the directory on the hard disk, and you will be in the root directory for the mounted file system. For example, most systems provide a default mount point at **/mnt** (for mount). Normally this directory is empty, as in this example:

```
$ ls /mnt
$
```

When you mount a floppy disk at that point, the root directory of the floppy disk becomes the contents of the **/mnt** directory, as shown here:

```
# mount -F ufs /dev/dsk/f13dt /mnt
# ls /mnt
data        sample
#
```

Note that you must specify the file system type with the **-F** option to the **mount** command.

If there are any files in the mount point directory before the floppy is mounted, those files will be hidden by the mount, and will not be visible until the mounted file system is unmounted. Although the files will not be lost or disturbed, it is best to use an empty directory as a mount point.

The mount point can be any directory location you choose within the file system, but usually a standard mount point is used. The directory **/mnt** is provided in SVR4 systems to mount floppy disks or tapes. Since you can only mount one file system at any mount point, you will need another standard mount point if you have more than one file system mounted, perhaps by two floppy disk drives. Create the directory **/mnt2** as the second mount point if it does not already exist in your root directory.

When you create the file system on the floppy with the administrative user agent, you can specify a *file system name* for **s5** file systems. If you do not mount the disk at this mount point, the **mount** command may give the error message

```
mount: warning: <fsname> mounted at <mount-point>
```

where *fsname* is the file system name and *mount-point* is the mount point. This is a friendly warning, and is not really an error.

While the disk is mounted, the UNIX system will follow normal procedures to keep the floppy disk up to date with any changes you make; in fact, it will act just like the hard disk in all ways (except speed!). The **mount** operation will add an entry to the system *mount table* in **/etc/mnttab**. The mount table is read by several system programs that work with mounted devices, such as **df**. However, no permanent record is made of which file systems are mounted, so if you reboot the machine while a floppy disk or tape is mounted, they will not be mounted after the reboot. Shutting down the machine while a floppy is mounted is only safe if the **shutdown** command is used. It is best to mount media only while they are in use, and to unmount them when you are through using them.

Using the mount Command

The **mount** command is used to mount a file system at a specific mount point. The device file to mount is given as the first argument, and the mount point is the second argument. Use the block device name, not the raw device, as shown here:

```
# mount -F ufs /dev/dsk/f0q15dt /mnt
```

This command will mount a 1.2MB floppy (drive 0) at **/mnt**. You cannot remove the diskette from the drive until it has been unmounted.

Once a device is mounted, you can **cd** to its directories through its mount point, and use it as a normal directory. Here is an example:

```
$ cd /mnt
$ ls -F
data      file1      file2
$
```

The mounted file system is writable as well as readable, so you must remove any write-protect tab from the disk before you mount it. The mount will fail if a disk is write-protected, unless you specify that the diskette be mounted *read-only*. This means that you can read the disk but cannot write to it. You should mount your precious archive disks read-only, to guarantee that they cannot be destroyed by mistake. Use the **-r** (for read) option with **mount** to mount a diskette as read-only. For example:

```
# mount -r -F ufs /dev/dsk/f0q15dt /mnt
```

You cannot write a file to, or change anything about a file system that was mounted as read-only.

While a diskette is mounted, the **df** command can report on its capacity, as follows:

```
# mount -F ufs /dev/dsk/f0q15dt /mnt
# df -t
/                  (/dev/root      ):   140248 blocks   63537 files
                           total:   294986 blocks   73632 files
/proc              (/proc          ):        0 blocks      73 files
                           total:        0 blocks     102 files
/dev/fd            (/dev/fd        ):        0 blocks       0 files
                           total:        0 blocks      66 files
/stand             (/dev/dsk/0s10  ):     7307 blocks      97 files
                           total:    10710 blocks     104 files
/mnt               (/dev/dsk/f0q15dt):    2356 blocks     285 files
                           total:     2400 blocks     288 files
#
```

This can help you track the use of space on your mountable media. The **du** command will also work as expected on directories in mounted file systems.

Unmounting a Diskette

When you are though using a mounted diskette or tape, you must unmount it before you can remove it from the drive. To do so, use the **umount** command, with the device file as argument, as shown here:

```
# umount /dev/dsk/f0q15dt
#
```

In SVR4 you can also use the mount point instead of the device file as an argument. For example:

```
# umount /mnt
#
```

These commands will remove the mounted file system, and you can then remove it from the drive. You must unmount the same device that you previously mounted. If the operation succeeds, **umount** returns silently to the shell.

If any user has an open file in the mounted file system, or has used **cd** to enter the file system, **umount** will fail. All the files and directories on the disk must be free before **umount** will work, as shown here:

```
# mount -F s5 /dev/dsk/f0q15dt /mnt
mount: warning: <> mounted as </mnt>
# cd /mnt
# umount /dev/dsk/f0q15dt
umount: /dev/dsk/f0q15dt busy
# cd /
# umount /dev/dsk/f0q15dt
#
```

All users must be "free" from a resource before it can be unmounted. Luckily, this protects you from unmounting your default hard disk!

Reporting on Mounted Media

You can give the **mount** command with no arguments. When used in this way, it will report on the devices that are currently mounted on the machine. Here is an example:

```
# mount
/ on /dev/root read/write/setuid on Sun Apr  8 09:53:41 1990
/proc on /proc read/write on Sun Apr  8 09:53:42 1990
/dev/fd on /dev/fd read/write on Sun Apr  8 09:53:42 1990
/stand on /dev/dsk/0s10 read/write on Sun Apr  8 09:53:43 1990
# mount -r -F ufs /dev/dsk/f0q15dt /mnt
# mount
/ on /dev/root read/write/setuid on Sun Apr  8 09:53:41 1990
/proc on /proc read/write on Sun Apr  8 09:53:42 1990
/dev/fd on /dev/fd read/write on Sun Apr  8 09:53:42 1990
/stand on /dev/dsk/0s10 read/write on Sun Apr  8 09:53:43 1990
/mnt on /dev/dsk/f0q15dt read only/setuid on Sun Apr  8 15:32:49 1990
# umount /mnt
# mount
/ on /dev/root read/write/setuid on Sun Apr  8 09:53:41 1990
/proc on /proc read/write on Sun Apr  8 09:53:42 1990
```

```
/dev/fd on /dev/fd read/write on Sun Apr  8 09:53:42 1990
/stand on /dev/dsk/0s10 read/write on Sun Apr  8 09:53:43 199
$
```

The report changes to *read/write* when the diskette is mounted without the **-r** option.

Copying Floppy Disks

The UNIX system provides two procedures for copying floppy disks. In both, you must format the new floppy disk before copying to it. You must also be sure that the disk you are copying *to* is as large or larger than the disk you are copying.

Manually Copying a Mounted Disk with cp

First, you can mount the floppy disk as described earlier, and copy all the files individually from it to a temporary directory on the hard disk. You can also use the **cp** command, perhaps in a shell script, to copy several files at once. Alternatively, you can use the **cpio -p** command, discussed at the end of this chapter.

Then, you must mount a new formatted floppy, with a file system, and copy the files from the temporary directory to the new disk using the same commands you used to create the temporary directory. If you have a second floppy drive you can then mount the new formatted floppy, with its file system, on the second drive (at a different mount point), and copy the files directly from the source to the target directory.

This procedure is tedious, and prone to errors. Take care to copy all the subdirectories and files whose names begin with a . (dot) correctly. In addition, this technique only works with mountable media. However, when you wish to delete or change the files during the move, this is the only procedure to follow.

The dd Command

Another command is available that makes an *exact* copy of a floppy disk, whether it is mountable or not. As usual, the new disk must already be formatted, and must be the same size and type as the original disk you are copying. However, you do not have to create a file system on the new disk; the copy procedure will do that as part of the exact copy.

The **dd** command is used to copy media exactly. By default, it copies its standard input to its standard output, so you can copy a file with this command line:

```
$ dd < in.file > out.file
```

If one of the files is a device, you can give the device pathname, as follows:

```
$ dd < /dev/rdsk/f0q15dt > /tmp/out.file
2400+0 records in
2400+0 records out
$
```

The **dd** command reports on the number of blocks it reads and writes. The number after the **+** is a count of partial blocks that were copied.

To copy a floppy disk, use **dd** to copy the disk device file into a temporary file, as in the previous example. Then replace the diskette with a new formatted floppy of the same type, and use **dd** again to copy the temporary file out to the disk, as shown here:

```
$ dd < /tmp/out.file >/dev/rdsk/f0q15dt
```

This procedure uses the raw device file to guarantee a complete, exact copy of the entire floppy disk. To finish the operation, delete the temporary file.

This procedure will work regardless of the floppy type or the number of files and directories on it, because the device as a whole is treated as a single large file. When the entire disk is copied, the end-of-file is read and the operation ends.

The dd Command Line

The **dd** command-line syntax differs significantly from most other commands. Options to **dd** are given as *keyword=value* pairs, where *keyword* is the option to set, and *value* is the value to use for that option. For example, you can give the input filename after the **if=** (for input file) option, and the output filename after the **of=** (for output file) option. These options, if present, will replace the standard input and output. For example:

```
$ dd if=/dev/rdsk/f0q15dt of=/tmp/out.file
```

By default, **dd** will make its copy by reading a 512-byte block, writing that block, reading another, and so on. This procedure can be slow, so options are provided to increase the block size. Changed block sizes should be multiples of 512 bytes for best performance. You can perform significantly faster operations by using a block size of 5120 bytes. Block size is specified with the **bs=** (for block size) option, as shown here:

```
$ dd bs=5120 </dev/rdsk/f0q15dt >/tmp/out.file
240+0 records in
240+0 records out
$
```

The block size is changed for both input and output operations, and the records copied counts will change, since the block size has changed. This is the most efficient form of the **dd** command for floppies (but try **bs=1024k** for copying magnetic tapes!).

You can also specify the block size separately for input and output operations. The **ibs=** (for input block size) and **obs=** (for output block size) options are used to set input and output block size, respectively. For example:

```
$ dd if=/dev/rdsk/f0q15dt ibs=5120 of=/tmp/out.file obs=51200
240+0 records in
24+0 records in
$
```

When **ibs** differs from **obs**, the counts of records in and records out will not match. This is relatively inefficient, because **dd** must construct the output blocks before writing them. If you are making a copy of a floppy, use the same block size for all four reads and writes, preferably with **bs=**.

In addition, **dd** provides conversion tools for changing data formats during the copy. The **conv=** (for convert) option specifies a conversion algorithm to use. Allowed are **ascii**, for conversion of files from EBCDIC to ASCII; **ebcdic**, for conversion from ASCII to EBCDIC;

lcase, for converting all characters in the copy to lowercase; and **ucase,** for converting all characters in the copy to uppercase. In addition, the **swab** option allows you to swap the order of each pair of bytes in the file. This option can be very useful when you are porting files from other machines that use a different byte-order for data than your machine does. Any of these options can be combined, providing they are separated by a , (comma), as shown here:

```
$ dd bs=5120 conv=ascii,swab < in.file > out.file
```

These conversion options can be very useful for file-to-file copies, but they are less useful for file to disk copies.

Finally, **dd** allows you to skip some blocks on the input or output before beginning the copy. The **skip**=n option is used to skip the first n blocks of the input file before copying, and the **seek**=n skips the first n blocks of the output file before beginning the output. Use these options with care, especially when you are writing, because they can easily destroy a file system if they are misused.

Raw Device Access—The cpio Command

The **mount** procedure allows the convenience of file system access to floppy disk and tape devices. However, mounting a diskette is relatively slow, and the standard file system takes space on the floppy that you might wish to use for your data. Furthermore, you cannot expand your files beyond the disk space available on the mounted disk. A complete file must fit onto the mounted disk; you cannot split files across multiple file systems.

To solve these problems, the UNIX system allows *raw* access to a diskette without mounting it. The **cpio** (for copy in/out) command provides this raw access. The **cpio** command is actually an archiving program that takes a list of files and copies those files into a single large output file, inserting headers between the individual files so they can be recovered. The **cpio** command has options that allow you to create archives, and other options that let you read the archives and reload the files in them. The program can be used to create archives directly on the machine's hard disk, but it is most often used to create archives on a floppy disk or tape.

Archives created with **cpio** can span multiple diskettes, allowing efficient backup of large directory hierarchies. In addition, **cpio** preserves file ownership and modification times, and can archive both text and binary files. Using **cpio** is the most efficient way to store files on a floppy disk, and a **cpio** archive is usually somewhat smaller than the original files that make up the archive. The system software and most other installable floppies are usually in **cpio** format.

Using Media for cpio Operations

Before you use **cpio** with a floppy disk or tape, you must format the media as usual. However, you can skip the **mkfs** step, because **cpio** will overwrite the file system as it creates its archive on the floppy. In fact, once you have used a diskette with **cpio**, you will need to create a new file system on the disk before you can mount it; **cpio** disks are not compatible with file system diskettes, and creating a file system with **mkfs** will destroy any data stored in **cpio** format.

You must use the raw device file for **cpio** operations, because **cpio** does not use the file system. Since **cpio** sends its archive to its standard output, you should use a command of this form when writing to a floppy disk:

```
$ echo filename | cpio -o > /dev/rdsk/f0q15dt
```

Before executing this or any other **cpio** command line, be sure that you have a formatted floppy disk in the correct drive with the drive door closed. The diskette must be write-enabled to allow output, but it can be write-protected for reading.

Creating cpio Archives

When creating an archive, **cpio** takes a list of files or pathnames on its standard input, and writes the archive on its standard output. This output is almost always redirected to a normal file or to a device file.

The filenames must be given one per line in the standard input stream. The **-o** (for output) option instructs **cpio** to create an archive from a list of files, as shown here:

```
$ echo "$HOME/myfile\n$HOME/yourfile" | cpio -o > output.file
```

The **ls** command is often used to archive a complete directory, as follows:

```
$ ls | cpio -o > output.file
```

You can also execute **cpio** with the filename list redirected from a file, like this:

```
$  cpio -o > output.file < file.list
```

This creates a single output file that contains all the files in the input list.

Several other command-line options are often used with **cpio -o**. The **-a** (for access) flag resets the file modification times associated with each file. By default, the original time stamps are preserved on all the files. The **-c** (for character) option causes **cpio** to produce its internal headers in character form instead of binary format. This is required for portability, and should be the default. Make a habit of using the **-c** option with all your **cpio** commands. Most **cpio** files you receive will also use it.

cpio Compatibility

In SVR4, the **cpio** command was changed in such a way that archives *created* with the SVR4 version of **cpio** may not be readable on older UNIX systems. To avoid this problem, and some others, **cpio** allows you to create archives in several different *header* formats in addition to the **-c** format. The **-H** (for header) option allows you to select several formats. For compatibility with older UNIX systems, use this command line, and omit the **-c** option:

```
$ cpio -o -H odc < file.list >output.archive
```

Also allowed after the **-H** option are **crc** for additional checksums, and **tar** for compatibility with the **tar** command discussed later in this chapter. When you use one of the -H options to create an archive, it may also be required to read the archive.

The **-B** (for block) option instructs **cpio** to create data blocks rather than a data stream. If the **cpio** file will reside on the machine's hard disk, or will be moved via **uucp,** the -B option is not required. However, if the archive will reside on a floppy disk or tape, the **-B** option should be used to speed disk access.

The **-v** (for verbose) option tells **cpio** to echo the names of all files as it reads them. This output comes to standard error.

By default, **cpio** does not follow symbolic links. This is usually desirable, because the targets of symbolic links will probably not exist when the archive is restored, and **cpio** will not create them. If you wish to include these files in your archives, add the **-L** (for link) option when you create the archives, and be sure the links exist when you restore the archives.

Using cpio

Frequently **cpio** is paired with the **find** command to generate archives. The **find** command will search a directory for files that meet its command-line arguments, and write the pathnames to its standard output. This output is piped to **cpio** for archiving, as follows:

```
$ cd
$ find . -print | cpio -oc >/tmp/home.cpio
113 blocks
$
```

The **cpio** command reports the number of blocks written if there are no errors. The previous example creates an archive containing all the files and subdirectories in your home directory, and leaves the archive in **/tmp/home.cpio.** You could write the output to a diskette by naming the correct device file instead, as shown here:

```
$ find . -print | cpio -ocvB >/dev/rdsk/f0q15dt
```

Of course, you can vary the **find** part of the command to change the filename list that is included in the archive. For example, to create a **cpio** file with only files that have changed within the last week, you would use

```
$ find . -mtime -7 -print | cpio -ocv > /tmp/home.cpio
```

Be sure to include the **-print** option on the **find** command line, or no names will be written to **cpio** for archiving.

If you wish, you can use **cpio** to archive a file that is already a **cpio** archive, and **cpio** will keep track of the levels correctly. However, you must not create an archive by redirecting the output into a file in the same directory you are archiving, because this will create an infinite loop and a very large archive! Although this command is "allowed" it will cause serious problems:

```
$ find . -print | cpio -oc > ./arch.cpio
```

Do you understand why this command is incorrect?

Reading a cpio Archive

The **cpio** command provides the **-i** (for in) option to read the archives produced by its **-o** option. The archive to be read is the standard input to **cpio**, which re-creates the files according to the pathnames given when the archive was created, as follows:

```
$ cpio -icv < /tmp/home.cpio
```

If the archive was created with relative pathnames, such as **find . -print**, the input files will be built as a directory tree within the current directory when the **cpio -i** command is executed. On the other hand, if the archive was created with absolute pathnames (beginning with /), the same absolute paths will be used to re-create the file. Using absolute pathnames can be dangerous, because you cannot easily move the input directory tree, and your **cpio -i** operation may attempt to overwrite the original files.

The **-c, -v, -B** and **-H** options have the same meaning for input as they do for output. If the archive was created using the **-c, -B** or **-H** options, you must use them when the archive is read back in, or the **cpio** command will fail, as in this example:

```
$ find . -print | cpio -o >/tmp/home.cpio
113 blocks
$ cpio -ic </tmp/home.cpio
cpio: ERROR: This is not a cpio file. Bad magic number.
$
```

If you don't know what **cpio** options were used when an archive was created, experiment with different combinations of **-c, -H** and **-B** until **cpio** reads the file correctly.

When you direct a **cpio** archive to a device, you must specify the correct raw device file according to the diskette format used. Similarly, when you read the archive back in, you must use the same device, as shown here:

```
$ find . -print | cpio -ocB >/dev/rdsk/f0q15dt
113 blocks
$ cpio -icB </dev/rdsk/f0q15dt
113 blocks
$
```

When a file is reloaded, its original permissions are retained. However, the owner and group of the file will be changed to your user id and group, unless you are logged in as a superuser, in which case the original owner and group will be retained. Since the user and group id are encoded, you should take care when you move files from one machine to another as a superuser, because the same user and group ids may belong to a different user on the new machine. After loading an archive with **cpio -i**, check the permissions with **ls -l** to be sure they are correct, and reset them if they are not. Things can get quite confused if user and group ids are incorrect, especially when you are moving important system files like **/etc/passwd!**

cpio Command-Line Options for Input

The **cpio** command provides many command-line options to control the reading of files from the archive. By default, it will not create directories needed to rebuild the pathnames of files in the archive. The **-d** (for directory) option forces **cpio** to create any necessary directories for files it is reading in. It looks like this:

```
$ cpio -icBd </dev/rdsk/f0q15dt
```

Existing directories will still be used, but if necessary **cpio** will make new directories to complete the specified path.

Similarly, **cpio** will not overwrite an existing file with the same name as a file read from the archive, unless the **-u** (for unconditional) option is given. This option should be used with great care, because the archive might contain a corrupt or out-of-date version. Usually, you will wish to create archives with relative pathnames, and then reload the archives into a temporary directory to avoid clashes with existing files.

You can also avoid this problem by using the **-r** (for rename) option. As **cpio** reads each file out of the archive, it will prompt you for a new name for the file, as shown here:

```
$ cpio -icBr </dev/rdsk/f0q15dt
Rename <data1>
```

You can enter a pathname if you wish, or if you enter newline the file will be skipped. Each file in the archive is prompted this way, so it can be tedious to reload a large archive.

The **-m** (for modification) option instructs **cpio** to retain the file modification time of the original file. By default, the file is created with the current time.

Displaying a Table of Contents for an Archive

You can examine the contents of a **cpio** archive without actually reloading it. Although this can save disk space, it is no faster than completely reloading the archive, because the entire archive must be processed. Use the **-t** (for table) option with **-i** to list the file names and other information. No files are created when **-t** is given. As usual, the **-c** and **-B** options must be correct to read the archive. Here is an example:

```
$ ls -l
total 155
-rw-r--r--    1 root     other         535 Apr  8 17:44 data1
-rw-r--r--    1 root     other        4282 Apr  8 17:45 data2
-rw-r--r--    1 root     other       68528 Apr  8 17:45 xx
$ find . -print | cpio -ocv >/tmp/arch.cpio
```

```
xx
data1
data2
152 blocks
$ cpio -ict </tmp/arch.cpio
.
xx
data1
data2
152 blocks
$ cpio -icvt </tmp/arch.cpio
drwxr-xr-x   2 root     other    0        Apr  8 17:45 1990, .
-rw-r--r--   1 root     other    535      Apr  8 17:44 1990, data1
-rw-r--r--   1 root     other    4282     Apr  8 17:45 1990, data2
-rw-r--r--   1 root     other    68528    Apr  8 17:45 1990, xx
$
```

The output will differ significantly if you use the **-v** option with **-t**; it will look more like the output from **ls -l**.

Selecting a Subset of Archived Files

Finally, you can instruct **cpio** to reload only a subset of the files in the archive by giving a *pattern* in the format of shell wildcard operators after the command-line flags. The **cpio** command will find all files whose names match the pattern, and reload only those files. The patterns should be enclosed in quotation marks to prevent the shell from expanding them before **cpio** sees them. For example:

```
$ cpio -icvB "*file" < /dev/rdsk/f0q15dt
```

This command will reload all files that have pathnames ending in the string *file* from the archive on the 1.2MB floppy disk.

Multiple patterns are allowed, but each must be surrounded by double quote marks, as shown here:

```
$ cpio -icvB "*file" "*[0-9]hello*" </dev/rdsk/f0q15dt
```

In addition to files with pathnames that end in *file,* this example will reload all files that include a digit 0 through 9 followed by *hello* anywhere in the pathname.

Archiving to a Floppy Disk or Tape

When you create a **cpio** archive to a diskette or tape, the archive can be larger than the capacity of the medium. The **cpio** command is smart enough to detect this condition, and will prompt you to replace the diskette with another formatted diskette. You can continue your archive onto two or even more diskettes this way.

When the first diskette is full, **cpio** will prompt you to replace it, as follows:

```
$ ls | cpio -ocB >/dev/rdsk/f0q15dt
Reached end cf medium on "output".
To continue, type device/file name when ready.
```

You must enter the full pathname of the device to use. Normally you will use the same device that you started with. In this case, replace the diskette with another of the same type, which has been correctly formatted. Then type the full pathname of the device file, and press newline; the **cpio** operation will continue. With this style of **cpio** prompt, you can switch device types in the middle. You can mix diskettes of different formats, switch between two drives, and so forth. However, you should usually keep the media format constant for an entire archive. If you do switch formats in the middle of a **cpio** operation, be sure that you carefully mark each diskette with its format.

In SVR4 systems you can use the **-O** (uppercase letter *o*) or **-I** (uppercase *i*) options, followed by the name of the device you are using. These options cause **cpio** to use the device named instead of the standard output or input, respectively. For example:

```
$ find . -print | cpio -ocvB -O /dev/rdsk/f0q15dt
```

This option has another effect as well: instead of prompting for the device name when the diskette is full, it causes **cpio** to produce a different prompt, as shown here:

```
$ find . -print | cpio -ocB -O /dev/rdsk/f0q15dt
Reached end of medium on "output".
Change to part 2 and press RETURN key. [q]
```

To continue, insert a formatted disk of the same type, and press new-line. You can repeat this step until the archive is complete. Be sure to mark and number the media correctly.

Similarly, when you read a **cpio** diskette, you must feed the media in the order it was written, replacing each disk with the next one as needed. You will be prompted to change disks, or for the device name as before:

```
$ cpio -icBd -I /dev/rdsk/f0q15dt
Reached end of medium on "input".
Change to part 2 and press RETURN key. [q]
```

Remember, you must match the devices and the order of diskettes used when the archive was created.

If you wish to stop the **cpio -i** operation in the middle, you can press **q** (for quit) at the prompt, and the operation will end, returning you to the shell. Files that have already been copied will be retained. It is difficult to begin reading in the middle of a sequence of floppies, however, so you should start from the first disk each time. Similarly, you can end your **cpio -o** operation in the middle, but you cannot restart output where you left off. In either case, there may be a partial file in the archive when the **cpio** operation does not complete normally.

Backing Up and Restoring Your Files

In addition to tools in the system administration user agent, several manual procedures are provided for backing up and restoring your files. The simplest uses the **cpio** (or **tar**) command, for which you name a list of files to archive, usually in a shell script. This is the most direct and efficient method for small "working" sets of files, an important consideration that encourages frequent backups. System administrators responsible for large systems or many users may choose to use the **backup** and **restore** commands, which allow *incremental* backups. These are the commands used in the **sysadm** user agent. Additional procedures are available with **ufs** file systems.

Backups Using cpio

Figure 18-1 shows a sample shell script that will back up a list of files and directories, including all the files in any subdirectories of the named directories. This script backs up files to a high-density diskette. You can edit the script to include the files and directories you wish to back up routinely, and to use tape or another medium instead of a 1.2MB diskette. The command needed to read the archive is given at the beginning of the script.

Many users maintain several scripts like that shown in Figure 18-1 to back up different areas of their work. The files in Figure 18-1 are a sample of system files that might be modified on a machine. Other scripts might back up an individual user's home directories or the databases for an application.

```
#! /sbin/sh
echo "Backing up key system files...."
echo "Restore with:  'cd / ; cpio -icvBdu -I /dev/rdsk/f0q15dt'"
echo "Insert formatted high-density floppy and hit return."
read DUMMY
cd /

find etc/passwd \
etc/shadow \
etc/inittab \
etc/ttytype \
etc/profile \
etc/uucp/Sys* \
etc/uucp/Permissions \
etc/uucp/D* \
etc/conf/pack.d/kd/space.c \
etc/conf/node.d/osm \
etc/default/login \
home/steve/lib \
sbin/cleanup \
etc/saf/ttymon/_pmtab \
usr/spool/cron/crontabs \
.olinitrc \
.olprograms \
.olsetup \
.Xdefaults \
.profile \
etc/conf/node.d/asy \
etc/conf/sdevice.d/asy \
.kshrc -print | cpio -ocvB -O /dev/rdsk/f0q15dt
```

Figure 18-1.   A sample shell script for backing up a list of files and directories

Backups Using backup and restore

The commands **backup** and **restore**, along with several support commands such as **bkhistory**, **bkoper** and **bkreg** are used within the system administration user agent to control system and *incremental* backups. Using tables of files and methods in the directory **/etc/bkup**, these commands allow development of comprehensive backup strategies and procedures, including exception lists of files to be skipped during routine backups. The user agent provides excellent access to these tools, but manual access is also allowed for custom backup procedures. To use these tools, consult their man pages and browse through the existing methods in **/etc/bkup**. If you use these tools manually, experiment with restoring the archives before you rely on them to preserve your valuable data.

Backups Using ufsdump

In addition to the procedures discussed so far, another incremental backup tool is available for **ufs** file systems. The **ufsdump** and **ufsrestore** commands allow regular dumps at different *dump levels*. This simply means that an individual backup at a given level will pick up all files in a file system that have changed since the last backup at a lower level. This procedure is often used by professional administrators of large systems, because it is comprehensive, easy to administer, and uses less tape or disk space for large backups. There is one caveat, however: with this procedure restoring the materials is more difficult than it is with the procedure discussed earlier. If you have only **ufs** file systems, and if you have experience with these tools from using BSD systems, you may find them helpful. Consult the **ufsdump(1)** and **ufsrestore(1)** man pages for additional information.

A Note on Backups

In general, it is better to perform several small backups than a single large one, because small backups are quicker and easier than large ones, and you will be less likely to neglect them. Even more important, if the first or second disk in a large multidisk **cpio** archive goes bad for some reason, the rest of the disks will be difficult to recover (see the section on damaged archives later in this chapter). Thus, maintaining several small archives will significantly improve the reliability of your backup procedure, and reduce the loss when a catastrophe occurs.

The most important rule in backing up data is do it *early* and *often*. You cannot back up your data too frequently! On busy days, consider making backups as often as hourly, but they should always be done at least daily. Inactive data need not be backed up as rigorously, but be sure you try to reload your backup media occasionally, because the disks might be writable but not readable. In this case, you can create the backup successfully, but you may not be able to read it. Also, keep in mind that floppy disks and tape *do* wear out after frequent use. A disk may stop being readable after it has been used for a few months.

On a multiuser machine where you do not have access to the backup facilities as often as you wish, you can sometimes copy your files to another file system on another physical disk. Thus, if one disk fails, your files are still protected. Consult with your system administrator to discuss procedures and security considerations.

System failures have an annoying tendency to occur only when you have not backed up recently, causing painful loss of data. Even if a failure never occurs, frequent backups will give you confidence that your valuable files are safe. Remember, the cost of creating the files and data is *always* much higher than the cost of the disks and time required to perform regular backups. A little "paranoia" in backing up your data can save months of work if a disaster does occur.

Care of Floppy Disks

Floppy disks are not immune from damage; magnetic fields are especially dangerous. Keep your diskettes well away from large electric motors, magnets of all sorts, and magnetized tools. Even a modern CRT display can cause problems if a disk is stored near it. In addition, you can destroy a diskette by heating it or freezing it. Don't leave media in the sun, or in a hot car. Keep diskettes in their paper envelopes, and store them in a clean, dust-free place. Naturally you should not spill food, liquids, or ashes on a diskette, and you should never remove a disk from its plastic cover.

Backup archives are usually stored at a site well away from the machine they are backing up. This prevents loss in case of a fire or other site-related disaster. Large corporations store their data in special environment-controlled vaults. Usually, this level of security is not necessary for smaller machines, but you should get into the habit of keeping backup data from your office machines at home, and vice versa.

Recovering Damaged Archives

If a backup archive is inadvertently damaged, it is still possible to recover *some* of the data on the disk. The SVR4 version of **cpio** includes the -k option for input, shown here:

```
$ cpio -icdkBI /dev/rdsk/f13ht
```

This option instructs **cpio** to attempt to skip damaged files and to ignore most I/O errors. Thus, if the damage is limited to a small portion of the disk (such as a bad block), you can usually recover the rest of the data on the disk, both before and after the error. The file or files that contain errors will be lost. This may not seem like much help, but older versions of **cpio** failed completely when a data error occurred.

Going Further

As you might expect, there are a great many more issues associated with media. The previous discussion focused primarily on diskettes, but many other types of media are used with UNIX systems. After disks, the most common medium is magnetic tape. Except for specific device pathnames associated with them, tape drives usually act just like disks; **cpio** and sometimes **mount** operations are associated with them.

Moving a Directory Hierarchy as a Unit

The **cpio** command also allows you to copy a list of files from one location in your file system to another. For this purpose, the **-p** (for pass) option is used with **cpio** instead of **-i** or **-o**. Rather than making an archive, this option just *passes* the files through the **cpio** command. This form of the command takes a path name as a target directory, rather than the redirected standard output that the other two **cpio** options use. For example:

```
$ ls | cpio -p /tmp/myfiles
```

As usual, **cpio -p** takes a list of files as its standard input. All the files in the current directory will be copied to the directory **/tmp/myfiles**, if it exists.

The **cpio -p** command also works with **find** to copy an entire directory hierarchy with one command line, as shown here:

```
$ find . -print | cpio -p /tmp/myfiles
```

This command differs from the previous one, because it moves the entire directory tree under the current directory.

The normal **cpio** options **-a**, **-d**, **-u**, **-v**, and **-m** can be used with **-p** to reset the file access times, create subdirectories as needed, overwrite existing files of the same name, display filenames as copied, and retain the original file time.

Note that the **cpio -p** command actually makes a copy of the files, so large directory structures can consume a lot of disk space. Where possible, use the **-l** (for link) option to instruct **cpio -p** to *link* the files rather than copying them. This can save significant disk space, assuming it's appropriate for your needs. Of course, you cannot link files across different file systems.

Creating Unusual File Systems

In addition to creating default **s5** and **ufs** file systems, **mkfs** can vary the number of inodes allowed in the file system, create special forms of interblock gap, allow you to select the number of blocks per disk cylinder, and establish other unusual configurations of file systems. This process can be quite arcane and difficult, especially when you are optimizing **ufs** file systems, so it will probably take several tries to get it right. Command-line options and allowed configurations differ between **s5** and **ufs** file systems; consult the **mkfs(1)** man page for more details.

For **s5** file systems, you can choose the number of inodes by adding the form :*n* after the block count, where *n* is the number of inodes to create. Here is an example:

```
# mkfs -F s5 /dev/rdsk/1s1 130000:30000
```

No whitespace is allowed before or after the colon.

You can also specify the interblock gap and the number of blocks per cylinder with additional command-line arguments. These parameters can improve the efficiency of disk I/O. Generally, they are only used with hard disks. After the *blocks:inodes* arguments, add the gap size and number of blocks per disk cylinder, as follows:

```
$ mkfs -F s5 /dev/rdsk/1s1 130000:30000 10 144
```

This will create a gap size of 10 and specify 144 blocks per cylinder. These values are optimal for a Micropolis 67MB hard disk. Consult the documentation for your disk to find the best values. In addition, you can specify a *prototype file* as an argument to **mkfs**. The prototype file gives the details of the file system you wish to specify. The prototype can contain names of directories to create on the file system, along with their permissions. See the **s5** man page for **mkfs** for details.

You can configure unusual **ufs** file systems using similar procedures. To do so, add a list of additional parameters after the device on the **mkfs** command line, as shown here:

```
# mkfs -F ufs /dev/rdsk/f0q15dt 18 9 4096
```

Consult the **ufs** version of the **mkfs** man page for more information.

Mounting a Second Hard Disk

Most small UNIX systems are supplied with a single hard disk, but probably you will eventually wish to expand your disk space. You can buy a larger hard disk to replace your original disk, or you can add a second hard disk to your machine. Be sure that the disk you buy is supported by the hard disk controller type you are using. Consult your hardware vendor to determine the correct disk and cables, and install the cables carefully on the controller card.

Many systems allow you to configure a second hard disk from the administrative user agent. If your system has this feature, you should use it, because hard disk configuration can be complex. Otherwise, look for the command **/sbin/diskadd**, a shell script provided by many systems that prompts you through the configuration procedure. Usually these procedures let you configure *either* an SCSI disk or a "fixed address" disk; however, command-line options may vary depending on which type you elect to install.

You can also use manual procedures to add a second disk. After installing the disk, run the command

```
# fdisk /dev/rdsk/1s0
```

to create a UNIX system partition on the disk. Then use the command **edvtoc** (for edit volume table of contents) to create disk slices for the UNIX system. Consult Table 18-2 for disk partition information. The **edvtoc** command replaces the older **mkpart** previously used for creating disk partitions. In addition, you can use the command **prtvtoc** (for print VTOC) to display the disk partitions for existing disks.

After the partitions have been created, you can use

```
# mkfs -F ufs /dev/rdsk/1s1
```

to create a file system on the first partition. Finally, mount the partitions as discussed in the following section. These are error-prone procedures that can permanently destroy data on disk, but they do allow full manual access to the disk and its partitions.

In every case, be sure you have carefully backed up the material on the first hard disk before you install the second one. Many gremlins inhabit this area of system configuration, and sometimes the contents of the first disk will be lost during the installation process, even when you use the administrative user agent.

Permanently Mounting a File System

The file **/etc/vfstab** contains a list of file systems that are mounted when the system is booted. These include both locally mounted resources, such as disk partitions, and remotely mounted resources from networks (see Chapter 24 for more information on remote mounts). Here is a sample listing:

```
# cat /etc/vfstab
/dev/root          /dev/rroot          /        ufs  1  yes  -
/dev/dsk/c0t0d0sa  /dev/rdsk/c0t0d0sa  /stand   bfs  1  yes  -
/proc              -                   /proc    proc -  no   -
/dev/fd            -                   /dev/fd  fdfs -  no   -
/dev/dsk/f0t       /dev/rdsk/f0t       /install s5   -  no   -
/dev/dsk/f1t       /dev/rdsk/f1t       /install s5   -  no   -
/dev/dsk/f0        /dev/rdsk/f0        /install s5   -  no   -
/dev/dsk/f1        /dev/rdsk/f1        /install s5   -  no   -
#
```

The fields for each line are the block device, the raw device, the file system location (mount point), the file system type, and a flag that indicates whether the file system should be automatically checked at boot time (1). The final two fields contain flags for indicating whether the file system should be mounted by the **mountall** command (**yes**), and for additional mount options that are used for remote mounts.

You can add new devices to the **/etc/vfstab** file when you wish to mount a device automatically. For example, this line might be added to mount a second hard disk at **/usr/src**:

```
/dev/dsk/1s1  /dev/rdsk/1s1 /usr/src  ufs  1    yes    -
```

Note the distinction between the **/etc/vfstab** and **/etc/mnttab** files. The **vfstab** file defines permanently mounted devices that are set up at boot time, while the **mnttab** lists *currently* mounted devices after a series of **mount** and **umount** commands. Manually changing the **mnttab** file will have no effect on the system, but changes made to **vfstab** will take effect on the next reboot.

File System Checking

The **/sbin/fsck** (for file system check) command is provided to check the correctness of a file system, and repair it if necessary. This is a complex tool that can damage a file system if it is used incorrectly, but can also save some of the data on a damaged disk. Only the superuser can use the **fsck** command. It is most often used to repair a hard disk after a system failure, as discussed in Chapter 21; however, it is also helpful to repair a mountable floppy disk or tape.

If you suspect that a floppy disk with a file system is damaged, you may be able to salvage some of its files with **fsck**. This command does not work on **cpio** archives, only on mountable media. If possible, you should always copy a diskette with the **dd** command before you use **fsck** on it. Some data will *always* be lost in repairing an inconsistent file system, but **fsck** does a good job of reducing your losses.

The **fsck** command takes a raw device name as argument, and checks that file system. It looks like this:

```
# fsck /dev/rdsk/f0q15dt
```

You can see some typical output from **fsck** in Figure 21-5.

Any incorrect "pieces" of files **fsck** finds are linked into the corrected file system in the directory **lost+found** below the root directory of the file system that is being checked. You can browse through these files after **fsck** completes to see if any of them are of value.

By default, **fsck** is an interactive tool that prompts for confirmation before making changes to the named file system. The **-y** (for yes) command-line option instructs **fsck** to answer all its questions itself, choosing good answers. This option is recommended, because the built-in **fsck** rules can usually provide better answers than most users can. The **-n** (for no) option instructs **fsck** to check the file system, without making changes. This option can be used to test the correctness of write-protected media.

Although **fsck** has many other options, they should not be used in most situations. Experiment with these additional options on a file system that you don't mind losing!

Magnetic Tape

The previous discussion has used the term *media* to refer to both diskettes and magnetic tape. Generally this is accurate, since some magnetic tape controllers can support tapes with file systems, and these *floppy tapes* can be mounted just as a disk can. The only difference will be in the names of the device files used for the tape drive.

However, some tape units do not support mounting, and these *streaming tapes* can only be used as raw devices. The manufacturer of the tape drive will include this information in the user's manual for the drive, and you must use the mode of access defined there. The standard SVR4 release supports a quarter-inch streaming cartridge in QIC format, and also a high-capacity SCSI-based DAT tape format. QIC-format tape capacities can differ; 60MB (QIC-24) and 150MB (QIC-150) are the most common for SVR4 systems. Higher capacity tape units may be unable to write at a lower capacity. If you wish to share data, consult your vendor to be sure that your tape unit is compatible with the other units involved.

Table 18-3 is a table of device names for the different functions supported on SVR4 tape units. If you are using the entire tape for a single archive, you will wish to use the *rewinding* device to reposition the tape to the beginning after the I/O operation completes. On the other hand, you can add a second or additional archives after the first one if you use the *no-rewind* device, which leaves the tape positioned at the end of an existing archive. To recover this second archive, you must position the tape correctly at the second "file" using the **tapecntl** command discussed in the next section. Then you can read multiple files in sequence using the no-rewind device name. Before the last operation on a tape, switch to the rewinding device so that the tape will be correctly positioned at the beginning before you remove it. Unfortunately, you cannot remove and then later replace a tape that is not at the beginning, because the tape controller automatically rewinds each tape when it is inserted.

If you find that tape operations fail with I/O errors, try using the *retensioning* device, which spins the tape to the end and back to the beginning before starting an I/O operation. This may cause the tape to run more smoothly across the read and record heads.

With streaming tape units, you can use **cpio** to create and read tape archives just as you can with a floppy disk. For example:

```
$ find . -print | cpio -ocvB >/dev/rmt/c0s0
```

For large archives, this can be a painfully slow process, but you can increase the *block size* **cpio** uses, as follows:

```
$ find . -print | cpio -ocv -C 1024000 >/dev/rmt/c0s0
```

The **-C** option replaces the **-B** option to specify a block size in bytes. Using 1MB blocks, as in this example, the transfer will go very quickly. Be sure you use the same block size to read the archive that you used to create it.

If you have a floppy tape drive in your system, you can use the device files in Table 18-3 to control it at the raw device level. Floppy tapes can also act like floppy disks; in fact the most common form of floppy tape uses the **f1** entries in **/dev/dsk** and **/dev/rdsk**. You can use all the file-system related commands with the tape unit, as discussed earlier. To use a floppy tape, you must first format the tape and place a file system on it.

The tapecntl Command

The command **tapecntl** is often available to retension or reposition tapes. The **tapecntl** command does not read or write a tape; it only positions the tape for normal read or write operations. Use the **-w** (for wind) option to rewind a tape, as shown here:

```
# tapecntl -w
```

The **-r** (for reset) option reinitializes the tape drive, rewinding the tape in the process. You can retension the tape with the **-t** (for tension) option, and you can completely erase an old tape by using the **-e** (for erase) option, as follows:

```
# tapecntl -e
```

Obviously, you should always use the **-e** option with care.

The **tapecntl** command is also used to *reposition* a tape to a specific archive or "file" on the tape. If you count the files on the tape from one to the end of the tape, you can read file number *n* with this procedure:

```
# tapecntl -w
# tapecntl -p n
# dd if=/dev/rmt/c0s0 of=/tmp/infile bs=1024k
#
```

The **-p** option takes a file number following it, and the **tapecntl** command will position the tape at the beginning of that file; then you can read that file (or write it) with **dd**, **cpio**, or **tar**. To continue reading the file directly following the file you just read, use the no-rewind device in your read command.

Note that if you write any file on a multifile tape except the last one, all the subsequent files will be lost. Thus, you must be extremely careful when you are writing tapes that contain multiple files.

The tar Command

In addition to **cpio**, the **tar** (for tape archive) program is also available. The **tar** command originated in the BSD release, and was designed primarily for archiving to nine-track tape reels. However, **tar** is frequently used to store archives on diskette or cassette tape, and many older systems support **tar** instead of **cpio**. While **cpio** does not let you *replace* a file in an archive with a newer version of the file, without completely recreating the archive, **tar** allows you to *add* new files to the end of an existing archive, and to replace files in the archive. You implement replacement in **tar** by writing the new file at the end of the archive. Then, when files are reloaded from the archive, the last file will overwrite all other files with the same name.

The **tar** program is a little more difficult to use than **cpio** because you must manage the archive on the media yourself. That is, if you create an archive with three versions of a file, you must take care that the last version is always the one you want, because **tar** cannot easily extract any but the last occurrence of a file. Of course, in backups the last version is usually the one you want, since it is the most recent version.

The **tar** command is noticeably slower in operation than **cpio**; however, **tar** can use either the raw device or the block device for its archives, and the raw device is significantly faster. Finally, **tar** cannot overflow onto a second disk when the first one fills up, so its archives are limited to the maximum size of your media.

The tar Command Line

The **tar** command takes a filename following **-f** (for file) as its major argument, and this is treated as the name of the archive to create. It can be a normal file or a device file. Arguments following the archive name are treated as filenames to archive. Unlike **cpio**, **tar** will automatically take all subdirectories of named directories. For example, this command will archive the directory trees **/home/steve** and **/usr/src**, with all their subdirectories, to a high-density floppy:

```
$ cd /
$ tar -cf /dev/rdsk/f0q15dt home/steve usr/src
```

If - (minus) is used as the archive name, **tar** will use standard I/O, so redirection is allowed.

The **tar** command can create, read, and update an archive. The options **-c** (for create), **-x** (for extract), and **-r** (for replace), respectively, control these operations. To create a new archive, use the **-c** option, along with **-f** and the archive device and input files. The preceding example will destroy the previous contents of the archive. If successful, **tar** will return silently. Like **cpio**, **tar** stores the pathname used when the archive was created. Thus, you should take care when you use absolute pathnames, because when you *extract* files from the archive, they may overwrite existing files. It is usually better to use only relative pathnames in your **tar** command lines.

To reload the archive, use the **-x** (for extract) option, and give the name of the archive you wish to reload, as shown here:

```
$ tar -xf /dev/rdsk/f0q15dt
Tar: blocksize = 20
$
```

This procedure will reload the archive into the current directory, providing the archive was created without full pathnames as in the previous example. Note that **tar** reports the block size in use when the archive was created.

If used with a list of filenames following the archive name, **tar -x** will reload only the named files. For example:

```
$ tar -xf /dev/rdsk/f0q15dt usr/src/steve/bsplit.c
```

Be sure to use the exact pathname that was used to create the archive.

Use the **-r** option as follows to replace a file in an archive, or to add new files to an archive, without destroying the existing archive:

```
$ tar -rf /dev/rdsk/f0q15dt usr/src/steve/bsplit.c
```

The **-x** option will find the newest version of a file when more than one verison is present in the archive.

You can display a table of contents for an archive with the **-t** (for table) option, as shown here:

```
$ tar -ft /dev/rdsk/f0q15dt
home/steve/data1
home/steve/data2
home/steve/cpio.out
usr/src/bsplit.c
usr/src/bsplit
$
```

The **-v** (for verbose) option produces a list of files written or read from the archive. Used with the **-t** option, it produces a table of contents similar to the output of **ls -l**.

Finally, the **-w** (for what) option instructs **tar** to prompt the user before taking any action. If you respond **y** to the prompt, the action is taken. If you enter any other character, the action is skipped and **tar** continues. The option looks like this:

```
$ tar -fxw /dev/rdsk/f0q15dt usr/src/bsplit.c
x usr/src/bsplit.c:
```

The **x** at the beginning of the prompt tells you that **tar** wants to extract the named file from the archive. You can retrieve an older version of a file with the **-w** option by accepting the version you want, and rejecting the later versions.

Mounting Your Hard Disk from a Bootable Floppy

Occasionally you may wish to boot your machine from a floppy disk. This might be required, for example, if you forget the root password on the machine. You can boot the machine off a floppy disk, mount the file system on the hard disk, and then edit the **/etc/passwd** or **/etc/shadow** file to remove the root password. After that, you can reboot from the hard disk, and log in without difficulty. The floppy boot procedure is discussed in Chapter 21.

Once the machine is running from the floppy (or a RAM disk), you can mount the default hard disk and examine or repair it. To do so, use this command:

```
# mount /dev/dsk/0s1 /mnt
```

Here, you are mounting the root file system of the hard disk onto a mount point on the floppy. All the files in this partition will be available for use. To access files in other file systems, consult Table 18-2 for the correct device name.

Quotas

The **ufs** file system type allows you to establish disk usage *quotas* for individual users. Unlike **ulimit** which controls the size of each *individual* file, quotas limit a user to a maximum disk usage for *all* their files within a file system. Quotas are not available for **s5** file systems, and these commands are restricted to the superuser.

You enable the quota system with the **quotaon** command, which takes a list of **ufs** file system names as arguments. You can also use **-a** to select all **ufs** file systems, as shown here:

```
# quotaon -v -a
```

The **-v** option reports on each file system as it takes action. Use **quotaoff** with the same arguments to turn off quota management.

To enable quotas for each user, you must create a file named **quotas** in the top-level directory of each file system on the machine. Then you can use the **edquota** (for edit quotas) command to create correctly formatted quota data in the file, as follows:

```
# > /quotas
# edquota steve
```

The **edquota** command is needed to convert the binary **quotas** file for each file system to a format that humans can read. The **edquota** command uses the **EDITOR** variable to select the editor it will use, and edits once for each user specified on its command line. Thus, you will have fewer errors if you use **edquota** for only one user per invocation.

For each file system on the machine that has a **quotas** file, one line will appear in the editing session, as shown here:

```
fs /mnt blocks (soft = 0, hard = 0) inodes (soft = 0, hard = 0)
fs / blocks (soft = 0, hard = 0) inodes (soft = 0, hard = 0)
```

This example specifies the file system name first, and then lists the resources in that file system that are subject to quotas for the user in question. For each file system you wish to control, change the *0* to a block or inode count. The *0* is a special value that selects unlimited space; be sure you set it to your desired value.

When quotas are enabled, the user will be prohibited from using more resources than you have specified, as this example demonstrates:

```
$ cp /etc/profile ./myfile
cp: cannot create ./myfile
cp: Permission denied
$
```

You can get a report of disk space usage with respect to the quotas with the **quota** command, which takes a user id as an argument. For example:

```
# quota -v steve
Disk quotas for steve (uid 104):
Filesystem  usage quota limit timeleft  files quota limit timeleft
/              86   100   100              14    0     0
/mnt            0     2     2               0    2     2
$
```

This command is often used in a regularly scheduled report to examine users' disk activity. The -v option gives a verbose report like the one just shown.

Finally, the **repquota** command will report on the disk usage and quotas of individual users, and **quotacheck** will verify the consistency of the quota system.

# NINETEEN

Using MS-DOS with the UNIX System

**N
I
N
E
T
E
E
N**

One of the most interesting innovations in the UNIX system in recent years has been the ability to use the MS-DOS operating system on UNIX machines. That is, machines based on the Intel 80386 and 80486 CPU chips are intrinsically able to execute these operating systems independently; however, most releases of the UNIX system for these machines will also allow you to execute MS-DOS *while* the UNIX system is running.

Versions of the UNIX system that run on other hardware architectures often support *coprocessor* boards that contain MS-DOS compatible microprocessors. Still other implementations provide *software emulation* environments that look like 80x86 processors to applications, but run on the machine's native processors.

These features, in whatever form they exist, allow your machine to *share* its resources between two operating systems that are running simultaneously. You can start an MS-DOS session from the UNIX shell, or in a *virtual console* within the UNIX system. While MS-DOS is running, you can jump to the UNIX system at any time, and execute commands as usual, by switching to another virtual console; then you can switch back to the MS-DOS session and continue under that operating system. When you are through using MS-DOS, you can kill that process and return your machine to the normal UNIX system. This *merged* MS-DOS process uses the same file system as the UNIX system, so you can easily share files and directories between the two operating systems, and run both MS-DOS and UNIX commands in the same session.

In some releases, especially those for 80386 and 80486 machines, it is possible to execute *multiple* MS-DOS sessions on the machine at the same time. You may also be able to execute MS-DOS sessions in multiple windows under the X Window System. However, only one of these sessions at a time will be able to access hardware devices, such as the diskette drives. Other releases, especially those based on software emulation, limit you to running *one* instance of MS-DOS on the machine at any time.

In addition to the Merge feature, nearly all SVR4 releases provide file system tools that allow you to read or write MS-DOS floppy disks directly into the UNIX system. If your machine has an MS-DOS compatible floppy disk drive, you can probably move files between the MS-DOS and UNIX systems. If there is a standalone MS-DOS partition on your machine's hard disk, you can also copy files between that partition and your UNIX system partition.

The DOS-under-UNIX feature is usually an extra-cost add-on to SVR4, especially when a coprocessor board is required. It may also demand more system RAM and faster CPU performance than you need to run the UNIX system alone. On the other hand, most SVR4 releases have the ability to read and write MS-DOS diskettes; thus, if you need access to MS-DOS disks but do not need to run MS-DOS applications, you may not need a Merge package or the additional hardware it entails.

Using MS-DOS Disks

If you do not need to run MS-DOS applications, you can read and write MS-DOS media directly with the SVR4 UNIX system. Thus, you can move data between the two operating systems without purchasing the add-on Merge package. Some releases of SVR4 will also allow you to mount MS-DOS media directly into the UNIX file system. To use this feature, your machine must have a disk drive that is capable of accessing MS-DOS diskettes. Usually common 1.2MB 5 1/4-inch drives and 1.4MB 3 1/2-inch drives have this capability, but other types of drives may not.

Several commands are provided to access MS-DOS file systems, as this example shows:

```
$ ls /usr/bin/dos*
/usr/bin/doscat
/usr/bin/doscp
/usr/bin/dosdir
/usr/bin/dosformat
/usr/bin/dosls
/usr/bin/dosmkdir
/usr/bin/dosrm
/usr/bin/dosrmdir
$
```

These commands perform as you would expect. For example, **doscp** works like the **cp** command to copy files between the MS-DOS and UNIX file systems, and **dosformat** formats an MS-DOS disk. In some versions of SVR4, these MS-DOS access commands may be included in the *Xenix Compatibility Package,* so you may need to add that package to get them.

Each command can take an MS-DOS drive designator such as **a:** or **b:** to specify the target of the action. For example, you can format an MS-DOS diskette with

```
$ dosformat a:
Insert new diskette for /dev/rdsk/f0t
and press <RETURN> when ready

Formatting...Format complete

   1213952 bytes total disk space
   1213952 bytes available on disk
$
```

In this example, drive **a:** is a 1.2MB, 5 1/4-inch drive. If you add the **-v** (for volume) option, **dosformat** will prompt you for a volume label to give the newly formatted diskette.

The **doscp** command, shown here, will copy a file between the UNIX and MS-DOS file systems:

```
$ doscp /etc/profile a:
```

You can also copy from a filename on the MS-DOS disk, as follows:

```
$ doscp a:/profile /tmp/file
```

With these commands, you use the UNIX style of directory naming, which separates the path elements with a **/** (slash), rather than the MS-DOS style, which uses a **** (backslash), for your file names on the MS-DOS disk. Also note that files created on the MS-DOS media must follow the rules for MS-DOS filenames: they can have up to eight characters followed by a dot and no more than three characters as an extension. If you exceed these limits, **doscp** will truncate the filename. All legal MS-DOS filenames are also legal under the UNIX system.

The **dosdir** and **dosls** commands report the contents of the MS-DOS disk. The output of **dosdir** looks like this:

```
$  dosdir a:
 Volume in drive A:  has no label
 Directory of  A:

PROFILE            1092  6-23-90  12:51a
          1 File(s)   1212416  Bytes free
$
```

The **dosls** command reports the result in a form similar to that produced by the **ls** command.

The commands **dosmkdir** and **dosrmdir** act like the normal MS-DOS commands **mkdir** and **rmdir** to create and delete directories on the MS-DOS disk. They take a directory name as argument. For example:

```
$ dosmkdir a:/subdir
```

Again, use the **/** in your pathnames on the MS-DOS disk. Similarly, the **dosrm** command, shown here, will delete a file from the MS-DOS disk:

```
$ dosrm a:profile
```

Finally, you can use **doscat** to write files from the MS-DOS disk to standard output without copying them.

As you would expect, these commands work with floppy drives **a:** and **b:**, but they also work on standalone MS-DOS partitions on the hard disk. That is, if you have configured your machine with an MS-DOS partition as well as a UNIX partition, you can use these tools to work with files on the MS-DOS partition. The hard disk partition devoted to MS-DOS is visible in the UNIX system as **/dev/dsk/0s5** or as **/dev/dsk/dos**. This partition is usually known as drive **d:** to these "DOS" commands. Thus, you can copy files between the UNIX system and the standalone MS-DOS partition just by using drive **d:** in your command. To see your MS-DOS partition, try

```
$ dosdir d:
```

You cannot directly execute MS-DOS commands from any of these drives, but you can perform file system operations from them.

The mapping between the MS-DOS drive letters and the UNIX file system location is kept in the file **/etc/default/msdos**. You can change the meaning of the MS-DOS drives or add new drive letters by editing this file.

Mounting MS-DOS Disks

In addition to these "direct" access commands, some releases of SVR4 allow you to mount MS-DOS file systems into your UNIX file system. Then you can use **cd** to move around in the directories and access the MS-DOS files with normal UNIX commands. The command

```
# mount -F dos /dev/dsk/f0t /mnt
```

may work to mount floppy disk **a:** at the **/mnt** mount point. Use **/dev/dsk/0s5** to mount the standalone MS-DOS partition on your hard disk.

If your system has the ability to mount MS-DOS disks, the mount will succeed. Once a disk has been mounted, you still will not be able to execute MS-DOS commands directly in the mounted partition, but you will be able to move and copy files. The mounted directory will follow UNIX system file manipulation rules, and you will not need the "DOS" commands discussed previously.

Converting Files

Due to conventions for ending text lines, the format of disk files differs between the MS-DOS and UNIX systems. Although the differences are most noticeable with text files, binary files and executable programs may also differ. Binary files that contain text lines, such as some word processor document files, may also cause problems.

In the UNIX system, each text line ends with the *newline* character, which is actually the ASCII character CTRL-J, or *linefeed;* however, under MS-DOS, each line ends with the carriage return and linefeed pair, or CTRL-M followed by CTRL-J. Thus, when you edit an MS-DOS file under the UNIX system, you will see a spurious CTRL-M at the end of each line. Similarly, when you use an MS-DOS command such as **type** to examine a file created under the UNIX system, each line will end with a linefeed but the next line will not begin at the left margin. For example, this UNIX system file

```
$ cat data
123 456 789
987 654 321
hello goodbye
$
```

might look like this under MS-DOS:

```
C> TYPE DATA
123 456 789
          987 654 321
                    hello goodbye
C>
```

In this example, each line in the file went to a new display line, but because of the missing carriage return, the cursor did not return to the left margin.

The "DOS" commands discussed earlier will automatically make the required conversions when a file is copied between file system formats (in either direction). Similarly, mounted files will be converted as needed. Both of these operations will take place automatically, so differences in the format of text files will not usually be a problem. However, executable programs or database files may not be converted as you expect; you must experiment with unusual file formats to make certain they are copied correctly.

To force a file to be copied without conversions, you can add the **-f** (for force) option to the commands **doscat** and **doscp**, as shown here:

```
$ doscp -f /tmp/myfile a:
```

This command will make an exact copy of the specified file.

A Note on Merge Packages

To go beyond disk access and execute MS-DOS applications under the UNIX system, you need to install the Merge package available as an add-on for many versions of SVR4. With this package, you can execute Version 3.x of the MS-DOS system. Some Merge packages specify a particular release of MS-DOS, often 3.3. You cannot use Version 4 of MS-DOS or the OS/2 system with a Merge package; however, almost all MS-DOS applications, including memory-resident TSR programs, communications applications, and mouse and screen intensive applications, will run correctly. The Merge package should provide a complete MS-DOS environment.

Merge capabilities have been independently marketed by several vendors, who have customized and adapted these features for specific machines. Thus, there are noticeable differences between implementations. Each implementation of the Merge feature looks a little different to the user, and wide differences in the configuration of the MS-DOS session are possible.

In this chapter we will focus on implementations that allow MS-DOS to share a CPU with the UNIX system. These implementations are primarily for 80x86 machines, although some software emulation environments also share the CPU with the UNIX system. Versions supported on coprocessor boards may look quite different.

In this chapter we can only survey the major features and pitfalls of a typical Merge subsystem. Much of the information presented here is drawn from the Locus DOS Merge package for the 80x86, which is sold with many SVR4 releases. However, most of the concepts and procedures discussed will apply to all versions of MS-DOS under the UNIX system. Consult the documentation specific to your Merge package for more information.

These "true" MS-DOS capabilities are simple in concept, but difficult in implementation. Simply put, a process is provided that gives MS-DOS an environment in which to work, in which MS-DOS applications believe they have complete control of the machine. The interface between this process and the underlying hardware is through a special *linkage,* or *bridge,* layer of software, which usually guarantees that the two systems will not experience any contention for resources.

Starting and Stopping MS-DOS

To use MS-DOS applications, you must first start the MS-DOS control process, which gives you access to its shell, the normal MS-DOS **command.com.** Then you can execute MS-DOS programs as you would on a standalone MS-DOS system. When you are through, you can stop the MS-DOS process and return to the UNIX system.

From the shell, you can start an MS-DOS process with

```
$ dos
```

The **dos** command is a UNIX system command that links to the MS-DOS system; although it executes under the UNIX system, the result of its action is an MS-DOS session that is a normal task within the UNIX system.

Following some banner material and copyright notices, the **command.com** prompt will appear, as follows:

```
$ dos
  .
  .
  .
C>
```

(The banner material is omitted in this example.)

The entire MS-DOS system is available from the C> prompt, and you can now execute almost any MS-DOS command or application.

The MS-DOS Startup Files

When the MS-DOS session starts, it will read your **config.sys** and **autoexec.bat** files, and initialize your MS-DOS session just as if you had booted a standalone MS-DOS system. Thus, you can use the *profile* features of **autoexec.bat** to set up your preferred environment within the MS-DOS session. Consult the MS-DOS documentation for more information on starting MS-DOS. You can include MS-DOS *device drivers* such as **ansi.sys** or TSR applications in your **config.sys** as desired. These configuration changes are local to your MS-DOS sessions, and will not affect any sessions in progress under the UNIX system.

Usually the files **config.sys** and **autoexec.bat** in the **/** (root) directory are executed first, followed by files of the same name in your home directory. Thus, there are two sources of profile material used when the MS-DOS session starts. Device drivers that are specified in the **config.sys** file, such as **ansi.sys**, can reside in any directory under the UNIX system, but you should give the full pathname in the **device =** line in your **config.sys** files. Use normal MS-DOS system path naming rules when you create your **config.sys** file. For example:

```
$ cat config.sys
device=c:\usr\dbin\ansi.sys
device=c:\usr\lib\merge\mouse.sys
device=c:\usr\lib\merge\emm.sys D000 208
$
```

Take care when you change the **config.sys** files, because some devices are required for the correct operation of the Merge session. Do not delete or change the **config.sys** entries that were installed when the Merge package was loaded.

Ending the MS-DOS Session

To kill the MS-DOS session and return to the shell, use the **quit** command at the MS-DOS prompt, as follows:

```
C> QUIT
$
```

Unlike the shell, you cannot end an MS-DOS session with CTRL-D, CTRL-C, or CTRL-BREAK, because these keys are not treated the same by MS-DOS as they are by the UNIX system. In many implementations of the Merge feature, you can end an MS-DOS session by entering the three-key combination CTRL-ALT-DEL (hold down the CTRL and ALT keys, and then press the DEL key). This combination may not work with all implementations of the Merge feature, so you should experiment on your machine.

Background Execution of MS-DOS

Two procedures, supported in different versions of the Merge feature, allow you to switch between MS-DOS and UNIX sessions. The simplest of the two uses the *virtual console* service. After you start the virtual console feature with the **vtlmgr** command, you can access multiple sessions from *hot keys*—usually the sequence ALT-SYSREQ followed by a function key (usually F1 through F8). You activate this sequence by holding down the ALT key, pressing the SYSREQ key, and then pressing the desired function key to select one of the sessions. Some merge releases use the key sequence CTRL-ALT-SYSREQ followed by the desired function key, while others may have a special key marked "window" to replace the multikey combination (different OS sessions are called windows, even though they take the full screen). Each function key will start a new shell session in a separate window, or you can execute the command **newvt** to start a new session in a new window. You can switch between sessions by pressing the hot key sequence followed by a function key. This causes the screen to switch to the session that is logically attached to that function key.

Normally, you start an additional UNIX session using this feature; then you can start an MS-DOS session in that virtual console. After that, you can jump between the UNIX and MS-DOS systems as necessary, starting more sessions whenever you wish.

The second procedure for switching sessions, which is often supported in older Merge releases, allows you to start a *background* MS-DOS session and sidestep the **vtlmgr/newvt** procedure. If this version is supported, you can start your MS-DOS sessions by executing the **dos** command in the background, like this:

```
$ dos &
```

The MS-DOS session will take over the current screen, but you can use the hot key sequence discussed earlier to switch back to the UNIX system, where you can start additional MS-DOS sessions or execute applications in the UNIX system.

Screen Switching

When you select a different session, the screen contents switch to that session. When you switch back, the former contents are again displayed. The contents of the screen are not lost when you switch sessions.

You can switch sessions while a command is executing in either operating system. That is, you need not be at the command prompt to switch sessions, because the hot key is interpreted at a very low level of the machine, and not at the shell level.

If a command is in progress when you switch sessions, output from that command may *block*. That is, the program may stop executing and wait until you return to that session. The type of display you are using, and the needs of the application running in that MS-DOS session, will often determine whether the suspended session blocks or continues to run. When an application uses EGA or VGA capabilities, it will block until its session is current. Applications that only use CGA capabilities, such as **command.com** itself, will continue to run in the background. Some Merge releases allow you to control whether or not the background session blocks by setting an option when you start the MS-DOS session. Blocking guarantees that no output will be lost when you switch away from an active program, but it may not be what you want in every situation.

Of course, in all cases, the application in the background will stop when it expects user input. When a session is blocked or waiting for your input, you can restart it by switching back to that session.

Invoking MS-DOS Applications Directly from the Shell

In addition to accessing MS-DOS by switching screens as discussed in the previous section, you can also execute MS-DOS commands and applications directly from the shell. You can use two procedures for this purpose.

First, you can give the name of the MS-DOS application as an argument to the **dos** command, as shown here:

```
$ dos ws
```

This will execute the MS-DOS system and immediately start the Word-Star application program. When you quit from the named application program, the MS-DOS session will end and you will be returned to the UNIX system.

Second, you can type the name of an MS-DOS command just as you would name a command under the UNIX system. As a result, the MS-DOS *environment* will start, and the named application will execute. When the MS-DOS command completes, you will be returned to the UNIX system as before. For example,

```
$ ws
```

will run the WordStar application.

These "indirect" invocations of MS-DOS are simpler but less efficient than a continuing **dos** session, because the MS-DOS environment must be started for each command you execute; it does not continue to exist between commands.

When using the second procedure, you should give pathname arguments in the UNIX system format. That is, pathnames should be specified with the **/** (slash) character separating directory elements, and not with the **** (backslash) separator used in MS-DOS. For example, you can use the MS-DOS **dir** command to get an MS-DOS style directory listing from the shell, as follows:

```
$ dir /home/steve/mydosdir
```

When you use an MS-DOS command directly like this, you must take extra care to quote any special characters to protect them from the shell. This applies to special characters for both the MS-DOS and UNIX systems, because either can be interpreted or expanded by the shell before being passed to the MS-DOS system. For example, you might use the command

```
$ dir *.bat
```

to list the names of all the batch files in the current directory. This command is correct when it is executed directly from MS-DOS. However, if it were used from the UNIX system, the shell would expand the wildcard character ***** before passing the command to MS-DOS. This would be an error, because the **dir** command allows only one name on its command line. You can avoid this type of problem by quoting command-line arguments that contain special or wildcard characters, as shown here:

```
$ dir "*.bat"
```

Be careful; mistakes with these special characters can easily destroy files.

Pipelines and Shell Scripts

You can sometimes create pipelines that contain a mixture of UNIX system and MS-DOS commands. If the MS-DOS command is *well-behaved*, it will read its standard input and write to standard output, just as most programs do under the UNIX system. In this case, you can combine commands from both operating systems into a single pipeline, like this:

```
$ dir a: | sort
```

This example will use the **sort** command under the UNIX system on the directory output from the MS-DOS **dir** command. *Ill-behaved* programs, which do not use MS-DOS standard I/O, should not be used in pipelines. Any program that reads or writes directly to the machine's hardware without using the MS-DOS BIOS conventions will be ill-behaved.

Some Merge implementations allow only one MS-DOS session per machine, which means you can only execute a single MS-DOS command at a time. That is, you can execute only one MS-DOS command in a pipeline, and only one user can execute the pipeline at any time. In most SVR4 implementations, more than one MS-DOS command can appear in a pipeline. Of course, pipelines like this can be quite inefficient, because the whole **dos** environment must start when each MS-DOS command is executed.

You can also include MS-DOS programs in shell scripts or other programs. The rules described in this and the following sections also apply within scripts.

MS-DOS Command Extensions

Unlike commands in the UNIX system, MS-DOS commands have a *command extension*. The extension follows the dot in the command name, such as the **exe** (for executable) in the name **ws.exe**. Other extensions include **.com** (for command) and **.bat** (for batch file). Under normal MS-DOS usage, you do not have to give the extension when you execute a command. For example, the two commands

```
C> WS
C> WS.EXE
```

are equivalent. Other commands such as **del** and **dir** are built into **command.com** directly, and have no extension.

When you run an MS-DOS command under the UNIX system, the **dos** linkage will usually figure out the extension just as **command.com** would, so you do not need to add the extension or worry about it at all. You can execute a command from the UNIX system just as you would under MS-DOS.

Usually add-on software and applications such as WordStar or Lotus 1-2-3 can also be executed from the UNIX system as **ws** or **123** without their MS-DOS extensions, *providing they have been installed with tools supplied in the Merge package.* If you install applications under an MS-DOS session using the application's own installation script, you may not be able to execute it from the shell unless you add the extension to your command line, and unless the application resides in the normal MS-DOS bin directory. If possible, be sure to install MS-DOS application software with the Merge tools to eliminate these problems. Installation is discussed at the end of this chapter.

PATH and Other Environment Variables

Both the MS-DOS and the UNIX systems use a PATH environment variable to define directories to search when a command is typed. Since MS-DOS commands must be accessible under the UNIX system, and vice versa, the same PATH is often used for both sessions. This PATH must include the Merge bin directories, usually **/usr/dbin** and **/usr/ldbin**. Be sure these directories are included in your PATH under the UNIX system. For example:

```
$ echo $PATH
/sbin:/usr/sbin:/usr/bin:/usr/X/bin:/usr/dbin:/usr/ldbin:
$
```

The **dos** command will usually reuse the UNIX PATH variable when you start an MS-DOS session, first changing it to MS-DOS format, and then adding it to your MS-DOS environment.

Alternatively, you can set the PATH environment variable in your **autoexec.bat**, so it will be picked up when your MS-DOS session starts. In addition, some Merge releases provide the *DOSPATH* environment variable under the UNIX system, which becomes your PATH under an MS-DOS session. Take care to retain the Merge directories and the normal UNIX bins in your MS-DOS PATH, or various parts of the Merge system will fail.

Some releases allow you to pass other environment variables to the MS-DOS session if their names are the values of the *DOSENV* environment variable. That is, **dos** looks at the contents of the variable DOSENV, and puts any named variables into the MS-DOS environment, as shown here:

```
$ PROMPT="hello:"   ; export PROMPT
$ TERM=AT386        ; export TERM
$ DOSENV=PROMPT,TERM ; export DOSENV
$
```

The variables PROMPT and TERM will be added to the MS-DOS environment when the **dos** command starts. Use the DOSENV feature carefully, because environment space may be limited in the MS-DOS session.

The Merge system will also create *TEMP* and *TMP* environment variables under the MS-DOS session for use by applications that need them. These are normally set to **C:** but you can change them by setting (and exporting) them under the UNIX system, or by using the DOSENV mechanism.

Executing UNIX System Programs from the MS-DOS Session

Similarly, you can run UNIX programs from the Merge session. The command **on unix**, or sometimes **rununix**, allows this. This feature differs significantly between Merge implementations as to the treatment of output, whether or not the session blocks, and the use of command names. Some Merge releases allow you to name certain UNIX system commands directly, without a preceding **on unix** command. The most common commands such as **cat, ls, cp, lp, mv, pr, grep** and **chmod** are usually supported. For details, consult the documentation for your particular implementation.

Other UNIX system command lines must follow the command **on unix,** as shown here:

```
C> ON UNIX SORT /TMP/DATA.FILE > SORTED.FILE
```

Use the file naming conventions of the UNIX system for commands and arguments. Output comes to the MS-DOS session. You can press CTRL-C to exit from commands run with the **on unix** facility.

In some implementations, you can only use the **on unix** procedure with commands and pipelines that are *noninteractive.* To execute any command that requires user input, you may have to return to a normal UNIX session with the hot key. Other releases provide a special form of the **on unix** command, called **ion unix** (for interactive **on**) that supports interactive applications.

Job Control

You can execute background, or *detached,* jobs with the **on unix** facility, by adding the **&** operator to the end of the command line, as follows:

```
C> ON UNIX CAT DATA.FILE &
```

You must put a space before the **&** or the **on unix** command will treat it incorrectly.

When you create these detached tasks, the MS-DOS **C>** prompt reappears, and you can continue with your session or create more detached jobs. Some Merge implementations provide a pop-up menu to *reattach* a detached job. Other releases provide a **jobs** command from the MS-DOS session to list the detached jobs you have created, and their current status. For example:

```
C> JOBS
JOB   HOST     STATE    EXIT STATUS    COMMAND
[ 1]  my_sys   Done     exit(0)        cat /etc/profile
[ 2]  my_sys   Running                 ps -ef
C>
```

If there is nothing to report, the **jobs** command returns silently.

In the previous example, the JOB column lists the job identifiers, small *job numbers* similar to those used by the job control features in the UNIX system. The STATE column gives the current status of the job, which can be *running, done, unknown, signal, coredump,* or *err3. Running* and *done* are normal. *Signal* reports that the command exited after receiving a signal, and *coredump* implies an error in the command that caused it to fail. *Unknown* and *err3* are errors internal to the **on unix** system.

Completed jobs continue to appear in the **jobs** output until you flush them. To clear all completed jobs, use - (minus) as an argument to jobs, as shown here:

```
C> JOBS -
```

Once a job has been cleared from the **jobs** list, you can no longer access it or its output.

You can use the job number to *reattach* a detached job and view its output. Use the **jobs** command with the job number as an argument to request that the job be reattached. Precede the job number with % (percent) as you would in the UNIX system job control. For example:

```
C> JOBS %1
```

To save the output of a job that has completed, redirect the output from the **jobs** command to a file, as follows:

```
C> JOBS %2 > OUTPUT
```

You can kill a detached job before it has completed if you wish. To do so, use the **kill** command from the MS-DOS session, with the job number as an argument, as shown here:

```
C> KILL %1
```

This command acts like the **kill** command under the UNIX system, and can take a signal number if desired. For example:

```
C> KILL -9 %1
```

The **on unix** facility has many more features. One allows you to replace the keyword *unix* with the name of a machine connected to your LAN. In this case, the command will be executed at the remote machine, and the results will be returned to your local machine. Consult your Merge documentation for details.

Disk Usage Under the Merge Session

Under normal conditions, MS-DOS and the UNIX system will share the system's hard disk; that is, both sessions will use it simultaneously, and the full file system will be visible to both sessions. Drive designations often vary dramatically between implementations of the Merge feature, but the hard disk will usually be accessible under the Merge session as drive C. The first floppy disk will be drive A, and a second floppy disk will be drive B.

You can navigate the file system with the **cd** command under the UNIX system, or with the equivalent MS-DOS command; however, if you change your working directory under one operating system, and then use the hot key to switch to the other operating system, the directory change will *not* follow. Remember, use the **/** (slash) character to separate directory tree arguments under the UNIX system, and the **** (backslash) character to separate them under MS-DOS.

In most implementations, the starting directory for a new MS-DOS session will be the current directory when you start the **dos** session. You can include a **cd** command in your MS-DOS **autoexec.bat** file to force a return to your home directory or to some other place.

By default, the **dos** command looks on the system's hard disk for any commands given as its arguments. The command

```
$ dos ws
```

is equivalent to

```
$ dos c:ws.exe
```

You can execute programs from a floppy disk by explicitly naming the drive where the program resides. For example:

```
$ dos a:123
```

will run the LOTUS 1-2-3 program from floppy disk drive A. You can use this procedure to run copy-protected applications that have a *key disk*, such as LOTUS 1-2-3. Alternatively, you can sometimes copy the application to the hard disk, and then insert the key disk in the floppy drive before starting the application. Some applications will read the key disk correctly when they start.

File and Directory Naming

The file naming scheme used in the two environments can be a problem. Under the UNIX system, filenames can be as long as necessary, while MS-DOS filenames can have no more than 11 characters, with an 8-character limit on the *name* section and a 3-character limit on the *extension* section. Also, some characters that are legal in filenames under the UNIX system are not allowed under MS-DOS rules. Thus, when you use the MS-DOS **dir** command to view a directory created under the UNIX system, the filenames may not be acceptable under MS-DOS. All legal MS-DOS filenames are acceptable under the UNIX system.

In some implementations of the Merge feature, the MS-DOS session ignores filenames that do not meet MS-DOS naming requirements. Better implementations provide *conversion rules*, which guarantee that all filenames acceptable to the UNIX system will be unique under the MS-DOS session. In this case all files will be accessible under both MS-DOS and the UNIX systems. When you use a file or directory under MS-DOS, you will sometimes see filenames that differ from those that appear under the UNIX system. To use a file under MS-DOS, you must give the name as it is displayed by the **dir** command, even though it may differ from the familiar name used under the UNIX system. Sometimes unusual characters or numbers will appear in converted names. The following conversion rules are used for SVR4 systems; older versions may have different rules.

First, all filenames that contain lowercase characters are converted to uppercase. If the UNIX system filename is shorter than eight characters, it will be the same under MS-DOS. If it has no more than eight characters, followed by a . (dot) and no more than three characters, it will be the same under the MS-DOS rules (but uppercase). However, longer filenames will be changed. If the unacceptable name contains a dot, the rules will be applied separately to the parts before and after the dot. Finally, the **dos** linkage layer examines all the filenames in the directory for duplications. If any are found, it substitutes a new combination of characters that is unique and follows the MS-DOS rules.

For example, this directory might be present in the UNIX system:

```
$ ls /tmp/SS
1234567890.dat        2234567890.dat        short.txt
1234567891.dat        longerthan8           small.large
$
```

Viewed under MS-DOS, the same directory might look like this:

```
C> DIR

Volume in drive C is my_sys
Directory of   C:\TMP\SS'F8U

.              <DIR>        7-21-90    3:02p
..             <DIR>        7-21-90    3:01p
1234'F84 DAT        0       7-21-90    3:01p
1234'F9T DAT        0       7-21-90    3:01p
2234'F9U DAT        0       7-21-90    3:02p
LONG'F9V            0       7-21-90    3:02p
SHORT    TXT        0       7-21-90    3:02p
SMAL'F95 LAR        0       7-21-90    3:02p
      8 File(s)   43339776 bytes free
```

As you can see, filenames can change substantially if they violate the MS-DOS naming rules.

When you are naming directories within the UNIX system, take special care to choose directory names that are legitimate under MS-DOS as well. Otherwise, you may have trouble using **cd** to change directories under MS-DOS. In the previous example, the directory name **SS** was changed by the **dos** linkage to **SS′F8U**. This occurs because the conversion rules change lowercase characters under the UNIX system to uppercase characters under the MS-DOS system. Thus, a name that contains uppercase characters in the UNIX system will be converted. If you create a directory or file named **SS** under MS-DOS, it will display as **ss** under the UNIX system.

If you create a filename that obeys the MS-DOS rules, its name will not differ when you use **ls**. Similarly, if you edit or otherwise use a file whose name has been changed under the MS-DOS session, its name will not change when you return to the UNIX system. However, if you delete a file under MS-DOS and then recreate it under the name **dos** uses, the *new* name rather than the old one will appear under the UNIX system.

The udir Command

A new MS-DOS command, **udir** (for UNIX system **dir**) will list both unconverted and converted filenames, so you can check the conversions that have been performed. For example:

```
C> UDIR

Volume in drive C is my_sys
Directory of c:/tmp/SS

.                .               root  drwxr-xr-x <DIR>   7-21-90  3:02p
..               ..              sys   drwxrwxrwt <DIR>   7-21-90  3:03p
1234567890.dat   1234'F84.DAT    root  -rw-r--r--      0  7-21-90  3:01p
1234567891.dat   1234'F9T.DAT    root  -rw-r--r--      0  7-21-90  3:01p
2234567890.dat   2234'F9U.DAT    root  -rw-r--r--      0  7-21-90  3:02p
longerthan8      LONG'F9V        root  -rw-r--r--      0  7-21-90  3:02p
short.txt        SHORT.TXT       root  -rw-r--r--      0  7-21-90  3:02p
small.large      SMAL'F95.LAR    root  -rw-r--r--      0  7-21-90  3:02p
      8 File(s)           43331584 bytes free
C>
```

The **udir** command can also handle wildcard arguments to restrict the output to a subset of the available files, but the wildcard rules follow MS-DOS conventions, not the UNIX system conventions. You can also add the **-h** (for hidden) option to display UNIX system files that begin with a dot. Note that **udir** is a UNIX system command, so its options begin with a - (minus) instead of the **/** (slash) used under MS-DOS.

A Note on Multiple Access to Files

Files on the machine's hard disk are usually visible to both MS-DOS and UNIX system programs. Neither operating system protects you against editing a file in one operating system, and then switching sessions before the changes have been written. If you attempt to edit the file in the other operating system, you will see the original, unchanged file. There is no *concurrency control* between changes to the file in the two sessions; it is your responsibility to be sure that files are *consistent* between the sessions. It is usually sufficient to write a file back to disk from your editor before you switch sessions. In more complex cases, you can set up application programs in both operating systems that process a file at the same time. It is easy to forget that you have such tools, and in this case your files may become corrupted.

File Conversions

Recall that end-of-line conventions differ between the MS-DOS and UNIX systems. The Merge package provides two utilities for converting files to the format of the other operating system: **unix2dos** and **dos2unix**, which convert files from UNIX system format to MS-DOS format, or from MS-DOS format to UNIX system format, respectively. These command names and the specific options they provide may differ, but the conversion operation is usually required when you are moving files from one operating system to the other. Both programs are available under MS-DOS and the UNIX system.

By default, both **unix2dos** and **dos2unix** read their standard input and write the converted data to standard output, as in this example:

```
$ unix2dos < unix.file > dos.txt
$
```

These filters return silently if there are no errors.

If one filename is given as an argument, that file is used as the input file, and output comes to standard output, as shown here:

```
$ dos2unix dos.txt > unix.file
```

If two filenames are given, the first is the input file and the second is the output file. For example:

```
$ unix2dos unix.file dos.txt
```

If you use one of the filters on a file that is already in the target format, the file will not be changed.

These utilities support several command-line options. Remember that options under the UNIX system begin with the flag character - (minus), while arguments under MS-DOS begin with a **/** (slash).

By default, **unix2dos** and **dos2unix** make the output data 7-bit ASCII characters. The **-b** (for binary) option preserves any 8-bit characters in the data. You can also convert files to all uppercase or all lowercase using the **-l** (for lowercase) or **-u** (for uppercase) option. The **-b**, **-l**, and **-u** options are mutually exclusive, so you can only use one of them on a single command. You can get a list of all command-line options with the **-?** option.

Both programs remove any *extra* newline characters at the end of each line. When you are converting UNIX system files, this will make all output files single-spaced. If you want to preserve the spacing of the input file by converting all newlines to return-linefeed pairs, use the **-f** (for force) option, as follows:

```
$ unix2dos -f double.space > double.spc
```

Remember, you should use these programs only on 7-bit or 8-bit ASCII text files, not on binary files; it is difficult to convert binary files such as the files produced by some word processors. The **dos2unix** and **unix2dos** commands allow you to specify a *conversion table* for converting each character, which makes it possible to convert binary files correctly. Experiment on copies of your word processor files before you assume that they will convert successfully.

MS-DOS Directories

The MS-DOS commands and tools have their own bin directory within the merged file system. This may be **/usr/dbin** or **/usr/vpix/dosbin**, depending on your Merge release. Any locally installed applications may be in **/usr/ldbin** or **/usr/vpix/dosapps**. Other supporting materials may be in other subdirectories of **/usr/vpix** or in **/usr/lib/merge**. The **/** directory often contains the primary **autoexec.bat** and **config.sys** files; but device drivers that are installed by **config.sys** often reside in **/usr/dbin** or **/usr/lib/merge**.

MS-DOS Memory Allocation

When an MS-DOS session starts, some of the machine's RAM is allocated to that session. In many Merge implementations, an MS-DOS session cannot be swapped or removed from memory until it ends. Thus, memory given to MS-DOS may be unusable by the UNIX system. This can cause problems if you have too little real memory on your machine, because the UNIX system will slow down dramatically when an MS-DOS session is running. In severe cases, your UNIX system commands may appear to start incorrectly. In this case, use the hot key to switch back to the MS-DOS session, and **quit** to exit from the session; your programs should then resume their normal behavior under the UNIX system. If you encounter these problems, you must add more memory to the machine to improve its performance.

The amount of real memory *grabbed* by the MS-DOS session is an argument to the **dos** command. You can instruct the **dos** command to take only as much memory as you need, up to 640K, the MS-DOS maximum. To do so, use the **+m** (for memory) option on the **dos** command line, as shown here:

```
$ dos +m400
```

This command will allocate 400K to the MS-DOS session. You can specify any amount between 64K and 640K. The **dos** command will try to allocate the specified amount of memory, but if it is not available, **dos** will do the best it can. You can sometimes get more memory for an MS-DOS session by reducing the number and size of processes running in the UNIX system when you start the MS-DOS session. If you have plenty of memory and ask for 640K, the **dos** program will probably give you only about 600K, because some memory is required for the *linkage* between the MS-DOS and UNIX systems.

Most MS-DOS applications can determine if the amount of memory available is inadequate, and display an error message if it is. You can use this information to determine the correct value for the **+m** option. You should usually use the minimum necessary.

The default memory allocation, which applies in the absence of the **+m** option, is a configurable parameter that can be set according to your needs. Configuring the MS-DOS session is discussed later in this chapter.

The **dos** command allows you to use *expanded memory* if an application needs it. You can allocate memory that will simulate expanded memory by adding the **+aems** option to your **dos** command line, as follows:

```
$ dos +aems
```

This command line will allocate 1MB of expanded memory. You can add more memory in 1MB chunks by appending a digit to the **+aems** option, like this:

```
$ dos +aems4
```

This line will allocate 4MB of expanded memory.

Expanded memory is supported by a line in your **config.sys** file. For example:

```
device=c:\usr\lib\merge\emm.sys D000 208
```

Do not delete this line if you wish to use expanded memory.

Most Merge versions do not support MS-DOS RAM disks, such as **ramdrive.sys**, so you should not add these to your **config.sys** file.

Other Command-Line Options for the dos Command

In addition to the **+m** option, the **dos** command supports many more command-line options that configure the MS-DOS session and regulate the MS-DOS environment. The options vary widely between implementations of the Merge feature; consult the **dos** man page for details specific to your machine. These options often follow the format -*x* to turn the option off, and +*x* to turn the option on. You can usually use +**h** (for help) to display a list of options available to your version of the **dos** command.

You can *grab* hardware devices (see the next section) with the +**a** (for assign) option, and release them with **-a**. You can send arguments directly to **command.com** without interpretation by the **dos** command with +**c** (for command). The +**u** (for UNIX system) option changes the pathname separator and switch character to their UNIX system equivalents: the MS-DOS **/** (slash) character becomes -, and the **** (backslash) character becomes **/** in command lines. This option does not work with all MS-DOS programs, so use it with care. Many other options are also available; try the +**h** option to see the full list for your machine.

Device Sharing Between the MS-DOS and UNIX Systems

When either operating system has full control of the machine, it allows you to access any hardware device. Because the rules for device management differ between the two operating systems, problems with devices may occasionally arise when both operating systems are running simultaneously. These problems do not affect the hard disk, but floppy disks, printers, and communication ports may behave oddly at times.

Floppy Disk Management

Both MS-DOS and the UNIX system allow you to use the floppy disk drives, but the two systems cannot share the floppy disk. The diskettes themselves differ in format, and the low-level device drivers that read and write the diskettes also differ. Thus, only one system at a time can use the disk drives.

When MS-DOS starts, it does not grab the floppy drives until you use them under the MS-DOS session. That is, you can switch from the MS-DOS session back to the UNIX system, and then use normal media commands to access a floppy under the UNIX system. However, if you do use a drive from MS-DOS, the MS-DOS session will grab the drives: if a drive is in use under the UNIX system, the MS-DOS command that accesses the drive will fail; if the drive is idle in the UNIX system, the MS-DOS session will use the drives as expected. Note that the grab will often take *both* floppy drives if you have more than one, even when you only requested one in your MS-DOS session.

In some Merge implementations, the grab will be released after the drive is idle for a short time (usually five seconds). In other releases, the drive will continue to be *owned* by MS-DOS after it is used, and the UNIX system will not have access to the drive until the MS-DOS session is killed. To release a disk drive back to the UNIX system after it has been used under an MS-DOS session, you may have to quit from the MS-DOS session; then you can restart the MS-DOS session and the disk drives will again be accessible by the UNIX system.

Printing Under MS-DOS

The same considerations apply to attached printers as to disk drives, because both operating systems could try to send output to the printer simultaneously. There are two solutions to this problem in most Merge implementations.

If the **lp** subsystem is in use, the MS-DOS **print** command will send output to the **lp** print queue instead of directly to the MS-DOS print spooler. This prevents conflicts, because **lp** manages the spool intelligently. Similarly, the MS-DOS *print screen* function works by sending the screen dump into the **lp** print queue. In either case, a printer named **doslp** (as specified in your **lp** configuration) is used for the output. Use normal **lp** tools to reassign the name **doslp** to the printer you wish to use for MS-DOS output. Some Merge versions also provide a command called **lpinstall** to change the printer configuration.

Alternatively, you can specify that the normal MS-DOS printer drivers be used instead of the **lp** queue. A special MS-DOS command grabs the printer away from the **lp** spooler and reserves it for the MS-DOS print utilities. From the MS-DOS session, use

```
C> PRINTER DOS
```

to grab the printer for the MS-DOS session. You can return the printer to the UNIX system with

```
C> PRINTER UNIX
```

After assigning the printer to the MS-DOS session, you may need to use the **mode** command to set the printer configuration correctly, especially if you are using a serial printer.

While the printer is being used by MS-DOS, the **lp** spool will be *disabled* so that the queue can grow but no output will be printed.

Using Communication Ports

Many Merge implementations require you to grab serial ports COM1 and COM2 when you start a Merge session. You cannot use serial ports on the fly as you can the diskette drives; you must reserve these devices when you start the session. When you grab a serial port like this, it will be unavailable to the UNIX system until the Merge session ends. Before using a COM port under a Merge session, you must stop any port monitor or **getty** process running on the port.

To grab the COM1 device, use the command

```
$ dos +acom1
```

This command assigns the COM1 device (tty0) to the Merge session. Similarly, use **+acom2** to grab the COM2 device. You can also use more than one **+a** option if necessary.

If you have a Merge session running and you wish to use the serial ports, you must end the **dos** session and restart it with the **+a** option.

Going Further

As you might have imagined, there are a great many more issues associated with sharing a single machine between two operating systems. In fact, it is remarkable that the Merge facility is available at all!

Unusable MS-DOS Commands

While the Merge feature is running, some MS-DOS commands will not be available, because they can destroy the Merge environment. Do not use the MS-DOS commands **fdisk** or **ship**, or any other commands that park the fixed disk heads. Do not use the MS-DOS **chkdsk, format,** or **sys** commands on the shared hard disk partition, although you can use them on floppy disks.

Running Merge from a Terminal

Most versions of the Merge capability allow you to run the MS-DOS session from a terminal as well as from the system console. You can run the MS-DOS session as usual, and the Merge bridge layer will handle output to the terminal if your TERM variable is set correctly. However, only well-behaved MS-DOS commands will work on a normal ASCII terminal; Ill-behaved applications, which write directly to the console display hardware, will not work on a terminal.

On a terminal, the special keys available on the AT-style keyboard will usually not be present. The function keys, PrtSc, and even the cursor control keys may not be available. Thus, the Merge system supplies special *escape sequences* to simulate these keys from an ASCII-only keyboard. For example, to simulate the F1 key, press the key sequence ESC followed by the digit 1. The PrtSc key is simulated by pressing ESC followed by the letter *r*. Other escape sequences are provided to redraw the screen (ESC-CTRL-R), and to create a new instance of the UNIX shell (ESC-CTRL-F). The sequence ESC-CTRL-K kills the MS-DOS session, and returns you to the UNIX system. This can be helpful when an MS-DOS program is hung, and you cannot use the **quit** command.

If your terminal supports only 24 lines, you cannot easily see the full 25-line MS-DOS display. The sequence ESC-CTRL-U causes **dos** to redraw the screen showing the *bottom* 24 lines. The top line is not displayed. Use ESC-CTRL-U again to shift the screen back to the *top* 24 lines.

If you use Merge from a terminal, look for a complete table of these escape sequences in your Merge documentation.

Running Merge Under the X Window System

Similarly, you can run the Merge system under the X Window System if it is installed on your machine. When you start an MS-DOS session, the **dos** command will determine that you are using X, and will create a normal MS-DOS display within a new X window. When you exit the MS-DOS session with **quit**, the X window will disappear. Most Merge releases allow you to have multiple MS-DOS windows within your X session.

To use **dos** under the X Window System, set and export the XMERGE environment variable. Its value should be the type of display you are using. For example:

```
$ XMERGE=vga
$ export XMERGE
```

Acceptable displays include *mono, cga, ega, herc,* and *vga.* Set this value in your X startup file (usually **.olintrc** or **.xinitrc**) not in your normal **.profile**, because some Merge releases will not work correctly if the variable exists *outside* the X environment.

By default, the MS-DOS window is a normal 25-by-80 console window. Well-behaved MS-DOS applications will run as expected within this window. In addition, the X session supports MS-DOS graphics applications that normally use the mouse and graphics console. To use these features, you may need to assign the mouse to the MS-DOS session, a process called *focusing* the mouse on an MS-DOS window. If the application demands the full resolution of your display, you can *zoom* the MS-DOS window to take over the full display screen. The Merge system will warn you if you try to run an application that requires zooming.

Both of these functions are handled by a pop-up menu that is available under X. To see the menu, press ALT-D from the MS-DOS window. Select the Focus option to assign the mouse to the MS-DOS session. This will make the mouse unusable in other X windows until you bring the menu up again and select the Unfocus option. Actually, this is a grab procedure similar to grabbing the printer or diskette drive.

Select Zoom from the menu to assign the full screen to the MS-DOS session. Then you can run high-resolution graphics applications. When you are through, just press ALT-D again to unzoom the window, and restore your X display. Naturally, you can have only one window focused or zoomed at any time, although you can run multiple applications in virtual consoles outside the X Window System.

Screen colors in the MS-DOS window may differ from those used in normal MS-DOS applications, because the *colormaps* of X and MS-DOS conflict. You can solve this problem by adding a new X resource to your .Xdefaults file. To do so, add the line

```
dos*installcolormap:     true
```

When you move your mouse pointer into the MS-DOS window, the screen colors will change to the MS-DOS standards (the rest of the screen will probably also change colors). Colors are always correct for console windows or zoomed windows. Several other normal X resources, including border colors, fonts, and so on, can also be set for the **dos** window.

Microsoft Windows Under Merge

Most releases of the Merge feature allow you to run MS-DOS session managers such as Microsoft Windows (and the applications available for Windows). However, you must use versions of Windows designed for *real mode*. You cannot use *protected mode* versions such as Windows/386 or the extended options of Windows Version 3. This limitation arises because the UNIX system uses the protected mode of the 80386 and 80486 processors, and this conflicts with similar usage in the Windows product. You must use the real-mode versions of Windows in a Merge session. Other session managers will have similar limitations.

Communications and Interrupts

Since the MS-DOS session runs as a process under the UNIX system, it does not really have full access to the machine's hardware resources. In fact, hardware events and interrupts are monitored by the UNIX system even while the MS-DOS session is active. Interrupts are passed through the UNIX system to the MS-DOS session, and MS-DOS applications that turn off interrupts really only stop their own virtual interrupts. This situation has several implications. First, rogue MS-DOS programs cannot destroy the UNIX environment, although some Merge releases will kill the MS-DOS session when interrupts are disabled for too long. Deranged MS-DOS applications are protected well enough that they cannot damage the executing UNIX system. Second, communications devices that cause frequent interrupts cannot run as fast under the Merge session as they can under a standalone MS-DOS session. Usually 4800 or 9600 baud is the fastest a serial device can run under an MS-DOS session.

Standalone MS-DOS on a UNIX Machine

If you have configured your machine with a separate MS-DOS partition, as discussed in Chapter 25, you can use MS-DOS as a standalone system without the Merge feature. When MS-DOS is running as a standalone system, you cannot access the hard disk partition used by the UNIX system, but must use the separate MS-DOS partition established when you formatted your hard disk. This lets you use the full speed and power of the MS-DOS system when necessary, without the UNIX system sharing the CPU.

There are two ways to use standalone MS-DOS. First, you can boot the machine from a floppy MS-DOS system disk. When you do this, the standalone MS-DOS partition of the hard disk will be known as drive C. This drive C is not the same partition as the drive C known to MS-DOS while it is running in the Merge session. The latter is the normal file system shared by the MS-DOS and UNIX systems, while the former is the standalone MS-DOS partition.

Before you can use this standalone drive C, you must format it as usual for MS-DOS disks. This format operation is only done *once*, the first time you use the partition. After booting the machine from an MS-DOS floppy disk, use the command

```
A> FORMAT C: /S
```

to prepare the partition for use. This format command may give an error message such as

```
Warning:  this will destroy all the data on the hard disk.
```

In fact, the command only erases the files in the MS-DOS partition, not all the data in the merged partition.

After it is formatted, you can load the MS-DOS operating system or applications onto this drive C as usual, and the files will not clash with the UNIX system on the merged file system. Then, when you reboot the machine from the hard disk, the UNIX system will come up as usual.

The second way to access the standalone MS-DOS partition is to use the **fdisk** command from the UNIX system to change the *active partition* to the MS-DOS only partition. For this purpose, execute **fdisk** from the UNIX system and not from the MS-DOS session. You should never use **fdisk** from the MS-DOS session within the Merge system. When you reboot the machine, the MS-DOS partition will have control, and the machine will boot under MS-DOS. Whenever you reboot the machine after that, the MS-DOS partition will be active. When you wish to change back to the UNIX system, use **fdisk** under the standalone MS-DOS system to change the active partition back to the merged partition. Thereafter, the UNIX system will start at boot time.

The E Drive

When you are using the merged session, you can access the "MS-DOS only" partition with a logical drive letter. In some implementations, this will be drive E. In others you may name the drive as you wish. Drive E is only available under an MS-DOS session within the Merge system; use drive D to access the standalone MS-DOS partition with the **dosdir** and **doscp** commands. You cannot access the the merged partition from a standalone MS-DOS system.

Several MS-DOS sessions can *read* data from drive E simultaneously, but *writes* to drive E usually cause a grab, so that only one MS-DOS session can write at any time. The drive becomes free when the first process exits.

The D Drive

Another logical disk drive may also be available when you start the merged MS-DOS session. This is drive D. Drive D differs from drive C in one respect: the "root" of drive D is your home directory, not the real root of the shared file system. You cannot see "above" your home directory on drive D. You switch to drive D in the normal way, as shown here:

```
C> D:
D>
```

Drive D is useful for applications that try to create files in the **/** (root) directory. When you install such applications on drive D, they will make their files in your home directory instead of in the real **/** directory, thus avoiding conflicts when more than one person uses these applications.

The J Drive

In addition to drive D and drive E, the **dos** command may also give you a drive J when it starts. Drive J is used when you execute an MS-DOS command directly from the shell, as follows:

```
$ ws document
```

Drive J will have a working directory that is the directory in which the executable program was found. This can differ from the working directory under the UNIX system, which will be drive C. Some versions of MS-DOS applications, especially older programs, require your data files to be in the same directory as the executable program. Drive J points to the executable program, while drive C points to the data file; thus, these older programs will work correctly. Otherwise, drive J isn't very useful, and it usually points to the MS-DOS local bin directory, **/usr/ldbin**.

Virtual Disk Files

You can create files in the merged file system that act like floppy disks or that act as MS-DOS hard disk partitions. These files can then be accessed with MS-DOS drive letters. They are called *virtual disks* because they are actually single files in the merged file system, but under MS-DOS each one can contain many files and be treated as a disk. Although virtual disks actually have few uses, they give you the ability to copy the contents of a floppy into a virtual disk file, which you can then access just as though it were a floppy disk. This can speed startup of applications that must start from a floppy, such as some copy-protected applications. Other copy-protected applications will not work correctly using this procedure; you must experiment to be sure.

You can copy the contents of an MS-DOS (or bootable) floppy into the merged file system with the **dd** command (under the UNIX system), as shown here:

```
$ dd if=/dev/rdsk/f13dt of=/home/steve/dosapp1
```

This command is appropriate to copy a 720K, 3 1/2-inch floppy located at drive B. When the command completes, the exact contents of the floppy will reside in a file on the hard disk. Then you can start the MS-DOS session, assigning the virtual disk file as drive B, like this:

```
$ dos +ab:=/home/steve/dosapp1
```

This command line assigns the file to drive B under the MS-DOS session so that you can see the contents of drive B with normal MS-DOS tools. For example:

```
C> DIR B:
```

You can read, write, or create new files in the virtual floppy disk as needed. When you assign drive A or B to a virtual file like this, you cannot access the real floppy disk without starting a new **dos** session. Note that virtual floppy disk files must use the drive letter *A* or *B*. As with a normal MS-DOS session, other letters are reserved for hard disk partitions.

A similar procedure allows you to create virtual hard disk partitions. Just create a large file (perhaps by copying an existing file) and attach it to a virtual drive letter, as shown here:

```
$ dos +ak:=/home/steve/virthd
```

When the MS-DOS session starts, you must format the partition just as you would any other hard disk partition under MS-DOS. Then you can use the assigned drive (drive K in this case) as another MS-DOS partition. This can be useful when several users wish to have private partitions within the MS-DOS session, because individual files inside these virtual partitions are not visible from the UNIX system.

Often a menu-oriented user agent supplied with the Merge package includes tools to create virtual disk files.

You can start applications that reside on the virtual disk by giving its name at the end of the **dos** command, as follows:

```
$ dos +ab:=/home/steve/dosappl b:appl
```

This command will start the application **appl** on virtual disk file **dosappl**.

Booting the MS-DOS Session from a Floppy Disk

When you execute the **dos** command, the MS-DOS session is started from the *MS-DOS Image* on the system's hard disk. This is the fastest method, and is usually what you want. Occasionally, however, you may want to boot the MS-DOS system from a floppy disk. Some applications cannot be installed on the hard disk, and some games are configured on standalone floppy disks that do not have a true MS-DOS system. You can use these applications with the Merge feature by booting the MS-DOS session directly from a floppy disk.

Place the bootable diskette in drive A, and execute the command **dosboot** from the UNIX system, as shown here:

```
$ dosboot
```

The operating system will start from the floppy disk. When you boot from a floppy in this way, drive C on the hard disk will not be available; you can only use the standalone system on the floppy. You can also use this feature to boot other operating systems, such as CP/M-86 or even OS/2.

When you are through with the **dosboot** session, press CTRL-ALT-DEL to end the session and return to the UNIX system prompt. Since drive C is not available, the normal **quit** command will not work.

Using MS-DOS as a Login Shell

You can set up users' login ids so that they get an MS-DOS session instead of a normal shell when they log in to the machine. Just add the **dos** command at the end of the user's normal **.profile**, as follows:

```
$ tail -2 /home/dosuser/.profile
dos
exit
$
```

With this setup, users will be switched to the MS-DOS environment when they log in. The **exit** after the **dos** command is required to ensure that users are logged off when they finish their MS-DOS session with **quit**.

The dosopt Command

When you start an MS-DOS application directly from the UNIX system, the **dos** program runs first to create the MS-DOS environment for the application. Because you are not running **dos** directly in this case, you cannot specify any command-line options for that invocation of the MS-DOS session. The **dosopt** (for MS-DOS options) command is used to permanently associate some **dos** options with an application program, so that the chosen options will be in effect when the command is executed directly from the UNIX system. Parts of the **dosopt** function are often included in a menu-oriented tool called **dosadmin**. Use **dosadmin** if it is present, otherwise use

```
$ dosopt [options] command
```

to install the named *options* with the *command*. The list of available options is the same as it is for the **dos** command. For example, to set the memory to the largest possible size when you execute the LOTUS 1-2-3 application, use

```
$ dosopt +m640 123
```

Then, when you execute

§ 123

the maximum available space memory will be allocated. This command may vary between implementations of the Merge feature, so check the documentation for your system before using it.

The stored options can be found in the files **/etc/dosenv.def**, **/etc/dosapp.def**, **$HOME/dosenv.def**, and **$HOME/dosapp.def**.

Installing the Merge Feature

Another area of great variability is the installation of the Merge feature. In most cases, your UNIX system vendor will provide a special user agent to help with its installation, and this tool will prompt you through the installation procedure. Consult the documentation provided with your Merge system for exact instructions.

Usually, you install the Merge feature with normal UNIX system software installation procedures, and then execute a special **dosinstall** command to load the MS-DOS operating system. The **dosinstall** command must be executed before you can use the Merge facility. You must have the appropriate disks for the MS-DOS system available for loading by **dosinstall** when you are prompted. Part of the procedure involves the creation of the MS-DOS Image for your hardware configuration.

After the Merge utilities and the MS-DOS system software have been loaded, you can install MS-DOS application programs onto the hard disk. Applications should be installed with the Merge feature to avoid problems with MS-DOS command extensions, and to allow you to execute the applications directly from the UNIX shell. Do not use the installation procedures provided with the application software unless you are installing an application into the standalone MS-DOS partition. Instead, use the **dosadmin** user agent provided with the Merge system, which provides menu-oriented tools for installing MS-DOS applications. It installs applications in the normal **dos** bin directory where they can be accessed by both the Merge and the UNIX systems. You can later use **dosopt** to associate special options with an application.

The MS-DOS Image

The *MS-DOS Image* is a file that contains the exact configuration of the MS-DOS session that is started when you execute the **dos** command. It is a snapshot, stored on disk, of the **dos** configuration. The image will usually reside in **/usr/lib/merge/*.img;** one image will be present for each display type available on the machine. The presence of these files allows fast startup of the MS-DOS session, because they are already configured and can be loaded quickly into the machine's memory by the **dos** command.

The MS-DOS Image is created when you install the Merge feature. However, the MS-DOS Image must change whenever you change the hardware configuration on the machine by adding or removing disks, display cards, system ROMs, and the like. You can remove the Merge feature before changing the hardware configuration, and reinstall it after you have upgraded the machine.

Alternatively, you can use the **dosadmin** command to create a new MS-DOS Image. Make sure all the hardware changes are completed, and then execute

```
$ dosadmin
```

from the UNIX system. A menu item named Create MS-DOS Image will create the new image for you. If you neglect this operation, the MS-DOS session will not work correctly after you make hardware changes in your machine.

Much of the system-specific data used by the image creation process is stored in the file **/etc/dosdev.** Browse through this file to see how the Merge system uses the machine's hardware resources.

# TWENTY

Timing and Scheduling

A Note on Timesharing Vs. Real-Time Performance
The UNIX System Is Designed to Operate All the Time
The date Command Revisited
File Times
The at and batch Commands
The cron Facility
Going Further

An important concern in any multitasking operating system is the *scheduling* of tasks. For multiple processes to receive fair access to the single CPU of the machine, there must be *timing* mechanisms within the operating system that switch to a new process when another has used its share of CPU resources. Indeed, the UNIX system includes excellent tools for timing and scheduling, with a time scale that ranges from milliseconds through years. The basic timing mechanisms are built into the operating system itself, and the commands and tools based on these mechanisms perform administrative functions regularly, without much attention from users or the system administrator.

Timing is so important under the UNIX system that nearly all UNIX machines have built-in battery operated clock and calendar hardware that keeps time correctly while the machine is turned off. However, the correct operation of administrative functions usually depends on the machine being "up" nearly one hundred percent of the time. Many functions are scheduled by the system to run once a day, usually in the small hours of the night. Other functions are scheduled to execute once a week, and others may operate only once or twice a year. In this chapter we will review some of the user-level timing considerations, and mention some of the administrative operations that are scheduled by the UNIX system.

A Note on Timesharing Vs. Real-Time Performance

When several users or processes share the machine, the responsibility for allocating CPU resources is held by the operating system. Thus, under normal circumstances, users cannot control how much CPU time they get during an interval. This means that *real-time* problems may occur. For example, a high-speed I/O device may be *starved* or *flooded* with data if the system is heavily loaded. In the past, this was a serious problem, which prevented the UNIX system from being used in many real-time applications. However, in SVR4 a new scheduling system has been introduced that allows the user (or administrator) to designate some or all of the processes as real-time. This means that some parts of the system get an unfair amount of system resources. See Chapter 11 for more information on *priority control* and related issues.

The UNIX System Is Designed to Operate All the Time

Historically, the UNIX system was used on timesharing systems with nearly one hundred percent availability. In these machines the only available CPU time was late at night when few users were active on the system. Therefore, a lot of *background* administrative tasks were scheduled for these late-night hours, and over the years tools evolved to provide for their automatic scheduling. In fact, many machines were only turned off for occasional hardware maintenance. Over the years, many subtle assumptions concerning high availability have crept into the UNIX system, so that today it is preferable to keep machines operating as much as possible. In addition, high availability also allows your electronic mail and **uucp** data transfers to take place at night, when telephone rates are low and the machine is lightly loaded.

Of course, the UNIX system will run successfully if it is only turned on occasionally; keeping the machine up and running is not truly required. However, if the machine is in daily use, it is better to keep it powered up all the time, than to shut it down overnight (this is much easier if you can turn off the console monitor independently of the CPU). In the discussion of the **cron** function later in this chapter, you will learn when activities are scheduled on your machine. You can tune the machine to do its administrative work at a time of day when it is usually turned on.

The date Command Revisited

The UNIX system maintains an internal date that is available to users. In its raw form, this date is actually a count of the total number of seconds that have elapsed since January 1, 1970, which (at least in myth) marks the dawn of the UNIX system era. Intervals longer than one second are kept in this format within the UNIX system. There is no easy way to get at this raw time value from the command line, but the number is fairly large—at least *660,000,000,* and growing fast!

Most commands that use the current time convert this value into a friendlier format. We discussed the basic functions of the **date** command in Chapter 7. As you'll recall, **date** provides the basic user-level access to the timing functions. For example,

```
$ date
Wed Jun 6 18:50:06 MDT 1990
$
```

displays the current date and time as known by the machine.

In addition, **date** can format its output in different ways. The format is specified as an argument to **date**, beginning with **+** (plus). Almost any output format is possible if you define *fields* in the argument. The **%** (percent) operator introduces a field, and a single character follows the **%** to describe the date element desired. For example, **m** requests the month of the year (1 through 12), as follows:

```
$ date +%m
06
$
```

In this case the month is 06 or June. Other operators that can follow the **%** are **d** for day of the month (1 through 31); **y** for the last two digits of the year; **H** for the hour of the day; **M** for minutes, **S** for seconds; **w** for the day of the week (Sunday through Saturday); **h** for the month (January through December); and **r** for the time in A.M./P.M. notation. Any of these formats can follow the % operator. Characters that do not follow % in the argument are treated as normal characters, so **date** can print complex expressions that include the date and time. For example:

```
$ date "+Today is %h %dth. The time is now exactly %r"
Today is Jun 10th. The time is now exactly 06:26:32 PM
$
```

In addition, **%n** can be used to request a newline, allowing multiline **date** output, as shown here:

```
$ date +"Month: %m%nDay: %d%nTime: %T"
Month: 06
Day: 10
Time: 19:02:58
$
```

These specially constructed **date** commands are often used in shell scripts to produce a display, or assigned to environment variables. The possibilities are only limited by your imagination; 29 different % operators are allowed with the **date** command.

Setting the System Date

The **date** command is also used to *change* the system's idea of the current date and time, although this privilege is reserved for the super-user. If you give **date** an argument that is not preceded by **+**, the argument is interpreted as a current date and time to be set as the system date. This argument must be of the form *mmddhhmm*, where the first *mm* is a two-digit month, *dd* is a two-digit day of the month, *hh* is a two-digit hour of the day in 24-hour format, and the second *mm* is the minute of the hour. The command

```
# date 06071647
Thu Jun  7 16:47:00 MDT 1990
#
```

will set the current date to June 7, 4:47 P.M. The new date is returned to verify the change. If necessary, a two-digit year can be added to the end of the argument to also set the year. For example,

```
# date 0607164791
```

will set the same date in the year 1991.

In practice, changing the date is discouraged unless it is necessary, because discontinuities in time counting can cause problems with some software. It is best to change the system date only when the system is lightly loaded. The ideal time is immediately after a reboot. In machines with built-in clock and calendar hardware, you very rarely need to reset the system date. However, the correct time is important to proper system operation, so you should make an effort to keep the system time accurate.

The Time Zone and Daylight-Saving Time

The **date** command works in local time, and correctly converts the date and time to *universal time* (or GMT), the internal time format of the system. The local time zone and the difference in hours between it and GMT is stored in the file **/etc/TIMEZONE**, and is usually also available in the environment variable **TZ**. These entries have a form like *EST5EDT*, where the time zone name is first (*EST*), followed by the number of hours away from GMT (*5*), followed by the name of the time zone if daylight-saving time is used (*EDT*). Usually the **TZ** environment variable is set by the system from the **/etc/TIMEZONE** file, so if you move your machine you can change **/etc/TIMEZONE** and then reboot. However, to be safe you should set the time zone through the administrative user agent provided with the machine.

The system provides a built-in algorithm for switching between standard time and daylight-saving time, and this algorithm may not be completely correct, since governments often change the daylight-saving time rules. Be sure to check your system's time after daylight-saving time begins and ends.

File Times

The UNIX system maintains several time-stamps for all files in the system, and one of these is displayed for each file with the output from

ls -l. This is the *modification time* of the file, the time at which the file was last changed. This time is used by several commands to determine if a file is up-to-date, and some commands detect whether a file has changed since the last time the command looked at the file. In addition, the system keeps two other times associated with a file. These are the *creation time* and the *access time* of the file. The creation time records when the file was originally created, and the access time records the last time a user or program read the file. The creation and access times of a file are not easily displayed by user commands, but some commands such as **find** and **test** can key on these times if desired. Normally you will be most interested in the modification time.

The touch Command

The **touch** command is used to change the time-stamp associated with a file. The command takes a filename list as arguments, and by default it changes the access and modification times of a file to the current time, as shown here:

```
$ ls -l old.file
-rw-rw-rw-  1 steve     users       539 Jan 15 04:15 old.file
$ touch old.file
$ ls -l old.file
-rw-rw-rw-  1 steve     users       539 Jun 10 21:02 old.file
$
```

The **-m** (for modification) option causes **touch** to change only the modification time, and the **-a** (for access) option causes **touch** to change only the access time.

The **touch** command can also set the time of a file to any other time if it is given an additional argument. For example:

```
$ ls -l old.file
-rw-rw-rw-  1 root      users       539 Jun 10 21:02 old.file
$ touch 03211541 old.file
$ ls -l old.file
-rw-rw-rw-  1 root      users       539 Mar 21 15:41 old.file
$
```

The new date follows any flags, but precedes the filename list. This new date is in the same format discussed earlier for setting the system date:

mmddhhmm, where the first *mm* is a two-digit month, *dd* is a two-digit day of the month, *hh* is a two-digit hour of the day in 24-hour format, and the second *mm* is a two-digit minute of the hour. An optional two-digit year can be appended to the end of the new date string if desired.

You can also use **touch** to create an empty file that did not previously exist, as in this example:

```
$ ls -l new.file
new.file not found
$ touch new.file
$ ls -l new.file
-rw-rw-rw-  1 root     users        0 Jun 10 21:06 new.file
$
```

This procedure is often used in shell scripts to ensure that a file exists. Alternatively, you can use your favorite editor to create a file, or the shell command > (right angle bracket), which will also create an empty file, if it is given alone on a command line, like this:

```
$ >new.file
```

The **-c** (for create) option *prevents* **touch** from creating a file that did not previously exist.

As with other aspects of time control under the UNIX system, it is undesirable to change the times associated with files unless it is really necessary to do so. Some procedures, such as automated backup tools, may not work as expected if the modification times of files have been changed.

The at and batch Commands

The **at** command allows you to schedule jobs for later execution. Any command line or shell script can be *queued* using the **at** facility. If necessary, a shell script can include another **at** command within it that allows scripts to reschedule themselves. The **at** command is available to normal users of the system, and includes appropriate security to allow or deny its use by individuals. The command works in addition to the systemwide scheduling mechanism called **cron**, which is intended for use by system processes and the system administration facilities. The **at** command is present in SVR4 and other recent releases, but some older versions may not include it.

Execute **at** by giving a time and date as a command-line argument; **at** will read its standard input for the text of the command or script to execute at that time. For example:

```
$ at 11:45 < script
job 660414980.a at Thu Jun 14 11:45:00 1990
$
```

This will execute the commands in the file **script** at 11:45 A.M. today. The **at** command responds with a job id and the time it will execute the job, written to its standard error. The job will be executed at that time, even if you log off the machine, or if the machine is rebooted before the scheduled time. You might recognize the job id number as an example of the "seconds since 1970" time format the system uses. Of course, if the machine is not turned on when the scheduled time arrives, the command will not be executed.

The **at** command is fairly intelligent about the shell environment in which the script is executed. It provides the same environment variables that were exported when the **at** command was executed, and restores the current directory, the **umask**, and the **ulimit** for the script. The standard output and standard error for the shell script are sent as mail to the user after the script is executed, allowing you to see its messages and output. If the script reads from its standard input while it is running, it receives an immediate end-of-file indication.

Specifying a Date for the at Command

The **at** command allows several formats for the time specification, including formats that specify a date later than today. A time may be specified as an hour with one or two digits. For example,

```
$ at 17
```

will execute the command at 5:00 P.M. local time. Unless *am* or *pm* follows the time, 24-hour time is assumed. The command

```
$ at 5pm
```

will also cause the script to be executed at 5:00 P.M. No space is allowed between the numeric value of the time and the *am* or *pm* string. In addition, a four-digit time is allowed with a : (colon) between the hour and minute, as shown here:

```
$ at 4:35pm
```

If the *am* or *pm* is omitted, the time is again interpreted in 24-hour format. The special strings *now, noon,* and *midnight* are also allowed. For example:

```
$ at noon
```

A job can be executed at an increment in time if the + (plus) operator is included after the time. The command

```
$ at now + 15 minutes
```

will execute the job in 15 minutes. In addition to *minutes,* the time specifiers *hours, days, weeks, months,* and *years* are allowed with the + operator. For example,

```
$ at 3:15pm + 6 months
```

provides an alarm clock that will ring one-half year from 3:15 P.M. today!

In addition to the time, a *date* can be added after the time for execution on that date. The command

```
$ at 2:15pm Jul 16
```

will cause the job to be executed on July 16. After the time, the optional date is composed of a month name and then a day of the month. You can also use a day of the week instead of the month and day if you wish. The month name and the day of the week must be either fully spelled out or abbreviated to three letters. A year can follow the month if a , (comma) follows the date, as shown here:

```
$ at 2:15pm Jul 16, 1991
```

The + operator is allowed with these longer date specifications if it follows the rest of the date. For example,

```
$ at 2:15pm Jul 16, 1990 + 3 years
```

will execute the job three years after 7/16/90, providing the machine is still running then!

These date specifications seem complex, but actually the format is fairly natural and intuitive; most of your normal ways of writing a date will work as expected. Otherwise, **at** provides a terse error message, as in this example:

```
$ at 6:15 pm Satur
at: bad date specification
$
```

Displaying the at Job Queue

The **at** command provides two options for managing the list of jobs you have scheduled. The **-l** (for list) option will list all your jobs by their job id numbers, giving the date and time each is scheduled, as follows:

```
$ at -l
660503300.a    Fri Jun 15 09:35:00 1990
660503360.a    Fri Jun 15 09:36:00 1990
$
```

The **-r** (for remove) option, with a list of job ids as an argument, will remove the named jobs from the queue, as shown here:

```
$ at -r 660503300.a
$ at -l
660503360.a    Fri Jun 15 09:36:00 1990
$
```

Of course, you are limited to removing jobs that you have created. Only the superuser can remove any of the jobs on the queue. Jobs created by

at are temporarily stored in the directory **/usr/spool/cron/atjobs** until they are executed, and if necessary a specific job can be deleted from that directory directly, instead of using **at -r.**

The contents of the shell script that **at** will execute are determined by your needs, but only scripts that you can normally execute from the shell are allowed. That is, **at** executes the script with the execution environment that was in force when the **at** command was given, so you cannot use **at** to do something that you would not be permitted to do at the terminal.

Normally, **at** only executes the script *once,* at the specified time; however, you may wish to create a script that executes regularly, such as once a day or once each hour. This is possible if a new **at** command is included in the script, so that the script effectively *reschedules* itself to execute again. Usually, the relative time operators available to **at** are used for this purpose, such as

```
at now + 1 day
```

This command will execute a script tomorrow at this time. If you include this command in the script that **at** executes, you have a command that will run once each day. An easy way to do this is by placing the command

```
at now + 1 day < $0
```

near the end of your script. The shell evaluates $0 to be the name of the script. This will work if the original **at** command that starts the schedule is executed from the directory in which the script resides. If it is not, $0 will not work and a full pathname will be needed.

Self-scheduling jobs like this can cause headaches in your system if they are incorrect. You must take care to debug a script carefully before you allow it to be self-scheduled. Furthermore, if the script ever disappears from the disk or its pathname changes, **at** will fail and the job will no longer be rescheduled, possibly producing extremely large log files in the process. The **crontab** facility, discussed later in this chapter, is generally preferable for regularly scheduled jobs.

The batch Command

Another command related to **at** is **batch**. This command acts like

```
$ at now
```

except that it schedules the job to run as soon as the system load is low enough. (In addition, **at now** will respond *too late* while **batch** will work as expected). The **batch** command uses an internal algorithm to decide when a job will be executed. This is useful when you wish to execute many large jobs at once. If these jobs were simply executed in the background using the **&** command-line operator, they would all try to execute at the same time, possibly clogging the CPU. As a result, they would all take longer, because each one would only get a small time-slice from the operating system before another took control. The **batch** command prevents this *thrashing* by letting you schedule all the jobs at once, but allowing only a few to start at a time. Thus, the first jobs complete relatively quickly, and the later jobs are spaced as system load permits. The overall time for completion of all the jobs will actually be shorter with **batch,** and total CPU usage will also be lower. In addition, the first jobs will complete much more quickly.

The **batch** command takes no command-line arguments, since the job is always executed as soon as is practical. Like **at, batch** reads the script from its standard input, and sends the standard output and standard error from the script to the user as mail. For example:

```
$ batch < script
job 660501560.b at Fri Jun 15 09:06:00 1990
$
```

The **batch** command writes the job number to its standard error, in the same format used by **at.** The **at -r** command can be used to delete a job scheduled by **batch,** providing you catch it before it begins to execute.

Security Considerations with at and batch

Both the **at** and **batch** commands provide security mechanisms that prevent users (other than the superuser) from scheduling jobs without prior authorization. If you try the examples given in the previous section on your system, you might be prohibited, as follows:

```
$ at 16:35 < script
at: you are not authorized to use at. Sorry.
$
```

Users can be individually authorized to use these tools or prohibited from using them.

The list of authorized users is maintained in the directory named **/etc/cron.d**, as shown here:

```
$ cd /etc/cron.d
$ ls -F
FIFO         at.deny      cron.deny    queuedefs
at.allow     cron.allow   logchecker*
$
```

FIFO is used as a communication channel between the **crontab** and **cron** program, and **queuedefs** contains information used internally by the **cron** facility. The **logchecker** is a tool used to truncate log files that grow too long. The two files in this directory that are of interest for **at** and **batch** are **at.allow** and **at.deny**. These files contain a list of user ids that are allowed to use or prohibited from using these commands, respectively. Here is an example:

```
$ cat at.allow
root
sys
adm
uucp
steve
jim
pat
$
```

As you can see, the user ids are listed one per line in the file.

Only the superuser is allowed to modify the **at.allow** and **at.deny** files, so keeping these files up-to-date with changes in the user ids on the machine is quite a job for the system administrator. However, administration can be simplified by using some additional rules: if the file **at.allow** is present, only users listed in the file are allowed to execute **at** or **batch** commands; this rule is observed whether or not **at.deny** exists. If the file **at.allow** is not present, **at.deny** is checked to see if a user is explicitly prohibited from using the commands. That is, if **at.allow** is not present, any user not listed in **at.deny** can execute the commands. If neither file is present, only the superuser can execute the commands. So, to open up **at** usage to all users, you can delete the file

at.allow, and then be sure that **at.deny** is empty, but present. You should also be sure that the user ids **root, sys, adm,** and **uucp** are always included in the file **at.allow**, if the file is present.

In addition, the **at** and **batch** commands use a *prototype* file that is merged with the user's script to generate the "real" shell script executed when the scheduled time arrives. The file **/etc/cron.d/.proto** contains this prototype file. The superuser can modify this script to enforce stricter security for all scheduled jobs. Consult the **proto**(4) man page for more details about customizing the environment for scheduled jobs.

The cron Facility

The **at** and **batch** commands use the services of a more fundamental scheduling mechanism that is always running within the UNIX system. This is the **cron** (for chronograph) facility, which you encountered when you learned about the command **ps -ef** and its output. In fact, **cron** is the name of a system *demon* that is executed early in the boot-up sequence of all UNIX systems. The **cron** process is present constantly while the system is running. Once every minute it wakes up, looks in a control file to see if there are any jobs to be executed at that minute, and then executes them. If no jobs are scheduled for that time, **cron** goes back to sleep until the next minute has passed. This is a very powerful scheduling mechanism that depends on the multitasking nature of the UNIX system. Fortunately, **cron** does not use many CPU resources even though it is always present.

The **cron** command is kept in the file **/usr/sbin/cron**, which is executable. However, **cron** is not a user command and should not be executed directly, even by the superuser. If two copies of **cron** are running on the machine, the system will be quite deranged. If **cron** is not running on your machine, you should reboot the system rather than executing **cron** directly. If **cron** is still not running after a reboot, there is something seriously wrong with the machine. Usually you will need to reload the operating system from the original disks to repair the problem. However, some versions of the UNIX system include timing mechanisms named something other than **cron**, so if a machine is not running SVR4, it is possible that no process named **cron** will appear in the output from **ps -ef**. However, the functions performed by **cron** are basic to the operation of all UNIX systems, and will always be present under some name unless the machine is deranged.

In addition to the systemwide use of **cron** functions, mechanisms are provided by which individual users in addition to the superuser can schedule jobs for regular execution at intervals of one minute or longer. This facility differs from **at** primarily because **at** schedules a job for one-time execution, while **cron** schedules jobs to execute *regularly* at some interval that you specify.

crontab File Format

The control file used by **cron** is known as the **crontab** (for cron table). It was originally a single file with the pathname **/etc/crontab**. Only the superuser was permitted to modify this file, and thus change the system schedule. Some older releases still use this file location. However, SVR4 and other recent versions of the UNIX system provide an expanded **crontab** facility within the directory **/var/spool/cron/crontabs**, shown here:

```
$ ls -F /var/spool/cron/crontabs
adm      root     sys
$
```

Each user who has specified some jobs for scheduling by the **cron** facility will have a file in this directory named for the login id who created the file. The files listed in the previous example will be present on nearly all SVR4 systems, and each is intended for a specific system-wide scheduling application. The **sys** file is often used to collect system performance data if the **sar** performance analysis tools are installed on the machine. The **adm** file is usually used to schedule performance profiling from **sar** data.

Most of the systemwide scheduling is usually located in the **root** file, which often contains several comments describing the file format for all the **crontab** files. Figure 20-1 shows a typical **root crontab** for a small SVR4 system. Yours will probably differ from this example, but it does show the required file format and some of the administrative tasks scheduled in the system as a whole. Later in this chapter we will discuss how individual users can create scheduled jobs.

Comment lines in the **crontab** files begin with #. These lines are ignored when **cron** reads the file. Lines that do not begin with # name commands to be scheduled, one per line. If the newline is escaped with \ (backslash), the command can continue onto subsequent lines. The first five fields of the line give the date and time to execute the command. Each of these fields is separated from the other fields by whitespace. A number in a field gives the date or time to schedule the job, and entries consisting of * (star) are translated to *every* by **cron**. The first field in the line specifies the minute of the hour to execute the job: *00* means on the hour, *30* means thirty minutes after the hour, and so on. The second field of the line specifies the hour of the day, in 24-hour format: *2* is two o'clock A.M., *14* is two o'clock P.M., and so forth. The third field specifies the day of the month, from *1* to *31*. The fourth field gives the month of

```
# This file will be scheduled via the cron command
#
#        Format of lines:
#min  hour  daymo  month  daywk    commandline
#
#        min  - time(s) of day
#        hour
#        daymo - day(s) of month (1, 2, ... 31)
#        month - month(s) of the year (1, 2, ... 12)
#        daywk - day(s) of week (0-6, 0 = sun)
#
#        Example:
#17 5 * * 0 /bin/su root -c "/sbin/cleanup > /dev/null"
#
#        At 5:17am on Sunday during any month of the year,
#        sweep the file system performing administrative cleanup
#
#======================================================================
#
17 5 * * 0 /bin/su root -c "/sbin/cleanup > /dev/null"
48 11,14 * * 1-5 /bin/su uucp -c "/usr/lib/uucp/uudemon.admin \
   > /dev/null 2>&1"
45 23 * * * ulimit 5000; /bin/su uucp -c "/usr/lib/uucp/uudemon.cleanup \
   > /dev/null 2>&1"
40 * * * * /bin/su uucp -c "/usr/lib/uucp/uudemon.poll > /dev/null"
26,56 * * * * /bin/su uucp -c "/usr/lib/uucp/uudemon.hour > /dev/null"
0 2 * * 0,4 /etc/cron.d/logchecker
```

Figure 20-1.   Typical root **crontab** for a small SVR4 UNIX system

the year, from *1* to *12,* and the fifth field gives the day of the week, from *0* for Sunday through *6* for Saturday. These time specifications can be combined, so that a specification of

```
30 5 * * 1
```

is interpreted as 5:30 A.M. on every Monday, while

```
30 5 * * *
```

means 5:30 A.M. every day of the week, and

```
30 * * * *
```

means 30 minutes past every hour, every day.

Lists of times are allowed within each field, separated by commas, as follows,

```
00 17 * * 1,2,3,4,5
```

providing there is no whitespace between entries in the same field. This example specifies a command to run at 17 minutes past midnight, Monday through Friday.

The rest of the line after the schedule is the name of the command to execute, along with any redirection of input or output. In the first noncomment line in Figure 20-1, the command **/sbin/cleanup** is executed at 17 minutes after 5 A.M., with its standard output redirected to the system garbage can. This entry is executed as if it were run by the **root** user. In Figure 20-1, the **su** command is used to switch the user id to its first argument, usually **uucp**.

The % (percent) operator has special meaning to **cron**. The % instructs **cron** to take the rest of the line as the standard input of the command named before the %. With the \ operator used to escape newlines, it is possible to include large shell scripts directly within the **crontab** files, although this is rarely done, and most scripts remain in their own files.

In Figure 20-1, the first command performs some regular system-wide cleanup. Its output is discarded. If the redirection to **/dev/null** were deleted, the output would be sent by mail to **root**. Like **at, cron** will use electronic mail to report the standard output and standard error of the commands back to the user.

The next four commands are administrative tasks performed regularly by the **uucp** communications programs. These run at different times, depending on their function. The **uudemon.admin** command generates a regular status report; it is scheduled for 11:48 A.M. and 2:48 P.M. every weekday. This script usually reports on possible **uucp** security violations and jobs that have been queued for sending during the last week, but have not yet been sent.

The next line, scheduled for 11:45 P.M. every day, is a cleanup script for the **uucp** system. This script usually flushes old jobs and log files from the **uucp** system.

The next two lines in Figure 20-1 are the hourly **uucp** schedules, which look for unsent outgoing jobs every hour, and attempt to send them if necessary. Since **uucp** uses an incremental algorithm to determine if a connection to a remote machine should be attempted, the hourly demon may not always cause a connection to be attempted even though a job may be waiting. These **uucp** schedules should be present in a system **crontab** file if you use the **uucp** or **mail** facilities to communicate with other machines. If they are not present, your mail may not be sent correctly.

The last line in Figure 20-1 is executed at 2:00 A.M. each Sunday and Thursday. It runs a script to clean up the log files produced by the **cron** facility itself.

These entries, or some like them, are usually present on active UNIX systems, but their content may differ depending on the work normally done on a given machine. In any case, there are usually routine administrative tasks that are delegated to **cron**, such as deletion of old log files in **/var/adm**, deletion of old **core** files, and so on.

The crontab Command

Often skilled administrators will edit these **crontab** files directly to change the system schedules. However, individual users can create scheduled jobs with the **crontab** command. The **crontab** command is provided to aid in creating and changing individual **crontab** files.

To create a new **crontab** schedule, create a **crontab** file with your editor, or copy an existing **crontab** file to a new file for editing. When the file is correct, it can be added to the **crontab** directory with the command

```
$ crontab filename
$
```

where *filename* is the new file you have created. As usual, the command will return silently if the installation is successful. The schedule is created under the user id of the user who executes the command, so different users can have their own schedules without interfering with one another. Only one **crontab** file is allowed per user. The **crontab** command can also read its standard input for the schedule, so redirection is allowed. However, if you enter the **crontab** command with no filename and no redirected file for input, you must take care to exit with the DEL key rather than CTRL-D, because the end-of-file mark will cause **crontab** to load an empty file into your schedule, which is probably not what you intended.

The **crontab** command will remove a schedule if the **-r** (for remove) option is given, as follows:

```
$ crontab -r
$
```

If there is no file to remove, **crontab** will complain. In addition, the **-l** (for list) option will list your **crontab** if one has been created.

cron Permissions and Security

The materials associated with use of the **cron** facility are located in two directories. The directory **/var/spool/cron/crontabs** contains the **crontab** files. The directory **/etc/cron.d** includes the control information for the scheduling mechanisms. The files **cron.allow** and **cron.deny** in this directory serve the same functions that **at.allow** and **at.deny** serve for the **at** command, as discussed earlier. If the file **cron.allow** is present, it is checked for a list of users who are authorized to use the **crontab** command. If **cron.allow** is not present, the file **cron.deny** is checked to see if a user is prohibited from using the **crontab** command. If neither **cron.allow** nor **cron.deny** is present, only the superuser is authorized to use the **crontab** command. User ids in both **cron.allow** and **cron.deny** are listed one per line in the files.

Going Further

Many of the timing-related tools in the UNIX system are designed for developers to use in optimizing the system and its applications. Although these are of little interest to most users, we will quickly mention a few of them here.

The cron Log File

The **cron** facility maintains a log of all jobs executed with **at, batch,** or **cron**. On SVR4 systems, this is the file **log** in the directory **/var/cron**. However, older versions of the system may have another location for the log, often **/usr/lib/cron/cronlog**. The log can be useful for tracing mysterious problems associated with scheduled jobs. The file format is not particularly verbose, but it can be understood. Here is an example:

```
$ tail log
<  sysadm 229 c Wed Jun 13 17:00:02 1990
<  sys 230 c Wed Jun 13 17:00:02 1990
! *** cron started ***    pid = 75 Thu Jun 14 08:18:45 1990
>  CMD: /usr/lib/sa/sa1
>  sys 86 c Thu Jun 14 08:20:00 1990
<  sys 86 c Thu Jun 14 08:20:01 1990
! *** cron started ***    pid = 75 Thu Jun 14 08:41:45 1990
>  CMD: 660414080.a
>  root 98 a Thu Jun 14 08:48:00 1990
<  root 98 a Thu Jun 14 08:48:03 1990
$
```

On older releases, the file format may differ from this SVR4 example. The lines that contain *cron started* are generated by the **cron** program when the system is rebooted and **cron** starts up. A date-stamp is included, and each command executed by the **cron** demon, either via **at** or a **crontab** file, has a section that begins with *CMD:* and the name of the command to execute. The last entry in the previous example, *CMD: 660414080.a,* is a familiar name for a command scheduled by **at**. All the lines following the *CMD:* and up to the next command, are log entries produced by **cron** as it executes the commands. In fact, **cron** executes commands by *forking* another copy of itself, and the child process actually executes the commands. However, both processes write to the log; lines that begin with a > (right angle bracket) are written by the original **cron** program before the command is executed, and lines that begin with a < (left angle bracket) are written by the child process, one per additional program executed by **cron**. The effective user id for the process is given first, followed by the PID of the process. Next is the job type, **a** for an **at** job, or **c** for a job scheduled by **cron**. The date and time when the process was executed come last on the line.

This log information can be useful if you suspect **cron** of creating or changing files incorrectly. Often the date or ownership of a file as revealed by **ls -l** can be traced back to an entry in the **cron** log, and then associated with the CMD that changed the file. This is only necessary in rare cases when scheduled jobs are causing problems. You might suspect such problems if mysterious changes in your machine or the file system occur at regular times but are obviously not under user control.

The log file is regularly moved into **/var/cron/olog** by the **logchecker** program discussed earlier, and is then deleted the next time **logchecker** runs.

Measuring Command Execution Time

When you are creating new shell scripts or executable programs, it is often desirable to estimate the system resources used by the command. This information can help you understand the relative expense of commands, and thus optimize them. However, in a multitasking operating system the *real* time, or clock time, a command takes may not be a reliable estimate of the system resources it consumes. Consequently, the UNIX system provides several tools for computing the time a command takes to execute. The simplest of these tools is the **time** command. A command or pipeline you wish to measure is given as an argument to **time,** as follows:

```
$ time sleep 100
real      1:39.4
user      0.0
sys       0.1
$
```

This example simply sleeps for one hundred seconds. The **time** command writes its output to standard error. The output from **time** reveals the amount of system resources consumed by the **sleep** command. These times are expressed in seconds and tenths of seconds. The *real* time is the total elapsed time consumed from the beginning of the command's execution until it ends. In this case, 1 minute, 39.4 seconds has elapsed. As you know, **sleep** can be inaccurate by up to one second, and in this case it is 0.6 seconds off. The *user* time is the amount of time the program spends executing its own code. In this example, the user time is below the limits of measurement. The *sys* time is the amount of time used directly by the UNIX system in the service of the command, 0.1 second in this example.

The CPU time used by a command is actually the sum of the sys and user time measurements, but the **time** command shows them as separate so that developers can determine whether the program is using kernel resources or spending time within its own code. The difference between the real time and this sum is a measure of the CPU time that is going to other programs executing on the machine while you are making the measurement. It is apparent that the CPU time used by a command can be much less than the real elapsed time. Under lightly loaded conditions, most commands will show a real time that is very close to the sum, as in this example:

```
$ time cat /unix >/dev/null
real      6.5
user      4.5
sys       1.0
$
```

This command takes 5.5 seconds of CPU time, and completes in 6.5 seconds of elapsed time. One second went to other work in the system. In a heavily loaded system, this same command would take almost the same amount of user and sys time, but the real time would undoubtedly be much longer.

The sync Operation

For purposes of internal efficiency, the UNIX system keeps data in *buffers* in its memory, and only updates the buffers to disk when necessary. That is, although you might change a file with your editor, and then write the file and quit back to the shell, the file may not actually be written to the disk, so that if you immediately turn off the power to the system your changes may not be preserved. SVR4 systems include special processes whose job it is to update the changed buffers to the system hard disk occasionally. These processes are named **pageout** (for page output), and **fsflush** (for file system flush). They are present in the output from **ps -e**, and update the disk regularly, often every 30 seconds. However, older releases of the UNIX system may not include this automatic update procedure, so you must be careful that the disk is correct with respect to the system buffers before you shut down the machine. A special program called **sync** (for synchronize) is available to manually update the memory buffers. You can execute this program whenever you want to force a buffer update, though in SVR4 systems this is rarely necessary. The command looks like this:

```
$ sync
$
```

The **sync** command may return to the shell before its job is done, so normal practice is to execute **sync** twice or three times to assure that the disk has been updated correctly before you proceed. For example:

```
$ sync
$ sync
$
```

System Usage Accounting for Individual Users

Large public UNIX systems often include *accounting* procedures so that individual users can be charged for their connect time, CPU usage, and disk space usage. When these tools are installed, they are usually kept in the directory **/usr/lib/acct**, and log files of all processes executed are kept in **/var/adm/acct**. Additional data is kept in **/var/adm/utmp** and **/var/adm/wtmp**. If accounting is used on a machine, the system administrator must take care that the accounting summary tools are executed regularly, perhaps through the **cron** facility, or these data files may become very large. You should routinely check these files and truncate them (but not delete them!) when they grow too long.

As the following example shows, many accounting commands are available, and these accounting tools make a coherent package that allows professional billing of resource use by individual login ids.

```
$ ls -F /usr/lib/acct
acctcms*    acctmerg*   chargefee*   lastlogin*   ptecms.awk*   turnacct*
acctcon*    accton*     ckpacct*     monacct*     ptelus.awk*   utmp2wtmp*
acctcon1*   acctprc*    closewtmp*   nulladm*     remove*       wtmpfix*
acctcon2*   acctprc1*   diskusg*     prctmp*      runacct*
acctdisk*   acctprc2*   dodisk*      prdaily*     shutacct*
acctdusg*   acctwtmp*   fwtmp*       prtacct*     startup*
$
```

Accounting can be turned on and off with these tools. They allow detailed analysis of system usage by time of day, disk and process use, and connect-time usage. It takes a skilled system administrator to use these tools fully, and they are not widely used with smaller personal UNIX systems. You can disable their entries in the **crontab** if they are present but you wish to stop their activity.

Process Accounting with the sar Package

Finally, fully configured systems include the **sar** (for system activity reporting) package, which gives a complete *profile* of all activity in the UNIX system during an interval of time. The **sar** package includes data logging tools for CPU and disk utilization, buffer usage, activity counters for disk and tty devices, file access measures, and other internal measurements. Interpreting this data is a task for an expert, but if the **sar** tools are present, they will be located in the directory named **/usr/lib/sa**, and the various logs produced by the **sar** tools will be in the directory **/var/adm/sa**. You should browse through these directories occasionally to be sure that the log files do not grow too large and consume excessive disk space. The **sar** tools are usually executed via the **cron** facility, and the **crontab** files may include one or more commands related to **sar**. Usually the sys **crontab** is used, and lines executing the commands **sadc, sa1,** or **sa2** are related to the **sar** tools. Logging of **sar** activity can also be turned off by commenting out the appropriate lines in the **crontab** files.

The **sar** package includes a timing program called **timex** that is similar to **time;** however, **timex** provides better diagnostic information than **time** does, especially for shell scripts that spawn child processes. Note that the **sar** package must be present on the machine for **timex** to provide this detailed output. By default, **timex** produces the same real, user, and sys times that **time** produces; however the additional options **-p, -o,** and **-s** are available with **timex** to display the process accounting data (**-p**), the disk block usage (**-o**), and the total system activity (**-s**) associated with the command executed after **timex.** Here is an example:

```
$ timex -o cat /etc/profile >/dev/null

real       0.93
user       0.00
sys        0.26

CHARS TRNSFD = 145216
BLOCKS READ  = 76

$
```

The other options are correspondingly verbose.

Boot and Shutdown

The Ongoing System Environment
Shutting Down the Machine
The Boot Sequence
init States
The /etc/inittab File
Going Further

There are usually several processes executing in a UNIX machine at any time. Consequently, it is very dangerous to simply turn off the machine's power when you are done using it. The UNIX system provides tools expressly designed to create an orderly sequence of events when you turn off the machine. This sequence is known as the *shutdown* procedure, and you should follow it carefully to assure the system's sanity when you start the machine again. The startup procedure is also complex, and tools are provided to *boot* the machine correctly when you turn it on. In this chapter we will review the steps the system goes through during the power-off and power-on procedures, and briefly mention some of the system *states* that are possible, as well as some common problems that can occur as a result of boot procedures.

The Ongoing System Environment

When the UNIX system is running correctly, many processes are likely to be active on the machine. Of course the system *demons* will always be running, and a system administrator logged into the system console will have a shell and possibly some other programs associated with the session. In addition, other users may be logged in to the machine from remote terminals, and these users may be executing programs. Also, there may be background electronic mail or **uucp** data transfers running at any time, and print jobs may be in progress. Finally, lack of synchronization between the in-memory *buffers* and the system hard disk means that the *real* contents of the disk and its *logical* contents will often differ. That is, when you write a file from the editor, that file will probably not be updated to the disk until seconds or minutes after the write is complete, and you are back at the shell executing new commands.

All of these factors, and several others discussed in this chapter, make it vital that you take care when shutting down the machine. Tools are provided to help with these tasks, and you should use them whenever possible. Of course, sometimes the power will go off unexpectedly; the building's power may be interrupted, for example. Modern versions of the UNIX system can withstand power outages and incorrect shutdowns, but with some risk of system failure or of losing the contents of the system disk. You can avoid such problems by reducing the likelihood of inadvertent shutdowns as much as possible.

Shutting Down the Machine

In principle, a correct shutdown warns other users to log off before the system goes down, carefully kills all nonessential processes, updates various system files and logs, synchronizes the disk with the in-memory buffers, and finally kills any remaining processes. Some systems can automatically park the disk heads under software control, as part of the shutdown. In fact, some UNIX machines include a software-controlled power switch so that the last step of the shutdown procedure is physically turning off the machine.

The *shutdown* Command

Several tools can be used to shut down the machine, and using any of these tools is preferable to simply turning off the power. The **shutdown** command is the safest of these tools, but it is also the slowest. The **shutdown** command is a shell script located in **/sbin/shutdown**, and you can browse through it to get a better understanding of its actions. Like all tools related to turning the machine on and off, **shutdown** is reserved for the superuser. It can be only be run at the system console, and only from the root directory, **/**. If these conditions are not met, **shutdown** will complain and refuse to take action.

The shutdown procedures, and the messages displayed during shutdown, vary widely among different versions of the UNIX system. In many systems, a menu-oriented tool for shutting down the system is available in the administrative user agent.

The **shutdown** command was originally intended to be interactive, with the superuser controlling the actions taken during the shutdown procedure. The command can still be used interactively, but recent releases of the UNIX system provide the **-y** option, which instructs **shutdown** to answer all questions itself, as follows:

```
# shutdown -y
```

This form of the command is much easier to use than the form without the **-y** option. Before you run this command, it is courteous to check with other users to be sure they are not doing something critical. You can use the **who** and **ps -af** commands to determine the current system activity. In addition, you should check that no job is being printed and no **uucp** data transfers are in progress, because these activities will restart from the beginning after a reboot if they are interrupted by the shutdown.

When executed, **shutdown** warns all users that the machine will be coming down soon, and they should log off before the machine dies. Figure 21-1 shows a typical console display during a shutdown sequence. Some of these messages are sent to all current users of the system, and others are limited to the system console. The warning message beginning "Broadcast Message..." is sent to all users currently logged into the machine. It is sent directly to the terminals of all users by the **/usr/sbin/wall** (for write to all) command soon after the shutdown process begins. Then the **shutdown** command sleeps for 60 seconds before continuing with the shutdown process. Users are expected to respond immediately, close any open files, secure their session, and then log off. All users (except the **root** login on the system console) must take immediate action.

After these messages, the **shutdown** command stops all active processes, updates the disk correctly, and gracefully brings the operating system to a halt. Finally, the system arrives at a point where the

```
# cd /
# shutdown -y

Shutdown started.   Mon Jun 11 20:29:49 MDT 1990


Broadcast Message from root (console) on my_sys  Mon Jun 11 20:29:49 MDT 1990
THE SYSTEM IS BEING SHUT DOWN NOW ! ! !
Log off now or risk your files being damaged.

Changing to init state 0 - please wait.
#
INIT: New run level: 0
The system is coming down. Please wait.
System services are now being stopped.
Print services stopped
xntad: received signal 15

The system is down.
Reboot the system now.
```

Figure 21-1.   Typical console display during the shutdown sequence

power can be turned off or a reboot can be initiated. Always wait for the
"Reboot the system now" message, or its equivalent, before you actually
turn off the power or reboot the system, to ensure that the shutdown
process has completed successfully.

By default, **shutdown** allows 60 seconds between the warning message and the actual beginning of the shutdown sequence. You can
change this interval by adding the **-g** (for grace) option to the **shutdown**
command line. The number of seconds to wait before beginning the
shutdown sequence follows the **-g** option. For example,

```
# shutdown -y -g300
```

will wait five minutes after the warning message. You can lengthen the
period to allow users to complete their activities before the shutdown
begins, or you can shorten it to allow a faster shutdown when it is safe.
In extreme cases, **-g10** can be selected to reduce the waiting interval.
Although **-g0** is allowed, it often does not clear all processes correctly,
so the system may not come down cleanly if you use this setting. Short
intervals should only be used if you are certain there is no activity on
the machine, because users should always have ample opportunity to
end their sessions before a shutdown.

The Boot Sequence

When the power is turned on, the machine goes through a complex process to start up. This *boot* sequence can take several minutes depending on what hardware and software is installed on the machine, and there is no way to make it go more quickly. The boot process includes several *sanity checks,* and often tries to repair any damage it finds, especially damage to hard disk files. Most UNIX machines have built-in procedures to minimize this error-checking if the previous shutdown was completed correctly. Thus, the boot sequence following a power outage or other inadvertent shutdown is likely to be more complex and thorough than a reboot after a normal shutdown. In any case, the boot sequence often helps repair system problems. Your first response to any derangement of the machine should usually be to reboot.

Figure 21-2 shows a typical boot sequence as displayed on the system console. This output will vary depending on the type of CPU in use, the version of the UNIX system installed, and any additional hardware or software on the machine. The example in Figure 21-2 is from a typical SVR4 machine.

Not shown in Figure 21-2 is the initial hardware test most small computers make before beginning the boot. This test, which is already familiar to users of most PCs, may include a memory test as well as a display of installed hardware. These come from the system's ROM hardware, and do not depend on the operating system in use. Some ROM software may also require a password before the boot procedure is initiated.

The first part of the boot procedure is also missing from Figure 21-2. A *ROM loader,* whose responsibility is to load the first parts of the operating system off the disk, executes first. In fact, the ROM loader loads another loader program whose job is to load the UNIX system itself. This additional *software loader* is stored on the system disk, so it must be loaded by hardware and ROM that exist permanently. Generally, all operating systems, including MS-DOS, OS/2, and the UNIX system, keep their loader programs at the same relative disk location within their disk *partition,* so the ROM loader can find the software loader. Thus you can switch between operating systems by simply changing the default partition from which ROM loads the software loader.

```
Booting the UNIX System...


total real memory   = 8388608
total available mem = 7122944

AT&T UNIX System V/386 Release 4.0  Version 2.0

Copyright (c) 1984,1986,1987,1988,1989,1990 AT&T
Copyright (c) 1987,1988 Microsoft Corp.
All Rights Reserved

Wangtek PC-36/EV-811 cartridge tape controller was found at address 00000300H
PC586 v2.7 Copyright(c) 1987,1988,1989 Intel Corp.,  All Rights Reserved
PC586 board 0 was found, Ethernet Address:  00:00:1c:00:02:f0
Node:  my_sys
The system is coming up. Please wait.
System V Streams TCP Release 1.0
(c) 1983,1984,1985,1986,1987,1988,1989,1990 AT&T
(c) 1986,1987,1988,1989,1990 Sun Microsystems
(c) 1987,1988,1989,1990 Lachman Associates, Inc. (LAI)
    All Rights Reserved
Print services started
The system is ready.

Welcome to the AT&T 386 UNIX System
System name: my_sys

Console Login:
```

Figure 21-2.   Typical console display for a simple boot sequence

After the software loader is brought into memory, ROM turns control over to it, and it starts executing. At this point the machine is committed to running the UNIX system, because the software loader can only deal with its own operating system. When the software loader begins, it displays the message

```
Booting the UNIX System...
```

and then loads the operating system *kernel,* which is normally **/stand/unix.** You can press a key on the keyboard while the "Booting..." message is displayed, and the loader will let you enter the name of an alternate kernel to load. If it is used, this alternate kernel must reside in the **/stand** directory; in SVR4 you cannot enter a full pathname unless it is under **/stand.** Normally you do nothing further at this point, and after a short interval the loader begins to load the standard kernel.

The file **/stand/unix** is visible on the hard disk. It is the kernel, the actual memory-resident portion of the UNIX system. The software loader reads it from the disk and installs it into the machine's memory. Then the software loader gives control to the newly loaded kernel, and the UNIX system begins to initialize itself.

As part of the initialization sequence, the kernel may display its idea of how much real memory is installed in the system. Older versions often required the memory information to be compiled into the system, but SVR4 can configure itself based on how much memory is actually installed. If more memory is added, the display will change and the UNIX system should adapt correctly. If the amount of *total real memory* differs from the amount of physical memory you know is installed in your machine, there is undoubtedly some hardware problem that should be addressed before you use the machine. The *total available memory* is the real memory the system has available after the UNIX system takes what it needs. In SVR4, the difference between these two numbers is the real memory used by the kernel. In addition, the kernel allocates a significant amount of memory for its *buffers*, which act somewhat like a RAM disk. Some releases of SVR4 display the number of buffers allocated at this point in the boot sequence. If present, this information will appear in this form:

```
buffers=900K
```

The number of buffers allocated during the boot sequence is a *tunable parameter* in SVR4, and it can be changed if necessary. However, the default value is usually appropriate for most needs.

The available memory, reduced by the buffers, can be used by normal programs when they execute. However, modern UNIX systems can *swap* or *page* segments of memory from RAM to disk when the system needs more memory. Thus, there can be many more programs executing than you might expect from the amount of available memory. As usual, the more real memory you have available, the more effective the UNIX system can be, because the frequency of swapping to disk is reduced.

Next, the UNIX system begins the initialization of itself and any installed hardware devices. The first series of copyright notices shown in Figure 21-2 comes from this device initialization. Additional, or at least different, copyright notices will probably appear on other versions that have different installed software and hardware.

As part of the initialization process, the kernel analyzes the *device drivers* associated with installed add-on boards, and the "Wangtek..." and "PC586..." messages appear at this stage. Usually one message of this type will appear for each installed device.

When initialization is complete, the UNIX system will actually be up and running, although several more steps must be completed before the system is ready for users to log in. The material in Figure 21-2 from the "Node:" line until the appearance of the login prompt is the result of boot-time shell scripts that you can browse. These will be discussed after a short digression.

In a correctly operating system, no action is required between turning on the power and the eventual appearance of the login prompt. However, if the machine crashed just previous to your rebooting it, this additional prompt will often appear in the boot sequence:

```
There may be a system dump memory image in the dump device.
Do you want to save it? (y/n)
```

This memory dump or *core image* is used in debugging the kernel. Choose **n** to bypass this step.

init States

The boot procedure for the UNIX system is complicated by the possibility of bringing up the system in different *states*. That is, the system can take several modes of operation known as *init states,* after **/sbin/init**, which is the program responsible for keeping the system running correctly. These states are very different from each other, and the system can be *in* only one of the states at any time. The shutdown and reboot procedures actually control which state the machine is in. The most commonly used state is *multiuser mode*. This is the system state used for nearly all the interactions discussed in this book, and the only one that allows more than one user. Another state that was historically important, although it is seldom used in small modern systems, is *single-user mode*. The single-user state is a multitasking version of the UNIX system, so it allows multiple processes, but not multiple users. That is, only the system console is active when the machine is running in single-user mode. Single-user mode is rarely used today, although it can be handy when you want to use the machine but prevent other activity such as network access or remote logins. The *UNIX User's Manual* often recommends that such tasks as setting the system date and time be executed only in single-user mode, but in modern UNIX systems these chores can also be done in multiuser mode.

There are several other states in addition to the single-user and multiuser modes. All the possible states are named by special identifiers, as shown in Table 21-1. Init state 0 is used to bring the machine down and stop the UNIX system. Single-user mode is known as init state 1, or as s or S, depending on whether the single active terminal is the system console or a remote terminal. Multiuser mode is init state 2, and 3 is used in SVR4 systems when most of the networking features are active. Some network support may also be present in state 2, but state 3 is really required to use networking effectively. State 4 is almost never used, but states 5 and 6 are used on some machines to mean shutdown the boot ROM and shutdown and reboot, respectively. Most SVR4 machines based on the 80x86 CPU do not use state 4, while 5 and 6 both cause a reboot.

Changing the Init State

By default, **shutdown** takes the machine to state 0, thus preparing to turn off system power. However, the **-i** argument allows you to explicitly

State	Function
0	Power off the machine
1	Single-user mode
2	Multiuser mode
3	Multiuser with networking
4	Not used
5	Shutdown to ROM (or shutdown and reboot)
6	Shutdown and reboot
s	Single-user mode
S	Single-user mode with remote console

Table 21-1.   init States for SVR4 UNIX Systems

set the init state to some of the available states. The command

```
# shutdown -y -g45 -i0
```

will take the system down, while

```
# shutdown -y -i6
```

will reboot the machine. Most versions of the **shutdown** command only support **init** states 0, s, 5, and 6.

Normally the system will be in state 2 unless you are using the networking facilities, in which case it will be in state 3. The **telinit** command is provided to change between these *operating* states. For example, this command will turn on networking from state 2:

```
# telinit 3
```

You can subsequently return to state 2 with the command

```
# telinit 2
```

The /etc/inittab File

After completing the internal initialization, the system starts the **/sbin/init** (for initialization) demon, which takes control of the bootup sequence. The **init** process remains active for as long as the system is running. It serves several very important functions, the most important of which is to make sure that all the other system demons are executing when they should be. For example, when you log in on the console, the **vtgetty** program is replaced with your shell, and the **vtgetty** process no longer exists. However, when you log off the machine your shell dies, leaving a dead port that cannot be used. It is **init**'s job to recognize that your shell has died and to *respawn* the **vtgetty** for the console, which results in a new display of the **Console Login:** prompt. Actually, when the shell dies, **init** is informed via a system *signal* and then takes appropriate action. In fact, **init** has this role in regard to several other system demons as well, and, in general, it is responsible for assuring that important system processes are running. Of course, if **init** itself dies there will be no process to respawn it, and the system will gradually become more and more deranged until it crashes. Luckily, it is very difficult to kill **init**!

The **init** process takes its instructions from the file **/etc/inittab** (for init table). The contents of this file control all the init states, and the file also determines which processes get respawned when they die. The **inittab** file is a typical UNIX system database, with lines that consist of several fields, each separated by a : (colon). Figure 21-3 shows a typical **inittab** from a small SVR4 system. The contents of **inittab** will differ greatly depending on what software is installed on the machine, how many remote terminals are allowed, and what version of the UNIX system is in use. When **init** starts up, it reads the lines of the **inittab** file in order, and takes action depending on the contents of each line.

The first field of each line is an identifier that effectively "names" each line, and it should be unique. The second field defines the init states for which the line is active. This can be more than one state, as in 23, which defines the line as active in init states 2 and 3. If this field has no content, as in the first several lines in Figure 21-3, that line will be active in *all* init states.

The last field on the line gives a command line that is executed by **init** when the machine is in the states named in the second field. This is

---

```
$ cat /etc/inittab
cc::sysinit:/sbin/chkconsole >/dev/sysmsg 2>&1
ap::sysinit:/sbin/autopush -f /etc/ap/chan.ap
ak::sysinit:/sbin/wsinit 1>/etc/wsinit.err 2>&1
ck::sysinit:/sbin/setclk </dev/console >/dev/sysmsg 2>&1
bchk::sysinit:/sbin/bcheckrc </dev/console >/dev/sysmsg 2>&1
is:2:initdefault:
r0:0:wait:/sbin/rc0 off 1> /dev/sysmsg 2>&1 </dev/console
r1:1:wait:/sbin/rc1  1> /dev/sysmsg 2>&1 </dev/console
r2:23:wait:/sbin/rc2 1> /dev/sysmsg 2>&1 </dev/console
r3:3:wait:/sbin/rc3  1> /dev/sysmsg 2>&1 </dev/console
r5:5:wait:/sbin/rc0 reboot 1> /dev/sysmsg 2>&1 </dev/console
r6:6:wait:/sbin/rc6 reboot 1> /dev/sysmsg 2>&1 </dev/console
sd:0:wait:/sbin/uadmin 2 0 >/dev/sysmsg 2>&1 </dev/console
fw:5:wait:/sbin/uadmin 2 2 >/dev/sysmsg 2>&1 </dev/console
rb:6:wait:/sbin/uadmin 2 1 >/dev/sysmsg 2>&1 </dev/console
li:23:wait:/usr/bin/ln /dev/systty /dev/syscon >/dev/null 2>&1
sc:234:respawn:/usr/lib/saf/sac -t 300
co:12345:respawn:/sbin/vtgetty console console
$
```

Figure 21-3.   Typical /etc/inittab file for a small SVR4 system

a normal shell command line, and redirection of input or output is supported, as shown in several lines in Figure 21-3. Since **init** creates a shell process to execute the command, either shell scripts or executable programs are allowed, and command line expansion will be performed if necessary.

Init Actions

The third field describes the action that **init** should take when it is in one of the states given in the second field. There are several possibilities. The **off** command instructs **init** to kill the named command if it exists, while **once** instructs **init** to execute the program when it enters the named state, without waiting for it to complete. Thus, **init** will continue with its work, not noticing whether the command exits or continues to execute. The **wait** command causes **init** to execute the program when it enters the named states, but to wait until the process completes before continuing. Thus, it is possible to execute commands in a specific sequence through **init**, because the **wait** command causes the command in one line to finish before the next line is executed. Commands specified with **boot** and **bootwait** are executed only when **init** reads the **inittab** file at boot time, and not when it reads the file at other times. They differ in that **bootwait** causes **init** to wait for the command to complete, while **boot** does not. The **initdefault** entry has a special meaning, and will not include a command field. It instructs **init** to enter the named state when it first starts up. Lines with **sysinit** are executed at system initiation, and are completed before the first **Console Login:** prompt appears. Finally, the **respawn** command instructs **init** to start the process when it enters the named states, and to restart (respawn) the program whenever **init** detects that the program is no longer running. Several other commands are possible in the second field, but these are rarely used in most machines.

Boot-Time Processing

With this information, you can read the **inittab** file to see how the boot-up process and the normal activity of the on-going UNIX system will work. Since **init** reads the file sequentially, the entire boot sequence can be understood. In the example in Figure 21-3, the first lines (**chkconsole, autopush** and **wsinit**) begin the boot sequence by establishing a correct device driver environment for the console. These commands are used in the *streams* system to *push* new modules according to the display type in use. The **setclk** command loads the UNIX system date-and-time clock from the hardware clock. File system checking and verification is performed by **/sbin/bcheckrc** (for boot check run control; you might see the **rc** in other contexts as well). This file is used in all **init** states, and is executed only at system boot time. It produces the "Node:" line seen in Figure 21-2. The **bchkrc** script has the function of checking the file system for sanity before it turns the operating system loose with it. Because of a preliminary test to determine whether the file system is thought to be sane, this script will not have much effect when the system has been shut down correctly. However, if the system went down because of a power outage or because of some internal error, the **fsck** (for file system check) command will be executed to clean things up. The **fsck** command is discussed later in this chapter.

The next line is the **initdefault** line, which instructs this machine to boot into state 2. From here to the end of the boot sequence, only lines that contain a 2 in the second field will be executed by **init**. If no **initdefault** line is present, **init** will prompt at the system console for a state to enter. Since this is usually undesirable, the **initdefault** entry is almost always present.

You can configure the machine to boot into state 3 by simply changing the 2 in the **initdefault** line to a 3.

rc Scripts

The next few lines specify scripts to execute when specific states are requested. They are all shell scripts, and can be browsed if you wish. Often **/sbin/rc2** (for run control for state 2) will be executed, because state 2 is frequently used. Again, **init** will wait for the script to be completed before it continues. The script **/sbin/rc2** contains much of the specific initialization code used to create the normal operating environment. The contents of this script differ between versions, but in SVR4 systems its primary function is to examine the directory **/etc/rc2.d**, shown here:

```
$ ls -F /etc/rc2.d
K20nfs          K89xdaemon*      S11uname       S70uucp*      S88smtpd*
K30fumounts     S01MOUNTFSYS*    S15mkdtab*     S75cron*      S89xdaemon*
K40rumounts     S02PRESERVE      S20sysetup*    S75rpc        xS21perf*
K50rfs          S05RMTMPFILES*   S69inet        S80lp*
$
```

The contents of your directory will probably differ from this example. In any case, **/sbin/rc2** will execute the scripts in that directory in a specific order. All files that have names beginning with *K* are executed first, in sequence sorted by their names. Then, all files that have names beginning with *S* are executed, also in sorted order. Generally the K entries are used to *kill* activity, while the S entries are used to *start* things. This arrangement allows developers to add new functions that are active during changes of the **init** state by simply adding new files to the directory **/sbin/rc2.d**. You can browse through this directory to get an understanding of the normal boot process on your machine. In the previous example, the K scripts start by clearing any networking configuration that may exist. This is necessary because the machine may have been in state 3 previously. The scripts **K20nfs** through **K50rfs** handle these chores. These entries will not be present in **rc2.d** if the networking features are not installed on your machine.

The **xntad** demon, a *nameserver* used by the X Window System, is killed next (**K89xdaemon**). Later, near the end of the sequence (**S89xdaemon**) it is restarted so that you can run X across a network.

The S scripts are executed next. They remount the local file systems (**S01MOUNTFSYS**), clean up files in the system temporary directories (**S02PRESERVE** and **S02RMTMPFILES**), clean up the **uucp** directories (**S70uucp**), set up the part of local area networking that is active in state 2 (**S69inet**, **S75rpc**, and **S88smtpd**), and start the **cron** program (**S75cron**). Only files that begin with K or S are executed by **/etc/rc2**, so the file **xS21perf** is ignored.

This same scheme is used when **init** enters states 0, 1, 3 and 6. The script **/sbin/rc0**, **/sbin/rc1**, **/sbin/rc3**, or **/sbin/rc6** is executed as appropriate, which in turn scans the directory **/etc/rc0.d**, **/etc/rc1.d**, **/etc/rc3.d**, or **/etc/rc6.d**. By following the sequence of these scripts and the contents of the directories, you can trace the complete sequence of actions the UNIX system goes through when it changes state.

Once the **rc** scripts have completed all the activities in their respective directories, the process environment of the machine has changed.

This is really all that is involved in moving between **init** states 1, 2 and 3. However, if the user wishes to reboot the machine (states 0, 5, or 6), an actual reboot must be initiated. This is the function of the **uadmin** lines in Figure 21-3. The **uadmin** command takes several arguments that actually force the machine to reboot.

The Service Access Facility

Access to the machine from remote devices, including terminals and modems as well as LAN access, is supported by the new *Service Access Facility* (SAF) in SVR4. The SAF replaces both the **getty** and the old-style **listen** processes on older releases of the UNIX system. The SAF works in several layers. At the top is the **sac** (for service access controller) process. It manages several *services,* including terminal port monitoring (formerly the domain of **getty**) and net access for **uucp** and other nonlogin services. The **sac** program, started from the **inittab**, consults a table of active, or *enabled,* services, and starts service-specific demons to monitor the ports in their respective domains. Typically, **sac** starts **inetd** (the basic Ethernet demon), a new **listen** (network listener), and **ttymon** (terminal port monitor). These services in turn start specific *handler* processes, such as **login,** when activity is detected on one of the devices under their management. This scheme is much more general and efficient than the old **getty** architecture, since one handler process can manage multiple ports. The entry point for this whole system is the single **sac** line in the **inittab.** You can trace this chain of events by examining the process and parent pids in the output of **ps -ef.**

The SAF moves the management of devices out of **init**'s control and into the control of the specific services. Thus, the specific needs of individual services can be met in logical and consistent ways.

One special case is the system console, which must be active in *all* **init** states. Since **sac** is only active in states 2 and 3, the "port monitor" for the console must be a separate process controlled directly by **init.** The **vtgetty** at the end of the **inittab** handles this task. It produces the **Console Login:** prompt. When a user logs in, **vtgetty** disappears, to be replaced by the user's shell. When the user logs out, the shell disappears and **init** respawns a new instance of **vtgetty** to wait for the next login.

Making Changes to the inittab File

Since the port management tasks are under the control of the SAF, there is very little reason to ever change the **inittab** in SVR4 systems.

In older releases, **inittab** was used for individual **getty** lines for each terminal port, lines that look much like the **vtgetty** line in Figure 21-3. If your system has these lines you can disable them by changing the **respawn** action to **off**, and then reenable them by changing the **off** to **respawn**. You may also wish to modify the speed field of a **getty** line. These changes can only be made by the superuser, who can edit the **inittab** file as desired. Note that on many systems changes made directly to **inittab** will not survive the addition of new hardware or software, so you must check your changes whenever you update the system configuration.

The **init** program reads the **inittab** file only once, when it starts up. If you make changes to the file, those changes will not take effect until you inform **init** that the file has changed. You do this by using the **telinit** program, as follows:

```
# telinit q
```

The **q** argument instructs the **init** process to reread the **inittab** file, and take actions based on any *changes* in the file since the last time **init** examined it. There is no change in the init state.

Going Further

The boot and shutdown procedures for a UNIX system can be very involved. Usually when things are just slightly wrong, the system as a whole will not act correctly. Rather than manually debugging the boot procedure and the sequence of events needed to change **init** states, it is usually easier to reload the system software from the original disks. If your data has been backed up correctly, nothing important will be lost when a reload is required. Luckily, the boot sequence is usually quite robust, so things rarely get deranged unless you experiment too much with the **inittab** file or the boot-time scripts processed via **rc0**, **rc1**, **rc2**, or **rc3**.

A Shorter Shutdown Procedure for SVR4

You should rarely try to make the boot-up procedure faster, although you might often wish it would take less time. Indeed, once you come to appreciate the many complex tasks being carried out at boot time, it is easier to tolerate the relatively long boot-up sequence. However, this is not the case with the shutdown procedure. Often there are no users on the machine, and you may understand the processes on the machine well enough to know that none will be unduly affected by being killed abruptly. If you know that the machine is in a relatively quiescent state, you can bypass the **shutdown** command and bring the machine down very quickly. Basically, three actions are required. First, the UNIX system buffers must be synchronized to the disk, so that the disk is up to date; second, any additional file systems beyond the root file system must be unmounted; and third, the disk sanity marker must be correct so that the file system check will not be required the next time you start the machine. This abbreviated procedure is only available on SVR3 and SVR4 systems, and not on earlier versions. Of course all these procedures are reserved for the superuser.

The first requirement is handled by the **sync** command, which updates the machine's hard disk so that it is correct. Normally, this command is executed two or three times in succession, as shown here:

```
# sync
# sync
#
```

To meet the second requirement, you can unmount any mounted file systems beyond the root file system with the **umount** or **umountall** commands. This action safely removes the additional file systems.

The third action is handled by the **uadmin** command, which appears in the **inittab.** The **uadmin** command can also be executed directly by the superuser. It takes two arguments to specify its actions. The first argument 2 causes a shutdown, and the second argument of 1 or 2 causes the machine to immediately reboot with a *hard* reset. Use the second argument 0 (zero) to turn off power to the machine, as follows:

```
# uadmin 2 0
Reboot the system now.
```

When the "Reboot..." message appears, you can turn off the machine. This usually takes only two or three seconds. The arguments to **uadmin** are *not* init states, but special codes used only by **uadmin**. This shortened shutdown sequence should be used with care, and only when you know that system activity is extremely low, with no users, no print jobs, and no remote data transfers in progress.

The fsck Command

There is one more important action usually associated with the boot-up procedure. This is *file system checking.* Since the UNIX system depends so much on the sanity of the file system, a special tool exists to check and repair it. This is the **/sbin/fsck** (for file system check) command, and it is reserved for the superuser. Its functions are many, and its usage is complex. At boot time, the **/sbin/bcheckrc** script tests whether the file system sanity flag was written as part of the shutdown sequence. The **uadmin** command will write this flag correctly, but unexpected shutdowns will not. When the flag exists, the boot-up procedure assumes that the file system is correct (even if it is not!). In this case, the **fsck** command will not be executed, and the boot-up sequence will be noticeably faster. If the flag is not set correctly, the **bcheckrc** script will assume that the file system may have been damaged, and will automatically execute **fsck**. When **fsck** is executed, additional output appears in the boot-time console display.

The **fsck** command can also be executed at the console by the superuser, with the name of a file system to check as an argument, as in Figure 21-4; however, in unskilled hands, this procedure can cause great damage to the file system. It is better to reboot the machine when a file system check is desired, unless you know exactly how to use **fsck**. When you use **fsck** manually, it is desirable to execute it on an *unmounted, raw* file system rather than on an actively mounted file system. In addition, you should specify the file system type you are checking with the **-F** option. Usually the type will be either **s5** or **ufs**, and you can use **fsck** on floppy as well as hard disks. The output will differ depending on which of these is types being checked, but the basic scenario will always be the same.

The **fsck** command executes five different *phases,* or separate parts of the file system check; first, it checks the internal tables of file sizes against the actual sizes of the files on the disk; second, it checks the sanity of the pathnames of directories and files; third, it checks for correct connectivity between files and their parent directories; fourth, it checks the link count between files and their names to be sure that the files are correctly referenced; and fifth, it checks to be sure that all unused disk blocks are correctly entered on the file system *free list*. When errors appear, **fsck** either displays an error message, or prompts the superuser to dispose of the file in some way, either by deleting it or by relinking it into the file system. The **y** responses to the questions shown in Figure 21-4 are examples of manual responses to these prompts. When **fsck** is executed as part of the boot-up procedure, it makes intelligent guesses about the action to take in each case, and does not prompt for your assistance. Generally, the boot-time **fsck** procedure is executed on *each* file system that was in use when the system went down.

```
# fsck -F ufs /dev/rdsk/0s1

** /dev/rdsk/0s1
** Last Mounted on /
** Phase 1 -- Check Blocks and Sizes
INCORRECT BLOCK COUNT I=76 (1 should be 0)
CORRECT? y

INCORRECT BLOCK COUNT I=68199 (1 should be 0)
CORRECT? y

** Phase 2 - Check Pathnames
** Phase 3 - Check Connectivity
** Phase 4 - Check Reference Counts
UNREF FILE I=68199 OWNER=uucp MODE=0
SIZE=0 MTIME=Apr 15 14:56 1990
CLEAR? y

** Phase 5 - Check Cyl groups
BLK(S) MISSING IN BIT MAPS
SALVAGE? y

10244 files, 160869 used, 134117 free (4661 frags, 16182 blocks,
1.6% fragmentation)
/dev/rdsk/0s1 FILE SYSTEM STATE SET TO OKAY

***** FILE SYSTEM WAS MODIFIED *****
#
```

Figure 21-4.   Typical output from **fsck**

When **fsck** finds a file or part of a file that is not correctly linked into the file system, it relinks that file into the system at a special place. This is the **lost+found** directory, and one of these directories should appear in the root directory of each file system that is mounted. Usually these will be **/lost+found** and **/usr/lost+found** if the machine has two file systems. The **lost+found** directory will also appear on floppy disks that contain a file system.

After the boot-up has completed, the superuser can browse through the files or parts of files in the **lost+found** directories to see whether they contain anything of value. Remember, any files in these directories were put there when **fsck** found the files to be in error. Thus, you should watch for files appearing in the **lost+found** directories, because they came from some other place in the file system. Sometimes these files are stray linkages that have no useful contents, but they may be critical system files that were in the process of being updated by the system when the machine went down. The **lost+found** directories can get very large, so you should browse through them occasionally to delete unknown files; however, treat the **lost+found** files very carefully, because it is always difficult to determine what they mean and where in the file system they originated.

Security

Because the UNIX system is designed to support multiple users, it provides many ways for users to access the system, and many tools for communication between users and between different machines. In today's world, however, there are reasons for unauthorized persons to break into a computer system, ranging from the simple thrill of the hunt to malicious damage or commercial theft of data and programs. Thus the many communications-related tools available in the UNIX system are a mixed blessing; you must balance ease of access for your "friends" with preventing access to your "enemies".

The UNIX system was originally developed to serve small groups of people who shared the machine fully. There were no rigid limitations on the access of one user to the files and commands of other users, or even to the most sensitive data used to keep the UNIX system running. Any user could easily delete or change files, or even bring the system down.

Over the years there has been a definite shift in philosophy toward greater security, and the SVR4 release can be made very secure. A skilled system administrator can totally control access to the system, and the UNIX system is now as secure as most other operating systems. Versions of SVR4 have been certified at U.S. Department of Defense B2 and B3 security levels. However, issues of security are complex, because there are so many subsystems, and everything must be correctly tuned for optimal security.

In this chapter we will review the issue of computer security and explore some related tools and commands. As you grow more and more dependent on your UNIX machine and the files and data it contains, the security of the system becomes more important. You can take steps to prevent unauthorized access, but the natural tendency of a complex operating system is toward less security over a period of time; you must be constantly alert for security loopholes, and quick to defend your system by plugging those holes.

If security is *truly* a concern, you can get the *UNIX System V/MLS* (for multilevel security) software from AT&T, which implements the B2 or B3 security levels.

A Security Policy

Within a machine or network of machines, the system administrator or the user group as a whole should establish a consistent security *policy* to guide the assignment of new user ids, the amount of password protection required within the system, and the amount of connectivity the machine allows to LANs and the outside world. The policy should be published for new users, and regular *sweeps* of the file system should be made to assess compliance with the policy. If the system is relatively isolated and has a small group of users with the same community of interest, the security policy can be relatively lax. On the other hand, if the system is large and has several user groups, a high public profile, or contains especially sensitive or proprietary data, the security policy must be more restrictive. The primary responsibility for compliance belongs to each individual user, although system administrators can develop a procedure of regular audits with feedback to the user community.

Beyond the security policy, the most important rule is *know your system.* If the system administrator and users frequently use the **ps, who, ls** and other system information commands, they become familiar with normal day-to-day activity on the machine, and alert to the *state* of the system at all times. Then, deviations from the norm are quickly noticed, so that the system administrator can take appropriate action to plug loopholes.

Security issues fall naturally into several general categories; first is protecting your private files and data from other users; second, is protecting the key operating system files from damage, either intentional or accidental; third, is the physical security of the machine; and fourth is protecting the system against determined attacks by skilled "hackers" bent on breaching or destroying the system. We will discuss each of these topics in the following sections.

Protecting Your Data from Other Users

When you share a machine with other users, you must make decisions concerning how much you want the other users to share your data. As discussed in Chapter 4, files in the file system have three levels of permissions: those for the individual user, those for the *group* the user belongs to, and those for all the other users on the machine. Normally, in a small machine where users share a strong community of interest, the system administrator will establish a single group for all users, so that users can share files at the group level while individual users can protect files for their own use. In larger installations where several unrelated communities exist, there may be many different groups.

As you may recall from Chapter 4, the command **ls -l** displays the permissions on a file or directory, as shown here:

```
$ ls -1 /etc/inittab
-r--r--r--  1 root     sys         526 Apr 10 19:49 /etc/inittab
$
```

The file has three sets of permissions for each of the three security levels; that is, it has read, write, and execute access for the owner, for the group, and for all other users. Each file is owned by a login id, and belongs to a group. In the previous example, the file owner is **root** and the group is **sys**. The file is readable by all, but is not writable or executable by anyone.

When you create a new file, you are the owner of the file, and your group is assigned as the group id. You can give away ownership of the file with the **chown** command, and you can change the group of the file with **chgrp**, but only if you own the file. Normally you cannot reclaim ownership once you have given it away, although if a file is readable you can make a new copy of it with your ownership restored. Only the superuser can change the permissions of any file in the system.

Default Permissions for File Creation

After you create a file, you should check the permissions with **ls -l** to be sure the permissions are what you want. Is it acceptable for everyone in your group to have access to the data? Should anyone else be allowed to read or write the file? You must ask these questions and set the permissions for each file you create.

The UNIX system automatically gives the creator of a file ownership of the file, and assigns the file to its creator's group. Although this cannot be changed, you can set a system variable associated with your login id that will set the *permissions* of a file without explicit action on your part. This system variable is called the **umask** (for user file-creation mask), and it is accessed with the **umask** command. You can determine the current value of the **umask** by executing the command with no arguments, as follows:

```
$ umask
000
$
```

Here, the result is three octal digits that refer to the owner, the group, and the other permissions, from left to right. This number is called a *mask* because each digit is subtracted from a systemwide default permission that all new files get. Normally this systemwide permission is **-rw-rw-rw-,** but individual systems and programs may differ. Because the user's **umask** is subtracted from this default value, you cannot use the **umask** to turn on permissions that are normally turned off, but you can turn off permissions that are normally turned on. Of course, you can explicitly turn on permissions with **chmod** if you own the file.

Each octal digit in the **umask** contains a binary bit that *clears* a permission: a 1 will clear the execute permission, a 2 will clear the write permission, and a 4 will clear the read permission. Thus, if a digit is zero, the default is used; for example, the previous **umask**, 000, means don't change any of the default values. The **umask** value 022 would create files with no write permission for the group or for others. For example:

```
$ umask
000
$ > def.perm
$ ls -1 def.perm
-rw-rw-rw-  1 steve     other        0 May 10 14:57 def.perm
$ umask 022
$ umask
022
$ > no.write
$ ls -1 no.write
-rw-r--r--  1 steve     other        0 May 10 14:58 no.write
$ umask 777
& > no.perm
$ls -1 no.perm
----------  1 steve     other        0 May 10 14:58 no.perm
$
```

The default **umask** of 000, creates files with the default permissions. When you reset your **umask** to 022, you create files with no write permission for other users. The **umask** 777 turns off all permissions for all users, so the last file in the previous example is not accessible at all!

To set your **umask**, use the **umask** command with the octal code as an argument. This setting does not survive after you log out, so if you want to permanently change your **umask**, put the **umask** command in your **.profile**. This way you do not need to consider the permissions for each file you create.

File Encryption

You can further protect files that require special treatment by *encrypting* them. Most UNIX systems in the United States provide tools to scramble files according to a password that you provide; only by reentering the correct password can you access such a file. File encryption is not available in implementations sold outside the United States.

Editors such as **ed, vi,** and **emacs** give you the ability to create and edit encrypted files. You can tell your editor to *decrypt* a file when it loads it, and encrypt it again when you write the file out to disk. The **-x** option specifies encryption, as follows:

```
$ vi -x crypt.file
Key:
```

Here, the editor is prompting for the encryption password or *key*. Enter the key just as you enter your password when you log in. Any password is acceptable when you encrypt a file, but of course you must use the same password to decrypt the file. As usual, the password is not echoed. If you enter the password correctly, the file will be decrypted and will come up in your editor. When you write the file back out during or after your editing session, it will be encrypted again. You can use this procedure to create a new file or to edit an existing file.

Versions of the UNIX system sold in the United States also provide a filter to do encryption and decryption. The **crypt** command reads its standard input and writes to its standard output. If the input is in *plain text*, the output will be encrypted. If the input is encrypted, the output will be decrypted. Like the editing procedure, **crypt** prompts for a password, as shown here:

```
$ cat plain.text | crypt
Enter key:
```

As usual, the password is not echoed.

Unfortunately, the algorithm by which files are encrypted under the UNIX system is a little too well known, and programs that can break the encryption algorithm are available. Thus, it is not safe to put excessive trust in encrypted files, especially in a hostile environment. The crypt-breaker programs work by analyzing the frequencies of characters in the encrypted files, and comparing them to character frequencies in normal English text. To defeat them, you can change the character frequencies of the plain text before encryption with another filter such as **pack** or **compress.** For example:

```
$ compress plain.text
$ crypt < plain.text.Z > out.file
```

The compressed file cannot be analyzed by any known crypt-breaker. Of course, when you decrypt the file you must remember to unpack it, as follows:

```
$ crypt < out.file > plain.text.z
$ uncompress plain.text.Z
$
```

Remember, you must compress before encrypting, and uncompress after decrypting.

Of course, the most successful file protection scheme is to write the file to a floppy disk or tape, delete the file from the machine, and keep the magnetic media with you.

Login Ids and Passwords

The heart of the UNIX system's security scheme is the individual user's login id and password. If potential attackers can be kept off the system completely, they can cause no damage. Unfortunately, in many machines password security is so poor that even an unskilled attacker can get to a shell. It is the responsibility of each user to defend his or her password, and to change it regularly.

Many user ids on a typical small system have no password at all, or their password is so similar to their login id as to be ineffective for security. Unfortunately, most users do not like to use the kind of arcane password that is really required for security, so over time passwords often become detectable. Every user should be forced to have a password, and the password should be *aged* so that the user is forced to change it regularly. Because the password is stored in encrypted form, even the system administrator cannot determine what it is. Luckily, the letter frequency attack mentioned earlier is not possible with a very short sample of text like a password.

The tool for changing your password is the **passwd** command. As discussed in Chapter 2, it prompts you for your current password before allowing you to change it. Then it requires you to enter the new password twice before it takes effect.

In most UNIX systems, there are rules that describe an acceptable password, and even if these rules are not enforced by the system software, they make good guidelines for creating your own password. A good password has at least six characters, of which at least one (preferably two) is a numeric or other nonalphabetic character. A mix of uppercase and lowercase characters is good, and any unusual or nonintuitive sequence of characters is also helpful. Some examples of unacceptably *trivial* passwords are your login id, your name, your child's name, your room or telephone number, your astrological sign, your address, and so on.

Login History

Most SVR4 releases provide a display that shows the *last* time your login id was used. The display appears when you log in to the machine, as follows:

```
login: steve
Password:

Login last used: Wed Oct 24 15:11:02 1990

$
```

This display is intended to alert you if someone else is using your login id. If the time differs from your recollection of your last login, your login id is being misused, and you should immediately take steps to change your password.

This feature is maintained by the **login** program when it verifies your password. It keeps a zero-length file called **.lastlogin** in your home directory. The last login date and time are the modification date of this file. The **.lastlogin** file is owned by the system, not by the individual user, and its permissions make it difficult to change, as you can see here:

```
$ ls -1 $HOME/.lastlogin
-r--------    1  root      sys          0 Oct 28 15:11 .lastlogin
```

This is not a strong security feature, but it can warn you if your login id has been compromised.

The Superuser

Each normal user is restricted to their own files and data, and those of their group. However, the **root** login id is provided on all UNIX machines to allow full read, write, and execute access to all files and directories. This user is known as the *superuser* (for super permissions). You can also use the **su** (for superuser) command to switch to superuser status without logging off and logging on again as **root**, as shown here:

```
$ /sbin/su
Password:
#
```

Chapter 12 discusses the superuser in detail.

The Password File

The critical information that controls user logins is maintained in a simple database in the file **/etc/passwd**. As you can see here, this file is readable by all users, but is not writable:

```
$ ls -1 /etc/passwd
-r--r--r--  1 root     root       526 Apr 10 19:49 /etc/passwd
$
```

These permissions should be carefully maintained; if the **/etc/passwd** file is writable by anyone, system security is easily breached.

Each user has a line in the password file, and there are also several standard systemwide login ids that are required for correct functioning of the system. Figure 22-1 shows a sample **passwd** file for an SVR4 system. Each line in the password file consists of several fields, each delimited by a : (colon). The user's login id comes first on the line, and a placeholder for the user's password (**x**) is the second field. The third field is the numeric representation of the *user id*, and the fourth is the numeric representation of the *group id*. These two fields work with file permissions to determine who can access each file in the system. The fifth field is a comment that usually contains the user's name and address. The next-to-last field contains the user's home directory, and the last field contains the full pathname of the user's login shell. If the last field is blank, it defaults to **/sbin/sh**.

In older releases of the UNIX system, the second field contained the actual encrypted password for each user. In SVR3, however, a second file was introduced into the system to contain the encrypted password and some other data. This file is **/etc/shadow**, and it should only be readable by **root,** as shown here:

```
$ ls -1 /etc/shadow
-r--------  1 root     root             187 Apr 10 19:49 /etc/shadow
$
```

```
$ cat /etc/passwd
root:x:0:1:0000-Admin(0000):/:
daemon:x:1:1:0000-Admin(0000):/:
bin:x:2:2:0000-Admin(0000):/usr/bin:
sys:x:3:3:0000-Admin(0000):/:
adm:x:4:4:0000-Admin(0000):/var/adm:
uucp:x:5:5:0000-uucp(0000):/usr/lib/uucp:
lp:x:7:8:0000-LP(0000):/home/lp:/sbin/sh
nuucp:x:10:10:0000-uucp(0000):/var/spool/uucppublic:/usr/lib/uucp/uucico
listen:x:37:4:Network Admin:/usr/net/nls:
sync:x:67:1:0000-Admin(0000):/:/usr/bin/sync
install:x:101:1:Initial Login:/home/install:
sysadm:x:0:0:general system administration:/usr/admin:/usr/sbin/sysadm
vmsys:x:102:100:FACE executables:/home/vmsys:/sbin/sh
oasys:x:103:1:Object Architecture Files:/home/oasys:/sbin/sh
steve:x:104:1:Steve:/home/steve:/usr/bin/ksh
pat:x:105:1:Pat:/home/pat:
jim:x:106:1:Jim:/home/jim:/usr/bin/ksh
$
```

Figure 22-1.   A typical **/etc/passwd** file

The **/etc/shadow** file contains the users' login ids, their encrypted passwords, a numeric code that describes when each password was last changed, and the minimum and maximum number of days required between password changes. For example:

```
# cat /etc/shadow
root:k2kLQBmtvd3Xw:7337::::::
daemon:NONE:7337::::::
bin:NONE:7337::::::
sys:NONE:7337::::::
adm:NONE:7337::::::
uucp:NONE:7337::::::
lp:NONE:7337::::::
nuucp::7388::::::
listen:np:7337::::::
sync:NONE:7337::::::
install:q20ahnOya9Dwg:7337::::::
sysadm:SYfb81BvwtwgA:7388::::::
vmsys:*LK*:::::::
oasys:*LK*:::::::
steve:R3cNOStpwogNA:7388:1:1000:900:::
pat:w4royOD17CX1y:7388:1:1000:900:::
jim:Ry09pLJkadskm:7394:1:1000:900:::
#
```

There will be one line in **/etc/shadow** for each line in **/etc/passwd**. When **/etc/shadow** is present, the password field in **/etc/passwd** is replaced by the single character **x**. Otherwise, the second field in **/etc/passwd** will look like the second field in the previous example of **/etc/shadow**.

The **/etc/shadow** file is created by the command **pwconv**, which reads **/etc/passwd** for the necessary information. Whenever you change **/etc/passwd** manually, you should immediately execute **pwconv** to be sure the changes are updated to **/etc/shadow**. The password and shadow files should not be writable, so only the superuser can change them.

A Typical /etc/passwd File

Figure 22-1 shows a typical **/etc/passwd** file for an SVR4 machine. Even before you begin adding users, several login ids are included in the default system. These login ids are required for the correct operation of the machine, and you cannot delete or change them substantially without damaging the system. The login ids, the user and group ids, the home directory, and even the default shell should not be changed on any login that does not belong to a real user.

The login **root** is the superuser. This is user id zero, and its home directory is the **root** directory **/** (slash). The **root** login should *always* have a password. An unprotected **root** login is the very worst security violation possible in the UNIX system, because the **root** user has complete access to everything in the system. The next few login ids are for other administrative tools, and in large installations these are used by individuals who are responsible for the administration of the different subsystems. Normally on a small machine with a single system administrator, you can disable these login ids by editing the string *NONE* or some other plain-text string into the password field in **/etc/shadow**. Since the password is decrypted from the entry in **/etc/shadow**, a plain-text string here will be decrypted into a nonsense string that users will not be able to guess when they try to log in.

The functions of these disabled login ids should be performed by the **root** user. All the login ids with a password of NONE or *LK* in the previous **/etc/shadow** example are of this type.

Because add-on software often adds administrative logins, the logins on a system may differ depending on the hardware setup on the machine.

The login **nuucp** is used by remote machines that wish to log in to send you mail. The shell for this login is **/usr/lib/uucp/uucico**, the program that handles data transfer for the **uucp** subsystem. Since this is not a normal shell, and the **uucico** program is very secure, you do not need a password to use the **nuucp** login. The similar login id **uucp** is for administration of the **uucp** subsystem, and should be disabled.

The individual users are listed near the bottom of Figure 22-1. There are three users on this system: **pat, jim,** and **steve**. These users each have their own user id number in field 3, but they all belong to the same group, group 1, as indicated in field 4. They should all have passwords in **/etc/shadow**. Note that **pat** uses the default shell, but **steve** and **jim** get a different shell when they log in to the machine.

To reiterate, all login ids should have passwords except **nuucp**. These should be either legitimate encrypted passwords for real users and **root**, or plain-text passwords for all other logins.

Adding and Deleting Users

Although it is usually easy to add or remove users, only the superuser can do so. The tools **useradd, userdel,** and **usermod** are designed for these jobs, and using them is much preferable to adding a user manually or to using the obsolete **passmgmt** command. If you do change user control files such as **/etc/passwd** manually, take care to retain the original permissions and ownership of the files.

Recall that each user has a login id, a numeric user id, a home directory, a default shell, and a password. When you create a new user, you must specify values for all of these items. The **useradd** command, which is designed to add new users to the system, keeps default values for some of these items, but you need to select the others when you add a new user. Use the **-D** (for display) option of **useradd** to display the defaults, as follows:

```
# useradd -D
group=other,1  basedir=/home  skel=/etc/skel
shell=/sbin/sh  inactive=0  expire=
#
```

This example shows the normal defaults that are assigned to new users if you take no specific action. New users will belong to group **other**, with group id (gid) 1. Their home directory will be under the **/home** directory, and they will get the standard shell as their default. The *inactive* and *expire* entries refer to password aging parameters, which are discussed later in this chapter.

Actually, these defaults are saved in the directory **/etc/skel**. You can change them by using the **-D** option of **useradd**, with a command-line argument to set the value of each default. This procedure is not recommended in smaller systems.

To add a new user, give the user's login id after the **useradd** command, as follows:

```
# useradd jim
#
```

This will create the user's entry in **/etc/passwd** and **/etc/shadow** using the default values, and will also create a home directory for the user.

If things work right, **useradd** will return silently. If the login id already exists, **useradd** will complain, as shown here:

```
# useradd jim
UX: useradd: ERROR: jim is already in use. Choose another.
#
```

Each login id must be unique, but the home directory, numeric user id, and other information can be shared among users, although this is not usually a good idea. Accountability in the system is much improved if each user has an individual environment. The only exception is the group id, which is intended to be shared among users.

Normally when you create a login id, you should add a *comment* that gives the user's name, affiliation, and other relevant information. This comment will appear in the user's **/etc/passwd** entry, and will help you keep track of users, especially on a large system. To add a comment, use the -c option in your **useradd** command line followed by the quoted comment, as follows:

```
# useradd -c "Jim, 555-1234, Suite 320" jim
```

By using additional command-line arguments to **useradd**, you can override the other defaults as well. You can select a specific user id (**-u**), a group id (**-g**), a home directory (**-d**), and a shell (**-s**), as well as other parameters associated with the login. With the **-e** (for expire) option, you can select an *expiration date* for the login. This allows you to create a temporary login that becomes invalid after a specified date. For example:

```
# useradd -e "12/31/90" -c "Temporary login for yabu project" jim
```

Several different date formats are acceptable with this option.

Password Aging

When you create a login id using **useradd**, the entry in **/etc/shadow** has a *locked* password, so the new user is not yet allowed access to the system. You must enable the login by selecting some *password aging* parameters before the user can use the system.

The password software allows (nearly requires!) the system administrator to set up a password aging procedure that forces all users to change their passwords regularly. When a password is established, a clock is started, and when the established interval passes, the password is discarded and you are required to choose a new one. When a new login is created, the superuser enables password aging using the **passwd** command. This procedure also clears the locked status of the password given to a new user. These features are limited to the superuser, and are supported by several command-line options to the **passwd** command.

To set the maximum number of days a password can be active before it must be changed, use the **-x** option with a number of days, as shown here:

```
# passwd -x 120 jim
#
```

To set the minimum number of days a password must be active before it can be changed, use the **-n** option, as follows:

```
# passwd -n 7 jim
#
```

These options will return silently if there is no error. You must set the maximum interval before you are allowed to set the minimum interval, or you can place both options on the same command line.

The **passwd** command can also report on the status of a user's passwd with the -s (for status) option. Here is an example:

```
# passwd -s jim
jim LK 00/00/00 7 120
#
```

As you can see, the user id comes first, followed by a status: LK means locked, PS means correctly password protected, and NP means no password. Next comes the date on which the password was last changed (00/00/00 if the login is new), followed by the minimum and maximum intervals discussed earlier.

After you have set the password aging parameters, you can remove the locked status with the **-d** (for delete) option, as follows:

```
# passwd -d jim
#
```

The **-d** option can also delete the password for a normal user. This option should be used with extreme care, because a login with no password is a security risk.

No one can create a new password for another user, so when a new user is added to the system the best procedure is for the administrator to immediately log in using the new login id, and set a starting password manually. Then the administrator can log back in as **root**, and execute

```
# passwd -f jim
```

(for force), which immediately expires the newly created password. When the intended user logs in for the first time, he or she will use the starting password, but will be required to change that password immediately, as shown here:

```
login: jim
Password:
Your password has expired.  Choose a new one
Old password:
```

This message will also appear for established users when the maximum time allowed for their passwords has elapsed.

In general, password aging is helpful for maintaining security, because users' passwords tend to become publicly known after they have been in use for a while, and requiring them to change regularly can reduce security violations. Forcing users to change their passwords two or three times a year is usually sufficient. One weakness of password aging is that users often alternate between two favorite passwords that are merely trivial permutations of each other. This practice should be discouraged, for the reasons discussed earlier.

Deleting a User

When a user has finished with the system, for whatever reason, the system administrator should take immediate action to *delete* the user's access to the system. This can be done in two ways, depending on the goal. First, you can lock the user's password, retaining the user's home directory and login. This prevents the user from entering the system, but later you can unlock the login without loss of the user's data. Use the **-l** (for lock) option of the **passwd** command, as follows:

```
# passwd -l jim
```

Alternatively, you can fully delete the user from the system. Use the **userdel** (for user delete) command, shown here, for this purpose:

```
# userdel jim
#
```

This command will return silently if it succeeds, but it cannot be used if the user is currently logged in. The **userdel** command will retain the user's home directory so that you can save the materials in it if you wish. To delete the user and the home directory (along with its subdirectories), add the **-r** (for remove) option, as shown here:

```
# userdel -r jim
```

You can change the parameters associated with an existing user, without deleting and then reestablishing the user, with the **usermod** command.

You must take care to keep up-to-date with deleting users. Often when a user leaves the system, for whatever reason, the system administrator does not immediately disable the login id. This is especially common in large systems with hundreds of users, and it presents a serious security risk, because ex-users may harbor a grudge, and can cause serious damage to the machine. You should take unusual care to peruse the password file regularly, and to disable users who are no longer active.

Adding Groups

When you add a new user to an existing group id (or accept the defaults), no further activity is needed after you run the **useradd** and

passwd commands. However, if you wish to create a new group for the user, or if you wish the user to appear in *multiple* groups, you must edit the file **/etc/group**. You can use the command **addgrp** (for add to group) or **delgrp** (for delete from group) to create new groups. Examine the file **/etc/group**, shown here, to see what groups are in use:

```
$ cat /etc/group
root::0:root
other::1:steve,pat,jim
bin::2:root,bin,daemon
sys::3:root,bin,sys,adm
adm::4:root,adm,daemon
mail::6:root
tty::7:root,tty
lp::8:root,lp
daemon::12:root,daemon
uucp::5:root,uucp
vm::100:
$
```

This file is a typical database that has fields delimited by colons. The group name in the leftmost field, and the group numeric id in the third field will appear in **ls -l** output. If users are allowed to change groups using the **newgrp** (for new group) command, the second field will contain an encrypted password that the user must enter before changing groups. Such changes of group should normally be disabled.

The final field in **/etc/group** contains a comma-separated list of user ids that belong to each group. A user may be in more than one group, and thus have access to files that belong to different groups. To redistribute users among groups, you must edit **/etc/group** manually, limiting your changes to the last field. The file **/etc/group** should be readable by all, but not writable or executable by anyone.

The Restricted Shell

The standard shell provides a great many capabilities that allow a user to move around in the file system, execute commands, change the PATH, and so forth. However, an additional shell called **rsh** (for restricted shell) is provided in most UNIX systems. This is usually the same executable program as the normal shell, which exists under two names in the system; it just acts differently depending on the name used to invoke it. In SVR4, the restricted shell is often located in the **/usr/lib** directory. Note that this is not the *remote shell* used with LANs, which usually resides in **/usr/sbin/rsh**. The restricted shell allows many fewer capabilities than the normal shell. You can set **/usr/lib/rsh** as a user's shell with the command

```
# useradd -s /usr/lib/rsh jim
```

Then the user will get the restricted shell instead of the standard shell.
    The **rsh** differs from the normal shell in these ways:

1. The user cannot use **cd** to change directories. The user is limited to the home directory.

2. The user cannot change the PATH variable, so only commands in the PATH set up by the system administrator are allowed.

3. The user cannot name commands or files using a complete path-name, so only files in the home directory and its subdirectories can be accessed.

4. The user cannot redirect output with > or > >.

These restrictions are enforced after the user's **.profile** is executed. The system administrator will set up a restricted environment in the user's **.profile**, including a PATH that points to a limited **bin** directory, and will then change the ownership of the **.profile** to **root** and make it readable by all, but writable or executable by no one. The user with the restricted shell will then be limited to the home directory and the commands allowed in the PATH.
    The **rsh** limits naive users from straying too far from their intended environment into the system files. Normally, the **rsh** is given to users who have a limited reason for logging in to the machine. For example, a bulletin board system might use the **rsh** for its users, or a word processing clerk might be limited in this way. Usually, you do not want to limit skilled users with **rsh**, because it interferes with their work needlessly. Also, the **rsh** is not completely secure, and any skilled attacker can break through it into the normal shell without difficulty. You cannot

depend on **rsh** as a security tool for hostile attackers, but it is useful for keeping unskilled users from inadvertently injuring themselves or the system.

Protection of the UNIX System and Files

Even skilled users can damage the UNIX system if they have too much access to key files, such as **/etc/passwd** or the **uucp** data. You must take care to prevent the system from becoming less secure as a result of the normal changes that occur during its lifetime. The method is easy to explain, but difficult to accomplish: just keep all file permissions and ownership the same as they were when the system was installed. Normally, the initial load of a UNIX system sets all the files and directories to the correct, secure, permissions. The only exception may be the system login ids in **/etc/passwd**, which often have no passwords by default. Inevitably, over time, the permissions will gradually become less secure, because no one is perfectly attentive to security. Files become more accessible, passwords disappear, inactive user logins accumulate, and so on.

Since no one is perfect in this regard, it is usually good policy to regularly reload the machine from the original system software. This places a burden on users, and on the system administrator who has no doubt *customized* the machine, but when security violations are suspected, it is the only way to assure a safe system. Normally, reloading once or twice a year is sufficient for most machines. When you reload, you can also assure that the password file is current, and clean up a lot of unused commands and files that may be clogging your disks. Of course, a good data backup procedure makes reloading the system much simpler.

A second approach is to conduct regular *sweeps* of the machine and its file system, possibly using an automated script to verify that file permissions and ownerships are secure. No such tool is officially provided in SVR4, but several samples have appeared on the net. In fact, some commercial *inoculation* products work on this principle to detect various forms of file corruption. Such a tool is necessarily dependent on the specific installation, but a clever system administrator could create a useful tool.

Physical Security

In the previous discussion, we have focused on user login ids and how to establish security for normal users. However, there are many potential security hazards other than those caused by users you allow into the system. You must also be concerned with direct access to the machine by people who can walk up to it in your absence.

In all cases, the primary form of security for a UNIX system is *physical security.* If you can prevent access to the machine, by keeping it in a locked room, or by making sure there are no external connections like modems or LAN connections, you can guarantee that security will not be breached. A truly secure system has no external data connections except for hard-wired terminals in locked rooms. If all login ids are correctly protected with passwords, no unauthorized access is possible.

Many UNIX systems can be accessed by rebooting them from a "master" floppy disk or tape. Many recent machines have password protection in ROM to retard such reboots, but even these are not completely secure. An attacker who is able to get to the machine can often reboot it and enjoy full privileges from their own version of the operating system on their bootable disk. Therefore, you must take care that the machine itself is not accessible.

Another, more devious, kind of attack on physical security originates with the software and applications that you load. Any disk or application package you load onto the machine may have security traps added by the developer or by an enemy who might have held the software before you received it. In a typical scenario the software is loaded correctly, but some part of it contains a security breach that is activated when that part of the program is executed. Either the program itself causes damage to the machine, or some modification is made to the system so that an attacker can break in. These problems do not usually occur with commercially available packages, but any "uncertified" software should be regarded with suspicion. Free software available from bulletin boards or pirated software circulated by hand is especially suspect. You cannot usually detect these problems until after the damage is done, so it is wise to be extremely leery of adding unknown software to your machine. In the worst case, security-conscious system administrators will demand access to the source code for applications, examine it carefully in a secure environment, and then compile it directly for the target machine. This isn't usually possible, but in any case you can be alert for suspicious behavior on the part of your software sources.

Local Area Networks

Environments in which many machines are connected via a Local Area Network (LAN) are especially dangerous security risks, because if attackers can get into any one machine on the network, they can usually "jump" to the other machines. It is important that users of all machines on a network understand the importance of secure passwords.

Since they usually are associated with a single project, many LANs have tools, such as the NFS or **rlogin** tools, that allow easy sharing of files and data between machines. Naturally this is risky, but it is usually acceptable if the individual machines are kept secure. Sometimes an additional password is required before access to the network is allowed. This may slow users' daily activities, but it can provide additional protection when security is a major issue.

Most LANs allow *domains,* which are groups of machines that can easily share files or remote logins. Machines outside a particular domain may be restricted from accessing that domain. With domains, the security of one machine on the LAN can be compromised without corrupting the entire LAN. Thus, domains can significantly ease the security burden. Consult with your net administrator to establish a security policy for your LAN.

uucp Security

The **uucp** data communications subsystems are a potential security risk, since these tools are expressly designed to *allow* remote access from the outside world. When **uucp** works, it connects to another machine and executes commands remotely on that machine, reading and writing files as requested. If security is weak, an attacker or just an honest mistake in the use of **uucp** can seriously damage your machine. However, the modern **uucp** software is very secure and robust, *providing security precautions are observed.* Like other aspects of the UNIX system, **uucp** security naturally degrades over time. You must be vigilant in monitoring the **uucp** tools.

The major security issue associated with **uucp** is the permissions of the **uucp** files. The materials in the directory **/usr/lib/uucp** must keep the permissions that they had when you initially loaded the software on the system. It is good practice to list these files with **ls -la** soon after you load the machine, and then to check their correctness carefully whenever you change anything in the **/usr/lib/uucp** or **/etc/uucp** directories.

The **uucp** system is designed so that a machine has a *public* directory hierarchy in which all **uucp** activity normally takes place. This public area is required if you allow any **uucp** activity on the machine. In addition, there is a list of commands that can be executed by a remote machine running the **uux** command. Normally, the public directory location is **/var/spool/uucppublic** (also known as **/usr/spool/uucppublic**) and the command list available remotely is only the mail command **rmail**. You cannot receive mail from remote machines unless you allow other machines to execute your **rmail** command.

The uucp Permissions File

Permissions related to **uucp** can be customized. The control data is kept in a file that is read by the **uucp** programs when they are executed. If a request is made that is not allowed by the control data, the request is refused and the **uucp** connection is broken. If the request is within the acceptable list, it is honored. The file **/etc/uucp/Permissions** (also known as **/usr/lib/uucp/Permissions**) contains this information, but only the superuser and the **nuucp** login should be able to read it.

The permissions can range from quite open to very restrictive. Usually the default established when the machine is loaded is quite limited. A typical wide-open **Permissions** file is shown here:

```
# cat /etc/uucp/Permissions

# This entry is wide-open....
```

```
LOGNAME=uucp:nuucp  REQUEST=yes SENDFILES=yes READ=/ WRITE=/
MACHINE=OTHER COMMANDS=ALL REQUEST=yes READ=/ WRITE=/
#
```

The format is a normal ASCII file, where lines beginning with a **#** (pound sign) are treated as comments, and the remaining lines contain data. The basic layout is a series of lines that contain *keyword = value* pairs, where the keywords describe the capabilities to be controlled, and the values set the permissions allowed. If there is more than one value for a keyword, you must separate the items with a : (colon), as in the **LOGNAME = uucp:nuucp** entry above. Each line can control a specific set of permissions, determining either how the machine acts when it calls other machines, or how other machines are treated when they call your machine. You will frequently use several lines of both types to tailor your **uucp** system to your needs.

The Default Permissions

By default, **uucp** permissions are relatively restricted, so a very simple entry will give good security. You can simply use

```
LOGNAME=nuucp
```

as the entire contents of the **Permissions** file. The keyword *LOGNAME* is used to refer to the login ids that may request **uucp** services. This is not for real users local to your machine, but rather refers to remote machines that may call your machine and request **uucp** services.

The simple entry **LOGNAME = nuucp** restricts remote access to the **uucp** system to the login id **nuucp**, which is normal. Recall that the default "shell" for this login is **/usr/lib/uucp/uucico**, a secure program for data communications. With this simple **Permissions** file, the **uucp** system is restricted to file transfers to and from the public directory **/usr/spool/uucppublic**, and only the default **rmail** command is allowed.

Customizing the Permissions File

You can add more lines to the **Permissions** file to customize **uucp** security to your needs. In a more complex **Permissions** file there are two types of lines: those that modify the actions of the system for incoming calls, and those that modify the actions for connections to specific machines that you call. The line that begins "LOGNAME = . . ." affects all incoming calls, and any line that begins "MACHINE = . . ." refers to specific machines that you call. There can be only one line that begins LOGNAME= in your **Permissions** file, but as many MACHINE= lines as you need. As you modify these **Permissions** lines, add additional *keyword = value* pairs on the same line. If the line grows too long, you can break it by ending the line with \ (backslash) to escape the newline.

Controlling Incoming Calls with the LOGNAME Line

When another machine calls you, you can allow jobs queued to it to be sent, or you can force your machine to call that machine before outgoing jobs are sent. The second choice is more secure, because a calling machine can lie about its **uname**, and take files not intended for it. This lying is called *spoofing* the **uucp** system, and the only certain way to prevent it is to make your machine call another machine whenever you have jobs spooled for it. Add the keyword SENDFILES= to the LOGNAME= line to control whether or not jobs are sent when your machine is called. For example,

```
LOGNAME=nuucp SENDFILES=yes
```

will allow such transfers, while

```
LOGNAME=nuucp SENDFILES=no
```

will prevent these transfers in all cases. By default, **SENDFILES = call**, which means files will only be sent to another machine when your machine calls it, not when it calls you.

Similarly, you can add the keyword REQUEST= to control whether or not your machine allows a remote machine to request files from your system. For example,

```
LOGNAME=nuucp SENDFILES=yes REQUEST=yes
```

will allow a remote machine to grab files from you, whether or not you have queued them for sending. This feature can be very dangerous and should usually be set to **REQUEST = no**.

You can also specify what directories you allow remote machines to use when they read or write files, by adding the READ = and WRITE = keywords to the LOGNAME = entry. The directory you specify names a complete substructure, so that any directory *under* the named directory can also be written or read. If you use **READ = /** and **WRITE = /**, you allow reading and writing from all directories on the machine. This is definitely not recommended. By default, the values **READ = /var/spool/ uucppublic** and **WRITE = /var/spool/uucppublic** are used. This is the recommended public directory.

When a machine calls you, you can set the **uucp** system to refuse the call, but to trigger your machine to immediately call that machine back. Use **CALLBACK = yes** on the LOGNAME = line to force this callback behavior. By default callback is not required (that is, **CALLBACK = no**).

Controlling Outgoing Calls with the MACHINE Lines

You can modify these permissions for a specific machine or list of machines by using the MACHINE = entry at the beginning of the line. Any change to the command list from the defaults is associated with a specific machine that you must name explicitly in the MACHINE = entry. If you want all calling machines to have the same permissions, you can use the special string *OTHER* following MACHINE = to refer to all machines, or you can name specific machines if you wish. REQUEST =, SENDFILES =, READ =, and WRITE = can appear in the MACHINE = line, as well as in the LOGNAME = line.

In addition, you can change the list of commands that other machines can execute on your machine, either when you call them or when they execute **uux** requests on your machine. To change the commands, add the keyword *COMMANDS =* to the MACHINE = line, followed by a list of commands each separated by a : (colon). For example:

```
MACHINE=OTHER  COMMANDS=rmail:news:lp
```

In this case, incoming **uux** jobs can use the **rmail, news,** and **lp** commands. The **rmail** command is always required, but in this example you can allow the **lp** command so that remote machines can send jobs to your printer via the **uucp** system. All commands given in the COMMANDS= list must be located in the directories **/sbin**, **/usr/sbin**, or **/usr/bin**. You can use **COMMANDS=ALL** if you want to allow a remote machine full access to all commands. Use of **COMMANDS=ALL** is not recommended unless you trust the remote machine completely, and it definitely should not be used with **MACHINE=OTHER**.

The uucheck Command

The **Permissions** file setup can be verified with the **/usr/lib/uucp/ uucheck** command, which checks the **uucp** subsystem for correctness, paying special attention to the **Permissions** data. The **uucheck** command is restricted to the superuser, since **uucp** permissions should be kept secret. Use

```
# /usr/lib/uucp/uucheck -v
```

to see a verbose display of how the **uucp** permissions are configured. The **uucheck** command is a very useful tool that can substantially reduce confusion in establishing **uucp** permissions. Figure 22-2 shows typical output from the **uucheck** command, when it is executed on the permissions setup given in the "wide-open" **Permissions** file listed earlier. The check is run in two phases: first the correctness of the **uucp** files and directories is checked (no output is provided in Figure 22-2 because the files are correct); second the **Permissions** are listed in an easy-to-understand, verbose format.

Unknown Remote Machines and Polling

If an incoming call is found to be from a machine that your system does not have in its **Systems** files, the call can be accepted as normal, or a shell script can be executed by the **uucp** system that is used to log calls

```
# /usr/lib/uucp/uucheck -v
*** uucheck:  Check Required Files and Directories
*** uucheck:  Directories Check Complete

*** uucheck:  Check /etc/uucp/Permissions file
** LOGNAME PHASE (when they call us)

When a system logs in as: (uucp) (nuucp)
        We DO allow them to request files.
        We WILL send files queued for them on this call.
        They can send files to
            /
        Sent files will be created in /var/spool/uucp
         before they are copied to the target directory.
        They can request files from
            /
        Myname for the conversation will be my_sys.
        PUBDIR for the conversation will be /var/spool/uucppublic.

** MACHINE PHASE (when we call or execute their uux requests)

When we call system(s): (OTHER)
        We DO allow them to request files.
        They can send files to
            /
        Sent files will be created in /var/spool/uucp
         before they are copied to the target directory.
        They can request files from
            /
        Myname for the conversation will be my_sys.
        PUBDIR for the conversation will be /var/spool/uucppublic.

Machine(s): (OTHER)
CAN execute the following commands:
command (ALL), fullname (ALL)

*** uucheck:  /etc/uucp/Permissions Check Complete

#
```

Figure 22-2.   Sample output from the **uucheck** command

from unknown machines, or for similar security precautions. This capability is not supported in the **Permissions** file; it works a little differently: if the file **/usr/lib/uucp/remote.unknown** is executable, the incoming call from a remote machine is terminated and the **remote.unknown** command is executed; if the file is not present or is not executable, the call is accepted in the **MACHINE=OTHER** category. Normally you disable the **remote.unknown** feature because you want to receive mail from machines that might know about yours, but which you do not know. However, when security breaches are suspected through the **uucp** system, this feature can be enabled by making **remote.unknown** executable. For security reasons **remote.unknown** is a binary program in SVR4, but you can replace it with a shell script if you wish to customize its actions.

In addition, the **uucp** subsystem can be configured to *poll* another system. This means that one machine can call another system and request any jobs that are intended for it. This feature is often used when a machine cannot call you for some reason, but you can call it. For example, a machine may have only incoming call support.

When a machine calls another machine, the "callee" can transfer any waiting outgoing jobs for the "caller." Usually this capability is disabled by the default value **SENDFILES=no** in the **Permissions** file of the recipient machine. When **SENDFILES=no**, a machine that wishes to send data must call the recipient machine, and the recipient cannot "pick up" messages when it calls the sending machine. Set **SENDFILES=yes** on a machine if you wish to allow it to transfer outgoing jobs when it is called.

Going Further

The security issues discussed in this chapter are central to any well-run public UNIX system. The UNIX system's security measures can be quite strong if they are administered with care and attention, but they really cannot defeat a skilled, devious, malicious attack. There is an amazing amount of UNIX system skill in the world, and some of it is directed solely toward unauthorized entry into UNIX machines.

System Attacks

Usually a malicious attack starts with "hackers" who only wish to stretch their skills at your expense. Frequently an attacker will break into the machine, snoop through the file system, get bored quickly, and leave without damage. However, occasionally attackers wish to steal your data or damage the system. Typically, an attack scenario goes something like this: An attacker gets a telephone number for your modem (or LAN) through a network of other attackers, or even by random dialing. Then the attacker experiments to discover an unprotected login id that provides access to the machine. The attacker then can browse the machine at leisure, until an opportunity to switch to the **root** login id arises. An attacker will often change system files, rearrange permissions, and add corrupted commands to the system that make it easier to break in again later. Network connections are then explored to locate "nearby" machines to attack. When your machine has been digested, the attacker will often cause some damage just for fun. Finally, the access information will be passed to another attacker and the process will start again.

You can learn a lot about malicious attacks from this scenario: first, password security is critical to prevent entry at the beginning; second, once an attacker gets into the system it can be extremely difficult to detect and prevent the attack; third, once the system is violated it is very likely to be attacked again, and attacks will often spread to "nearby" machines; fourth, if you take inadequate action against an attack, the attacker will learn of your changes, and continue to defeat them.

Defender Behavior

Almost invariably the first reaction to a suspected attack on your machine is to deny that it happened. You can almost always think of good rationalizations to explain why file permissions were changed, or even how your password file was suddenly modified. Often you really don't remember what the system should look like. Naturally a malicious attacker will take advantage of this confusion and denial to dig deeper into your machine. When you are sure that an attack has occurred, you may try to deny its importance. Even when unknown logins are active, you will often try to contact the users with **mail** or **write**, to politely ask why they are using your machine. Of course, this warning is just what attackers want. In the next stage, you might announce to all users (usually by **news!**) that your machine is under attack. Again, this warns attackers that they are no longer unknown. Then you may take some tentative steps to improve your security, like changing your passwords (usually to other trivial passwords similar to those the attacker may have used to break into the machine!). Finally, after repeated attacks, you may overreact, totally closing down all connectivity to the machine.

It is not difficult to see that this defender behavior only trains a more skilled attacker. You have repeatedly warned the attacker that you know the machine is compromised, and you have made security changes at such a slow pace that he or she can usually keep ahead of your precautions. Attackers may even plant *Trojan horse* software that traps passwords as people log in, change file permissions, and so on. Eventually, you may take such drastic action against an attack that it hinders your own use of the machine.

The behavior described earlier in this chapter will work much better. Usually if you detect an attack it is best not to change the system at all while you plan your defense. It is especially unwise to issue a **news** announcement describing the changes you are going to make! Your first overt act should be to suddenly and completely change the system: change the telephone numbers for modems, reload the system software from the beginning, change all the passwords and login ids, and then reestablish your **uucp** connections with other machines. If your defense is silent and strong enough, you will have solved the problem. In no case should any evidence that you are aware of an attack or notification of impending changes appear on the machine under attack!

Detecting an Attack

Unfortunately, detecting an attack can be difficult, because most attackers are more skilled than most defenders. Key places to look for an attack are in changes to permissions of the security-related files discussed in this chapter, or to **/etc/inittab**, **/etc/profile**, the **cron** data files, and the Service Access Facility control files. A change in the contents of any of these files is also suspicious, especially in **/etc/passwd**, **/etc/uucp/Permissions**, the **uucp** Systems files, and **/etc/profile**. The **uucp** log files can provide information on unusual **uucp** connections to other machines that may be unknown. Unusual users logged in to the machine during late-night hours are also a clue. The file **/var/adm/sulog** contains a record of all uses of the **su** command, which is often used by attackers.

Attackers usually try to cover their tracks. A skilled attacker can edit files like **sulog** to remove their traces, but the permissions and modification date of the files may give away the fact that they were changed. Detecting an attack can be a job for Sherlock Holmes! This is an ideal place to use a security monitoring tool, as discussed earlier in this chapter.

Trojan Horses, Viruses, and Worms

The most devious and unpleasant form of attack occurs when the attacker changes your machine by replacing some key pieces of software with corrupt copies that allow the attacker access. Usually, this only happens when you have warned attackers that you know they are present on the machine, and it can be very difficult to detect. You might use your routine backup procedures to copy the corrupt program to your archive. Then, when you rebuild the system in defense, your natural tendency would be to restore the backup rather than to reload the system from scratch. Often this simply restores the corrupt program, and once again, you have only helped train your attacker. When you suspect an attack, your backup data may be unreliable, and you must take care when you restore this material. It is good practice to back up only your user data, and not the system software. When you reload the system you should use the original system software that was purchased with the machine.

Virus and *worm* programs work by the same principles as hackers, but they can usually spread and infect other machines without the direct action of an attacker. A virus is a program that somehow attaches itself to an existing piece of software, while a worm is a standalone program that survives due to the multitasking nature of the system. Usually, executing an infected program or mounting an infected disk activates a virus or worm, which then infects the host machine. The infection may cause immediate damage, but more likely, the virus will wait for a period of time while it infects more diskettes (or your LAN!). Then, at some trigger date, it will awaken and destroy the host system.

These infections can be extremely difficult to detect and repair. The best defense is to prevent them. Be *extremely careful* with your connections to other machines and with the software you load.

System V/MLS

The *Multilevel Security* system is a version of SVR4 that meets U. S. government Security Class B2 or B3. The specifications for these classes include file-by-file access lists, individual user and group checks before file access is allowed, and hierarchical security levels, such as secret and top secret. Level B2 also requires a formal security model that can be verified from design through implementation. These systems are definitely secure, but they impose significant overhead on system performance. If you need this level of security, consult your UNIX system vendor.

The X Window System

A major innovation in recent years has been the incorporation of the *X Window System* as an industry-standard part of the UNIX system. The X Window System, often called simply *X*, provides a full-screen environment that allows multiple windows or applications on the screen simultaneously. New applications can be developed to take full advantage of the windowing environment, which includes high-quality graphics, color support, and use of a mouse or other pointing device. Older applications can continue to run in special *terminal emulator* windows that act like old-style ASCII terminals.

X provides a standard development and user environment across nearly all versions of the UNIX system, allowing excellent portability of applications. This, in turn, makes it easier and less expensive for developers to provide applications. Thus, several different *GUI* (for graphical user interface) systems based on X have been created for SVR4, and most UNIX system vendors choose one of these for their release. The most common choices are the *OPEN LOOK* system supported by AT&T and Sun Microsystems, and the *Motif* system supported by the Open Software Foundation. However, several other GUIs exist. The *Open Desktop* and the *Looking Glass* systems are marketed by UNIX/386 vendors SCO and Interactive Systems, respectively. Several other options are also available. The user environment shared by NeXT and a

TWENTY-THREE

few other systems is the major exception to the use of X in the UNIX world. On the other hand, X is becoming so pervasive that versions are now offered for nearly all computers and operating systems, even those outside the UNIX system. X support is available for Macintosh, larger MS-DOS machines, and OS/2 systems.

As a large and complex software environment that requires high-performance hardware to run, X places extensive new performance requirements on your machine. You need a high-resolution graphics display (color or monochrome, but at least EGA quality, preferably VGA or better) and a mouse or other *pointing device* to take advantage of the X features. If you are using a terminal (rather than the system console), you need a high-speed data link to the host machine; even a 9600 bps modem connection is not sufficient. These are the minimum requirements for running X; to get *usable* performance from X, your machine must have better CPU performance, more disk space, and more real RAM memory than you would normally need. If you are doing graphics-intensive work, hardware floating-point support is very helpful, although many X applications (such as **xterm**) do not require much floating-point arithmetic. Consult with your UNIX system or X vendor for recommendations.

Basic X Concepts

The X Window System is oriented around a logical *display*. A display is generally a regular graphics device like a CRT, but includes a keyboard and a pointing device, usually a mouse. A display must also have computing power, so a simple terminal cannot be a display. A display may have more than one CRT; that is, one keyboard and mouse may be shared between multiple CRTs. Multiple CRTs within a display are called *screens,* but most displays have only one screen. Commonly, the system console with keyboard, mouse, and CPU constitutes a display with one screen.

Each application gets its own *window* (or multiple windows if it needs them) on the screen, and output from that application goes only to that window. An application can create, change, move, or delete its own windows, but cannot usually affect windows owned by other applications.

The user can select which window the keyboard or mouse input will go to. Output from multiple applications can appear in their windows simultaneously, but input can go to only one window at a time.

The X Server

The software provided to manage the display is a major part of the X package. This software is called the *display server* or simply the *server*. Its job is to interpret key presses and mouse clicks, and to draw on the display device. The server has very little application-specific knowledge; separate processes handle most requirements of specific applications. The server must be running throughout your X session, and applications communicate with it to display output or read input. The server can communicate with multiple applications simultaneously, and send keystrokes to the appropriate *client*, so that you can execute several applications at a time without difficulty.

Client Applications

The specific work of the application is performed by *client* programs that communicate with the server as necessary. Thus, X divides the world into two realms, one display-specific and the other application-specific. The most important implication of this division is that applications need not understand the hardware that handles I/O operations, and so become portable. The server can be developed once by each hardware vendor, and the clients can be easily ported between computers. Another important implication is that the server and client can run on separate machines, and communicate via LAN. The X Window System is *network capable*. This means you can run your X server on a "small" local machine, while running your clients on a faster (and more expensive) remote host, thus reducing the overall cost of your computer installation.

Window Managers

In the X model, neither the server nor the client knows much about the *look-and-feel* of the window system. The window borders, mechanisms for creating and moving windows, on-screen menus, and many other general features are provided by a third part of the X architecture. The *window manager* is a special type of client application designed to perform these services. When a client wants to create a window, the client and the server consult the window manager to figure out how the window should be displayed. Since the window manager is a client, you can easily change the look-and-feel of your X installation by changing the window manager you are running. Individual users can work in different X environments simply by using different window managers.

Three major window managers are offered with SVR4 systems. Each of them provides very different services as well as a very different look-and-feel. You can choose the one you prefer. The OPEN LOOK window manager (**olwm**) is the official standard for the SVR4 release. It implements a user interface recommended by AT&T and Sun Microsystems, who jointly developed the standard. The Motif window manager (**mwm**) provides a look-and-feel very similar to the OS/2 Presentation Manager. It was developed by the OSF consortium as an alternative to OPEN LOOK that would port the OS/2 and Microsoft Windows look-and-feel to X. If you have experience with OS/2 or Windows, you may prefer Motif. Either option provides a fixed look-and-feel that follows (different) published standards, although screen colors and a few other features are configurable. The third alternative, *Tom's Window Manager* (**twm**), was named after its creator, Tom LaStrange, but is often called the *Tab Window Manager*. It is a fully configurable tool that allows users broad latitude in creating the environment that *they* prefer. Of course, configuring **twm** is much more difficult than accepting a predefined standard; the designers of both **olwm** and **mwm** did extensive user testing to find an optimal look-and-feel that is easy to learn and use. A fourth alternative, the *Generic Window Manager* (**gwm**) is a new window manager that is even more configurable than **twm**, but is not as widely available. It is possible to configure **gwm** to emulate both **mwm** and **olwm**, although **gwm** uses a LISP-like control language that is quite difficult to master. Older window managers like **awm** and **uwm** are essentially obsolete, and are unlikely to be well maintained in the future.

Actually, some parts of the user interface may be embedded in the applications themselves, instead of in the window manager. You can often buy commercial applications that are designed to be used only with **mwm** *or* **olwm**. These use special X *toolkits* that help the developer meet user interface standards. When you purchase commercial X applications, be sure to get the version that is intended for your preferred window manager.

The remainder of this chapter assumes an OPEN LOOK environment, but most OPEN LOOK commands have equivalents in the Motif system, and also generic X equivalents. If you are using another implementation of X, consult your documentation for the specific command names chosen by your vendor.

Starting X

Normally X is started from your login shell, but some users set up their **.profile** to start X automatically when they log in to the machine. The **olinit** (for OPEN LOOK initialize) command starts an X session in the SVR4 system. The **xinit** (for X initialize) command is the generic equivalent, although many vendors include it inside a shell script that is often called **xstart**. All of these commands perform basically the same functions: they start the X server, establish an environment that is hospitable to the X system, and execute a startup shell script in your home directory. You can place any additional commands or startup data that you wish in this shell script. You'll find more information on configuring X startup later in this chapter.

Before starting OPEN LOOK for the first time on a new login id, the superuser should establish an initial X environment with the **oladduser** command, as follows:

```
# oladduser loginid
```

Here, the *loginid* is the user name for which to configure the OPEN LOOK environment. The **oladduser** command places several files in that user's home directory. Thereafter, you can start X simply from the shell using

```
$ olinit
```

You can place the startup command in your **.profile** to enter X immediately when you log in; however, if you ever use dial-up terminals, be sure to configure your **.profile** to bypass X unless the terminal is sufficiently powerful to handle it.

After X starts, you will see a multiple window display that typically looks something like Figure 23-1. You can move the arrow pointer on the screen by moving the mouse.

The light background is called the *Workspace,* the *desktop* or the *root window.* Individual applications have their own windows on this background. At the bottom-right of the screen are two applications, a clock (the **xclock** client) and a mail notification tool (**xbiff**). The large window near the top is a *terminal emulator* (the **xterm** client) that allows you to run normal shell processes, and thus any old-style UNIX application. The large window at the bottom-left is the OPEN LOOK *File Manager,* a directory and file browsing tool that borrows many ideas from the Macintosh and Presentation Manager systems. You can have as many windows on screen simultaneously as you need, although overall performance will suffer if you have too many.

To kill X and return to the shell with this default setup, move the mouse pointer into the root window, and press and hold the right mouse button. The *Workspace menu,* shown in the upper-left of Figure 23-1, will appear. Move the mouse so the pointer is over the Exit item, and release the button. You may be prompted to confirm the exit with another mouse click, and then the X session will end. You will be returned to your login shell, or directly logged off the machine.

The DISPLAY Environment Variable

Since X is network capable, there is no reason to assume that X clients will display their windows on any specific display in a network. That is, you can run a client on one machine and expect the windows to appear on another machine. Thus, you must inform X what machine (and display) you are using by setting and exporting the *DISPLAY* environment variable, which contains the name of your X server, on the host machine. To do this, use the form

```
$ DISPLAY=hostname:0.0
$ export DISPLAY
```

where *hostname* is the name of the machine on which the X server is running. Most often, when the server is running on the same machine as the client applications, this will be the **uname** of your machine. The first digit after the colon is the display number for that server machine (usually zero), and the digit after the dot is the screen number for that display. In most situations both will be zero. You may also see

```
$ DISPLAY=hostname:0
```

Here, the screen number defaults to zero. If the DISPLAY environment variable is not set, X will try to open the console for the system you are using, and a DISPLAY value of

```
$ DISPLAY=unix:0.0
```

will be assumed. If X cannot open this device, it will complain, as shown here:

```
$ olinit
olinit: Can't open display
$
```

When you see this message, check to be sure your DISPLAY variable is set correctly.

Often error messages like this will not appear directly on the console, but will be sent to the file **$HOME/.oliniterr** instead. If you don't see any error messages, but **olinit** is not working as expected, look for the **.oliniterr** file.

Managing Windows

Once X is running, you can create, move, or kill windows as necessary. Because the methods used to manage windows are mostly a function of the window manager you are using, these procedures will differ. Here we assume you are using **olwm**.

The X Window System contains an automatic *screensaver* that blanks the display screen whenever ten minutes pass without keyboard or mouse activity. This is completely normal, and no output directed to the screen will be lost. To reenable the screen, just move the mouse slightly.

Input Focus

Output that is intended for a window will appear whenever the application writes; this is a *nonblocking* output scheme. Input from the keyboard or mouse, on the other hand, must be directed to a specific window by a user. Only one window can be selected for input at any time. If no window is selected, or if the root window is selected, input will be discarded by the X server. The selected window will have a highlighted title bar or a different border color than the nonselected windows.

You can choose one of two methods for telling X which window you want to receive this *input focus*. The first method, called *click-to-type*, requires you to position the mouse pointer within the window, and then click the left mouse button. This *selects* that window to receive input, and the border of that window will usually be highlighted in a contrasting color to mark it as selected. You can now move the mouse anywhere on the screen and the selected window will continue to receive input. This is the default method with OPEN LOOK.

The second method, called *focus-follows-mouse*, is not available in some releases of OPEN LOOK. When you are using this method, you must position the mouse pointer within the desired window for input to go to that window. When you move the pointer to another window, the focus will change. To select this method, execute **olwm** with the **-f** (for focus) command-line option in your **.olinitrc** or **.xinitrc** file, as discussed later in this chapter.

Each of these methods has its fans; if both are available experiment to decide which one you prefer.

Controlling Window Position

The multiple windows on the screen can *overlap*, and you can change the size and position of windows to suit your needs. You can also *iconize* a window, which makes it small and moves it out of the way without killing the application. These operations differ depending on the window manager you are using.

With **olwm** you iconize a window by moving the mouse pointer to the small box in the upper-left corner of the window border, and then pressing the left mouse button. The *Window Menu,* shown in Figure 23-1, will appear. While holding the mouse button down, move the pointer to the Close option, and then release the button. The actual window will disappear, and a small representation of the window will replace it. This icon will usually appear on the bottom-left side of the screen. If you iconize an **xterm** window, the icon will contain a small picture or the name *xterm.*

To restore an icon to full size, *double-click* the left mouse button while the pointer is on the icon, or choose Restore from the Window menu associated with that icon.

In addition to iconizing a window, the Window menu allows you to expand a window to fill the entire screen, push a window to the back of the stack of windows, redraw a window and its contents, and exit from the application. You can also invoke the Window menu by clicking the right mouse button anywhere in the window border.

To move a window on the screen, place the pointer on the window border (any border will work, but the top border is easiest); then press the left mouse button and hold it down. As you move the mouse, a *wire-frame* representation of the window will move around the screen. Position the wire-frame where you want it, and then release the mouse button. The window will jump to the new location.

Clicking the left mouse button in the window border also causes the window to rise to the top of the overlapping stack of windows, exposing the entire window for your use.

Selecting Multiple Windows

In OPEN LOOK terminology, pressing the left mouse button in the window border performs a *select* action; it selects a window and deselects any other windows. This also raises the selected window to the top of the stack. Pressing the middle button in the window border performs an *adjust* function; it toggles the selected state of the window without raising it or deselecting other windows.

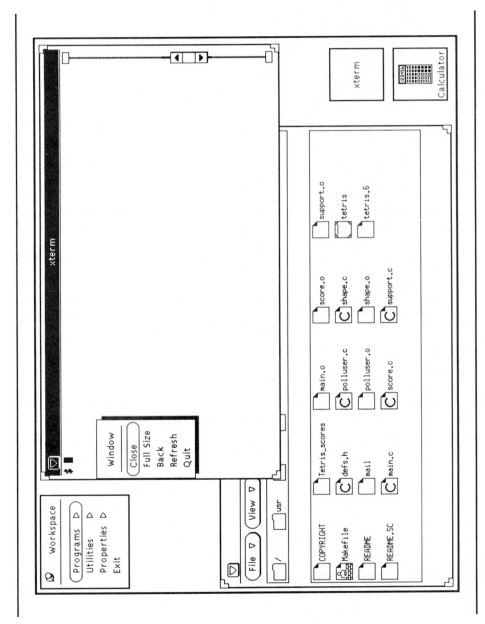

Figure 23-1. The OPEN LOOK window menu

By using these two buttons, you can select multiple windows. Select the first window by clicking the left button in the window border. Then select a second window by clicking the middle button in its border. Now you have two windows selected. If you press and hold the left button in the border of either of the selected windows, you can move them both. As you'll learn later in this chapter, some other functions associated with the Workspace menu also affect all selected windows. You can deselect a window by clicking the middle mouse button in its border. To deselect all but one window, click the left mouse button in its border.

Resizing a Window

The small L-shaped areas in the corners of the window border are used to *resize* the window. If you position the pointer on one of these corner areas and press and hold the left mouse button, you can stretch or shrink the window before releasing the button. The wire-frame will appear to show the new size and shape of the window. Note that the opposite corner remains fixed, so you cannot resize and move a window in the same operation. Nor can you resize an icon.

The Workspace Menu

When you move the pointer to the background area outside any window and press the right mouse button, the *Workspace* or *Function* menu, shown at the upper-left of Figure 23-1, will appear. This menu gives you the opportunity to start new applications, exit from the X environment completely, change your preferences, and perform other functions.

The Workspace menu, and many other OPEN LOOK menus, can be *pinned* on the screen so that they will not disappear after you make a selection. Just hold down the right mouse button, and move the pointer over the drawing of a pin in the upper-left corner of the menu. The pin will move, and the menu will stick on the screen. To *unpin* the menu, click on the pin with the left mouse button.

The Exit function kills the **olwm**, and thus the entire X session, returning you to your login shell.

Items on the Workspace menu may contain *submenus*. These are additional menus associated with the main menu items. When you slide the pointer to the right near the arrowhead on one of the main menu items, the submenu will appear over the Workspace menu. You can then select items from the submenu before releasing the mouse button.

The Programs menu item contains a list of applications that you can execute directly, without using the shell (**xterm**) to start them. Usually these are X client programs that perform useful services. When you start one of these applications by clicking on its menu item, its window will usually appear on the screen, and you can then use the application. To kill the application, use its own quit procedure.

You can configure some of the contents of the Programs submenu, or sometimes of the entire Workspace menu, by editing the **.olprograms** or **.openwin-menu** file (whichever exists) in your home directory; however, the Properties menu usually includes an item to change the list of programs.

The Utilities submenu provides several useful services. A typical list is given in Table 23-1. If present, the *Lock Screen* item starts the X client **xlock**. It blanks the screen and displays a mathematical pattern until you type your password. This allows you to keep your terminal logged in, but still secure. Note that the **xlock** application consumes significant CPU resources, so its use is not recommended when you are running large jobs. The Print Screen application contains several submenus that let you select a subset of the X display for printing, while the Network Administration item lets you change the list of remote machines (hosts) that can create windows on your display. If you have a LAN, and wish to run X clients on other machines, but view their

Label	Description
File Manager	Invoke the OPEN LOOK File Manager
Network Administration	Change host access to your X display
Refresh	Redraw entire screen
Print Screen	Screen dump to printer
Lock Screen	Start **xlock**

Table 23-1.   Typical OPEN LOOK Utilities Submenu

windows on your display, you must list those host names in this entry. This menu item executes the **xhost** application.

The Properties menu item, which appears on several OPEN LOOK menus, is used to change the configuration or properties of individual menus or of the overall display. These functions are usually part of the **olwsm** (Workspace Manager) application, although they may be included in a separate **xproperties** or **xset** program. From this menu, you can select your favorite font, display color, icon position, and other configurable elements. Available properties differ widely between releases, so you must experiment to see what is possible.

Scrollbars

Some windows may have horizontal or vertical *scrollbars*. This feature allows you to move the contents of the window *inside* the window border. Figure 23-1 shows a large **xterm** window with a vertical OPEN LOOK scrollbar. The scrollbar includes several areas that function differently when you touch them with the mouse pointer. At the top and bottom are *cable anchors,* which are connected to the central *elevator* by a *cable.* On the elevator, an *up-arrow* and *down-arrow* surround a small central *drag area.* To move the contents of the window within its scrolling region, position the pointer over the drag area and press the left mouse button. You can then drag the elevator up and down (or left and right) to move the contents of the window. You can jump the window one line by clicking on the up-arrow or down-arrow, or move immediately to the top or bottom of the scroll region by clicking on the top or bottom cable anchor. To move the window by one full screen, click in the cable area. For these techniques to work, the application must usually support the OPEN LOOK scrollbar format. Some applications may use a format that differs from that shown in Figure 23-1, but most OPEN LOOK applications will use a similar left-button-drag-and-release scrolling style.

The application itself determines the *size* of the scroll region, or the "history" recalled by the application. Some applications remember a large region, but you can only scroll within the limited area the application can remember.

Some OPEN LOOK applications allow you to *split* a window into separate *panels* that are controlled by individual scrollbars. Usually you are allowed to split a window either horizontally or vertically. Consult your OPEN LOOK documentation to see if this feature is available for each application.

The Help System

OPEN LOOK and many other X environments include a window-based help system that provides information and advice when you need it. Usually help is associated with the F1 function key, but this can be changed through the Properties menu or the X *resource database*, discussed later in this chapter. To access help, move the mouse pointer over a window or other on-screen object, and then press the F1 key. The result will resemble Figure 23-2. The help system provides information on most objects, but if no help is available the system will often be silent. At other times you will see a message saying "No help available." Usually the help window will be pinned on screen when it appears. Click on the push-pin to unpin it and dismiss the window. Pop-up menus often have help available, but you may need to pin the menu on screen for the Workspace manager to locate the window and find its help.

The File Manager

The *File Manager* provides a graphically oriented entry into the UNIX file system. A sample File Manager display appears at the lower-left of Figure 23-1. This is the OPEN LOOK File Manager, but most X packages include a similar application, as mentioned briefly in Chapter 4. You can start the File Manager from the Utilities submenu of the Workspace menu.

The File Manager lets you move around in the file system, select a subset of the files in a directory for an action like moving or deletion, and successively open subdirectories. If you click on an object with the left mouse button, you will select that object for some action, which is in turn selected from the menus in the upper-left of the File Manager window. You can select multiple objects for an action with the middle button.

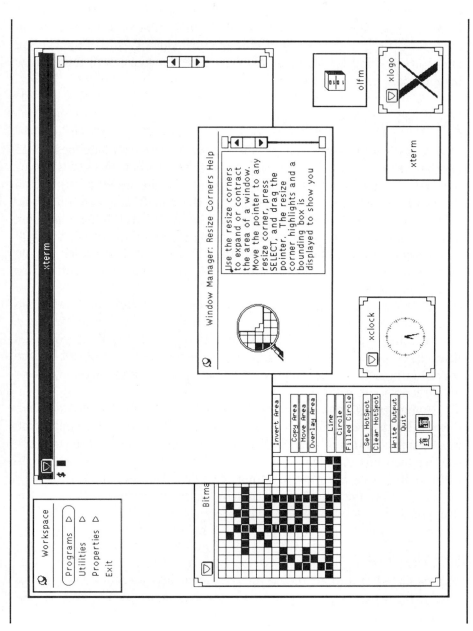

Figure 23-2.   OPEN LOOK help menu

By double-clicking the left mouse button on an object, you cause that object to be *opened*. If it is a directory (folder), the contents of the directory will replace the contents of the large window, and the directory's name will appear in the list at the middle of the File Manager window. Other objects cause different actions. A text file is edited in its own window, using your EDITOR environment variable, and an executable program is executed in its own window. When an application ends (or is killed by the Quit item in the Window menu), its window disappears.

Drag-and-Drop Operations

A *drag-and-drop* feature allows you to copy objects from one location to another. For example, try clicking the left mouse button over a file or directory, and then move the mouse pointer while holding the button down. The mouse will drag the object to the new folder, and when you release the mouse button, the object will be copied to this new location. You can make copies of individual files or of entire directories, but in many releases the adjust (middle button) function will not work. If you hold down the SHIFT key along with the select button, the object will be moved instead of copied.

If you drag a directory into the Workspace (background), and then release the button, you will create a new instance of the File Manager. This window will contain the directory that you dragged. If you then drag an object between these File Manager windows, the object will be moved or copied. You can have as many separate File Manager windows on screen as you want.

Some applications also allow objects to be dropped into their windows. This feature will not work with all applications; the application must support it. If the drop feature is supported, the application will use the dropped object as its argument. For example, a Wastebasket application will delete a file or directory that you drop into it. Consult the documentation for each application to determine whether it supports dropping.

Name Matching

The Directory line at the top-right of the File Manager window lets you type a pathname, and then click the Match menu item to jump to that directory. You can select a subset of files in the selected directory if you type a filename wildcard pattern (using the familiar * and ? operators) in the Pattern field before you click Match.

More complex file system features are available through the File, View, and Edit menus. The File Manager is really a straightforward interface to the UNIX file system.

The xterm Client

The most important client application is the **xterm** (for X terminal) program. It provides a *terminal emulator* window in which a normal shell listens for your commands. You can execute any UNIX command or shell script inside an **xterm** window; you can even start other X clients as you need them. Normally, when you start the X environment, at least one **xterm** is started for you. You can create additional **xterm** windows, either through the Workspace menu or from the shell (running in another **xterm** window!), and then run applications in these windows. To start an **xterm** window from the shell, you can use

```
$ xterm &
```

After a noticeable delay, the new window will appear in the default size and position. The shell specified in your SHELL environment variable will be run inside the window. Note that X applications run from the shell in this way are normally executed in the background (with &), because X applications are usually killed from menu items rather than directly with CTRL-D. You can kill an **xterm** window by exiting from its shell, either with CTRL-D or with the **exit** command, or by selecting Exit from its menu.

When an **xterm** window is created, the X server places a TERM entry for that window into the UNIX environment, so normal full-screen applications like **vi** will run correctly. The **xterm** client emulates the DEC VT102 and the Tektronix 4014 terminals, and often emulates the native mode of the system console, although emulation is not perfect. The value

```
TERM=xterm
```

is preferred over the standard console or VT102.

You can move or iconize the window without affecting any applications running in it, but if you kill the window any applications in it will also be killed (unless you specify **nohup** when you start the application). You can also resize the **xterm** window, but currently running applications will not be notified that the window has changed size. If you kill an application, resize its **xterm** window, and then restart it, the application will get the correct window size.

xterm Menus

Like most X clients, **xterm** has its own set of menus to manage its behavior. These menus will appear in different ways in different releases. In some, you can bring up a menu by pressing the right mouse button while the pointer is inside the **xterm** window. If this works, you will have only one menu. In other releases, you must hold down the CTRL key and press one of the mouse buttons. In this scheme, there are three **xterm** menus, one bound to each mouse button. SVR4.0 supports the former model, so only one **xterm** menu is usually available, but it contains most of the items in the three-menu version. This menu, shown in Figure 23-3, allows you to send signals to processes running in the window, to *redraw* or refresh the contents of the window, to set specific properties, and to perform other functions.

Select the Show Tek menu item to switch to the Tektronix 4014 graphics display. The 4014 mode has its own submenus. You will probably not need this capability unless you have specific software that uses the 4014 terminal. The 4014 window usually appears in addition to the normal window, so when you kill the 4014 window, you do not kill the **xterm** client.

Cut and Paste with xterm

The **xterm** application allows you to *select* or *cut* a block of text from one window and *paste* it into another **xterm** window or to another location in the same window. This is the function of the Edit submenu shown in Figure 23-3. Some other X clients support this cut-and-paste

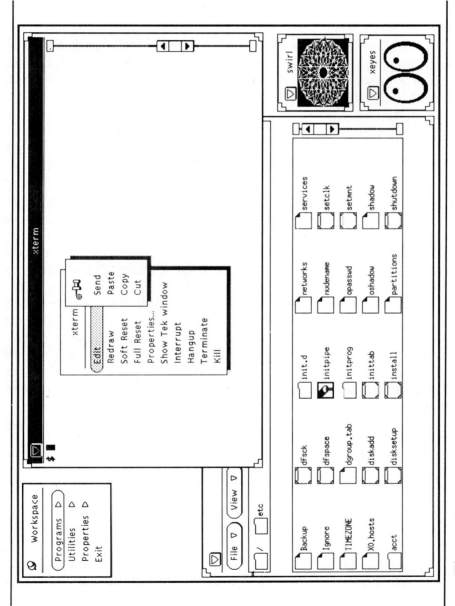

Figure 23-3.   SVR4.0 OPEN LOOK xterm menu

mechanism as well. When you are running those clients you can cut or copy and paste between different applications.

The *syntax* of the cut-and-paste and copy-and-paste functions differs greatly among X implementations, and even in different versions of the OPEN LOOK specification. Experiment to see how these functions work in your system.

If you have scrollbars enabled on the **xterm** window, you can scroll back to a previous section of text, select it, and then reenter it in an editor or at the **xterm** command line. The selected text block is highlighted in a color different from that of the surrounding text.

Use the left mouse button to select a block of text by pressing the button, *sweeping* across the desired text, and then releasing the button. Move the pointer to the window you want to paste the material into, and press the right mouse button to bring up the menu. While holding the right button down, pull up the Edit submenu, and select Send to copy the selected text into the target window at the cursor position. Alternatively, you can choose Copy, which copies the selected text into an internal *clipboard*. If you select Cut the selected material will be deleted from the window where it originally appeared. All three of these options place the text on the clipboard. You can use Paste or Send to retrieve the clipboard's contents into the current window.

There is only one internal clipboard, so each Copy, Cut, or Send operation will discard the old text and save the selected text. However, you can *adjust* your text selection while it is highlighted on the screen by pressing the middle mouse button and sweeping a new area. This text will be added to the previously selected text before it goes to the clipboard. You can deselect a region of text or select a new region at any time by pressing the left mouse button.

xterm Command-Line Options

When you run **xterm** from the command line (of another **xterm** window!), you can add various command-line options. The **xterm** client supports the client command-line options discussed in the next section, plus some additional options that are specific to **xterm**. Consult the **xterm**(1) man page for more information.

The most important option allows you to select a command to execute inside the **xterm** window, instead of the shell. Type the command line after the **-e** (for execute) option. The **-e** and its associated command must be the *last* argument, because **xterm** uses the end of the command line to mark the end of the command to execute. For example, to run **xterm** and start the **vi** editor in it at the same time, you can use this command:

```
$ xterm -e vi filename &
```

When it is used with the **-e** option, the **xterm** application exits when the associated application finishes, so the window created in the previous example will disappear when you quit the editor. This feature is often useful in shell scripts or in networked environments, where you might use the **rlogin** command after the **-e** option to start a session on a remote machine.

Generic X Command-Line Arguments

The **xterm** client, and most other X clients, support many command-line options that control the appearance of their windows. You can specify the window *geometry* (the size and position of the window on the screen), the colors of the window, the font to use for text in the window, the label on the window border and icon, and many other attributes of the window. You can use these command-line arguments with most X clients, not just with **xterm**. These command-line options are very handy for customizing the Programs submenu on the Workspace menu.

Window Geometry

To select the window size and position, use the **-geometry** argument, followed by a specification of the form

```
COLSxROWS+XLOC+YLOC
```

where *COLS* and *ROWS* are the size of the **xterm** window, expressed in characters, and *XLOC* and *YLOC* give the initial position of the window measured in pixels from the top-left corner of the screen. For example, a 24-row by 80-column window, placed horizontally 100 pixels and vertically 200 pixels from the top-left corner, would be specified as

```
$ xterm -geometry 80x24+100+200 &
```

To select the default values for either of these two classes of information, just leave that section out of the specification. For example, to create a 24x80 window in the default position, you could use

```
$ xterm -geometry 80x24 &
```

and to create a window located at $+200+300$ in the default size, you could use

```
$ xterm -geometry +200+300 &
```

The previous window location specifications create a window offset from the upper-left corner of the screen. Alternatively, you can offset the window from any other side of the screen. The + (plus) in the specification uses the left side for the horizontal zero point, and the top of the screen for the vertical zero point. You can switch to the right side or the bottom by using a - (minus) instead. For example,

```
$ xterm -geometry -200+300 &
```

will place the window 300 pixels from the top of the screen but 200 pixels from the *right* side. Any combination is allowed; experiment to become familiar with the geometry specifications.

Note that most X clients other than **xterm** require you to specify the window size in *pixels* rather than character counts, so if you make a mistake the window may appear in a strange size.

Fonts

The character font used inside the client window can also be set on the command line. Use the **-font** option followed by the name of the font you wish to use. For example:

```
$ xterm -font 8x13bold &
```

Here, *8x13bold* is the name of a font known to X. Since most X implementations support many fonts (up to 600 in some cases), selecting a font can be difficult. The **xlsfonts** (for X list fonts) client lists all the font names known to that implementation of X, as shown here:

```
$ xlsfonts | tail -15
-adobe-courier-bold-o-normal--14-100-100-100-m-90-iso8859-1
-adobe-courier-medium-o-normal--14-140-75-75-m-90-iso8859-1
-adobe-symbol-medium-r-normal--12-120-75-75-p-74-adobe-fontspecific
-bitstream-charter-bold-i-normal--19-180-75-75-p-117-iso8859-1
-bitstream-charter-medium-i-normal--19-180-75-75-p-103-iso8859-1
6x10
8x13
8x13bold
9x15
cursor
fixed
pc12x20
pc6x10
vrb-25
btbold
$
```

As you can see, font names come in several different forms. The long names in the first five lines of the previous example contain an encoding of the font size, dot density, and other information. The shorter names below them tend to be *aliases* for fonts with longer names, so there may be some repetition in font appearance even when names differ.

When you wish to use a font that has a long name, you can specify it with a wildcard syntax. For example,

```
*-courier-bold-o-normal--*-100-*
```

is an acceptable name for the first font in the previous list. The **X(1)** man page usually explains more about the rules for naming fonts, and the way the X server resolves wildcard names.

To examine a specific font, you can use **xfd** (for X font display), as follows:

```
$ xfd -fn font-name &
```

Give the font name as listed by **xlsfonts** after the **-fn** (for font name) option. This application will show a grid of all characters from the named font. Most users spend some time testing candidate fonts in their **xterm** windows to find their favorite.

The fonts themselves reside in one or more directories that **xlsfonts** and other applications search when a font is named. These directories are given in the *XWINFONTPATH* environment variable, shown here:

```
$ echo $XWINFONTPATH
/usr/X/lib/fonts/Xol,/usr/X/lib/fonts/misc,/usr/X/lib/fonts/100dpi
$
```

This is a comma-delimited list of directories that contain fonts. You can change the fonts that are available by simply changing this environment variable, but many applications expect to find specific fonts, and some applications will not survive changes to XWINFONTPATH. Actually, when a font name is used, the X server will search these directories to find the first font that matches the name. Thus, you may be surprised at the results when you use font names that include wildcards.

Colors

Use the **-fg** (for foreground) and **-bg** (for background) options with **xterm** and most other X clients to set foreground and background colors. Both of these options take a normal color name as an argument. For example,

```
$ xterm -fg white -bg blue &
```

creates an especially restful white-on-blue screen. Use the **xcolors** client to see a list of all the available colors and their names supported on your display. If your system does not include the **xcolors** client, the colors can be displayed through the Workspace Properties menu. If you have a monochrome display, about the best you can do is

```
$ xterm -fg white -bg black &
$ xterm -fg black -bg white &
```

You can use the command

```
$ xterm -rv &
```

as a synonym for one or the other of the two previous commands. The
-rv (for reverse video) option switches the foreground and background
colors.

Titles and Names

You can specify the label in the top border of most windows with the
-title, **-tl** or **-T** option, which takes a quoted character string as an
argument. You can give a label for the window's icon with **-n** or **-in** (for
icon name), as shown here:

```
$ xterm -title "The main window" -in "master shell" &
```

Usually the client's icon name will be the window title, but some applications use the application name as the icon name.

Icons and Help

The **-iconic** argument instructs the client to start as an icon rather than
as a full window. In addition, many X clients support the **-help** argument, which prints a help message listing the command-line arguments
allowed by that client. Once the list is printed, the client will exit.

X Clients

Many client programs are available for X, and many of these are
publicly available (usually in source form). New clients appear regularly.
Among them are toys and games, X-related utility programs like
xlsfonts, and full-scale applications like multimedia editors, drawing
tools, and spreadsheets. Table 23-2 lists many of the most useful client
programs. This exact list will probably not be available on your machine,

Name	Type	Description
olwm	Window Manager	OPEN LOOK
mwm		Motif
twm		Official X11R4 wm from MIT
gwm		Generic LISP-like wm
xauth	Utility	Manages an authorization list of users' access to machines
xev		Displays the contents of each X event
xfd		Displays fonts
xhost		Manages the list of hosts that can create windows on your display
xlock		Locks the screen; password to reenable
xlsfonts		Lists the names of all available fonts
xmodmap		Loads an X keyboard map into the environment
xperfmon		Displays a graph of CPU and net load
xpr		Processes a window dump for printing
xrdb		Loads an X Resource Database into the environment
xrefresh		Redraws the entire screen
xset		Sets user preferences (properties)
xuwd		Displays a window dumped by **xwd**
xwd		Dumps a bitmap of a window to a file
olam	OPEN LOOK	Net access control
olfm		File manager
olpixmap		Pixmap (colors) editor
olprintscreen		Dumps window to printer
olwsm		Workspace manager
bitmap	Application	Bitmap editor
hexcalc		Calculator with hexadecimal arithmetic
tgif		Drawing tool
xbiff		Displays a "Mailbox" window; signals arrival of mail
xcal		Desk Calendar
xcalendar		Desk Calendar
xcalc		Mouse-oriented mathematical calculator
xclipboard		Temporary clipboard for cut-and-paste operations
xedit		Simple mouse-oriented text editor

Table 23-2.   Common X Client Applications

Name	Type	Description
xmag		Displays "fatbits" for a section of display
xman		Displays man pages
xmail		Reads and creates mail
xmessage		Displays a window containing a text message
xmh		Reads and creates mail
xpic		Drawing tool
xps		Previewer for PostScript files
xrn		Reads and creates news
xsetroot		Changes background display parameters
xtroff		Previewer for ditroff output
aquarium	Toy	Displays moving fish on the background
ico		Displays a bouncing "ball"
kaleid		Displays a continually changing kaleidoscope in a window
xclock		Displays a clock
xdemo		Displays various demonstrations of X
xeyes		Displays moving eyes that follow the pointer
xgranite		Display a granite pattern on the background
xloadimage		Displays image in a window or background
xlogo		Shows the X Window System logo in a window
xphoon		Displays an image of the phase of the moon on the background

Table 23-2.   Common X Client Applications (*continued*)

so experiment with the applications in the X **bin** directory (usually **/usr/X/bin** or **/usr/bin/X11**) to see what clients are available. Only a few are discussed here.

The xhost Client

The **xhost** client is a security tool that is useful if you are using X on a LAN. The **xhost** client, also known as **olam,** controls the other machines on the network that are allowed to display windows on your display. That is, you can run the X server on one machine, and run an X client on another machine on the network. If it is enabled by **xhost**, the client will be able to display its windows on your screen.

To see which other hosts can create windows on your machine, use **xhost** with no command-line arguments, as shown here:

```
$ xhost
access control enabled (only the following hosts are allowed)
localhost
yoursys
$
```

You can enable access by all other machines with

```
$ xhost +
all hosts being allowed (access control disabled)
$
```

or disable access to all other machines with

```
$ xhost -
all hosts being restricted (access control enabled)
$
```

To add or subtract individual hosts from the access list, name them after the + or - on the **xhost** command line, as follows:

```
$ xhost + yoursys
yoursys being added to access control list
$
```

When the X server starts, it consults the file **/etc/X0.hosts** on the local machine. This file contains a list of hosts (one per line) that are granted access by default. For example:

```
$ cat /etc/X0.hosts
yoursys
othersys
$
```

The zero in the filename stands for display number zero on that host, and corresponds to the zero in the DISPLAY name, shown here:

```
DISPLAY=hostname:0
```

If you have more than one display on the machine, you can create additional **/etc/X?.hosts** files as necessary.

The xset and xsetroot Clients

The **xsetroot** client is one of the most fun to use. It allows you to establish properties for the root or Workspace background, which is the unused space *behind* the windows on the screen. It takes the usual X command-line arguments for setting foreground and background colors, and so on. In addition, it can take a bitmap file after the **-bitmap** argument to select a picture to display on the background. Try this command, for example:

```
$ xsetroot -rv -bitmap /usr/X/lib/bitmaps/nights -fg blue -bg red
```

Many pictures are available. Most of them are in the public domain, and on most systems they are kept in **/usr/X/lib/bitmaps** or in **/usr/include/X11/bitmaps**. If a bitmap is smaller than the screen area, **xsetroot** will *tile* multiple copies of the picture onto the screen, producing some interesting effects.

You can set a solid background color with

```
$ xsetroot -solid color
```

where you replace *color* with the desired color name.

The **xset** application is similar to **xsetroot**, but it sets generic preferences such as font paths, mouse parameters, and so forth. The command

```
xset -q
```

(lowercase *Q*, for query) will display the currently selected preferences supported by **xset**.

Actually, both **xsetroot** and **xset** are called by the Workspace Properties menu when you change your preferences, but the commands usually have more capabilities and options than the Properties menu.

The xcalc Client

The **xcalc** client is a mouse-oriented calculator that acts like a pocket calculator. It usually allows you to select either an algebraic (normal) or reverse polish notation. The **hexcalc** version includes the hexadecimal number base.

xbiff and Reading Mail

The **xbiff** client (so named because the developer had a dog that chased mail carriers) displays a mailbox in a small window. When new mail arrives, the flag on the icon is raised, the display beeps, and the window often switches to reverse video. After you read your mail, **xbiff** automatically returns the flag to the down position. If you click on the raised flag, the icon will also be reset.

Unfortunately, **xbiff** does not include a *mail reader*. You must go to an **xterm** window and run your normal **mail** program to actually read incoming mail. Mail reading tools are available in some X releases, but all releases include **xbiff**.

Usually, you can change the bitmap for the displayed **xbiff** icons, but the procedure varies between versions of the program. Often you can set an X resource to point to the desired bitmap file. Consult the man page for details.

Going Further

The X Window System is a rich and highly configurable environment. Instead of using the default SVR4 setup discussed so far, you can take full control of the X environment and customize it to your liking. In addition, there are many features and clients that we have not yet mentioned.

In most X systems, you can use the raw X Window System if you bypass **olinit** and use **xinit** instead. This may eliminate the OPEN LOOK environment, but it gives you control over the parallel tools designed for a generic X Window System. Most OPEN LOOK and Motif programs and procedures have been adapted from these generic tools, and the original generic procedures still work.

The xinit Command Line

The **xinit** command allows you to use command line options that customize the **xinit** command itself, and also lets you include options that are passed on to the X server (usually called **X** in the *User's Manual* and **ps** listings). Thus, the **xinit** command line can be quite complex. Its basic form is

```
$ xinit [[client] options] [-- [server] [display] options]
```

A similar complete command form is allowed with the **olinit** command, but this is rarely used.

You give options that are intended for **xinit** itself first on the command line, and then add -- (hyphen-hyphen), followed by specific options for the server. When present, the first set of options usually includes a client to execute and its arguments. If the client name is omitted, **xterm** is used as the default client. This part of the command line may also let you specify screen colors and other properties for the client. The second set of options (for the server) lets you select a display, change to a different server, and so forth. Consult the **X(1)** man page for details on configuring the server. As an example, consider these two commands, which are nearly equivalent:

```
$ olinit
$ xinit -geometry 80x24 -- :0 -vdctype vga800x600
```

This direct command-line form is not usually necessary unless you wish to start the server on one machine from another machine in the network.

The xinit Startup Script

When **xinit** runs, it starts the X server for your display, and then executes the file **$HOME/.xinitrc** (for init run control). The equivalent

OPEN LOOK version is **$HOME/.olinitrc**. Both files are shell scripts that can contain any commands you choose. They are normally used to start your favorite X clients, to run commands that customize the X session, and to start your favorite window manager, as shown here:

```
$ cat $HOME/.olinitrc
olwm &
olfm &
xclock - geometry 40x40-0+0 &
xbiff -rv -geometry 40x40-2-2 &
xmodmap .Xmodmap
xterm -geometry 80x24+10+0 &
$
```

This is a simple example of an **.olinitrc** file. You'll see a more complex example later in this chapter.

If the file does not exist, **olinit** or **xinit** will set up a simple default environment. This will usually result in a working X environment, but without a window manager it probably won't be usable. The **olinit** command normally runs the **olwsm** client by default, however, so you may have the Workspace menu available.

Ending the X Session

When you kill **olwsm** through the Exit menu item, the entire X session ends. On the other hand, **xinit** works by starting the server, and then executing the shell script in **.xinitrc**. When this shell script exits, **xinit** assumes you are finished with the X session; thus, it kills the server and returns you to the login shell. This means that the **xinit** program (or a program replacing **xinit** via **exec** in the **.xinitrc** file) must be running all through your X session, and the **.xinitrc** shell script should not exit until you are through with the X session. These requirements are normally met by running all the commands in your **.xinitrc** in the background (that is, ending with the **&** operator), *except for the last command.* You should arrange things so that the last command is one you wish to kill to end your X session. Usually this will be your window manager, because it provides menus and commands for the entire session. For example, Figure 23-4 shows a fairly complex **.xinitrc** file that distinguishes between different machines, starts different clients depending on the machine, and starts the window manager last. This

```
#!/bin/sh
# A sample .xinitrc

HOST=`echo $DISPLAY | cut -d: -f1`

# Comment these out if you aren't using them
userresources=$HOME/.Xresources
usermodmap=$HOME/.Xmodmap
#sysresources=/usr/X/lib/xinit/.Xresources
#sysmodmap=/usr/X/lib/xinit/.Xmodmap

# merge in defaults and keymaps
if [ -f "$userresources" ]; then
    xrdb -merge $userresources
fi
if [ -f "$sysmodmap" ]; then
    xmodmap $sysmodmap
fi
if [ -f "$sysresources" ]; then
    xrdb -merge $sysresources
fi
if [ -f "$usermodmap" ]; then
    xmodmap $usermodmap
fi

# choose your wm!
# WMCMD="exec twm -f $HOME/.twmrc"
WMCMD="exec olwm -f"
# WMCMD="exec gwm -f mwm"
# WMCMD="exec mwm -f"
export WMCMD

# special setup depending on what machine we're on
if [ $HOST = "my_sys" -o $HOST = "unix" -o $HOST = "localhost" ]
then
    xphoon
    xperfmon -geometry 200x300-4-4 user system input output collision &
    xclock -geometry 50x80-1+1 &
    xbiff -geometry -1+90 >/dev/null &

    xterm -title $HOST -geometry 80x30+120-4 -fg white -bg blue \
    -font -adobe-courier-bold-r-normal--18-180-75-75-m-110-iso8859-1 &

    xterm -geometry 80x30+0+0 -name login -fg white -bg blue \
    -C -font -adobe-courier-bold-r-normal--18-180-75-75-m-110-iso8859-1 &

    xterm -title yoursys -geometry 80x12+1-4 -fg white -bg blue \
    -font -adobe-courier-bold-r-normal--18-180-75-75-m-110-iso8859-1 \
    -e rlogin yoursys &

    $WMCMD

else     # monochrome display -- don't set colors
    xclock -geometry 50x50-1+1 &
    xperfmon -geometry -200x300-4-4 user system input output collision &

    xterm -geometry 80x30+0+0 -name login -C \
    -font -adobe-courier-bold-r-normal--18-180-75-75-m-110-iso8859-1 &

    $WMCMD
fi
```

Figure 23-4.   A more complex **.xinitrc** file

.xinitrc also configures the user session with the **xrdb** and **xmodmap** programs, two utilities that are discussed later in this chapter.

The window manager is started last with **exec** so that the **.xinitrc** script does not linger, but it is the *only* command that is not started in the background; thus, when you select **exit** from the window manager menu, the entire X session will exit.

The Resource Database

The X Window System maintains an internal database of resources that can be consulted by applications to set the values of parameters useful to that application. Usually, window geometry, fonts, colors, and other X-related information is kept in this *resource database,* but any application-specific data or information is allowed. The resource database is used by the Properties menus to change the default fonts, colors, and all the other properties of your session (and of individual windows). When you make changes to the Properties menus, you are actually changing these resources.

Keeping information in this resource database allows you to set your preferences without attaching a long list of command-line options to your commands. There are usually many more resources than are represented in the Properties menus. In fact, resources can be specified on a per-window basis if an application supports this level of detail, so some multiwindow applications allow different colors or fonts for each window.

Resource information is usually kept in a normal text file in your home directory, and this file is read when X starts. Then the information is available to any application that requests it, and the individual application need not read the file. Actually several files may be consulted in sequence so that some systemwide defaults can be established, and then *merged* with your own defaults.

The **.Xdefaults** file in your home directory is read first; then the *XENVIRONMENT* environment variable is consulted, and if it contains the pathname of another resource file, that file is read. If there is no XENVIRONMENT variable, a file named **$HOME/.Xdefaults-host name** is consulted; the *hostname* is the name of the machine where the client (not necessarily the server) is running. Information in files that are read later overrides resources in files that are read first.

The content of all these **Xdefaults** files follows the same format: a list of *name-value* pairs. These pairs are specific to the application, but they may include wildcard entries in the name that allow you to choose global as well as specific resources. The names often include unusual combinations of upper- and lowercase, and you must get both the case and the wildcard values correct for the client. Actually, the names beginning with uppercase letters define *classes* of resources, while lowercase names define specific *instances* of the resource for that client. This distinction is not often useful unless you want to set the value of a resource once, and then override it for a specific window.

Here is part of a simple **.Xdefaults** file:

```
$ tail -21 $HOME/.Xdefaults

! set up a path to search for bitmap files
*bitmapFilePath:        /home/steve/bitmaps:/usr/X/lib/bitmaps

*selectBtn:     <Button1>
*admustBtn:     <Button2>
*menuBtn:       <Button3>
*beep:    always
*borderColor:   red
*iconGravity:   south
xterm*background:       blue
xterm*boldFont:8x13bold
xterm*cursorColor:      white
xterm*font:     8x13bold
xterm*foreground:       white
xterm*geometry:80x24+0+40

xbiff*fullPixmap:       xbiff.xbm
xbiff*fullPixmapMask:   xbiff_mask.xbm
xbiff*emptyPixmap:      xbiff_empty.xbm
xbiff*emptyPismapMask: xbiff_empty_mask.xbm
```

Each entry in this file appears on a separate line, and blank lines are ignored. Comments can follow the ! (bang) operator and continue up to the end of the line. Names appear on the left, ending with a : (colon). One whitespace character (a tab in this example) follows, and the rest of the line is the value for that resource. Note that trailing whitespace is part of the resource value; is not ignored by the application. Thus, you should end the line directly after the end of the resource value. You can continue a value on the next line of the **.Xdefaults** file if you end the line with a \ (backslash) to escape the newline.

The names are composed of a hierarchical specification in which the client name comes first, followed by a window name, and then by the resource name. Thus, you can name resources independently for each client, or even for each window within a client. You can replace any component except the resource name with a * (star) to mean *any* for that component. For example, the line

```
*bitmapFilePath:     /home/steve/bitmaps:usr/X/lib/bitmaps
```

will use the named resource for all applications, while

```
Xterm*Foreground:   white
```

will make the foreground color for all the **xterm** windows white. It is not usually easy to determine the specific window names, so the central components of the name will often be * unless the defaults file was originally created by the application developer. You can sometimes find a list of common resources in the man page for the client, or in simple cases you may be able to construct such a list by experimenting with the Properties menus.

The xrdb Command

In addition to reading the **.Xdefaults** file when X starts, you can load additional files or change the defaults file while X is running. However, you must instruct X to add or reread a file. Use the **xrdb** (for X resource database) command, followed by a filename, to *replace* the current contents of the resource database with the contents of the named file. You can also use the standard input instead of giving a filename. When used with the **-merge** option as follows, **xrdb** will *add* the contents of the file to the current database, rather than replacing it:

```
$ xrdb -merge .Xresources
```

You can see the current contents of the database with the **-query** option, as shown here:

```
$ xrdb -query
```

Except for a few standard resources such as window geometry, colors, and fonts, X clients differ widely in their use of resources and in the names they expect. Consult the man page for a specific client to see how (or whether) that client uses resources.

In addition, many applications have their own private resource files that specify systemwide default values for most of the resources supported by the application. These resource files are located in the directory **/usr/X/lib/app-defaults**, or sometimes in **/usr/lib/X11/app-defaults**. You can change these systemwide defaults if you want to change the application's behavior for every user. In any case, these application defaults can suggest many ideas for the use of resources in your own **.Xdefaults** file.

The Keyboard Map and the xmodmap Command

Another important area of configurability in the X Window system is the *keyboard map*. Keystrokes and mouse clicks are actually defined at the hardware level by numeric *keycodes,* which are converted to generic *keysyms* (for key symbols) by the X server. In turn, these keysyms are translated into characters or *strings* for forwarding to the client application. You can modify these *translation tables* to reorganize your keyboard. A set of translations for the *Dvorak Keyboard* has been published, but more likely, you might want to exchange a few keys on your keyboard, or make an otherwise unused function key (or CTRL or ALT key) send a specific key sequence to ease your use of the system. The **xmodmap** (for modify keymap) command takes a filename as an argument, or reads its standard input, and uses the contents to reorganize the keymap.

Using a command language in the file gives you full control over your keyboard. The control file is a normal text file, with one command per line. Blank lines or lines that begin with a ! (bang) are ignored. Each line begins with a command; the most useful commands are **keycode**, which assigns a keysym to a key code number; **keysym**, which assigns a new keysym to an existing keysym; **remove**, which deletes a keysym from the map; and **add**, which adds a new keysym. The target keysym or keycode comes next, followed by = (equal) and the new name. For example:

```
$ cat $HOME/.Xmodmap
! swap ESC and grave
! note that these keycodes are machine-dependent; check your
! own system with "xev" or "xevent" to see what keycodes are used
keycode 9 = quoteleft
keycode 49 = Escape

! switch functions of left CTRL key and CAPLOCK key
remove Lock = Caps_Lock
remove Control - Control_L
keysym Control_L = Caps_Lock
keysym Caps_Lock = Control_L
add Lock = Caps_Lock
add Control = Control_L
$
```

The keycodes used for specific key presses may differ on your system, but on this system 9 is the keycode for the ESC key, and 49 is the keycode for the ` (grave) key at the upper-left of the keyboard. The second set of commands switch the meanings of the left CTRL key and the CAPSLOCK key. First the old definitions are removed from the map; then the new keysyms are assigned, and finally the new values are added to the table.

The keycodes can be determined by using the **xev** or **xevents** (for x events) command, which displays the contents of all X *events* directed to a window. You can run **xevents**, and then press keys to see which keycodes are used for which keys. Also displayed by **xevents** is the current keysym name associated with each key. With a little detective work, you can figure out how the keyboard is mapped on your system, and then change it as desired. Some data may be found in the **kbd(7)** man page.

Since it changes the X server, **xmodmap** reorganizes the keyboard for *all* clients, but it can only map single keystrokes to (other) single keysyms.

Another procedure is provided that uses the resource database to change the meaning of keys for a specific application, if the application supports these *translations*. This procedure also allows you to define *strings* and attach them to a key, as shown here:

```
$ cat .Xresources
xterm*VT100.translations: #override <Key>F4: string ("troff -mm") \n \
    <Key>F5: string( "rlogin yoursys") \n
$
```

This is a complex definition, but basically it overrides the meanings of the F4 and F5 function keys, so that **xterm** sees the given strings when those keys are pressed. You can reassign any keys in this way. Take care to copy the above example exactly, placing the characters **\n** (backslash n) at the end of each separate translation, and adding an additional **** to escape any real newlines, as in this resource definition. The *F4* and *F5* in this example are keysym names used by **xmodmap.** Use

```
Shift<Key>F4
```

to define the shifted F4, or

```
Ctrl<Key>F4
```

to define CTRL-F4. Some X users have defined a whole private keyboard environment using these translations. However, the translations resource may not work correctly on all SVR4 versions of X; check your system to be sure.

Programming the olwm Workspace Menu

You can configure the menus of most window managers so that they contain the commands you normally use. Procedures vary among window managers, but most use a text file that contains the configuration. When the window manager starts, it reads the file and builds the menu. The OPEN LOOK window manager uses the file **.olprograms** or sometimes **.openwin-menu** in your home directory to configure the Programs menu and the Workspace menu, respectively. Your system will probably have only one of these files. In general, each line in the file specifies one item on the menu. If you have **.openwin-menu**, you can also define the "pull-right" submenus.

The **.olprograms** file contains a list of *name-value* pairs, separated by a : (colon). The left-hand part appears in the Programs menu, while the right-hand part is executed when the specified menu item is selected. The first item will be the default. For example:

```
$ cat $HOME/.olprograms
Xterm...:        exec xterm -fn 8x13bold -geometry 80x24+20+30
Tetris: exec xterm -geometry 80x24 -e /usr/src/tetris/tetris
Lock Screen:    exec xlock
Calculator:     exec xcalc
$
```

The Workspace manager acts by creating a window, and then executing the application named on the right. When the application ends, the window is destroyed.

Using X with Virtual Consoles and DOS

The X Window System is well integrated with the other screen-oriented tools in SVR4. If you have a machine that supports these features, you can run an X session under a *virtual terminal* on the console. You cannot usually run multiple X sessions under multiple virtual terminals, but you can maintain one X session and simultaneous console sessions. As usual, you can run full-screen DOS sessions in other virtual consoles. You can use the normal *hot key* sequence (frequently ALT-SYSREQ-*function key*) to switch between sessions, and you can return to the original console with ALT-SYSREQ-H (for home). This will usually work even if you did not start the **vtlmgr** application. If **vtlmgr** is running, you can also switch to other virtual terminals that contain DOS sessions or other activities.

In addition, you can run DOS sessions inside one or more **xterm** windows, and you can run Microsoft Windows inside the DOS sessions within an X session. You may need to experiment to see how to configure the **xterm** window so that it is the correct size and shape for a DOS session.

Of course, all these multiple sessions use extreme amounts of real memory, swap space, and CPU time. You may find system performance inadequate to do many things at once.

Authorizing Users for X

In most SVR4 versions of X, users are *not* allowed to use X unless they have been authorized by the system administrator. This is partially for security reasons, but mainly because the **.profile**, PATH, and other parts of the users' environments must be modified to create a working X environment.

Although the administrative user agent often includes a selection for administering X, many of them do not. Other releases provide the programs **oladduser** (to add a user), **olremuser** (to remove a user), and **olsetvar** (to set OPEN LOOK environment variables). These programs usually reside in the directory **/usr/X/adm**. If neither of these options is available, the system administrator must configure each user's X environment manually.

All these procedures work by modifying the users' **.profile** or by installing the **.olinitrc** and other files discussed in this chapter. You can trace the changes by examining your **.profile**, running **oladduser**, and then looking at the file again.

Often the line

```
. $HOME/.olsetup
```

is added to your **.profile** to establish the correct environment variables when you log in to the machine. The **.olsetup** file is usually quite simple, but it contains the critical environment variables used by X, as shown here:

```
$ cat .olsetup
OLINVOKE=no export OLINVOKE   #!@ Do not edit this line !@
DISPLAY=unix:0 export DISPLAY #!@ Do not edit this line !@
XNETACCESS=on                 #!@ Do not edit this line !@
PATH=$PATH:/usr/X/bin export PATH       #!@ Do not edit this line !@
XWINFONTPATH="/usr/X/lib/fonts/Xol,/usr/X/lib/fonts/misc,\
/usr/X/lib/fonts/75dpi, /usr/X/lib/fonts/100dpi" export XWINFONTPATH
if [ "$OLINVOKE" = "yes" -a -r /usr/X/bin/olinit -a -x \
 /usr/X/bin/olinit -a -r /usr/X/bin/olwsm -a -x /usr/X/gin/olwsm ]
then
     /usr/X/bin/olinit /usr/X/bin/olwsm -- -xnetaccess $XNETACCESS
fi
$
```

This file just sets up the correct environment, and then tests the OLINVOKE variable to determine whether or not to start the X environment.

The **oladduser** procedure also copies default versions of **.olprograms**, **.olinitrc** and **.Xdefaults** into your home directory. If you use **xinit** instead of **olinit**, you can make these additions to your **.profile** manually.

Session Management and X Terminals

A relatively new product is the *X terminal*. These are terminals with high-quality graphics screens and extensive memory, but no general-purpose CPU or disk. They usually contain an implementation of the X server in ROM, and clients can connect to the terminal via a LAN. X terminals are optimized to run the X server, and so they can be much less expensive than an equivalent computer that has the capability to run both the server and the client.

On the other hand, the UNIX system must be specially administered to support X terminals, because they log directly into the X system and may not go through a normal login procedure. In this configuration, a special X process named **xdm** (for X display manager), or sometimes **xsm** (for X session manager), replaces the Service Access Facility to manage logins from X terminals. The **xdm** process (or its equivalent) is a demon that must be running on the host used by the X terminal. You can configure X terminals to change the desired host.

In operation, **xdm** listens for connect messages from X terminals. When the X terminal is reset or powered on, it sends a message to the display manager, which displays the equivalent of the **login:** and **Password:** prompts. If the login is accepted, **xdm** runs the user's **.olinitrc** or **.xinitrc** file, and then steps out of the way. When the user ends the session, **xdm** notes that fact, and resets things for the next login.

The display manager may differ between releases of X or even between manufacturers of X terminals, so you will have to follow the procedures that are specific to your system.

Networking

Access to Remote Machines
Network Information Commands
Access to Remote Files
Determining Mountable Resources
Mounting Resources from Remote Machines
Automatic Mounts
A Note on Clients, Servers, and init States
Sharing Resources with Other Machines
Going Further

Support for *local area networks* (LANs) is much improved in SVR4, compared to older releases of the UNIX operating system. In addition to low-level *driver* support in the kernel, simple and friendly software is provided to connect the two major LANs available in the UNIX world, Ethernet and StarLan.

Ethernet was originally developed for BSD versions of the UNIX system, and it has become an industry standard for connecting many kinds of machines with divergent operating systems. The worldwide Internet, a *wide area network* (WAN), can easily connect to Ethernet networks. Full support for Ethernet and its services only appeared in Release 4 of System V. This means that SVR4 can now fully participate in networks of machines using the TCP/IP communications protocols, whether all machines in the network are System V systems or not.

The alternative network, StarLan, was developed by AT&T using its own hardware and communications protocols. StarLan support was added to System V in Release 3, and it is still very well supported in Release 4. Other net implementations, such as token-ring and some PC nets, are not as common under the UNIX system, although many alternatives do exist.

These networks are all relatively high-speed, at least 1Mb and often 10 to 20Mb per second. This allows the use of software tools that require fast response and high performance, such as the ability to *mount* file systems on remote machines so that they appear as if they were on a local disk. Remote mounts can be very valuable because they allow fewer copies of a file or directory to exist in a network of machines, simplifying maintenance of the files and reducing the possibility that some machines will have outdated copies. If properly used, remote mounts can also save significant disk space in the network as a whole. In fact, remote mounts have allowed the development of *diskless machines,* again pioneered in the BSD environment, where the entire file system is located remotely. Additional tools allow logins on remote machines at a performance level far surpassing the abilities of terminal emulators like **cu**. The X Window System and other networked windowing environments also depend on the high speed LANs.

Three general classes of software use these two LAN designs. The *Network File System* (NFS) is primarily oriented toward the Ethernet environment, and the *Remote File Sharing* (RFS) system is primarily oriented toward StarLan. With SVR4, however, it is possible to use either LAN architecture with either software system, though this is rarely done. A third class, the *remote access* commands, are transparent to the network type, and make no distinction between networks. Thus, they run equally well on either type of network.

Use of the commands and ideas in this section requires that your machine be connected to one or the other of these two LANs. If you have neither of these LAN types, or yours is a *standalone* machine, this chapter will not be useful; consult your LAN vendor for information on connecting and using SVR4 machines with your network.

Access to Remote Machines

If your network is already up and running, you can use several commands that make it easy for you to log in to another machine on your LAN. These tools allow you to execute commands on the remote machine. They are similar in concept to the various **uucp** tools, but they are designed for high-performance LANs rather than slower telephone lines. To use these *remote access* tools, you must have a valid login id on the remote machine you wish to use.

The rlogin Command

The **rlogin** (for remote login) command allows you to start a normal login session on a remote machine. It takes the *hostname* or *uname* of the remote machine as its argument. For example:

```
my_sys$ rlogin yoursys
yoursys$
```

Assuming you are authorized to use the machine *yoursys*, after a short delay you will see a prompt for the remote machine, and you can then execute commands on that system. When you are through, you can use CTRL-D or **exit** to end the remote session, as follows:

```
yoursys$ exit
Connection closed.
.my_sys$
```

You will then be returned to the local machine to continue the session there. You can also use the ~. (tilde dot) sequence to close a remote session.

By default, the **rlogin** command establishes an environment on the remote machine that is similar to the environment you would see if you log in to that machine directly; you are even placed in your home directory on the remote machine. The TERM value and a few other environment variables are also passed from the local machine, so that full-screen applications will work as expected.

If you do not have a login on the remote machine, **rlogin** will prompt you for a password. You can bypass the password prompt by entering a newline, and **rlogin** will prompt you for a login. Then you can enter another login id if you have one. Alternatively, **rlogin** allows the -l (for login) option, which takes another user id as an argument. The **rlogin** command will try this login id, and will request a password, as shown here:

```
my_sys$ rlogin -l jim yoursys
Password:
```

While your remote session is active, all your commands will be entered at the remote machine, and your local session will wait until you exit from the remote system. If you are using a shell with job control, you can temporarily *suspend* the remote session by entering a ~ (tilde) followed by the suspend character, CTRL-Z. This stops the **rlogin** session until you restart it with job control. If you enter CTRL-Z without the tilde, **rlogin** will pass the CTRL-Z character to the remote machine, where its shell will attempt to suspend a job there.

The rcp Command

You can use the **rcp** (for remote copy) command to copy files between systems. It acts very much like the normal **cp** command, except its arguments take the form

```
machine:path
```

A missing *machine:* part defaults to the local machine. The filename can be omitted for the target if you wish to use the same path used for the source file. For example, to copy the file **/tmp/doc.file** from the local machine to a remote machine you would use

```
my_sys$ rcp /tmp/doc.file yoursys:
```

If you give the **-p** option, **rcp** will attempt to retain the file's permissions and time-stamps after the move. If you use the **-r** (for recursive) option, **rcp** will copy the entire directory subtree below the named path. In this case, the target must be a directory name.

The **rcp** command allows you to copy files from the local machine to a remote machine, from a remote machine to the local machine, or between two remote machines. Just use the *machine:* part of the filename where it is needed. However, you must have login access to each of the machines, and all files to be copied must be readable by you. Other netwide restrictions on file copying may apply on your network. Consult your net administrator to resolve any problems that arise.

The rsh Command

The **rsh** (for remote shell) command connects to a remote machine and executes a command specified on its command line. The command copies its standard input to the remote command, and copies the standard output and standard error of the remote command to the local standard output and standard error. It takes the remote hostname as its first argument, followed by the command line to execute on the remote machine. For example,

```
my_sys$ rsh yoursys cat /tmp/doc.file
```

will display the file **/tmp/doc.file** from the **yoursys** machine. You can use redirection or pipelines to mix local and remote commands, as shown here:

```
my_sys$ cat /tmp/doc.file | rsh yoursys wc -l > /tmp/size
```

This allows you to distribute long-running programs to the most lightly loaded machine on the network. If you omit the command part, and use only

```
my_sys$ rsh yoursys
```

rsh will act like **rlogin**, and create a shell on the remote machine.

If you *quote* any redirection operators in your command line, these will be interpreted on the remote machine rather than the local machine. For example,

```
my_sys$ cat /tmp/doc.file | rsh yoursys wc -l ">" /tmp/size
```

will create the file **/tmp/size** on **yoursys** instead of on the local machine.

As with the other remote access commands, to use **rsh** you must have a valid login on the remote machine, and have sufficient permissions there to execute your commands.

The *remote shell* should not be confused with the *restricted shell,* although both are named **rsh**. The restricted shell is **/usr/lib/rsh,** or sometimes **/sbin/rsh,** while the remote shell is usually **/usr/bin/rsh.** Take care not to get the wrong command; you may wish to use the full pathname or make an alias for **rsh** to avoid confusion. On some systems the remote shell command has been renamed; often to **nsh** or **remsh.** Check your own machine to be sure.

Because the remote shell can be renamed as the host to call, you cannot rename it yourself. That is, if you try

```
# ln rsh remsh
# remsh hostname
remsh: unknown host
#
```

the remote shell will try to connect to the host *remsh,* probably not what you intend. On the other hand, this ability can be a positive feature, because it allows you to link **rsh** to a hostname, and then write commands such as

```
$ yoursys cat /tmp/myfile
```

to execute commands on **yoursys.**

Network Information Commands

Several commands are available that provide information about the network and its users. These can tell you where a user is logged in or how busy a machine on the network is.

The rusers Command

The **rusers** (for remote users) command lists the users currently logged in to each machine on the network, as follows:

```
my_sys$ rusers
my_sys      steve
yoursys     jim pat root
my_sys$
```

This command line will usually report on all the users on all machines in the network, although some SVR4 versions require that a hostname be given on the command line. A machine will not appear in the output if no one is currently logged in on it; use the **-a** (for all) option to force idle machines to appear in the output.

To get a report on only a specific machine, give the hostname as an argument, as shown here:

```
my_sys$ rusers yoursys
yoursys   jim pat root
my_sys$
```

This option is often helpful if you have a large network.

To get a longer listing that includes the terminal ports users are on, the time they logged in, and their usage of CPU time on their host, use the **-l** (for long) option, as follows:

```
my_sys$ rusers -l my_sys
steve     my_sys:console         Apr 28 10:45       35
my_sys$
```

The last column gives the time in minutes since the user entered a command.

A similar command called **rwho** may not work unless a special **rwhod** demon is enabled on a machine. In any case, the **rusers -l** command is preferable.

The finger Command

A widely used net information command is **finger**. This command reports on each user, what terminal port each is using, and when he or she logged in to the machine. By default, **finger** reports on each user on the local machine, as in this example:

```
my_sys$ finger
Login      Name            TTY       Idle    When    Where
root       0000-Admin(0000)  console    58 Sat 10:45
steve      Steve            pts011          Sat 11:44 yoursys
my_sys$
```

The **Idle** entry gives the time in minutes since the user last entered a command. If the user entered from a remote host with **rlogin**, that machine is reported in the **Where** column.

If a login id (or list of login ids) is given as an argument to **finger**, a more verbose report is provided for that user only. For example:

```
my_sys$ finger steve
Login name: steve                        In real life: Steve
Directory: /home/steve                   Shell: /usr/bin/ksh
On since Apr 28 11:44:50 on pts011         from yoursys
3 minutes 50 seconds Idle Time
New mail received Mon Apr 16 15:32:46 1990;
 unread since Sat Apr 28 11:44:19 1990
No Plan.
my_sys$
```

The mail lines report when the user last received and read mail. The *Plan* is the contents of the user's **$HOME/.plan** file, if one exists. If you or your group use **finger** frequently, you can leave your schedule or other information in the **.plan** file for the use of others. If that file does not exist, **finger** reports "No Plan." Another file, **$HOME/.project**, is also displayed if it exists.

To get information about users on remote machines, you can use these formats:

```
$ finger user\@machine
$ finger \@machine
```

Be sure to escape the @ (at) sign with a \ (backslash) or the command line will be discarded in SVR4. The first form will try to find the *user* on the *machine* given, and the second will report on all users on that machine.

The **finger** command allows several display variants, which are selected by command-line arguments. You can use **-l** to get a long output format, **-s** to get a short format, or **-q** to get an even shorter *quick display*. The **-h** option suppresses the project output, and the **-p** option suppresses the plan output. Finally, you can use **-f** to suppress the header output, making it easier to use **finger** in a shell script.

Like many of the information commands, **finger** requires that a special demon be running on the target machine; the command will fail if the demon is not present.

The ping Command

The **ping** command attempts to send a message to a remote machine. If the machine is up and listening for net activity, it will answer the message. Thus, you can determine if a machine is alive on the net, as follows:

```
my_sys$ ping yoursys
yoursys is alive
my_sys$
```

If you add the -s (for statistics) option, **ping** will send a sequence of messages, and report the effectiveness of the data transfer between machines, as shown here:

```
my_sys$ ping -s yoursys
PING yoursys: 56 data bytes
64 bytes from yoursys (130.0.17.32): icmp_seq=0. time=10. ms
64 bytes from yoursys (130.0.17.32): icmp_seq=1. time=180. ms
64 bytes from yoursys (130.0.17.32): icmp_seq=2. time=0. ms
64 bytes from yoursys (130.0.17.32): icmp_seq=3. time=0. ms
64 bytes from yoursys (130.0.17.32): icmp_seq=4. time=10. ms
64 bytes from yoursys (130.0.17.32): icmp_seq=5. time=0. ms

----yoursys PING Statistics----
6 packets transmitted, 6 packets received, 0% packet loss
round-trip (ms)  min/avg/max = 0/33/180
```

With the -s option, **ping** will continue to send packets until you press DEL; then it will report the summary statistics and exit. This can be useful if you suspect that your network is not working properly.

Access to Remote Files

The UNIX SVR4 system provides tools for using files physically located on media attached to remote machines. Using these tools, you can mount directories that are located on remote machines into your local file system. You can then use remote disk resources as if they were your own. In practice, using these tools is very much like using a mountable floppy or a local hard disk, except when you use remotely mounted files, the system fetches the data across the LAN.

These remote access commands differ internally depending on whether you are using the Network File System (NFS) or the Remote File Sharing (RFS) system, but user-level tools are provided to reduce or eliminate the differences where possible.

The local machine can only use resources from a remote machine if the remote machine allows this access. That is, the system administrator on a machine must *share* directory subtrees with the other machines on the network before remote access to those files is allowed. Once the directory is shared, other machines can mount those directories, using the familiar **/sbin/mount** command.

All of these tools work on a directory as a whole; you can mount a directory (and all its subdirectories), but you cannot mount an individual file. Each directory must be mounted at a specific place in the local directory tree, called a *mount point*. This mount point is an empty directory somewhere in the file system. You must have a separate mount point for each directory you are mounting simultaneously, but you can reuse a mount point if you *unmount* one directory before trying to mount another. The system will allow you to mount one directory over another directory that is not empty, but this is not usually a good idea. If you frequently use remote mounts, it is best to create dedicated empty directories as mount points. Once a remote directory is mounted, you can use it almost as if it were a normal local directory.

Determining Mountable Resources

After another machine has shared some directories (as discussed later in this chapter), you can mount these directories on your machine when you need them. You can easily determine the shared resources on the net by using **dfshares** (for distributed file shares). Without arguments, **dfshares** lists all the resources available to your machine throughout the network, as shown here:

```
my_sys$ dfshares
RESOURCE                      SERVER   ACCESS   TRANSPORT
    my_sys:/export            my_sys   rw       tcp
    yoursys:/usr/src/access   yoursys  ro       tcp
my_sys$
```

You can select a specific machine by giving the hostname as the argument to **dfshares**. This is usually preferable on a large network. Note that some SVR4 versions require your machine to be in init state 3 (discussed later in this chapter) for the **dfshares** command to work correctly.

Mounting Resources from Remote Machines

When you know the pathname of a remote resource, you can mount a remote directory at a local mount point. Remote mounts are limited to the superuser on the local machine. Be sure to use an empty directory as your mount point, or if necessary create a new directory as follows:

```
# mkdir /usr/src/remote
# mount -F nfs yoursys:/usr/src/access /usr/src/remote
```

Give the remote hostname, followed by a : (colon), and then the remote pathname with no intervening whitespace. Last, give the local mount point. If the command succeeds, the remote directory will appear in your local file system.

When mounting a remote resource, you must specify the *file system type* used for the resource you are mounting. This is the purpose of the **-F** option. For networking, the possibilities are **nfs** and **rfs**. Some releases of SVR4 may allow you to omit the **-F** option, but you are less likely to make errors if you get in the habit of using it. The value after the **-F** option must match the network type in use on both the local and the remote machines.

With this usage, the remote resource will be mounted with the permissions set as they were when the resource was shared (read-only or read-write). You can ask for *fewer* permissions by giving the **-o** option, as shown here:

```
# mount -F nfs -o ro yoursys:/usr/src /usr/src/remote
```

You cannot ask for more permissions than were specified when the resource was shared.

Mounting Several Resources

You can mount a series of directories with the **mountall** command, or place a series of **mount** commands in a shell script for execution as a group. By default, **mountall** picks up its instructions from the file **/etc/vfstab** (for virtual file system table), shown here:

```
# tail -2 /etc/vfstab
/dev/dsk/f1             /dev/rdsk/f1   /install      s5 - no -
yoursys:/usr/src/access -              /usr/src/remote nfs - yes ro
#
```

There is one line for each mount, with several fields on each line (separated by whitespace). The fields are the file system location (block and raw devices); the local mount point; the file system type (**nfs, rfs, s5,** or **ufs**); a flag indicating whether a password is required to mount the resource; **yes** or **no** depending on whether the resource should be *automatically mounted*; and finally, the options for the mount.

You can create your own file describing the mounts you wish to make. Give the pathname of this file as an argument to **mountall**. Its format should be the same as that of **/etc/vfstab**.

Listing Mounted Resources

You can examine a list of all mounted resources by giving the **mount** command with no arguments, which lists all the mounted file systems, both local and remote. This use of the **mount** command is not limited to the superuser.

Unmounting Remote Resources

A resource, once mounted, stays available until it is unmounted or until your machine is rebooted. You can use the **umount** command to release the resource. Give the local pathname as argument to **umount**, as follows:

```
# umount /usr/src/remote
```

You can unmount all your mounted resources at the same time with the **umountall** command. This will unmount all your remote resources, but it may also unmount some local resources, such as floppy disks, so use **umountall** with care.

Automatic Mounts

The sixth field in the **mountall** command is not used when **mountall** is given on the command line, but you can place lines of **mountall** format in the **/etc/vfstab** file so that resources get mounted at boot time. In this case, the **yes** or **no** in the sixth field is used to determine whether the resource is mounted when the machine is booted. Examine your current **/etc/vfstab** file for more information on the existing boot-time mounts. The **vfstab** file is used to control both local and remote mounts.

In addition, you can configure NFS (though not RFS) to *automount* a remote directory when a user requests access to it. That is, the directory will not be mounted until it is needed, but then it will be mounted without superuser intervention. The **automount** command is a demon that listens for attempts to open a file in a list of named directories. When it notices such an attempt, **automount** consults a database to determine how to mount that file system, and then performs the mount. After the user leaves the mounted directory, **automount** waits for an interval, and then unmounts the resource. This facility can be very helpful, because the local machine will often be adversely affected if a mounted NFS resource is on a machine that is down, or if a LAN segment is down. On the other hand, this feature does slow overall file system access, even for directories that are not in the **automount** list. Consult the **automount**(1) man page for more information on using this service.

A Note on Clients, Servers, and Init States

In SVR4, some aspects of remote file access are intended for *clients*, or machines that mount resources from other machines, and other aspects are intended for *servers,* or machines that provide files for clients to mount. A machine can be a client, or it can be both a client and a server, but there is no server only condition. The **rlogin, finger,** and other commands discussed earlier in this chapter are available to both clients and servers.

Generally, servers are faster machines with large disks, while clients tend to be personal workstations. However, this distinction is not conceptually important. You can make any machine a server when you want to share some files, and then return it to client status when you only wish to mount files from other machines. In this sense, the networking tools in the UNIX system implement a *peer-to-peer* LAN scheme.

In practice, however, there is a definite performance difference between machines used as clients and those used as servers. Servers require many additional processes whose job is to "listen" for mount requests from other machines on the net, and to act on those requests. A client, on the other hand, does not have to listen, it only has to make requests when it wants something. Thus, client-only machines perform better than servers.

In SVR4, the distinction between client and server is implemented in the *init state* a machine is in at any time (see Chapter 21 for more information on init states). Init state 2 is used for standalone and client-only machines; init state 3 is reserved for servers. From init state 2, you can mount resources from another machine, but to share resources your machine must be in init state 3.

The **who -r** (for run-level) command reports the init state the machine is currently in, as follows:

```
# who -r
   .        run-level 2  Mar  6 05:07    2    0    S
#
```

As you can see, this command also reports the date and time the machine was booted, and several other items.

To change to init state 3, use

```
# telinit 3
```

When you are ready to return to client mode, use

```
# telinit 2
```

If you are using the RFS system, you should use **rfstart** to switch to init state 3.

```
# rfstart
```

Use **rfstop** to return to init state 2.

If you try to mount a resource from another machine, and you see an error such as

```
mount: yoursys:/export server not responding:
RPC: Program not registered
```

check to be sure that the remote machine is running and is in init state 3.

Sharing Resources with Other Machines

To give other machines access to your directories, you must be in init state 3, and you must also *share* the resources. This is a security precaution that provides extra control in addition to that provided by the normal file permissions.

The **share** command enables other machines to mount your directories; it is restricted to the superuser. The **share** command takes several command-line options to specify the type of remote access allowed. You can specify a directory subtree as *read-only,* or allow *read-write* access. Use the **-o** (for only) option to select either **rw** (for read-write) or **ro** (for read-only). Give the directory you wish to share following the **-o** option. Finally, you should give a *resource name*; a label that you can use to refer to the resource when you wish to unshare it. For example:

```
# share -o ro -d "Normal Exports" /export MYFILES
```

This command will share the **/export** directory tree under the name *MYFILES*, but will restrict remote machines from writing anywhere in the tree. If you wish, you can add a quoted text description of the resource following the **-d** option.

It is also possible to specify this information for each individual machine that might mount the directory. That is, you can provide different access levels for different machines on the network. As used in the previous example, **share** will allow any machine on the network to have the requested access level. To limit the access level to a particular machine, just add the form $=machine$ after the argument to the **-o** option, as shown here:

```
# share -o ro,rw=yoursys /export MYFILES
```

This restricts all machines to read-only access *except* **yoursys**, which is allowed read-write access. You can list as many machines as you wish. Separate individual entries with a comma, and be sure there is no whitespace in this argument, or **share** will become confused.

Listing Shared Resources

The **share** command with no arguments lists the directories currently shared on your machine. For example:

```
my_sys$ share
MYFILES        /export         rw              "Normal Exports"
SRC1           /usr/src/access ro,rw=yoursys   "My Source Tree"
my_sys$
```

The first column of the output gives the resource name that was set when the resource was shared. Next comes the directory that is shared, followed by the permissions. The last column gives the description, if one was specified. This use of **share** is available to all users, not just to the superuser.

Sharing Several Resources

You can share a group of resources with the **shareall** command, as follows:

```
# shareall cmdfile
#
```

Here, the file *cmdfile* contains a series of **share** command lines, as discussed previously.

If no file is given on the **shareall** command line, the default file **/etc/dfs/dfstab** (for distributed file sharing table) is used. The **dfstab** file usually contains comments that give instructions for setting up the table.

Directories shared with **share** or **shareall** will not remain shared when the machine leaves and then reenters init state 3, unless you add entries for them in **dfstab**. The **dfstab** is processed whenever the machine enters init state 3, so you can initialize your sharing environment once, and thereafter it will be used whenever the machine is used as a server. Be sure **dfstab** contains *only* directories that you *always* wish to share; use another (personal) file for occasional sharing.

Unsharing Resources

To remove a resource from the list of shared directories, use the **unshare** command. It takes the resource pathname as an argument, as shown here:

```
# unshare /export
```

The command returns silently if it succeeds in unsharing a resource. Some versions of **unshare** may use the resource name instead of the pathname to identify the resource to unshare.

If some user on a remote machine has used **cd** to enter that directory, or is currently using a file, **unshare** will still succeed, but the user will get an error when he or she next accesses the unshared resource. For example:

```
yoursys$ ls /mnt
ls: /mnt: Stale NFS file handle
```

This can be annoying for your remote users, so take care that resources are idle before you unshare them.

The **unshareall** command will make *all* of your currently shared resources unavailable to other users.

Reporting on Shared Resources in Use

The **dfmounts** (for distributed file mounts) command reports on what other machines have mounted your shared resources. This is often useful detecting other users before you try to **unshare** a resource. With no arguments, **dfmounts** will list the users of all your shared resources, as follows:

```
# dfmounts
RESOURCE      SERVER PATHNAME              CLIENTS
MYFILES       my_sys /export              yoursys
#
```

The output format will differ depending on whether you have NFS or RFS, but in either case it lists the resource name and the client machines that have mounted the resource.

A Note on Security Considerations for Sharing

Usually, network policy determines how much sharing is allowed. The policy is determined by the needs of the users and by security considerations. In a friendly environment where everyone needs access to other users' data, most directories (or directories that are high in the file system hierarchy) will probably be shared. In a more secure environment, where public data is controlled in a small directory tree, only a few directories might be shared. In SVR4, the **/export** directory tree is designated for sharing. This directory may be empty in a default configuration, but you can add to it as you discover material that should be shared.

Remember, once a machine shares a resource, many machines on the network can access that resource. It is wise to unshare resources as soon as they are no longer needed on the net.

Going Further

As you might imagine, networking can be a complex and difficult subject. The previous discussion mentioned only the most generally useful commands and procedures. With the merger of NFS and RFS, these issues have grown even more complex. You need a lot of experience to become a true network expert, and the following sections are just an introduction to some of the issues involved. Configuring a new network is not discussed here; we assume that the network is already up and running, and only describe the procedure for adding a new machine to an existing network.

The rdate Command

The **rdate** (for remote date) command allows you to set the local date from a remote machine on your LAN. This *master* time source is called the *date server.* If you use any tools that compare the modification times of files on various machines, a single centralized date is very useful. The **rdate** command takes a hostname as an argument. It reads the time from that machine, and then sets the time on the local machine to match. For example:

```
# rdate yoursys
Sat Apr 28 11:59:03 1990
#
```

If it is successful, **rdate** returns the new time it set. Although you must be a superuser to use **rdate,** it is often included in a boot-time script to assure that the time is synchronized when the machine starts.

The telnet Command

The **telnet** command is similar to **rlogin** in its function, but it can be used in situations where **rlogin** is inappropriate. For example, **rlogin** can only be used between UNIX systems, while **telnet** can communicate across a LAN between different operating systems. Also, **telnet** uses a different communication path than **rlogin,** so it can often be used when **rlogin** is not working for some reason. Some X terminals use **telnet** to make the initial contact with the X client machine that starts the first **xterm** for a session. The command has several other uses as well. However, because it provides fewer services than **rlogin, telnet** should be reserved for special situations.

The **telnet** command takes a hostname or Internet address as an argument, and connects to the **login** service on that host, as follows:

```
$ telnet yoursys
Trying 127.12.0.30 ...
Connected to yoursys.
Escape character is '^]'.

yoursys login:
```

You must login normally at the remote machine. All your typed characters will be passed to the remote system for handling, and you can execute commands as usual on the remote machine.

Note that unlike **rlogin**, the **telnet** command does not pass your current environment to the remote host when the connection is made. You must explicitly set up your environment there in your **.profile**. The **telnet** command may emulate a VT102 terminal internally, so experiment with your **TERM** variable for best results. Usually, you will set **TERM** to VT102, VT100, or ansi for correct operation of the remote session.

The **telnet** command contains a *command mode* that offers many features and options. You can switch from *terminal mode* to command mode with the **telnet** *escape character*, which defaults to CTRL-] (control left bracket), as shown here:

```
$  CTRL-]
telnet>
```

The new prompt comes from the local **telnet** command mode. At this point, you can enter any of several **telnet** commands. Use **close** to end the session with the remote host but remain in the **telnet** command mode. Alternatively, **quit** will close the remote session and end the **telnet** command, returning you to the local shell, as follows:

```
telnet> quit
Connection closed.
$
```

You should log out of the remote host before using the **quit** command; but sometimes logging out will end the **telnet** command and return you to the local shell.

The **?** (question mark) command provides a concise help display that lists the available commands. From command mode, a simple newline (with no command) will return you to the shell at the remote host.

Networking Demons

Many of the services discussed here require that *demon* processes be running on the server machine. These demons are typically started when you enter init state 3. You can examine the differences in your process environment by comparing the output of **ps -ef** when your machine is in init state 2 versus init state 3. In addition to these "normal" demons, some of the remote access commands require additional demons that are not started by default. If commands like **rusers** or **finger** do not work, it is probably because their specialized demons are missing. Consult with your network administrator to set up these demons if they are not present in your network.

Setting Up a New Machine on a Net

To add a new machine to an existing LAN, you must *configure* the networking tools correctly. These procedures differ among networks, but you should complete them soon after you physically plug your system into the net.

If you are using only one of the network types NFS or RFS, you must inform the networking tools which network is in use. The file **/etc/dfs/fstypes** (for file system types) contains this information. When the system is installed, it usually contains *both* types, as shown here:

```
# cat /etc/dfs/fstypes
nfs     Network File System Utilities: 2.0
rfs     RFS Utilities: 2.0
#
```

You can comment out the unused network type by adding a # (pound sign) at the beginning of the line you are not using. If you do not do this, the system will assume you have both networks, and many DFS commands will become confused.

Setting Up NFS

Once you have physically connected your network, you must configure the NFS system. This is relatively easy, but it must be done correctly.

Before starting, you must have three pieces of data for your machine: its *Internet address*, its *physical address*, and its uname or hostname. The Internet address is a four-part number that defines the machine with a logical address that should be unique in the world. The hardware physical address is determined from the Ethernet controller hardware, and is also unique in the world. The Internet address is assigned by your network administrator in accord with the worldwide hierarchical numbering scheme, and the physical address is usually displayed when the machine is booted.

The Host List

All these networking commands use *logical* machine names, which are the hostnames or unames of the machines on the network. Internally, however, the network uses a *numerical* addressing scheme when it communicates between machines. This numerical address is the Internet address. The file **/etc/inet/hosts** (linked to **/etc/hosts**) contains the mapping between these two forms, and the networking commands must consult that file before they can connect to the remote machine. The file looks like this:

```
# cat /etc/inet/hosts
# If the yellow pages is running, this file is only used when booting
#
# Internet host table
0.0.0.0         anyhost
127.0.0.1       localhost
130.0.17.35     my_sys
130.0.21.37     yoursys
#
```

The **/etc/inet/hosts** file contains the hostname and the correct four-part Internet address of each machine on the net. Each system should be described by a line in the file that has the form

```
130.0.17.35     my_sys
```

In the previous example, the lines

```
0.0.0.0         anyhost
127.0.0.1       localhost
```

are special entries. The **anyhost** entry gives a generic address for any machine, or more correctly for machines that do not know their address. This address is often used for *broadcast* messages to all machines. The **localhost** entry is another generic term that refers to *loopback* communications between applications on the local machine. The comment at the top of the **/etc/hosts** file is a reminder that this file is not used when the *Yellow Pages* system is running. This system is discussed at the end of this chapter.

NFS Setup Procedures

Many modern Ethernet boards automatically report their physical address to the UNIX kernel when the machine is booted. Otherwise, the file **/etc/bootptab** is consulted at boot time to assign the logical Internet address from the physical address. Check to see if this file is present on your system, and if it is, add your machine's Internet address and physical address to it.

Next, add your hostname and Internet address to the file named **/etc/inet/hosts**. If your machine is a diskless workstation or boots off another host rather than its own disk, you may also need to update the file named **/etc/bootparams** so that your machine will know which *boot server* to ask for services. This should be sufficient if your network is already functioning. Remember, though, these procedures will *not* be used if the Yellow Pages service is running on your network. Your machine should appear on the LAN after a reboot.

You can test the configuration with

```
# ping localhost
```

This will work if the networking hardware is operating correctly on your machine. The command

```
# ping hostname
```

where *hostname* is your own machine name, will work if the network addressing is correct. Use the name of another machine on your net for the *hostname* to determine whether or not your machine can communicate across the net.

Setting Up a Machine on RFS

Setup procedures differ between RFS and NFS. Be sure you are using the correct procedures for your network.

To use RFS, you must configure the domain and your machine's appearance in the domain, or you can join an existing domain. A *domain* is a separate partition of a larger net, and is controlled by demons that run on a *name server* for that domain. If you are starting a new domain, your machine may be a primary or secondary name server, or a normal machine that can share and mount resources. You can limit your machine to a specific domain on the network, or protect access to resources with passwords. Since many optional procedures are associated with RFS and its domains, including sophisticated security considerations, you should consult the RFS documentation and your network administrator before configuring a new domain or starting RFS on your machine for the first time.

Domains and Name Servers in RFS

A domain is a group of machines that allow RFS networking among themselves, but may exclude machines that are not domain members. NFS networks can also have domains, and this is usually controlled by the net administrator. Here we will discuss only RFS domains.

A large LAN with many RFS machines can have several separate domains that do not conflict with each other. A machine can participate in more than one domain, but machines in one domain usually do not access files on machines in another domain.

Each domain has exactly one *primary name server*. This machine is responsible for administering the domain as a whole, and it usually belongs to the network or domain administrator. In addition, you can establish one or more *secondary name servers*. These are usually not used for administration of the domain, but can take over routine name server duties if the primary server is down for some reason. The primary name server executes special demons that manage the domain and its activities. Other machines can join the domain to share or mount files without being name servers.

Establishing a Domain

If you are establishing a new domain, you must set up the primary name server first. If you are joining an existing domain, you should ask your domain administrator to add your machine to the domain database if your machine is to share resources, or if client verification procedures are in force in your domain. Then you can start RFS networking and mount remote resources as necessary.

Several steps are required to start a new domain. The following procedures are executed on the machine selected to be the primary name server for the new domain. Establish the *domain name* with the command

```
# dname -D domain
```

where *domain* is the unique domain name you have chosen. A domain name must have 14 or fewer characters, and must be unique on your network.

Because a machine can be attached to more than one network, you must assign a network for the domain, as follows:

```
# dname -N starlan
```

In this example, **starlan** is the special file in **/dev** that connects to the network you wish to use, and coincidentally is also the name of the network. Use **tcp** instead if you wish to use RFS on an Ethernet.

The **dname** command can also report on the domain name and network type of a machine. Use the command

```
# dname -a
```

(for all) to see this information once the domain is created.

Establishing Name Servers

Next you must create a file that contains a table of name servers for the domain. A domain must have only one primary name server, but can have several secondary name servers. The primary name server executes administrative demons that manage the domain and perform security checks. The secondary name servers take over these tasks when the primary name server is down. Since name server duties add an additional load to the machine, only a few secondary name servers are usually specified on a domain.

On the machine to be designated as the primary name server, create or edit the file **/etc/rfs/starlan/rfmaster** (for remote file master). This is the master list of name servers for the domain, and when RFS is running, this file will appear on all the servers in the domain; however, at this point you must create it on the machine designated as the primary name server. Use the same network name for the third part of the path (**starlan** in this example) that you used when you named the network.

The **rfmaster** file lists the name servers, tells whether each machine is a primary or secondary name server, and gives the network address of each server, as shown here:

```
my_sys$ cat /etc/rfs/starlan/rfmaster
# the primary and secondary name servers are listed first
local p local.steve
local s local.my_sys
# the domain and network addresses follow
local.steve a steve.serve
local.my_sys a my_sys.serve
my_sys$
```

Each line consists of three fields separated by one whitespace character. Some releases allow only a single blank or tab; multiple whitespace characters may cause the file to be processed incorrectly.

There are two types of lines in the **rfmaster** file: those that describe name servers and those that give network addresses for the name servers. The first field is the domain or machine name, the second is an action code, and the third is a network or domain address. In the previous example, the domain is called **local**, and the primary (**p**) name server is the machine **steve** at domain address **local.steve**. The machine **my_sys** is the secondary (**s**) name server, and its network address is **local.my_sys**. There can be only one **p** line, but several **s** lines are allowed.

Network addresses are mapped to domain addresses (**a**) in the rest of the lines. Only name servers need be mentioned in the **a** lines. The first field is the domain address and the third field is the network address. Network addresses of the form *uname.serve* are typical of StarLan networks. Comment lines in the **rfmaster** file begin with a **#** (pound sign). Once **rfmaster** is correct, write it and leave your editor. Verify that **root** owns the file, and that the permissions are 0644.

Adding Machines to the Domain

At this point you can add machines to the domain. To do so, use the **rfadmin** command with the **-a** (for add) option, as follows:

```
# rfadmin -a domain.hostname
Enter password for hostname:
```

Here, *domain* is the domain name and *hostname* is the name of the machine you wish to add. The **rfadmin** command prompts for a password, which must be entered by the administrator on the *hostname* machine when networking is started on that machine. You can press newline to skip the password, but be sure to respect your network security policy when you add new machines.

To remove a machine from the domain use **rfadmin** with the **-r** (for remove) option, as shown here:

```
# rfadmin -r domain.uname
```

To display the current name server for the domain, use

```
# rfadmin
```

with no argument. The current name server must be your machine, or you will not be able to perform any of the domain administrative tasks.

Now you can start RFS on the primary name server with **rfstart**. Then, execute **rfstart** again on the secondary name servers, and your domain should be up and running, and available for other machines to use. To work with remote resources, use the **share** and **mount** commands.

You can determine the current status of RFS at any time with the **-q** (for query) option of **rfadmin**, shown here:

```
# rfadmin -q
RFS is running
#
```

If things are not working properly, check to be sure RFS is running.

Changing an Existing Domain

You can switch the primary name server responsibilities to a secondary name server with the command

```
# rfadmin -p
```

You might use this command before bringing the primary down for maintenance. This is only intended to produce a temporary change in name servers. As soon as the primary is back up, execute

```
# rfadmin -p
```

on the current name server to restore responsibilities to the primary. To permanently change the primary name server, you must edit the file **rfmaster**. Be sure to stop RFS on all primary and secondary name servers in the domain with **rfstop** before changing name servers. Then edit **rfmaster** on the new primary, start RFS there with **rfstart**, and finally start the secondaries.

When the name servers are operating correctly, the primary server regularly distributes the key administrative files to the secondary servers. If the primary name server crashes, responsibilities automatically pass to the first secondary name server in the **rfmaster** file. The crash will not affect any mounted resources in the domain, unless they reside on the crashed machine. However, the secondaries cannot perform the full name server duties, so if the primary does not come back on line soon, you should switch the primary responsibilities to another machine, usually to one of the former secondaries. Carefully check the **rfmaster** file and the shared resources for errors, because the secondaries do not always have completely current administrative files.

More RFS Issues

RFS allows *mapping* of users on remote machines into user ids and group ids on server machines. Thus you have complete control of permissions granted to remote users of your resources. Mapping can be complex, and you should study the RFS documentation before using it.

Finally, several tools are available for measuring RFS usage, and *tuning* its performance to your needs. The **fusage** (for file usage) command allows you to study how clients are using your resources, and the **sar** (for system activity reporting) command reports on how much CPU time is being used for remote file access. You can change the servers and their responsibilities to minimize CPU usage on the domain as a whole. In addition, you can adjust the values of RFS *parameters* to control values such as the maximum number of people using your resources, and the maximum number of processes associated with RFS. These are all complex functions that should be used with care.

Using Both NFS and RFS on a Machine

Normally you will choose *either* NFS or RFS, or another compatible communications protocol, for your network. This decision is based on the need for your machine to fit into an already existing network that uses one of these systems. However, SVR4 allows many different protocols to be used on a single network, though this is rare. To make it work, you must configure all the networks correctly as discussed earlier; then you can selectively share and mount resources from any of them. You can obtain information about resources available with individual networking systems, and start and stop them independently (although both NFS and RFS require that a machine be in init state 3 for sharing).

The **share, mount, unshare, umount, shareall, unshareall, umountall,** and **dfshares** commands can all take the **-F** command-line argument that specifies *which* system is intended when you give these commands. Here is an example:

```
# share -F nfs -o ro /usr/src
```

This added command-line argument is required when you are using both NFS and RFS, but, except with the **mount** command, it is not needed when you are using only one of these sytems.

SVR3 RFS Commands under SVR4

In addition to the new **share** and **mount** procedures, SVR4 still supports the commands used to manage an RFS network in SVR3. Because the new commands are much simpler to use and support both

RFS and NFS, it is preferable to use them whenever possible, but if you wish to run several RFS domains on your network, you will need the older commands to get individual control over the domains and their members.

You can use the **nsquery** command to list available RFS resources, as shown here:

```
my_sys$ nsquery
RESOURCE    ACCESS       SERVER          TRANSPORT  DESCRIPTION

DATA        read/write   local.my_sys    starlan    Real database
DATA_BKUP   read-only    local.my_sys    starlan    Backup database
SCRATCH     read/write   big.my_sys      starlan    For temp moves
STEVE       read/write   big.steve       starlan    steve's public dir
BILL        read-only    local.yoursys   starlan    bill's public dir
my_sys$
```

In this example, there are three machines in two different domains. The domains are called *local* and *big*, and the machines are **my_sys**, **yoursys**, and **steve**. You can limit the **nsquery** output to resources on a subset of the total list by naming the machine or the domain as an argument, as follows:

```
my_sys$ nsquery local.my_sys
my_sys$ nsquery my_sys
my_sys$ nsquery big.
```

The dot is required when you are naming a domain.

The **/usr/sbin/fuser** (for file system users) command will report current users of your shared RFS resources. The **fuser** command takes a directory as an argument, and reports the process ids of processes that are using that resource. Use the **-u** (for users) option to list the login ids of the people who own the processes, as shown here:

```
# fuser -u /export
/export:    121c(steve)   123p(jim)   135c(jim)
#
```

In this example, three processes are using the resource **/export**, and their PIDs are 121, 123, and 135. The user ids are given in parentheses after the process. The letter **c** (for current directory) signals that the users have the resource as their current directory. The **p** (for parent) marks the resource as the parent directory for the process, and **r** (for root) marks the resource as the root directory for the process. For remote resources, the report will be for any file within the mounted resource. The **fuser** command can also report on use of local resources, such as mounted file systems, which can help identify users of floppy disks and other removable media.

In an emergency, you can use the **fumount** (for forced unmount) command to force a resource to be unmounted even though users are accessing it. Because this procedure can seriously inconvenience remote users, it should be used with care. The **fumount** command takes a resource name as an argument, and allows an optional delay if the **-w** (for wait) flag is given with a number of seconds, as follows:

```
# fumount -w 30 DATA
```

The **fumount** command starts an **rfuadmin** (remote file user administration) process on each client machine that is using the resource, and this process has the task of unmounting the resource from that machine. The **rfuadmin** process gives a warning to client users with the **wall** command if the **-w** option is given, and then waits the delay time before using **fumount** locally to unmount the resource.

Processes accessing the resource will be killed, so if you are a client user and receive a message such as

```
DATA is being removed from the system in 30 seconds.
```

you should immediately relinquish your use of the resource by ending programs that access it, or by using **cd** to move out of the resource directory. This procedure is also executed automatically when the host is shut down.

The **adv** (for advertise) and **unadv** (for unadvertise) commands work like **share** and **unshare**; however, they can take a resource name and a pathname as arguments, as in this example:

```
# adv DATA /usr/steve/my.data
```

The resource name is assigned when the resource is shared, or advertised, and the pathname is the local directory that you wish to share.

The **adv** and **unadv** commands can also take flags and other command-line arguments, including one that chooses a specific domain for the resource. Consult the relevant man pages for more details.

Many additional RFS administration commands are supported, but most of them are used primarily to administer networks that have extensive security restrictions.

Configuring mail for a Network

LAN-based electronic mail frequently does not use the **uucp** transport service discussed in Chapters 14 and 15. Instead, a special protocol and demons are used on most LANs. The **smtp** (for simple mail transport protocol) command is used internally to send mail across a LAN, and the **smtpd** demon listens for incoming mail. Neither of these programs is intended for users. Instead, the normal **mail** program can be configured to search both the **uucp** data files and the network hosts table (**/etc/inet/hosts**). It will use whichever delivery route it finds *first* for the machine.

In SVR4 systems, the control file for this search process is **/etc/mail/mailsurr** (for mail surrogate). When **mail** runs, it reads this file to *rewrite* an address and execute the appropriate mail *transport agent* program for that piece of mail. The **mailsurr** file contains a list of complex rules that look something like regular expressions. Each mail address is matched to one of these rules, and the associated command is executed. The order of the rules in the **mailsurr** file is significant, because the first match that contains an agent command ends the search.

In many standard releases of the SVR4 system, the lines in **mailsurr** that support **uucp** mail transport are enabled, but the **smtp** lines are disabled. For example:

```
# tail -13 /etc/mail/mailsurr

# For remote mail via uucp and smtp. Uucp is first because
# it is more universal and handles binary mail properly.
#
'.+'    '!([^!]+)!(.+)'    '< /usr/bin/uux - \1!rmail (\2)'
#'.+'    '!([^!]+)!(.+)'    '< /usr/lib/mail/surrcmd/smtpqer %R \1 \2'

# If none of the above work, ship remote mail to a smarter host.
```

```
# Make certain that SMARTERHOST= is defined in /etc/mail/mailcnfg.
# If there is no smarter host, then routed mail fails here.
#
'.+'    '!(.+)'              'Translate R=!%X!\1'
#
```

Comment lines begin with a # (pound sign). In the previous example, **uucp** transport is enabled, but **smtp** transport is disabled. You can enable LAN mail by deleting the # at the beginning of the line below the **uux** message, as shown here:

```
# tail -13 /etc/mail/mailsurr

# For remote mail via uucp and smtp. Uucp is first because
# it is more universal and handles binary mail properly.
#
'.+'    '!([^!]+)!(.+)'    '< /usr/bin/uux - \1!rmail (\2)'
'.+'    '!([^!]+)!(.+)'    '< /usr/lib/mail/surrcmd/smtpqer %R \1 \2'

# If none of the above work, then ship remote mail to a smarter host.
# Make certain that SMARTERHOST= is defined in /etc/mail/mailcnfg.
# If there is no smarter host, then routed mail fails here.
#
'.+'    '!(.+)'              'Translate R=!%X!\1'
#
```

Note that this example tries the **uucp** rules before the **smtp** rules. You can switch the order of the two lines to reverse this behavior.

The last line in the previous example allows the **mail** system to send the message to a *gateway* host on the LAN if it cannot resolve the address itself. This line should also be uncommented if your LAN has such a gateway machine.

In addition, you may need to create or add lines to the file **/etc/mail/mailcnfg** to describe your domain and the hostname of the gateway, as follows:

```
# cat /etc/mail/mailcnfg
DOMAIN=.mydomain.com
SMARTERHOST=yoursys
#
```

Ask your net administrator for the names of the domain and gateway machine.

If you have the BSD compatibility package, you can configure **mail** to use the **sendmail** version instead of the **mailsurr** version. You will need to replace the **/usr/bin/mail** and **/usr/bin/rmail** programs with their BSD equivalents (**/usr/ucblib/binmail** and **/usr/ucblib/binrmail**, respectively). Move the program **sendmail.cf** to **/etc**, and also replace **/etc/mail/mailsurr** with **/usr/ucblib/mailsurr**. It will take some experimentation to integrate this process with your normal usage of **mail**. As usual, your net administrator will probably have more information about setting up the **sendmail** system.

A Note on Commercial Networked Applications

Most commercial *networked applications* such as databases are based on concepts implemented in the UNIX utilities discussed in this chapter. Most will use a local process that makes a *service request* across the net to a single centralized *server process* on a server machine. This server process is usually a demon on the server machine that "listens" for requests from clients and processes them as they happen. Often the local *client process* manages the user interface, the connect, and the communication procedures, while the server does the real work of the application. If the centralized server process or the net as a whole is not running correctly, the local process will fail.

Some commercial applications use a centralized *license server* demon, which is consulted before a local application starts. The license server controls how many instances of the application are allowed to run simultaneously in the net as a whole. If that number has not been exceeded, a new user is allowed to use the application, the count is incremented, and the application starts as expected, usually on the local machine. When the application ends, the license server is again consulted, and the user count is decremented. The cost of the application depends on how many instances of the application can run simultaneously, or on a cumulative count of how many times the application has been used.

Device Sharing

The RFS system, unlike the NFS system, allows the sharing and mounting of remote *devices*. A device is a special file in the **/dev** directory that connects to a hardware device like a printer or disk. You can mount the **/dev** directory of a remote machine at a mount point in the local file system, and use the remote devices connected to that machine just as if they were local devices. Be sure not to mount a remote **/dev** directory on your local **/dev** directory, because this can damage your UNIX system. Once it has been mounted, you can usually open, read, and write to a remote device just as you can to a local device. However, all devices in SVR4 do not support remote access, so you should experiment with specific devices to see how they respond under RFS.

More Networking Concepts

Network support is built on three features recently added to System V: the *Virtual File System* (VFS), *streams,* and *sockets.* The VFS provides a general capability within the kernel that allows mapping between any file system types. That is, you can set up an MS-DOS or an NFS file system as a file system type, and then use this "foreign" file system just as you would use a normal file system; redirection and all the other commands will be available. The complexity involved in this process is hidden within the kernel, and is not visible to users. In turn, the VFS is built on streams, a general device driver facility that allows run-time configuration of communications channels. Sockets are abstract communications interfaces that are built from capabilities of streams. They allow applications to communicate, while hiding the actual communications from the applications.

These low-level networking facilities in the UNIX system allow the development of *protocol stacks,* which implement the actual communications across a network. The most popular of these is TCP/IP (Transmission Control Protocol/Internet Protocol), which is used with the NFS system. Another is the ISO (International Standards Organization) protocol stack for Open Systems Interconnect (OSI), which is used by RFS. The purpose of these multiple layers of software is to separate logically distinct operations into discrete parts that can be maintained and updated independently. Fortunately, most of this complexity is hidden from users.

You can examine the system's use of protocols and sockets with the **netstat** command. This command has many options, and the output can be quite complex. Consult the **netstat(1M)** man page for more information.

The primary interface to the lower levels of the NFS and TCP/IP systems is the **ifconfig** (for interface configuration) command. This command allows you to add or delete protocols and change the machine's *net mask* and *broadcast address*, as well as several other parameters. Your net administrator can explain how **ifconfig** is used in your network.

Yellow Pages

The *Yellow Pages* system is a centralized *database server* that can manage user login ids, hostnames and addressing, mail addresses, and several other kinds of administrative data in the UNIX system. The **yp** system was developed by Sun Microsystems, and is now included with many releases of SVR4.

The decision whether or not to use **yp** is made by the network administrator, but it is frequently used on Ethernet LANs that use NFS. It allows network administrators to maintain a single centralized copy of much of the key data needed to run a UNIX system. When individual machines (and applications) need the data, they consult the central Yellow Pages rather than the local data files. This *redirection* is transparent to the applications, which act the same whether or not **yp** is running. The Yellow Pages system supports many features, including the creation of domains similar to RFS domains.

The following local files are usually replaced by their **yp** equivalents:

```
/etc/passwd
/etc/shadow
/etc/hosts              (/etc/inet/hosts)
/etc/bootparams
/etc/ethers
/etc/group
/etc/networks           (/etc/inet/networks)
/etc/protocols          (/etc/inet/protocols)
/etc/services           (/etc/inet/services)
/etc/netgroup
/etc/hosts.equiv
/.rhosts
```

That is, the local version of these files is *not* used when **yp** is in operation, so you cannot edit the local files to change the local environment. Instead, you (or the net administrator) must change the centralized database. Additional files may be replaced in some **yp** installations.

For users, the most useful command in the **yp** system is **ypcat** (for yellow pages **cat**), which displays the contents of one or more of the **yp** databases. The command

```
my_sys$ ypcat hosts
```

will list the hostnames available in the network, and

```
my_sys$ ypcat aliases
```

will list the mail alias list for net users.

You can list the available databases, also called *maps,* with the **-x** option, as follows:

```
my_sys$ ypcat -x
Use "passwd" for map "passwd.byname"
Use "group" for map "group.byname"
Use "networks" for map "networks.byaddr"
Use "hosts" for map "hosts.byaddr"
Use "protocols" for map "protocols.bynumber"
Use "services" for map "services.byname"
Use "aliases" for map "mail.aliases"
Use "ethers" for map "ethers.byname"
my_sys$
```

The **ypinit** and **ypbind** commands are used to initialize and start **yp** services for a network. The **ypbind** command is a demon that must be running on each machine in the **yp** domain.

When the net is down for some reason, access to the **yp** system will be blocked, and many applications that use the data (such as some mail systems, machine reboots, and even remote logins) will be unavailable. Consult your net administrator for more information if your net uses **yp**.

System Configuration

When you acquire a new computer and a UNIX software package, the first step is to *load* the software onto the machine's hard disk. During this loading process there are several decisions to make, decisions that affect the *tuning* of the machine. Modern releases of the UNIX system make loading relatively easy; all decisions can be made by accepting the default values suggested during the load process. However, the default values tend to be compromises that cover the majority of situations, and you can change the defaults to tune your machine to your specific needs.

In this chapter we will discuss the issues concerned with *building* a UNIX system, including both hardware and software configuration. We will focus primarily on SVR4 systems running on powerful microcomputers, but most of the issues, if not the exact numbers, will apply to other releases on other hardware.

Hardware and the UNIX System

Because the UNIX system was originally designed for large minicomputers, and only recently ported to microcomputers, it makes significant demands on the computer hardware environment in which it runs. For this reason, implementations of the UNIX system on the smallest machines have not been an outstanding success.

Only with the continuing drop in hardware prices has the UNIX system really become viable on personal computers. The SVR4 release is a large and complex operating system that requires significant machine resources; a machine with 32-bit *word size* is required to run it.

The 80386 and Other Machines

The Intel 80386 processor is an ideal hardware environment for a personal UNIX system. It provides the raw CPU speed a sophisticated system demands, and includes efficient support for *virtual memory* and other features required for optimum performance. Machines based on the Motorola 68020 processor and other 32-bit microprocessors also make excellent UNIX systems. Higher performance CPUs such as the Intel 80486, the Motorola 68030 and 68040, and most RISC CPUs make excellent multiuser systems, but the most cost-effective personal system is still the 80386 PC/AT class machine. Machines based on the 80386/SX can run the UNIX system, but the system's performance usually suffers; if you have a choice, select an 80386/DX with cache memory and a CPU speed of 20MHz or higher.

Larger sites that support more users or act primarily as *servers* may need faster systems at correspondingly higher prices.

Of course, you must buy the correct software for a specific machine; versions of the UNIX system designed for 80386 machines will not work with 68020 or other CPU chips, and vice versa. However, versions of the UNIX system designed for the 80386 will run on the 80486 (and vice versa), and some software designed for the 80286 UNIX system may run on the 80386 and 80486 machines, although the resulting performance will not be equivalent to native implementations. Most versions of the SVR4 system will automatically detect the differences between the ISA (for industry standard architecture) bus and the newer EISA (for extended ISA) architecture, but MCA (for micro-channel architecture) or other bus configurations may require a special version of the SVR4 system. Most RISC systems will require their own versions of SVR4.

Machine selection is often complicated by the need for specific application software, such as CAD packages or desktop publishing systems, which may be supported on only a few hardware *platforms*. Before you buy a machine, be sure that any software you intend to use is available for it.

Memory (RAM) Considerations

The UNIX system requires significant *real memory*, or RAM, to be installed in the machine. The SVR4 version requires at least 4MB of real RAM, and more memory is desirable. The system's true potential does not become apparent until 6 to 8MB of real memory are installed. For very heavily loaded file servers or multiuser systems, even more memory is preferable, and it is not unusual for a busy system to contain 16MB or more of real memory. This much memory is not necessary for a typical personal system, of course, but at least 4MB is always required to run SVR4 successfully. The UNIX system can determine the amount of memory installed on the machine when it boots, and automatically uses all the memory available. Make sure that any switches are set correctly so the power-up diagnostics can find all the memory in your machine.

Memory for the UNIX system is not the *bank switched* or *expanded* memory used under MS-DOS for expanding beyond its 640K limit. The UNIX system uses a *linear* type of memory management, so any switches on expansion memory cards should be set at *nonpaged* or *extended* settings. If switches are set to allocate any memory to the paged type, the UNIX system will not use that memory, and it will be wasted. Often hardware retailers will set up the memory correctly when you buy the machine, if you let them know that the machine will be using the UNIX system.

Disk Considerations

At least one floppy disk is usually required to load the system software. In addition, floppy disks are very useful for backing up your data, and for moving files easily from machine to machine. Several floppy disk formats are currently available, including 5 1/4-inch floppies and 3 1/2-inch disks in plastic cases. Most SVR4 releases are provided in either of these popular disk formats. You cannot easily copy the UNIX system floppies from one format to the other, because the *floppy boot* procedure, which starts the UNIX system from a floppy disk, is usually tied to a specific disk format. The floppy boot must be performed at least once, when the machine is initially loaded with the system software.

You must usually configure the machine so that the type of floppy you are using for the system boot is on drive 0 (called drive A in the PC/AT).

The UNIX system requires at least one hard disk to operate as designed. The UNIX system is installed on a hard disk, and boots and runs primarily from it. Floppy disks are generally used for initial software loading and for backing up your data. The UNIX system can read and write from floppies just as it can from hard disks, but the system is optimized for hard disks, and floppy access is painfully slow by comparison.

Most SVR4 releases support several types of hard disks (at least SCSI, ESDI, ST506, IDE, and IDI are usually supported), but sometimes multiple types are not supported on the same machine. Be sure you get the correct disk controller to match your disk type, and verify that your UNIX system supports that disk type. Multiple disks of the same type are allowed, although sometimes the maximum number is two.

The larger the hard disk installed on the machine, the better. Experience shows that disk usage eventually rises to fill all the available space, and it is cheaper to begin with a larger disk than to change the disk later. The SVR4 system requires at least 60MB of hard disk space for its own use, and this is the bare minimum; an 80MB or larger disk is preferred. With the X Window System and the development set, you may need up to 140MB, and you must add to this the disk space required for any standalone MS-DOS system sharing the disk. In busy machines, 200MB and larger disks are not unusual. The UNIX system can support all the disk space available, and has no artificial limitations.

In addition, the UNIX system allows multiple disks, and large minicomputer versions of the system may have three or four disks, each with 400 to 600MB capacity. However, smaller personal computers may be limited to a single hard disk controller card, which in turn may be limited to controlling only two hard disks. Again, consult your hardware vendor for more information about a specific machine. Two large hard disks are usually sufficient for most needs. Furthermore, you can buy the second disk when the first one fills up, and cable it to the existing hard disk controller without reloading the first disk.

The hard disk is controlled by a software *device driver* that is specific to the hard disk controller, and the controller may not be able to access some disks. Thus, it is usually futile to add a new hard disk controller card to an existing UNIX system unless you are sure the correct device driver is included with the card. Disk controller software designed for MS-DOS or other operating systems will not work with the UNIX system. Again, before buying an add-on disk, you should consult a reputable dealer to verify that the disk is usable with your controller.

If you intend your SVR4 system to be attached to a *Local Area Network* (LAN), you may be able to use a *diskless* machine. Diskless machines get all their data not from a hard disk attached to the machine, but from a remote disk attached to another machine on the LAN. The diskless machine boots across the net, and all its files and commands reside on the remote disk. Consult your network administrator for more information on diskless machines, but note that a machine with a local disk will always outperform a diskless machine.

The Console and Monitor

All UNIX systems must have a *system console*. On larger systems this is usually an inexpensive printing terminal that is permanently attached to the machine, and is rarely used. On smaller personal machines, however, the built-in console is configured as the system console, and serves double duty, both as the system console and as a user's terminal. The system console is used to display boot-time messages and system error messages. Furthermore, SVR4 restricts the use of the **root** login id to the system console.

A device driver is also used to control the console, so you probably cannot change the display adapter and monitor without installing a new display driver. For example, 80386-based SVR4 releases usually have drivers to support the EGA and VGA display standards, and the display adapter must support these standards. In addition, some releases provide special-purpose graphics drivers for high-resolution displays. Once .

more, the best solution is to consult your hardware vendor to be sure that a machine is compatible with the version of the UNIX system you are using.

Ports and Terminals

Remote terminals used for UNIX machines have historically been serial, ASCII, character-only devices that can attach to a **tty** *serial port,* usually called COM1 or COM2 in PC/AT-style machines. These asynchronous communications ports cannot support graphics terminals without special device driver support, but many different types of ASCII terminals can be attached to UNIX machines if the **terminfo** database includes a description of the terminal in question. In addition, external modems can be attached to these ports, so that remote users with modems can dial into the UNIX system. In either case, no additional software or device drivers are required.

Most microcomputers include only one or two serial ports. You should definitely have at least one serial port with your UNIX system to take advantage of its best features.

Having only one or two asynchronous communications ports may prevent you from attaching your machine to some local area networks that use the machine's serial port, because these networks will take one of the available ports. Similarly, a serial printer or serial mouse will each use one of these communications ports. You should carefully analyze your expected use of serial ports before investing in a machine or a specific implementation of the UNIX system. Experienced users of the UNIX system find that there are never enough serial ports on a machine to allow freedom of expansion. Some *multiport* add-on cards that may include four or eight ports per card are available, but you should consult with the vendor to make sure the UNIX system supports a particular ports card, before you buy the system.

With SVR4, you can also run the X Window System from a remote terminal if it has sufficient intelligence. These *X terminals* have high-speed connections to the host machine, usually over a LAN; thus they will not usually use a serial port. X terminals will have an attached mouse, a high-resolution graphics display, and built-in X server software.

SVR4 Licensing Restrictions

Microcomputer versions of SVR4 are sold in two forms: a two-user version and a more-than-two-user version. Some vendors may also sell a sixteen-user version. The operating system software is restricted in the two-user version so that only two users can be logged in simultaneously, although more than two ports are allowed; one user may be on the console, and the other on a serial port. Alternatively, two users can use the machine simultaneously through serial ports if the console is unused. To support two simultaneous remote logins you will need two serial ports. The two-user version of SVR4 is less expensive than other versions, and is usually adequate for personal UNIX systems.

The larger, *unrestricted,* version allows as many simultaneous users as there are ports or LAN connections on the machine. The restricted two-user license does not limit the ports for printers, local area networks, and so on, but only for simultaneous user logins.

Printers

Because of the (potential) shortage of serial ports, most microcomputers using the UNIX system have *parallel printers* rather than serial printers. Most modern microcomputers include a parallel port, and a second parallel port can be added on an expansion card (LPT1 and LPT2, respectively). These parallel ports cannot be used for terminals, so only one is usually needed unless you have more than one printer on the machine. The **lp** system can support many different types of printers, both parallel and serial. However, this is another area where you should confirm that your UNIX system and machine hardware can support the specific printer devices you wish to use. Generally, common dot-matrix or letter-quality printers are supported without difficulty, but sophisticated laser printers or uncommon devices may need expert coaxing to work correctly.

Printers that speak the PostScript page-description language, and also the popular HP LaserJet printers, are supported in SVR4, and these often use serial ports. If you have one of these printers and wish to connect it to a serial port, you must be sure that enough serial ports are available for your needs.

Networking

Because of the economies associated with sharing printers and other devices, many modern UNIX systems are attached to LANs. Most networks use their own plug-in cards and special device drivers, rather than either parallel or serial ports, thus saving these ports for other uses. In addition, some networks allow incoming telephone calls to a special network modem, which can then switch the caller to a specific machine on the network. This setup can be noticeably less expensive than providing extra communications ports and modems to each machine. Ethernet is the dominant network for UNIX systems, and most vendors of UNIX systems support it.

A network also allows the establishment of *file server* machines that have larger disks than most machines on the network, resulting in additional savings. These file server machines can be used to store large databases or data backups from the "personal" machines, which is actually the principle underlying the diskless workstation.

LANs that use serial ports on the attached machines may be more expensive than buying modems and communicating at lower speeds over dial-up telephone links, but balancing all the considerations in the networking area is not easy.

Magnetic Tape

As the UNIX system grows larger, and as hard disk capacity rises, the use of floppy disks as a tool for initial loading of the UNIX system (and for backup of user files), becomes ever more difficult. Consequently, SVR4 is often shipped on magnetic tape, and the system is then loaded from that tape. After the system is up, the tape drive can be used as a high-capacity backup device. As the price of tape units continues to drop, they will become an even more attractive alternative to disks. However, to load the machine from tape, you may need to start by booting it off a floppy disk, so a tape unit may not entirely replace a floppy disk drive.

Several tape formats and tape controller cards exist. As usual, you must verify that your UNIX system vendor supports a specific tape unit before you purchase it. Most common are the QIC (for quarter inch cartridge) format and the very high-density DAT (8mm) formats, but ask before you buy! Even these formats have subcategories: QIC-24 (60MB) and QIC-150 (150MB) are the most common. If you wish to use tape to transfer data between machines, you must also verify that both machines read and write the same format.

A Minimal Configuration

A standalone personal UNIX system can be configured with a single serial port and attached modem, and a parallel printer. The serial port with modem will allow both incoming and outgoing telephone calls, although not both at the same time. One remote user can call in while a user is active on the console, and printing is simultaneously supported on the parallel port. Recall that at least 4MB of real memory is required, and also at least 60MB of hard disk space. Later you may be able to add additional ports or network cards if you have verified that your machine and implementation of the UNIX system can support them.

   If you wish to use the X Window System, you will also need a mouse and a minimum of 80MB of disk space.

Setting Up the System

The procedure for physically attaching the parts of a system together is so dependent on the specific machine and associated devices that little of value can be stated here. Generally you should lean heavily on your hardware vendor to be sure that the correct cables are provided for attaching your devices. There are great differences in the cables required for various devices, and even "standard" RS-232 cables and devices can differ in many frustrating ways.

   Experts usually set up a machine with the minimum hardware configuration, load the software, and get the machine up before trying to attach additional devices like printers or terminals. This incremental

approach lets you become familiar with the machine before you introduce new problems with recalcitrant cables or the **lp** subsystem. The
best approach is to get one component working first; then add more
elements gradually, keeping each element running after it is installed,
until the full configuration is achieved.

One issue to watch for is the *sex* of the connectors on the machine
and the peripheral devices. You should purchase compatible cables after
you've examined the machine and peripherals, so that you don't have to
use a sequence of "gender-bender" plugs to achieve cabling compatibility.

In addition, cables designed for attaching an external modem to a
serial port may not work when you are attaching a hard-wired terminal
instead. This is because the modem and the terminal use different pins
to signal that they are active. A special *null modem* cable may be
needed to attach a terminal to a port designed for a modem. A null
modem is usually required to connect a PostScript printer to a serial
port. Again, consult with your vendor regarding the correct cables to
avoid unnecessary frustrations.

Many machines include some configuration in nonvolatile memory.
Often total RAM size, disk number and types, display adapters, and
other information is stored in this battery-supported memory. While the
UNIX system does not usually make much use of this information, the
machine may not boot properly if these settings are not correct. As you
add hardware, be sure to update this memory.

Finally, don't neglect the *human factors* of your working position at
the computer. Arrange the display screen, the floppy disk mechanism,
the keyboard, and your chair and work table for your comfort. This
seems obvious, but it is amazing how many uncomfortable and even
painful workstations are built around computers. If you become stiff or
sore, or get a headache from your use of the machine, it is probably not
because the UNIX system is so difficult, but because your chair is the
wrong height for your keyboard!

Testing the Initial Configuration

Before loading any software on the hard disk, you should verify that the
machine is operating correctly. Most machines are sold with a *diagnostics* disk, and you can boot the machine with this disk in the floppy drive.

Other systems have sophisticated diagnostics in battery-supported non-volatile memory, and these provide a procedure for entering the diagnostics subsystem.

If the machine comes up with a diagnostics prompt on the display, you can be sure that it is at least partially functional. However, it is good practice to perform many, if not all, of the tests available through the diagnostics procedure before going further. Convince yourself that things are working at this level before you load any software.

Usually the diagnostic disk boots to a menu that allows you to select from several tests, including floppy disk formatting and hard disk surface tests. You can often set the machine configuration at this level, although the UNIX system does not use the BIOS found on most PC/AT machines after the beginning of the boot procedure.

Figure 25-1 shows a typical display after the diagnostics disk comes up. If the diagnostic disk does not boot, or you cannot enter the ROM diagnostics, the system is probably deranged beyond recovery, although the diagnostics disk itself may be bad.

In the diagnostics disk used in Figure 25-1, options 1 and 2 allow formatting and copying of floppy disks. You can use these features to copy the *floppy boot disk* (the first and second disks of the System Installation Set) before you load the UNIX system for the first time. This is a safety precaution, but is not required in SVR4, where the floppy boot disk can be write-protected. In SVR3 and older systems, the floppy boot disks must be write-enabled. In either case, you should make copies of these disks as soon as possible, because they can easily be destroyed by careless handling.

```
SELECT AN OPTION

0 - SYSTEM CHECKOUT
1 - FORMAT DISKETTE
2 - COPY DISKETTE
3 - PREPARE SYSTEM FOR MOVING
4 - SETUP
9 - END DIAGNOSTICS

SELECT THE ACTION DESIRED
?
```

Figure 25-1.   Typical display from a diagnostics disk

Option 4, Setup, allows you to set the system date and time. This feature is unnecessary, because there are better tools for performing these tasks in the software configuration procedures and in the running UNIX system.

Option 3, Prepare System for Moving, is used to *park* the heads on the hard disk to secure it from damage when the system is moved or disassembled. Most modern systems park the disk heads automatically when the machine is powered off. If your disk does not park the heads automatically, you should do it manually *whenever* you move or disassemble your machine. Don't take chances with disk damage!

Option 0, System Checkout, allows you to examine the installed hardware and the switch settings that enable RAM memory, disks, and other hardware. Select this option to verify the system's record of your hardware configuration. Usually, a mismatch is the result of incorrect switch settings on the machine's system board (or in a ROM if your machine has one). If you have changed the machine's hardware configuration, which includes adding new RAM memory, you will probably need to change the switch settings on the system board to reflect the new hardware. Some machines no longer use physical switches for hardware configuration, but have a software-controlled ROM that can be set from a *Setup* option in the diagnostics. Follow your vendor's instructions carefully when changing these "switches."

Occasionally some hardware will be inoperative. If the System Checkout option works at all, the fundamental hardware configuration is operating correctly. However, this does not guarantee completely correct machine operation, and does not test the integrity of the software in any way. Failures in the System Checkout will usually require that you return your machine for repairs, unless you can fix things by changing switch settings on the system board or an add-on card.

An especially important part of the diagnostic procedure is the *hard disk surface test*. This verifies that all parts of the disk are working correctly by writing data to each disk block, and then reading the data back. Any failed operations mean that a particular disk block is bad, and the bad area will be added to a *bad track table* on the disk. A few defective tracks are normal on a disk. These bad blocks will not be used while the machine is running. The disk surface test may take as long as an hour to complete, but it is strongly recommended whenever you reload the system software. The UNIX system can become seriously deranged if bad disk blocks are available for its use, and you can avoid many problems by taking care to keep the bad block table up to date. Perform the surface test *every* time you reload the system software. Note that the surface test overwrites the entire contents of the partition, so it cannot be used when the system has already been loaded.

When you are through with the Diagnostics Disk, select option 9 or shut down the machine. Then remove the Diagnostics Disk before rebooting the machine, either from the UNIX system if it is installed, or from the floppy boot disk if you are just beginning the software installation.

Hard Disk Partitions

Once the hardware is configured and correctly connected, you must load the UNIX system onto the machine's hard disk. There are several decisions involved in loading the system software, and these revolve around the configuration of the hard disk. A disk can be divided into several separate parts, or *partitions,* which can be used for different operating systems, such as the UNIX and MS-DOS systems. Usually these separate partitions are not "visible" from each other. That is, when you are using one part of the disk with one operating system, the other parts cannot be accessed. The **fdisk** command is provided to change the *active* partition, and following a reboot the newly selected partition will be used, allowing another operating system to be booted. The partitions are established when the machine is first set up, and cannot be changed without erasing the hard disk. Consequently, you must decide how many disk partitions to establish on your machine before you load the UNIX system.

Most SVR4 versions for 80x86 machines allow multiple partitions, so that one can be used for the UNIX system and another for the MS-DOS or OS/2 operating system. If you wish to use any other operating system in addition to the UNIX system, you will need a second partition. The disk space used for any additional partitions will not be available for the UNIX system, so you should make sure that enough space is available on your hard disk for additional partitions. Generally about 5 to 10MB are reserved for an MS-DOS partition, or more if you have large storage needs under MS-DOS or wish to run OS/2. If you never use any operating system other than the UNIX system, you will not need a second partition.

A partition dedicated to MS-DOS or OS/2 is separate from and in addition to a *Merge* capability that might allow you to use the MS-DOS operating system under the UNIX system. That is, the Merge software shares the file system between the UNIX and MS-DOS systems, so an additional partition is not required. You will only need a separate partition if you plan to execute MS-DOS or OS/2 as a standalone system.

If you have multiple hard disks, the DOS partition (if one exists) and the basic UNIX system partition must both be on the first hard disk.

Swap and Dump Space

Another consideration in disk configuration is *swap space*. When processes fill up the entire available real memory, the UNIX system automatically *swaps* some idle processes to disk, in order to free real memory for active processes. This swapping is done without user intervention, and the disk space used for swapping does not come from the normal file system. Swap space is in the partition used by the UNIX system, but is a logically separate disk area. The desirable amount of swap space depends on the amount of real memory installed and on how heavily the machine is used: if there is more real memory, the system will need to swap less; if the machine is very heavily used, with many processes active simultaneously, more swap space will be needed. Disk space devoted to swapping is not available for files, even if it is not being used for swapping. The UNIX system will crash heavily if swap space becomes full, with a *panic* error message directed to the console, so it is usually better to err on the side of too much swap space than too little. Most SVR4 systems default to a swap size about *double* the amount of real RAM, and this is a good compromise for most situations. If you have a very heavily used server machine with insufficient real memory, more swap space may be desirable, but this is unusual. If the machine is a personal workstation with few simultaneous processes, and you have an unusually large amount of RAM but a shortage of disk space, you can get by with less swap space.

SVR4 also allows you to establish some *dump space*, which is used to store a copy of the operating system when it crashes. Like swap space, this is taken from available file space in the UNIX system partition; but unlike swap space, dump space is not really required for running the system. Unless you are involved in device driver or kernel development work, you do not need a separate dump partition.

File Systems

Finally, the disk space available to files can be further subdivided into separate *file systems*. The concept of file systems is really intended for machines that have two or more hard disks; one file system is usually installed on each disk, which allows the UNIX system to manage access to the separate physical disks efficiently. On machines with only one disk it is usually better to configure fewer file systems. SVR4 systems that have one hard disk can run well with only two file systems: one for booting the machine (**/stand**) and the other for all the rest of the system (the **/** file system).

With fewer file systems, it is much easier to manage your disk space budget. A file or directory cannot be split across file systems, but must be wholly contained within a file system. When you have too many file systems, there is an irritating tendency to run out of space on one file system while a large amount of unusable space remains on another file system. Juggling many tiny file systems can be frustrating and can also encourage errors.

There are some advantages associated with separate file systems, because a general corruption of one file system does not affect the others. For example, if one file system fills up, it will not steal space from the others. If you need more isolation of users or files, and care less about pooling your disk space, more file systems may be desirable. With symbolic links, it is possible to make a physical file on one file system look like it belongs to another directory hierarchy.

The configuration process may establish several file systems on a single hard disk by default, especially if you have a large hard disk. You may need to take action during the installation process to reduce the number of file systems. If you have multiple hard disks, it is best to create only one file system on each disk. This is the minimum allowed, because you cannot split file systems across disks.

File System Types

In SVR4 you can also select the *type* of file system to install. Two types are supported: the **s5** type is the standard System V file system inherited from SVR2 and SVR3; the other type, **ufs**, is adapted from the BSD system. Some application software may expect one type or the other; consult your application vendor to be sure. If not, the **ufs** type is preferable; it offers better performance and also allows filenames up to 256 characters, eliminating the old 14-character limit that still exists in the **s5** type.

A Note on Software Packaging

The SVR4 release is often shipped in several packages. If you know the intended use of the machine, you can select a subset of the available packages and only load the ones you need. Table 25-1 shows the major independent packages in SVR4, although some releases may combine the listed packages into larger sets. In general, if you select a package from Table 25-1, you should install *all* the parts associated with that package, or the system may fail in mysterious ways. On the other hand, the fewer packages you install, the less disk space you will consume and the fewer extraneous demon processes will reside on your system. A system will boot faster and perform better when fewer packages are installed.

There are definite dependencies in the order of installation. Follow your vendor's documentation carefully to avoid an incorrect loading order. At best, an incorrect loading sequence will cause the installation process to abort with an error; at worst, the machine may become deranged.

Loading the System Software

With this background, you can configure your machine to your needs as you load the UNIX system. Some differences exist between the installation procedures for various implementations of the UNIX system, even within SVR4, and several steps in your installation may differ from the examples given here.

The basic scenario is to boot the machine off the first floppy disk in the *Foundation Set*. The installation procedure will prompt for disk configuration information, format the hard disk correctly, and load a kernel from the floppy. Then you must remove the floppy disk and reboot off the hard disk. The installation process will continue by prompting for your machine's hardware configuration, and will then load the rest of the UNIX system from the floppy disks or magnetic tape. You will be led through an initial setup for the UNIX system, which allows you to set the date and time, install passwords for the system logins, and add new login ids for the system's users. You will then reboot the machine again. At that point, you can log in to the machine and load any add-on software packages using the normal system administration tools. When this process is complete, you can load the Merge software and the MS-DOS operating system if you have it. Then, if you have established an MS-DOS partition you can reboot from an MS-DOS floppy, access the dedicated MS-DOS partition on the disk, and load the MS-DOS operating system for the standalone version of MS-DOS. The entire loading process can take several hours, especially if you include a disk surface test at the beginning of the procedure.

Begin the installation by inserting the first floppy disk in the machine's drive; then turn on the power. The correct disk is called the *System Installation Disk* or the *Floppy Boot Disk*. It may be the first disk of the *Base System Package*. In some versions of the UNIX system, the Floppy Boot Disk must not be write-protected, but in SVR4 it *should* be write-protected. Use a copy of your boot disk, rather than your original, if possible. Some releases may require you to change to a second floppy disk after the first disk has been digested.

A special installation version of the UNIX system will boot off the floppy, and prompt you through the rest of the installation procedure. Do not remove the floppy until you are prompted to do so.

Full or Overlay Installation

Some releases allow you to *overlay* an existing UNIX system with the new load. If this is the case, one of the first prompts after the machine boots will be

```
Do you wish to overlay your existing UNIX System (y or n)?
```

If you have an existing system on the disk, you can select **y** to accept the overlay. This choice will overwrite your system software without touching existing user files. Options are limited with the overlay installation, and you cannot change the disk or partition setup without a full system load. Also, SVR3 and older releases cannot accept an overlay of a new SVR4 system. Overlay is designed primarily for updating an older SVR4 version with a new one. In any case, system integrity and overall performance will be better if you do not use the overlay installation, even when it is allowed.

Hardware Selection

Many versions start by immediately prompting you for your machine's hardware configuration and for the software packages you wish to install. Generally the hardware settings for basic machine type (EISA, MCA, and so forth) and display type (VGA, etc.) are included here, although some releases will automatically detect hardware configuration. These autodetection procedures may not work correctly; for example, a super VGA (800x600) display may be reported as normal VGA (640x480). Always set the hardware configuration manually if you have a choice. Usually interrupt and memory address settings for add-on boards such as network controllers are selected when you install the specific software package, not at the beginning of the install procedure. In any case, you must answer the hardware questions correctly or your machine will not work properly. If you have any doubts, stop the installation procedure and verify the type of boards you have and their switch settings before you continue.

Selecting Software Packages

At this point some releases will prompt you to select subparts of the full SVR4 release to install. Other releases (especially those delivered on floppy disks) may omit the queries here. In this case, you will have to install each package separately after the basic system is running. If you have the selection, you will see a prompt, such as

```
Do you wish to install any of these packages (y or n)?
```

Consult Table 25-1 to make your decisions; then select the appropriate subset of packages. You may find that your vendor has packaged the release slightly differently from the arrangement in Table 25-1.

fdisk Installation Procedure

If you have chosen a complete installation rather than an overlay, prompts will lead you through a disk configuration sequence. In some releases the first display is from the **fdisk** (for fixed disk) command, which is used to configure the partitions on the hard disk manually. In other releases there is an initial series of prompts that request partitioning information. Then the **fdisk** command is executed automatically by the installation scripts to set up the partitions.

Before continuing, you should map out your intended use of the machine's hard disk. If you want space for a standalone MS-DOS or OS/2 partition, you must decide how much space to allocate. Usually only a few megabytes are devoted to the MS-DOS partition, especially if you have a Merge package that can share file space between the UNIX and MS-DOS systems. It is simplest to think of the different disk partitions in terms of the *percentage* of the disk they will use. For example, if you have a 100MB disk, you may wish to allocate 10 percent for exclusive use by MS-DOS, and preserve the rest for the UNIX system. A standalone MS-DOS partition of about 10MB is plenty for most uses.

If your installation starts with the **fdisk** program, some initial copyright notices will appear, followed by the message

```
WARNING: A new installation of the UNIX System will destroy all files
currently on the system.
Do you wish to continue (y or n)? y
```

Press **y** at this point to continue, or you can immediately reboot if you do not wish to reload your hard disk.

Name	Subsets	Comments
Foundation		
	Base	Required; includes **uucp**, disk drivers, etc.
	Editing	**vi**
	terminfo	Full set of terminal descriptions
	termcap	Backward compatibility; often not needed
	lp	Needed for printing
System administration		
	FMLI	Form interpreter; needed for OA&M
	OA&M	Administrative tools; can be large
Networking		
	nsu	Support utilities; required for all networking
	dfs	Distributed file system; recommended with **nsu**
	inet	TCP/IP, Internet utilities
	Ethernet driver	Hardware specific; required for Ethernet
	StarLan driver	Required for StarLan
	RPC	Remote procedure calls
	NFS	Network file system
	RFS	Remote file sharing
Security		
	Crypt	File encryption; only available in U.S.A.
	Users	License for more than two users
	Enhanced security	Add-on security features
X Windows		
	Mouse driver	Required for X
	geus	X user system; required
Development		
	scde	ANSI C compiler, make, SCCS
	gpp	X development tools
	Kernel debugger	Not recommended

Table 25-1.   Software Packages for SVR4

Name	Subsets	Comments
Documentation		
	man	On-line manual; may not be available
	Help	May not be available
Document preparation		
	ditroff	Base **troff** system
	pic, grap	Enhanced features
	wwb	Writer's Workbench; may not be available
MS-DOS		
	Simultask or Merge	Features and packaging may vary
	DOS server	Required to support DOS machines on a LAN
Compatibility		
	BSD	Required to use BSD commands
	XENIX	Required to load existing XENIX applications
Miscellaneous		
	FACE	Office menus for ASCII terminals
	DMD windowing	Only if you have the supported terminal
	Cartridge tape driver	Needed for cartridge tapes
	Floppy tape	Floppy tape hardware needed

Table 25-1.   Software Packages for SVR4 (*continued*)

Now the **fdisk** program will start, and your screen will look like Figure 25-2. Figure 25-2 shows two partitions already established, but in your initial load the partition table will probably be empty. This screen is for a 200MB disk; the number of cylinders will differ for disks of different sizes.

You can select an operation from the menu to proceed with the partitioning of the disk, or you can select 5 to exit without changing anything. Make your selections by typing the selection number followed by a newline.

```
            Total hard disk size is 815 cylinders

                                       Cylinders
    Partition  Status    Type      Start  End   Length   %
    =========  ======    =========  =====  ===   ======  ===
        1                DOS          2    111     110    13
        2       Active   UNIX       112    814     703    86


SELECT ONE OF THE FOLLOWING:

    1.   Create a partition
    2.   Change Active (Boot from) partition
    3.   Delete a partition
    4.   Exit (Update disk configuration and exit)
    5.   Cancel (Exit without updating disk configuration)
Enter Selection:
```

Figure 25-2.   fdisk display for disk partitioning

To create a partition, select option 1. The **fdisk** command will prompt you for the starting and ending cylinders for the partition. Use the total disk size as displayed at the top of your screen and your selected disk percentage for the partition to compute the size to enter. The first partition should always start at cylinder 1 or 2 (never cylinder 0), and the last should end at one less than the total hard disk size as displayed for your system. Each partition after the first should start at the next cylinder following the end of the previous cylinder. When you are creating partitions, use partition number 1 for MS-DOS or OS/2; the UNIX system should be on the *last* partition you create, as in Figure 25-2.

If you make an error in setting up a partition, you can delete any or all partitions with option 3, and then start again. Be sure the partitions are correct at this point, because once they are established you cannot change them without destroying the contents of your hard disk.

The *active* partition is the one that will boot when you turn the machine on: if you want the machine to start in the UNIX system, it should be the active partition; if you want the machine to boot under MS-DOS, that system should be the active partition. To load the UNIX system, and later to use it, be sure to make its partition active at this point. Select the active partition with option 2 on the menu. When the MS-DOS partition is active, you can only access the UNIX system by executing the MS-DOS version of the **fdisk** command to set the active partition to the UNIX system, and then rebooting.

If you create a standalone MS-DOS partition with **fdisk**, the MS-DOS partition will not be formatted. To use it, you will have to enter MS-DOS and follow normal procedures there for setting up the hard disk. The partition devoted to the UNIX system will be formatted during the loading procedure, as discussed in the following sections.

Prompted Installation Procedure

In some versions of the UNIX system, the configuration is prompted and **fdisk** runs automatically. In these versions, the initial display after booting the Floppy Boot Disk will resemble Figure 25-3, although the

```
. . . . . . . . . . . . . . . .
boot: /unix


UNIX System V/386 Release 4.0
Node intel
total real memory  = 4194304
total available memory  = 3289088

Copyright (c) 1984, 1986, 1987, 1988, 1989, 1990  AT&T
Copyright (c) 1987, 1988 Microsoft Corp.
All Rights Reserved

386/ix Drivers Copyright (c) 1986 Interactive Systems Corp.
All Rights Reserved

About to install UNIX on your hard disk.  This process will destroy
any and all data currently on that disk, INCLUDING DOS FILES!
If you have DOS files you would like to back up before proceeding
with system installation, enter n<RETURN> to the following question.

Do you wish to proceed with UNIX installation (y/n)?
y

Do you wish to (re)format your hard disk (y/n)?
y

Do you wish to do a complete surface analysis?  Answer 'y' to write
and read every sector, 'n' to just read every sector.  NOTE: writing
the whole disk takes a while... (y/n)?
y
```

Figure 25-3.   Prompted configuration procedures

copyright and other notices may differ on your machine. After loading, the system will pause at the "Do you wish to proceed" prompt. Presumably you will enter **y** here, and press newline. The system will respond "Do you wish to (re)format your hard disk?" Select **y**, because this guarantees a clean disk for the installation. The system will next prompt "Do you wish to do a complete surface analysis?" Again, respond **y** to verify that all the bad blocks are included in the disk's records. The surface test is not actually done at this time; it will be performed later in the installation process.

Figure 25-4 continues the configuration dialogue. The *Disksetup* program allocates the various disk partitions and subpartitions. When it

```
Welcome to the Disksetup program.  This program will allow you to
specify certain parameters about your
hard disk, as well as partitioning
the disk into Unix volumes and a DOS area (if desired).

This system uses 17 512-byte sectors per track.

Disk parameters currently configured are as follows:
Number of heads: 8.  Number of cylinders: 940.
Is this correct (y/n)? y

Your disk drive will have 1 cylinder used for alternate sectors.

This leaves 939 cylinders (65384448 bytes) available, 69632 per
cylinder.

Do you wish to allocate any of your disk
to exclusive use by DOS (y/n)? y

Enter number of cylinders for DOS (0-577): 50

FDISK will be run to create the following disk allocation:
DOS starting at cylinder 1 for 50 cylinders, and
UNIX starting at cylinder 51 for 889 cylinders.

Is this the partitioning you want (y/n)?

You will now have the opportunity to enter known bad areas on
your disk.  To do this, you will need to know the cylinder, head,
and byte offset from the index mark of each defect.  This data
can usually be found on a label on the disk drive or on a defect
list which is shipped with the drive.  If you have no such list,
only those sectors found to be bad during surface analysis will
be marked.

Do you wish to enter any more defect information (y/n)? n
Are you sure you've entered all defects (y/n)? y
```

Figure 25-4.   Prompted system installation dialogue, part II

starts, it reads information directly from the disk, and reports on the disk sector parameters with the message that begins "This system uses . . . ." The example in Figure 25-4 is for a 67MB hard disk. The numbers may vary if you have a different type of hard disk on your machine, but you can usually trust the displayed message. If you are sure the disk parameters are reported incorrectly, respond **n** to the prompt "Is this correct (y/n)?" If the reported values are incorrect, there is usually some mismatch between the hard disk's *low level format* and the disk controller card. You may need to change some settings on the controller card if you suspect the disk size information to be incorrect as reported. Normally, however, you should accept the values by responding **y** to the prompt.

The next prompt allows you to dedicate some disk space for exclusive use by MS-DOS. If you wish to do so, enter **y** at this prompt, and the system will ask you to indicate the amount of disk space to reserve. You enter the amount of disk space by giving a number of *cylinders* to reserve. To compute this number from your chosen disk percentage devoted to MS-DOS, divide the total disk size in cylinders by your percentage. Only 50 cylinders (3.48MB) are reserved in this example. The system will report on its computations, and prompt you to verify the results, with "Is this the partitioning you want?" If you enter **n** here, the prompts will be repeated from the beginning.

The next section of the installation process allows you to manually enter bad blocks. These would be blocks listed as bad on a label attached directly to the hard disk case inside the machine's cover. This list is the result of a rigorous disk test given at the factory where the disk was produced, and many of the listed bad blocks will only be marginally bad. Most users let the surface test find "real" bad blocks. In some installation procedures the original bad block table on the disk is retained, and you do not have to enter the list from the top of the disk manually.

Other types of hard disks, such as SCSI or IDE disks, use a logical block number scheme so that the system never sees any bad blocks that might exist. In this case, you can skip the entry of the bad block table. Otherwise, enter *both* the list of bad blocks on the disk itself, *and* the bad blocks found as a result of the surface test. Better to be conservative now than sorry later!

In Figure 25-4, the entry of bad blocks has been bypassed by responding **n** to the prompt. After that, another verification prompt appears, and you can then enter **y** if you are really through entering bad blocks.

```
The following hard disk elements are required and
must reside on your primary (disk 0) hard disk:
Drive   Name                     Type    File System/Slice
0       Boot File System         bfs     /stand
0       Swap Slice                       /dev/swap
0       Root File System         s5, ufs /

Please select the File System Type for / (Root File System   ) from
the following list:
            s5, ufs
Please press ENTER for the default type, s5.
```

Figure 25-5.   File system partitioning

File System Partitioning

For both the manual and prompted configurations, the installation procedure continues with the partitioning of the UNIX file systems, shown in Figure 25-5. For each file system you choose beyond the fixed-format *Boot* and *Swap* file systems, you must select a file system type. The **ufs** type is preferable, but some application software may require you to use **s5**. Otherwise, **ufs** is recommended for all file systems you establish. Enter the selected file system type after the prompt that begins "Please press ENTER . . . ."

Next, you can specify additional file systems if you wish. The prompt looks like this:

```
Do you wish to create any optional
disk slices or filesystems (y or n)?
```

If you wish to add any other file systems, enter **y**, and the system will prompt you through a list of available choices. In a personal system, you should rarely have additional file systems on your primary hard disk. If you select **n** at this point, all the rest of the disk space will be assigned to the root file system. When you are through with the list of available file systems, the system will prompt for verification, as follows:

```
The hard disk layout you have selected is:

Drive   Name                     Type    File System/Slice
-----   ----                     ----    -----------------
0       Boot File System         bfs     /stand
0       Swap Slice               -       /dev/swap
0       Root File System         ufs     /
```

```
Is this correct (y or n)?
```

If you've changed your mind, you can select **n** and the whole process will be repeated. Otherwise, select **y**. The system will now perform the hard disk surface analysis, shown here:

```
Checking for bad sectors in the UNIX System partition...

Checking cylinder: xxx

The following slice sizes are recommended for your disk.
A / filesystem of 616 cylinders (153 MB)
A /dev/swap slice of 65 cylinders (16 MB)
A /stand filesystem of 21 cylinders (5 MB)

Is this configuration acceptable? (y/n)
```

Now you can verify the *size* of the various file systems. The defaults will usually be acceptable. You will need about 5MB for the **/stand** file system, and the swap space should be set at twice the real RAM present in the machine. The other file systems (if there are any) can be set at a size you choose, although the **root** (**/**) and **/usr** file systems may have minimum required sizes. Usually the defaults will be the best selection, but if you select many file systems on a small disk (less than 100MB), the defaults may not be sufficient to hold all the files the system will try to install.

After the surface check is completed, the system will actually create the file systems, as follows:

```
Filesystems will now be created on the needed slices
Creating the / filesystem on /dev/rdsk/c0t0d0s1
Creating the /stand filesystem on /dev/rdsk/c0t0d0sa

A UNIX System will now be installed on your hard disk
Please standby.

When you are prompted to reboot your system,
remove the floppy disk from the diskette drive,
and strike CTRL-ALT-DEL.
Please wait for the prompt.

Reboot the system now.
```

When you reboot, the disk will be configured.

Loading the Foundation Set

When the system reboots, it will be executing a special installation version of the UNIX system, and the first prompt after the reboot will be something like this:

```
Please indicate the installation medium you intend to use.

Strike "C" to install from Cartridge TAPE
or "F" to install from FLOPPY DISKETTE.

Strike ESC to stop.
```

Select the correct choice for your software and hardware. You'll be prompted to insert the correct medium, and to press **go** or ENTER when you're ready. Be sure to use the correct Foundation Set diskette or tape.

If you have floppy disks, start with the first disk in sequence *after* the Boot Disks; then feed the rest of the system software floppy disks into the machine one by one. The system will read each disk and prompt you for the next one. While a disk is being read, you cannot remove it. Do not interrupt the load procedure in any way or you will have to restart the installation process from the beginning. If you are using tape, the process will read the entire Foundation Set off the tape.

If you entered the packages to install, as discussed earlier, those choices will now be recalled; otherwise, the system may prompt for them here. Then the tape will be read and you will see prompts for any package-specific questions. You may be asked for Ethernet addresses, security restrictions or authorizations, or other package-specific material. If you do not have the answers to the queries, accept the defaults. You can usually change your mind using system administration tools after the machine is running. If you are loading the system from floppy disks, you may need to enter the system after it is running, and load each floppy package as discussed later in this chapter.

When all the disks in the Foundation Set have been loaded, or the entire tape has been digested, the UNIX system will start.

The Setup Procedures

Now the system will begin a special setup environment that allows you to perform the initial administrative tasks necessary for a well-behaved machine. These procedures are well prompted and are quite straightforward, but may differ significantly between releases of the system. In some releases you have to log in to the system with the special **setup** login id, while in others the setup procedures are automatic once the Foundation Set has been installed. You should complete the setup procedures now while they are prompted rather than returning later to perform them with manual procedures.

The first part of the procedure sets the date and time in the system's internal clock. UNIX systems generally depend on the correct time, so it is important that it be set accurately. Some releases prompt you for a new date and time, while others assume that the time is correct. At least, you will see a display of the time. If the time is not correct, you should change it at the first opportunity.

The next prompts in the setup procedure allow you to create passwords for the **root** and **install** users. Sometimes you can also add login ids for other users at this point. In this case, you should at least create a login id for yourself, because the **root** login should be reserved for performing system administration and maintenance tasks. Each new login id requires several items of information, including the desired login id, the user's name, and a starting password. You can use any login id you wish, as long as it begins with a lowercase letter (a through z) and contains from two to eight characters. Most users use their names or initials, or a whimsical name chosen by them. Usually you should accept the default values for the user id number, group id number, and user's home directory, because the system can do a better job of determining correct values for these entries. All login ids should have passwords, so you should always select an initial password when you install new login ids. The password must be entered twice to guard against errors. Be sure to follow good security practices, as discussed in Chapter 22, when you create new passwords.

The final step in the setup procedure is to establish a unique system name. This is known as the *node name*, or system **uname** (for UNIX name). The machine name should be unique, so that other machines can send you mail unambiguously. A default **uname** may be hard-coded into the system, but you should always change this name to something unique. Select a machine name that has 4 to 8 characters, and begins with a lowercase letter. You only need to set the machine name once, and you should very rarely change the name because users on other machines will use it to send mail to your machine. If the name is changed, the **uucp** subsystem will not work correctly unless all your correspondents also change their **uucp** data.

The **uname** is the last item in the setup procedure. If you wish to stop the load process at this point, you may do so, and continue loading at a later time. If you stop the load process, it is important to reboot the machine immediately, so that the new system configuration can be permanently established. When you reboot, you should see a message such as

```
The UNIX Operating System will now be rebuilt.
This will take some time. Please wait.

The UNIX Kernel has been rebuilt.

Reboot the system now.
```

This message tells you that the UNIX kernel is being *relinked,* and that any new drivers or devices will be installed. You will see this message after all but the simplest software packages are loaded.

Installing Additional Software Packages

Instead of rebooting at this point, the system may prompt you to begin loading any additional packages that you selected previously. If you did not make any selections earlier, you can do so here. The system will present a prompt something like this one:

```
Insert a cartridge tape into Cartridge Tape Drive.
Type [go] when ready,
or [q] to quit:
```

If you have been loading from diskette, the prompt will also ask for a floppy disk. If you select **q** here, the machine will rebuild the kernel and reboot.

You can load all the desired packages that are on the same type of media before finishing this step. If you have some packages on tape and others on disk, you will need to reboot when you are ready to switch from one form to the other, and load the rest of the packages from the shell.

Loading Software from the Shell

When the machine comes back up after rebuilding the kernel, you can log in as **root**, and run **sysadm** or another system administration *user agent*. Most include a software loading option. Alternatively, you can execute the command **pkgadd** or **installpkg** to load more software; however, it is most efficient to load as much software as possible during the initial setup, because this significantly reduces the overall loading time.

Whether you should use **pkgadd** or **installpkg** depends on the specific software package you want to load. Try

```
# pkgadd -d diskette1
```

if the package is on a floppy disk, or

```
# pkgadd -d Ntape1
```

if it is on tape. Try **pkgadd** first; if you get an error message, try **installpkg**. These commands will prompt you through the installation procedure for the software package you are installing. Consult the specific documentation for your machine and for the software package to determine whether any special or additional steps are needed.

Using the Installation Commands

The **pkgadd** and **installpkg** procedures often involve many additional prompts designed for security purposes. For example, in the middle of the install procedure, you may see prompts like these:

```
The following files are already installed on the system and are being
used by another package:
        /usr/lib <attribute change only>

Do you want to install these conflicting files [y,n,?,q]

This package contains scripts which will be executed with super-user
permission during the process of installing this package.

Do you want to continue with the installation of this package [y,n,?]
```

These prompts are designed to improve system security, but you must answer all of them with **y** or that installation will be aborted. If the packages are coming from original media provided by the vendor, the best procedure is to accept all the offered queries, and proceed with the installation regardless. Usually, software that *intentionally* breaks security rules can easily bypass these checks anyway.

Some packages may prompt you to select various hardware configurations, such as choosing interrupt or memory addresses for add-on boards. If you see these messages and do not know the answers, you can record the query and abort the installation. Then you can power off the machine, check the jumpers or hardware documentation, and restart the installation later. The installation procedure will usually clean up correctly when it is aborted.

Because of the complexities inherent in integrating so many packages into a single system, installing one package may create conflicts with others. These situations are officially "bugs," but they do happen. You may see several messages of the form

```
Installation of <pkg> partially failed.
```

or its equivalent. In this case, you will not have a one hundred percent correct installation, but there is often nothing you can do to avoid these messages. If you do get one, try continuing with the installation anyway. The system will generally remain usable until you can get a corrected version of the package from the vendor.

Terminal Setup

One additional capability is often configured immediately after setting up the system. This is the *Service Access Facility,* which allows users to log in to the system from remote terminals over the asynchronous communications ports. In SVR4, this procedure is supported through the **sysadm** system administration tool, discussed in Chapter 12.

After you have completed this step, the terminals or modems will be available for incoming connections. Also, you will probably wish to configure the **uucp** subsystem to allow your machine to call out to other machines. This procedure is discussed in detail in Chapter 15.

Going Further

System configuration is properly an expert's job, because tuning the system for optimal efficiency is a complex task. However, most microcomputers are not very sensitive to changes in configuration and tuning, so few requirements are critical. With the exception of file system size, most users can accept some small reductions in system performance, if in return they don't have to think too much about the details of system configuration; however, a few more issues should be addressed.

PANIC Messages

When the UNIX system and the kernel are not operating correctly, the system can occasionally crash unexpectedly. This is not a normal event, and only occurs as the result of a bug or problem in the deepest parts of the operating system. You should never see this condition when things are operating correctly, although it may appear if you add new hardware or expansion cards to your machine incorrectly.

When a crash occurs, the system will display a message at the console, and then die. For example:

```
PANIC: system error type 0x0e
Attempting to dump 512 pages.....
```

After such a message appears, the machine will be inoperative until it is rebooted. The specific message may differ, but the key word *panic* will appear somewhere in it. You should record the message completely, and then reboot the machine. If it does not reboot, you have probably encountered a failure of some hardware, such as the disk or mother-board.

If the machine boots but the panic message reappears, it is usually because some switches or jumpers on add-on boards have been set incorrectly. Be sure that all your additional hardware is operating correctly, either by removing the cards one by one and observing the state of the system, or by carefully examining the card's documentation and switch settings.

If the panic message appears only once and does not recur, there is probably no need to worry unduly. You have simply uncovered a (rare) bug in the UNIX operating system! Historically, experts judged the quality of a release of the UNIX system by the frequency of panics, but modern UNIX systems should *never* panic unless the hardware fails.

Booting from a Floppy Disk

When the UNIX system is running correctly, the machine will boot from the hard disk whenever there is no floppy in the floppy drive. However, if a floppy disk is in the drive and the drive door is closed, the machine will try to boot off the floppy. If the floppy in the drive is not *bootable*, the boot procedure will generally switch back to the hard disk and the machine will come up as usual; however, in some cases the machine will hang, and the boot will not complete. If this happens, remove the floppy and try rebooting again.

In addition, you can intentionally reboot the system off the System Installation Disk if necessary. You might do this when the system will not boot correctly from the hard disk, and manual repairs to the hard disk are needed. Simply boot off the first System Installation Disk, just as you would if you were reloading the UNIX system. Be sure to use a copy of the disk rather than your original. The first time the floppy boot procedure pauses for a prompt, press the DEL key immediately. This aborts the installation process, and leaves you in a normal shell; however, instead of running off the hard disk as usual, the system will be running off the floppy disk, or sometimes from a temporary RAM disk.

There are several differences in the environment when the system is running from a floppy disk. First, it is much slower than usual, because the fast hard disk is not in use. Second, you cannot remove the floppy without crashing the system. Third, the list of available commands is much reduced because they must all reside on the relatively small floppy disk. Fourth, the system is running in single user mode, so the process environment will be much different. This floppy boot procedure is not intended for regular machine use; it should only be employed by a skilled user for rare tests and repairs.

Once the machine is running, you may be able to mount the hard disk to gain access to its files and directories. The command

```
# mount -F ufs /dev/dsk/0s1 /mnt
```

will mount the hard disk partition with the **root** file system. You can then **cd** to **/mnt** to access the **root** directory on the hard disk, and move around the hard disk file system from that point. You can execute commands from the hard disk by giving their full pathnames, including the leading **/mnt**, or you can change your PATH to pick up the hard disk **bin** directories. Thus, you can repair any files that you suspect are bad. Unfortunately, you cannot remove the floppy to copy files from a backup floppy onto the hard disk, nor can you use the **uucp** subsystem or LAN tools to move files over a network, so the floppy boot procedure is quite limited. It may have more value for maintenance if your system has two floppy drives.

When you boot from a floppy disk in this way, you must take care to shut down the machine correctly. Although the **shutdown** command will probably not be available on the floppy disk, this short procedure will work:

```
# umount /mnt
# sync
# sync
# uadmin 2 0
Reboot the system now.
```

At this point, you can power off the machine or reboot from the hard disk as usual.

Upgrading from Older Releases to SVR4

If you are currently using an older version of the UNIX system, you should plan carefully before beginning an upgrade to SVR4. You will need to reinstall the system software, and probably repartition the disk to meet the additional swap space requirements of SVR4. Therefore, you will probably wish to reformat the hard disk and rebuild the disk from scratch. Furthermore, many key system files have changed, sometimes markedly, between older releases and SVR4. You cannot use an overlay installation when you are upgrading. Only a completely new installation is supported.

The first step in upgrading is to scrupulously back up your system to some safe media such as disk or tape. Back up the complete system, because if the upgrade fails for some reason you will want to reinstall the older version. The upgrade could fail, for example, if one of the floppy disks containing the new release is bad, and will not load correctly. Be sure to back up *all* your files and any materials that you will want later. The best way to perform this backup is to back up each individual directory onto a separate floppy disk. Later, when you are ready to bring the materials back in the new release, you can load each disk separately into a temporary directory, carefully move the files to their destinations, and then delete the copies. This procedure keeps excess disk utilization to a tolerable level, because you probably cannot support two separate versions of the entire system on your machine at once. Furthermore, you cannot simply overwrite the older version of the system onto the SVR4 release, because this will corrupt the system. At the least, you should back up your personal files and those of other users separately from system files, because you cannot restore *any* system files or directories safely. This includes **uucp** files and anything in the **/etc** and **/var** directories, such as **/etc/profile**, **/etc/passwd**, **/etc/shadow**, or **/etc/inittab**.

After backing everything up, begin the load as described previously. When the load is complete, you can log in to the system and begin to restore your backed up materials. If you are now using SVR3, the conversion is relatively straightforward, but releases older than SVR3, or older XENIX releases, will require substantial changes. In these cases it is probably not worthwhile to try to save any of the older materials; you will have to build up the machine as you discover things that are not to your taste. However, your text files, spreadsheets, databases, and so on, can be reloaded without harm, and many of their executable programs may work correctly.

It is very important that you restore the old system into a temporary directory, and then manually examine the materials and use **mv** to put them into the target directory location. If you are unsure of yourself, *do not* overwrite existing system files outside your home or other private directories. You will have to examine each file carefully and decide how to treat it. Usually you *cannot* restore system files from older releases.

SVR3 executable applications and data files, if moved from an 80286 or 80386 machine, *may* continue to work correctly on a 80386 or 80486 SVR4 system, but you should test them carefully. If possible, you should recompile any applications moved to SVR4 machines from older releases.

System Defaults

In most SVR4 systems, the directory **/etc/default** includes several files that contain configuration data for the machine, as shown here:

```
# ls -F /etc/default
boot            default.att512   login          tar
cron            default.cpq      msdos          workstations
default.at386   dump             passwd         xrestor
default.att     init             su
#
```

These files hold configuration information for the specific hardware and environment of the machine. The files that begin *default* contain specific memory maps and other items that differ among machine types. The remaining files control other system variables. You can browse through these files and change individual entries. When the machine is rebooted, the changes will take effect.

Examine each file to get a feeling for what kinds of changes are possible in each area, but *be careful* when you make changes. Test each change carefully before inflicting a new configuration on your users. In some cases the range of alternatives is limited, and you cannot randomly change these files.

The most important file for system administration is **login**, which contains several important configurable parameters. For example:

```
$ cat /etc/default/login
TIMEZONE=MST7MDT
HZ=100
```

```
ULIMIT=80000
CONSOLE=/dev/console
PASSREQ=YES
ALTSHELL=YES
$
```

The *TIMEZONE* and *ULIMIT* values should be set explicitly for your system; be sure that you also set **/etc/TIMEZONE** when you change the *TIMEZONE* value in **/etc/default/login**. The *CONSOLE* value can be changed to a tty device if you want to run the machine from a remote console; the other variables should not usually be changed.

You can set a value for the default *TERM* variable for each individual port in the file **/etc/ttytype**. Normally it is preferable to set *TERM* in each user's **.profile**, but if you have a hard-wired terminal permanently attached to a serial port, or if you often use the virtual console feature, a default can be set for that terminal in **/etc/ttytype**. Examine **/etc/ttytype** if you want to use this feature.

Finally, you can generally reorganize or *remap* the position of characters on the console's keyboard. This is often done to make the AT-style keyboard friendlier to UNIX system users. Frequently the CAPSLOCK and left CTRL keys are switched, and the ESC key is swapped with the ` (grave) key. Other keyboard reorganizations are also possible. The **mapkey** command performs these actions, but note that changes made by **mapkey** do not propagate into sessions under the X Window System. If you use X, you will need to make changes with **mapkey** for the console, and also with **xmodmap** for the X session.

To use **mapkey**, dump the current keyboard map to a file with

```
# mapkey -d > file
```

Edit the map to meet your needs, and then reload it with

```
# mapkey < file
```

Consult the **mapkey(1)** and **kbd(7)** man pages for more details, but note that changes to the map do not survive a reboot, so you will have to make these changes again every time you boot the machine.

Tunable Parameters

Many UNIX systems allow a skilled system administrator to vary some *tunable parameters* within the kernel. These are variables that specify the size of some key data areas within the operating system. Their values can be set for special purposes, if necessary. Microcomputer versions of SVR4 usually provide some tools to change a few of these tunable parameters, and others may appear somewhere in **/etc/default**. Often **nbuf** (the number of system buffers), **nclists** (the number of system character I/O buffers), **nproc** (the number of simultaneous processes allowed for a user), and **nfile** (the number of open files a process is allowed) are tunable on small SVR4 systems. However, these values should not be changed from their defaults unless you are installing a special application package that requires the change. Follow the vendor's instructions carefully, and do not change these values unnecessarily.

Going Further

You've learned that the UNIX system provides an extraordinarily rich and varied computer environment. The title of this book may be *The Complete Reference,* but as you've probably realized by now, no single book can hope to cover the UNIX system *completely,* or even to adequately survey the entire range of its commands and associated lore. In this book we have attempted to discuss the Foundation Set in enough detail that a moderately experienced microcomputer user can become a competent user and administrator of a personal UNIX system.

In addition to the Foundation Set, there are several other pieces of the UNIX system in the complete SVR4 release. The *Documenter's Workbench* and the *C Compilation System* are two of the most important of these. Many "semistandard" packages that are not included in most vendor's products are also part of the official AT&T SVR4 software release. The *Writer's Workbench,* a package of additional tools built on top of the Documenter's Workbench, the *System Activity Reporting* (**sar**) tools, and the *Remote Job Entry* tools are examples.

Another type of add-on software consists of applications supported by the legions of UNIX system devotees in the world. The EMACS text editor, the news network, and some popular games are examples of this class. These programs are available for nearly all versions, although some are not available for purchase, but only exist in source code form.

T
W
E
N
T
Y
-
S
I
X

Many public-domain bulletin boards provide executable or installable versions of popular programs, and a little exposure to the *UNIX system community* will provide the information you need to find them.

Finally, there are a great many commercial software products available for the UNIX system. Contrary to the popular impression that "no software exists for the UNIX system," in fact thousands of popular applications are available. These include many spreadsheets and word processors, a large number of sophisticated scientific and engineering programs, graphics tools, and a rich set of communications packages. Today, most software and hardware vendors are writing their applications in the C language, and most of them support the UNIX system. With the growing popularity of the UNIX system, new applications are appearing on the market regularly. Since developers usually prefer the UNIX system over any other operating system, this rich and varied software base will continue to grow!

Games and Toys

One of the most popular "unofficial" areas of software is games and toys. As is true for most computing environments, a great many innovative games have been developed for the UNIX system over the years. In keeping with the philosophy of supporting remote ASCII terminals a large majority of these are character-oriented toys. The best of the games are almost legendary in the computing world, and it is often said that they have consumed more CPU resources on UNIX machines than any other category, including software development and word processing.

Games, when they are available, are usually kept in the directory **/usr/games**. The content of this directory varies widely on different machines, since games are no longer delivered as an official part of the UNIX system. However, the UNIX system did include some games at one time, and Section 6 of the manual is reserved for games and toys. This original set of games still forms the foundation for the **/usr/games** directory. The original games are mostly simple children's toys like "tic-tac-toe" and "hangman," but several more sophisticated games are also included. The UNIX system **chess** game can beat average chess players, but it has been superseded in recent years by state-of-the-art programs, such as the freely available **gnuchess** program from the Free Software Foundation, which is an excellent master-level player.

The most popular game in the original set is **adventure**. Known by the name "Zork" in the MS-DOS world, **adventure** is an exploration of a predefined dungeon, for one player. Its user interface is not graphical, but language oriented. That is, the user moves around in the dungeon by entering short command sentences like "Go West" or "Pick up the knife."

During the early 1980s, **rogue** displaced **adventure** as the king of the UNIX system games. While **rogue** is also a dungeon-oriented game, it improves on **adventure** in many ways. It includes a full-screen display of the dungeon, adds many dungeon levels, and requires the "hero" to fight 26 kinds of monsters in a quest for gold and the fabled *Amulet of Yendor*. Although **rogue** is so difficult that only a few players have been able to win, it remains a peculiarly fascinating and addictive pastime.

In the mid- to late-1980s, **rogue** spawned several popular children, each offering more complexity and features than the last. For example, **hack** is a sort of "super rogue" with much greater intricacy, but the same basic style of play as **rogue**.

Presently, games with bit-mapped graphical user interfaces are beginning to appear for UNIX systems that can support them. Multi-player games are also appearing. Some of these are high-action games based on real-time communications between users, and others are strategy games that are similar to chess, but take special advantage of the multitasking features of the UNIX system. The foremost example is **mazewar,** in which players wander in a maze, gaining points from shooting other players. Many others are also available. Several work with the X Window System and/or the Internet. One of the most popular is **nethack**, a multiplayer version of the **hack** game. Such graphical and multiplayer games will surely come to predominate over the next several years. Some of the best creativity in the computer business is devoted to games and toys, and these games are well worth trying. Thousands of users have been enchanted by (if not addicted to) them!

The Worldwide User Community

Over the history of the UNIX system, a tight-knit user community has appeared, fostered in part by the ease of communicating with **uucp** and

mail, and in part by the mystique the UNIX system has always held for developers. There are several independent users' groups, the foremost of which is called *Uniforum* (formerly **/usr/group**). In addition, several national conventions and meetings are devoted to discussions of the UNIX system, the largest of which is the *Usenix* meeting, which is held regularly. These organizations are excellent sources of information and contacts. Most of the real advances in UNIX system technology have been disseminated by word-of-mouth (or electronic mail!) between interested users, and only brought into official releases after being well accepted by the user community.

In addition, users of the UNIX system support a worldwide *bulletin board* and electronic mail system that serves several thousand machines and hundreds of thousands of users. Known by various names such as *netnews, usenet, readnews,* or simply *the net,* this network is based primarily on dial-up access between nearby machines, which exchange electronic mail messages known as *news items.* These news items can be grouped into over three hundred categories, or *newsgroups.* Nearby machines *feed* the messages to other machines, and thus a message eventually propagates from its originator to all the other machines in the network. A person working on one of the machines uses special *news reader* software to see the messages, and can set up a profile that limits retrieval to only desired news groups. Users can browse through, save, or reply to messages. The news network has *gateways* that link it to several other popular networks such as the Internet, a large-scale wide area network, and BITNET, a network of computers in colleges and universities.

Over a thousand messages per day cross the news network, on every subject imaginable. Especially fertile subjects are the UNIX system and C language lore. There is a constant flow of new public-domain source code for everything from games to new algorithms and full-blown expert systems. There are interesting discussions of new technologies and new products, and nontechnical news groups discuss politics, music, sports, and many other topics.

The news network is a completely self-sustaining operation that is supported by each machine, which pays the telephone bills associated with forwarding messages to its neighboring machines. However, recent experiments with satellite-based communications and a paid *backbone* network for communications between central *hub* machines may change the freelance character of the net, because these costs cannot easily be shared by individual machines. Netnews software is provided in the public domain by creative developers who are constantly improving the tools. Several popular news readers are available, but they are usually distributed in source code form.

To add your machine to the news network, you will need news management software in addition to the normal **uucp** package. Also, you must allocate a significant amount of hard disk space for the news messages, and find a nearby machine that is willing to feed your site. As much as 2 to 3MB of news per day can be delivered to your machine if you include all the different newsgroups. An alternative is to subscribe to one of several *public access* systems that provide news, bulletin board, and mail services for a fee. Once you begin receiving a news feed, you can be attached by a multi-hop connection to nearly every other UNIX machine in the world!

Reading the News

If you have the news system on your machine, you can use one of several public-domain programs to read the news. One of the best is **rn** (for read news). A version for the X Window System, called **xrn**, is also available. These programs, like the news system as a whole, are not an official part of SVR4, so they may not be present on your system.

The **rn** program displays news items, allows the user to search through news items, and provides tools to create and *post* news items. In addition, **rn** manages a list of active newsgroups and keeps track of unread news items. It can take many command-line options, but its simplest form, shown here, is most often used:

```
$ rn
```

The **rn** program will switch into an internal command mode with many subcommands. If you use the **xrn** version, most **rn** functions will be available via mouse clicks instead of through the command set.

When it starts, **rn** reads a personal file in your home directory, **.newsrc** (for news run control). The first time you run **rn**, it creates this file if it doesn't exist. The **.newsrc** file contains a list of all newsgroups supported on the machine. Each newsgroup has its own line in the **.newsrc** file, as shown here:

```
$ tail -6 .newsrc
comp.unix.wizards: 1-11402,12974-13606
rec.games.go: 1-1395
comp.unix.i386: 1-4476
comp.os.mach: 1-161
sci.virtual-worlds! 1-9
rec.arts.startrek.info!
$
```

Since there are several hundred newsgroups, **.newsrc** can become large. Each newsgroup belongs to a hierarchy of class names. The **comp** groups cover computer technology, **rec** includes many forms of recreation, and so forth. Within each of these classes, there are subclasses, such as **unix** or **arts**. Further subdivisions are also common. Each news item received by a machine is assigned a number, and the entire history of the netnews system on that machine is represented by the list of numbers following the newsgroup name. For instance, there have been 4476 news *articles* received in the **comp.unix.i386** newsgroup on the machine in the previous example. As you read news items, this count is updated, and **rn** uses the count to display only unread articles. A : (colon) or ! (bang) after the newsgroup name tells **rn** whether to show you that newsgroup. The ! tells **rn** that you do not *subscribe* to that newsgroup. For example, the line

```
sci.virtual-worlds! 1-9
```

means that this user examined the first nine articles in this newsgroup, and then unsubscribed from the group.

Typically, news items are only maintained on a machine for a short time (usually a week or two), so it is possible that you will not see all the news items if you unsubscribe from a group or neglect to read your news for a while. The line

```
comp.unix.wizards: 1-11402,12974-13606
```

shows a gap in the list of items that have been read. These items were deleted from the machine before this user saw them.

You do not have to edit or change the **.newsrc** file manually; that is done by the **rn** command.

Actually, **rn** is a complex program with several different modes and a separate command set for each. It can work at the *newsgroup level*, in which it manages the list of newsgroups you subscribe to, allowing you to add or delete newsgroups as your interests change. When you delete a newsgroup at this user level, it is not really eliminated from the machine, but **rn** no longer displays news items from it. You can resubscribe to a group at any time. The *article level* manages access to articles within a *current* newsgroup, allowing you to select or reject specific articles. The *paging level* manages the display of individual articles, allowing you to page forward or backward in the article, search for information, and so forth. In addition, **rn** provides modes for creating and posting a news article, replying by mail to an article, and configuring your session.

When you enter **rn**, it starts by comparing the articles in the news tree (usually **/usr/news** and its subdirectories) with the listed articles in your **.newsrc**. If more articles are present than you have read, **rn** will display the number of unread articles in each newsgroup that you subscribe to, in the order that they appear in your **.newsrc** file, as follows:

```
$ rn
Unread news in comp.sources.games        2 articles
Unread news in comp.unix.wizards         1 article
Unread news in comp.windows.x           16 articles
Unread news in rec.games.go              1 article
Unread news in alt.sources               1 article
etc.

********   2 unread articles in comp.sources.games--read now? [ynq]
```

To reduce the amount of output, **rn** only displays the first few newsgroups, and then prompts you to decide whether or not to read the first newsgroup now. At this point you are in newsgroup mode. You can press **y** to enter article mode for that newsgroup, **n** to skip to the next listed newsgroup, or **q** to exit the program and return to the shell. Many other possible commands are also accepted in newsgroup mode. You can see a list of these commands by entering **h** (for help). You can skip to a named newsgroup with **g group.name**, unsubscribe to that newsgroup with **u**, search for a newsgroup whose name matches a pattern with

/pattern, or take many other actions, all related to newsgroup management. You can list the subjects of all unread articles in a newsgroup by entering = (equal). You can enter **c** (for catch up) to mark all the articles in a newsgroup as read if you do not wish to read them.

To read the articles in a newsgroup, select an article number (if you used = to see the list), or just press **y** to display the first unread article, as shown here:

```
********   2 unread articles in comp.sources.games--read now? [ynq] y

Article 493 (1 more) in comp.sources.games (moderated):
From: steve@my_sys.com (Steve)
Subject: v98i085:  go -- the oriental board game
Message-ID: <146@my_sys.com>
Reply-To: 6 Feb 90 17:43:12 GMT
Sender: steve@my_sys.com
Lines: 1989

Follows is a version of the game of "go" for UNIX SVR4.

The following is a "shar" archive; unpack with "/bin/sh" NOT csh

========================= Cut here ==============================
--MORE--(2%)
```

At the beginning of the article are a number of *article headers* that give information about this article. The headers are much like mail headers, although they are more numerous than those produced by most mail programs. Included is the sender, the date and time the message was created, the subject, and a message id that was assigned by the news system when the message was created. Note that this number differs from the local message count maintained on the *receiving* machine. The "Reply to:" field will usually give a correct UNIX mail address at which to contact the creator of the message, although sometimes the reply address will not work even though the news has reached your machine.

In the previous example, the message contains more lines than the screen can hold. The **rn** program detects this, and stops with the "MORE" message when the screen is full. You are now in page mode, and can enter commands similar to the **more** functions. If you enter a space, the message will scroll to the next page, or you can step through the message line-by-line by entering newline. Enter **h** at the **MORE** prompt to see a full list of page mode commands. You can also enter **n** (for next) to mark this article as read and go on to the next article, or you can search for a string within the article. Finally, you can enter one of several commands that will take you to the end of the article.

When you reach the end of the article, either because you have read the whole article or because you have jumped there from within page mode, you enter article mode, as indicated here:

```
End of article 493 (of 494)--what next? [npq]
```

You can enter **n** (for next) or press the SPACEBAR to see the next article in the newsgroup, enter **p** (for previous) to see the previous article or enter a - (minus) to repeat the last article you saw. Enter **q** (for quit) to leave the current newsgroup and move on to the next one. If you enter **h** (for help), you will see the full list of article mode commands. You can search for the next article with (approximately) the same subject line by entering CTRL-N, or search backward for the same subject with CTRL-P. Enter **s** (for save) to save the article in a file in your directory. The **s** command can take a pathname as an argument, and **rn** will try to save the article in the specified location, as follows:

```
End of article 493 (of 494)--what next? [npq] s $HOME/go.shar
File /usr/steve/go.shar doesn't exist--
        use mailbox format? [ynq]
```

As you can see, **rn** tries to save the article as if it were a mail message, appending it to the filename you give. The **rn** program can save files in two formats: if the file already exists, **rn** uses the same format; otherwise, **rn** prompts you to select the file format. The only difference between the two formats is that the mail format can be read by the **mail** program, but the other format cannot. If you wish to abandon the save operation, enter **q** (for quit), and **rn** will return to article mode. If you do not give a name for the save file, **rn** defaults to a file in your **$HOME/News** directory, which it will create if the directory does not already exist. The filename will be the name of the newsgroup.

You can also save an article to a pipeline instead of to a file. This allows you to process an article with a series of commands or to print it. Just use | (pipe) after the **s** command, and then enter the pipeline as usual. For example,

```
End of article 493 (of 494)--what next? [npq] s |pr|lp
```

will process the article with **pr**, and then print it with **lp**.

Replying to an Article by Mail

If you enter **r** or **R** (for reply), you can reply to an article through normal UNIX **mail** channels. The **rn** program will pick up the "Reply-To:" address, and will then start an editing process for the message. When the process has completed, **rn** will send the message and then return to article mode for more news.

The reply procedure uses message setup procedures internal to **rn**, but you can escape to your favorite editor to write the message. The first thing **rn** does is write message headers that include some of the key information from the article headers. This provides some reference to the original article, as shown here:

```
End of article 493 (of 494)--what next? [npq] r
To: steve@my_sys.com (Steve)
Subject: Re: v98i085:  go -- the oriental board game
Newsgroups: comp.sources.games
In-Reply-To: <146@my_sys.com>
Organization: Human Interface Design Consulting
Cc:
Bcc:

(Above lines saved in file /home/steve/.rnhead)

(leaving cbreak mode; cwd=/home/steve)
Invoking command: mail -h /home/steve/.rnhead

Prepared file to include [none]:
```

In this example, the program explains what it is doing as it builds the mail message, and then prompts you for the name of a previously prepared file. If you enter a pathname, that file will be included, or you can just enter newline to skip this part. Then, **rn** will start the editor given in the EDITOR environment variable, with the current version of the message as text. You can edit the message and headers, but some of the headers will be included even if you change them in the editor. When you write the file and quit the editor, **rn** will prompt for your next action, as follows:

```
Send, abort, edit, or list?
```

You can **send** the message, **abort** the reply altogether, reenter **edit**, or **list** the message. When you finish, **rn** will return to article mode for the next article.

Introduction to xrn

If you have the X Window System, you may find **xrn** more friendly than the keyboard-oriented **rn**. The **xrn** program has the same functions and modes as **rn**, and uses the **.newsrc** file in the same way. Figure 26-1 shows the initial screen for **xrn**. The top of the screen lists newsgroups in newsgroup mode, or article subject lines in article mode. The bottom area is used for page mode, and displays selected articles. You can select a newsgroup with the mouse, and then click on the **read group** button. The top display will switch to a list of unread articles (in article mode). The top group of menu buttons will change to a command set appropriate for article mode, and you can then select individual articles for display in the lower window. By using the mouse and the scroll bars on the left edge of the window, you can move around in the article. When an article is displayed, the gray buttons at the bottom of the window become active, allowing you to save or reply to an article. In addition to mouse versus keyboard control, **xrn** differs from **rn** in more subtle ways. Experiment with both programs to get a feel for their operation.

Creating an Article

When you are in article mode, you can enter the **f** or **F** (for followup) commands to create a *followup article*. Two commands are provided because **rn** includes the original article in the message when you use **F**. Instead of creating a private mail message to the sender of the original message, a followup article is posted to the net just as the original article was. Creating a followup message is very much like creating a mail message, and the procedures given earlier for reply mail will work. When you enter your editor to create the file, you can tailor the message headers to suit your message instead of the original. Often you will wish to change the keywords, the subject, and the references. You can also use the f command to create a new article that does not refer to any previous article by deleting the "References:" line from the header and creating a new subject. Note that you cannot alter some of the headers, because **rn** will override any changes you make to them in your editor. The "From:" and "Organization:" lines cannot be changed, which prevents you from *spoofing* the news system by falsifying your name or address. The **rn** program will assign the message id.

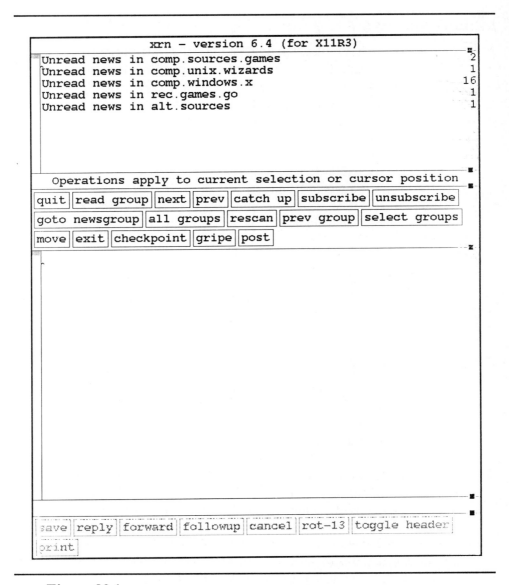

Figure 26-1.   **xrn** screen appearance

At the end of your newly created article, **rn** will append the contents of the file **$HOME/.signature**. You can create a personalized signature in this file that will be appended to your postings to the net.

The signature can be as long as you like, although short signatures are preferable.

The "Distribution:" line restricts articles to a subset of the net as a whole. You can usually select your own organization with the organization name, your state, your country, and a few other destinations. Consult your local news guru for the exact list.

A Note on News Etiquette

Unlike most things that can go wrong with the UNIX system, which affect only your login id or your machine (or at worst your LAN), posting an article sends the article into the worldwide news network. There, it can be copied to thousands of machines worldwide, and read by a great many users. Because posting has such a wide scope, it is appropriate to limit your posting to articles of *general interest* and *importance.* Select as limited a distribution as possible, and keep your articles short and concise. Resist the tendency to *flame* another message that you do not agree with, keep your signature short, and think carefully before posting. Of course, you should always use good taste in all aspects of your messages. Some of the most respected voices in the UNIX world *never* post to the net, but rather conduct their correspondence in private, though **mail**.

If you create an article mistakenly, it is very difficult to stop its distribution; however, the Cancel option in **rn** attempts to retract an article. If you read your article and decide that it should not distributed, cancel it. Only the creator or a few trusted net administrators can cancel an article. Canceling may not be effective if an article has propagated too far into the network, and note that canceling an article causes *another* net message to be sent, thus doubling the net traffic.

Many newsgroups are *moderated,* meaning that when you post an article, it is really sent by mail to a designated moderator for the newsgroup. The moderator reads the article and decides whether or not it should be posted to the net as a whole (or to a distribution list). Sometimes you can contact the moderator to retract an article before it has been distributed.

The news system is a powerful free service; treat it with respect.

The Internet and the ftp Command

The *Internet* is a worldwide, high-speed *Wide Area Network* (WAN) originated as a DARPA research project by the U. S. Department of Defense. In recent years it has moved into general use, and DARPA has reduced its participation as the Internet has become self-sustaining. Thousands of machines are connected to the Internet, and most can be contacted using the unique four-part *Internet address* discussed in Chapter 24. If your machine (or your LAN) is attached to the Internet, you can use applications that work like **rlogin** to connect with machines worldwide. Naturally, security on the Internet is higher than that within most LANs, but many useful services are available. Much of Internet's work is carrying mail and news articles between individual users, but real-time communication across the Internet is also provided. Consult your local net expert to determine if you have Internet access, and what restrictions have been placed on its use.

One of the most useful tools for Internet access is **ftp** (for file transfer protocol), which allows a user to log in to another system across the Internet, and copy files between the systems. It functions much like **cu**, except at much higher speed. In addition, **ftp** can transfer binary as well as ASCII files between machines. The **ftp** program can also connect you to other machines on your LAN as well as across the Internet, but since **rlogin, rcp,** and other tools are easier to use and more efficient, **ftp** is primarily used for Internet connections. You can experiment with **ftp** on your own LAN before attempting to use it with the Internet. Conversely, you can use **rlogin, rcp** and other tools on Internet connections as well as on your LAN, providing the remote host allows this level of access.

ftp Addressing and Login

The **ftp** command takes a hostname as its major command-line argument, and attempts to connect with that host. If no hostname is given, **ftp** will enter its command mode and wait for you to select a host. The hostname takes the same form as that used by **rlogin**; it can be either a logical hostname or a four-part Internet address. The logical hostname is looked up in the **/etc/hosts** file (or its **yp** equivalent) and the numerical address is actually used. Thus, if your machine does not know the host you wish to contact, you will need the four-part numerical address. These are all acceptable command lines:

```
$ ftp yoursys
$ ftp gateway.hid.com
$ ftp 127.0.0.1
$ ftp
```

If **ftp** can connect to the named host, it will attempt to log you in to that host, as follows:

```
$ ftp yoursys
Connected to yoursys.
220 yoursys FTP server (UNIX System V Release 4.0) ready.
Name (yoursys:steve):
```

You must give a login id and password. If **ftp** knows you, it will default to your current login id. You can accept this by entering newline, or you can enter a different login id. In the latter case, you will usually need to enter your password. If it is accepted, you will be logged in to the remote host, and **ftp** will enter its command mode; otherwise, **ftp** will complain. For example:

```
$ ftp yoursys
Connected to yoursys.
220 yoursys FTP server (UNIX System V Release 4.0) ready.
Name (yoursys:steve): nouser
530 User nouser access denied.
Login failed.
ftp>
```

In either case, you will be left in command mode.

To exit the **ftp** program, close the connection to the remote host, and return to the shell, just enter **quit** at the **ftp>** prompt, as shown here:

```
ftp> quit
221 Goodbye.
$
```

Many Internet hosts allow you to **ftp** into the machine and copy archived files to your own system. These sites and the files they contain are often posted on the net and other places. Since unknown users may try to *scoop* files with **ftp,** most hosts that allow this access provide an *anonymous* login capability. Permissions for *anonymous ftp* are generally greatly restricted compared to those for normal logins, but they usually allow you to move around in a limited directory tree, copy files, and use a few simple commands. To use anonymous **ftp,** give the id **anonymous** at the login prompt, and enter your name and machine at the password prompt, as follows:

```
$ ftp yoursys
Connected to yoursys.
220 yoursys FTP server (UNIX System V Release 4.0) ready.
Name (yoursys:guest): anonymous
331 Guest login ok, send ident as password.
Password:
230 Guest login ok, access restrictions apply.
ftp>
```

Use a password of the form

```
login@machine.net
```

where *login* is your login id, and *machine.net* is your logical Internet or **mail** address. You can also use the four-part numerical address if you wish. The purpose of the anonymous password is to allow the administrator of the host to track users of the host, and to contact them if necessary.

When you successfully connect to a remote machine, you are not connected to a normal shell on that machine, but to a special **ftp** *server process* that is quite different than a shell. This process does not support the full set of UNIX commands, but only a small set of commands provided by the **ftp** command mode.

ftp Command Mode

At the **ftp>** prompt, many commands are available to control your session and copy files between machines. The most important is **quit,** which closes the connection to the remote host before exiting back to the shell. You can also enter ! (bang) followed by a command line to execute on the *local* machine. If you enter ! with no command line, **ftp** will start an interactive shell. When you exit from that shell, **ftp** returns to its command mode. You can also enter **help** or a **?** (question mark) to get a list of all **ftp** commands. The form

```
ftp> help cmd
```

will provide a short explanation of the *cmd* name given.

The **ftp** program allows you to change directories on the remote host, and to list the contents of directories. Use the **ftp** command **cd** to change directories on the remote host, and the **ls** command to display the contents of a directory. You can change the current directory on the *local* machine with **lcd** (for local **cd**). Since these commands may be internal to **ftp**, they may perform slightly differently than you expect them to. Here is an example:

```
ftp> cd pub/src
250 CWD command successful.
ftp> pwd
257 "/pub/src" is current directory
ftp> ls
200 PORT command successful.
150 ASCII data connection for /bin/ls (127.0.0.1,2390) (0 bytes).
mystuff
patches
contrib
226 ASCII Transfer complete.
170 bytes received in 0.08 seconds (2.1 Kbytes/s)
ftp>
```

As you can see, **pwd** displays the current directory.

Lines of the form

```
200 PORT command successful.
```

will appear frequently in **ftp** output; these are messages from **ftp** as it creates and breaks separate communication *channels* within the connection to transfer the data.

File Transfer with ftp

The **ftp** program provides several commands for file transfer between machines. You can copy both binary (executable or compressed) and text (ASCII) files between machines. The program has two modes for the file types; use the commands **binary** and **ascii** to switch between them, as shown here:

```
ftp> binary
200 Type set to I.
ftp> ascii
200 Type set to A.
ftp>
```

The default is ASCII mode, so be sure to change modes before you try to copy binary files. Binary mode will usually copy ASCII files correctly, so you can enable binary for all transfers, especially when you do not know the file type.

To copy a file from a remote machine, use the **get** or **mget** (for multiple get) commands. The **get** command takes an argument that names the file to copy from the remote to the local machine. For example:

```
ftp> get file.name
```

The **mget** command allows you to copy multiple files with the familiar wildcard naming rule, as follows:

```
ftp> mget *xbm*
mget xwatch.xbm?
```

The **mget** command will prompt you for each file to copy. If you answer **y**, the file will be copied to the current directory on the local machine, as shown here:

```
ftp> mget *xbm
mget xwatch.xbm? y
200 PORT command successful.
150 ASCII data connection for xwatch.xbm (127.0.0.1) (1886 bytes).
226 ASCII Transfer complete.
local: xwatch.xbm remote: xwatch.xbm
1913 bytes received in .11 seconds (17 Kbytes/s)
mget xwatch_empty.xbm?
```

A lot of tracing information is provided, but the file transfer is completed. As you can see, **mget** can move data quite quickly (17K per second in this example).

If you wish to copy several files at once, you can disable the prompting for each file with

```
ftp> prompt
```

The **prompt** command toggles the prompting; to turn prompting back on, execute the command again.

You can **put** files from the local to the remote machine using a similar procedure. The **put** and **mput** commands take a filename (or a list or a wildcard specification with **mput**) as an argument, and copy the file or files from the local to the remote system. The **mput** command uses the **binary** and **prompt** features just as **mget** does. Of course, you may not be permitted to create files on the remote machine; in any case you should use this feature with care.

The **ftp** command includes many features designed for experts, including the ability to create *macros*, which are named lists of frequently used commands. You can control whether **ftp** performs filename expansion as in the previous examples, or treats the names given to **mget** literally. Furthermore, you can explicitly control the creation of communication channels (the PORT commands), and other features. Most users will rarely use these advanced features. Consult the **ftp(1)** man page if you need more information.

Software Development

Perhaps the richest area within the UNIX system is software development. The C programming language and an excellent support environment make the UNIX system very popular with developers. Nearly all the tools and the majority of the kernel are written in the C language. C has recently taken hold in environments other than the UNIX system, and C compilers and tools are now available for almost all operating systems. C is widely regarded as one of the best systems programming languages in use, because it allows the developer a great deal of flexibility in spanning the range from assembly-level code to very high-level, abstract programming concepts.

The official SVR4 Standard C Development Environment implements a new high-performance compiler capable of producing code that usually executes 10 to 20 percent faster than older System V releases. In addition, the new tools support the recent ANSI specification for the C language in a way that is particularly compatible with older software.

You can use **make** to reduce the compilation time required for development of large projects. The **make** program uses a predetermined list of *dependencies* between source files and the target application to determine the minimum recompilation needed to regenerate the application after any part has changed. The file system modification date is used to determine which files are newer than their dependents. Then **make** efficiently rebuilds these modules and reconstructs the application. In large software projects that consist of many source files in several directories developed by different people, **make** can significantly reduce the development effort.

The **make** program has many applications outside software development. It can be useful in any application where the output depends on several input files, or where there are several different "recipes" for creating the output. The **make** program is often used in documentation projects; it can serve small as well as large projects.

The standard development set includes two tools for *lexical analysis* and development of programs from linguistic descriptions of the *effects* the programs should have. The **lex** (for lexical analysis) and **yacc** (for yet another compiler-compiler) programs are *fourth-generation* development tools that allow programmers to develop lexical state machines and compilers by describing *how* the applications should act, rather than specifying *what* they should do. These are sophisticated tools designed for experts, and considerable experience is required to use them successfully.

FORTRAN compilers and other languages and development systems are available for the UNIX system from several sources. Almost any development tool you might desire is available for UNIX systems, including full-scale statistics and graphics packages, and many spreadsheets and full-screen calculators for various terminals and displays.

The official C Development Set is usually an extra-cost add-on to the basic SVR4 system, but the popular **gnu C** is available free from the Free Software Foundation. It is distributed in source form, so you need access to a C compiler to get it running, but it is a solid and cost-effective alternative to the standard development set. The **gnu C** package includes many additional development tools including versions of the **c++** and **yacc** tools. Furthermore, **gnu C** supports the ANSI C language as well as the older "K&R" syntax.

Many vendors support diverse programming systems for the UNIX environment, such as LISP, ADA, Prolog, and even COBOL. Database query languages, shell-like interpreters, expert systems, and user interface development tools are also available. On the other hand, it can be quite difficult to find an implementation of BASIC for SVR4.

Although development is beyond the scope of this book, there is a great deal of literature that discusses the subject. If you have an interest in programming, you will find the UNIX system well suited to your needs.

The Source Code Control System

One part of the software development environment that has general utility for users is the *Source Code Control System*, also called SCCS. Originally designed for software management, the SCCS tools also provide *document management* or *version control* services for any text documents. As documents change over time, it can be difficult to archive *all* versions, along with their dates, comments and the *parent* document they were changed from. The SCCS makes this process easier by administering a single file that contains all changes to a document. You can add changed versions, or *deltas*, to the file at any time without destroying older versions. Then you can *get* any of the versions from the master file as necessary for further changes, printing, or compiling. SCCS is not provided with the basic UNIX Operating System, but is in the C Compilation System.

SCCS works by keeping *version numbers* for each new delta added to the database. When the file is created, it is assigned version number 1.1. When you get that version from the database, edit it, and return the new version to the database, the new version will be marked 1.2. Next time it will be 1.3, and so forth. Thus, all previous versions remain available, and you can get them at any time. SCCS also provides a *comment* facility to annotate the versions, so you can keep track of the reasons for the changes.

The SCCS database for a file is the name of the file preceded by **s.** (ess dot). For example, if a file is named **mydoc**, its SCCS database will be named **s.mydoc**. If your system has the 14-character filename limit, you will have to give your original documents names of 12 characters or less.

To create a new SCCS database for a file, use the **admin** command. The arguments **-n** (for new) and **-i** (for input) followed by the original filename are required. Last, give the SCCS filename, as follows:

```
$ ls
mydoc
$ admin -n -imydoc s.mydoc
No id keywords (cm7)
$ ls
mydoc      s.mydoc
$
```

No whitespace is allowed between the **-i** option and the filename.

The file **s.mydoc** contains the original contents of the file in SCCS format. The *keywords* message is a friendly warning, not an error; keywords are discussed later in this section. The **admin** command is a general-purpose tool for administering SCCS files, and has a great many additional functions (and command-line arguments!) that are not discussed here. Its features include the ability to get reports about the delta history of a file and the ability to patch a corrupted database.

To retrieve the original text from the database, use the **get** command with the SCCS filename as an argument. For example:

```
$ rm mydoc
$ get s.mydoc
1.1
12 lines
No id keywords (cm7)
$ ls
mydoc      s.mydoc
$
```

This operation creates a file with the original name that contains the contents of the original file; the SCCS database is unchanged.

By default, **get** retrieves the *latest* version in the database, but you can get a previous version (if it exists) by using the **-r** (for release) option followed by the version number, as shown here:

```
$ get -r1.1 s.file
```

This operation is intended to give you a *snapshot* of the file that you can use for printing, compiling, or other purposes. You are not expected to delta this file back into the SCCS database. In fact, to remind you not to change it, the file as created does not have write permission. The SCCS database file is not writable either, so you must always use the SCCS tools (which override the permissions) to make changes. If you wish to get the file for editing and then return it to the database, use the **-e** (for edit) option with **get**, as shown here:

```
$ get -e s.mydoc
1.1
new delta 1.2
12 lines
$ ls
mydoc      p.mydoc      s.mydoc
$
```

In this case, the file **mydoc** will be writable. The extra file created in this operation, **p.mydoc**, is a control file that tells the SCCS system a file is *out* for editing. Version control requires that only *one* user at a time be allowed to edit a given version, so you are prohibited from getting a version that someone is already editing. Be sure never to delete the p-files, or SCCS will become confused.

If you wish to create a *new* version of the file, rather than one that simply increments the *minor* version number, use **get** with the **-r** option and the version you want to create, as follows:

```
$ get -r2.0 -e s.mydoc
1.2
new delta 2.1
12 lines
$
```

The next version will now be 2.1, not 1.3.

To return an updated version to the SCCS database, use the **delta** command. You can only use **delta** if you previously got the file for editing. Here is an example:

```
$ ls
mydoc      p.mydoc      s.mydoc
$ delta s.mydoc
comments? incorporated boss's suggestions
No id keywords (cm7)
1.2
1 inserted
0 deleted
12 unchanged
$ ls
s.mydoc
$
```

Give the name of the SCCS file (**s.mydoc** in this example) as the argument to **delta**. As you can see, the original writable file and the p-file are both deleted, but the SCCS database is updated to contain the latest version. The *comments* prompt gives you a chance to annotate the new version, and then **delta** reports on the changes to the file.

The SCCS deltas can form a complex hierarchy of versions. For example, if you have versions 1.1, 1.2, 2.1, and 2.2 in your SCCS database, you are allowed to get version 1.1, edit it, and delta it back into the database. SCCS knows about the other versions, and instead of replacing version 1.2 it will create a version 1.1.1. When you subsequently edit version 1.1.1 and delta it back in, the new version will be 1.1.2. If you get version 1.2 and delta a changed version back, version 1.2.1 will be created. There are really no limits on the number of versions allowed.

The SCCS system also supports *keywords,* special strings you can put into your file. When you get a version from the database, SCCS automatically replaces the strings with their current values. This allows you to place the correct version number in the file itself. For example, the string **%M%** (percent M percent) will be replaced by the filename; **%R%** will be replaced by the major release number, and **%I%** will be replaced with a useful SCCS *identification string* that contains the date, the version number, and other information. The full list is in the **get(1)** man page. You can use these strings as necessary in your text. Note that when you use **get -e** the keywords are not replaced; they are only replaced when you do not expect to delta the file.

The Expanding Influence of the UNIX System

Along with the software development tools, the UNIX system itself has proved to be an extremely fertile source of ideas and algorithms for developers. Most modern microcomputer software has borrowed liberally from concepts that first appeared in the UNIX system. For example, the OS/2 operating system gleaned much from the UNIX system, from its kernel through **cmd.exe**, its version of the shell. On the other hand, the X Window System adapted many ideas from the Macintosh user interface and the Microsoft Windows products. You will find that knowing the UNIX system makes it easier for you to use almost any other computer system, although you may occasionally become frustrated when familiar tools and procedures from the UNIX system are not available in other computing environments.

Bibliography

If you wish to pursue any aspect of the UNIX system in more detail, many sources of information are available. Over the years, the user community has favored some documents over others; some of the best are listed here.

Aho, A. V., B. W. Kernighan, and P. J. Weinberger. *The awk Programming Language.* New York: Addison-Wesley, 1988.
An in-depth treatment of the **awk** tool that focuses on the recent **nawk** variant.

Anderson, G., and P. Anderson. *The UNIX C Shell Field Guide.* Englewood Cliffs, N.J.: Prentice-Hall, 1986.
An excellent users' guide for the C Shell.

AT&T, Intel, and other vendors. *UNIX System V Release 4 Programmer's Guide.* 1990.
The official document for programming in SVR4. Unlike the *User's Manual,* this guide gives descriptive information on using the system calls and subroutines available in SVR4.

AT&T, Intel, and other vendors. *UNIX System V Release 4 User's Manual.* 1990.
The official reference manual for all commands in the UNIX system. Be sure to get the version prepared by your vendor for your specific release of the system. The *User's Manual* is published in several volumes, each covering a different part of the full UNIX system.

Bach, M. J., *The Design of the UNIX Operating System.* Englewood Cliffs, N.J.: Prentice-Hall, 1986.
The definitive look at system internals, including extensive detail on the kernel and its design.

Bolsky, M. I., and D. G. Korn. *The Korn Shell.* Englewood Cliffs, N. J.: Prentice-Hall, 1989.
The definitive guide to the Korn Shell.

Coffin, S., *UNIX System V Release 3—The Complete Reference.* Berkeley, C.A.: Osborne/McGraw-Hill, 1988.
A user's reference to the predecessor of SVR4. This book is appropriate if you have SVR3, because SVR4 introduces extensive changes.

Comer, C., *Internetworking with TCP/IP.* Englewood Cliffs, N. J.: Prentice-Hall, 1988.
Everything you ever wanted to know about the TCP/IP protocol, the Internet, and networking under the UNIX system.

Harbison, S. P., and G. L. Steele, Jr. *C: A Reference Manual.* 2d ed. Englewood Cliffs, N. J.: Prentice-Hall, 1987.
Provides excellent coverage of the C language, including the ANSI variant, and is somewhat more accessible than Kernighan and Ritchie.

Harrington, J., *The A/UX Handbook.* New York: Simon & Schuster, 1989.
Describes the Apple Macintosh version of System V.

Kernighan, B. W., and D. M. Ritchie. *The C Programming Language.* 2d ed. Englewood Cliffs, N. J.: Prentice-Hall, 1989.
The final word on the C language. The second edition covers the latest ANSI specification for C, but does not discuss the new variant C++, which is used by an increasing number of developers.

Libes, D., and S. Ressler. *Life with UNIX.* Englewood Cliffs, N. J.: Prentice-Hall, 1989.
An entertaining book, full of lore for fans of the UNIX operating system.

Moore, M. L., *Working with Xenix System V.* Glenview, IL.: Scott, Foresman and Company, 1986.
This book gives a user-level view of the XENIX version of the UNIX system.

Nutshell Handbooks. Newton, MA.: O'Reilly & Associates.
Short essays that each cover a specific topic related to the UNIX system. You can order one or more from the publisher. Write to O'Reilly & Associates, Inc. at 981 Chestnut Street, Newton, MA 02164, or call 1-800-338-NUTS for a current list.

Wood, P. H., and S. G. Kochan. *UNIX System Security.* Indianapolis, IN.: Hayden Books, 1985.
Provides excellent coverage of security issues, but does not review topics unique to SVR4.

Of course, many additional books and documents on the UNIX system are available. Local bookstores and libraries usually have a selection.

A Few Last Words

At last, you have reached the end of the book. If you have arrived here the hard way—through all the intervening chapters—by now you are surely a competent user who can stand on your own and make the UNIX system work for you, now and in the future. We hope you have joined the rest of the worldwide user community in its enthusiasm for the UNIX system. Remember, learning the UNIX system is a continuing process, and even the most established guru can know only part of its rich environment. You can always continue to develop your skills if you are not afraid to experiment with new ideas and procedures on your own machine. As you join the community of users, pass your knowledge on to the beginners you meet, and help to make others as skilled as you have become. See you on the net!

The manuscript for this book was prepared and submitted to Osborne/McGraw-Hill in electronic form. The acquisitions editor for this project was Roger Stewart, the associate editor for this project was Laurie Beaulieu, the technical reviewers were Bill Corwin and Stuart Goossen, and the project editor was Madhu Prasher.

Text design by Judy Wohlfrom and Mary Abbas, using Century Expanded for text body and Eras Demi for display.

Cover art by Bay Graphics Design Associates. Color separation and cover supplier, Phoenix Color Corporation. Screens produced with InSet, from InSet Systems, Inc. Book printed and bound by R.R. Donnelley & Sons Company, Crawfordsville, Indiana.